A New View of
Comparative Economic Systems

A NEW VIEW OF
COMPARATIVE ECONOMIC SYSTEMS

DAVID KENNETT

Vassar College

HARCOURT COLLEGE PUBLISHERS

Fort Worth   Philadelphia   San Diego   New York   Orlando   Austin   San Antonio
Toronto   Montreal   London   Sydney   Tokyo

PUBLISHER	Mike Roche
MARKET STRATEGIST	Janet Morey
DEVELOPMENTAL EDITOR	Amy Porubsky
PROJECT EDITOR	Jon Davies
ART DIRECTOR	Van Mua
PRODUCTION MANAGER	Holly Lewerenz

Cover images: © PhotoDisc™

ISBN: 0-03-018959-4
Library of Congress Catalog Card Number: 00-101402

Requests for permission to make copies of any part of the work should be mailed to the following address: Permissions Department, Harcourt, Inc., 6277 Sea Harbor Drive, Orlando, FL 32887-6777.

Address for Domestic Orders:
Harcourt, Inc., 6277 Sea Harbor Drive, Orlando, FL 32887-6777
800-782-4479

Address for International Orders:
International Customer Service, Harcourt, Inc.,
6277 Sea Harbor Drive, Orlando, FL 32887-6777
407-345-3800
(fax) 407-345-4060
(e-mail) hbintl@harcourt.com

Address for Editorial Correspondence:
Harcourt College Publishers, 301 Commerce Street, Suite 3700, Fort Worth, TX 76102.

Web Site Address:
http://www.harcourtcollege.com

Printed in the United States of America

2 3 4 5 6 7 8 9   039   9 8 7 6 5 4 3 2 1

Harcourt College Publishers

HARCOURT SERIES IN ECONOMICS

Baldani, Bradfield, and Turner
Mathematical Economics

Baumol and Blinder
Economics: Principles and Policy
Eighth Edition
(also available in Micro and Macro
paperbacks)

Baumol, Panzar, and Willig
*Contestable Markets and the Theory
of Industry Structure*
Revised Edition

Breit and Elzinga
*The Antitrust Casebook: Milestones
in Economic Regulation*
Third Edition

Brue
The Evolution of Economic Thought
Sixth Edition

Callan and Thomas
*Environmental Economics and
Management: Theory, Policy,
and Applications*
Second Edition

Edgmand, Moomaw, and Olson
Economics and Contemporary Issues
Fifth Edition

Gardner
Comparative Economic Systems
Second Edition

Gwartney, Stroup, and Sobel
Economics: Private and Public Choice
Ninth Edition
(also available in Micro and Macro
paperbacks)

Gwartney and Stroup
*Introduction to Economics:
The Wealth and Poverty of Nations*

Hess and Ross
*Economic Development:
Theories, Evidence, and Policies*

Hirschey
*Fundamentals of Managerial Economics:
Theories, Evidence, and Policies*
Sixth Edition

Hirschey
Managerial Economics
Revised Edition

Hyman
*Public Finance: A Contemporary
Application of Theory to Policy*
Sixth Edition

Kahn
*The Economic Approach to
Environmental and Natural Resources*
Second Edition

Kaserman and Mayo
*Government and Business: The
Economics of Antitrust and Regulation*

Kaufman
The Economics of Labor Markets
Fifth Edition

Kennett
*A New View of Comparative
Economic Systems*

Kennett and Lieberman
*The Road to Capitalism: The Economic
Transformation of Eastern Europe and the
Former Soviet Union*

Kreinin
International Economics:
A Policy Approach
Eighth Edition

Mankiw
Principles of Economics
Second Edition
(also available in Micro, Macro, Brief
Macro, and Essentials paperbacks)

Nicholson
Intermediate Microeconomics
and Its Application
Eighth Edition

Nicholson
Microeconomic Theory: Basic
Principles and Extensions
Seventh Edition

Ramanathan
Introductory Econometrics
with Applications
Fourth Edition

Rukstad
Corporate Decision Making in the World
Economy: Company Case Studies

Rukstad
Macroeconomic Decision Making in the
World Economy: Text and Cases
Third Edition

Salvatore
Managerial Economics:
In a Global Economy
Fourth Edition

Samuelson and Marks
Managerial Economics
Third Edition

Santerre and Neun
Health Economics: Theories, Insights,
and Industry Studies
Revised Edition

Scarth
Macroeconomics: An Introduction
to Advanced Methods
Third Edition

Sexton
Exploring Economics: Pathways
to Problem Solving
(also available in Micro and Macro
paperbacks)

Stockman
Introduction to Economics
Second Edition
(also available in Micro and Macro
paperbacks)

Walton and Rockoff
History of the American Economy
Eighth Edition

Welch and Welch
Economics: Theory and Practice
Sixth Edition

Yarbrough and Yarbrough
The World Economy: Trade and Finance
Fifth Edition

To Lily and Michael

INTRODUCTION

The area of comparative economics, it is safe to say, has altered a great deal in the past decade. The largest change was prompted by the political and economic revolutions that swept the Soviet Union and its satellite states in the late 1980s. The system of centralized command planning that had served since the 1920s as the polar alternative to market capitalism first faltered, then attempted to reform itself, and ultimately collapsed. The establishment of about two dozen independent economies, all trying to move to more liberal market regimes, focused an enormous amount of attention on the methodology, direction, and pace of institutional change. Multilateral organizations like the IMF, the World Bank, and the EBRD turned their attention as never before on the formerly centrally planned economies. The problems of transition forced economists to look with new intensity at the functioning of their own market economies and the institutions necessary for fostering efficient functions.

While it was clear that change led toward some form of market solution, its ultimate destination was open to doubt. Some economists advocated a market solution pure and lacking in government intervention to a degree unseen in any Western economies. Others favored a liberal Anglo-Saxon model, while a more *dirigiste* solution, as seen in continental Western Europe, was also proposed. At the point in time that transition from socialism to market began, the East Asian economies, particularly Japan and Korea, enjoyed much apparent success, and state-led capitalism presented a plausible model for the formerly socialist states: a strong relationship forged between government and a few powerful industrial groups with the potential to promote growth while retaining political control. As we will see in the text, the debate over the direction of change and the accompanying research on the relationship of institutions and performance has informed and enlivened the study of comparative economics.

PURPOSE

This book introduces students to the systems of capitalism seen in both Europe and Asia, before launching into a fuller discussion of centralized planning, its downfall, and the problems of transition. It also integrates issues that have become an important part of contemporary economic thought; in particular, law and legality, corruption, principal/agent problems, market contestability, the problem of regulation, and the consequences of government failure are part of this discussion.

The book is designed to be taught in a 13-week semester at a rate of roughly two chapters a week. While it can "stand alone," a course for upper-level students would benefit from supplementary readings such as those suggested at the end of each chapter. Moreover, both students and faculty are welcome to visit my Web site at http://irving.vassar.edu/ComparativeEconomics/index.html where they will be able to access some material electronically, and be guided toward useful resources of data and information.

ORGANIZATION

Part 1 gives a basic introduction to the study of comparative economics. Chapter 1 looks at how economic systems may be compared and contrasted, while chapter 2 gives a perspective on how and why economic institutions have changed over time. Part 2 deals with the broad outline of how a market economy functions, the principal sources of market failure, and the potential benefits and costs of government intervention. While it is possible to read this section with little or no formal economic training, I have assumed that most students will have had at the very least an introductory course in microeconomics that will give them a broader knowledge of competitive economies than I am able to provide in this space.

Part 3 covers capitalism in Europe, discussing the French and the Swedish economies, as well as the evolution of the European Union, certainly one of the most important economic and political events of our times. The studies of the two countries are included for particular purposes. Chapter 6 looks at France with a focus on a possible source of market failure, the absence of information, and its amelioration through the use of indicative planning. In chapter 7, Sweden is studied for its aggressive attempts to establish an egalitarian distribution of income while leaving the ownership of production in private hands. The evolution of the institutions of the European Union is handled in chapter 8, while the economic consequences of the EU are more thoroughly discussed in chapter 9.

Part 4 is devoted to the Asian economies, starting with the first of the "late industrializers," Japan, and moving on to Korea (chapters 10 and 11). Reform in China, an immense and important topic, is covered in chapter 12. As the world's most populous state and the largest practitioner of central planning, China's dramatically rapid economic growth and the singular path of its movement toward a market economy make it a compelling object of study. Less fully than some courses may require, chapter 13 covers smaller Asian economies including Taiwan, Singapore and Indonesia. Chapter 14 is an evaluation of the phenomenon of the "Asian Miracle" that attempts to assess how much of the performance of these economies was "out of this world" and how much is explicable by the more extensive use of factors of production.

Part 5 is a retrospective look at Soviet planning with a particular eye to the system of incentives that led to its failure. Chapter 15 reviews Russian economic history and may be omitted by students with a good background, while chapter 16 assesses the performance and problems of centralized command planning as practiced in the USSR. Chapter 17 assesses the "participatory economy," both in theoretical terms and through the economic history of the Yugoslav state. Chapter 18 looks for the third way—some form of accommodation for socialism and the market. Part 6 evaluates the issues of transition, starting in Western Europe. Margaret Thatcher's reforms and their consequences are dealt with in chapter 19 and the reunification of Germany is studied in chapter 20. General issues of transition are introduced in chapter 21 and discussed in the Russian context. Finally, chapters 22 and 23 cover Poland and the Czech Republic.

ACKNOWLEDGMENTS

I want to acknowledge some intellectual and personal debts, with the usual thanks, while assuming all responsibility myself. I took my first classes in comparative economics from Herb Levine, and had my initial exposure to Soviet planning from Aron Katsenelinboigen, who I will always remember for his graphic depictions of human struggle in that outwardly technical process. Fate and my first job put me in an office next to Igor Birman, who tried to teach me about the Soviet system while I occasionally helped him to interpret Samuelson's *Economics*. My wife, Susan, first took me to Russia and let me see the system first hand. My children have suffered from my preoccupation over the years; to them the book is dedicated. Francis Lees of St. John's University, Ed Stuart of North Eastern Illinois, Berhanu Abegaz of the College of William and Mary, and several other reviewers evaluated my drafts with necessary good humor and patience. They made many good suggestions, some of which are reflected in the final text, and others probably should have been. Finally Cristina Carp served as typist, research assistant, and proofreader, and designed and constructed the Web page; without her I do not think I could have finished this project. Needless to say all errors of fact and interpretation are mine alone.

David Kennett
Vassar College
Poughkeepsie, N.Y.
kennett@vassar.edu

CONTENTS IN BRIEF

CONTENTS

CHAPTER 12
THE PEOPLE'S REPUBLIC OF CHINA 276

PART FIVE SOCIALIST ECONOMIES 350

CHAPTER 15
THE COMMAND ECONOMY 352

CHAPTER 16
THE OPERATION OF THE SOVIET PLANNED ECONOMY 371

A New View of
Comparative Economic Systems

INTRODUCTION TO
COMPARATIVE ECONOMICS

TYPES OF ECONOMIC SYSTEMS

INTRODUCTION

The study of comparative economics has changed a great deal in recent years. The principal reason for this has been the collapse of the Soviet **centrally planned economic system** in the late 1980s. Soviet central planning had served for many years as the clear polar alternative to the variety of capitalist systems that exist in the West. At the same time reform swept the Soviet Union, the various offsprings of the Soviet system also underwent large-scale reform from within or change brought about by external forces. In China, economic restructuring and liberalization, although largely without the political counterpart so visible in the Russian experience, have transformed that economy in recent years into one of the fastest changing and most rapidly growing on earth. Yugoslavia, the most frequently studied model of collectively owned, **worker-managed socialism,** has broken apart and much of its economy lies in ruins. Even Cuba, the bastion of socialism in the Western Hemisphere, deprived of support and subsidy from the Soviet Union, has ruefully been contemplating change.

In one sense market capitalism has emerged the victor in a war of competing economic ideologies that has been waged for much of the 20th century. Whether this will be a permanent state of the world, an irreversible and linear evolution in economic and political arrangements, or merely a short-lived development is too soon to judge. A drift of popular sentiment back toward the former Communists has been a feature of recent elections in Eastern Europe and the former Soviet bloc, suggesting that it may be premature to assume that central planning is buried forever. Moreover, at the same time that economies based on centralized planning were faltering and forced toward reform, new variants of the capitalist model were emerging, especially in East Asia, as alternatives to the western model. Japan long ago joined the ranks of the "developed nations," and its success in terms of growth and world trade led to great interest in its institutions, its economic culture, and its policies. These features of the Japanese economy are significantly different from the capitalist economies of Europe and North America.

Interest in **Pacific-rim capitalism** has been reinforced by the emergence of the new **Asian Tigers.** Nations that only a decade ago were universally regarded as "developing" have made a leap into late industrial development. The economies of South Korea, Taiwan, Singapore, and Thailand—until the recent Asian financial crisis—exemplified rapid and sustained growth, and western nations looked to learn lessons from their success. Scrutiny of their systems of economic organization increased accordingly, and investigation of the root causes of their present difficulties will doubtless provide further insights into the operation of alternative systems.

Even within the core of Western Europe there has been substantial change. Sweden was for the entirety of the postwar period the nation whose economic system best exemplified the concept of **social democracy** and the **welfare state.** However, faced with slow growth and a deteriorating trade position, the Swedish system underwent considerable change in recent years, moving away from the extreme of egalitarian social democracy toward more liberal capitalism. At the same time, the evolution of the original 6-member European Common Market into the 15-member European Union is a development of the greatest importance. The melding together of the various economies of western Europe, which had until recently quite disparate institutions and traditions, is in itself a bold step. The replacement of the national currencies of 11 of the member countries of the European Union with the "Euro," and the necessary constraints on national fiscal and monetary freedom, will require substantial institutional change. Moreover, the proposed expansion of the European Union to include current economies in transition, which less than a decade ago were fully centrally planned, is a major challenge. The strong interventionist spirit of the European Union is itself a product of the active role of government traditional in the continental member states. This will reinforce the contrast between the American (or Anglo-Saxon) concept of the relationship of government and business and the European concept, sometimes called the **Rhine model.**

These changes, far from making the study of comparative economics redundant, have provided us with a new and incisive way of looking at how economies are organized and how they function. The process of transition in Eastern Europe, to take one example, has forced us to compare the institutions of capitalism and socialism in a new and very fundamental way. The dramatic and almost uniformly experienced collapse of output in the economies of the former Soviet bloc and the unexpectedly slow pace of recovery have forced us to evaluate very carefully the differences in institutions, culture, history, and policy that have made this transition more painful than had been predicted.

WHAT IS AN ECONOMIC SYSTEM?

In every society, whatever its structure, size, wealth, or level of development, certain economic decisions must be made. The most important of these decisions may be reduced to three types:

> First, it must be decided *what* goods and services are to be produced, and in what quantities. This is generally referred to as the **production decision,** often represented in stylized form as the familiar "guns versus butter" choice of elementary textbooks. Such a two-dimensional representation simplifies society's choices and obscures the fact that decisions must be made between a huge array of goods. Nevertheless, the choice of the mix of goods that are to be produced must be faced and made in some way.

Second, a decision must be made about *how* these goods will be produced: what combination of factors of production (generally speaking labor, land, and capital—though all of these are not homogenous) will be used, and through the agency of what organizations this will be achieved. This is the **choice of technique** decision.

The third set of choices relates to *who* will receive the benefit of this production. This is the **distributional decision.** It is important to note that all three of these broad types of decision have a temporal dimension to them. Since we can, through saving and investment and through the choice of how rapidly we deplete or exhaust our scarce resources, alter the time pattern of consumption, we have a choice of whether to consume now or later, and implicitly whether to benefit the current population or their descendants.

The mechanism by which these decisions are made within any economy is referred to as the economic system. The study of how such systems differ between economies, and how differences in systems determine economic outcomes, comprises the field of study of comparative economic systems.

The concept of a **system** has been borrowed, albeit rather loosely, from the physical sciences. In those disciplines, a system is thought of as a collection of objects essentially closed to outside forces, within which the behavior of the objects is subject to physical laws. An economic system consists of analogies to the same essential ingredients. On the one hand are the objects, in this case economic institutions, and on the other hand are the "laws" (which in economic analysis include not only formal laws but also rules, procedures, and customs) that govern the interaction of these institutions.

Although broadly analogous, there are important differences between the physical sciences and what we observe in economies. First, the institutions within an economic system do not always merely respond passively to the forces acting on them. Rather, many institutions (which are organizations of human beings) are not merely inert, but have specific objectives that they seek to further. (In addition, these objectives may change over time.) Second, while the laws that govern physical behavior are immutable, the "laws" that govern interaction within economies are by and large observed regularities and subject to change as culture and customs evolve.

ECONOMIC INSTITUTIONS

The kinds of institutions that characterize a modern industrial economy, whether that of the United States or any other developed market economy, will be familiar to most students from their courses in introductory economics, but some review is useful to set the stage. All economies do not, of course, possess identical sets of institutions. Different histories, cultures, ideologies, and priorities have led to different institutional forms and also lead to differences in the way that these institutions interact.

HOUSEHOLDS

The most fundamental components of almost any economic system are the **households.** On the one hand, households are the suppliers of labor, and on the other, they are the ultimate consumers of the bulk of the goods and services produced in the economy. In most systems (the prime exceptions being primarily socialist economies), households are also responsible for the supply of capital and land to the productive sector. The household in some form is common to practically all economies, developed, less developed, and socialist, though the size, composition, makeup and decision-making responsibilities differ substantially, even within industrial economies.

Households must be regarded as having objectives or goals. Mainstream economists generally consider that the household is a "utility maximizing" institution and make assumptions about what factors enter into its utility function. We should note that utility maximization cannot be equated with a desire to maximize income or even material well-being, although today we seem to have a general belief that more material output is better than less. Other objectives, such as a desire for prestige, gaining satisfaction from leisure, patriotism, or a preference for an equitable distribution of income, may form important arguments in a household's utility function. Moreover, the nature of the utility function will vary from society to society, bearing the stamp of history, culture, and ideology.

GOVERNMENT

Common to all economies, except the most primitive ones (or theoretical conceptions of anarchy), is some form of government. In a modern industrialized economy, the government is complex and its authority far-reaching. All contemporary governments are, to some extent, involved in the establishment and protection of economic and individual rights, the regulation of business and industry, the provision of goods and services, and the redistribution of income. Because the government embodies a powerful set of agencies, and because it can make and change the rules by which the economy operates through legislation, it ranks, even in quite liberal societies, as one of the important institutions for answering the fundamental economic questions—*what, how,* and *for whom?*—that were introduced earlier. Clearly, the means by which a government derives its power, and the degree of control that it exercises over the behavior of its citizens and the other institutions that constitute the economy, varies greatly from country to country.

The goals, or objectives, that the governments choose to pursue may also vary a great deal. When we speak of goals we are generally talking of something quite broad. For example, goals may be such vague objectives as "an accelerated rate of growth of output," "a more even distribution of income," "an increase in expected longevity," and so forth. A shift in these goals, or in the strategy of their pursuit, can take two forms: either a thorough-going reform of the system itself (as we are witnessing in Eastern Europe and the former Soviet Union) or the application of different **policies** operating within the existing system. The boundary between systemic reform and a radical policy initiative is necessarily a gray area. For example, many countries have embarked on extensive privatization by selling large parts of publicly owned (or "nationalized") industry to the private sector. Clearly when this takes place on the scale of the mass privatization that occurred in Russia, it constitutes systemic change. But the sale of some public corporations within the context of the French economy is a different matter. Even the most radical "western" privatization, that of Margaret Thatcher in Britain in the period of roughly 1981 to 1989, is generally regarded more as shift of policy within the mixed capitalist system than as a systematic change.

Policies may be defined as the actions that a government takes within an existing system in pursuit of its objectives. Examples of policies are the establishment of a fiscal deficit in an attempt to stimulate growth in national income, the use of taxes and expenditures to redistribute economic well-being from one group to another, the commitment of government to provide investment funds for industry, the creation of a national health service, and so forth. Such policies are facilitated by the use of **instruments** like the income tax, the money supply, government expenditure, or the structure of tariffs. Changes in these instruments are usually called **measures.** Thus a government of a mixed capitalist economy (system) might decide to reduce (measure) the income tax (instrument) to create a fiscal deficit (policy) to reduce unemployment (objective).

In the real world, things are necessarily more complex than depicted here, and more incisive analysis can help us understand how a system operates. For example, it is generally an oversimplification to view the government as a monolithic entity with a single objective. All governments consist of different ministries and agencies, each with different powers and functions. In all likelihood the agencies of government also have different objectives. This occurs because agencies cater to different constituencies, and they are likely to become "captured" by those interests and serve them rather than some larger conception of the public good. For example, one arm of government might be responsible for furthering industrial growth, while another might have responsibility for the environment. There are likely to be frequent occasions in which the interests of these agencies are in conflict, and the outcome itself is a matter of political interaction.

ENTERPRISES

The third broad group of institutions is composed of economic enterprises that produce goods and services. These may be owned privately, cooperatively (by a small group, usually consisting of the workforce), or socially (by society as a whole, through the agency of some level of government). Even within a market economy enterprises may take on a wide range of institutional forms, and this affects their nature and performance. For example, they may be "incorporated," a form that carries with it the important characteristic of limited liability and a particular tax treatment. In turn, privately owned corporations fall into two groups. They may be "public" in that their shares are traded freely, generally on a stock exchange, or "privately held," whereby ownership is limited to a small group of individuals and shares are not available for purchase or sale beyond that group.

Other forms of enterprise in a market economy are partnerships or wholly owned proprietorships.

Economic enterprises, like households, have to pursue objectives. Economists commonly assume that in a free-enterprise economy, privately owned firms are profit maximizers, at least in the long-run. However, a growing body of research on the actual behavior of firms, and managers within firms, suggests that this may be too simple a view. Conflicting goals such as maximizing market share, rapid sales growth, employment maximization, or management's well-being may all play a role, at least in the short term.

Moreover, even if profit maximization is the clear and overt objective, all firms that are more complex than a single proprietorship with no employees are beset with **principal/agent problems.** These arise because of the difficulty of getting workers, or management for that matter (the *agents*), to act in the way that best serves the interests of the owners (the principal). Thus, although the ultimate owner of the firm (that is, shareholders) might favor profit maximization, the management and the workers pursue their own goals (leisure, prestige, income), which might well be in conflict with this.

LABOR ORGANIZATIONS

A fourth important set of institutions is composed of labor organizations, which may have a substantial influence on employment, workplace technique, and compensation. By uniting and solidifying the interests of individual workers and asserting a degree of monopoly power in labor negotiations, labor unions can have important influence in decision making in the economy. Moreover, across economies unionization has taken on different forms, and this has resulted in various methods of political expression. One clear distinction is between **company unions** (which are common in Japan) and the **craft** or **occupational unions** (which are the norm in several European economies). In most of continental Europe it is generally accepted that labor has an important role at the governmental level. In some countries (for example, Sweden), labor is an actor in national negotiations to determine wages, while in others (like France) the unions have an official status in setting the objectives and priorities of governmental policy and the National Plan.

In the socialist, centrally planned economies, labor unions were largely powerless. The ideology of socialism asserted that since the means of the production were owned by the people, there was, in theory, no need for workers to organize to protect their interests. Free labor organizations were therefore frequently repressed and only unions licensed by the state or party were allowed. Almost paradoxically the collapse of the "Workers' State" in Poland was brought about largely by the growth of Solidarity, the "alternative" labor union opposed to the state.

NONGOVERNMENTAL ORGANIZATIONS

There is a growing recognition by economists and political scientists of the importance of a fifth set of institutions that play an important role in modern economies. These are the nongovernmental organizations (or **NGOs**), and they have attracted considerable attention in recent years. The NGO sector is composed of organizations that are not only nongovernmental, but are also nonprofit-making, distinguishing them from firms in a capitalist economy. Broadly speaking, NGOs fall into three groups: organizations that exist to provide services (like the United Way in the United States or various developmental and health agencies that operate in the developing world), organizations that serve as centers of common interest (hobby groups and church organizations), and lobbying groups (like the AARP).[1] They may fulfill some of the functions that are also served by government (in education, poverty relief, health care, and so on). Given the determination to reduce the size of the governmental sector, which seems to be common to all developed market economies, the role of NGOs may be expected to expand. Most people would regard this increase in voluntarism to be beneficial to welfare; an NGO can replace some of the functions of government without needing to raise taxes or encountering the excess burdens that accompany taxing and spending. However, NGOs serve mainly the interest of a particular group and cannot be relied on to preserve the interests and well-being of minorities, and they frequently do burden the public purse because of the tax-exempt privileges extended to donors.

MARKETS

A final set of institutions that must be noted in almost any economy is made up of the markets within which these institutions interact. In broad terms, these are the goods market: the labor market, the financial markets, the stock markets, and the commodity markets. However, any "market" economy is characterized by many thousands of markets. These are organized in different ways in different economies, and the study of how they differ is generally termed comparative economics. The depth, complexity, and richness of markets is an important factor in determining economic outcomes.

RULES

While this is far from an exhaustive inventory of the institutions found in a modern economy, it provides an idea of their range and variety. These institutions interact with each other in answering the production, distribution, and choice of technique decisions. Let us now turn to the rules that govern these interactions. It is important to take note from the outset that the rules that govern any society are complex and hybrid. They consist of both *formal rules,* which are embodied and codified as **laws** and **regulations,** and *informal customs,* **practices** and **beliefs,** which influence behavior. While at first glance it might seem that laws should be the more important, the force of custom and tradition is decisive in many issues.

FTN

[1] The American Association of Retired Persons is the powerful organization that lobbies on behalf of senior citizens in the United States.

Moreover, custom, culture, and tradition determine not only the nature of the rules by which institutions interact, but they also shape the nature of the institutions themselves.

THE LEGAL FRAMEWORK

All institutions within a society must operate under the rule of law. Laws are, by definition, those rules that are made by some level of government[2] and rely on the power of the government, which we may think of as having a monopoly on force in most societies, to ensure that they are obeyed. In a modern economy the system of laws has a very wide range. As well as constituting a criminal code, laws also determine a variety of factors that are vital for the functioning of the economy. These include such things as the establishment and enforcement of contracts, the nature of property and property rights, the obligations of firms and individuals under the tax system, environmental regulations, health codes, the minimum age of workers, (in some societies) the minimum wage that must be paid to workers, what firms must disclose to their stockholders and potential owners, and how firms and individuals may enter bankruptcy.

Such laws help to determine both the character and the behavior of economic institutions. For example, the structure of the U.S. financial system has been shaped by a series of federal and state regulations that limit the activities of commercial banks, investment banks, brokerage houses, and other institutions. These regulations mean that the organization and functioning of U.S. banking will be different from that in, for example, Germany, where different laws apply. Germany has no equivalent to the Glass-Steagall Act, which mandates the formal separation of the activities of investment and commercial banks. Consequently, in Germany **universal banks** (sometimes referred to as U-banks), which perform a wide range of functions, are the norm, and the relationship between the financial and productive sectors is quite different from the one in the United States. Laws concerning the incorporation of firms and the liabilities of partnerships dictate the type of enterprises that may exist and the extent of their activity.

Laws mean little unless they are enforced. We can be quite deceived about the nature of a society, or an economy, if we only look at the laws as they are on the books and not at how they are actually administered. Later in this book we will discuss the nature of **legality** within society, a state which requires not only a comprehensive set of mutually consistent laws but also the expectation that those laws will be generally and impartially enforced.

---

[2]Some clarification of the idea of making laws might be in order here. Laws are often made by active legislative initiative, but in many societies they evolve through precedent and may be codified after the fact or remain in force without any real form of codification. The example of this most familiar to most readers is the evolution of English Common Law.

RULES WITHIN ORGANIZATIONS

The behavior of economic institutions is not wholly determined by the laws and their enforcement. Institutions must operate within an externally imposed legal framework, but they also have self-imposed rules that limit their behavior. This is true for government departments, stock markets, corporations, charities, or labor unions. Organizational rules are generally written and codified and must be subsidiary to the laws of society, at least as far as those laws are enforced; they have a pervasive effect on the organization of economic activity.

PROCEDURES

On a level less formal than rules, the day-to-day running of all organizations tends to be governed through procedures, which have less formal force than laws or the regulations by which organizations define themselves. It is tempting to presume that because they are less formal than laws or regulations, such procedures might be more easily changed; but in reality they might be more enduring. Some examples may be employment practices, systems of promotion, the way purchasing proceeds, and so forth.

CUSTOM, CULTURE, AND TRADITION

Also determining the nature of economic outcomes and the behavior of economic actors within an economic system is the force of custom. Different societies do things in different ways and have particular beliefs and prejudices, which may be just as powerful in their effect as formal regulations or even procedures. These customs can influence a wide range of economic variables. For example, in some societies custom discourages girls from receiving anything above the most rudimentary education, a fact that greatly changes the supply of labor, productivity, and, in turn, per-head incomes. Some societies are, by custom, high consuming, while others have deep-seated prejudices favoring saving and accumulation.

Such factors are frequently neglected but they can have a decisive influence on the direction and performance of an economy. In a recent book,[3] Francis Fukuyama made the case for the vital role of social institutions and cultural values in determining economic outcomes. He argued that a distinction can be drawn between "high-trust" societies (among them Japan, Germany, and the United States), which have developed the flexible civic institutions that a modern economy demands in greater abundance, and "low-trust" (or "familistic") nations like China, France, and Italy. The presence of these institutions reduces the costs of economic interchange and this greatly facilitates commerce and leads to more rapid growth. It is, on the face of it, an interesting argument, although Fukuyama's premises may be questioned. For example, why is the United States (the most lawyer-ridden and

---

[3] Francis Fukuyama, *Trust: The Social Virtues and the Creation of Prosperity* (New York: Free Press, 1995). See also the review in *The Economist*, 2 September 1995.

litigious society in the world) classed with Japan (which is the developed economy with the fewest lawyers) as "trusting societies"?

Economies differ not only in their institutions and the rules that govern the interaction of those institutions but also in the endowments of wealth that they possess. Each economy has at any point in time a stock of capital and resources, which is in part the result of the geography, geology, and climate of the country and in part the consequence of the cumulative impact of actions taken by individuals, productive enterprises, and governments in the past. These actions consist of the myriad savings, consumption, and investment decisions that determine the stock of human and physical, human-made capital that is inherited from previous generations. While this wealth exists in many forms, it is convenient and useful for our current purpose to group it into three broad types.

NATURAL ASSETS

The most fundamental part of the wealth base consists of the **natural resources** of the economy. These consist primarily of minerals (like coal, oil, natural gas, ores), which are located within the ground of a nation's economy, and the naturally occurring vegetation, like forests, which are found on it. Also included in an inventory of natural resources should be water resources and certain topographical features that facilitate communication (harbors, navigable rivers, and the like). In addition, we should consider the weather and such naturally occurring features that might, for example, attract tourism.

Closely linked to natural resources is the stock of productive agricultural land. The value of this to the economy is determined by both the generosity of nature and the incidence of human-made improvements on it that create or enhance productivity. These are composed of infrastructural developments (like irrigation in the American West or the terracing of rice paddies in Asia). Agricultural land is in fact a combination of nature and human-made resources, although some of the improvements (clearing forests, canalizing rivers) are so ancient as to defy any normal scheme of asset valuation that would dissociate the improvement from the value of the natural resource itself.

PRODUCED ASSETS

Economists, in their analyses, have tended to focus a lot of attention on an economy's stock of produced assets, the extant accretion of man-made capital that was created in previous periods.[4] The most easily envisaged examples of this stock are

---

[4]Marx in fact referred to capital as "dead labor."

the machines, the factories, and the inventories of finished goods and goods-in-process in **industry capital.** That, however, is only part of the picture. We must also take notice of the social capital embodied in roads, bridges, dams, schools, universities and the like.

HUMAN CAPITAL

The most important form of resources on a global level are embodied as **human capital** in the skills and education of individuals. A recent World Bank Study found that almost two-thirds of the value of accumulated wealth in the world lies in human capital. The importance of human capital is most obvious in the highly developed industrial nations. Japan's land and natural resources are of trivial consequence compared to the value of its human capital, which is overwhelmingly the reason it ranks third in the world in resource wealth on a per-head basis. The same is true of Germany. Similarly, Singapore, an island state with few natural resources (though its location gives the land value), is wealthy because of a highly educated and enterprising population.

HOW WEALTH VARIES AMONG NATIONS

There have been several recent attempts to quantify the distribution of these resources, which represent the stock of wealth available to an economy, and to compare the relative endowments of different economies, as well as the changes within an economy. The World Bank's Environmentally Sustainable Development Project embarked on the bold step of attempting to quantify the wealth in each of 192 nations.[5]

The explicit recognition that a country's wealth is the combination of various forms of capital—produced, natural, and human resources—led to new thinking on what constitutes wealth and how it might be measured. The figures that the World Bank comes up with are necessarily somewhat rough, and there will always be debate on the accuracy and appropriateness of some of the estimation procedures. However, the results are interesting.

In the World Bank analysis, produced assets (fixed capital and infrastructure) have been estimated using a perpetual inventory method, using flow data on depreciation and investment to estimate the current stock of capital. The value of natural resources has been estimated by classifying the land into cropland, grassland, forests, and other uses, valuing each as a multiple of per-head income in the country where it is located. (This means that an acre of cropland in Latin America represents less "wealth" than an acre in, say, the Netherlands purely because of location.) Adjustments were made for subsoil assets and standing timber.

---

[5]See *Expanding the Measure of Wealth: Indicators of Environmentally Sustainable Development* (Washington, D.C.: World Bank, 1997), and *Monitoring Environmental Progress: A Report on Work in Progress* (Washington, D.C.: World Bank, 1995).

■ **TABLE 1.1**

ESTIMATES OF THE WEALTH OF NATIONS, DOLLARS PER HEAD: SELECTED NATIONS, 1995

Rank for Total Wealth	Country	Total Wealth	Human Capital	Produced Capital	Natural Resources
1	Australia	835,000	175,350	58,450	592,850
11	United States	421,000	248,390	67,360	105,250
21	United Kingdom	324,000	268,920	45,360	9,720
22	Singapore	306,000	260,100	45,900	0
31	Saudi Arabia	184,000	51,520	33,120	101,200
39	Greece	142,000	106,500	19,880	15,620
54	Russia	98,000	14,700	14,700	68,600
61	Mexico	74,000	54,020	8,140	11,840
71	Estonia	55,000	39,050	7,700	7,700
87	Iran	38,000	12,920	14,060	11,020
96	Turkey	34,000	24,480	5,100	4,420
117	Romania	17,000	11,900	2,890	2,210
161	China	6,600	5,082	990	528
175	Kenya	3,800	2,128	1,216	456
181	Rwanda	2,900	2,030	638	261
192	Ethiopia	1,400	560	294	546
	World Average	86,000	55,040	13,760	17,200

SOURCE: World Bank, *Sustainability and the Wealth of Nations,* 1995.

In this analysis, human resources were valued as the residual, after allowing for the effect of natural resources and produced capital. Such a measure includes therefore not only the human capital embodied in individuals by virtue of the education, experience, and training, but also the economic value of the social institutions. Also included in this residual effect would be any cultural factors that might make that society more productive than another. Significantly for the issue at hand, the measure of human capital is conflated with the efficiency of the economic system. Notwithstanding these problems, the results of the study give considerable food for thought. Figures for some selected nations are provided in Table 1.1.

1. As a global average, almost two-thirds, 64 percent, of total wealth is embodied in human resources composed of individual human capital and social institutions.

2. The wealthiest nation on a per-head basis is Australia, which possesses large natural wealth distributed among a small, but highly educated population.

3. Most of the "top 25" nations in terms of aggregate wealth have natural assets comprising less than 10 percent (and most of these less than 5 percent) of total wealth, further suggesting that accrued human capital rather than initial resource endowment is the key to prosperity.

4. The variation in per-head wealth between nations is even more pronounced than the variation in per-head income. Australia, at the top, has about 500 times the wealth of Ethiopia, the bottom country.

THE DETERMINATION OF ECONOMIC OUTCOMES

By economic outcomes we mean measurable consequences like per-head income, the distribution of income, employment, inflation, and even demographic factors like life expectancy. These outcomes are the result of the interaction between the available resources, the institutions, and the rules that govern the system. This might be easy to envisage in terms of a functional statement:

$$O_i = F_i(NR_i, PA_i, HC_i)$$

where O represents the economic outcomes, NR the natural resources, PA the stock of produced assets, and HC human capital. In structure it is very like a production function,[6] but what differs is that the economic systems and indeed the goals of all of the observations under review (the economies) are different. Thus, the F_i are different for all economies. In part, comparative economics is concerned with how the goals of different economies vary, and how the systems of different economies contrast, such that wealth endowments result in different outcomes. Our problem, in fact, is why some societies use their factors of production more efficiently. In Mancur Olsen's words, we would like to know why some economies inefficiently "leave five dollar bills on the sidewalk" while other systems are much more adept at picking up such windfalls and using their resources productively.

SOME FUNDAMENTALS OF ECONOMIC SYSTEMS

Even a cursory glance at the world shows us that economic systems are complex and hybrid, embodying a range of features. However, there are some fundamental approaches that we may use to distinguish between different systems. There are three important dimensions in which economic systems differ from each other: the extent of individual rights (particularly as they pertain to property), the means of coordination of economic activity, and the incentive systems that influence the response of individuals.

THE NATURE AND EXTENT OF INDIVIDUAL RIGHTS

All systems of government put some constraints on the rights of individuals in economic matters, although the range and force of restraint differs dramatically. The extent of the rights that the government allows, either actively or passively, to

---

[6] Indeed, some in the World Bank look forward to the arrival of a general production function.

remain with the individual, coupled with the degree to which the state effectively protects and guarantees those rights against the incursions of other individuals (and possible incursions by the state itself), is of great importance in determining the shape and functioning of the economic system.

PROPERTY OWNERSHIP AND PROPERTY RIGHTS. The character of a society is determined largely by the extent of rights and freedoms that are allowed to individuals within it. From the point of view of studying the functioning of an economic system, one of the most significant of these rights is the right to own property. In practical terms almost every society, even the most collectively or socialistically organized, allows individuals the right to own some personal property, possibly limited only to food for consumption, clothing, and furniture. From an economic perspective, the most important issue is whether individuals (or groups of individuals) are allowed to own "the means of production"—the enterprises, organizations, tools, and inventories that are used to make goods and services.

The existence or otherwise of private ownership of the means of production is the basis for distinguishing between the two great "isms" that have dominated the study of comparative economic systems in this century. **Socialism** is a system predicated on the means of production being owned by the state. **Capitalism,** often taken as synonymous with "free enterprise," is predicated on the means of production being owned by individuals or freely associated groups of individuals.

However, on closer inspection *ownership* is not the simple matter that it might initially seem to be. What is commonly called ownership actually involves a series of potentially separable qualities or **property rights.** Of these, three are particularly important. The first of these is the right *to use* a good or resource in the way that the "owner" of the property sees fit. In some discussions, especially those pertaining to the debate on the efficacy of privatization, this is also known as the **control right.**[7] The second is the right *to receive income* or other benefits generated by the use of the property, also known as the **cash-flow right.** The last is the right *to exchange or sell* property at a price deemed appropriate by the seller—the **disposal right.** If these rights are together vested in individuals, they constitute the "right to engage in economic activity," since they confer the right to establish or acquire businesses, the right to manufacture goods, and the right to buy and sell goods.[8]

However, it is important to note that even in societies regarded as "free enterprise" or "capitalist" these rights are seldom unrestricted. For example, zoning restrictions and environmental regulations frequently constrain the nominal

---

[7]See, for example, Maxim Boycko, Andrei Shleifer, and Robert Vishny, *Privatizing Russia* (Cambridge, Mass.: MIT Press, 1995).

[8]This right to engage in economic activity was one of the fundamental rights demanded by Gregory Yavlinsky and Stanislav Shatalin, in the somewhat over optimistic "five hundred day plan," and defined in many ways the emergence of Russia from a socialist to a market economy.

owner's use of property. Such regulations take away some of the property rights of the owner and confer them upon others. An individual's right to use her property as she sees fit might be balanced by property rights of others, who have rights to clean air, light, or unpolluted water. Licensing prevents the entry into some industries, while other industries may be restricted as a governmental or private monopoly. Most developed market economies have systems of taxation that tax away some part of both corporate and personal income, an infringement of an individual's unrestricted right to income from property.

With respect to disposal rights, many societies with market-oriented economies choose at times to prevent owners from selling property, goods, or services to whomever and at prices that they see fit. Such restrictions might be short term and quite limited. In the United States, for example, there are laws that can be used to control prices in order to prevent "profiteering" after a natural disaster. However, some controls may be of longer duration. Recent history has produced examples of both general restrictions on price changes with a view to fighting inflation (which occurred under the Nixon administration), and on specific goods (e.g., gasoline, which happened during the oil crises of the 1970s). Rent control is a familiar feature in many western economies, and all market economies regulate the pricing behavior of privately owned utility companies to counterbalance monopoly power.

Across societies there is a spectrum of such restrictions on individual economic freedom. At one polar extreme are countries, fewer since the demise of the Soviet Union, who have adopted socialist economic systems and in which the economic rights of individuals are reduced to a minimum. For example, in the Soviet Union, before its dissolution and the subsequent economic liberalization in the successor states, virtually all of the means of production were owned by the state. As late as the 1980s it was estimated that 97 percent of total economic output in the Soviet Union, as well as East Germany and Czechoslovakia, was in the control of the state. This was not the result of the state outcompeting private enterprise, but rather the consequence of the denial of the right of individuals to own productive resources and to establish enterprises. At the other extreme are the highly laissez-faire states, for example Hong Kong under British rule, in which governmental restrictions on enterprise and the labor force were minimal.

Despite the fact that under such socialist systems practically all property rights are formally vested in the state, there is *de facto* a complex of property rights of individuals, established by practice and custom. Even in the most completely centrally planned systems, the management of enterprises and the political leadership did, in practical terms, have a species of ownership in the fruits of the enterprise. They had both some control rights (although most were held by the planners) and some cash-flow rights, since they could cream some income from the enterprises. It was well established that the *apparatchiks* in the Soviet Union had access to goods and privileges by virtue of their positions in the enterprises.[9]

---

[9] The property rights of the bureaucrats and enterprise managers constituted a recurrent barrier to the reform of centrally planned systems. As we will see when we look at the issues of transition, the success of any liberalization agenda is contingent on the ability to ensure the participation of key players

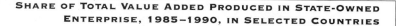

■ FIGURE 1.1

SHARE OF TOTAL VALUE ADDED PRODUCED IN STATE-OWNED
ENTERPRISE, 1985–1990, IN SELECTED COUNTRIES

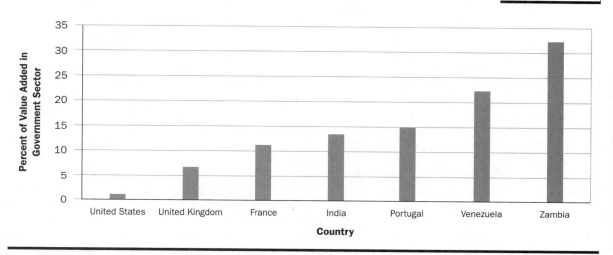

SOURCE: World Bank Development Report.

Freedom of Mobility and Employment.   Property rights are an important dimension of the economic system, but not the only set of rights that play an important role. Another relates to an individual's freedom to work and his or her choice of occupation and location. The ability to enter a profession or establish a business is an important right, the denial of which has a profound effect on the economic system.

Extent of Government Ownership.   A crude measure of economic freedom can be provided by the extent of government ownership of industry, services, and infrastructure. This varies greatly from country to country. Even within "free market" economies, governments control varying amounts of industry. Figure 1.1 shows the value added produced in the government sector in selected economies for the time period 1985–1990. It shows a considerable range. In the United States only 1.1 percent of total value occurred in the public productive sector, which is limited to a modest share of transportation (Amtrak), the U.S. Postal Service, and some utilities. In Europe there is a stronger tradition of government production. In

in the bureaucracy and enterprise management. They must be induced to give up the property rights and income that they held in the *status quo ante.* See, for example, Jan Winiecki, "Why Economic Reforms Fail in Soviet Type Systems: A Property Rights Approach," *Economic Inquiry* 28, no. 2 (April 1990): 195.

Britain, at that time undergoing the "Thatcher reforms," the share was 6.7 percent. Across the channel the French public sector had been expanded by the Socialist Mitterand government, which had nationalized several major corporations in the early 1980s and stood at 11.2 percent. In general, less developed countries are likely to have a larger government sector because the government promotes industry in an attempt to accelerate development. In oil-rich Venezuela, government-owned enterprise produces almost a quarter of total output, and in Zambia the comparable figure is almost one-third. It is important to recall that in centrally planned economies this figure at this time would have been close to 100 percent. These differences between countries apply not only to government production. There is also substantial variation in the range of services that public authorities provide. In some countries the government is a major supplier of health care, transportation, and financial services that are in other countries the province of private operation.

A better index of the role of government would be a measure of the degree of government interference in the economy, since government regulation of private industry can be a substitute for public ownership. Privatization, the transference of assets from the government to the private sector, is often accompanied by an increase in regulation. Consequently countries with a high degree of private economic activity may be among the most heavily regulated. However, though such an index would be informative, the extent of government interference is hard to quantify.

COMMAND VERSUS THE MARKET

Another dimension in which we may compare the structure of economic systems is the degree of reliance on planning, on the one hand, or the market, on the other, as means of coordinating economic activity. Under planning, the government determines, or at the very least seeks to influence, the answers to those important economic questions of *what, how,* and *who* discussed earlier. Under a market system, in contrast, it is the action of individuals, acting through the institutions that they comprise, each pursuing their own objectives, which leads to the set of outcomes. This process was called **the invisible hand** by **Adam Smith,** the great Scottish philosopher and economist, in his seminal book *An Inquiry into the Nature and Causes of the Wealth of Nations.*

COMMAND PLANNING. Planning can, of course, vary considerably in its scope and comprehensiveness. At one extreme we have the kind of economic organization established in the former Soviet Union, in which the government controlled almost all economic activity, and nearly all production was within enterprises owned and controlled by the government. In that system, detailed plans guided the flow of all resources, materials, and finished goods. Moreover, when those plans were finalized they were endowed with the force of law, and the economic actors on the production side were required to follow the procedures laid down, and achieve the targets prescribed, under threat of legal sanction. For obvious reasons this compulsive, top-down planning is called command planning. However there are gentler variants.

INDICATIVE PLANNING.   A different form of planning was pursued, and to a lesser extent is still practiced, in many Western European nations (particularly France) and in Japan. In those countries the government relies primarily on the voluntary and uncoerced response of the private sector to a set of guidelines produced as a result of discussions between government, industry, and labor. The objective of the planning exercise is largely to establish a common information base and a consensus on the broad direction of the economy. The expertise of the government in marshaling statistics and producing forecasts is important, and it is the government that provides the forum and formalizes the outcome. On the whole, this form of planning seeks to coordinate, unify, and identify "bottlenecks" and initiate remedial action. The powers of the government may be used to favor particular outcomes, but the scope of direct intervention is circumscribed (frequently limited to some intervention in credit markets) and scant scope for coercion. Because the main purpose of this planning is to lay out the likely course of the economy, this form is called **indicative planning,** and it is designed to function in parallel with, rather than to the exclusion of, the market.

CHOICE AND THE MARKET SYSTEM.   One of the most important features of the market system is such a limitation of coercion. The overall outcome of the economy must be determined primarily by the voluntary actions of individuals, and therefore the absence of bureaucratic constraints and the consequent maximization of the role of choice are essential features. As we will see in later chapters, the market cannot always be relied on to lead the economy to an optimal use of resources, nor are the distributional aspects of a market system always universally approved of. In particular, the market may lead to a pattern of income and access to basic consumer goods that might be considered unacceptable by some societies. The final distribution of income in a market and welfare are contingent on the initial distribution of wealth, position, and ability. There are also a variety of well-known instances of market failure in which government intervention may plausibly lead to higher levels of social satisfaction. These issues will be more fully discussed in chapter 4.

CENTRALIZATION VERSUS DECENTRALIZATION

Another way to classify economies is by looking at the centralization of the decision-making system. Again, we may take the example of Soviet-style planning, in which a single plan governing the use of all resources and the production of output was prepared, codified, and formalized as law. At the opposite pole we can conceive of close to pure market systems in which all of the important decisions are taken by individuals or private institutions and the function of government is largely to provide a framework and stability within which markets can operate. Between these two poles is a continuum of decentralization of power; where a particular economy lies on this continuum is a very useful way of gaining insight into how its system operates.

Later when the difficulties of centralized planning are more fully examined, we will see that one of the major problems in the implementation and maintenance of a centralized planning system is the quantity of information that must be gathered and accurately reported to the center. Only when the planners are well informed does the plan have a chance of using resources efficiently. This is more than a mechanical problem and involves important issues of incentives. There are certainly well-documented examples of situations in which incentives may motivate the actors at the periphery (plant managers, etc.) to gain advantage by systematically misreporting information to the center. A simple example is to overestimate the need for capital or raw materials in order to be sure to have plenty on hand to meet the output quotas that the planners assign.

INCENTIVES: MORAL, MATERIAL, AND COERCIVE

This leads us into a more general discussion of incentives. In all economic systems above the level of a totally individualistic economy we encounter what economists call principal/agent problems. As the name implies, this set of problems is concerned with the difficulties of creating a structure of incentives in order that someone appointed as the "agent" to act for a "principal" does indeed pursue the principal's interest rather than his or her own. At the simplest level, an agency problem may be represented as: "If I hire a worker how can I ensure that he works as hard and as well for me as I would for myself?"

This problem is pertinent from a **Robinson Crusoe economy** to the largest corporation, and to the most complex centrally planned economy. Why should Friday work hard when Crusoe is out of sight? Why should the management of IBM act in the interest of shareholders, who are ultimately the owners, rather than in their own interests? Why should workers or management in a factory pursue the targets that the architects of a central economic plan lay down, rather than act to maximize their own welfare?

There are three general ways to address the agency problem. One is to use **moral persuasion** to exhort actors to maximum performance. In such a scheme the management or government (principals) expect people (the agents) to behave appropriately because that is the "right thing to do," and perhaps find some way of granting prestige to those who conspicuously do well. This kind of incentive has frequently been found to be quite effective in the short run. In crises (wars, disasters, changes of regime), people are capable of making immense and seemingly irrational sacrifices because they have been exhorted to do so. Encouragements like "for the fatherland," "for the glory of God," or even John F. Kennedy's "ask not what your country can do for you, ask rather what you can do for your country" have all proved effective to some degree. Communist regimes, especially during their early stages, asked for and often received large sacrifices from significant sections of the population who worked "for the revolution" or "for the Party." Moral suasion can even be effective within enterprises and corporations. A high degree of identification with the company has often been cited as one of the causes of Japan's success. Governments can berate firms and achieve a modification of behavior, and sometimes rhetoric will even seem effective against other countries. However, in the longer run, moral incentives tend to be relatively ineffective unless they are backed up by the prospect of material improvement or, on the other hand, by the likelihood of **coercion.**

Material incentives apply when people work, and adjust the level and intensity of their work, because of the rewards, including advancement and promotion that are proffered. On the whole we tend to think of market economies relying almost exclusively on material incentives, and the consequent absence of coercion is commonly regarded as one of that system's strengths. Each actor in a pure market system enters only into economic exchanges or contracts willingly, whether it is as a consumer or a supplier of factors of production. Work represents leisure sacrificed and will be performed only when the material compensations of work outweigh the loss of utility resultant from reduced leisure. Were it generally a reality, this aspect of choice ensures that welfare is maximized under a capitalist system. In fact, not all capitalist systems are as market reliant as may be initially assumed. First, as we have noted, the initial endowments of factors are crucial in determining incomes, and the need to survive acts as an element of coercion. The "whip of hunger" does serve as a coercive element in many "market" societies. Second, within the workplace capitalism frequently resorts to coercion, through time-clocks, piece rates, supervision, and so forth. This may be less draconian in the developed market economies than it once was, but quite overt workplace coercion is common in the developing world.

We often consider planned economies to be more reliant on coercion than market systems, and this is true to some extent. Obviously under a command system of central planning, entry into many economic activities is limited since in general citizens cannot establish firms or form independent professional practices. Buying articles for resale, which in market economies would be regarded as healthy and necessary arbitrage or speculation, is illegal. In some command economies the government has a tight grip on the labor market giving the individual little choice in occupation, location, hours worked, or many other significant aspects of employment. However, this may not always be the case. Highly structured materials balance planning can be associated with a fair degree of liberalism in labor markets. For example, in the former Soviet Union it was illegal to be unemployed, and indeed there was no source of support for those who were able bodied and of working age if they did not work. However, there was a reciprocal responsibility to provide a job for everyone, no matter how inept a worker he or she may have been. There were restrictions on movement, and the central determination of wages made the market for labor clumsy and unresponsive, but on the whole workers responded to material incentives just as in the developed market economies. Workers performed because of piece rates, bonuses, or the prospect of advancement as well as supervision, the same as in the West. Management operated largely in its own best interest and indulged in what economists refer to as "rent-seeking behavior." Truly coercive systems of labor allocation and job performance are those that rely on slavery, serfdom, indenturement, or peonage.

Experience seems to suggest that the best system of labor incentives is an eclectic one. There is evidence that higher productivity results when workers feel less alienated from their job, the organization that employs them, and the products that they produce. This heightened sense of identification stems in part from security of job tenure if minimum performance requirements are met. It is hard to identify with a firm if it is about to fire you. In addition, it is useful to give workers a material stake in the enterprise, either through stock ownership or bonus systems, which encourage them to be personally interested in the firm's success. Such an approach combines the moral and the material, but it also has a coercive element since the pressure of interested coworkers is frequently an excellent source of peer supervision.

MEASURING THE DIFFERENCES IN ECONOMIC SYSTEMS

In recent years the clear contrast between the centrally planned and free market economies has been eroded by the changes that have swept through Eastern Europe and other planned economies. These developments have reinforced the recognition that the degree of economic freedom seen in various economies should be seen as a continuum rather than as polar extremes. In turn, this has led to attempts to measure the economic restrictions imposed in various economic systems and to compound the many dimensions of these restrictions into a single index. Such attempts must always be open to the criticisms that the methodology adopted, the grading methods, and the means of aggregation into an index are all highly subjective and therefore prone to manipulation.

Nevertheless, the results can be interesting and revealing if viewed with caution. We will consider here two aggregate indices, both of which really seek to measure the degree of economic freedom and the extent to which economic and political institutions support economic growth and integration into the global economic system.

ECONOMIC FREEDOM

Table 1.2 shows the indices of **economic freedom** for 1997 that have been prepared by the Heritage Foundation, a conservative United States–based organization. The index is computed by assessing the performance of the economy on each of 10 dimensions scoring on a 5-point scale, with 1 being "free" and 5 being "restricted." The 10 dimensions are as follows:

1. Trade policy
2. Taxation policy
3. Government consumption of output
4. Monetary policy
5. Capital flows and foreign investment

6. Banking policy
7. Wage and price controls
8. Property rights
9. Regulation policy
10. The presence of a black market

The relevance of most of these variables is self-evident. Low levels of tariffs and taxes, limited government consumption, an absence of price controls, a few restrictions of incoming foreign investment, and limited regulation in both banking and goods markets are all generally considered indicative of high degrees of economic freedom. A restrictive monetary policy is considered favorable because growth of the money supply may produce inflation, which acts as a hidden tax. Well-defined and well-enforced property rights are seen as essential to free enterprise, while the absence of a black market is another indicator of freedom to pursue market activity, since black markets prosper when socially beneficial activity is prohibited.

While most people would agree that the majority of these factors are correlated with economic freedom, there is room for dispute on some particulars. For example, the regulation of business might reduce the freedom of the capitalist, but it might enhance the freedom of the consumer if it is directed at limiting market failure resulting from limited information and externalities. A capitalist's freedom to pollute might at some point collide with a citizen's freedom to breathe, and the issue of whose rights and freedoms are paramount becomes central. In addition, simply averaging the scores on these many dimensions to arrive at the "final score" is a questionable practice. It is possible to argue that, say, a highly government-controlled banking structure is a bigger curb on domestic enterprise than high levels of import tariffs.

With that reservation in mind, some of the implications of the table are quite interesting. The five "freest" nations are all small with an average population of less than four million. The first three of them (Hong Kong, Singapore, and Bahrain) are really only city states with the specific function of serving as a free trade and banking area for a larger hinterland. It is hard to draw lessons for the design and conduct of an economic system from the experience of these countries, no matter how rapid their recent growth experience. It is simply not realistic to assume that Russia or India will undergo sustained growth by adopting the same policies as Hong Kong or Singapore.

ECONOMIC COMPETITIVENESS

Quite similar to the attempt to measure economic freedom have been the efforts to quantify the **competitiveness** of various economies. At least two international

■ TABLE 1.2

HERITAGE FOUNDATION INDICES OF ECONOMIC FREEDOM

Rank	Country	Score	Rank	Country	Score
1	Hong Kong	1.25	39	Malaysia	2.60
2	Singapore	1.30	40	Portugal	2.60
3	Bahrain	1.60	41	Spain	2.60
4	N. Zealand	1.75	42	Argentina	2.65
5	Switzerland	1.90	43	Belize	2.70
6	United States	1.90	44	Jordan	2.70
7	United Kingdom	1.95	45	Uruguay	2.70
8	Taiwan	1.95	46	Paraguay	2.75
9	Bahamas	2.00	47	Morocco	2.75
10	Netherlands	2.00	48	Oman	2.75
11	Canada	2.05	49	Tunisia	2.75
12	Czech Rep.	2.05	50	Costa Rica	2.80
13	Denmark	2.05	51	Barbados	2.80
14	Japan	2.05	52	Guatemala	2.80
15	Luxembourg	2.05	53	Israel	2.80
16	Belgium	2.10	54	Philippines	2.80
17	UAE	2.10	55	Saudi Arab.	2.80
18	Australia	2.15	56	Switzerland	2.80
19	Austria	2.15	57	Turkey	2.80
20	Ireland	2.20	58	W. Somoa	2.80
21	Germany	2.20	59	Bolivia	2.85
22	Chile	2.25	60	Botswana	2.85
23	Finland	2.30	61	Greece	2.85
24	Thailand	2.30	62	Indonesia	2.85
25	Estonia	2.35	63	Zambia	2.85
26	Kuwait	2.40	64	Hungary	2.90
27	Norway	2.45	65	Peru	2.90
28	So. Korea	2.45	66	Uganda	2.90
29	Sri Lanka	2.45	67	Benin	2.95
30	Sweden	2.45	68	Gabon	2.95
31	France	2.50	69	Latvia	2.95
32	Iceland	2.50	70	Lebanon	2.95
33	Panama	2.50	71	Malta	2.95
34	El Salvador	2.55	72	Namibia	2.95
35	Trinidad	2.55	73	Djibouti	3.00
36	Cyprus	2.60	74	South Africa	3.00
37	Italy	2.60	75	Ecuador	3.05
38	Jamaica	2.60	76	Kenya	3.05

Note: Only countries for which four or more surveys were extant are included.

SOURCE: The Heritage Foundation: Economic Freedom 1997.

Rank	Country	Score	Rank	Country	Score
77	Slovak Rep.	3.05	115	Albania	3.65
78	Colombia	3.10	116	Lesotho	3.65
79	Mali	3.10	117	Russia	3.65
80	Lithuania	3.10	118	Bangladesh	3.70
81	Papua NG	3.10	119	Croatia	3.70
82	Pakistan	3.10	120	India	3.70
83	Slovenia	3.10	121	Niger	3.70
84	Honduras	3.15	122	Zimbabwe	3.70
85	Poland	3.15	123	Congo	3.75
86	Fiji	3.20	124	Burundi	3.80
87	Ghana	3.20	125	Chad	3.80
88	Nigeria	3.20	126	China	3.80
89	Algeria	3.25	127	Mauritania	3.80
90	Madagascar	3.25	128	Belarus	3.85
91	Senegal	3.25	129	Georgia	3.85
92	Tanzania	3.25	130	Sierra Leone	3.85
93	Mongolia	3.30	131	Yemen	3.90
94	Brazil	3.35	132	Haiti	4.00
95	Ivory Coast	3.35	133	Mozambique	4.00
96	Mexico	3.35	134	Suriname	4.00
97	Moldova	3.35	135	Ukraine	4.05
98	Romania	3.40	136	Rwanda	4.20
99	Cape Verde	3.44	137	Sudan	4.20
100	Armenia	3.45	138	Syria	4.20
101	Dominican R.	3.45	139	Zaire	4.20
102	Guinea	3.45	140	Myanmar	4.30
103	Egypt	3.45	141	Angola	4.35
104	Burkina Faso	3.50	142	Azerbaijan	4.60
105	Guyana	3.50	143	Iran	4.70
106	Cambodia	3.55	144	Libya	4.70
107	Malawi	3.55	145	Somalia	4.70
108	Bulgaria	3.60	146	Vietnam	4.70
109	Cameron	3.60	147	Iraq	4.90
110	Ethiopia	3.60	148	Cuba	5.00
111	Gambia	3.60	149	Laos	5.00
112	Nepal	3.60	150	North Korea	5.00
113	Nicaragua	3.60			
114	Venezuela	3.60			

■ **TABLE 1.3**

THE WORLD ECONOMIC FORUM INDICES OF ECONOMIC COMPETETIVENESS, 1998

1	Singapore	2.16	28	China	−0.15
2	Hong Kong	1.91	29	Israel	−0.17
3	United States	1.41	30	Iceland	−0.18
4	United Kingdom	1.29	31	Indonesia	−0.19
5	Canada	1.27	32	Mexico	−0.23
6	Taiwan	1.19	33	Philippines	−0.31
7	Netherlands	1.13	34	Jordan	−0.42
8	Switzerland	1.10	35	Czech Rep.	−0.47
9	Norway	1.09	36	Argentina	−0.48
10	Luxembourg	1.05	37	Peru	−0.50
11	Ireland	1.05	38	Egypt	−0.52
12	Japan	0.97	39	Viet Nam	−0.53
13	New Zealand	0.84	40	Turkey	−0.57
14	Australia	0.79	41	Italy	−0.69
15	Finland	0.70	42	South Africa	−0.84
16	Denmark	0.61	43	Hungary	−0.85
17	Malaysia	0.59	44	Greece	−0.87
18	Chile	0.57	45	Venezuala	−0.98
19	Korea	0.39	46	Brazil	−1.10
20	Austria	0.37	47	Colombia	−1.12
21	Thailand	0.27	48	Slovakia	−1.17
22	France	0.25	49	Poland	−1.18
23	Sweden	0.25	50	India	−1.61
24	Germany	0.15	51	Zimbabwe	−1.70
25	Spain	0.02	52	Russia	−2.02
26	Portugal	−0.02	53	Ukraine	−2.51
27	Belgium	−0.03			

organizations produce such indices on an annual basis: the World Economic Forum and the Institute for International Management Development in Lausanne. Table 1.3 reproduces the World Economic Forum's (WEF) ranking of competitiveness, which is designed to assess the ability of the institutions embodied in that nation to produce long-term growth. Jeffrey Sachs, director of the Harvard Institute for International Development and cochairman of the Advisory Board of The Global Competitiveness Report, has described the concept this way:

In the [World Economic Forum] approach, "competitiveness" refers to the fitness of a country's economic institutions and structure to produce growth, in view of the overall structure of the world economy. In our meaning, an economy is "internationally competitive" if its institutions and policies will support sustained and rapid economic growth. Nations "compete" mainly in the sense of choosing alternative national economic institutions and strategies to promote more rapid growth and increases in living standards. Some efforts are successful, while other efforts end on "the scrap heap of history." The competitive nations are the ones that have chosen the institutions and policies that promote long-term growth. Our competitiveness index is designed to assess which countries have the best prospects for economic growth over the period of the next five to ten years, on the basis of each country's current economic conditions and institutions.

The basis of the WEF approach is therefore to evaluate a nation's institutions in terms of how well they fit the economy to compete in the international environment and to produce sustained economic growth.

Recent economic performance in terms of, say, growth in gross domestic product (GDP) is downplayed in order to highlight what the authors feel are the fundamental issues of strong institutional concern. The criteria examined include the following:

- The openness of the economy to international trade and finance
- The role of the government budget and regulation
- The development of financial markets
- The quality of the economic infrastructure
- The quality of business management
- The degree of labor market flexibility
- The quality of judicial and political institutions

The use of these criteria identifies those economies best suited to thrive in a capitalist world. Singapore topped the competitiveness list in 1998, followed by Hong Kong. The United States, in 3rd place, is the highest ranked of the large economies, well ahead of Japan in 12th place. The nations of the European Union, with high social expenditures and relatively inflexible labor markets, are generally further down the list. The United Kingdom, the member most at odds with overall EU policies, has risen to 4th place, well ahead of its fellows: France, Sweden, and Germany hold ranks 22–24. On this analysis Latin America still seems in urgent need of reform. The best-placed nation is Chile (18), but Mexico (32), Argentina (36), and Brazil (46), still face daunting economic challenges. Many of the most frequently discussed reforming and developing economies—the Czech Republic, Poland, India, Russia, and South Africa—fare quite badly and are all in the lower half. So too, interestingly, are many of the recent "growth stars" like China and Indonesia. This is largely because these economies at the moment are "competitive" only because they are able to exploit labor that is relatively cheap compared to other countries. In the view of the authors they have not established an institutional basis—a system—that will lead to sustained growth. Further reform and institutional change is therefore indicated.

THE EXTENT OF CORRUPTION

One important determinant of the real character of economic systems has been neglected in the economic literature until recently; this is the extent of **corruption,** which can result in the *real* system differing from the *nominally defined* system. "Whenever it is pervasive, corruption can deter investment, impede economic

■ **TABLE 1.4**

PERCEPTIONS OF CORRUPTION INDEX, SELECTED COUNTRIES, 1997

Rank	Country	Score	Variance	Rank	Country	Score	Variance
1	New Zealand	9.55	0.07	20	South Africa	5.62	2.35
2	Denmark	9.32	0.01	21	Portugal	5.56	0.66
3	Singapore	9.26	0.21	22	Malaysia	5.28	0.36
4	Finland	9.12	0.07	23	Taiwan	5.08	1.03
5	Canada	8.87	0.44	24	Spain	4.35	2.57
6	Sweden	8.87	0.11	25	Korea	4.29	1.29
7	Australia	8.80	0.54	26	Hungary	4.12	0.69
8	Switzerland	8.76	0.52	27	Turkey	4.10	1.33
9	Netherlands	8.69	0.63	28	Greece	4.04	1.65
10	Norway	8.61	0.78	29	Mexico	3.18	0.06
11	Ireland	8.57	0.17	30	Italy	2.99	6.92
12	United Kingdom	8.57	0.17	31	Thailand	2.79	1.69
13	Germany	8.14	0.63	32	India	2.78	1.63
14	United States	7.79	1.67	33	Philippines	2.77	1.13
15	Austria	7.13	0.36	34	Brazil	2.70	3.11
16	Hong Kong	7.12	0.48	35	Venezuala	2.66	3.18
17	France	7.00	3.32	36	Pakistan	2.25	1.62
18	Belgium	6.85	3.08	37	China	2.16	0.08
19	Japan	6.72	2.73	38	Indonesia	1.94	0.26

Note: Only countries for which four or more surveys were extant are included.

SOURCE: Transparency International.

development, and undermine political legitimacy."[10] The presence of corruption in an economy can deter economic growth in two ways. First, it acts like a tax, increasing the cost of doing business and transferring income from "legitimate" participants to illegitimate ones. This might not always be the case. For example, tax officials might agree to turn a blind eye to a tax liability in return for a "cut" of the tax savings. Thus the costs for the individual firm might be reduced, because the effective rate of tax is lower than the nominal rate. However, this in turn is bound to lead to further inefficiency because the tax rate becomes discriminatory, favoring corrupt firms and channeling resources into the corrupt sector.

Second, corruption increases the level of uncertainty for investors because it puts the firm in a situation in which substantial consequences might result were the letter and spirit of the law to be enforced. Furthermore, the existence and tolerance of corruption opens the door for what economists now term "rent-seeking behavior." This occurs when resources are expended in the creation of regulations the sole point of which is to invite the payment of bribes.

Table 1.4 shows the consolidated results of several surveys, largely of foreign businessmen who have experience in dealing with national bureaucracies. Thus

---

[10] Elliot, Kimberly Ann, *Corruption and the Global Economy* (Washington D.C.: Brooking, 1997), vii.

the data describe perceptions of corruption in various nations, rather than actual corruption, and there is likely to be considerable cultural bias. The scores have been standardized. A score of 10 indicates "totally clean" implying an incorruptible bureaucracy and enforcement of the letter of the law. A zero, on the other hand, indicates a totally corrupt country, with bribes to officials at all levels the normal way of doing business. Since the data are responses to questions about perceptions there is likely to be a high degree of variability dependent on each respondent's experience. The column labeled "variance" indicates the statistical variance of the results, and is, therefore, an index on how much agreement there was among the various sources.

New Zealand appears at the top of the list, with Singapore third. Recall that both of these countries scored highly on the competitiveness of their institutions in the results reported in Figure 1.1 and the extent of freedom detailed in Table 1.2. Generally speaking, Western European countries score well, and this might indicate to some observers the existence of a certain amount of cultural bias. Note that among these nations the variance is low, implying that the various surveys generally agreed on the status of these countries. There are exceptions among the European Union (EU) countries. The most obvious is Italy which ranks 30th with a score of only 2.99 against an average rank for the European Union of 12.5 and a score of 7.3. Also interesting is the position of the group of countries that the World Bank calls the high-performing Asian economies (HPAEs). Although many studies stress the importance of an "insulated bureaucracy" able to respond without undue influence of business, this study finds a high perception of corruption in these countries. The average rank is 24.5, and the average score is less than 5.

COMPARING OUTCOMES

As well as being classified by their structure, or some measure of competitiveness or freedom, economies may also be classified by the outcomes that the confluence of their history, endowments, and economic systems produce. We frequently speak of economies as being rich or poor, of having egalitarian or discriminatory income patterns, of achieving levels of human capital development, or of being environmentally sound with sustainable economies rather than tending to deplete resources. This is in some ways less analytically sound than examining the system, because it neglects the level of development and focuses on the immediate and obvious rather than the structural, but these are commonly made comparisons.

LEVELS OF INCOME

One of the most obvious and frequently made comparisons of different nations can be made by looking at income levels. Table 1.5 shows the division of most of the world's economies by level of recorded gross national product adjusted to dollars using 1993 exchange rates. An immediately apparent feature is that the global distribution of income is highly skewed. A few countries, representing less than 15 percent of the world's population, have very high income levels and account for about

■ **TABLE 1.5**

DISTRIBUTION OF WORLD ECONOMIES BY INCOME PER HEAD, 1993

Income Level of Economy	Number of Economies	Population (millions)	Per Head PPP GNP (1993)	Percent of Total Population	Percent of Total GNP
Low	45	3,092.7	$380	56.2	4.8
Lower Middle	41	1,095.8	$1,590	19.9	7.2
Upper Middle	32	500.5	$4,370	9.1	9.0
High	24	812.4	$23,090	14.8	77.1
Total	132	5,501.5	$4,420		

Note: Be aware that 132 economies are classified in this table. In fact the World Bank identifies and keeps some data on a total of 209. The 77 not included in this table are characterized either by populations less than one million or by sparse data.

SOURCE: The World Bank.

77 percent of the total of the world's gross product. At the other end of the scale, 56 percent of the global population lives in relative poverty and accounts for less than 5 percent of the world's gross product.

The group of the 23[11] countries that are richest in terms of national income per head is by and large the same as the group usually identified as "developed market economies." Only two oil-rich Gulf states fail to meet that criterion. The membership of this group is also very close to that of the Organization for Economic Cooperation and Development (OECD), the association composed of 29 of the world's most developed economies. Only eight OECD members fail to qualify for the World Bank's higher income economy classification.[12]

RECENT ECONOMIC PERFORMANCE

Another way in which we commonly classify economies is by their recent economic performance. The idea of division into high-growth or low-growth economies is quite common, and generally we assume that the faster the rate of growth the more successful the economy. As noted earlier, the World Bank frequently

---

[11] The 23 richest countries in terms of 1993 income converted to dollars at international exchange rates, in ascending order, are New Zealand, Ireland, Spain, Israel, Australia, Hong Kong, United Kingdom, Finland, Kuwait, Italy, Singapore, Netherlands, United Arab Emirates, Belgium, France, Austria, Germany, Sweden, United States, Norway, Denmark, Japan, Switzerland. Even within this group there is considerable variance. Swiss per-head GNP at over $35,000 is almost three times that of New Zealand.

[12] The eight are the Czech Republic, Greece, Hungary, South Korea, Mexico, Portugal, Spain, and Turkey. Iceland and Luxembourg make it in terms of per-head income but have populations of less than a million.

■ **TABLE 1.6**

ECONOMIC INDICATORS FOR SELECTED ECONOMIES

	United States	Japan	France	Sweden	Czech Republic	Russia	South Korea
Growth of GDP/head, 1985–1994	1.3	3.2	1.6	−0.1	−2.1	−1.2	7.8
Inflation, annual rate, 1984–1994	3.3	1.3	2.9	5.8	11.8	124.3	6.8
Unemployment, 1995	6.1	2.6	12.5	8.0	3.0	0.9	2.4
Current account balance (as % of GDP, 1994)	−2.1	3.0	1.8	1.2	0.0	0.7	−1.1

SOURCE: World Development Report 1996, International Financial Statistics, December 1996.

identifies the more successful Asian economies by the acronym of HPAEs, which stands for the "high performing Asian economies," thus distinguishing them by their performance rather than by their systems. Some possible comparisons are shown in Table 1.6.

Similarly, we can look at economies in terms of their negative features—high rates of unemployment or high rates of inflation. We can also group economies by their economic relations with the rest of the world. We describe some economies as open, others as closed. This classification can be ambiguous. On the one hand "closed" might mean that the economy is largely self-sufficient and has relatively little need for trade, but it might also imply tight and inefficient control over trade via tariffs and quotas. We can also look at whether these economies are in deficit in their balance of payments, a typology which divides the economies of the world into capital importing or capital exporting nations.

THE STRUCTURE OF OUTPUT

We often also distinguish between economies by looking at the ways in which value is added in the economy. Some economies are relatively heavily agricultural in nature, in others manufacturing activity predominates. In other economies (generally but not exclusively highly developed market economies), it is the service sector that provides the greatest amount of employment and value added. While there are clear exceptions, we observe that there is a transition that occurs in parallel with the general level of development, the least developed societies being more agriculturally based.

In Table 1.7 we see that India has a high proportion of agricultural output and a relatively small manufacturing sector. As per head incomes rise and the level of development increases, we see first a movement toward manufacturing and industry, and ultimately toward services. This general association of

■ TABLE 1.7

THE STRUCTURE OF OUTPUT IN SELECTED ECONOMIES, 1995
(% OF GDP ORIGINATING IN EACH SECTOR)

	Agriculture	Manufacturing	Other Industry	Services
India	31	17	10	41
China	19	38	10	33
Brazil	11	38	10	52
Korea	7	29	14	50
United Kingdom	2	25	8	65
Sweden	2	26	5	67
France	3	22	7	69
Japan	2	36	11	57

SOURCE: The World Bank.

development with falling agriculture and rising services is true both in cross sectional and historical analyses.

THE DISTRIBUTION OF ECONOMIC WELL-BEING

Another way of comparing the economic systems of societies is by looking at how they answer the distributive question, "for whom?" Table 1.8 gives some summary data on the distribution of income in selected countries. The countries are ranked in ascending order of incomes, and the share of income for each quintile of the population is given. In general there is a discernible tendency for a more even distribution of income as income rises. Thus it is in the highly developed and rich market economies that we see the most even distribution of income and within that group in the welfare state societies of Western Europe—Sweden, the Netherlands, and Germany. Japan has a fairly even distribution because of low unemployment rates.

The most inegalitarian nation shown in the table here is Brazil, where the richest 20 percent of society account for 67.5 percent of the income, while the poorest 20 percent only receive 2.1 percent of the product. Thus the average "rich individual" in the top 20 percent of society is more than 30 times better off than the average "poor" person. The situation is very similar in Guatemala, although per-head incomes are only at 50 percent of Brazil's level. The People's Republic of China, despite its communist heritage, has a distribution very similar to India. Russia, after 50 years of socialism, has a distribution less egalitarian than "capitalist" South Korea, and every sign concerning the impact of transition and privatization in the Russian economy indicates that the distribution is becoming more skewed. Sweden and the Netherlands vie for the title of the most egalitarian in terms of income distribution. In both countries the richest quintile accounts for about 37 percent of

■ **TABLE 1.8**

DISTRIBUTION OF ECONOMIC WELL-BEING (% OF GDP PER QUINTILE)

Country	Quintile					PPP*
	First	Second	Third	Fourth	Fifth	GDP/Head
India	8.8	12.5	16.2	21.3	41.3	$1,220
China	6.4	11.0	16.4	24.4	41.8	$2,330
Guatemala	2.1	5.8	10.5	18.6	63.0	$3,350
Russia	4.2	9.8	15.3	22.8	48.0	$5,050
Brazil	2.1	4.9	8.9	16.8	67.5	$5,370
Korea	7.4	12.3	16.3	21.8	42.2	$9,630
Hong Kong	5.4	10.8	15.2	24.3	44.3	$21,560
United Kingdom	4.6	10.0	16.8	24.3	44.3	$17,100
Netherlands	8.2	13.1	18.1	23.7	36.9	$17,330
Germany	7.0	11.8	17.1	23.9	40.3	$16,850
Sweden	8.0	13.2	17.4	24.5	36.9	$17,200
United States	4.7	11.0	17.4	25.0	41.9	$24,470
Japan	8.7	13.2	17.5	23.1	37.5	$20,850
Switzerland	5.2	11.7	16.4	22.1	44.6	$23,660

*PPP denotes purchasing power parity.

SOURCE: World Development Report, 1995.

income, the lowest quintile for about 8 percent. They are closely followed by Japan, whose system, as we will discuss later, depends on a great deal of consensus.

The United Kingdom once had a more uniform income distribution, but it has been transformed by a sharp move away from the all-embracing welfare state, an ideological shift that we now refer to as "Thatcherism." A series of economic changes privatized most of state-owned industry, reduced the progressivity of the tax system, and reduced the coverage of the social safety net. The income profile of the United Kingdom now resembles much more that of the United States than the European social democracies. One of the more surprising features of these figures is that Hong Kong now has both a higher income per head and a more even distribution of income than the United Kingdom. However, summary figures of income distribution are very incomplete descriptors of economic systems. The figures for Russia and the United Kingdom, for example, are (with the exception of income per head) quite similar.

Economists often use either diagrams or summary statistics to represent the important aspects of the distribution of income. The most frequently used graphical device is the **Lorenz curve,** illustrated in Figure 1.2. The curve consists of a graph of the cumulative amount of wealth or income enjoyed by some cumulative breakdown of the population. Complete equality would be represented by a straight line across the diagonal of the box, and increasing degrees of inequality are expressed by the amount that the actual curve "bows away" from the diagonal. Hence the

■ FIGURE 1.2

LORENZ CURVE FOR BRAZIL AND SWEDEN

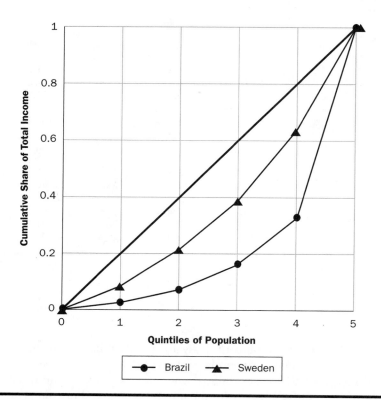

SOURCE: Data from Table 1.6.

relatively egalitarian Swedish income distribution is represented by being closer to the diagonal than the more uneven distribution of income in Brazil. Another way of summarizing the income distribution is by the **Gini coefficient,** which is defined by the ratio of the area between the diagonal and the Lorenz curve and the total area under the diagonal. Perfect equality would lead to the Lorenz curve and the diagonal being coincident, and hence the Gini coefficient would be zero. Complete inequality (one individual having all of the income) would lead to a Gini coefficient of 1.

OTHER CLASSIFICATIONS

There are many other ways in which we can classify economies. In an age when we are increasingly concerned about the environment and the future of the planet one increasingly popular approach is to look at economies in terms of the sustainability of their resource base and ecosystems. Does this economic system and the income flow it generates depend on expending nonrenewable resources or the over-exploitation of resources that are potentially renewable? This would give us an indication of how far into the future a system dependent on the use of such resources could be sustained and might be important in viewing economies that exploit mineral or other naturally occurring wealth, like old growth forests. The issue of environmental sustainability will increase in importance in the years ahead.

CAN WE EVALUATE?

In comparative economics it is tempting, and perhaps appropriate, to look at economies in terms of success and failure. In doing this we must exercise the greatest care. As discussed earlier, an economy is not reducible to simple "production function" terms. The ultimate objective of human endeavor is to achieve well-being, and that has characteristics that transcend the economic. Economists have tended to focus their attention on measurable concepts—like material income per head—and have left the indicators of the social fabric to sociologists. Now we are coming to better appreciate the costs of growth on society and on the environment. This is not to say that growth and social welfare, or growth and the environment, must always be in conflict. There are rich societies with low suicide rates, high life expectancy, and a stable environment. It is merely to note that we must look at a wide range of outcomes when we attempt to evaluate success and failure.

KEY TERMS AND CONCEPTS

Asian Tigers	European Union
beliefs	Gini coefficient
Capitalism	households
cash-flow right	human capital
centrally planned economic system	indicative planning
choice of technique	industry capital
coercion	instruments
company unions	the invisible hand
competitiveness	laws
control right	legality
corruption	Lorenz Curve
craft or occupational unions	material incentives
disposal right	measures
distributional decision	moral persuasion
economic freedom	natural resources

NGOs

Pacific-rim capitalism

policies

practices

principal/agent problems

production decision

property rights

regulations

Rhine model

Robinson Crusoe economy

Smith, Adam

social democracy

Socialism

system

universal banks

welfare state

worker-managed socialism

QUESTIONS FOR DISCUSSION

1. Discuss the nature of national wealth. Where do you believe the greatest source of long-term increase in wealth will lie?
2. Why might a high measure of economic freedom lead to a high growth of GNP?
3. Corruption is often compared to a *tax*. Why?
4. Why is a more even distribution of income considered an advantage for a society? Can you think of negative aspects of an even distribution of income?
5. Why are NGOs increasing their scope of activity?
6. Why is the contemporary fixation of achieving a favorable balance of trade sometimes called "new mercantilism"?

RESOURCES

The most useful resources to accompany this chapter are those that will give the reader access to comparative data on a range of characteristics for the economies of the world.

WEB SITES

Some of the most valuable resources to a researcher, because they are current, easily accessible, and by and large free, are the Web pages of the major international organizations. The most useful single link that I have found is the page of links for the United Nations System, which can be found at http://www.unsystem.org/. This will link you to the Web pages of all of the organizations of the United Nations system. All of these links are useful in researching the economic structure and system of a country but the most relevant for the economist, and likely to be among the most durable links, are the major multinational organizations.

MULTILATERAL AGENCIES

The International Monetary Fund (IMF) . . . . http://www.imf.org/
Now one of the most useful sites around. Particularly valuable are the downloadable full-text versions of the working paper and country reports series. This is a necessary first stop for any research project whether topical or country based. Current data and some interesting studies are available through the access to a free downloadable version of *World Economic Outlook.*

The World Bank (IBRD) . . . . http://www.worldbank.org/
Another useful site for research on developed and developing economies. Clicking on "publications" will connect the reader with the Digital Library, an online library of full-text publications and summaries of major World Bank publications, feature articles, and abstracts from World Bank journals.

The World Trade Organization (WTO) . . . . http://www.wto.org/
Not as valuable a resource as the other United Nations organizations for the study of comparative economics, but a good place to check on issues like the environment, intellectual property disputes, and regional trade issues. A first-rate document dissemination facility (DDF).

The United Nations Development Programme (UNDP) . . . . http://www.undp.org/
A really excellent Web page largely because of the access it gives both to the Human Development Report (HDR) and to the a large number of national Human Development Reports. The HDR gives access to the Human Development Index, an important supplement to GDP statistics and indices of competitiveness in evaluating economic success. The nations reports are useful because they generally include background pieces and descriptions of economic structure and recent economic history. Coverage is, however, patchy—very good for Europe east and west but poor for Asia and the Pacific.

Organization for Economic Co-Operation and Development . . . . http://www.oecd.org/
Unlike the preceding sites, the OECD is not a part of the United Nations system but it is probably the best site available for information on developed countries. The statistical series are comprehensive and standardized, and the OECD Surveys give a wealth of information on economic systems, institutions, policies, and prospects.

REGIONAL COMMISSIONS OF THE UN

The Regional Economic Commissions of the United Nations are responsible for monitoring and analyzing economic developments by region. They provide useful country data and analysis, much of which can be obtained from their Web sites.

Economic Commission for Africa (ECA) . . . . http://www.un.org/Depts/eca/
A good starting point for work on liberalization and reform in Africa. The site allows free access to the ECA's annual report, a useful library, and good links.

Economic Commission for Europe (ECE) . . . . http://www.unece.org/
An excellent site for research on recent developments in both the transition economies of Eastern Europe and the member nation of the European Union. Much of the annual survey of the ECE, which covers both western and eastern Europe, is accessible from this site as well as important selected charts and tables.

Economic Commission for Latin America and the Caribbean (ECLAC) . . . .
. . . . http://www.eclac.cl/
A good jumping off point for research on Latin America. *The Annual Survey* is available here and is a thoughtful document, with useful statistical appendices and tables.

Economic and Social Commission for Asia and the Pacific (ESCAP) . . . .
. . . . http://www.unescap.org/
The Annual Survey provides a good overview of the region, and the downloadable publications are an excellent source for country-by-country analysis of financial sector reform in the wake of the Asian financial crisis.

For studies on particular aspects of comparative economics the following Web sites of specific UN agencies with functional rather than general responsibilities are valuable:

Food and Agriculture Organization of the United Nations (FAO) . http://www.fao.org/

International Labour Organization (ILO) . . . . http://www.ilo.org/

Multilateral Investment Guarantee Agency (MIGA) . . . . http://www.miga.org/

UN Conference on Trade and Development (UNCTAD) . . . . . . http://www.unctad.org/

UN Development Fund for Women (UNIFEM) . . . . http://www.unifem.undp.org/

UN Educational, Scientific and Cultural Organization (UNESCO) . . . .
. . . . http://www.unesco.org/

UN Environment Programme (UNEP) . . . . http://www.unep.org/

UN Foundation . . . . http://www.unfoundation.org/

UN Industrial Development Organization (UNIDO) . . . . http://www.unido.org/

UN Research Institute for Social Development (UNRISD) . . . . http://www.unrisd.org/

UN Centre for Human Settlements (UNCHS (Habitat)) . . . .
. . . . http://habitat.unchs.org/home.htm

World Intellectual Property Organization (WIPO) . . . . http://www.wipo.int/

OTHER WEB SITES
Columbia International Affairs Online . . . . http://www.ciaonet.org/

European Bank for Reconstruction and Development . . . . http://www.ebrd.com/

Heritage Foundation . . . . http://www.heritage.org/

Transparency International . . . . http://www.transparency.de/

World Economic Forum . . . . http://weforum.org/

BOOKS AND ARTICLES

Brademas, J., and F. Heimann. "Tackling International Corruption." *Foreign Affairs,* September 1998, 17–23. Assessment of the consequence of corruption and the possibilities of reform to tackle it.

Elliot, Kimberley Ann. *Corruption and the Global Economy.* Washington, D.C.: Brooking, 1997. Collection of good readings concerning corruption. Particularly good is Paulo Mauro's "Cross Country Analysis," chapter 4. Comprehensive references and data sources.

Fukuyama, Francis. *Trust: The Social Virtues and the Creation of Prosperity.* New York: Free Press, 1995. Argues that social capital is vital for rapid economic development.

Johnson, Brian, Kim R. Holmes, and Melanie Kirkpatrick. *The 1999 Index of Economic Freedom.* Washington, D.C.: Heritage Foundation, 1999. The source of the Index of Economic Freedom.

Pearce, David W., and Jeremy J. Warford. *World without End: Economics, Environment and Sustainable Development: A Summary.* Washington, D.C.: World Bank, 1998. A summary is available at the World Bank Web site, http://www.worldbank.org/html/extpb/reports/worldEnd2.html

Stapenhurst, Rick, and Sahr J. Kpundeh, eds. *Curbing Corruption: Toward a Model for Building National Integrity.* Washington, D.C.: World Bank Institute Development Studies, 1999.

Tanzi, Vito. "Corruption Around the World Causes, Consequences, Scope, and Cures." Downloadable from the IMF site at http://www.imf.org/external/pubs/CAT/longres.cfm?sk=2583.0

United Nations Development Programme. *Human Development Report.* New York: Oxford UP, 1998. A wealth of comparative data, excellent references, and each year tackles a different theme; 1998 dealt with consumption patterns and how to change them.

World Bank. *Helping Countries Combat Corruption: The Role of the World Bank.* A downloadable synopsis is available from the World Bank site at http://www.worldbank.org/html/extdr/corruptn/coridx.htm

World Bank. *World Development Indicators.* Washington, D.C.: World Bank, 1999. Very useful compendium of data for developing countries.

World Bank. *World Development Report.* New York: Oxford UP, 1998. Excellent source for all sorts of data. Excellent bibliography and each year a different theme. 1998 was concerned with the creation of knowledge.

Worldwatch Institute. *State of the World, 1998.* New York: W. W. Norton and Company, 1998. An annual assessment of environmental developments from a very environmentalist viewpoint. Some good country data.

2

THE ROOTS OF ECONOMIC SYSTEMS

WHY AND HOW DO ECONOMIC INSTITUTIONS CHANGE?

Economic systems are not static. A glance at history, even the history of merely the past decade, shows us that systemic change is relatively frequent. New institutions may be created, and old ones terminated, and the rights of the various constituent groups and individuals of society with respect to property, economic activity, or mobility may be altered. The extent of government ownership in the productive sphere is by no means constant and varies with "privatization" (the current trend) and its converse "nationalization." Governments can change, sometimes in dramatic fashions, and new governments may bring with them an entirely new philosophic approach to the objectives of the system or the new ways of addressing those objectives. Consequently they set about altering the web of laws and regulations that govern economic activity. Industries are taken into public ownership, or "privatized." Controls over output and prices may be tightened or relaxed.

Two questions are of great and enduring interest to students of comparative economics:

Why do economic systems change?

How do they change?

The answer to the first question is often considered to lie within two dynamics: **technological change** and **population growth.** However, neither of these is truly exogenous to the economic system, and therefore they cannot be regarded wholly as external agents of change. In fact, we can see that often both the direction and pace of technology and population dynamics are influenced to a considerable degree by the nature of the economic system. For example, it can be argued that *laissez faire* capitalism rewards the kind of technical change that favors small enterprise, and therefore, as a system, it tends to foster relatively small-scale technology. Socialism, on the other hand, has been criticized both for being inimical to economic change, and where change has occurred it has been biased to large-scale technology.

On the population side, we know that relatively less-developed societies with little provision for a social safety net tend to be characterized by high birthrates, because parents need some surviving offspring to provide care in their old age. Therefore the introduction of even modest public health measures leads to rapid population growth, at least in the short run, before societies adjust their behavior and lower the birthrate in response to changed circumstances. In subsequent sections we will look at how changing technology and population have been historically linked with substantial shifts in the economic system.

EVOLUTIONARY AND REVOLUTIONARY CHANGE

Studying development and change in economic systems in historical context prompts the observation that at certain points in time and space change seems to be rapid, while at other points it is much slower and more even, in line with our understanding of evolution in natural history. Two schools of thought about economic change have emerged. Adherents of the **evolutionary school** stress the gradual nature of change. They see shifts in an economic system as a process of gradual accommodation to the movements in technology, the resource base and population through small continuous innovations in the institution of the system and the laws that govern their interaction. Problems are resolved by incremental adjustments. Societal progress is slow and, as once observed about evolution in nature, tends to "make no leaps."

In contrast to the gradualism of the evolutionist we have the revolutionary **laws of motion** that were put forward by the 19th-century philosopher and economist Karl Marx. His vision of social dynamics, like that of evolutionists, was linear. Each form of social organization gave way to a successor, in a progressive and irreversible way, but in Marx's view change tended to occur discontinuously, with periods of rapid change punctuating periods of relative constancy.

Marx's conception of the causality of social change lay in material factors. As populations grew and technology advanced, the growth of material output became constrained by the existing system of economic and social organization. This led to a growing tension between the societal groups that dominated the established economic system and those who would benefit from a new set of arrangements. This produced antagonism, struggle, and eventually (generally after a series of crises and false starts) rapid revolutionary change. The old social order was overthrown and replaced by one better suited to maximize social output in the changed situation.

As a result of this revolution originating in material factors, the whole **superstructure** of society was changed. This included not only political relations (who held the power and who governed?) but also law, culture, custom and even religion. The development of the social system had its genesis in economic change. We can see in the thought of both the evolutionists and Marxists parallels to the theories of biological evolution propounded by Darwin. As conditions alter, the existing economic system becomes ill adapted to the maximization of output and the consequence is growing social stress. In both cases change results, although in one view it is creeping and may be tenuous, reversible, and experimental. In the other, the Marxian view, it is sweeping and total. Of course, the significant departure from biological Darwinism is that economic systems are humanmade and involve therefore some human design and thought. While natural selection occurs as the result of unplanned changes favoring the randomly evolved species that happen to be better suited, the change of economic system can be conscious, thoughtful, and imitative of changes that have occurred elsewhere.

ECONOMIC SYSTEMS IN HISTORICAL PERSPECTIVE [1]

As a precursor to the study of the economies that exist today, it is useful to review, if only in bare outline, the procession and variety of economic systems that have existed through history. In each instance we will try to not only briefly outline the structure of each system but to also ask the following questions: What forces led these systems to change? How did that change occur? How did that resolve the problems that had been faced?

HUNTER-GATHERER SOCIETIES

To start we look at the most primitive economic organization—the hunter-gatherer society. While our knowledge of the precise social organization of this prehistoric world is imperfect, we can make some generalizations. We know that it was in this form of social organization that humankind has existed for most of its time on earth. All successive forms of social and economic organization have been crowded into the last 9,000 years or so. In fact, a few isolated hunter-gatherer societies have even managed to survive into our present age.

At the heart of a hunter-gatherer system must lie the sustainability of the environment in which it exists. If the natural vegetative resources of the land are over-picked, or if the animal stocks are overhunted, then the equilibrium of such a system will be threatened. Such overexploitation of renewable resources has two roots. One lies in advancing technology; superior hunting techniques and more advanced tools and weapons take a greater toll of animal stocks and may perhaps encourage waste. The other cause lies in the growth of population. Greater numbers will place greater demands on resources. Of course, these two are closely related. The higher productivity associated with superior technology allows the population to enjoy living standards above subsistence, and consequently it expands. However, when overexploitation is encountered the greater difficulty of gathering food and hunting in a depleted environment causes productivity to fall. When average social productivity falls below subsistence level, the population will shrink. This, in turn, will allow resources to replenish, generating a new cycle of potentially increased productivity. This cycle of growth and contraction of human, and animal, population was the rule for many thousands of years.

PASTORAL AND AGRARIAN SOCIETIES

However, around 9,000 years ago, we know that some hunters began to make the switch to settled farming. This may have taken the form of scratching a cultivable garden within the forest and tending edible plants. It also involved the primitive domestication of animals. Initially such enterprise provided a living that was barely above subsistence, but it did enable survival in the face of increased demands on

---

[1] This section is concerned with the evolution of societies in historical perspective and can be omitted without damaging the overall flow of the text. It is recommended that any reader rejoin the discussion with "Contemporary Economic Systems" on page 57.

natural resources. Over time experience led to improved technique, and the development of better seed and livestock resulted in rising productivity. In turn, the growth in agricultural communities accelerated.

It was at this point in history that a series of social innovations could occur. First, the population engaged in agriculture generated a surplus that enabled a greater division of labor. Artisans, priests, soldiers, lawyers, and doctors could be supported by the excess produce of the farmers. The economic system and the legal framework had to become more complex. A settled agricultural society requires a different set of institutions and more comprehensive laws than those that governed the hunter-gatherer societies. Whereas in the earlier society property was largely communal, and resources open to all, in a farming society property rights are important. Some tenure on the land is essential, if only between the planting season and harvest, and much longer is desirable if land improvement is to be effected. Some authority competent to enforce property rights and adjudicate disputes is vital. Settled agriculture also allowed the creation of a greater social surplus than had been feasible in hunter-gatherer societies. This, in turn, allowed the creation of a nobility, an artisan class providing consumer goods and services, a religious establishment, and a permanent military.

"ORIENTAL DESPOTISM"

As the population of agrarian societies grew, pressure on resources increased. In many areas water was a vital resource required to maintain the highly productive agriculture necessary to support the population. The social order and high productivity in agriculture depended on the preservation of the water supply for irrigation and clear definition and enforcement of water rights. In the view of Marx and others,[2] this dependence on irrigation was the explanation of the durable, wealthy but inequitable states of Asia.

In the nations of South and Eastern Asia, the organization and management of the water supply was especially important. Successful irrigation meant the difference between a highly populous and productive community and a sparsely inhabited and precarious subsistence economy. Irrigation projects were characterized by large economies of scale and required considerable, though well-rewarded, social investment. Consequently, a large public works bureaucracy was required, with the resources and expertise to develop and maintain this water. It was precisely the great social return to these projects that accounted for what Marx called **Oriental despotism** in Eastern **"hydraulic" societies.** The ruler and the associated bureaucracy were able to expropriate the greater part of the produce of society because that produce was dependent on the success of the irrigation project. The populace, aware of the importance of hydraulic organization and the great benefits provided, was powerless in the face of a bureaucracy that had a monopoly

[2]See especially Karl August Wittfogel, *Oriental Despotism: A Comparative Study of Total Power* (New Haven: Yale University Press, 1957), which embodies his seminal views on the relevance of water to political structure.

on organization and expertise as well as military power. It was forced to acquiesce to confiscatory rates of taxation.

CLASSICAL SLAVE ECONOMIES

In Europe the great classical societies of Greece and Rome were less dependent on irrigation for agriculture. They relied to a much larger degree on the institution of slavery. Although the Greek city-states are frequently touted as the cradles of democracy, in fact participation in political decision making was very circumscribed. Most residents of Greek cities had no say in their policy or destiny. There may have been as many as 18 slaves per freeman in Athens at the height of its prosperity. In Rome, which was a highly centralized empire with a large urban population to support, production in agriculture was dominated by the *latifundia*. These were large farms that operated on a slave-labor plantation system. Slaves also formed the basic labor supply in mining, construction, and manufacturing, as well as supplying services within the household.

Although now we regard the institution as morally deplorable and therefore nonviable under any circumstances, the economic efficiency of slavery depends on certain specific conditions. The objective of a slave system is to obtain labor at rates below those that would pertain under a market system. Where markets are competitive and labor is mobile, each worker is paid a wage approximate to his or her marginal productivity. Where labor is plentiful relative to land and capital, the marginal product of labor will be low and the wage will tend in the long run to move toward subsistence, the wage that ensures the survival and replication of the labor stock and no more. In such a situation slavery will not be viable since "free labor" may be had for the subsistence wage. In contrast, slavery is likely to flourish in circumstances where labor is in short supply relative to capital and land, because then the marginal product of labor is high. Under such circumstances the potential savings in labor costs are likely to be the greatest.

However, slavery does involve costs that the employment of contract labor does not. These are principally the cost of purchase and the cost of supervision. Purchase can be regarded as a form of capital investment. Supervisory costs have two components. The first involves protecting the investment from flight, theft, and illness. The second can be looked on as a form, albeit an extreme one, of the "agency problem," that was briefly discussed in chapter 1. All users of labor face agency problems in getting workers to perform, to work as hard as if they could appropriate all of the income from increased productivity. Overseers, timeclocks, and the practice of piecework have all been used as a solution for the agency problem in a free market. Under slavery these problems are more acute.

The centrality of supervision costs means that slavery is likely to be most enduring where there is a strong centralized authority, no refuge for slaves within or close to the slave society, and where the enslaved group is racially or ethnically distinguishable from the "free" population. When the Roman empire was well ordered, the power of the state minimized the private costs of supervision. However, as centralized authority in Rome began to collapse under the weight of incursions by wandering tribes apparently propelled by a population explosion in the Eurasian heartland, the private costs of supervision and enforcement rose and the slave problem contributed considerably to Rome's difficulties and ultimate fall.

THE FEUDAL SYSTEM

In the aftermath of the collapse of the western Roman empire, Western European society became highly disordered. The institution of slavery was replaced by that of serfdom within the context of the **feudal system.** Feudalism was the dominant system of political and economic organization in western Europe for a period of roughly a thousand years. Although the duration of feudalism differed in different territories or regions, in broad terms we can think of it as persisting from the fall of Rome and the onset of the so-called "dark ages" of western Europe (in the 5th century) until the establishment of nation-states in about the 16th century. Feudalism therefore thrived in a situation where centralized control was absent and most of the restraints on individual behavior had vanished.

The basis of feudalism was one of hierarchical personal obligation, which, although largely determined by power, was to some extent reciprocal. In return for the provision of protection, which was necessary in such a chaotic society, individuals occupying the lower ranks of the social pyramid were required to pay rent in goods and service to those higher up. The rapaciousness of the higher-ups was curbed only by the potentiality of revolt by the lower orders and the necessity of at least preserving the population and social capital for replication in the next time period. An additional constraint in some circumstances may have been the moderating doctrines of religion.

In feudal theory, all land was ultimately at the disposition of the monarch, but the effective title of estates was parceled out to the nobility as a reward for past services rendered and to ensure future loyalty. The upper echelons of the nobility enjoyed substantial autonomy from the monarchy in the control of their locality and its microeconomy. They in turn delegated property rights and political jurisdiction to a lower level of aristocracy, as a reward for tribute, loyalty, and service.

The nobility was to a great extent a self-appointed class that relied on power and coercion to secure its position. Herman Schwartz has somewhat flippantly typed them as

> [A] kind of dispersed biker gang: armor, horses, and their propensity to resort to violence elevated them above most of the rest of the population in the same way as leather and Harleys elevate movie bikers where State authority is absent.[3]

At the bottom of the social pyramid was the peasantry. In "typical" European society this class comprised about 90 percent of the rural population. Substantial variation was due to the differential productivity of the land and the peasants. Broadly speaking, the higher the productivity, the more superstructure (nobles, warriors, priests, etc.) that could be supported. The peasantry itself was not a

---

[3] See Herman Schwartz, *States Versus Markets: History, Geography, and the Development of International Political Economy* (New York: St. Martin's Press, 1994).

monolithic class; within it lay distinct gradations. The serfs (also called villeins) constituted the most numerous group but had only highly limited property and personal rights. Serfdom as an institution differed from slavery (as, for example, in the United States) in that the serfs were regarded as part of the property of the *demesne,* or manor, and since they could not be alienated from it they could not be sold in the market. Consequently the family under serfdom was a rather more stable institution than under slavery, but the lives and very existence of serfs depended on the frequently capricious and arbitrary rule of the lord. Above them in the social pyramid lay a stratum of free or landed peasants, who had rights to a small plot of land, but who also owed service to the aristocrat and were just as dependent on his rule and protection.

The feudal economy was a command economy in most of its attributes, but it had both centralized and decentralized aspects. At the state level, the monarch was responsible for a limited but important set of decisions. This was particularly true of external trade, which was almost always under direct state control and was usually organized as a licensed or sanctioned monopoly of the monarchs. In addition, the monarch also frequently designated the monopoly producer of certain important productive activities, or issued monopoly licenses for others to engage in them. These arrangements usually covered industries like shipyards, ceramic factories, and armories. Resources flowed to the crown via monetary taxation, in-kind tribute of goods, and conscripted labor for military and other service. The high frictional cost of transportation meant that most economic activity was very local. Both economic hinterlands and political jurisdictions tended to be restricted to the feasible limit of a day's travel on foot or by wagon, a radius of roughly 10 miles in all directions around a central point. The manor and the village were relatively self-sufficient units in which economic activity fell largely under the direction of the lord of the manor or in many cases church authority (since the religious establishment was a major landowner).

The business of the manor and the village was largely agricultural. The basic organization of the northwest European manorial system will be familiar to most readers. The arable land of the village was commonly divided into three fields, one of which lay fallow each year. The land within the fields was divided into strips, which were allocated among the landed peasantry. Livestock was grazed on common land.

The landlords extracted their income in two ways: by appropriating goods in kind, as rent, and in return for services, especially milling grain, and by labor service provided as work on the aristocrat's lands. Market activity was limited, but landed peasants were able to sell the surplus produced in excess of the demands of the lord, the church, and their own subsistence, and could through purchase or barter acquire those goods (clothing, tools, etc.) that they were unable to produce themselves.

In summary, the important economic decisions were made by the command of monarchy and nobility: they controlled what should be produced, how it should be produced, and who should glean the benefit. In terms of incentives, the dominant mode was coercion, although elements of both moral and material incentives may be found. Some form of sharecropping was frequently practiced so the peasantry had an incentive to maximize output in order to retain the most they could for consumption and sale in the market. Such a system did embody a material incentive, though the heavy "tax rate" tended to dull it. Great stress was placed by society, and especially by the Church, on social order, and therefore an element of moral incentive was added. However, when all was said and done the peasant worked for, and gave goods to, the lord of the manor because he had no alternative. The nobility had a monopoly on force, which could be used to coerce him or to protect him from the predations of others.

Feudalism was a static economic and social system that evolved following the wreck of the Roman empire and the collapse of imperial order. There was little within the system oriented to, or supportive of, economic growth or development. The nobility were consumers rather than investors and such economic surplus as was generated found its way into castles, churches, and military adventurism rather than into capital improvements to increase economic output in the long run. The uncertain status of the peasant and the absence of long-term tenure of any given piece of land under the strip system made land improvement by the peasant pointless. The authority of the monarch was limited by the power of the nobility and little impetus could come from the center.

Commercial activity as we know it today was largely incompatible with feudalism. The greatest European commercial center in the early Middle Ages was Venice, which had, from its very foundation, taken steps to separate itself from the feudal states of Western Europe both by its insular location and the maintenance of a deliberately and strategically vague allegiance to Byzantium. Within Venice commercial activity, markets, and banking all began to thrive and to throw out seeds that were to provide the impetus for a broader commercial revolution.

MERCANTILISM

Although it had proved a durable system, lasting for about a thousand years in parts of western Europe, feudalism's basic economic weaknesses put it under attack from two directions. On the one hand, monarchs sought to consolidate their own power and to increase their own wealth by controlling more fully the territories that were nominally under their rule. On the other, the growth of market economies challenged the established system of labor servitude.

The extension of the control, and therefore the wealth, of the monarch could only be achieved by breaking the grip of the nobility on the microeconomies that existed within the state. In this respect the monarchy was assisted by change in military technology. The power of the feudal nobility to resist a centralized state had two roots: the fighting potential of the armored, mounted knight and the defensive strength of the castle. The one enabled the wealthy aristocrat to be the physical superior of the unmounted fighter; the other gave the aristocrat the ability to withstand sieges and therefore to flaunt the authority of the monarchy. The arrival of gunpowder devalued both of these advantages. An aggressive monarch with a professional army and an artillery siege train was in a position to reduce any disruptive and defiant magnate. This cleared the way for the creation of nation-states, which had common currencies, standardized weights and measures, and uniform laws. Such states also had fewer internal obstacles to trade. Costly transportation still posed a problem, but much more effective division of labor was possible under a unified state. Similarly, the use of firearms became the great equalizer, because the knight became an easy prey of the foot soldier.[4]

Feudalism was also under attack from within. As trade slowly revived, the potential to create wealth by arbitrage and exchange was seen and grasped by a growing merchant class. Feudalism—static, consumption-oriented, and organized in geographically limited microeconomies—was antithetical to this growth of trade. Commercialism defied the existing social order by putting this wealth in the hands of commoners, and the barony frequently attempted to confiscate the growing wealth of the merchants. Merchants turned directly to the monarch for protection, and as a result, commercial activity became increasingly located in towns whose royal charters set them apart from the power of the nobility.

The growth of towns brought with it a surge in the demand for labor, and this put a stake into the very heart of feudalism: the servile system. The marginal productivity of urban employment was certainly greater than that of the serf on the manor, and town-based employers were inclined, and had an incentive, to pay a worker more than he received from the rural aristocrats. Before the growth and independence of towns, a serf had no alternative to remaining on the manor, depending on his albeit meager income and on the protection of the lord. With the emergence of urban centers, flight to towns brought the prospect of freedom, independence, and a higher real standard of living. Furthermore, the *bourgeoisie*[5] were reluctant to return the serf to the manor for punishment and defied the feudal magnates. In Germany there arose the phrase *Stadtluft macht frei*—the air of the cities makes one free, and indeed the growing towns afforded new opportunities to the peasant classes.

This competition between town and country, between capitalism and feudalism, was intensified by the epidemics of the "Black Death" in the 14th century. In many districts of Europe half of the population was lost, producing an acute shortage of labor. The surviving serfs were the beneficiaries of the competing needs of the countryside and the town. Land was so plentiful relative to labor that much fell out of production. Rural labor was in such short supply that the solidarity of the system broke down. Runaway serfs became welcome even in the countryside on the land of other aristocrats and were seldom returned to their own manors. In the towns, which had been even harder hit than the countryside by the pestilence, labor shortages pushed up wages and increased the lure to former serfs. Serfdom declined and was replaced by a much more freely operating labor market in much of Europe.[6] The simultaneous movement toward the establishment of markets and the blending of the microeconomies into a larger economic space produced the collapse of feudalism.

---

[4] In Japan, feudalism lasted longer in part because firearms were prohibited and the *samurai* had their life as a social class extended until the late 19th century by this measure.

[5] Literally this means the townspeople, although it later came to have class connotations.

[6] Further east in Europe less change was seen in the institution of serfdom. In Russia the serfs were not freed until the 1860s.

MERCANTILISM DEFINED.   The confluence of the state-building activities of the monarchy and the growing power and influence of the trading classes characterizes the system that we call "mercantile." The term **mercantilism** can be interpreted as meaning "the doctrine of merchants," and this is perhaps its most literal rendering, but it has come to mean something more complex than that, although the term has been often loosely applied and this has resulted in a rather confused discussion.

Some of this confusion is due to the fact that there was no systematic statement of mercantilist theory by its adherents. Important arguments were laid out by pamphleteers usually working on behalf of a merchant lobby,[7] but they are incomplete and often conflicting. Our own understanding of mercantilism stems from the straw man created by Adam Smith in the *Wealth of Nations,* a rather coarse caricature intended to be easily demolished. In this work Smith advocated a new system better suited to the needs of an increasingly industrialized society. As a result of Smith's work, many people consider "mercantilists" as rather foolish people who failed to distinguish between real national wealth and a heap of precious metal.

What then do we mean by the term *mercantilism?* First, it involves an internal project, the *creation of an integrated economic space* above the size of the microeconomies that had characterized the feudal system. In this sense the problems were really quite similar to those faced in the construction of the European Union today, inasmuch as mercantilism involved the removal of fiscal and physical barriers to trade, the acceptance of a common legal code, a movement toward a common currency, and the use of a common language. Second, mercantilism is usually thought of as supporting *state involvement in the development of the national economy.* Thus it fell to the state to establish industries where they were lacking, especially where there was the potential for import substitution, as well as to grant subsidies and monopolies to key industries.

Third, a *positive balance of trade was desirable.* In the eyes of the monarch the purpose of overseas trade was to increase national wealth, which could be directed to exert strategic influence. While today it might be said that the object of trade in such a system is to raise living standards by bringing plentiful cheap goods into the country and to effect a more efficient global division of labor, this was not the case under the mercantilist system. Thus a prime element was the achievement of a "favorable" **balance of trade.** This meant that there would be an inflow of precious metals into the country because the difference in the value between exports and imports would be settled by an inflow of precious metals. This stock of bullion was considered important because it could be taxed, borrowed, or otherwise acquired by the state and used to finance statecraft, conspicuous consumption, or military expenditure. This is the origin of the famous phrase that mercantile policy "put power [of the State] before plenty [for the individual]."

---

[7] *England's Treasure by Foreign Trade,* by Thomas Mun, a merchant, is one of the best known of these. While mainly directed to attacking legislation suggested to curb bullion export, it lays out a clear picture of the benefit of trade in national development. See the Web site at http://socserv2.socsci.mcmaster.ca/~econ/ugcm/3ll3/mun/treasure.txt

This preoccupation with the trade balance was one of the features of mercantile thought that attracted Adam Smith's derision in the *Wealth of Nations,* in which he accused mercantilists of confusing money with national wealth. Smith was at pains to explain in his seminal work that the wealth of nations lay in productive capacity, not in fallow stocks of precious metal. As a doctrine, trade fetishism was also taken to extreme by two branch "schools" of the mercantilist tree. "Bullionists" genuinely thought that the real source of a nation's wealth was the stock of precious metal within the country, rather than the productive capacity. "Cameralists" focused their attention on the fiscal position of the state, judging well-being to be measured essentially by the ability to tax and the accumulated stock of fiscal surpluses.

Merchants, however, were not generally adherents of either of these extremes, and in England they lobbied against legislation advanced by bullionists that would have outlawed the export of precious metals. Rather, merchants favored the positive trade balance because it alone acted to expand and therefore, in modern terms, "loosen" the money supply. A growing money supply led both to low interest rates and a higher rate of inflation than otherwise would prevail. Both of these factors were advantageous to mercantile interests, since traders were generally debt-financed and held a substantial inventory of goods.

The policy of promoting a positive balance of payments led in part to the aggressive acquisition of overseas possessions and colonies that characterized the mercantile system. By incorporating into the home country, or "metropolis," territories that could produce raw materials that were not available at home (for example, tropical produce), costly imports that would have to be financed with bullion might be avoided. The preoccupation with trade balance also led to the widespread use of subsidies (or "bounties") for production and export. Goods that cost more to produce than the prevailing market price became profitable for producers and saved bullion from foreign exchange while requiring taxation to raise the necessary subsidies.

A fourth premise of mercantilism was the establishment of a positive **balance of employment.** In simple terms, this prescribed that the labor content of exports should be greater than that of imports. Correspondingly, the most advantageous form of trade was to exchange domestically produced manufactured goods for foreign produced raw materials. In contemporary terms we can see this as a desire to maximize value added and skilled employment in the metropolis. Such a policy would lead to a maximization of both the domestic population and the skill level embodied in that population. It led therefore to a policy of restricting, or in some cases reversing, the economic development of colonial possessions. To take two examples from the British empire, extensive legislation (the Iron Act, the Woolen Act, and the Hat Act) sought to curb development of the manufacturing industry in the American colonies and so to retain them as export markets for goods made in Britain itself. Parallel policies actually led to the "undevelopment" of the possessions in India, by the destruction of textile production and the conversion of India into a producer of raw material alone.

Of central importance in mercantilist practice to this strategy of maximizing growth at the center were the measures that sought to control the direction of trade and the means by which trade was to be conducted. In England these took the form of a series of "navigation acts," but parallels are to be found in Spain, Portugal, and France. The earliest navigation acts in England determined that all trade to and from the nation should be carried in vessels of English registry; this had the effect of strengthening demand for, and therefore the size and profitability of, the merchant marine. Subsequent acts ensured that all colonial imports and exports (often including those with other colonies) should be conducted through the metropolis.

It was also thought economically sensible to discourage economic development in the colonies, keeping them as suppliers of raw materials alone and not as competitors in the production of finished products. To this end, there were often laws prohibiting the development of manufacturing industry and even certain kinds of agriculture in the colonies.[8]

While Adam Smith was able to attack the mercantile system to good effect, at least as far as England was concerned, the basic ideas of mercantilism have been pursued by many nations, among them late industrializing nations who have successfully crossed the divide from "less developed" to "developed" status.[9] The essential ingredients that we have introduced here (economic unification, state promotion of industry, favoring exports, discouraging imports, and an attempt to foster high value-added manufacturing) are all policies that are espoused today. Indeed mercantilism seems to be something of a policy for the second best. The preeminent power of the 17th century was the Netherlands, which had little use for the close management of trade or state promotion of industry that lay at the heart of the mercantile system as practiced by the Spanish and the English.

The policy of establishing the Low Countries as an entrepôt of free trade was highly successful and the most competitive prices for many commodities were those on the Amsterdam market. Consumers in countries wrapped in mercantile regulations usually had to pay more for products and were taxed more for subsidies than where market rates pertained. However, the costs of the mercantile system fell hardest on colonial possessions, since these were treated rather as providers of raw materials and markets for the metropolis. Active policy to discourage development was the norm, and this proved most injurious to the long-run economic health of colonies.

The routing of all trade with any of the colonies through the metropolis was also burdensome since it raised both the costs of exporting and the prices of imports. As a counterbalance, however, the colonies benefited from a protected market in the metropolis and from subsidies designed to encourage the production of many goods. There have been many attempts to estimate the economic cost of these trade acts with respect to British North America, and the maximum figure arrived at was about 3 percent of annual colonial gross domestic product (GDP), a figure thought by most to be scarcely significant.

---

[8] In English legislation these included the Hat Act, the Iron Act, and the Woolen Act. Spain prohibited the growth of olives and the production of wine in its American possessions.

[9] The most notable of these were Japan and Korea, which followed used regulation to good advantage while pursuing a "market friendly" approach.

THE INSTITUTIONS OF COMMERCIAL CAPITALISM

While we can regard mercantilism as an overarching but general belief system espoused by the classes that effectively controlled society and the economy, the day-to-day economic system that prevailed between the end of feudalism and the advent of the industrial system is more descriptively called **commercial capitalism.** The title is appropriate because the dominant wealth-creating activity, at least as far as western Europe was concerned, was commerce, and it was conducted by entrepreneurs who controlled capital and were interested in its accumulation.

This period was important in terms of institutional change because it saw the development of two innovations that were vitally important for subsequent capitalist development: the practice of incorporation of businesses and the emergence of banks as true financial intermediaries. Incorporation involves the creation of a legal entity with two very important features. First, it is an efficient means of commingling the funds of individuals, thereby gathering together the means for large investments. Second, the liabilities of corporations are limited by the extent of their assets. Consequently it encourages risk taking, because the downside is limited, while the upside is not. Banks facilitate the pooling of saving and the lending of funds to individuals with ideas and enterprise but limited startup capital.

INDUSTRIAL CAPITALISM

Just as changing technology and a widening world had first threatened and then destroyed the feudal order, supplanting it with mercantilism, by the end of the 18th century the commercial capitalist system was itself under threat. The proximate cause in this case was the growth of mass production and the rise of industrialized manufacturing, which was brought about by what we have historically called the Industrial Revolution. Recent scholarship tends to dispute the idea of a short explosive burst of innovation and tends to settle on a more extended and evolutionary series of innovations and institutional changes.[10] However, we can characterize the shift in productive technique as embodying four broad sorts of changes that were effected in the process of industrialization:

1. The replacement of muscle power (whether animal or human) by machine power, first water power and then steam

2. The replacement of skill and craftsmanship by the artificial and repetitive precision of the machine

3. The replacement of organic sources of raw materials by inorganic ones

4. The replacement of natural "time" by the clock (This last development was especially important for the creation of workforce discipline in the factory system.)

---

[10]The debate on this issue continues to be lively, and an interested reader might want to look at Peter Temin's "Two Views of the British Industrial Revolution," *Journal of Economic History* 57, no. 1 (March 1997): 63–82, which addresses the issues with clarity.

These developments made possible a factory system much as we know it today. In Britain, which was the first country to undergo substantial industrial urbanization, the system that developed was by and large highly competitive. Especially in the textile trades, which were the lead sector of technological change and were located largely in Northern England, the industrial structure approximated the model of competitive capitalism that is now embodied in the textbook treatments of the theory of the competitive firm. The product was close to totally homogeneous, there were many buyers and many producers, and labor was largely undifferentiated. Decisions were made primarily by an entrepreneur who both managed the firm and had a substantial part of his own capital at risk. Government policy at that time was best described as "laissez faire, laissez passer."

The largest shifts in the economic regulation happened because mercantile restrictions adversely affected the long-term competitive prospects of manufacturing. At the beginning of the industrialization process, political power had remained in the hands of the land-holding and commercial classes, who had a strong interest in the retention of relative comprehensive trade regulations. However, the increasing economic power of the manufacturers led, in 1832, to their enfranchisement, and within 15 years this growing political power resulted in sharp changes in the economic system.

The most visible of these changes was the outcome of the popular and parliamentary debate over the reform of the corn laws. The **corn laws** were variable levy tariffs that restricted the import of cereal grains into Britain and hence led to both higher food prices and increased returns to the owners of agricultural land. The manufacturers' interests, however, lay in minimizing costs, and higher food prices forced them to raise wages, ultimately hurting the competitiveness of British goods on international markets. After considerable pressure, the corn laws were repealed and Britain was able to freely import food and other materials. This represented in some ways recognition for the economic doctrines of David Ricardo, as well as Smith. Ricardian thought rejected the idea of mercantile restrictions and presented a cogent case for the rise of the free trade movement.

The onset of British industrialization saw further changes in the role of government. Urbanization produced a plethora of problems associated with growth and the government was called on to deal with the issues of public health and pollution control (albeit in a very rudimentary form). Unacceptable workplace dangers and the widespread use of child labor occasioned laws that governed factory practices. The government also became involved in the development of human capital, in the form of education for the less privileged classes, which had a strongly positive effect on productivity.

Industrialization also enabled labor to organize to an extent that had not been seen hitherto. Unions began to spring up and were at first resolutely opposed by manufacturers and the government. The first union organizers were prosecuted under "combination acts" and imprisoned or deported. However, over time the legality of labor organization was confirmed and the stage was set for the emergence of mass unions representing the working class. In Britain these unions were modeled on the old craft guilds and were structured around occupations rather than around specific employers. This had long-term consequences for the nature of collective bargaining in the British context, which will be discussed later.

THE INDUSTRIAL SYSTEM IN CONTINENTAL EUROPE

Industrial development in continental Europe differed from that in Britain because of two factors. First, the role of government was by and large greater—this owed much to a different and generally less liberal political tradition. Second, European nations were playing catch-up. Consequently, they had the opportunity to adopt technologies that had already been pioneered and tested elsewhere. This was especially true after Britain abandoned all attempts to control the export of machines and machine tools in the late 1840s. Continental industrial structures were from the start less competitive than those in Britain. Their industries, and often specific favored firms, enjoyed both more overt government support and closer relations with the banking sector than was true in Britain. This was the genesis of a political/economic system that involved much closer management of industry by government than was seen in Britain, at least prior to World War II. This close relation of government and business is in one respect a holdover from earlier mercantile practices. As one observer, Charles Tilly, has put it, mercantilism appeals to the second best, or at least the latecomers, who require government support, direction, and protection against competition. This model of late industrialization that pertained to continental Europe in the late 19th century has substantial echoes in the policies and practices of the East Asian late industrializers in the late 20th century.

The different role of banks on the continent was also significant. Banking had played only a small role in the creation of credit in the British Industrial Revolution. A surprisingly large amount of capital had been generated through retained earning and the granting of interfirm trade credits. Banking had been especially useful in overseas trade and the financial sector had developed in a differentiated pattern with a variety of specialized banks. On the continent banking was much more central, largely because the average enterprise at inception was much larger than in Britain. Large firms did not grow from small startups but were created from whole cloth. This was necessary in order to take advantage of the scope of latest technology and to grasp the economies of scale required to compete with existing suppliers. Banks played a great role in providing startup capital, and because of the size of their stake, the banks became closely associated with the management of the venture. Continental banks were not specialized but were "universal" in nature providing loans, owning capital, granting trade credits, and being responsible for brokerage services.

FINANCE CAPITALISM AND IMPERIALISM

The close relationship between the banks and business that had always been the case in Europe, and which was evolving in Britain and in the United States,[11] led neo-Marxian observers to see a new stage in the evolution of economic systems. Following Bruno Hilferding, an Austrian, this system became labeled as **finance**

---

[11] In the United States the most obvious example of this closeness was the takeover of the U.S. steel industry by J. P. Morgan.

capitalism and differed from early **industrial capitalism** in the role that was played by financial capital. In Hilferding's conception, which was significant to Lenin, a small coterie of bankers were capable of dominating the system. This resort to monopolization was a defensive technique employed to delay the inevitable decline in the rate of profit.

In Marxian analysis this same close group of financier/industrialists was potentially also influential on government policy. This became especially important, since Marx believed that the capitalist system would face repeated crises. The root cause of these was the basic tendency toward accumulation, the replacement of labor by ever-deepening capital. This meant that capitalist societies would ultimately always be faced with problems of declining profits and insufficient demand. Monopolization of production and the elimination of competition was one strategy that afforded some relief from these pressures. The other was to look abroad, outside the capitalist system. Colonies could provide both fields to invest capital at higher rates than applied at home and a source of demand for finished products. This was another way in which the fatal crisis might be postponed.

CONTEMPORARY ECONOMIC SYSTEMS

SOCIALISM AND COMMUNISM

Marx believed that capitalism would face repeated crises. These would be caused by the long-run decline in the rate of profit and ever-increasing problems of excess supply as demand failed to keep pace with production. These economic problems would be played out against a backdrop of growing worker alienation. The confluence of these forces would present the crucial limitation on capitalist production and the means by which the system would change. Like other systems before it, it would be swept away. The system that would replace it in his conception of history would be socialism.

The simplest definition of **socialism** is that the ownership and control of the means of production should be held by the community as a whole and administered for the good of all. In Marxian terms, the advent of socialism is characterized by a *dictatorship of the proletariat* and the continued existence of scarcity. Thus it represented in Marx's terms a transitional stage on the way to communism. There are other conceptions of socialism. For example, utopian socialists in Britain saw a much more limited shift in society and the economic organization they envisaged and saw in effect that communities like New Lanark had much in common with worker-owned cooperatives. Socialism also came to be largely identified with the existence of a high degree of centralized planning.

Communism was to be the final culmination of Marx's successive revolutions. In such a society, class was to have vanished and the state as such would largely be unnecessary. Each would contribute according to his or her ability, and each would take according to need. Clearly no society approached this definition of communism and instead the term has come to be largely synonymous with the socialist societies of the Soviet Union and China.

THE GROWTH OF THE WELFARE STATE

While Marx was confident that the crises of capitalism would lead to socialist revolution in the most advanced capitalist societies, this has not been the case. Britain, the United States, and Germany, with large manufacturing workforces, would, at the end of the 19th century, have seemed to be the prime candidates for revolution. However, all of these "escaped." Rather than a revolutionary shift to total public ownership and the dictatorship of the proletariat, these states instead evolved into societies that generally carry the label of **welfare state.**[12] In these nations the government assumed a much greater range of responsibilities, including responsibility for the management of the economy and the creation of what has come to be called the social safety net. Labor got to share to a much greater degree in the increase in productivity that followed technical change, and consequently the revolutionary potential of working class discontent was diffused.

These shifts were gradual; the original impetus in Britain started before World War I, accelerated between the world wars, and culminated with a far-reaching social program immediately following World War II. This included the creation of comprehensive social security, nationalized health care, and the assumption of public ownership of a large swath of industry. In the United States the key dates are the creation of the New Deal by the Roosevelt administration after 1933 and the Great Society program of Lyndon Johnson in the late 1960s.

CORPORATISM AND FASCISM

At various points in this book we will refer to economic systems as "corporatist." This label is a rather loose one and refers to a system of economic organization where the various institutions of labor and capital are licensed by and operate under the close supervision and coordination of the state. Thus **corporatism** combines the market institutions of private property and ownership of the means of production with the idea that the government is responsible for shaping and steering the actions of both labor and capital for the social good. It is a term that has been used to describe Sweden, where the government brings together labor unions and employers' federations to determine national wage settlements. It has been used to characterize Japan, where a triumvirate of politicians, bureaucrats, and industrialists jointly forge a national industrial policy. In its most extreme form it takes on the rather pejorative label of "Japan Inc."

Corporatism has also been closely associated with the political system of **fascism,** which represented the state as being dominated in all aspects of life. In fact, a model of the corporate state was pioneered by the Mussolini regime in interwar Italy.[13] In this conception, under state aegis all industries in the country were

---

[12] Evolution is perhaps too mild a word for the metamorphosis in Germany, which throughout the 1920s teetered on the brink of revolution before falling to the Fascists in the 1930s. After World War II, the occupying powers were highly influential in restructuring the economic system by decree. Only after this can the German development of the welfare state be regarded as gradual evolution.

[13] See Rondo Cameron, *A Concise Economic History of the World,* 2d ed. (Oxford: Oxford University Press, 1993), 363.

organized into 12 "corporations," controlled by boards on which representatives of labor, business, and the Party served. In reality, they were government sponsored trade associations, or cartels, with the responsibility for allocating output among members, fixing prices, and regulating wages. Although the objective was to promote state control of industry and rapid growth, in fact the monopolistic organization resulted in corruption and a loss of efficiency. In Germany a less structured system gave the government a high degree of control of business and replaced free unions with the National Labor Front. Businessmen were coerced into cooperation by the prospect of relief from the labor strife that had characterized the previous decade.

ECONOMICS AND ISLAM

In the past couple of decades there has been considerable interest in the ideas of **Islamic economics** and attempts to introduce ideas into the economic life of primarily Islamic societies. Its proponents argue that the practice of Islamic economics could unite the strengths of both capitalism and socialism. There are three fundamental precepts: first, an opposition to the use of interest, based on an interpretation of the Qu'ran; the adoption of the *zakat,* a form of voluntary redistribution; and the filtering of all economic decisions through Islamic moral norms. The most important of these ideas in practice is the prohibition on interest. Other societies have attempted to do without the use of interest but none very successfully.[14] Although no entire economies are based on Islamic principles, Islamic banking, as an alternative to the capitalist variety, is present in dozens of countries.

Timur Kuran[15] argues that the prohibition of interest is in fact due to a misinterpretation of the Qu'ran, which sought only to outlaw a particularly grievous practice, whereby the principal was doubled in the event of a default. However, the latter day adherents have insisted on this idea and justify it by the notion that it is immoral to earn income from capital without assuming risk. Instead of the use of loans, therefore, business finance has to be placed exclusively on a basis of shares or "equity" participation. Thus the Islamic Development Bank, which was founded in 1974 by the Organization of the Islamic Conference to promote Koranic principles in the economies of member states, makes no loans but finances development projects in return for participation in terms of a share of the profits, or in return for a "commission rate." This is not unknown, of course, in Western economies. Indeed, the entire venture capital industry, which financed much of the high-tech small company growth in the United States, relies on equity participation rather than loans.

---

[14]Similar restrictions on "usury" were placed by the Roman Catholic church, and this is thought to have been one of the factors that impeded economic growth in the predominantly Catholic countries of the Mediterranean. See, for example, R. H. Tawney's *Religions and the Rise of Capitalism: a Historical Study,* (New York: Harcourt Brace, 1926).

[15]Timur Kuran, "Islamic Economics and the Islamic Sub-Economy," *Journal of Economic Perspectives* 9, no. 4 (fall 1995): pp. 155–173.

However, as we will see in this book, modern economics tends to stress the role of interest as "the price of capital" and it is considered necessary for the efficient operation of an economy, especially in the intertemporal context. In some ways the problem for Islamic systems is parallel to that experienced by centrally planned economies, which, too, eschewed interest rates on principle. Without a market for finance, both the savings/investment decision and the choice of technique decision become more complex and prone to an inefficient outcome.

KEY TERMS AND CONCEPTS

balance of employment

balance of trade

commercial capitalism

communism

the corn laws

corporatism

evolutionary school

fascism

Feudal system

finance capitalism

"hydraulic" societies

industrial capitalism

Islamic economics

laws of motion

mercantilism

Oriental despotism

population growth

superstructure

technological change

socialism

welfare state

QUESTIONS FOR DISCUSSION

1. Why does technological change frequently cause changes in the economic system? Can different economic systems be compatible with a single technology?

2. Why did the system of irrigated agriculture practiced in much of South and East Asia allow the surplus to be appropriated by the state?

3. How did the revival of trade and the advent of the Black Death undermine the feudal system?

4. What economic rationale might there be for a merchant class to favor a balance of payments surplus?

5. In what ways did the repeal of the corn laws in Britain represent a victory for the manufacturing classes over the landowners?

6. In what ways did economic development on Continental Europe differ from development in Britain?

7. Distinguish between socialism and communism as economic systems.

8. What defines a corporatist state?

9. In what ways have Islamic economies found alternatives to handle the restriction on the use of interest rates?

WEB SITES

This chapter is largely concerned with economic history and the history of economic thought. A good starting point for any research into the history of economic thought is the "History of Economic Thought" Web site, which is currently at http://www.econ.jhu.edu/people/fonseca/het/hethome.htm, although it is in the process of relocation. It provides links to Web information on all major economists (living and dead), providing access to biographies, critiques, and their work that is downloadable from the Web. Two particularly useful sites in the context of this course are the following:

1. A searchable and downloadable copy of Adam Smith's *An Inquiry into the Nature and Cause of the Wealth of Nations*, which is at http://www.duke.edu/~atm2/SMITH/

2. The Marx/Engels Internet Archive has links to all of the Web-accessible work of Karl Marx and Friedrich Engles, as well as a lot of commentary. It is at http://csf.colorado.edu/psn/marx/

BOOKS AND ARTICLES

Cameron, Rondo. *A Concise Economic History of the World*, 2d ed., 363. Oxford: Oxford University Press, 1993.

Coleman, D. C. *Revisions in Mercantilism*. London: Methuen, 1969.

Farouqui, Mahmood, ed. *Islamic Banking and Investment: Challenge and Opportunity*. New York: Kegan Paul, 1998.

Fei, John C. H., with Gustav Ranis (Contributor). *Growth and Development from an Evolutionary Perspective*. London: Blackwell, 1997.

Hodgson, Geoffrey M. *Evolution and Institutions: On Evolutionary Economics and the Evolution of Economics*. White Plains: Edward Elgar, 1999.

Presley, John, and John Sessions. "Islamic Economics: The Emergence of a New Paradigm," *Economic Journal* 104 (May 1994): 584–596.

Schwartz, Herman. *States Versus Markets: History, Geography, and the Development of the International Political Economy*. New York: St. Martin's Press, 1994.

Timur, Kuran. "Islamic Economics and the Islamic Sub-Economy," *Journal of Economic Perspectives* 9, no. 4 (Fall 1995): 155–173.

PART TWO

THE OPERATION OF A MARKET ECONOMY

$ vs. DM

Bank

and Indexes

DM

CURRENCY CROSSRATES

Germany   Italy

	Dollar	Pound
Belgium	.517	49.91
Canada	1.369	
ECU	.8261	
France		

3

HOW A MARKET SYSTEM WORKS

ADAM SMITH AND THE INVISIBLE HAND

Ever since Adam Smith described the operation of a private property market system in his seminal work *An Inquiry into the Nature and Causes of Wealth of Nations*,[1] the functioning of markets has inspired a kind of awe rooted in the apparent paradox of his "invisible hand" theorem. In Smith's conception, individuals act only to benefit themselves, yet, given certain preconditions, such behavior results in a social optimum. Selfish individuals collectively generate a level of efficiency and economic well-being that more "rational" systems of central planning have been unable to match. In this chapter, we take a closer look at the operation of market capitalism. How, exactly, does a market system work? What are its essential features? Why has it performed so well in some areas—growth, allocative efficiency, technological innovation—and what are its shortcomings?

Much of what we know about the market system today was well understood by Smith in 1776, although the tools that we use to analyze it differ. Smith argued that the ability to exchange and barter was both fundamental and universal to humankind. It was also unique, one of the things that set humans apart from the animals. In *The Wealth of Nations* he wrote:

> [T]he propensity to truck, barter, and exchange one thing for another . . . is common to all men, and is to be found in no other race of animals, which seem to know neither this nor any other species of contracts. Nobody ever saw a dog make a fair and deliberate exchange of one bone for another with another dog. Nobody ever saw one animal by its gestures and natural cries signify to another, this is mine, that yours; I am willing to give this for that.[2]

Another of Smith's important insights was the need for specialization and **division of labor** if the social product were to be maximized. Rather than meet all of their own needs, individuals are better served by concentrating on what they do

---

[1] Smith (1723–1790) was an 18th-century Scottish political economist and philosopher who laid the foundations of our understanding of the workings of competitive economies in his 1776 book *An Inquiry into the Nature and Causes of the Wealth of Nations*.

[2] There are so many versions of *The Wealth of Nations* that to give the page number of a particular edition might not be helpful to the reader. It is probably clearer to cite the book, chapter, and rough line number. This quote is from book I, chapter 2, line 4 and following. Links to very useful hypertext version are given at the end of this chapter.

best and relying on exchange in the marketplace to meet their needs and to improve their welfare. In Smith's own language, it was

> the certainty of being able to exchange all that surplus part of the produce of his own labour, which is over and above his own consumption, for such parts of the produce of other men's labour as he may have occasion for, encourages every man to apply himself to a particular occupation, and to cultivate and bring to perfection whatever talent or genius he may possess for that particular species of business. The difference of natural talents in different men is, in reality, much less than we are aware of; and the very different genius which appears to distinguish men of different professions, when grown up to maturity, is not upon many occasions so much the cause, as the effect of the division of labour.[3]

The ability to specialize and exchange, coupled with the single-minded pursuit of their own interests, leads individuals to serve the public good in a much more effective way than if they had altruistically sought to benefit others. This is Smith's **invisible hand,** one of the most compelling and important metaphors in modern social thought. It can be seen as both paradoxical and beautiful, in that individual self-interest leads to a social optimum much more effectively than when people try to promote the general well-being. In fact, as the last two sentences of this quotation reveal, Smith had a deep cynicism of the motives of people who claimed to act in the public good:

> [An individual] intends only his own gain, and he is in this, as in many other cases, led by an invisible hand to promote an end which was no part of his intention. Nor is it always the worse for the society that it was no part of it. By pursuing his own interest, he frequently promotes that of the society more effectually that when he really intends to promote it. I have never known much good done by those who affected to trade for the public good. It is an affectation, indeed, not very common among merchants, and very few words need be employed in dissuading them from it.[4]

MARKETS IN A MODERN ECONOMY

Smith's insights into the operation of markets remain in many respects as valid today as in the 18th century when he first made them. However, the complexity of modern economies has increased. Today, every economy based on exchange consists of many thousands of individual markets. There are, for example, financial markets, labor markets (which exist for many different kinds of labor), agricultural markets, markets for intermediate goods, and so on. These markets do not function in isolation but are linked so that each one interacts in some way with the others. Changes in the taste for a single good require adjustment not only in its own market but also in all other markets; the present and future prices of labor, intermediate goods price, and factors of production will all change, perhaps only to some

---

[3] Book I, chapter 2, line 30 and following.
[4] Book IV, chapter 2, line 40 and following.

infinitesimally small degree. Because the consequences for other markets are in many cases small, economists often look at the impact of a disturbance on a single market alone. This approach is called **partial equilibrium.** However, we must always be aware that there are impacts on all other markets, on all goods and factors, in all places and times. The full effect is an adjustment to a new **general equilibrium.**

Acting together, these markets determine a price for all goods, factors, and services, and they also determine the quantities of each that will be supplied. It is instructive to consider the alternative to reliance on the market to make these decisions. If they all had to be made by a planning authority, the amount of information that would have to be gathered at the center of the economy would be huge. Planners would have to attempt to estimate the demand for products and gear the entire production process toward its satisfaction. One of the most appealing features of a market system is that it coordinates itself in the absence of a central coordinating authority.

GOODS MARKETS

To illustrate this, let us begin by looking at a single market for a good, depicted in Figure 3.1. The tools we will need are familiar to most students from their work in introductory and intermediate economic theory, and for more thorough treatment of the issues they would be advised to look over that material again. Here we will look only at some important features of competitive markets, focusing on issues of supply and demand. Dr. Johnson, Adam Smith's contemporary, acerbically observed that he could teach a parrot all that was essential about economics if he could get it to say the two words *supply* and *demand*. Although this overstates the issue, the important features of competitive markets can be illustrated using these concepts.

■ **FIGURE 3.1**

A SIMPLE MARKET MODEL

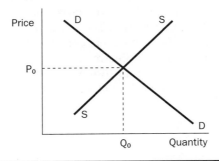

On one side of the analysis, we have a **market demand curve, D.** This is an array of pairs of prices and quantities that reflect how much of a good the individuals who compose the market would be willing to purchase at given prices. This market demand curve is an aggregation of the demands of individuals, households, firms, and government. It is in a sense an abstraction. It is valid only instantaneously and is based on the assumption that the prices of all other goods, as well as incomes and tastes, are constant. We expect and assume the demand curve to be downward sloping. This reflects the generally held principle that for all consumers the more of a good that they have the less they will value the last, or marginal, unit of that good.

On the other hand, we have the **market supply curve, S.** Like the demand curve, this is a collection of pairs of prices and quantities. This curve reflects how much the market participants would be prepared to sell at various prices. In the case of a good that can be newly produced (let us say agricultural products or manufactured goods), the supply curve is represented as upward sloping because marginal costs of production are assumed to rise (in the medium term at least) as production increases. The intersection of the supply curve and the demand curve gives us the equilibrium price—that price at which the consumers will be able to buy all that they wish to and the sellers will be able to part with exactly what they want to sell. For a market to be competitive, there must be many sellers and many buyers, and no one seller or buyer is important enough to affect the sale price. The price therefore moves to equilibrate the demand and the supply side of the market, without any one individual or firm decisively influencing the outcome.

Two things should be noted here. First, neither demand nor supply curves are readily observable. The point defined by the equilibrium price and quantity pair is the only one that we actually observe on either curve.[5] Second, because of the interaction of the many thousands of markets, equilibrium in any product market is likely to be a fleeting affair. Conditions in other markets will change, creating changes in all markets as the interactive system searches, constantly, for a general equilibrium.

An important feature of markets is that, under competitive assumptions, the market price of a good will be equal to its marginal cost of production. This follows because the equilibrium price lies on the supply curve, and the supply curve is the aggregation of the marginal cost curves of suppliers. Because the equilibrium price also lies on the demand curve, we can be sure that it will also be equal to the valuation that the marginal consumer puts on his or her last unit of purchase. Thus a competitive market ensures that goods will be produced up to, and not beyond, the point where the marginal cost of production is equal to the value that the marginal consumer places on it. If all markets were competitive, then all prices would be equal to their marginal costs. Economic theory further tells us that this would be an efficient outcome in the sense that no other allocation of resources could produce more of any one good without reducing the output of another. It also has a

---

[5] Using econometric techniques we are able, under certain conditions, to estimate both curves.

ADJUSTMENT TO DEMAND SHIFT IN THE SHORT RUN

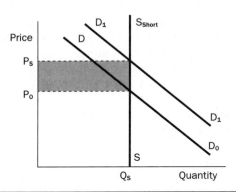

quality appeal to some people as being equitable. Those who consume goods must pay the marginal costs of production of those goods.

A SHIFT IN DEMAND.   What happens if the demand for a good changes as a result of some exogenous event? As a first example, consider a shift in consumer tastes favoring the good which is represented in Figure 3.1. The higher demand is represented by a shift in the demand curve to the right—more is demanded at every price of the good. The adjustment to this disturbance can be looked at in three phases. In the short run, the supply of the good is fixed, and the supply curve S_{short} will be perfectly inelastic, or vertical. The full response to the change in demand will be reflected by price change. The price of the good will increase sharply from P_0 to P_S reflecting the short-term scarcity. Those fortunate enough to have stocks of the good will be able to reap **windfall profits.** This is shown in Figure 3.2, where the shaded area reflects those windfall profits.

In the medium term, shown in Figure 3.3, the higher prices will encourage existing producers to increase their output, probably by hiring additional labor. Capital, which is normally regarded as invariate in the medium term, cannot be increased within this time frame. Only variable inputs (usually labor) can be changed. Therefore the supply curve S_{medium} is upward sloping and moderately elastic (responsive to price). The additional output $(Q_M - Q_0)$ is produced at higher marginal cost than the original output, because on average each worker is working with less capital than previously. The "law of diminishing returns" suggests that as variable inputs (labor) are increased against a fixed input (capital) the marginal product of labor will fall. However, the rate of return on capital will rise, because capital is now relatively scarce in this industry. The higher than average rates represent "economic profit" and will attract new capital to the industry, lowering marginal costs and establishing a new long-term equilibrium.

ADJUSTMENT TO DEMAND SHIFT IN THE MEDIUM TERM

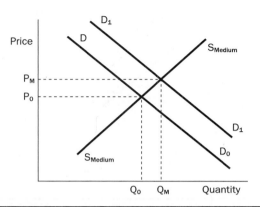

Economic profits, defined as returns on capital above the normal rate, are vital for the efficient functioning of a market system in responding to changes. Such profits, or their equally important counterpart economic losses, are generated in the short term and medium term when there are shifts in supply or demand. Profits and losses, therefore, are signaling devices in a market system. The existence in some industries or product lines of rates of return on capital that are above the economy-wide average, or normal, rate of return will cause capital to flow to those sectors. This will, in turn, lead to increased output, moderated prices, and the eventual complete erosion of the super-normal profits. Most important, capital will flow into those industries where its productivity is greatest, leading to a more efficient allocation of resources. Figure 3.4 illustrates the consequences of this capital inflow. The long run supply curve S_{long} is likely to be more elastic (flatter) than its short and medium counterparts. The increase in consumer demand results in increased output and only moderately increased prices, which reflect the marginal cost of the production of the good after new investment has entered the industry.

INNOVATION.   Let us consider now a second form of market disturbance. A single supplier makes an innovation in the production process that results in a lower marginal cost of production. Since initially he is the only producer to make this innovation, he will earn excess profits in the form of "economic rent." **Rent** is a return over and above the average rate of profit. This accrues to him because of ownership of a specific factor of production, in this case the productive innovation. The rent will be earned as long as the innovator holds the monopoly of this knowledge, and in all likelihood market share will increase. In the long term other producers will either have to match the cost savings that result from the innovation or go out of business.

■ **FIGURE 3.4**

ADJUSTMENT TO DEMAND SHIFT IN THE LONG RUN

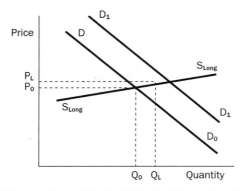

The market encourages innovation by providing unusually high rates of return to those producers that successfully introduce a cost-saving improvement. The same process in effect requires that all producers match the innovation, or improve on it, or they will lose their market share to more efficient competitors.

OTHER DISTURBANCES. We could show in a similar fashion how the market deals with other kinds of disturbance. A sudden exogenous reduction in supply (a shift of the supply curve to left) under conditions of constant demand will again yield windfall profits to the remaining producers and provide incentives to channel new investment into the industry. A sharp exogenous increase in supply (a rightward shift in the supply curve) will have the reverse effect. It will lower prices and the rate of return in the industry below the level of the economy at large. New investment will be diverted from the industry to other uses, and when the historically committed capital is depleted by depreciation it will not be replaced until average rates of return rise to the economy-wide level.

REQUIREMENTS FOR MARKET EFFICIENCY

Perfect markets require such an exacting set of preconditions that we can, by and large, dismiss their existence in the real world. For example, perfection would require that all participants in the market would need to know all prices for all goods and factors, both current and future. A more realistic concern is whether or not markets are reasonably allocatively efficient and handle the task of answering the essential economic questions in the fashion that is most prone to increase consumer welfare. Even this lesser standard requires a lot of preconditions, some of which may not be met, resulting in "market failures." We have mentioned some of these in passing. For example, efficient markets are characterized by many suppliers and many buyers so that there is no accretion of market power that may be exploited. Efficiency also requires good information. Buyers must be aware of the prices of all substitute goods and indeed have knowledge about the future movement of prices. Producers must be similarly well informed about the prices of other potential products, as well as raw materials and factors of production.

THE ROLE OF THE ENTREPRENEUR.   The existence of the **entrepreneur** is vitally important for the efficient functioning of markets. The establishment of super-normal profits as signals is effective only insofar as there is someone there to recognize, appreciate, and act on the signals. In the 18th-century world of Adam Smith, as well as in the 19th-century milieu of Alfred Marshall,[6] the ownership of capital and the management of business were by and large embodied in the same people. These entrepreneurs represented restless, potentially footloose capital, which was mobile enough to flow into industries in which profits were unusually high. One question that hangs over the analysis of contemporary markets is whether institutional change, particularly the separation of ownership from management, has led to the weakening of entrepreneurial activity, and a consequent reduction in market efficiency.

FACTOR MARKETS

So far we have discussed the functioning of markets for goods, but an efficient system also requires the market mechanisms to determine the allocation of factors of production (capital, land, and labor) between competing uses. Similar basic principles apply here as in the goods markets. In a free enterprise system individuals have the ability to offer their labor to any employer. Generally they will choose that occupation and employer who offers the highest wages or compensation package, although nonpecuniary factors like job satisfaction, working conditions, hours of work, and security of job tenure will also play a part in a worker's rational choice.

The employer in turn is free to hire as much labor as he or she chooses and will be indifferent between workers as long as they all contribute the same amount to output. It is a normal assumption of economics that, at least after a certain point, the marginal product of workers declines. This is the result of an important observed generality termed the law of diminishing marginal returns.[7] Employers will hire labor up to the point where the contribution that the marginal worker makes to revenues (termed the **marginal revenue product**) is equal to the wage that must be paid. If hiring proceeds beyond this point, under diminishing returns, additional workers will reduce profit. If all workers are indistinguishable in terms of

---

[6] Alfred Marshall (1842–1924), an Englishman, is regarded by many as the father of modern economics. Marshall's work pioneered the **marginalist** or neoclassical model of the functioning economy. A useful Web site for investigating the life of Marshall and for accessing many of his works is http://www.econ.jhu.edu/people/fonseca/HET/MARSHALL.HTM

[7] Like all economic laws, the law of diminishing marginal returns is a generalized assumption based on both reasoning and observation.

their contribution, and therefore interchangeable, then the wage will be the same for all and will be equal to the revenue product of the marginal worker.

This situation embodies again both efficiency and a form of fairness. The worker is paid the contribution that he or she makes to the revenue of the enterprise. If this "marginal revenue product" were greater in other employment the worker would, everything else being equal, change jobs and earn the higher wage. This would happen because the owner or manager of the firm in which the worker's marginal revenue product were greater would offer the worker a higher wage to leave his or her current occupation. No employer would offer more than its marginal product, but each would be prepared to pay up to that amount. The employer to whom the worker is most valuable would win out. This competitive process ensures that workers are employed in their socially highest value use. This will, in its turn, produce an efficient outcome for the economy as a whole. It can also be argued that this process is in a sense equitable, because each worker is paid the amount by which he or she increases the social product. While this feature of market systems is very appealing to some, it is to others a more problematic proposition and one that merits further examination in chapter 4 when we consider if the distribution of well-being that results in a market economy may appropriately be considered as a failure of the system.

CAPITAL MARKETS

In a modern market economy the **capital market** plays a particularly central role. In the 18th or 19th century, it was often true that a single entrepreneur was both the manager of the enterprise and the owner of the capital. Today, enterprises are larger and much more use is made of financial intermediaries to provide the funds for investment. Small savers place their money in banks for which they receive interest payments, and these resources are comingled and lent by the banks to firms. Alternatively, a firm can turn to venture capitalists for a loan (usually pledging some share of future profits) or issue instruments of debt, corporate bonds, in order to gather investment funds. A further avenue is provided by the sale of stocks or shares in the future profit stream of the enterprise.

The function of financial markets is to assess the combination of expected returns and potential risks and to allocate the capital to those ventures that offer the best combination of risk and return. In the case of a bank-financed startup, the entrepreneur must present a business plan and collateral and the loan officer of the bank must decide if the potential borrower is creditworthy. The bank wants to loan its limited resources to those borrowers with the highest probability of repayment. Alternatively, if the entrepreneur seeks finance by issuing stock, she or he will try to sell the shares into the stock market at an appropriate price. In this way the financial markets are the midwives for new ventures. Acting together, the individual actors will allocate society's scarce capital resources among potential users. It is important for the efficiency of the system that they act impartially, focusing solely on the hard financial facts, and remain unswayed by personal or political factors.

As well as providing means for the birth and growth of firms, the financial markets also act as undertakers, even executioners, by ensuring that existing firms whose prospects do not merit continued investment are culled from the system. By refusing to issue new loans, or by the protracted fall in the value of companies' shares, the financial markets are signaling to the management and ownerships of firms a judgment concerning the prospects and performance of the firm. In the short term this can just be a signal to mend its ways; in the longer term it is a death sentence. Michael Keren has expressed this idea well:

> The capital market as well as providing for the birth of firms, also provides for their death, and for changes in their course in midlife. It plays a Darwinian role of selection. As in Darwinian natural evolution, here too the role of chance is great and the dependence on time is paramount. What succeeds today may be what failed yesterday, because yesterday was not ripe for the idea, or because it was not properly packaged.[8]

Most important, the judgment of the capital market is an impartial one. It is not the opinion of an individual, a politician, or even a "National Board of Investment" that motivates the decision in a free market economy, but the result of the interplay of many groups. The verdict is a weighted one that takes into account the informed views of a range of people. Bankers, loan officers, fund managers, and individual investors must all make the best informed decisions that they can, otherwise the capital that they own or manage will be lost. If a loan officer shows protracted and systematic bias, his own job, and the future of the bank are at risk. If a fund manager favors pet theories that run counter to logic, her performance suffers and she will have less capital to manage. The dispassionate function of capital markets is one of the strengths of the market system.

As we shall see in subsequent chapters of this book, one of the drawbacks of centralized socialist planning is the pervasive influence of what has come to be called a **soft-budget constraint.** This phenomenon has long been observed. In the 1930s the Austrian Economist Ludwig von Mises[9] attacked the theory of socialism on the grounds that rational calculation was impossible without a clearly defined "bottom line."[10] However, the seminal work on the soft budget constraint, and the coining of the term itself, was by an "insider," the Hungarian economist Janos Kornai[11] who observed firsthand the operation of an economy without capital markets. He noted that in the absence of impartiality in credit and investment funds, and with the lack of a mechanism to gage and act on performance, an enterprise manager has little incentive to perform in a socially efficient way. Rather his time is better spent influencing those who hold the key to his fate by allowing his access to credit. Instead of being confronted by a "hard" budget constraint, where the amount that a manager could spend or borrow was performance related, he operated under a

---

[8] From "On the (Im)possibility of Market Socialism," *Eastern Economic Review* 19, no. 3 (1993): 333–344.

[9] Von Mises lived from 1881–1973. He was considered by Milton Friedman to have done more to spread the fundamental ideas of free markets than any other individual. The curious can start their search at http://www.econ.jhu.edu/people/fonseca/HET/mises.htm

[10] See Ludwig von Mises, *Socialism: An Economic and Sociological Analysis,* 2d ed. (New Haven: Yale University Press, 1951).

[11] See "The Soft Budget Constraint," *Kyklos* 39 (1986).

soft budget constraint, determined in large part by the degree to which he was fa-vored by his political masters.

ARBITRAGE AND SPECULATION

Profits are important in a market system because they attract the attention of en-trepreneurs and channel new capital into an industry. However, the quest for profit is also vital in keeping the markets themselves "orderly"—that is, consistent across space and time. The differential in price of a good between any two geo-graphical points should be no greater than the cost of transportation between those points. Orderly markets require the action of **arbitrageurs** who engage in a simul-taneous transaction of buying where the price is high and selling where the price is low, earning a profit at least enough to cover the transaction and transportation costs.

The orderly nature of markets is also furthered by the activity of **speculators.** Unlike arbitrageurs, speculators take a position concerning the direction that they anticipate prices to move in. Investing in shares traded on a stock exchange or the commodities traded on a mercantile exchange is classic speculative activity. It is a popular misconception that speculators increase the volatility of markets. Pure speculation will be profitable only if the speculator buys, and therefore increases the demand for the good, when the price is low and sells when the price is high, raising the supply. Thus speculation, in fact, reduces the amplitude of market swings and assists in the efficient operation of markets.

CHARACTERISTICS OF THE MARKET SYSTEM

A competitive market system has a number of advantageous features worth briefly reviewing here:

(1) UNDER A MARKET SYSTEM DISEQUILIBRIA ARE SELF-CORRECTING. Self-correction is certainly one of the most important features of a market system. Be-cause of the flexible prices, disequilibria created by supply shocks or demand shifts invoke a coordinated and automatic response. Any disturbance in the system will set in train a series of reactions that will adjust the entire system to take account of the changed circumstances, resulting in **self-correcting disequilibria.** Consider a rise in demand. As a first-order effect the price of the good itself will rise, as will the factors of production and materials that go into making it. The prices of sub-stitutes will rise too, those of complements will fall. Thousands of prices will change in thousands of markets without any central authority directing it. Under central planning the whole menu of prices would have to be adjusted, relying on *ad hoc* decisions, or models, to arrive at a new equilibrium.

An example of this process of adjustment was provided by the market response to the oil shocks of the 1970s. As an example it is complicated by the fact that some "free market" governments (including the United States) acted to impose price controls that prevented the market mechanism from adjusting swiftly and fully to the shock. However, what we did see was a restriction of supply, creating short-run profits. This set in train a series of further adjustments. Higher prices encouraged reduced consumption of oil and oil products. Homes became better insulated, thermostat sales increased, car engines became smaller. Industry sought new, less energy intensive techniques. The prices of energy substitutes rose, and returns to capital and labor in those industries increased. New sources of supply were brought on line; new capital was invested in oil exploration, production, and oil field rehabilitation. What to some had seemed a potentially catastrophic blow to the global economy had by the early 1980s been absorbed and corrected for by market action. Government policy, whether price controls or promotion of alternative fuels, had little impact on the resolution of the crisis. In the Soviet bloc countries, energy prices did not change substantially despite the shift in world prices. Those countries continued with cheap energy, energy-intensive production techniques, and waste until the end of the 1980s, with damaging consequences for their competitiveness when they ultimately emerged into the world economy.

(2) MARKETS MINIMIZE THE NEED FOR INFORMATION FLOWS. For a planning agency to engineer the complex adjustment to prices, quantities and production techniques across the board that the response to the oil shock produced, and to get the response right, it would have to be both extremely well informed and rather lucky. The market system requires no such centralization of information. The individual actors in the system need only to know the information required for each to maximize its own welfare. No one individual or agency needs have access to all price and cost information, and no one needs have a full understanding how the whole system works. Thomas Schelling put it this way:

> The dairy farmer doesn't need to know how many people eat butter and how far away they are, how many other people raise cows, how many babies drink milk, or whether more money is spent on beer or milk. What he needs to know is the prices of different feeds, the characteristics of different cows, the different prices [for milk], the relative cost of hired labor and electrical machinery, and what his net earnings might be if he sold his cows and raised pigs instead.[12]

This economy of information is valuable. It saves expense in having to collect and relay data, and the resource cost of the bureaucracy to process it, issue directives, and monitor the fulfillment of the objectives. Perhaps most important, the market offers very few opportunities to gain advantage by falsifying data or misrepresenting a situation. As we shall see when we discuss the economic consequences of the centrally planned economy in more detail in chapter 15, the information gathered by central planners is frequently flawed because there are incentives for the enterprise managers in planned systems to provide inaccurate information to the center. In some cases they might deliberately understate their potential output, enabling them to limit their production quotas. In other cases

---

[12]Cited in Richard Lipsey, Peter Steiner, Douglas Purvis, and Paul Courant, *Economics,* 9th ed. (New York: Harper and Row, 1990), 423.

they might overstate their need for material inputs. Gathering data is expensive, and checking the accuracy of data may be prohibitive. A system that minimizes information demands and decentralizes decision making avoids the problems of a whole system orientating itself on data that are themselves faulty.

(3) A MARKET SYSTEM PROVIDES STIMULUS TO INNOVATION. Under a market system **innovators** who pioneer new, lower cost processes or new products that appeal to consumers are rewarded in the short run by **super-normal profits,** or **economic rent.** It costs resources to develop new processes or goods, and in a market system this investment is made in the expectation of gain through profit. Many innovative ventures fail, and the would-be innovator loses the investment, but some that have marked impact on our well-being are successful.

A planned system on the other hand leaves the development of new products largely to the research agencies of the state. An enterprise manager has little incentive to research new techniques or goods other than those that he or she has been charged to adopt or produce by the planners. Attempts at innovation could only prove a distraction, taking the manager's attention and budgeted resources away from the prime task of meeting his or her physical production targets.

(4) UNDER A MARKET SYSTEM RELATIVE PRICES REFLECT RELATIVE COSTS. Under a competitive system there is a tendency for the price of a good to be driven toward the marginal cost of its production. At the margin of his or her consumption, therefore, the consumer must be prepared to pay the costs of the inputs and factors that have gone into the production of the marginal unit of the good. The relative prices of goods thus reflect the relative costs of the production. This is sometimes expressed in microeconomic terms as the marginal rate of substitution in consumption is equal to the marginal rate of transformation in production. This is an allocatively efficient outcome. Society's scarce resources are directed toward the production of goods that have the highest values in the eyes of the consumer. Therefore social welfare is maximized. An increase in the cost of a resource will raise the cost of the good in whose production it is used. When governments intervene and determine either the quantities of goods to be produced or the prices that shall be charged for them, it is more than likely that relative prices and relative costs of production will diverge. This is not a problem that is exclusively seen in centrally planned economies. Price controls are frequently used to depress the costs of goods or services that politicians, in the name of equity, think should be cheap, generally with unfortunate results for both long-term supply and allocative efficiency.

(5) A MARKET SYSTEM OPPOSES THE CONCENTRATION OF POWER. As we shall see when we look at the behavior of planned economies, their function requires combining political and economic power. The political masters not only control the lives of the citizenry through the legal system, but they also control their real incomes through the availability of goods and the prices that are charged. In a highly competitive market structure there is very little concentration of economic power. Again we should note that under the kind of capitalist market

systems that we actually confront there is considerable accretion of economic power. The leaders of industry and trade unions do have considerable power, both in the marketplace itself and through lobbying in the halls of government. In the late 19th century, economic power in the United States became so concentrated that it motivated the intervention of government to break up the mammoth trusts that had grown up. In the 1950s and 1960s there was considerable alarm that the economic and political systems of the developed market economies were evolving into a form of corporatism, but one in which the state was subsidiary to the needs of the corporations rather than vice versa.[13] The sovereignty of the consumer is constantly under threat, but compared to the concentration of power that occurred in the Soviet Union under communism or that is still observed in China today, the consequences were modest.

Even if the leaders of an authoritarian state are well intentioned and seek nothing but the general good of the population, the task of organization and coercion is so great that there is every probability that the relying on the enterprise of individuals will render a happier conclusion. This too was the belief of Adam Smith, and we conclude this chapter with another quote from his most insightful work:

> When all systems either of preference or of restraint are taken away, the obvious and simple system of natural liberty establishes itself of its own accord. Every man, as long as he does not violate the laws of justice, is left perfectly free to pursue his own interest in his own way and to bring both his industry and capital into competition with those of any other man or order of men. The sovereign is completely discharged from a duty, in the attempting to perform which he must always be exposed to innumerable delusions and for the proper performance of which no human wisdom or knowledge could ever be sufficient—the duty of superintending the industry of private people and of directing it toward the employments most suitable to the interest of the society. . . . [T]he sovereign has only three duties to attend to; three duties of great importance, indeed, but plain and intelligible to common understandings: first, the duty of protecting the society from the violence and invasion of other independent societies; secondly, the duty of protecting, as far as possible, every member of the society from the injustice or oppression of every other member of it, or the duty of establishing an exact administration of justice; and thirdly, the duty of erecting and maintaining certain public works and certain public institutions.

KEY TERMS AND CONCEPTS

arbitrageurs

capital market

division of labor

economic rent

entrepreneur

general equilibrium

innovation

invisible hand

marginal revenue product

market demand curve, D

---

[13] These ideas about the concentration of economic and political power in the United States were addressed in John Kenneth Galbraith's *The New Industrial State*.

market supply curve, S

partial equilibrium

self-correcting disequilibria

soft-budget constraint

speculators

super-normal profits

windfall profits

QUESTIONS FOR DISCUSSION

1. Describe the role of profit and the role of the entrepreneur in correcting disequilibria.
2. Why are arbitrage and speculation important for the orderly operation of markets?
3. Why are market systems economical in the need for centralizing data?
4. Why is it important for relative prices to reflect relative costs of production in general?
5. What economic functions does Smith conceive of as being the preserve of the sovereign?
6. Why is the capital market both a "midwife" and an "undertaker"?
7. How does a competitive market system oppose the concentration of power?
8. Is the tendency of the wages to reflect the marginal revenue product under competition a recipe for "fairness"?

RESOURCES

WEB SITES

The History of Economic Thought Web site . . . . http://www.econ.jhu.edu/people/fonseca/HET/
More about Smith, Marshall, and von Mises can be found at this site.

The von Mises Institute . . . . http://www.mises.org/
The von Mises Institute is a libertarian think tank and lobby group.

The Cato Institute . . . . http://www.cato.org/
A lot of other libertarian information and ideas can be found at this site.

The Adam Smith Institute . . . . http://www.adamsmith.org.uk/

BOOKS AND ARTICLES

Fry, Michael, ed. *Adam Smith's Legacy: His Place in the Development of Modern Economics.* New York: Routledge, 1992.

Galbraith, John Kenneth. *The New Industrial State.* Boston: Houghton Mifflin, 1971.

Keren, Michael. "On the (Im)possibility of Market Socialism," *Eastern Economic Review* 19, no. 3 (1993): 333–344.

Kornai, Janos. *The Socialist System: The Political Economy of Communism.* Princeton: Princeton University Press 1992.

Kornai, Janos. "The Soft Budget Constraint," *Kyklos* 39, no. 1 (1986): 3–30.

Smith, Adam. *The Wealth of Nations,* ed. D. D. Raphael. London: Everyman's Library Series, 1991.

von Mises, Ludwig. *Economic Calculation in the Socialist Commonwealth.* Auburn, Ala.: Ludwig von Mises Institute, 1990.

MARKET FAILURE
AND GOVERNMENT FAILURE

At the close of chapter 3, we saw that Adam Smith envisaged the task of government as highly limited and beneficent only in three areas: national defense, the administration of justice, and in certain large-scale infrastructural investments that private industry would not, or could not, assume. However, a glance at any modern market economy reveals that government activity is not confined to these areas but extends into production, regulation, and redistribution. In the wealthy countries of the Organization for Economic Cooperation and Development (OECD) governments take in and spend an average of about 40 percent of gross domestic product (GDP).[1] Despite the common political rhetoric of the 1980s and 1990s on the need to downsize government, the trend, measured in terms of governments' share of GDP, seems to be inexorably upward.[2] How is such widespread interference in the market economy explained? There are two main answers: the correction of "market failure" and redistribution of the social product toward disadvantaged, primarily economically inactive, groups.

MARKET FAILURE

One general justification for government intervention in the operation of free enterprise economy is **market failure.** While many modern economies are characterized by highly competitive markets for some products and factors of production, the conditions necessary to establish perfect competition in all markets are seldom encountered. Four phenomena considered to lead to serious inefficiencies are briefly listed here:

1. **Market power.** The possession of substantial market power by a single or small group of market participants creates conditions under which prices deviate from marginal costs, an allocatively inefficient outcome. Similarly we might encounter market power in the supply of labor through unionization, implying that the price of labor will differ from the value of its marginal product.

---

[1] Average general government receipts comprised 38.2 percent of GDP in the OECD nations in 1996. Disbursements averaged 41 percent, creating an average general government deficit of 2.8 percent of GDP.

[2] This apparently universal and irresistible trend has been dignified with the label Wagner's law, after the work of the 19th-century German political economist Adolph Wagner.

2. **Lack of information.** Any inability of relevant market participants to access relevant information at reasonable cost prevents them from acting in an economically rational fashion.

3. **Public goods.** Goods that are nonrival in consumption and for which the marginal cost of supply is zero will not be produced in efficient quantities by a private market.

4. **Externalities.** Outcomes based on private costs and private benefits are inefficient when social costs and social benefits are economically significant.

Government intervention has frequently been seen as a corrective to these problems, but there is a growing criticism that such action is often more harmful than the market imperfections that occasioned it. In this chapter we will first examine the rationale for such intervention and then we will assess to what degree government action is likely to benefit, rather than harm, the general welfare.

SOURCES OF MARKET FAILURE: MARKET POWER

Markets function efficiently only when no participant has substantial market power. Such power may be found on either side of the market. However, it is power on the supply side, monopoly (a single seller) and oligopoly (a few sellers), that has been seen as the most injurious to economic welfare and has been the target of most governmental legislative, judicial, and regulatory activity. Market power on the buying side (monopsony) is considered less harmful to public welfare and is rarely a target of regulatory activity.[3]

THE PROBLEM OF MONOPOLY

When markets are perfectly competitive, firms are **price takers,** facing a horizontal, or infinitely elastic, demand curve. Any deviation of price from that dictated by the market will result either in a lower than normal profit rate, untenable in the long run, or a total loss of sales to lower priced producers. Competitive pressures ensure that the market price is equal to the marginal cost of production. Whenever markets are not perfectly competitive, a firm's demand curve is not horizontal but slopes downward; the firm becomes a **price setter,** having some control over the prices that it charges.

Confronted by downward sloping demand curves, profit-maximizing firms restrict production, raise prices, and, therefore, generate economic profits, returns above the normal rate for all industries. The existence of barriers to entry prevents these super-normal profits from serving their usual function, which should be to

---

[3] In fact monopsony is most likely to lie with the government, which is often the sole purchaser of defense output and which in the welfare states of many European countries is the sole purchaser of health-related goods. There is little harm to the general welfare in this form of monopsony, which is frequently seen as a "countervailing power" to monopoly power.

MONOPOLY

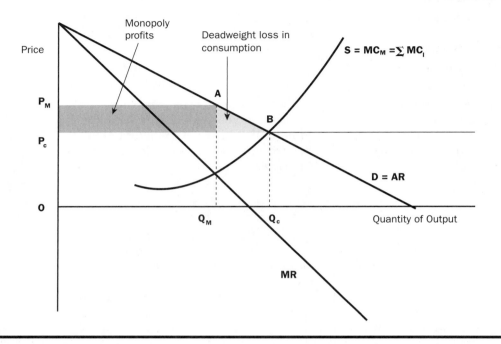

attract new entrants and capital into the industry that would, over time, return the profit rate to normal. Importantly, monopoly drives a wedge between the price that the buyer must pay and the marginal cost of production. Consumption is reduced and consumers' surplus is lost creating economic inefficiency. This is illustrated in Figure 4.1. The monopolist maximizes profit by setting output at the point where marginal cost is equal to marginal revenue. This results in a lower output than might be the case under competition Q_M as opposed to Q_c, and a higher price, P_M as opposed to P_c. The loss of welfare is denoted by the triangle labeled deadweight loss in consumption.

Monopoly also results in a transfer of welfare from consumers to the monopolist. This is shown in the diagram by the rectangle labeled monopoly profit. Such a transfer is not a loss to society, since both consumer and monopolist are members, but it is often seen as inequitable and it can be at least as important as the deadweight loss in motivating government action. Correction of this form of market failure, in order to promote efficiency and protect consumers, is considered in many countries a reason for government action.

NATURAL MONOPOLY. Economists have traditionally distinguished between two forms of monopoly. One, usually termed **natural monopoly,** occurs because of

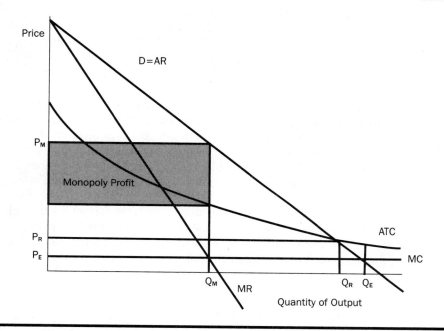

high fixed costs and declining or constant marginal costs, which cause the long-run average cost curve to be falling across the relevant output quantities. If competition can be created, it is only at the cost of the expensive and wasteful replication of facilities. In such cases monopoly is generally tolerated, but it is modified by government action, generally through the control of prices by a public agency.

Natural monopoly is common in industries that require very high fixed costs due to extensive initial capital investment. Electricity supply, telephone networks, and TV cable distribution are frequently cited as typical examples of natural monopoly. The existence of natural monopoly in fact involves a dual problem. As shown in Figure 4.2, in the absence of price regulation, a profit-maximizing monopoly would fix output at Q_M and price at P_M, thus earning profits in excess of the normal rate of return. This provides a rationale for government intervention to fix the price, usually through the activity of a public utility commission.

However, once the decision to regulate has been made, the appropriate price remains a subject of contention. From an efficiency point of view there is a case for regulators to fix the price at marginal cost. In Figure 4.2, we can see that in declining average cost industries marginal cost lies below average cost for all relevant output levels. Marginal cost pricing would give a price of P_E, and would require an output of Q_E. However, at such a price revenues would fail to cover the total costs of the enterprise. Such policy would require the granting to the utility of a subsidy (ideally in the form of a block grant) from the government to cover fixed costs. Subsidies of this kind are often politically unattractive, and a common "compromise" solution is for regulatory commissions to fix the price at average total cost, as shown in the diagram as P_R. This price is above the marginal cost and allows the utility to cover all fixed and variable costs including a "normal" rate of return on capital. This solution avoids the "gouging" potentiality of an unregulated monopoly, but it does dilute incentives to strive for optimal efficiency. It also presents the possibility of capture of the regulatory agency by the regulatee, a topic we will return to as an example of "government failure."

Natural monopolies do not represent a fixed and unchanging set of industries but are a function of the state of technology. They are a much less significant phenomenon in the long run than in the short run, and economists now regard them as less of an impediment to efficiently functioning markets than in the past. Changes in technology are capable of bringing about the emergence of competitors that may obviate the need for regulation, and sometimes regulation is a barrier to their emergence.

Consider, for example, long-distance telephone services. When all phone traffic had to be carried on fixed cables, the construction of the network was very expensive. There was an opportunity to earn monopoly profits because the high cost of establishing the network made the entry of a second or third supplier unlikely. Furthermore, in most people's minds it would be socially wasteful to replicate the network. The emergence of satellite technology to replace cables has had a profound effect on competitive structure and eased entry, obviating the need for regulation. However, it took regulatory changes (in the United States there was the breaking up of ATT, the telephone monopoly, and in much of Europe there was the end of state-provided phone service) to allow the wind of competition to blow through the communications marketplace. In electricity supply, a similar change has occurred, due to the realization that, although the grid of cables itself is a natural monopoly, there can be vigorous competition among the suppliers who serve users connected to the grid. Thus, rather than regulating the delivered price of electricity, most of the benefits of competition might be grasped through regulating the price of conveyance on the grid and allowing electricity suppliers to compete on a price basis.

In some cases, government's willingness to intervene in the market can lessen competition and act against the consumers' interest. For example, all transportation modes are gross substitutes and are to some degree in competition with each other. In a market context they can act as a limit on the price behavior of each other. Regulating transportation on a mode-by-mode basis, with mode-specific agencies, can tend to reduce competition in the broader industry and be counterproductive to consumer welfare.

ANTITRUST POLICY. The other form of monopoly (which can be termed unnatural or artificial) is created by the gathering of market share by a dominant enterprise, which then erects barriers to entry to forestall competition. This behavior is countered by what in the United States is termed **antitrust policy,** regulatory and legal action designed to promote freedom of entry and to prohibit the merger (or collusion) of competitive firms that would result in harm to consumers.

All developed nations have a government agency nominally charged with the maintenance of competition, although in some countries it is more vigilant than in others. In the United States the relevant agency is the Federal Trade Commission, an arm of the Department of Justice, empowered to investigate and bring suit in defense of trade. In the United Kingdom it is the Competition Commission, formerly known as the Mergers and Monopoly Commission. Such agencies are charged with reviewing competitiveness on an industry basis, assessing the impact of mergers on competition, and, in cases where the evidence merits, taking legal action because the public interest has been or might be harmed.

In doing so, such agencies are looking for accretion of economic power and its impact on economic welfare. In the past much attention tended to be focused on the existence of power as measured by "concentration ratios," defined as the share of domestic market consumption represented by a given number of firms. The logic behind this is that the greater the domination of the market by a small number of firms, the less likely is competition to be intense. The most usual index is the **four firm concentration ratio**—that is, the amount of total sales accounted for by the largest four firms. In the United States, using this basis, the most concentrated industries reported in the Census of Manufacturing were chewing gum and cigarettes (96 and 92, respectively). Another measure is the so-called **Herfindahl Hirschman index** (HHI, named for its originators, O. C. Herfindahl and A. O. Hirschman),[4] which takes account of the market composition among the four largest firms.

However, recent developments have led to a change of thought about how we should measure economic power or loss of welfare. First, there is skepticism of the view that either market share or concentration ratios are useful indices. Many economists today are of the view that what matters to keep a market functional, even if not perfect, is not how static market shares add up but the degree to which the market is **contestable**.[5] The threat of a competitor may be as effective as the existence of one in moderating excesses in pricing behavior. If there are few firms in the market and high **barriers to entry**, potential competition is certainly choked. However, even a total monopolist may be subject to restraint, and behave therefore more like a competitor, if entry into the market is easy. The issue therefore becomes not one of the size of market share at any moment in time but rather the height of the barriers to entry that determine the level of contestability.

Consider the position of Microsoft, Inc. In many areas of personal computer software, the company has a near total monopoly. However, historically, entry into

---

[4] A good discussion of these measures as well as issues of entry can be found in W. Kip Viscusi, John Vernon, and Joseph Harrington, *Economics of Regulation and Anti Trust*, 2d ed. (Cambridge: MIT, 1995).

[5] The original discussion on this topic can be read in William J. Baumol, John C. Panzar, and Robert Willig in *Contestable Markets and the Theory of Industry Structure* (New York: Harcourt Brace Jovanovich, 1982).

the industry has been relatively easy, and high product prices would serve to lure competitors into the industry. Consequently it is the threat, rather than the actuality, of competition that moderates Microsoft's pricing behavior. If, as has been alleged in the current antitrust suit, Microsoft can use its market power to restrict entry, the market is no longer contestable and loss of welfare can result.

The decline in reliance on domestic concentration ratios as indices of market power has been accelerated by the growing integration of the world economy and generally falling barriers to international trade.[6] In the past, domestic markets tended to be relatively closed to each other compared to the situation today. Tariff barriers were higher and frictional impediments to trade more significant because of high communications and transportation costs. **Trade to GDP ratios** were generally lower than they are today. Because of the relatively closed nature of national economies, power in the domestic market represented a definite threat to the welfare of domestic consumers. Now in general there is a greater volume of trade, lower average tariff levels, and an increasing number of regional free trade blocs, all of which make the structure of domestic concentration increasingly irrelevant. In such circumstances, domestic markets, although perhaps highly concentrated, may be highly contestable because of growing competition from abroad and relatively low barriers to entry to foreign firms. For example, the four firm concentration ratio for the U.S. automobile market in the late 1960s was very high, and one firm, General Motors (GM), represented over half the market. Conventionally measured market power was high, but the surge of imports in the 1970s showed how easily contestable the market was. The Federal Trade Commission closed its ongoing investigation of GM in the mid-1970s.

In some cases the existence of this high degree of contestability of domestic markets due to potential entry of foreign firms has led to the virtual abandonment of traditional antitrust policy. Many governments tolerate, encourage, or even help to create through merger **national champions** to monopolize the domestic market and control the resources to compete with foreign firms.[7] This policy is justified generally by the belief in substantial economies of scale in production or, more relevant recently, in research and development.

LABOR UNIONS

So far we have discussed only monopoly in the supply of goods and services. Labor organizations represent the monopolization of a factor of production with a view to restrict supply and raise its price. The consequence in general terms is

---

[6] On balance, trade barriers have been falling across the world due to unilateral tariff cutting and the action of the successive rounds of trade negotiations under the General Agreement on Tariffs and Trade (GATT) and now the World Trade Organization (WTO). One counter to this trend has been the increase in nontariff barriers to trade (NTBs) in recent years.

[7] French policy has often leaned in this direction, especially in the 1970s and 1980s when a policy of creating publicly owned national champions in key industries was espoused.

higher wages and better benefits for workers, and a higher level of unemployment than would exist otherwise.

Governmental policy toward labor unions varies widely from country to country and has changed a good deal over time. For example, in the first capitalist industrial society, 19th-century Britain, the government, elected by and largely beholden to property owners, took a dim view of the union movement because it sought to shift income from capital to labor. It was, therefore, criminalized through the Combination Acts,[8] and union organizers were arrested, imprisoned, and on occasion deported. After the extension of the electoral franchise to nonproperty owners in the 1880s, labor won the right to organize and formed its own political party to protect such gains. Other industrialized nations also saw violence and political upheaval in the birth of the movement.

Today most industrialized countries not only recognize unions, but also make organized labor part of the process of economic management. In Europe especially, organized labor has a prominent role in both politics and economic management as we will discuss more fully in the chapters on Sweden, France, and Germany. However, it should be noted that the decline of heavy industry and the growing surplus of labor in these economies, as indicated by secularly high rates of unemployment, has weakened the power of the union movement. Union power in the European economies is greatest now in the public sector, where it is resistant to market forces because of a clear link to electoral politics.

Later industrializing countries are still passing through the stage of union establishment. The Japanese miracles of the 1960s through 1980s were assisted by the repression of the labor movement in the late 1950s. After decades of opposition by employers and government, Korean unions are now emerging. In countries more remote in development terms, like Indonesia, independent unions are still banned.

LACK OF INFORMATION

Market systems can work well only if consumers have access to reliable information about the product that they are buying. In the case of simple commodities, reliance on the old maxim *caveat emptor* ("let the buyer beware") is probably adequate; information is relatively cheaply available and reputation is an important asset when repeat purchasers are frequent. However, in the case of more complex goods or goods that are purchased infrequently, information might be difficult, impossible, or expensive to obtain.

In such cases, governments frequently step in to "protect" the consumer. In some cases this is done by prescribing specific behavior for those who make and sell products to the public or by dictating specific product standards. Rules or laws

---

[8] The Combination Acts were legislated in 1800 and repealed in 1825; although unions were legal, leaders were still frequently prosecuted for specific job actions, such as strikes. See Rondo Cameron, *A Concise Economic History of the World* (New York: Oxford University Press, 1989), 218.

specify what information a seller must offer to the buyer and what recourse the buyer has in the case of disappointment. In other industries or professions, the government may create barriers to entry by limiting access to the industry to those who have "appropriate qualifications," preventing the unqualified from offering such goods or services. Such licensing is common in a wide variety of professions from lawyers to morticians.

This may provide an effective way of minimizing the consumers' need for expensive information. Consider, for example, a potential patient choosing a surgeon. In most countries only people who have attended medical school, served an internship, and passed examinations can hang up a shingle and offer surgical services. Performing surgery without such qualifications is forbidden. In contrast, there are few restrictions on who can offer to shave people or cut hair. In more remote times, such licensing was not considered essential for surgeons, and indeed barbers doubled surgery with their shaving duties.

Why is government intervention merited in one case and not the other? The answer lies in the availability of information and the consequences of not being able to get it. When it comes to hairdressing, we feel we can rely on reputation to weed out poor performers. One bad haircut does not kill and serves in itself to tell others about performance. One poor surgery can kill, and licensing, while not eliminating the problem entirely, does, it is argued, reduce the risk to the public.

The goal of protecting of the public has spawned a large regulatory industry. In the United States, the government hires inspectors to tell consumers what meat is "choice," requires product information on labels, looks for "misleading" advertising, requires approval of drugs, and so forth. Few people would argue that all of it is necessary, especially in view of the fact that there are market remedies in many cases. Frequently such licensing is the result of rent-seeking behavior, a phenomenon which we will discuss in greater detail later in this chapter.

PUBLIC GOODS

The third major class of market failure is due to the existence of "public goods." The qualities of public goods may best be understood by looking first at those of private goods. Private goods and services, whose supply is left to individual rather than collective action, have two important qualities: excludability and diminishability. **Excludability** enables producers or sellers to charge a price for private goods and services because they can deny access to those who fail to pay the price. **Diminishability** implies that one person's consumption of a good or service reduces the supply available to others. This is really another way of saying that the marginal cost of consumption is greater than zero. Efficiency, therefore, requires that private goods should have a price that is greater than zero as well. Excludability establishes there is a feasible mechanism to impose a charge.

In contrast, pure public goods are neither diminishable nor excludable. The marginal cost of additional unit of consumption is zero, and therefore efficiency requires a zero price. Anyway, there is no cost-effective way of charging for the service. The absence of excludability leads to the **free rider problem,** in which people are able to enjoy the service without payment and therefore make no financial contribution to their "fair" share of costs. Consequently, private institutions will fail to supply, or will chronically undersupply, such goods, and only the government, with its ability to coerce payment through taxation, has the potential to supply the goods at the optimal level.

Although pure public goods are theoretically important, in reality they represent a relatively small class. National defense, the system of administration of justice, and public health measures are salient examples. In none of these cases can an individual be excluded from benefit without fundamentally altering the nature of the good. In virtually all countries, these goods are provided by the government and are financed out of taxation. Moreover, such goods are probably essential for the existence of the modern state, and it is hard to imagine in these cases how a private substitute could be created.

The provision of lighthouses is a much-used example of public goods in the economic textbooks. Its frequency stems more from its tractability than its economic significance. Lighthouses are not as fundamental to an economy as defense or the law, but they obviously do have economic benefits. Use of the services of lighthouses is susceptible to free ridership, and they would therefore be undersupplied by private institutions,[9] who would have to rely on donations from shippers, sailors, and the general public to finance them. It requires a considerable step to assume that the government would get the level of provision right. To supply even pure public goods at an optimal level, the government must have some means of accurately estimating benefits or inducing consumers (in this case the shippers and sailors) to reveal their demand. It is quite conceivable that the government would err just as much as a private system based on subscription or contribution. In fact, the nature of politics and lobbying would probably lead to oversupply, for reasons which will be discussed later in the chapter.

In general, socially provided goods are not "public" in the rigorous sense. In most cases they are excludable, as we can see by looking at the examples of education, health services, highways, recreation facilities, and so forth, all of which have counterparts in the private sector. In most countries, services that are clearly diminishable (for example, postal services or garbage disposal) are provided by the government as well as the private sector. To justify government supply of such potentially private goods and services, market failure is not sufficient. The actual motivations might include distributive concerns, a need to establish equitable standards, or a conviction that government is superior in efficiency terms to private enterprise in some tasks. In recent years economists have focused considerable attention on public goods supply and have frequently arrived at the conclusion that it is determined at least as much by the lobbying activity of interested parties as by a concern for correcting market failure.

---

[9] In fact, despite the clear public good qualities of lighthouses, in the 19th century they were provided largely by private charities.

EXTERNALITIES

The final class of market failure to be introduced here consists of imperfections created by the presence of *externalities*, external economies and diseconomies (which are sometimes called spillovers). These are consequences to third parties (or bystanders) of the economic activities of others. Such consequences may be either positive, contributing to the welfare of the third party, or negative. Because externalities are unrequited (we do not receive compensation for negative effects, nor do we pay for the positive ones), they do not enter into the decision process of the individuals initiating the activity. Decisions by consumers and producers are made by considering private benefits and private costs. From a societal point of view, the appropriate considerations should be social benefit and social cost. This is illustrated in Figure 4.3.

In this diagram, the existence of a substantial externality (perhaps the ability of producers to emit smoke into the atmosphere without paying any pollution fee or compensation to those affected) causes a divergence between the **private marginal cost** and the **social marginal cost.** The consumer is confronted by prices based on the private, not the social marginal cost. Correspondingly, the market system with the imperfection of uncompensated externalities tends to overproduce the good, to the point Q_P in Figure 4.3, rather than the socially optimal position of Q_S.

One of the most obvious and pressing examples of externalities lies in the analysis of environmental issues. Consider a factory that emits air pollution as a by-product of manufacturing a good. In the absence of any control, the manufacturer considers only private benefit and treats the environment as a free resource, despoiling the air and reducing the welfare of others in the process.

■ **FIGURE 4.3**

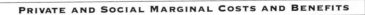

PRIVATE AND SOCIAL MARGINAL COSTS AND BENEFITS

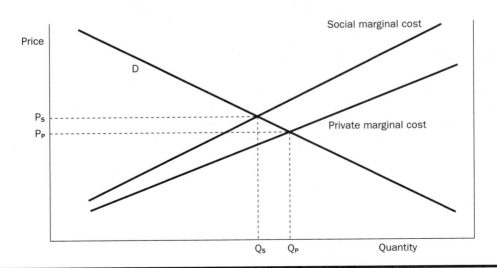

Government regulatory activity to counter pollution can be of several kinds:

- It can ban the polluting process entirely.
- It can establish minimum compliance standards for the manufacturer to meet.
- It can offer subsidies to the manufacturer to reduce pollution.
- It can charge the manufacturer a fee per unit of pollution emitted.

The first two remedies are generally held by economists to be allocatively inefficient. In the first case, banning the production totally will generally result in an undersupply of the polluting good; the loss of consumer welfare from the absolute nonavailability of the product may outweigh the gains of completely clean air or water. In the second case, establishing minimum standards for pollution leaves no incentive for manufacturers to press for a further reduction below the standard, even though an additional cut might be socially beneficial. The third and fourth courses of action can both lead to an economically efficient outcome. A subsidy to reduce pollution can have the same effect as a pollution fee since either can be designed to reflect the marginal cost of the polluting activity. What is obviously very different is the distributional impact of the two approaches. Policy 3 grants the right to pollute to manufacturers and bribes them to stop. Policy 4 gives the manufacturers no rights but forces them to purchase the ability to pollute from the state.

Some economists have argued that the problem of externalities is solely the result of the inadequate specification of property rights. Private individuals who have clear rights of ownership, and who live in countries where the legal system functions well, have recourse against the despoliation of their property or loss of health through a civil suit. The threat of litigation results in negotiation and in many cases a contract that will result in a mutually acceptable, and therefore efficient, solution to "externality problems." Consider, for example, a case in which my neighbor was about to reduce my welfare by building a skyscraper that would block the sun. If my right to access to light were clear and legally guaranteed, then he could only proceed if we were able to arrive at a contract whereby my permission to build was granted on the basis of some form of compensation. Alternatively, if he clearly has the right to use his site in any way he chooses, irrespective of third-party consequences, I might dissuade him from construction through a contract that appropriately compensated him for his lost opportunity and revenue. Either solution would be efficient although the distributional effects (who gained and who lost welfare) would be markedly different according to how the property rights were determined.

This approach to the problem of externalities is exemplified by the work of Ronald Coase.[10] His work suggests that the externality problem might be solved through the complete definition of property rights. Fully comprehensive and well-specified property rights would result in the "internalization" of externalities, and

---

[10] Ronald Coase, "The Problem of Social Cost," *Journal of Law and Economics* 3 (October 1960): 1–44.

the optimal solution would be arrived at through negotiation and contract. This happy result of the Coase theorem is, however, subject to some limitations. "Internalization" leading to mutually agreeable contracts, and therefore efficiency, might be the outcome in cases where the number of participants is small, but as soon as we get to a case where either the affecting or the affected party is numerous the costs of negotiating the appropriate contract may become prohibitively high. In such cases government intervention may achieve close to equivalent results at the cost of fewer resources. Most of the discussion about externalities relates to negative effects; this is partly because issues like pollution, global warming, and traffic congestion are very important issues and play a very prominent role in our lives. However, we should not discount the responsibility of governments to correct the market failure of the under-provision of positive externalities. Indeed, it can be argued that much of the benefit of public education lies in the production of external benefits stemming from educated and productive citizenry.

GOVERNMENT FAILURE

Each of the four phenomena previously discussed is real and each can cause markets to fail, leading to an outcome that is less efficient than would be the case if markets were perfect. Thus there is an initial rationale to consider the use of government action to address market failure. However, it would be imprudent to conclude that government intervention in such cases will always increase welfare. That would unwisely compare imperfect markets to a perfect government. In recent years, economists have taken a more skeptical view of the capabilities of government, recognizing that there are many sources of **government failure,** which can themselves be at least as damaging as the market failure that they seek to correct.

We cannot assume that governments will always be, in Anne Krueger's phrase, "benevolent, costless social guardians."[11] It is problematic even to consider a homogenous "public" interest, because only rarely will all members of the public be affected in a symmetrical fashion; there will always be those who gain more than others from any action. Government, even if it is motivated to increase aggregate welfare, will inevitably have problems in determining the preferences of citizens in the absence of markets and meaningful prices. Furthermore, like the rest of us, bureaucrats and politicians are subject to complex incentives. They will, in most cases, pursue their own interest, as do employers, workers, and households. Of course, this is nothing new. We are led back once more to Smith, who had a poor opinion of government, just as he had a poor opinion of manufacturers. He wrote in *The Wealth of Nations:*

> Great nations are never impoverished by private, though they sometimes are by public, prodigality and misconduct. The whole, or almost the whole, public revenue is in most

---

[11] Anne Krueger, "Economists' Changing Perceptions of Government," *Weltwirtschaftliches Archiv* 126, no. 3 (1990): 419.

countries employed in maintaining unproductive hands. Such are the people who compose a numerous and splendid court, a great ecclesiastical establishment, great fleets and armies, who in time of peace produce nothing, and in time of war acquire nothing which can compensate the expense of maintaining them, even while the war lasts. Such people, as they themselves produce nothing, are all maintained by the produce of other men's labor.

SOURCES OF GOVERNMENT FAILURE

We turn now to look at some of the specific sources of government failure.

AVAILABILITY OF INFORMATION. One of the beauties of the market system lies in its economy of information, since it operates in a decentralized way, with no participant needing to see "the whole picture." Government action, on the other hand, requires all relevant information to be centralized. Even if we make the contentious assumption that the objective of bureaucrats and politicians is to maximize public welfare, rational choices about what public goods to supply and in what quantity require an accurate picture of the total costs and benefits of that activity. Later in this book we will discuss the socialist planned economy more fully and examine in some detail the problems and the resource costs of maintaining a reliable flow of information from periphery to center. However, the problem of gathering accurate information is not unique to centrally planned economies. In a mixed market economy it is in the interest of groups that benefit from the provision of a publicly supplied good to overstate their demand by strategically misleading behavior. Government will only outperform even an imperfect market if it has access to all appropriate information, but this is at best expensive and at worst impossible when participants have an incentive to provide misleading information.

THE CAPTURE OF REGULATORS. We know that the presence of monopoly power can reduce social welfare and for this reason public policy to regulate monopolies is a staple of government activity. The main device for the control of monopoly power lies with regulatory agencies established to supervise pricing and output. However, there is a large body of literature suggesting that over time a regulated industry "captures" the regulatory body set to oversee it. Such bodies tend to identify more with those of the industry that they in theory control than with the public at large. In part this is due to a "revolving door" of personnel between the agency and the industry, in part it is due to a understandable absence of adversarial behavior between the regulator and the regulated.

Regulation may also impair dynamic performance. A regulated industry generally enjoys guaranteed profit margins set by the agency. Given this guarantee, firms tend to grow cautious about innovation and often pay too little attention to cost control. The industry actually comes to enjoy the protection of the agency that was set to constrain it. A comfortable symbiosis develops, characterized by high costs, excess capacity, and a lack of enterprise. Prices to the consumer, which are set to cover average costs, trend upward as increasing inefficiency and waste are accommodated. A soft budget constraint is established whereby the cost structure of the industry is legitimized by the action of the regulators at the expense of consumers. Anne Krueger points out "that the real truth of the capture theory is frequently revealed when deregulation is proposed: it is more often than not, those in the regulated industry themselves who are the loudest in protest against deregulation!"

COLLECTIVE ACTION. In his important book *The Logic of Collective Action*,[12] Mancur Olsen argues that small interest groups can organize much more easily and forcefully than large ones. Small groups with intense preferences will lobby hard for some types of expenditure, even if total costs well exceed benefits, precisely because the costs will be spread among large numbers, while the benefits are more compactly distributed. Members of beneficiary groups try to "free-ride" on the broader tax-paying population, and the consequence is that some public goods will be oversupplied. Moreover, in a process known as "log rolling" pressure groups band together to form coalitions and are thus able to receive the support of other small groups for their cause in return for reciprocal support of the other groups' schemes. The result of this process is a general oversupply of public goods.

The same lobbying phenomena have implications elsewhere in the sphere of government action. Consider, for example, the issue of trade protection. An industry and its workers may have very strong preferences concerning the imposition of a protective tariff and may lobby hard for it. They will frequently prevail although the impact on overall consumer welfare might be strongly negative, purely because they are easily organized and highly focused, while the "losers" are dispersed and disorganized. A good example of this is the U.S. motor industry in the 1980s, which was adversely affected by foreign (primarily Japanese) competition and a surging import market share. Extensive lobbying in Washington produced government sympathy, which in turn led to pressure on the Japanese to impose "voluntary export restraints," which curtailed the number of vehicles shipped into the United States (though not their value). It has been estimated that this action led to an increase of $960 in the price of each new automobile sold in the United States and a cost in extra burden on consumers of $160,000 per job saved.[13] Automobile company profits rose sharply, and motor executives earned record salaries, not for their leadership in production but for their persuasive lobbying. In short, the total costs of government action certainly exceeded the benefits, but a compact lobbying group for control overwhelmed a dispersed opposition and earned monopoly rents.

RENT-SEEKING BEHAVIOR. This example from the U.S. motor industry introduces us to **rent-seeking behavior** defined as the expenditure of real resources in the attempt to appropriate a surplus in the form of rent. Company executives

---

[12] See Mancur Olsen, *The Logic of Collective Action: Public Goods and the Theory of Groups* (Cambridge: Harvard University Press, 1971).

[13] Robert Crandall, "Import Quotas and the Automobile Industry: the Costs of Protection," *Brookings Review,* summer 1984, 8–16.

employ lobbyists (real resources) who convince the government to restrict competition (the "voluntary" export restraints), reducing supply and creating monopoly rents, which accrue to management, capital, and labor in the motor industry.[14]

A common form of government intervention, ostensibly motivated by a desire to protect the consumer, is to deny access to specific industries or professions to those who are not appropriately qualified. This reduces the supply in such activities and enables the successful entrants to earn a monopoly rent. The possibility of this reward encourages rent-seeking behavior, which can be defined as the expenditure of real resources in an attempt to secure a monopoly rent. Rent seeking has been frequently analyzed and discussed in the context of less developed countries where it appears in many forms, from the ability of customs clerks to generate bribes to the allocation of large-scale import licenses.

PORK BARRELING.   Politicians, whether democratically elected or not, are prone to use government expenditures to bolster their own position. James Buchanan was awarded the Nobel Prize in economics for work in political economy based on the premise that politicians in a democracy act to maximize the probability of their reelection.[15] Representatives of a particular district will lobby hard for specific expenditures that will benefit their own electorate. These may take the form of public expenditure on infrastructure or government facilities that benefit the locality but the cost of which is spread over the tax-paying population of the entire economy. We can also note that while they are less sensitive to the vagaries of public opinion, dictators or other authoritarian regimes are also likely to use the public exchequer to build coalitions of supporters.

We can find examples of politicians opportunistically using expenditures to enhance their future in many contexts. For example, in the runup to the Russian presidential elections in 1994, Boris Yeltsin acted to relax the relatively tight monetary policy of the central bank. This ensured that joblessness and the failure of enterprises to pay wages to their workers would have a minimal impact on electoral preference. U.S. presidential candidates may support higher levels of defense expenditure to capture votes in politically marginal areas where the local economy is highly defense dependent.

This "pork barrel" analysis has three general implications for government activity. First, voters, or groups of voters, that care a great deal about a specific issue are likely to be rewarded for their concern. This is especially true of "single issue" voters. For example, in the United States it would be difficult to reduce health care expenditure for the elderly largely because this is a decisive issue for a large group of voters. Second, in countries where politicians rely on contributions to

---

[14]Note that the Japanese motor industry shares in these rents that are extracted from the U.S. consumer. Also bear in mind that the government action produces a deadweight loss (due to reduced consumption) as well as the redistribution from consumers to the industry, which is due to increased prices.

[15]James M. Buchanan and Gordon Tullock, *The Calculus of Consent* (Ann Arbor: University of Michigan Press, 1989).

finance their election campaigns, the concerns of the check-writing rich are, *ceteris paribus,* likely to receive greater attention than those of the poor. Finally, because of log rolling, the creation of coalitions will result in a general oversupply of quasi-public goods.

AGENCY INERTIA.   Once created, bureaucracies tend to have a life of their own, and they will seek to perpetuate their existence by finding work to do. In 1935 the Roosevelt administration founded the Rural Electrification Authority to facilitate the provision of electricity to rural farms and households. Since practically all households now have power, and those who don't have a lifestyle so remote that they can be presumed to be avoiding it, its task is now finished. However, it stays in business, albeit under the new name of the Rural Utilities Service, by providing subsidized funds to ski areas and golf courses. This is not a unique oddity, but results when bureaucrats have little interest in cutting their own jobs and in some cases have a choke-hold on the information about their own activities.

DEADWEIGHT LOSS AND TAXES.   The case for "correcting" market failure rests on imperfect markets causing a **deadweight loss,** a fall in economic welfare that accrues to no one. However, government action is not costless and requires finance in one of three ways: taxation, borrowing, or the printing of money, any of which inevitably has an adverse effect on the operation of the market and therefore its own deadweight loss.

With the exception of lump-sum taxes (those levied on a base that is totally inelastic such as a **poll tax,** whose base is population),[16] all taxes influence economic choices by changing relative prices. They thereby impose an excess burden and reduce economic welfare. Taxes on income, for example, drive a "wedge" that distorts the household's choice between labor and leisure. Consumption, value-added, and excise taxes also change relative prices, distorting choice and creating deadweight losses.

Sometimes a particular tax results in a large excess burden while generating little revenue. In the late 18th century, for example, Britain imposed a revenue-raising tax on the improbable tax base of number of windows. The rationale behind this was that the number of windows in a dwelling was a rough approximation of the wealth of the occupant. It also had the advantage of being a highly visible tax handle. However, in order to avoid the tax, many occupants simply bricked up windows, hence, reducing the tax base. Any change in behavior occasioned solely by the imposition of a tax is an example of deadweight loss.

While less visible than taxes, the other means of finance for government also imply deadweight losses. An increase in government borrowing will tend to raise interest rates, thereby distorting the choice between saving and consumption, and will lead, it is frequently argued, to a crowding out of private-sector investment. Printing money has inflationary consequences that, even if anticipated, distort the

---

[16] In fact, even a poll tax can have an effect on the choice of family size and so will have a deadweight loss in the long run.

choice between present and future consumption and if unforeseen by some will have profound distributional consequences. It is therefore important to recognize that any government expenditure must be financed by means that impose welfare losses. Any efficiency gains that can be anticipated by the establishment of regulatory agencies or the provision of public goods must be weighed against the efficiency losses that are occasioned by raising the revenue to finance them.

GOVERNMENT AND REDISTRIBUTION

Government action is not limited to regulation nor is government expenditure limited to the provision of goods and services. A large part of government spending, particularly in industrialized countries, consists of redistributive expenditures. This is the part of the government budget that has grown most rapidly in recent years and that will, for the reasons of interest group politics outlined earlier, be difficult to contain or curtail in the years ahead.

Redistributive expenditures can take two forms. They may be direct **transfer payments** of cash (such as old age pensions, unemployment compensation, and cash welfare benefits). Alternatively, redistribution may take an in-kind form such as the provision of subsidized housing, free education, free medicine, and so on. These are all goods and services that may be provided by the market but to which the less well off have limited access since they are constrained by limited budgets. These redistributional expenditures have come to dominate the public finances of most of the developed market economies. In the cross-section of countries of Western Europe and the United States, subsidized housing and social security payments taken together represent between 38 percent and 60 percent of total government expenditure. However, statistics like this tend to overstate the redistributive stance of most government policy toward lower income groups. While many program expenditures are targeted toward the poor, these are by and large offset by **tax expenditures** that favor the better off. Such tax expenditures take the form of tax relief for *inter alia* pension contributions, insurance premia, mortgage payments, and property tax payments, all of which are expenditures that rise more than proportionally with income.

The justification of a role for government in reshaping the distribution of income that results from market interaction must be different from that which legitimizes the "correction" of market imperfections that reduce allocative efficiency. Although the income and wealth distributions that result from a market economy are frequently seen as one of its "failures," it is not apparent that a fall in efficiency results. A somewhat tenuous case can been made that a more even income distribution can enhance social cohesion, and thus "social productivity," but it is by no means universally accepted.[17]

---

[17]The "Swedish model," which we review in chapter 7, lays stress on social cohesion and egalitarianism.

The "justness" of the distribution of income that results in a market system depends on the idea that material reward should be directly related to contribution.[18] Given the appropriate assumptions, each factor of production in a market economy may be thought of as being appropriately rewarded when it receives its marginal value product; that is, each factor is paid what it contributes at the margin. An individual's, or a family's, income is therefore the sum of the contributions of the factors of production that it owns or controls. These factors derive from six sources:

1. *Natural talent and ability.* Ability is not equally distributed at birth. Some people have characteristics (intelligence, strength, stature) that are going to be more productive and therefore more rewarded than others.

2. *Acquired skills.* The earning power of congenital characteristics is qualified by the skills and experience acquired during education and working life. Economists generally regard this as the accumulation of human capital (investment in oneself) made by education and foregone earnings.

3. *Effort.* Inasmuch as effort is a determinant of productivity it should have an effect on earnings. Employers should hire the hard worker and pay him or her more than a time server. The ability to do this is conditioned on the ability of employers to pay different rates for the same job description, which is often organizationally difficult or in some cases legally prohibited.

4. *Inherited wealth.* In almost all of the countries for which we have good statistics, wealth is distributed less equally than income. Much of this is due to inheritance whereby blocs of wealth, represented by productive physical and financial assets, are passed from generation to generation. It is also important to note that human capital and inherited wealth are highly correlated. More affluent parents are more able to invest in the human capital of their offspring.

5. *Accumulated savings.* Not all physical and financial assets are inherited. One's stock of productive assets is also a function of savings and consumption decisions made over a lifetime. The more one foregoes in one time period, the greater will be the capital to be consumed in a later one.

6. *Related supply and demand considerations.* Finally, income has a lot to do with circumstances over which we have little control. The value of a worker's marginal product, for example, is a function of the supply and demand, and therefore the price, of the product that he makes. Consider a coal miner. His income would rise should the world oil supply be restricted, but it might fall were a technology for cheap solar energy devised.

Given these complex considerations (which are compounded by the many imperfections of both product and factor markets), it becomes difficult to sustain a

[18]For an interesting discussion of the justice of rewards in a market economy, see Arthur Okun, *Equity and Efficiency: The Big Trade-off* (Washington, D.C.: Brookings, 1975), 40–50. Reprinted in part as "Rewards in a Market Economy" in Bornstein *Comparative Economic Systems: Models and Cases.*

belief in the unique justice of market-based distribution. Most people would accept the premise that the amount of effort one puts into one's work, as well as the amount of saving and investment in one's own human capital, should be rewarded. These represent sacrifices that should be compensated, and be seen to be compensated, because of favorable incentive effects.

There is still strong disagreement on the ethics of inheritance. In the immediate post–World War II period, especially in the European social democracies, egalitarian sentiment supported the enactment of almost confiscatory estate taxation designed to break up inherited wealth and level the playing field for a new generation. However, loopholes enabled those who availed themselves of forward thinking estate planning to avoid the tax, and the incidence fell only on the unwary. Today, tax planners refer to the estate tax in the United States as "the voluntary tax."

Governments not only affect the income distribution by tax and transfer, but they may also attempt to influence the structure of wages. One frequently used policy is the institution of a minimum wage. The original justification was that all jobs should pay at least "a living wage." Within the United States at least this has clearly not been achieved, and many critics claim that the imposition of a non-market clearing wage has resulted in high levels of unemployment, especially among young people. Currently in the United States and in some nations of Europe, there is pressure on the government to influence the labor market through the imposition of a wage structure based on "comparable worth." In simple terms, this theory suggests that two jobs that require roughly similar effort, education, and qualifications should be paid similarly. It has been used to justify setting public-sector pay scales in line with private ones and was a part of the Swedish system of wage settlement. It has also been used as an argument to raise the rates of pay in typically "female" occupations to eliminate the gap between male and female average wages.

JUSTIFICATIONS FOR REDISTRIBUTIVE POLICY

What then are the cases that might be made for government intervention to amend or correct the income distribution determined by the market? Some of the most familiar are discussed next.

UTILITARIANISM. If we start from a generally held position in economics, that the more one has of a good the less it is valued at the margin, it can be argued that the intrinsic value of one dollar is greater to a poor person than a rich one. Consequently, taking a dollar from a rich person and giving it to a poor one would increase social well-being. This utilitarian (or "greatest happiness of the greatest number") principle makes a case for the maximization of social well-being through redistribution. It follows that an enlightened Benthamite social guardian might pursue redistribution on these grounds, subject always to the caveat that the disincentive effects on total output are less than the welfare gain. However, in reality such a picture of government is at variance with the views that we laid out earlier.

ALTRUISM. The development of extensive social welfare programs has been seen as an outgrowth of collective altruism. In such a view the welfare-promoting aspects are even greater than the utilitarian rationale. Under altruistic motivation, giving, like Portia's "quality of mercy," would be twice blessed, enhancing the welfare of both givers and receivers. Again, however, there seems little support for this as an explanation for the growth of major social programs.

SOCIAL CONTRACT. A more contemporary view of redistribution is that it is motivated by quasi-contractual relationships. In this conception citizenship, or residence, endows everyone with rights to a minimum standard of living. Thus it is the right of the old, the young, the halt, the lame, and the unemployed or others who have little to sell in the market system to be supported to some minimum level. A key question is where that minimum level should be located.

In early capitalist economies, the right was to subsistence alone, and no more. Support above that level was denied because it would reward indigence and, according to **vacuum theory of population,** attributed to Malthus, it would increase the number of paupers. Consequently, support for the poor whether "indoor" (that is in poorhouses) or "outdoor" using cash grants and in-kind support was minimal. The rise of the liberal welfare states and the extension of the voting franchise changed that. In contemporary European social democracies, the level of support is relatively high, and the income distribution that results is quite egalitarian. The income share of the richest 20 percent in Europe is generally around five times that of the poorest 20 percent, as opposed to about 8:1 in the United States. Such redistribution is criticized by "supply-side" economists because it reduces the incentive to find work and contributes to the high level of unemployment. On the other side of the coin, financing redistributive policies requires high rates of taxation, which lower the incentives to work and to save. Thus egalitarianism is seen as a root cause of economic stagnation. When transfers are regarded as rights or entitlements, demographics play a powerful role in determining the structure of expenditures. Low birthrates and a sharp increase in life expectancy have caused a pronounced aging of the population in industrial societies and require ever higher levels of transfer.

THE INCREASE OF SOCIAL PRODUCTIVITY. Redistribution has been justified as having a positive impact on social productivity. This might be achieved in two ways. By elevating social cohesion it might solidify institutions that are beneficial to growth. Moreover, redistribution can lower social problems, leading to savings on expenditures (like crime or remedial education).

SOCIAL CONTROL. A fifth view sees redistribution in contemporary market economies as a tool in a struggle to maintain social peace and stability. Potential disruptive elements of society are bought off by providing access to quite generous pensions and goods. This strategy certainly has a history. Imperial Rome secured the quiescence of the Roman unemployed through the provision of free "bread and circuses." The response to contemporary urban disturbances in industrialized countries has frequently been to increase the number and funding of social programs oriented toward the disaffected group. Redistribution can be regarded as a substitute for expenditure on more conventional aspects of law enforcement. The level of distribution is not determined by concern for, or by rights of, groups disadvantaged by the market process but rather by the potential power of disaffected groups to create problems.

SHARED GROWTH.   Economists are not unanimous about the relationship between income distribution and economic growth. Some see in egalitarianism a lowering of incentives and a consequent slower growth path. Others are adamant that sharing of the proceeds of growth is essential to maintain a growth trajectory; growth that benefits only a few is likely to be unstable because it leads to a loss of social unity. Each group has some merit; both extreme egalitarianism and extreme reliance on material incentives (which leads to an unequal distribution of income) are likely to present problems. Some commentators on the strong growth performance of East Asian economies have noted the sharing of growth as an important factor in sustaining economic expansion.

THE DEMOCRATIC PROCESS.   In modern democracies the key to the increased share of redistributional expenditure is likely to be found in the ballot box. Earlier we discussed how politicians act so as to ensure their subsequent reelection, and providing access to redistribution is one way of influencing voter behavior. This is an especially potent explanation when the potential group is unified and "single-issue oriented." This basic thought underlies much of the work of James Buchanan, Nobel laureate in economics.

DEMAND STABILIZATION.   Capitalist economies are subject to variations in the level of macroeconomic activity, and at times this has been ascribed to a systemic tendency toward underconsumption. Inasmuch as the less well off have a higher marginal propensity to consume than the better off, redistribution from rich to poor lowers the societal marginal propensity to save and reduces the chance of an "underconsumptionist trap." From the English liberal economist John Hobson onward,[19] some economists have advocated domestic redistribution as an antidote to recession. While it is hard to see such a clear espousal of a particular macroeconomic theory by the politicians who ultimately determine redistributive policy, it is a fact that developed nations have managed to steer clear of major recessions since the inception of mass redistribution programs.

CONCLUSION

Where does this leave us in evaluating the role of government in correcting the inefficient or unacceptable features of market logic? In the light of this discussion, few would assert that each and every market imperfection is a case for government

---

[19] Hobson anticipated many of Keynes's views on the dangers of underconsumption, although his main agenda was to restrain overseas imperialism, which in its relentlessness to attach for foreign markets by force was an alternative remedy to redistribution for domestic stagnation.

intervention. The particular failures of the market must be evaluated against cost and potential failures of government intervention before any action is initiated.

Even in those cases where market failure is so pronounced that some government intervention is merited, economists would be best employed in considering solutions that are designed to reduce the risk of government failure, rather than assuming that regulation along the old lines was necessarily beneficial. The new view of government suggests that policies that provide individuals with incentives and freedom to correct market failure might be best. At present we have few examples of these kinds of policies, which might be described as **incentive-compatible** or **market augmenting policies.** Promising approaches seem to lie in the use of **quasi-markets** to assist in the provision of services currently supplied largely by the government. This would allow the simultaneous addressing of the equity and the efficiency issue. Such a device would be the use of vouchers provided gratis by the government to eligible families with children, but which could then be used to pay for educational services. Market augmenting approaches have also been used in Asian countries as a means of determining which firms should receive government support, and these will be looked at again when Japan and Korea are presented in chapters 10 and 11 of this book.

It is sufficient at this point to suggest that the direction of future research should be to identify the areas of comparative advantage for government and to examine how the logic of the market and appropriately designed incentives may be used to better the performance of government.

KEY TERMS AND CONCEPTS

agency inertia

altruism

antitrust policy

barriers to entry

capture of regulators

caveat emptor

collective action

contestable markets

deadweight loss

diminishability

excludability

externalities

four firm concentration ratio

free rider problem

government failure

Herfindahl-Hirschman index

incentive-compatible policy

lack of information

market-augmenting policy

market failure

market power

national champions

natural monopoly

poll tax

pork barreling

price setter

price takers

private marginal cost

public goods

quasi-markets

rent-seeking behavior

social contract

social marginal cost

tax expenditures

trade to GDP ratio

transfer payments

utilitarianism

vacuum theory of population

QUESTIONS FOR DISCUSSION

1. Evaluate the arguments for and against the use of government power to curb monopolies.

2. How has the need to regulate "natural monopolies" changed in recent years?

3. Why are concentration ratios not thought of as good indices of the level of industry-wide competition? What may be a better approach?

4. How does lack of information impede the operation of a market system? How can a government act to correct this?

5. Define public goods. Are pure public goods an important category? Give some examples. Is information a pure public good?

6. Why may government action be required to correct externality problems like pollution? Which type of system, planned or market, would you expect to lead to most pollution?

7. Why is the government not a "benevolent, costless social guardian"?

8. Give some reasons why redistribution via both cash and in-kind payments is the fastest growing governmental activity.

RESOURCES

WEB SITES

U.S. Federal Trade Commission . . . . www.ftc.gov/
This site has useful information and downloadable papers on specific industries.

U.K. Office of Fair Trading . . . . www.oft.gov.uk/
This site gives the background, philosophy, and structure of U.K. policy against monopoly.

BOOKS AND ARTICLES

Baumol, William J., John C. Panzar, and Robert Willig. *Contestable Markets and the Theory of Industry Structure.* New York : Harcourt Brace Jovanovich, 1982.

Brock, Gerald W. *Telecommunication Policy for the Information Age : From Monopoly to Competition.* Cambridge: Harvard University Press, 1998.

Buchanan, James M., and Richard A. Musgrave. *Public Finance and Public Choice : Two Constrasting Visions of the State.* Cambridge: MIT Press, 1999.

Buchanan, James M., and Gordon Tullock. *The Calculus of Consent.* Ann Arbor: University of Michigan, 1962.

Coase, Ronald. "The Problem of Social Cost." *Journal of Law and Economics* 3 (October 1960): 1–44.

Crandall, Robert. "Import Quotas and the Automobile Industry." *Brookings Review*, summer 1984, 8–16.

Krueger, Anne. "Economists' Changing Perceptions of Government." *Weltwirtschaftliches Archiv* 126, no. 3 (1990): 419.

Musgrave, Richard A. *Public Finance in a Democratic Society: The Foundations of Taxation and Expenditure.* White Plains: Edward Elgar, 2000.

Okun, Arthur. *Equity and Efficiency: The Big Trade-off.* Washington, D.C.: Brookings, 1975.

Olsen, Mancur. *The Logic of Collective Action: Public Goods and the Theory of Groups.* Cambridge: Harvard University Press, 1971.

Train, Kenneth E. *Optimal Regulation : The Economic Theory of Natural Monopoly.* Cambridge: MIT Press, 1991.

Viscusi, W. Kip, John Vernon, and Joseph Harrington. *Economics of Regulation and Anti Trust,* 2d ed. Cambridge: MIT Press, 1995.

5

THE INSTITUTIONS
OF A MODERN MARKET ECONOMY

In chapter 1 we discussed in broad outline some of the institutions that comprise any economy and in chapter 4 we visited the issue of market failure and looked at some of the ways that the government acts to attempt to remedy this. In this chapter we will look in more detail at the framework of a "developed market economy," and how the institutions that have been established operate to shape and steer the functions of the economy. We start with a discussion of the various objectives of government policy and how they fit together, and sometimes conflict, in an overall picture of government activity.

THE OBJECTIVES OF GOVERNMENT POLICY

It seems almost too obvious to state, but in a mixed market economy the government is one of the most important institutions. Even in those countries that are popularly regarded as the bastions of "free enterprise" and capitalism, a large part of the gross domestic product (GDP) passes through the government sector and public employment represents a considerable share of the total. The revenues of industrial giants like General Motors, Exxon, or Microsoft are quite small compared to the receipts and expenditures of governments in developed industrial economies. The debts of banks, corporations, and households similarly pale when compared to government debt. Government regulations, civil, criminal, and administrative law control or shape almost every aspect of our lives. One way of viewing government activity is to see government as being divisible into three functions: allocation, distribution, and stabilization.[1] This functional distribution enables us to view the operation of government systematically. However, we must always bear in mind that policies implemented to achieve goals related to one function will inevitably have "spillovers" that impact the others.

THE ALLOCATION FUNCTION

Chapter 4 dealt with issues of market failure. The existence of such failures suggested the need for government intervention because the market alone either failed

---

[1] For a full discussion of this view of the responsibilities of government, see Richard and Peggy Musgrave, *Public Finance in Theory and Practice* (New York : McGraw-Hill, 1984).

to supply some goods altogether or supplied certain goods at allocatively inefficient quantities and prices. We also discussed the problem of government failure, which occurs when the costs of government intervention are greater than any potential social gain, or when the action of the governmental/political process frustrates the possibility of socially advantageous intervention. Nevertheless, governments of all mixed capitalist societies are involved in the production of goods and the regulation of business, with overt justification of improving the allocative efficiency of the economy. This is what we term the allocation function of government.

GOVERNMENT PRODUCTION OF PURE AND QUASI-PUBLIC GOODS. We established in chapter 4 that although pure public goods are theoretically important, operationally they are a rather limited class of goods. Most goods provided by the government could also be provided by the market. A list of what is actually produced, at least in part, by some level of the government in the United States, includes national defense, passenger rail transportation, urban mass transit, law enforcement, electricity supply, education, health services, information, public health measures, research and development, water supply, postal services, and housing. We would obtain a similar list if we looked at most of the developed market economies, in Europe or in Japan. As a general, but not universal, rule, the lower the overall level of development, the greater is the likelihood that the government assumes more extensive production responsibilities. What is striking, however, is that almost all of the goods produced by governments are either also produced at the same time in the private sector or have close substitutes that are.

Some of the goods or services on the list of government production can be justified by the fact that the market would supply the goods only in suboptimal quantities and at prices that are too high. These goods are the ones that generate substantial positive externalities, or spillovers, that are socially beneficial but are not captured in the private market. Production by the public sector causes these goods to be supplied closer to the optimal level and priced more efficiently through the operation of a public subsidy, or at least priced at less than the profit maximizing rate. Goods of this type might include information, education, electricity supply, public transportation, and water supply.[2] Finally, some goods are provided by the government as a form of income transfer—housing, health care, and to some degree education—fit this category.

Table 5.1 shows the structure of current government expenditure in 12 nations using standardized Organization for Economic Cooperation and Development (OECD) classifications. The first thing that strikes us is the wide variation in the scope of government as a percentage of GDP; Korea is the lowest followed by Japan and the United States. In general, the continental European nations have the highest levels of government activity, reaching a peak in the Scandinavian states of

---

[2]One element that often becomes a factor in these industries is the possibility of cross-subsidization. High-cost users are charged the same rate as low-cost users, facilitating a single pricing scheme and coverage.

THE STRUCTURE OF GOVERNMENT EXPENDITURE IN SELECTED COUNTRIES

	Total Current Government Expenditure, Percentage of GDP	Government Final Consumption Expenditure Percentage of GDP						
		Total	Defense	Public Safety	Education	Health	Social Security	Housing and Amenity
Australia	35.6	17.2	1.9	1.3	3.6	3.1	1.0	0.4
Belgium	51.7	16.5	2.5	1.6	6.1	0.5	1.0	0.2
Canada	45.8	na	na	na	na	na	na	na
Czech Republic	40.5	na	na	na	na	na	na	na
Denmark	59.6	25.2	1.8	1.0	5.6	5.0	6.7	0.2
France	51.6	19.8	3.1	0.9	5.2	3.4	1.5	1.4
Italy	49.5	16.3	1.7	1.7	4.2	3.4	0.7	0.5
Japan	28.5	9.9	0.9	na	3.2	0.5	0.7	0.7
Korea	15.7	10.3	3.0	1.3	2.6	0.2	0.5	0.2
Sweden	63.8	27.2	2.6	1.5	5.3	4.8	6.0	0.5
United Kingdom	42.3	21.3	3.2	2	4.5	5.7	1.9	0.6
United States	34.3	15.8	na	na	na	na	na	na

Note: na = not available.

SOURCE: National Accounts, OECD, Paris, 1998.

Denmark and Sweden. There is less variation between nations in terms of current expenditures, though the features of individual economies can be quite important. Some nations have especially high levels of particular social expenditures, for example, health, while others have relatively high levels of defense spending.

INFORMATION AS A PUBLIC GOOD.   The provision of information is an important function of a modern government. Without good information on a wide range of topics (from the weather to the unemployment rate), it is impossible for the economic actors to make informed and therefore rational decisions. Information is not, however, a pure public good. While the marginal cost of providing information to additional users is very low (especially in the age of television and the Web), it is quite possible to charge for information and exclude nonpayers from receiving it. A whole industry of consultants relies on the charging of a fee for "proprietary" information, at prices that reflect a monopoly rent rather than the cost of dissemination.

Nevertheless, information gathering is costly, and social resources can be saved if needless duplication can be avoided. Thus a government's role in the collation and dissemenation of information is justifiable on efficiency grounds. When information flows are improved, better decisions are made, and the overall efficiency of the market system is enhanced.

REGULATION OF PRODUCTS.   A large part of government activity is concerned with product regulation of one form or another. In the United States, for example, it sets standards for the safety, quality, and efficacy of many products. The economic basis for this, in terms of improving the allocative efficiency of the economy, lies in the fact that it economizes on information costs for consumers.

REGULATION OF INDUSTRY.   Moreover as we discussed in chapter 4, governments have extensive powers to regulate prices and outputs in industry and they use these powers most frequently to address market failure due to monopoly.

THE DISTRIBUTION FUNCTION

INCOME SUPPORT.   The second broad function of government lies in redistributing income. While this is not a new activity (even ancient Egypt and Rome had income support policies) it has grown enormously in importance in recent decades. A large part of government expenditure is directed toward some form of amelioration of income distribution. In previous centuries, assistance was oriented toward poverty relief and intended only to raise the indigent to the subsistence level.

In the 20th century the government assumed increased responsibility for stabilizing the economy. It also came to be held increasingly responsible for the individual as well as the aggregate consequences of joblessness. "Social security" became a common feature (and a burgeoning bureaucracy) in all developed economies during the 20th century. Support was provided not only for the unemployed but also for the elderly, single parents, and the disabled. As a result, transfer payments took a larger share of government expenditure.

The economic consequences of this steady progress toward guaranteed income are much debated. Today the prevailing orthodox view is that redistributive payments have sharply reduced the flexibility of labor markets. Providing support for people without jobs reduces the urgency of job search, lowers incentives to find work, and encourages higher wage demands. This in turn leads to higher levels of unemployment. In the countries of Western Europe, where the reduction in take-home income on losing a job can be as little as 10 percent, the cost of being unemployed is correspondingly low, and unemployment rates are high.

Concern over the disincentive consequences of income transfer schemes has grown. Steps to reduce unemployment benefits and tighten accessibility rules have been undertaken in some market economies. They have been accompanied by sharp falls in unemployment. Britain is a case in point, which following a trimming of the welfare state now experiences its lowest unemployment rate in decades. On the other hand, countries that have maintained high benefit rates have seen unemployment continue to grow (for example, France). While this suggests a strong link, evidence that transfer payments actually *cause* unemployment is slight. Some income support for the jobless can be justified in terms of raising the allocative efficiency of the economy since it allows a more rational process of job search and a better resultant fit.

REDISTRIBUTION IN-KIND.   Economic theory tells us that an individual's welfare is raised by increasing his or her ability to choose. Consequently, welfare-maximizing redistribution, at least from the recipient's viewpoint, should consist of unrestricted cash grants. However, much redistributive activity actually takes the form of public provision of goods that might well be supplied privately. These include health care, education, housing, and food. The adoption of such a system can be justified in two ways. First, it is claimed that these goods generate social externalities. Consequently, the loss of an individual recipient's welfare through constraining choice is compensated by a rise in the welfare of third parties. Second, some may argue that the recipients may be ill-informed or irrational and act against their own long-run welfare. If given free control over resources they would dispose of them in a fashion that would favor short-term gratification over long-term well-being. Hence an element of paternalism is used to justify the public provision of such goods, rather than providing cash to purchase the appropriate amount in private markets. This interference with individual preferences creates a class of goods that are referred to in the literature as **merit goods,** and they are widespread in most economies.

In recent years the state-owned industries and bureaucracies created by the public provision of these goods have come under attack because of their inefficiency and inflexibility relative to the private sector. In the United States criticism has focused on publicly provided education. In Britain the National Health Service has been under siege. One possible avenue of reform is use of **voucher systems.** Although these still involve interference with personal preferences, since they are (unlike cash) service specific, they introduce consumer choice between suppliers and therefore foster competition, leading, it is hoped, to greater efficiency.

THE STABILIZATION FUNCTION

The idea that governments should be responsible for the level of macroeconomic activity—the level of unemployment, the rate of inflation, and the rate of growth—is a relatively recent one. It had two sources. One was political reform that broadened the franchise and gave a louder voice to those most affected by unemployment. The second lay in the developments in macroeconomic theory and statistical collation that occurred in the 20th century, especially in the Depression-troubled 1930s, which made government management of the economy more feasible. Emphasis on government responsibility for the macroeconomy reached its height in the 1960s when it was widely held that the principles underlying economic activity were so well-understood that the economic task of government was merely to fine-tune the economy. However, faith in the ability of government to deliver low inflation and high employment faltered in the economically turbulent 1970s. Stabilization policy apparently failed and came to have negative connotations. Confidence in the effectiveness of fiscal policy waned, and government activity came to be seen by a growing number of economists as the cause of instability rather than its antidote.

While in the 1960s much of stabilization policy had been framed in terms of the judicious trade-off between inflation and unemployment, a new orthodoxy emerged in the 1970s suggesting that unemployment, at least below a threshold "natural" level, was, after all, not something that the government could do much about. Attempts to raise employment accelerated the rate of inflation, without having any long-term results. Slow growth was seen as the result of government interference in demand management as public expenditure crowded out private investment. Today we are back in the middle of the road. While confidence in our ability to guarantee stability has been shaken, most economists believe that economic policy is effective in shaping economic outcomes for the better.

THE INSTRUMENTS OF STABILIZATION. In most mixed market economies governments have at their disposal two distinct sets of policy measures: fiscal (those that involve the changing of tax rates and government expenditure) and monetary (those that involve the manipulation of the money stock in the hands of the public).

FISCAL POLICY. To be effective, fiscal policy requires a well-developed and defined tax system in which tax rules are both visible and enforced. This, in turn, presupposes that the government is supported by a well-established and competent bureaucracy. In less developed economies, and also in the transition economies of Eastern Europe, the lack of the essential infrastructure for tax-gathering limits the effectiveness of fiscal policy. Fiscal policy is concerned not only with the changing of taxes and tax rates, but also with the role of government expenditures on macroeconomic activity. Stabilization can be effected by shifts in government expenditures (for example, by the initiation of public expenditure projects or the curtailment of unemployment insurance payments). Government expenditures, like taxes, tend to have an automatic stabilizer effect, since even in the absence of policy shifts they rise as the economy contracts.

In modern mixed market economies, tax capabilities are by and large similar. Some countries have more efficient tax systems and greater degrees of tax compliance than others, and this affects economic performance. However, the larger differences lie in the kind of tax structure adopted. The United States, for example, relies heavily on income taxes, social security taxes, and corporate income taxes at the federal level.[3] State finance is predominantly based on sales taxes, supplemented by individual and business income taxes. Other economies rely much more heavily on indirect taxes at the national level. In Europe, for example, much greater reliance is on indirect taxation, largely through value-added taxes.

MONETARY POLICY. The other broad technique of macroeconomic stabilization is the use of monetary policy to influence the rate of interest, the rate of inflation, and therefore the price level. The implementation (and in many economies the determination) of monetary policy lies with the central bank whose functioning we will discuss more fully in the context of the financial system discussed later.

---

[3] In 1995, 44 percent of federal revenue came from the individual income tax, 36 percent from social security taxes, and 12 percent from corporate income taxes. The remaining 8 percent came from other sources, chiefly excise taxes. Source: *Economic Report of the President.*

THE TAX SYSTEM

What really sets the government apart from other institutions is that it has a monopoly on the power to tax. No other institution can demand that resources be transferred to it with no specific *quid pro quo* under the threat of sanctions that include imprisonment. This unique feature makes the activity of government of prime importance and the design and functioning of the tax system a decisive feature for the operation of the economic system. Taxes are generally divided into two types: those imposed on people or firms (direct taxation) and those levied on goods (indirect taxation). The most important direct tax measured in terms of the share of total revenue that it raises, is, in most economies, the personal income tax. Direct taxation also includes social security taxes, corporate taxes, expenditure taxes,[4] and some forms of wealth and estate taxation.

The degree of progressivity of direct taxation differs sharply between economies. Under a **progressive tax** the average tax rate rises as the individual's or household's base of the tax (income, expenditure, or wealth) increases. Progressivity was at one time almost universally considered a desirable characteristic in a tax system. It was justified by some on moral or ethical grounds arguing that equal sacrifice of welfare across the population required an increasing average rate of income tax because the marginal utility of money declines as income increases. To others it had the more pragmatic virtue of constituting an "automatic stabilizer," which would limit or dampen the cyclical behavior of the macroeconomy. As the economy expanded, under a progressive tax system, tax revenues would increase at a faster rate than national income. Thus the size of the government fiscal deficit would shrink (or the size of the surplus increase), hence slowing economic growth. The reverse would hold in cyclical downturns.

In more recent years, however, the consensus favoring progressivity has weakened, largely because the negative supply side effects of high personal taxation have attracted more concern. Equity and equal sacrifice are now thought of more in terms of proportionality (i.e., constant average and marginal rate taxation) rather than requiring progressivity. Consequently, we have seen a widespread decline in the number of tax brackets and lower tax rates more generally applied. This change has applied especially to the taxation of capital. In many economies, so-called unearned income (interest, dividends, properties, rents, etc.) was once taxed at higher rates. Sometimes these rates were close to confiscatory— 70 percent and higher. Today differential rates for earned and unearned income are largely a thing of the past, and in some countries the pendulum has swung toward the other extreme and income from capital is actually taxed at lower rates than that from labor. This is true in the United States where changes in the treatment of capital gains have resulted in some forms of capital income being taxed at a lower rate than wage or salary income. Lower marginal tax rates also

---

[4]Expenditure taxes are levied on an individual's or household's total aggregate consumption expenditure and should not be confused with sales taxes, which are indirect taxes imposed at the point of purchase.

■ TABLE 5.2

THE STRUCTURE OF THE TAX SYSTEM IN SELECTED COUNTRIES

Tax Structures as a Percentage of Total Tax Receipts

	Total Tax Receipts Percentage of GDP	Personal Income Tax	Social Security Contributions		Total Taxes on Income	Corporate Income Tax	Taxes on Goods and Services	Other Taxes
			Employees	Employers				
Australia	30.7	40.6	0.0	0.0	40.6	14.7	29.2	15.5
Belgium	46.5	31.5	10.9	20.1	62.5	6.7	25.9	4.9
Canada	37.2	37.3	5.4	11.1	53.8	8.1	25.5	12.6
Czech R.	44.3	12.4	9.7	26.4	48.5	12.3	33.1	6.2
Denmark	51.3	53.7	2.5	0.6	56.8	4.1	32.4	6.6
France	44.5	13.9	13.1	26.8	53.8	3.7	27.3	15.2
Italy	41.3	26.2	6.7	20.9	53.8	8.7	27.3	10.3
Japan	28.5	21.4	14.4	18.3	54.1	15.2	15.1	15.5
Korea	22.3	18.9	2.9	5.1	26.9	12.2	42.6	18.3
Poland	42.7	22.9	0.0	30.4	53.3	7.7	35.2	3.7
Sweden	49.7	35.3	3.5	24.9	63.7	6.1	24.3	5.8
Turkey	22.5	21.6	4.7	6.3	32.6	6.7	37.6	23.1
United Kingdom	35.3	27.4	7.4	9.6	44.4	9.5	34.7	11.4
United States	27.9	36.3	10.7	13.1	60.1	9.4	17.9	12.5
EU Average	41.8	26.4	10.4	16.3	53.1	6.9	31.0	9.0
OECD Average	37.4	27.0	8.0	14.1	49.1	8.0	32.4	10.4

SOURCE: *Revenue Statistics, 1965–1996*, OECD, Paris, 1997; *The Tax/Benefit Position of Employees, 1995–1996*, OECD, Paris, 1998; Fiscal Affairs Division.

have the beneficial effect of lowering the incidence of both tax evasion and tax avoidance.[5]

Taxes can be levied on objects as well as on individuals, and this constitutes indirect taxation. Imposing taxes on things (commodities, imports, exports, houses, land, and so forth) tends to be administratively easier than all but the simplest direct taxes on individuals. A glance at history tells us that states generally relied on commodity or land taxation for public finance. In modern mixed capitalist societies, commodity taxation is still widely practiced (Table 5.2). In the United States, local government is largely financed by taxes on real property, while some form of sales taxation predominates at the state level.

Countries in a lower state of economic development often rely on a relatively simple form of indirect taxation with highly visible "tax handles" that do not require a sophisticated enforcement mechanism (although evasion through an under-the-counter cash market is frequent). In history, several nations relied on "salt taxes," which, because the taxes fell on a good with a low price elasticity, were

---

[5] Tax evasion is the illegal concealment of tax liabilities from the authorities. Tax avoidance is the alteration of behavior to limit tax exposure; it involves a deadweight loss to society.

relatively efficient with minimal deadweight loss. However, such single commodity taxation cannot raise the volume of revenue required by a modern state. Consequently, a broader base is often sought. Unfortunately, simple turnover and gross receipts taxes, which are the easiest to administer, have the drawbacks of being inefficient and distortionary, and nondistortionary indirect taxes like the value-added tax (VAT) are preferable where possible.

We have distinguished to this point between direct taxes, which are levied on the characteristics of individuals or families, and indirect taxes, which fall upon objects or activities. Taxes that are levied on the profits of businesses, organized corporations, or public limited liability companies, are usually classed as direct, as if they fell upon an individual. Such taxes are a significant element of the overall public finance system of developed economies, and the tax base is the profit stream of incorporated business.

At the federal level, the United States depends heavily, almost exclusively, on direct taxation. The individual income tax constitutes 45 percent of total revenue, and the social security payroll taxes contribute 38 percent. Thus taxes on personal income comprise 83 percent of total revenues. Corporate income taxes constitute about 11 percent of total revenues, and the balance of about 6 percent is made up of excise taxes, gift and estate taxes, and custom duties. At the state level there is a much greater reliance on sales taxes and property taxes, which amount to more than half of the revenue. The tax systems of other nations differ in terms of the balance of reliance on direct versus indirect taxation. In Europe, for example, the value added tax, an indirect tax, is a very important part of central government revenue.

It is clear that both the design of the tax system and the overall tax burden have important effects on economic growth and performance. Taxes are not only distortionary, but also are frequently structured to favor particular groups or activities. However, just as important as the overt or nominal tax structure is the efficiency and even-handedness of tax administration. Healthy economies require honest and efficient tax administrations. Without them it is hard to prosper.

THE LEGAL SYSTEM

Any modern market economy depends on a clear and enforceable system of property rights, and the clarification and enforcement of such rights is the most important economic role of the legal system. A complex and resource-expensive system has grown up in market economies to control these functions. Some would argue that the role and scope of the law has become too broad and the cost of the legal system is too high. Nowhere is the focus on the law and the role of lawyers greater than in the United States, and in most market economies the percentage of national income accounted for by the legal system is smaller, but growing.

OWNERSHIP AND PROPERTY RIGHTS

In chapter 1 we discussed the concept of property ownership, and we saw that it is a rather more complex matter than might seem at first glance, embracing the issue of property rights, which extend beyond merely physical property. It is concerned with rights as varied as the right to clean air, the right to quiet, the right to access to sunlight, the right to earn income from an invention, and the right to broadcast over the airwaves. In the West, property rights have developed incrementally and have been adapted and extended to take account of new complexities, both by legislation and by precedent in law. New technologies and new external circumstances have required that new rights be defined. Environmental property rights, intellectual property rights, and the right of access to radio frequencies are three areas that have recently leaped to prominence.

While even the limited right of ownership and transfer of physical property will ensure the development of some forms of market relations, it does not go far in stimulating economic efficiency. Alone it will lead, in the words of Evgenii Yasin, a Russian reform economist, to a "bazaar" rather than a "market." A market *system* requires much more. The complex legal system of western nations has as one of its functions the promotion of efficiency and the economy of scarce resources. Of course, this is not the sole function of the law. It must also protect individual and group rights against a variety of incursions. Moreover, although many laws and regulations have evolved to contribute to the efficient operation of a market economy, a good deal of legislation serves the interest of quite narrow groups and does little either for economic efficiency or human rights.

FREEDOM TO ENGAGE IN ECONOMIC ACTIVITY

In order for prices of goods to even approximate resource costs, markets must be relatively competitive, and this requires individuals, and groups of individuals or firms, to have the right to engage in whatever economic activity they perceive as offering the greatest return. In simple terms, people must have the right to choose their own professions (among them being a self-employed entrepreneur) and choose the physical locations of where they pursue these professions. This is much the same as granting individuals the right to enter any business or industry that they choose and to live wherever they choose. Without a guarantee of free market entry, private monopolies, with their attendant inefficiencies, would arise. Under such conditions prices would not reflect the resource costs of production and monopoly rents[6] would be appropriated, harming efficiency. A major target of Smith's *Wealth of Nations* was the system of royal licensing and monopoly that restricted the action of the individual. If the state can prevent the entry of individuals into a trade or profession, then the consumer, and society as a whole, is the loser while the monopolist, or the official that grants it monopoly powers, is the winner.

Even today free entry into all economic activities is not guaranteed in overtly market systems. Many professions and trades require licenses or permits; this practice is usually defended as being efficient since customers cannot always gather all the information they need. Certifying lawyers, stockbrokers, or auto mechanics provides cheap information and protects the customer. Although market

---

[6]Monopoly rent is the margin above normal profit that results from the exercise of monopoly power.

radicals, like Milton Friedman, denounce such regulation as monopolistic and therefore inefficient, such barriers are an integral part of economic life in most market systems.

THE ENFORCEMENT OF CONTRACTS AND COMPENSATION

While ownership and entry will create an infrastructure in which rudimentary exchange can take place, such a market could operate only with a very short time horizon. Longer-term economic relationships are made viable by the use of contracts binding parties to specific performance standards. Contracts are an integral part of moving from the "bazaar," where already-produced goods are exchanged, into a longer-term system of stable interrelations enabling planning and foresight. A contract specifies what both parties must do, whatever the change in external circumstance, and provides for enforcement or compensation for nonperformance.

Some long-term relationships can be established even in the absence of enforceable contracts, since the market can produce its own remedies often through reputation effects. A supplier, for example, who persistently failed to deliver would have a great deal of difficulty finding future customers as knowledge of his persistent failure to perform became widespread. However, contract law removes part of the costs of gathering information from the contracting parties by providing general remedies and compensation for failure to perform and to deliver. This obviates the need for a socially expensive search, although it introduces costs of making and enforcing contracts.

To promote economic efficiency, contract enforcement need not always require strict performance to the letter of the contract, but it may instead give the injured party compensation for the losses incurred as a result of nonperformance. Strict enforcement would be burdensome and inefficient in some cases where expected circumstances have changed and fulfilling the contract in its literal terms is impossible. However, the law must provide both the means for the injured party to be compensated and an appropriate system of adjudicating damages resulting from nonperformance.

BANKRUPTCY LAW

Frequently overlooked in the discussions of infrastructure is the role of bankruptcy legislation. Capitalism is, in Schumpeter's words, a "gale of creative destruction." Company failure and the dissolution of corporations must be regarded as a normal aspect of the system. The efficient operation of that system, however, is highly dependent on the predictable disposition of the assets of the firm in the event of failure. A necessary condition for orderly capital markets is a full and enforceable set of defined property rights; bankruptcy law is one component of these rights.[7] The risks that lenders and materials suppliers assume in supplying a firm

---

[7] See J. Mitchell, "Managerial Discipline, Productivity and Bankruptcy in Capitalist and Socialist Economies," *Comparative Economic Studies* 22, no. 3 (fall 1990).

can only be assessed when there is full knowledge of the pecking order in which debtors will be arrayed should the firm go into bankruptcy.

Accounting and Financial Disclosure

The law plays a vital role by requiring that firms must report their financial results in a specified standard accounting system and that this information be made publicly available. The efficiency aspects of this are obvious if we consider the alternative: without required and standardized disclosure the costs of information to an individual or other firms, whether potential shareholders, suppliers, or customers, would be very high. Thus required disclosure has clear social efficiency in reducing information costs. This is of great importance in the operation of equity markets, where buying shares without access to accurate information on the financial state of the company would be undesirably risky and share prices would not reflect underlying values. It is also of great relevance to those who supply the company with raw materials and inputs and those who provide credit to firms in more direct ways.

A Clear Definition of Governmental Responsibility

Just as a lack of clarity and stability in tax regimes is a disincentive to business activity and investment, so is any imprecision or opaqueness in the role of government. Confusion about government restriction or subsidies, or which level of government has jurisdiction, can constitute an impediment to the growth of economic activity. As the size and scope of governmental activity has grown, the codification of governmental responsibility, and its limits, has become more vital. For example, a worker's rational behavior in the labor market is contingent on a clear understanding of his or her rights in the social security system. These rights must therefore be clearly and comprehensively stated, to avoid their arbitrary implementation. Firms need to know government's responsibilities in providing services, enforcing standards, and regulating labor, before they can optimize their behavior. In developed market economies, therefore, there is a large body of administrative law that has grown up to define governmental responsibility.

One area of the world where we can see a pressing need for a clear definition of governmental responsibility is in the countries now on the path of transition, where the state was once both all-powerful and all-responsible. There was no distinction between where the activities of government ended and the activities of enterprises began. The state was both the producer of almost all goods and the provider of social services. In such a situation it was understandable that the productive enterprises, as wholly owned agents of the state, should assume a much greater responsibility toward the social welfare of their employees. Now the smooth functioning of industry and the labor market requires a clear and comprehensive definition of a government-provided social safety net.

A SYSTEM OF CIVIL COMPENSATION

A functioning civil code is an aid to business. Just as incorporation[8] removes the shareholders from exposure to unlimited financial loss due to failure or the infliction of harm to third parties, so a civil compensation code removes businesspeople from the threat of criminal proceedings in all but the most blatantly negligent incidents. It might be argued that chief executive officers will be even more careful about the behavior of their corporations and underlings if they were liable to a jail term rather than merely dipping into the shareholders' profits to settle a suit. However, a system of criminal redress would have two consequences. First, it would affect the behavior of potential victims by encouraging untoward caution since they know that no monetary compensation will be available. Second, it would discourage quite legitimate business activity because of fear of criminal punishment.

We can better understand the significance of this by considering what would happen in the absence of civil compensation, a circumstance that existed in socialist economies where the law of liability was likened to military law. Blame, when it could be assigned, was a criminal matter and would be redressed by the punishment of the offender rather than by the compensation of the victim. **Tort law,** which deals with the redressing of private or civil wrongs through suit, did not exist in the centrally planned economies. Some may think that the United States suffers from a plague of lawyers, many of whom make their living through civil suits, and the prospect of a tort-free society might seem attractive. However, it is clear that the threat of suit can have positive consequences; a firm found guilty of injury will ameliorate its behavior in the future, the more so if it is forced to pay punitive damages. Consider a Western business engaged in, say, an extractive industry, wishing to start operations in say, Russia. The technique is not without risk either to the business's own workers or other nearby individuals. In the West, the businessperson would know that he or she is subject to civil suit in the case of accidents, but to criminal liability only in the case of gross negligence. In Eastern Europe and the former Soviet Union, it is quite possible that the redress would occur only through criminal proceedings. What is true for the Western investor is also true for the domestic Russian businessperson. Removing the greatest problems to investment while retaining some censure over dangerous behavior, and ensuring the ability of the victim to be compensated, requires the development of a civil liability code.

THE FINANCIAL SYSTEM

The role of a financial system in a mixed capitalist economy is paramount. While it can be argued that since it does not "produce" any final good, the financial superstructure of an economy is to some extent "unproductive," the evidence of

---

[8]See later in this chapter for a fuller discussion of the corporate form and its advantages.

recent years seems to be that those countries with the least regulated and most competitive financial systems have been the ones that have prospered. This is a sharp turnaround from the situation in the 1970s and 1980s, when the economies with highly controlled (Japan and Korea) or the noncompetitive (Germany) financial systems seemed to perform best in terms of economic aggregates.

THE CENTRAL BANK

At the heart of the financial system is the central bank. The linchpin of monetary policy, the central bank has several important functions to discharge. Generally speaking, these include the following:

1. To act as a clearing bank for the banks
2. To act as the promulgator and enforcer of financial regulation, designed to enhance the stability and efficiency of the financial system
3. To act as a lender of last resort
4. To control the overall stock of money in the economy, and hence the interest rate
5. To monitor the foreign exchange value of the currency

The central bank has at its disposal several tools with which it can influence the stock of money in the system:

1. Open-market operations, by which the central bank buys or sells government bonds to and from the public
2. The reserve requirements, which constitute controls on the minimum amount of liquid reserves that banks must hold against the liabilities that it owes its depositors
3. The discount rate, which is the interest rate at which the central bank lends money to banks to provide the reserve base against which banks can lend to borrowers

In addition to these tools of the central bank, the money supply can also be changed by the obvious device of printing more money, although that is usually the activity of the treasury or finance ministry rather than the central bank.

THE INDEPENDENCE OF THE CENTRAL BANK. A key issue in comparing economic structures lies in the relative degree of **Central Bank independence.** In the United States and, for example, Germany, the central banks have constitutions and powers that insulate them to a high degree from the government and the political system. In other countries, autonomy is not the case. The Bank of Japan and the Bank of France are highly controlled by the government. The Bank of England, which was for most of the postwar period an obedient arm of the British government, has now been granted a much higher degree of independence. Monetary policy in the United States is determined by a seven member board of governors.

Each governor is appointed by the president of the United States and confirmed by the Senate. Vacancies occur on average about every two years, and during a maximum of two terms in office a president is likely to appoint at most four governors. Thus a president can structure the board of governors to his ideological liking only at the point at which his second term ends.

The argument for independence largely rests on the fact that central bankers have a tough job to do. They have the expertise to make impartial decisions and will "do the right thing" if politicians are prevented from influencing them. The prime job of the central bank is, after all, to preserve the value of the currency, and therefore a central bank should frequently take a restrictive and conservative line on credit creation. If politicians were given control over the central bank, monetary policy would tend to be too relaxed. The hard job of squeezing credit and watching enterprises fail, while unemployment mounted, would be avoided.

The opposing argument is that a totally independent central bank is answerable to no one. In a market economy it is an institution of great significance,[9] and it is odd that in a representative democracy the people have no say in this vital dimension of policy making. In this view the central bank is responsive largely to the narrow financial community from which the board of governors are likely to spring. As such, an independent central bank might be unduly austere, placing burdens on the less well off, and hence jeopardizing political stability by pursuing its own brand of financial rectitude.

There is no right and wrong answer to this debate. Politicians are adept at judging the public will, and when they control the central bank we could say that a form of representative democracy prevails. On the other hand, politicians do tend to have a short-term outlook and are prone to shallow compromise, where the financial experts insulated from pressure might effect the correct long-term policies.

DEPOSITORY INSTITUTIONS

The important tasks of the financial system are the pooling of savings, the assessment of borrowers, and the lending of funds at appropriate interest rates. The gathering of the savings of small savers is largely a task of the depository institutions: commercial banks, savings and loans (also known as thrifts, building societies, etc.), credit unions, and (in many countries) the postal savings system.

COMMERCIAL BANKS. Commercial banks are characterized mainly by the fact that they accept deposits from individuals and firms, they allow the transfer of funds by check from account to account, and they lend out money to individuals and businesses. Within these broad parameters they can take a variety of institutional forms. In most market economies they are privately owned (rather than nationalized) institutions, they are organized as limited liability corporations, and

---

[9] If confirmation of this were required, we have only to take note of the army of "Fed watchers" in the United States, who are concerned with predicting the Fed's behavior.

they are profit seeking. However, a quick glance at the commercial banking structure of various countries reveals very wide differences. The United States is characterized by a very large number of commercial banks, and this is a product of regulation. Banking is governed by state law, and interstate branching of banks was for a long time prohibited. Consequently, while other countries witnessed their banking system consolidated by mergers and takeovers, in the United States a very large number of independent commercial banks survive to this day. There are some 12,000 commercial banks in the United States, contrasting substantially with the much more concentrated systems in, for example, England or Canada, where commercial banking is dominated by only a handful of institutions.

Depositors use commercial banks largely as a matter of convenience and security. Demand deposits usually carry no, or a low, interest rate, but this is offset by accessibility and the safety that is provided by the banks' diversified portfolio of assets. Borrowers use commercial banks as a source of funds because transaction costs are likely to be lower than having direct access to the stock or bond markets. In most industrialized countries commercial banks are the dominant form of corporation finance for small and middle-sized companies. Stability and probity are essential in the commercial banking system. That is why most commercial banking systems are heavily regulated, to avoid the prospect of bank failure, and the deposits of customers are often insured by the government to guard against runs on a bank.

SAVINGS AND LOAN BANKS. Savings institutions (otherwise known as thrifts or, in some countries, building societies) evolved largely as a means to finance home construction and ownership. They accept interest-paying deposits from savers and lend money to home buyers as mortgages. This can lead to a serious mismatch in the term structure of their assets and liabilities. Interest rates on mortgages are long-term [10] and represent illiquid assets. Deposits, the thrift's liabilities, on the other hand, are liquid, and in the United States in the late 1970s and 1980s flowed from the thrifts to the rapidly growing money market mutual funds.

CREDIT UNIONS. A growing alternative institution for savings and lending in the United States has been the credit union. One of the problems of lending to individuals is the difficulty of gathering information on the characteristics of the borrower and hence assessing the appropriate level of risk to assign. Credit unions tackle this problem by lending only to people who share some characteristics (generally occupation or employer). This familiarity reduces risk and makes the problem more tractable.

POSTAL SAVINGS BANKS. Although they are not found in every country, many economies have an extensive postal savings bank as a vehicle for mass banking. Such a system uses the wide distribution of post offices to create a highly accessible

---

[10] In the U.K. building society mortgages almost universally use a variable rate, and U.K. building societies were not placed in the squeeze that their counterparts in the United States experienced.

banking network, which provides a highly liquid form of savings but pays low interest. Post office banks do not make loans, but the accumulated and pooled saving is generally upward to the government. It is therefore either a way of subsidizing the general government deficit or a source of pooled savings to be used on some investment project. In Japan, for example, such saving is received from the post office and channeled by the Ministry of Finance to fund chosen industrial projects.

NONDEPOSITORY INSTITUTIONS

INVESTMENT BANKS.   Investment banks are not depository institutions. Their principal function is to assist larger businesses in acquiring new capital by issuing and underwriting new stock or bond issues into the primary financial markets. In this underwriting function, investment banks guarantee a price to the issuer and try to profit by selling the stock at a level above the guaranteed price. This is known as the "spread."

Investment banks increase the efficiency of the financial system by reducing information costs. A buyer of securities can rely on the name and reputation of the investment bank as a proxy for expensive research about the reliability of the issuer. Investment banks offer advice and help in the restructuring of firms and merger acquisitions. They also engage in merchant banking by lending their own capital to firms in the process of reorganization.

MUTUAL FUNDS.   Mutual funds are financial intermediaries that allow individual investors to take advantage of the returns and security offered by investing in stocks, bonds, or other instruments like short-term corporate debt. The mutual fund industry has seen enormous growth in recent years, especially in the United States, as smaller savers have used it to gain access to stocks with the security of diversification. This growth has had negative implications for other parts of the financial system. Thrift institutions (like savings and loans in the United States) have had to fight harder for deposits and have had to raise interest payments to compete with mutual funds.

VENTURE CAPITAL FUNDS.   In recent years venture capitalism has made a strong comeback and has been credited with providing much of the finance for the small and medium-sized firms that have powered the great expansion of the United States economy in the 1990s. Venture capital companies generally raise risk capital from private sources and grant it to startup firms in return for a portion of the share capital. In general, venture capital companies have proved more flexible and innovative than commercial or investment banks.

INSURANCE COMPANIES.   Although one function of insurance is to protect individuals and companies from risk, the accretion of the premiums paid by policy holders puts a great deal of capital in the hands of the insurance companies and makes them important players in financial markets. As Table 5.3 shows, in the

■ TABLE 5.3

OWNERSHIP OF COMMON STOCK: AN INTERNATIONAL COMPARISON (PERCENTAGE AT YEAR-END)

	United States	Japan	Germany	France	United Kingdom	Italy	Sweden
	1994	FY 1994	1993	1993	1993	1993	1993
Financial Sector	45	44	29	8	62	19	24
Banks	3	26	14	3	1	10	1
Insurance companies	4	16	7	1	17	2	8
Investment funds	0	0	0	0	0	0	8
Pension funds	26	0	0	0	34	0	0
Mutual funds	12	0	8	2	7	6	6
Other financial institutions	4	2	0	2	3	1	0
Nonfinancial Sector	55	56	71	92	38	81	76
Nonfinancial enterprises	0	24	39	59	2	32	34
Public authorities	0	1	4	4	1	28	7
Individuals	48	24	17	19	18	17	16
Foreign	6	7	12	11	16	5	9
Other	1	0	0	0	2	0	10
Total	100	100	100	100	100	100	100

Note: Due to rounding, the figures may not add up to the total. Pension funds in Japan are managed by trust banks and insurance companies. The assets in these funds are included under banks and insurance companies. No data are available on the extent to which mutual funds own shares. Security houses do manage such funds. These companies are included under other financial institutions.

SOURCE: *Flow of Funds*, Board of the Federal Reserve System. Round Table of National Stock Exchanges, "Survey of Stock Ownership Distribution," August 1995. Deutsche Bundesbank, Banque de France, CSO, Consob, Banca d'Italia, Statistika Centralbyran, Sweden. Quoted in OECD (1995b). Annual Security Statistics (1995). [OECD Economic Surveys, 1995–1996, Japan, p.152.]

United States insurance companies hold about 4 percent of all common stock. In other countries, Japan and the United Kingdom especially, the share is much greater.

THE MARKET FOR FINANCIAL ASSETS

The financial sector is largely concerned with the transfer of financial assets of one form or another: stocks (or shares), which are ownership of corporations, or bonds or other forms of debit instruments that may be issued either by corporations or by any level of government. The action of the financial markets by and large determines which companies should grow and which should contract or become defunct by regulating access to investment capital.

THE OWNERSHIP OF STOCK. Financial structures vary between countries. One aspect of this is how dispersed share ownership is within the population. Table 5.3

gives data on the major capitalist economies. One immediately apparent feature is the wide distribution of stock in the United States relative to other countries. Almost half (48%) of the total market capitalization is held by individuals and a further 12 percent lies in mutual funds, generally as a proxy for individuals. Only one-third is owned by financial institutions like insurance companies, banks, and pension funds. This "popular capitalism" is an important feature of the U.S. system. It ensures broad support for the capitalist system (implying, for example, a resistance to high rates of capital and capital gains taxation). It also means that stock market movements have a direct effect on the income and wealth of individuals, providing a much more direct link between financial performance and, say, consumer expenditure than in other countries. It also probably contributes to the stability of the system because a fall in the value of shares does not immediately endanger the financial well-being of other financial and nonfinancial corporations

In Europe there is a much lower level of stock ownership by individuals, roughly 18 percent of stock is held by the household sector. In Germany a sizable part of total share is held or controlled by banks, while in the United Kingdom pension funds and insurance companies predominate. In Japan the corporate sector is largely owned by banks and other corporations through cross-share holding within the large industrial groups, or *keiretsu*. In recent years this has proved a source of great instability for the Japanese financial system. A fall in the price of shares puts pressure on the balance sheets of banks and raises the risk of cumulative collapse, which was very nearly experienced in the crisis of 1997.

HOW FINANCIAL MARKETS PROVIDE CORPORATE GOVERNANCE. In most Western nations the exchange of both shares and bonds is handled through brokerage houses that are members of exchanges. Traditionally brokerages have performed not only the function of buying and selling for a customer, but have also had extensive research departments, as do the mutual funds companies and pension funds. In addition, specialist institutions exist that sell data useful to market participants. Of special note and importance are the bond-rating services, which are influential in determining the interest costs faced by corporations and government. These institutions focus on the performance of firms, agencies, and municipalities, and draw attention to missteps of management, providing therefore a constant check on management performance.

THE MARKET FOR CORPORATE CONTROL. Firms that are performing badly in the eyes of financial analysts face two problems. First, they face an inability to raise loans, either directly from banks or in the debt markets. This places a serious and hard budget constraint on the firm and may curb expansion, force it to improve the efficiency of its operation, or possibly drive it to bankruptcy if it cannot ensure the credit it needs to survive. The other consequence is that the value of a firm's shares is driven down on stock markets, making it vulnerable to an outside takeover bid. In such a case, the assets would fall under new management that would better realize the potential.

THE ORGANIZATION OF BUSINESS

THE CORPORATE FORM

One of the most important innovations of Western economies is the ability to create corporations, legal entities that can, through the sale of stock, raise capital from a large number of individuals, each of whom shares in the profits of the firm. The corporation has a second important feature; each investor is liable only for the amount of money that he or she has invested. Thus, the overall liabilities of the firm are limited to the net worth of the firm, rather than its total debts and obligations. Consequently, the downside in a corporate venture is less than that in an equivalent partnership or proprietorship, where the owners would be liable for the full value of the obligations.

The development of the corporate form in Western economies was crucial in providing a means to raise large sums of capital and limiting the risk of each investor, particularly when the number of investors is large and no one investor can be responsible for oversight of the operation of the firm. Without access to the corporate form it is difficult to gather the finances necessary to undertake large-scale operations. Corporations may be either privately held, in which the shares are not traded on stock markets, or publicly held, in which ownership is liquid and traded on stock markets. To be successful, economies in development or transition must establish stock markets and overcome the considerable barriers to their rapid expansion. It should be noted that although the corporation is efficient in encouraging large and risky ventures, its very presence does limit the effectiveness of contract law. A corporation's liability is limited to the extent of its assets, and situations may result in which its liability under a contract exceeds those assets.

THE BEHAVIOR OF FIRMS

There is no doubt that the corporation is the dominant form of enterprise in the major market economies. It accounts for most of output, most employment, and most research and development. In the United States, for example, some three million corporations make up almost 90 percent of total sales. Within that group large publicly held corporations constitute the majority of employment and output.

However, the very existence of the modern corporation presents the theory of the market economy with some serious problems. The first is that in a large corporation there is necessarily a separation between the ownership of the firm and its management. This causes what is known as a principal-agent problem. How can the owners of the firm, who are the shareholders or principals, be sure that management (the agents of the shareholder-owners) is in fact pursuing the shareholders' interests rather than its own? (This, of course, is in addition to a more general principal-agent issue—how do managers get workers to maximize their effort?)

This raises a further question. The whole paradigm of free enterprise and the market system relies for its efficiency on the idea of pursuit of profit maximization. If the corporate sector fails to ruthlessly pursue profit and settles instead for other objectives, then how efficient can the market system be? One clear way of resolving the issue is to make managers' interests more closely coincident with those of the owners. This in large part accounts for the rapidly growing popularity of stock options as a form of remuneration, since rising share prices earn money for the managers and hence ensure that they will tend to pursue policies that will maximize share values.

The other constraint on the behavior of management comes from a contested market for corporate control. In theory, shareholders can band together to get rid of management that is underperforming, but in reality such "revolutions" are rare. It is more likely that a corporation that is underperforming will find itself the target of takeover interest from other companies or entrepreneurs who feel that the assets are underused. Since top management is likely to be ejected as a result of hostile takeover, this provides a constraint on management behavior.

THE LABOR MARKET

An important set of institutions in most developed market economies are in the labor market. On one side we have the workers, who can join together to form unions; on the other side are employers, who frequently unite to form a collective bargaining agency. A third agent is the government, which can regulate the labor market by controlling the age of workers, the length of workweeks, and the minimum wages. It can also maintain institutions that improve the efficiency of labor markets through job exchanges and retraining policies. Also very relevant are government income support policies, which affect the reservation wage of workers and so can tend to increase the unemployment rate.

TYPES OF LABOR UNIONS

In all industrial democracies, union power grew with the rise of large-scale industrial enterprise. There tended to be a lag in this process, because in many countries unionization was opposed by employers and was initially illegal. Subsequently, unions were granted legal status, and in some countries they became important institutions in overall economic decision making. In the United States, the 1930s were decisive in union growth. The Wagner Act gave unions rights to organize, and the Congress of Industrial Organization (CIO) provided a powerful umbrella organization embracing all workers, skilled and unskilled. Union membership in U.S. nonagricultural employment rose sharply in the 1930s and 1950s, reaching a high in 1955 when about one-third of the workforce was unionized.

American unions tend to be organized along industry lines. Thus, for example, almost all unionized workers in the automobile industry are members of the United Automobile Workers (UAW). Wage negotiation functions on a firm-by-firm basis, rather than being determined for the entire industry. In other countries unionization has taken a different path. Although the picture has changed somewhat in recent years, unions in Britain are organized along occupational rather than industrial lines. Thus all electricians belong to an electricians' union, irrespective of the industry that they are actually employed in. This makes labor negotiation more difficult and labor peace more fragile because each employer must negotiate with several unions within an individual factory or work site. In Germany, as in the United States, unions are organized on an industry basis, but labor negotiations occur between a union and a confederation of employers. Thus wages and conditions are broadly the same across industries. In Sweden a similar system now exists, although until recently unions, through the national labor federation, were an important part of national wage determination procedures. In Finland and Portugal this kind of system is still in place. In Japan unions are organized along company lines and represent both white- and blue-collar workers. As an established part of the enterprise they are characterized by considerable docility.

RELATIVE RATES OF UNIONIZATION

The Scandinavian countries are the most highly unionized societies in the world, with some sources giving unionization rates in Sweden at over 90 percent. The United States in contrast has the lowest rates, with an aggregate economy-wide rate of 19 percent. Japan has an overall rate of about 28 percent, but, as noted earlier, its unions tend to be rather nonmilitant because they are company unions. Most other industrialized countries have rates for full-time workers of between 33 percent and 50 percent (Table 5.4).

■ **TABLE 5.4**

UNION MEMBERSHIP, SELECTED COUNTRIES, 1987–1989

	Membership as a Percentage of		
Country	Nonagricultural Employment	Full-Time Employment	Full-Time Manual Workers
Sweden	96	na	na
Austria	61	52	57
Australia	56	70	69
Ireland	51	48	49
United Kingdom	50	47	53
Italy	45	33	37
Germany	43	34	39
Canada	36	na	na
Netherlands	35	42	47
Switzerland	33	37	37
France	28	na	na
Japan	28	na	na
United States	17	19	27

SOURCE: David G. Blanchflower and Richard B. Freeman, "Unionism in the United States and Other O.E.C.D. Countries," *Industrial Relations* 31 (winter 1992): 56–79; Richard B. Freeman, "American Exceptionalism in the Labor Market: Union-Nonunion Differentials in the United States and Other Countries," in *Labor Economics and Industrial Relations: Markets and Institutions,* ed. Clark Kerr and Paul D. Staudohar (Cambridge, Mass.: Harvard University Press, 1994), 279.

In industrial countries the rate of unionization in the private sector has fallen sharply in recent years. In part this has been due to the decline of large-scale "rust-belt" industry—steel, textiles, rubber, ceramics—and the growth of the service sector, which has proved historically more difficult to unionize. An exception is federal, state, and local government, where unionization has increased sharply with important ramifications for overall political economy. One reason why it has proved hard to restrict the growth of the government sector is that government workers are now well organized and are opposed to initiatives designed to reduce public-sector employment.

INCOME SUPPORT

The extent and generosity of the "social safety net" varies considerably from country to country. In the United States, while it is comprehensive and relatively generous in supporting retired workers, the level of support for the unemployed (especially long-term unemployed) and single parent families has tended to decline, while in Europe the level of support for the unemployed remains high. In the European Union take-home pay after losing a job can frequently be as much as 80 percent of the working rate. Consequently, there tends to be little downward flexibility in wages, and a probable consequence is high unemployment. Japan's income support systems are not generous, but whether this is the cause or the effect of low levels of unemployment is debatable. What is clear is that the difficulties currently encountered by large corporations in maintaining the system of "nenko" or lifetime employment are particularly important, given the low level of income support.

INDUSTRIAL POLICY

Industrial policy is a general term that encompasses the involvement of the government in the promotion of economic growth. As such, it can have both macroeconomic and microeconomic aspects. In its macro form, industrial policy involves the successful pursuit of economic stabilization, the determination of exchange rates and interest rates calculated to support economic growth and due attention to infrastructure and human capital development. Normally, however, when we speak of industrial policy we have in mind particular policies that aim to affect the prospects of specific sectors of the economy or even individual firms within these sectors. This is the microeconomic form of industrial policy, and it is widely practiced in many countries, although there is considerable debate over its effectiveness. Industrial policy can either promote the growth of an industry, seek to stabilize against (for example) inroads of foreign competition, or assist in the orderly decline of an industry, mitigated by the consequences for unemployment or the waste of social infrastructure and human capital.

Government has at its disposal a variety of measures in the pursuit of micro industrial policy. These include direct subsidy payments to firms, government funding of research and development, discriminatory tax relief, government-subsidized or government-directed finance, and the use of tariffs or quotas to protect domestic products. The most aggressive example of industrial policy in recent years is found in the late industrializing countries of East Asia. Slightly earlier, comprehensive industrial policy was practiced in Germany and France. This points out immediately a relevant fact; the most successful industrial policy is practiced by those economies that are well behind the frontier of best practice and advanced technology and have ground to make up.

Consequently, Japan was able to successfully use industrial policy in its transformation after the Meiji restoration in the 1860s as well as in the post–World War II "miracle" period. Similarly, German industrialization relied a great deal on state intervention and direction in both the late 19th century and during the 1950s and 1960s. The success of Germany and France in the 1950s, Japan in the 1960s, and Korea in the 1970s attracted favorable attention to the concept of industrial policy, and some advocated the institution of more extensive industrial policy in the United States. However, the rationale behind any government intervention in the economy must be that there exists some form of market imperfection, and it is hard, in the context of the United States today, imagining the bureaucracy performing better than the market.

Thus while macroindustrial policy might be used to address, for example, the incompleteness of capital markets or failures of coordination due to poor information, justifying microindustrial policy is more difficult. When an economy is behind cutting-edge technology and the government can see the "state of the art" and is knowledgeable about its structure of comparative advantage, it might be able to outperform the market because it has superior information. However, the closer an economy gets to the "frontier," the more difficult the task of "picking winners" becomes. Moreover, intervention in credit markets, frequently a facet of industrial policy, carries with it the loss of the independent impartiality and of the financial system. Industrial policy might be valuable is in encouraging growth of specific geographical regions where the preservation of infrastructure might carry externalities that the market fails to reflect.

TRADE POLICY

In the postwar years there has been a concerted and sustained effort toward liberalization in trade. This has led to burgeoning of international commerce and practically all economies are more open than they used to be. Consequently, the implications of trade for growth and employment are greater than they used to be, and despite lower tariff levels, trade policy has become a very active part of economic diplomacy.

Trade policy has two clear dimensions: assisting exports and protecting the home market. Some countries have economic agencies that act very aggressively in export promotion. Japan, for example, has a very active ministry, the Ministry of International Trade and Industry (MITI), that plays a strong role in coordinating Japanese exports abroad. The other side of trade policy is the protection of the home market and employment. This kind of policy has its roots in the mercantile doctrines of the 16th and 17th centuries that sought protection for domestic industries against colonial and other competition. Economists generally believe that restraints on trade not only lower global welfare but also reduce the welfare of the countries that impose them. They are therefore explicable largely in terms of politically motivated redistribution.

DEVELOPING HUMAN RESOURCES

We saw in chapter 1 that the greatest source of the wealth of nations lies in the stock of human capital embodied in its population, and we should also give thought to the role of the institutions responsible for the development and maintenance of human capital—the educational system and the health care system.

THE EDUCATIONAL SYSTEM

In most developed market economies, much of the educational investment is made by the government. As we noted earlier, education is not a pure public good, since it is both excludable and diminishable, and its public provision is probably justified best on grounds of externalities. An educated individual provides **spillovers,** which increase the productivity of those around him or her (and often other measures of welfare, too). There is a high degree of variance even among the wealthier nations in the delivery of education: who pays, who sets standards, who evaluates, and who receives the greatest level of service. In most European nations education is seen as a social expense, and the school and university systems are almost entirely public. Access is frequently determined by national examination and purports to be largely meritocratic—though clearly class, background, and wealth play a role. In "Anglo-Saxon" nations a greater role is played by the private sector, especially in the United States, implying that education is seen more as personal rather than social investment.

The scope, efficiency, and finance of educational systems are vital because education is a major determinant of economic outcomes. The performance of the educational system is crucial in understanding the functioning of the larger economic system. A particular puzzle is the performance of socialist countries, where universal literacy and high participation in tertiary education was the rule, but economic performance lagged. Today we must ask what implications does the large stock of well-educated workers have for successful transition to a market economy?

THE HEALTH-CARE SYSTEM

The health-care system shares many characteristics with education. It is not a pure public good, but it is frequently supplied by the government, particularly in Europe, where national health services are the norm, and less so in the United States. There is a very current debate on the effectiveness of publicly provided universal health care versus private systems.

KEY TERMS AND CONCEPTS

allocation function

central bank independence

civil compensation

corporate control

corporate governance

depository institutions

distribution function

fiscal policy

industrial policy

investment banks

merit goods

monetary policy

progressive tax

quasi-public goods

redistribution in-kind

spillovers

stabilization function

Tort law

voucher systems

QUESTIONS FOR DISCUSSION

1. Tax systems are becoming less progressive in many societies, while transfers continue to rise. Can you account for these apparently contradictory trends?

2. Why is contract enforcement necessary for the functioning of a modern market system?

3. Why should central banks be independent of the political process?

4. Does the widespread holding of shares in the United States have an impact on the effectiveness of corporate governance in the United States? Why?

5. The corporate form enables businesspeople to escape the full consequences of their actions. Discuss.

6. The low level of unionization in the United States is a key reason for the low rates of unemployment relative to Europe. Discuss.

RESOURCES

WEB SITES

Mark Bernkopf's Central Banking Resource Center . . . .
. . . . http://adams.patriot.net/~bernkopf/index-nf.html
This site offers a very comprehensive series of links to almost every central bank and ministry of finance in the world, as well as ministries of Finance, research departments, and an excellent page on the history of central banking. The site is a certain first step for any research on comparative central banking.

The Cato Institute . . . . www.cato.org/
The home page of this conservative think tank and lobby organization has a lot of information and papers on the introduction of markets into public service provision (health and education), welfare reform, and the privatization of social security. All the work conforms to

the institute's agenda but it is comprehensive and useful, and much can be downloaded free of charge.

The Milken Institute . . . . www.Milken-Inst.org/
This site also has some useful books and position papers.

BOOKS AND ARTICLES

Alstenstetter, Christine, ed. *Health Policy Reform: National Variations and Globalization.* London: St. Martin's Press, 1997.

Blanchflower, David G., and Richard B. Freeman. "Unionism in the United States and Other O.E.C.D. Countries." *Industrial Relations* 31 (winter 1992): 56–79.

Crumper, George. *Evaluation of National Health Systems.* Oxford: Oxford University Press, 1991.

Freeman, Richard B. "American Exceptionalism in the Labor Market: Union-Nonunion Differentials in the United States and Other Countries." In *Labor Economics and Industrial Relations: Markets and Institutions,* ed. Clark Kerr and Paul D. Staudohar. Cambridge, Mass.: Harvard University Press, 1994.

Friedman, Milton, with Rose Friedman. *Free to Choose.* Fort Worth, Tex.: Harcourt Brace, 1990.

Goodhart, Charles. *The Central Bank and the Financial System.* Cambridge, Mass: MIT Press, 1995.

Kwoka John E., and Lawrence J. White, eds. *The Antitrust Revolution: Economics, Competition, and Policy,* 4th ed. New York: Oxford University Press, 1997.

Lippo, Francesco. *Central Bank Independence: Political and Economic Aspects of Delegating Arrangements for Monetary Policy.* White Plains, N.Y.: Edward Elgar Press, 1999.

McGroarty, David, and William J. Bennett. *Break These Chains: The Battle for School Choice.* Rocklin, Calif.: Prima Publishing, 1996.

Musgrave, Richard, and Peggy Musgrave. *Public Finance in Theory and Practice.* New York: McGraw-Hill, 1984.

Nester, William R. *American Industrial Policy: Free or Managed Markets?* New York: St. Martin's Press, 1997.

Okimoto, Daniel I. *Between MITI and the Market: Japanese Industrial Policy for High Technology.* Stanford, Calif.: Stanford University Press, 1990.

CAPITALISM IN WESTERN EUROPE

6

INDICATIVE PLANNING
AND THE FRENCH ECONOMY

THE THEORY OF INDICATIVE PLANNING

One of the failures of a market economy considered in chapter 4 resulted from lack of information. That discussion focused on the difficulty and expense of consumers acquiring full information about products, but market failure also results from enterprise managers knowing too little about the future economic environment to make optimal investment decisions. Informed investment choices require knowledge about a wide range of macroeconomic variables, among them the future prices and availability of inputs, the rate of growth of the economy, movements in the value of the currency, the inflation rate, and so forth. In a pure market environment, firms either have to estimate such movements based on their experience or purchase information from some proprietary source, such as consultancies. Even though the marginal cost of disseminating such information is very close to zero, it will tend to be undersupplied and incomplete under market arrangements.

Indicative planning is an attempt to bridge this information gap. The government's capacity to marshall information, and its ability to draw the actors in the economy into a dialogue about their needs and intentions, put it in a strong position to compile a comprehensive and consistent set of forecasts about the future direction of the economy. If these projections are accepted by leaders of industry, investment decisions will be consistent and based on a common set of assumptions and the forecasts have a better chance of being realized. In the words of one authority on French planning:

> The aim of pure indicative planning is to improve the performance of the economy by the provision of better economic information: forecasts or targets are published but compliance with them is voluntary. The underlying logic is that the plan, via collective action, can supply economically valuable information which, as a public good, the market mechanism does not disseminate efficiently.[1]

If there were complete and efficient forward markets there would be less need for indicative planning or any shared set of assumptions because enterprises could use such markets to hedge the risks attendant on their investment decisions. Pierre

---

[1] Peter Holmes, "Indicative Planning" in the *New Palgrave Dictionary of Economics*, ed. John Eatwell and Murray Milgate (New York: Stockton Press, 1987), 781.

Massé, the planning commissioner from 1959 to 1965, justified French indicative planning in terms of its capability to informally correct the absence of such forward markets. The market forecasts embodied in an indicative plan give both buyers and sellers confidence that the general levels of demand for products and supply of materials would be forthcoming. By identifying early the existence of oversupply or bottlenecks, investment behavior can be modified in a timely fashion and the incidence of market disequilibria reduced. Thus both business and consumers can benefit from an exercise in collective and consistent market research, which is freely distributed to all the relevant actors in the economy.

This view of the value of indicative planning is not accepted by everyone. Strong believers in the efficiency of market mechanisms insist that firms are better forecasters of the variables that affect their business than governments, precisely because they have a pecuniary interest in getting those forecasts right. Those most efficient at producing reliable estimates are in a position to earn super-normal profits, which provides an incentive for private firms that the government does not experience.

Such fundamental objections aside, the effectiveness of indicative planning depends to a large degree on the reliability of the estimates. The government may indeed have a better view of the overall economic landscape than individual participants, but as we shall see in the case of central planning, the government is largely dependent on information provided by the firms, who might have an incentive to mislead the government. Consider an example used by Peter Holmes to illustrate this problem. The users of, say, electrical components might have an incentive to overstate their demand for such components. This might produce over-investment by component suppliers, a corresponding artificial glut of components, and an opportunity for the user to take advantage of the cheap prices. Such strategic behavior can apply to a wide range of goods and factors of production including the supply of qualified labor. An overestimation of the demand for computer engineers, for example, might induce both public and private (human capital) investment in training to the advantage of employers but the disadvantage of newly qualified workers and society as a whole.

Even if successful in its objective of reconciling potential endogenous disequilibria, indicative planning may run into serious problems because of shocks to the external environment in which the economy functions. In theory it might be possible to bring endogenous supply and demand into closer equilibrium by the judicious use of indicative planning, but unless the economy is totally closed the projections can be made irrelevant by exogenous changes over which neither the government nor the internal actors have any control. For example, the best of indicative plans would have been confounded by the explosion in oil and energy prices that occurred during the 1970s. Investment projections based on the oil prices of 1971 would be nonviable given the increase in the real price of oil by 1978.

The more open the economy, and the greater the uncertainty concerning exogenous variables, the more difficult and the more hazardous becomes the indicative planning exercise. This can be dealt with to some degree by producing multiple projections based on different "scenarios." The problem here is that there are so many factors in the external environment, and the number of scenarios increases, literally, exponentially with the addition of each relevant factor. Even if there were as few as three exogenous state variables, each of which could assume two values (high and low), then eight different sets of estimates would be required for each year. If there were ten state variables, each of which could assume any one of three values in any given year, then the total number of scenarios to be investigated in a five-year planning period would be a staggering 24 million!

Proponents of indicative planning pragmatically overlook these theoretical problems. There are, they say, even within relatively open economies operating in an uncertain world, advantages to sharing, in Commissioner Massé's words, "a common view of the future." However, there is a temptation to make the plan embody as rosy a view of the future as possible in the hopes that it will induce the actors to operate in an expansionary fashion. Setting a growth forecast of 5 percent a year, for example, might cause the aggregate level of investment to rise by appealing to optimism and the "animal spirits" of entrepreneurs. The use of plans as self-fulfilling prophecies is attractive to governments interested in accelerating the rate of growth. Sir Roy Harrod, the pioneer of modern growth theory, suggested that an appropriate policy would be for the government to forecast growth at the **warranted growth rate,** and that this would tend to reduce the discrepancy between the actual and the warranted rates.[2] While this position has a sound theoretical underpinning, it presents the possibility of using the plan as undisciplined boosterism: forecasting a high rate of growth to induce a high rate of private investment. Such a practice might be successful in the short term, but it will only last as long as there is no great divergence between the outcome and the forecast. A highly visible shortfall might erode the credibility of the plan, and a plan that is perceived as being systematically misleading and overoptimistic might well be worse than no plan at all!

Even if the indicative plan is highly successful in forecasting key macroeconomic variables and the levels of demand in various sectors, this does not directly imply that an investment decision by a particular firm is legitimated. That would occur only if there were substantial collusion between the constituent firms of an industry, by which the total investment was systematically divided between them. This might be tolerated or actively encouraged by the government, but it shows the danger that indicative planning might be anticompetitive. Say, for example, there are four firms in the industry and demand is forecast to rise by 20 percent. It is tempting for a government to encourage each of the firms to increase their investment and output at the same percentage rate as industry growth and to tolerate some form of price fixing. This ensures that the investment required to meet the plan target is actualized. The dangers are that competition is eroded, a government-sponsored cartel is sanctioned, and less efficient firms are rewarded. This behavior is perhaps more prevalent in downturns, when the government might see fit to allocate shares of a shrinking pie equally among competitors.

[2] The warranted growth rate is the rate of expansion of GDP that equates planned saving with planned investment. It can be shown, under simple assumptions, to be equal to the marginal propensity to save to the capital output ratio.

Despite these problems, there is a pragmatic appeal in the practice of indicative planning to many people. At the very least, the process of planning requires the systematic collation and reconciliation of a large amount of data that is useful to government and business alike. Moreover, the preparation of the plan involves the exchange of information among the principle economic actors. Technocratic planners engage in a dialogue with labor unions, business associations, and the representatives of other branches of government, as well as any other groups that may be included. This process, known to the French as *concertation,* is a very important part of the exercise in itself. In the words of the First French Plan (1947–1952), it represents "a permanent exchange of ideas between the government and the public," but as well as that rather vertical arrangement it also facilitates horizontal exchange between, say, business and labor leaders and, often neglected but equally important, the various government agencies.

An important question is who should be included in the dialogue. If the participants are narrowly defined, we have a corporatist state where only those institutions sanctioned by the state have a role in formulating policy. In Japan, for example, the debate is largely limited to business leaders and bureaucrats, with the third side of the "iron triangle," the politicians, holding a watching brief. Labor and community groups are by and large excluded although the concerns of certain powerful lobby groups (like the farmers) are well known. Initially in France, a different, but equally corporatist, composition was established. The First Plan sought input only from unions, the civil service, employers' federations, and farmers' alliances. However over time, there has been considerable "dialogue broadening," and new participants representing women's groups, senior citizens, young people, and environmentalists have been given a seat at the table. This broadening has not always appealed to the original core participants, who see the newcomers as somewhat "soft," tending to distract attention from the "hard" issue of defining the relationship of labor, capital, and government.

There is no simple way to decide whether indicative planning is a worthwhile exercise. Perhaps the best test is to look carefully at the experience of the nations that have practiced it. Much of indicative planning's appeal to would-be imitators certainly lay in the conspicuous economic success of its two most prominent practitioners—France and Japan. In the 1960s, an envious glance at their growth records persuaded Britain to initiate a planning system very like the French, producing a so-called National Plan. In the British case, however, one important lesson was learned: plan targets cannot be set in isolation of macroeconomic constraints. In Britain the plan attempted to promulgate a growth rate of 4 percent, but this was derailed by one of many balance of payments crises and the targets had to be ignominiously abandoned.

INDICATIVE PLANNING IN FRANCE

THE BACKGROUND TO THE PLAN

In France there is a long history of state involvement in economic development that sets it at variance to the "Anglo-Saxon" tradition of **laissez faire.** Aggressive and comprehensive governmental policies were pursued by Jean-Baptiste Colbert, the finance minister under Louis XIV. **Colbertism** became a byword for interventionist state activity and constitutes a prime example of "mercantilism," state manipulation of industry and trade to maximize its power. Similarly in the 19th century, France was a "late industrializer" relative to the rapid start of Britain, and policy was directed toward nurturing and protecting of industry.

Because of this interventionist history, there was no sharp cultural or political discontinuity when, in the aftermath of World War II, France initiated a system of planning. French procedures contrasted sharply in philosophy and method to the highly formal centralized command planning adopted in the Soviet Union in the 1920s and 1930s. In France there was never an assumption that all of the means of production should be nationalized, nor that the power of coordination should rest exclusively at the center. Rather, the market was seen as the principal tool of coordination in a mixed economy where private production would dominate. The role of the government was to supply information, oversee a dialogue between the various actors, provide guidance and, where necessary, provide the infrastructure required to meet the targets of the plan. The essential principles of such a model, which involves a large element of industrial policy, were expressed in the First Plan:

> In our economy, made up of nationalized industries and as well as an extensive free-market sector, the Plan should provide guidance as well as directives. Its means of implementation, while laying down disciplines, should at the same time promote creative initiatives in all sectors and maintain within businesses both justifiable profits and risk-taking, which provide the necessary impetus and sanctions.[3]

Nor did the planning apparatus imply that French industry should be isolated from the world economy, but the centrality of trade and international competitiveness for success in a market economy was stressed. In fact, much of the emphasis in the first plan was on restoring France to a position of international competitiveness after the war.

THE ORGANIZATION OF PLANNING

One of the most obvious features of planning in France was the small number of people permanently employed in plan production. The agency responsible for the plan, the General Planning Commissariat for Equipment and Productivity (CGP), never employed more than 50 professional staff. Its power, however, has always been disproportionate to its size since it is attached directly to the office of the prime minister. Its function continues to be largely one of coordination and it draws the personnel to prepare the plans from other ministries—primarily from the Ministry of the Economy and Finance (MEF), especially from the forecasting directorate (DP) and the National Institute of Statistics (Insée). These agencies are responsible for the initial collation of basic economic data forecasts. The production

---

[3] From the *First Plan* cited by Bernard Cazes in "Indicative Planning in France" in *Comparative Economic Systems: Issues and Cases*, ed. Morris Bornstein (Burr Ridge, Ill.: Irwin, 1993), 161.

of the final plan consists of three distinct stages, and although the nature and objectives of the planning system have changed over time, these have been permanent features.

(1) INFORMATION GATHERING. An essential step in any planning exercise entails gathering basic data on the economy for use in forecasting. Equally valuable, however, is the assembling of research, both retrospective and forward looking, on the policy options and likely movement of exogenous factors that are important to the functioning of the economy. The forward-looking elements in this exercise have been characterized as "throwing a light on the future." They involve raising such questions as: What have been the major developments in technology and industry? How will these affect employment and industrial structure? What potential developments in the international economy will significantly affect the French economy?

As the plan has "softened" and more social considerations have become a part of the process, more "futurism" has been built into this phase. For example, in preparing the Tenth Plan (1989–1992), a group led by the historian E. Le Roy Ladurie was charged with engaging in long-range speculation on possible futures for society, technology, and the economy beyond the year 2000. This step also involves model building in order to forecast the movement of the economy across several time periods from the short- (one year) to the long-term (five years) to point out the potential difficulties that may be encountered.

(2) CONCERTATION (OR DIALOGUE). Much activity in French planning centers around a process known in French as *concertation,* usually translated into English as "dialogue," though it is rather more than that. The French regard their economy as one in which problems are resolved through a constant exchange of ideas between the government and the public. Thus rather than a guided economy (*economie dirigée*), they see a concerted economy (*economie concertée*), where through exchange of opinion and debate the participants arrive at a common conception of the future.

During this phase all parties with a role in plan preparation participate with civil servants in a series of about 30 "modernization commissions." Some of these are vertically structured and deal with specific productive sectors of the economy. For the Sixth Plan, for example, there were nine vertical commissions: energy, agriculture, food, transport, industry, communications, commerce, tourism, and handicrafts. Other series of commissions have a broader interest in national issues: finance, employment, social benefits, research, economic information, regional development, and the overseas departments. Another set of commissions deals with social issues.

In the early plans only the employers' groups, trade unions, and representatives of agriculture had a substantial voice in the *concertation* process. As noted earlier, this tended to give a very corporatist aspect to French planning; the only institutions that participated were those that were solicited and licensed by the state. Over time, however, the number of participants has been enlarged and less formal groups (representing young people, women's groups, consumers' groups, and so forth) have been allowed to have a role in the planning process. As the process became more inclusive, the nature of the plans necessarily changed and involved the development of various models of French growth in which quality of life and equity became important elements of the debate.

(3) CONSISTENCY.   After the modernization commissions have completed their discussions, and the broad outline of the plan has been determined, it is the function of the planners to provide consistency to the plan. This consistency has two dimensions: longitudinally (that is, across time) and cross-sectionally (that is, between the various sectors of the economy).

COMMITTING TO THE PLAN

Indicative planning does not involve compulsion or direction, and one immediate question about its effectiveness is whether or not the existence of the successive French plans has changed anything. In what sense do the participants of the plan "commit" to it, and what is the concrete result of their commitment?

COMMITMENT THROUGH PARTICIPATION.   One possible answer is that involvement in the production of the plan in the *concertation* stage binds the participants to the common vision of the plan. Early plans involved only a narrow constituency in their preparation (labor, business, and agriculture), and the exchange of views between these groups was intensive, or "deep." The participants, while not bound in any contractual sense to conform to the norms, had strong moral pressure to do so because they had been fully and actively involved in their establishment. These plans, produced from a narrow, corporatist constituency, might be called the State's Plan *(Plan de l'État).*

In later plans the constituency involved in *concertation* was broadened and though more participants had input in *concertation,* the exchange was less deep, possibly implying less commitment. To some the ideal would be to create a dialogue that is both broad and deep, that would produce a Nation's Plan *(Plan de la Nation),* to which, because everyone participated in its development, the entire nation would be committed. This is a utopian and questionable conception of the world. Extending participation to a broader constituency does not necessarily mean full acceptance of the fundamental assumptions and goals of the plan. In fact, the more groups that are represented in the discussion, the greater is the likelihood of conflict and failure to arrive at a consensus.

COMMITMENT TO EXPERTISE.   Another view of the plan is that it is a comprehensive "market research" document that throws a revealing light on the future. People accept the plan, and commit to its findings, because it is in some sense the best available vision of the future, one produced by pooled intelligence and hard work. Precisely because it is a well-produced document, authored by experts, it is rational for individual players to accept this common vision. Any other behavior would be suboptimal.

COMMITMENT BY CONTRACT.   The two types of commitment discussed up to this point are voluntaristic and therefore binding in only the loosest way. A third category of commitment to the targets of the plan involves the signing of contracts that will specify performance, particularly in terms of commitment to specific investments or infrastructural improvements. In theory such contracts could be undertaken by any of the principal actors, whether private or public. In reality, however, it is the public sector—state-owned enterprises, agencies of central government, or regional authorities—that are likely to make the commitment. Private firms might be induced to commit to specific actions in return for grants, loans, or concessionary tax treatment. In the 1980s the French introduced planning contracts *(contrats de plan)* as part of a revamping of the indicative planning process.

THE CHANGING NATURE OF THE PLANS OVER TIME

THE FIRST PLAN.   Since their inception in 1947, plans have been made on a five-year basis. The First Plan was generally known as the Monnet Plan after its chief architect, **Jean Monnet,** who moved on to play a vital and formative role in the development of the European Union. This plan was largely a recovery plan and was quite different in character from its successors. It focused on the reconstruction and modernization of industry after the German occupation, during which a lot of heavy capital equipment was expropriated to Germany and there was inadequate investment and maintenance. This plan emphasized long-run growth and development, rather than short-run stability, and focused on investment in basic industry: coal, electricity, steel, cement, railways, and agricultural inputs. The task of planning was made easier because at this time the majority of firms in all of these industries were nationalized and in many cases were sectoral monopolies. Thus planning was by and large a matter of rendering consistency to the investment plans of the nationalized firms.

The period of the First Plan coincided with inflow of capital under the Marshall Plan, the major American postwar reconstruction initiative in Europe. The central planning commissariat was the principle interface between the Marshall Plan administration and the French government. Over one-third of total capital investment covered by the plan originated from Marshall aid.

1952–1965: THE "HARMONIZING PLANS."   The next three plans[4] attempted to bring to the other sectors of industry the systematic investment and modernization fostered in the basic sectors by the First Plan. The environment was more difficult because Marshall assistance had been terminated. Moreover, the planners' emphasis on the long-term brought them into frequent conflict with the Ministry of Economics and Finance, which tried to refocus policy on short-term stabilization.

---

[4]Note that although this covers three planning periods, the elapsed time is only 13 years. The Third Plan was aborted after two years.

■ **TABLE 6.1**

PERCENTAGE ACHIEVEMENT OF PLAN IN FRANCE

France	Plan II, 1954–1957	Plan III, 1958–1961	Plan IV, 1962–1965
National income	103	98	100
Investment	110	100	105
Private consumption	106	97	101
Industrial production	115	105	na
Agricultural production	93	97	na
Steel	99	102	86
Coal	97	89	84
Oil	93	101	127
Electricity	104	101	93
Gas	95	na	92
Machine tools	75	91	88
Motor vehicles	147	91	93
Textiles	117	88	95
Meat	104	95	94
Milk	100	104	94

SOURCE: Vera Lutz, *Central Planning for the Market Economy: An Analysis of the French Theory and Experience,* Institute of Economic Affairs (Harlow, England: Longmans, 1969).

An attempt to resolve this conflict led to the planning commissariat being detached from the office of the prime minister and located with the MEF in 1954. It was restored to "independence" in 1962, but the problems of linking short-term stabilization policy to the medium- and long-term plan objectives of maximizing investment and growth remained. In terms of the continued development of the basic sector, the plan was quite successful until the 1960s. Outcomes for basic industries (steel, gas, coal, etc.) were usually within 10 percent of the target (see Table 6.1). However, the performance of the private industrial and service sector was generally widely off target, either over- or underperforming, depending on the sector, as can be seen from the performance of motor vehicles and machine tools in Table 6.1. Despite these problems, overall growth of national income was close to target, and investment was generally above it, reflecting perhaps the confidence that the planning framework gave to industrialists.

1965–1975: SOCIAL CONCERNS AND RISING COMPLEXITY. In the late 1960s two distinctly new features of the planning process evolved. First, social objectives (including regional policy) began to take a much more prominent role. These had been creeping into the process during the previous planning periods but their consideration became more explicit in the Fifth Plan. The range of representation on the modernization commissions increased and issues like income policy began to come to the fore.

The second change was an increase in the complexity and technical detail of the planning process itself. Complex macroeconomic models were featured for the first time in the Fifth Plan (1965–1970). This represented an attempt to get to grips with the problems of resolving the conflict of the short-term stabilization aspects and long-term growth aspects of government policy. This trend toward increasing complexity was further exacerbated in the Sixth Plan—implemented between 1971–1975, but in preparation from 1966. In this plan the technical modeling exercises became even more ambitious. In particular a physical and financial resources model (wittily and universally known as FIFI) took the center stage. Its main purposes were to reveal the medium-term macrodevelopment problem in the economy, to study over time the results of different policy options, and to get a long-term view of the problems of France as "a competitioned economy" (i.e., one that is highly open to world trade and therefore conditioned by international developments in costs). In this sense the plan had shifted from a **normative planning** model, with clear targets to be achieved, to what Holmes terms (with some understatement) "a modest forecasting exercise." Nevertheless, the idea of the plan as an attempt to reveal some kind of common consensual vision of the future remained.

The Late 1970s: The Decline of Planning and the Rise of Laissez Faire. The 1970s were a decade of turbulence for the global economy and, as we noted in earlier sections in this chapter, even endogenously consistent plans can be made irrelevant by sudden exogenous shocks. Sharp increases in oil prices, surging global inflation, and the collapse and restructuring of the system of international payments all occurred in the first four years of the decade and were sufficient to render the forecasting estimates of the Sixth Plan all but useless.

Moreover, French politics had taken a rather sharp lurch to the right with the advent of the conservative administration of Giscard d'Estaing. His administration was prepared to place a much greater faith than previous governments in the unfettered operation of the market. For these ideological reasons, the importance of planning receded. The plan continued to exist, and the formal mechanisms were largely unchanged, but it served only in a forecasting function.

The 1980s: The Socialist Reforms. In May of 1989 the Socialist François Mitterrand won the presidency and in the subsequent general election his party captured 285 of the assembly's 491 seats while the Socialists' Communist allies won another 44. This gave the left a powerful mandate and the parliamentary majority for a radical turn. The most obvious manifestation of this was the nationalization of a large part of French industry. Already a substantial part of productive activity was accounted for by the public enterprises. Nationalized firms held a virtual monopoly of electricity supply, coal, gas, public transport and air transport, accounting for about 5 percent of gross domestic product (GDP). In addition, there were several industrial enterprises (including Renault, the automaker, and SEITA, a tobacco company) that competed with private industry.

Mitterand added 12 major industrial firms to the public sector, among them seven of France's largest enterprises (employing more than 800,000 people). In addition, a large part of the private financial sector was added to the banks already under public ownership. As a result, 25 percent of industrial output, all of major utilities, and almost all of the financial sector was in public hands. This was a step in the opposite direction from the broad trends apparent in most other parts of the world, and it stood in particular contrast to the events on the other side of the English Channel, where Margaret Thatcher had two years earlier embarked on the denationalization of all publicly held enterprises in the competitive sector and a large part of public utilities as well.

The increase in the scope of the state in France provided an opportunity to revive planning and to give it a purpose above the primarily forecasting function to which it had been relegated during the 1970s. To further this end, the government created a new Ministry of the Plan and Regional Planning, to replace the old planning commissariat, and convened a national commission to investigate how the planning procedure might be improved. This commission recommended two reforms, both of which were embodied in the Planning Reform Law of 1982. The first was organizational, and aimed to promote a more democratic planning process by increasing the role of parliament and broadening the *concertation* under the coordination of a new National Planning Commission. The planning ministry was phased out, and the old system of a commissariat reporting directly to the prime minister was reestablished. A further feature of this reform, perhaps the one with the most enduring consequences, was the devolution of a substantial amount of power from the national level to the regional and provincial levels.

The second dimension of the reforms sought to increase the level of formal commitment to the plan. This involved the introduction of **planning contracts**—between the central government and regional governments and between the central government and the nationalized industries. These commit both parties to specific actions and levels of expenditure for certain priority projects defined in the national plan and the subsidiary regional plans. This is a step to answering, at least in part, the perennial question of who is committed to what in the framework of the plan. Of course, private industry is not involved in these contracts and the significance of the nationalized industries is likely to decline as reprivatization is on the agenda. However, the issue of government's commitment to the plan was largely resolved.

THE 1990s. The return of a conservative coalition government in 1986 reversed the fortunes of planning once more. Ideologically, the new administration saw the prime determinant of the vitality of the economy as lying in the competence and ambition of individual entrepreneurs rather than in the planning activity of the government sector. The increase in the scope of the nationalized sector was immediately halted and a privatization program initiated with particular emphasis on the liberalization of the financial sector. Industrial firms were to be sold off at the fastest pace that France's relatively shallow stock market would allow.

The conservative administration toyed with the idea of getting rid of the CGP, transforming it into the "office of strategy." Planning activity went into a hiatus during 1986 and 1987 but emerged with the Tenth Plan in 1988 to cover the four-year period 1988–1992 and make the plan period coincident with the completion of the internal market of the European Community (EC) in 1992. The commitment of the state to the plan was high, and some FF52 billion were pledged by the central government to completing regional planned projects.

It is significant that the planning process is now being coordinated with European objectives. In the production of the Tenth Plan, *concertation* was extended to private and public leaders in the other members of the European Union (EU), as well as to representatives of "young people" (aged 18–25) within France.

After some administrative reshuffling the planning commissariat is once more attached to the office of the prime minister, now a Socialist, Lionel Jospin, who must "cohabitate" with the conservative president Jacques Chirac. The conflicting philosophies within the government and the growing integration of the European Union, making independent economic policy increasingly difficult, have necessitated a change in planning's role. While the planning commissariat is no longer charged with producing a clear blueprint for economic action and change, it remains important in initiating debate and in the development of consensus. The current commissioner for planning, Jean-Michel Charpin, recently redefined the role of planning in France:

> The government deems it necessary to have a long-term vision of economic and social development to allow better coherence of action between institutions and economic actors.[5]

Lionel Jospin, the prime minister, recalled that the CGP had a special function in arriving at government decisions. It is, he wrote in his mission letter to the commissioner, "the animator of strategic and forward-looking analysis, a privileged place for debate and inter-ministerial cooperation, and the evaluation of public policy."[6]

Now the mission of the CGP falls within three aspects:

1. The development of the French economy in the context of globalization and European integration
2. The reinforcement of social cohesion, including the social safety net and the problems of young and old
3. The modernization of the institutions of government, including regulation of industry and the environment

WAS FRENCH INDICATIVE PLANNING SUCCESSFUL?

For 30 years or so after the inception of planning in 1946–1947, the French economy was one of the fastest growing market economies in the world. The growth of GDP was both high in the average and also quite consistent and steady over time. It would be tempting to ascribe this "miracle" of the 30 glorious years (*les trentes glorieuses*, as the French fondly remember them) to the planning effort. In truth there is little to separate the performance of the "French miracle" from the miracles in Germany, Italy, or the Netherlands where planning was much less a part of the

---

[5] *La Lettre du Commissariat du Plan*, P.I. no. 1 (November 1998).
[6] Letter of Mission from Jospin to the CGP (9 January 1998).

apparatus. There is no irrefutable cross-section or time series evidence of indicative planning's efficacy.

In its initial manifestation, say for the first 20 years, the plan set out a vision of the future. This was not merely a cold prediction of what was likely to occur, but it represented rather the consensus view of what should occur. It was therefore a normative exercise, not merely a positive one. This important observation affects what approach we can take in evaluating the failure or success of indicative planning. Pierre Massé put it this way:

> [T]he Plan is in principle normative, the projection [on which the Plan is based] is partly normative and partly predictional. Plan and projection not being identical, the invalidation of the projection does not mean failure for the plan. This is why the question to what extent are French Plans implemented is ambiguous. This ambiguity cannot be removed simply by comparing projection with reality. Falling short of the projection is not in itself significant. In measuring success or failure of the Plan, one must assess, to a certain extent subjectively, the underlying significance of falling short in any particular way.[7]

In some ways this normative exhortation for the leaders of industry to accept and conform to the targets of the plan is the most important aspect of planning. This common vision and shared market research might have salutary effects on investment planning and growth. As Charles Kindleberger has observed:

> Knowledge of income and industry projections and faith in the inevitability of expansion are communicated to firms at intra- and inter-industry meetings. This is perhaps the most powerful effect [of French planning] and one which has a faint resemblance to a revivalist prayer meeting.[8]

Of course, the danger of such an evangelical approach to planning is that any failure is likely to cause a crisis of faith. This became apparent during the 1970s when plan projections were somewhat cynically manipulated for political ends, and in this process confidence in planning as a disinterested and technical exercise was destroyed. Following that, planning held a more detached forecasting function, until its "revival" by the socialist administration of the early 1980s. In this new form planning does pack more of a punch, because the performance of some of the major players is guaranteed by the existence of the planning contracts. Thus private enterprise can see exactly what the government is committed to and can make its plans appropriately.

Indicative planning has operated in France for more than 50 years. Its durability throughout different governments and economic regimes suggests that the participants in the planning process thought that they had gained by their involvement

---

[7] Pierre Massé, "The French Plan and Economic Theory," *Econometrica* (April 1965): 267. Cited in Charles Kindleberger, "French Planning" in *National Economic Planning*, ed. Max Millikan (New York: Columbia University Press, 1967), 301.

[8] Charles P. Kindleberger, "The Postwar Resurgence of the French Economy," in *In Search of France*, ed. Stanley Hoffman, C. P. Kindlebeger, J. R. Pitts, and L. Wylie, J. B. Duroselle, and F. Goguel (Cambridge, MIT Press, 1963), 155.

in the exercise. If the exercise offered nothing, then there would be a reluctance on the part of the various participants to be involved, but in contrast, the list of groups seeking inclusion has been growing.

During the 1970s planning was in sharp decline. The integration of France into the European Communities and the external shocks that ripped through the international economy with many domestic consequences made the planning exercise seem obsolete. How could planning be effective when vital variables like energy prices were so far beyond domestic control? However, the advent of the socialist government in 1981 brought with it a rebirth in the confidence in planning, an increase in the extent of nationalized industry (and therefore state control of the economy), and a restructuring of the institutional mechanism of planning. The return of the conservatives, the relaxation of controls, and the reprivatization process undercut some of that momentum. It remains to be seen whether the return of a socialist administration will put another breath of life into the process. In some sense that is unlikely. Today the French involvement in the European Union, and the necessity of conforming to the broader structure and rules of the European Union, has reduced the importance of the plan.

For most of the period of indicative planning the French economy has been buoyant. In the past decade, however, economic performance has been significantly lower than the average for industrial nations. Growth has been slow, and unemployment has ballooned, particularly among young people. A new socialist administration was voted in during 1997, and the future of the plan lies in its hands. The debate is whether or not this is due to too much planning or too little. Proponents of planning can point to greater success when the process was more directed, had fewer participants, and produced specific targets rather than loose scenarios. They claim that a return to a more aggressive planning would pay dividends. In contrast, free marketeers feel that the poor French performance is due to the rigidities of French life and a reluctance to let the market pick winners. They see high levels of controls, an extensive public sector, a rigid labor market, and misguided industrial policy as well as the attempts at planning as the causes of the malaise.

PROSPECTS FOR THE FRENCH ECONOMY

The focus of this chapter has been on the role of the plan, and clearly there has been a shift away from traditional *dirigisme,* the control of the economy by the state, and a sharp reduction in the degree of government intervention.

Table 6.2 shows French performance compared to performance in both Germany and the G7 nations as a whole since 1970. It is a record of declining *relative* growth accompanied by rising unemployment and growing government deficits, for which the increasing burden of social expenditure must take much of the responsibility.

France today is in the process of repositioning its economic policy, from one in which the state played an almost completely dominant role to one in which markets and less formal institutions play a key part. An aspect of this has been the

■ TABLE 6.2

RECENT FRENCH ECONOMIC PERFORMANCE: AVERAGE ANNUAL GROWTH RATES

	1971–1980	1981–1990	1994	1995	1996	1997
Real GDP						
France	3.3	2.4	2.8	2.1	1.6	2.3
Germany	2.7	2.3	2.7	1.8	1.4	2.2
G7	3.3	2.9	2.8	2.2	2.8	2.9
Inflation						
France	9.7	6.4	1.7	1.8	2.0	1.2
Germany	5.1	2.6	2.7	1.8	1.5	1.8
G7	8.7	4.8	2.2	2.3	2.2	2.0
Employment						
France	0.5	0.3	−0.1	1.1	0.0	0.8
Germany	0.2	0.5	−0.7	−0.4	−1.3	−1.4
G7	1.3	1.2	1.0	0.8	0.7	1.3
Unemployment Rate						
France	4.2	9.3	12.3	11.6	12.4	12.5
Germany	2.7	7.3	9.6	9.4	10.4	11.5
G7	4.5	6.9	7.2	6.8	6.9	6.7
General Government—Overall Balance						
France	−0.5	−2.3	−5.7	−4.9	−4.1	−3.0
Germany	−2.0	−2.0	−2.4	−3.3	−3.4	−2.7
G7	−2.1	−2.9	−3.5	−3.4	−2.8	−1.4

SOURCES: INSEE, *Raport sur Les Comptes de la Nation*, 1999; and International Monetary Fund, *World Economic Outlook*, 1999.

rapid privatization since 1996 of much of state-owned enterprise, embracing not only manufacturing industry (Renault, Thomson, Péchiney), but also utilities (France Télécom), insurance (Assurances Générale de France), banking (Crédit Lyonais and Credit Foncier), and the defense sector (Aérospatiale). This represents an asset sale as great as Thatcherism in the United Kingdom and is remarkable in that the Socialists have pursued privatization with greater enthusiasm than did the Conservative administration that preceded them.

There is some skepticism about whether France has developed sufficient market institutions and supportive social organizations to thrive in the "new economy" for which state direction seemed ill suited. The universality of the French state has a long history and was much criticized by Tocqueville, while Francis Fukuyama characterizes French society as "low trust" and lacking the capacity for informal association that he believes the current economy requires. He wrote:

French *dirigisme,* or the active involvement of the state in economic life, was thus both the cause and the effect of the weakness of the French private sector and of its inability to create competitive large-scale enterprises of its own. That is, in the distant historical past, the centralized French state deliberately undermined the independence of the private sector through taxes and privileges in order to bring it under political control, which had the effect of weakening the entrepreneurial and organizational habits of businesses. But in later years, that very weakness of entrepreneurial spirit became a

■ **TABLE 6.3**

FRANCE: EFFECTIVE DURATION OF WORK FOR SELECTED COUNTRIES

	Average Effective Duration of Work per Employee in 1997 (hours per year)	Average Effective Duration of Work per Person Aged 15–64 (hours per year)	Duration of Work in Life Cycle of Men Aged 14–70 in 1992 (hours)
United States	1,976	1,458	61,343
Japan	1,990	1,408	71,123
New Zealand	1,838	1,307	—
Spain	1,745	856	62,257
United Kingdom	1,731	1,223	73,904
Canada	1,721	1,182	—
Italy	1,682	861	61,825
Switzerland	1,643	—	—
France	1,539	973	60,635
Germany	1,519	1,014	64,578
Netherlands	1,397	896	61,622

SOURCE: OECD, *Employment Outlook*, 1998, 207, and Commission d'Enquête du Senat sur les 35 Heures, 1998.

motive for the renewed intervention of the state, which sought to reenergize a cautious and unimaginative private sector. The willingness of the state to step in then perpetuated the dependence of the private sector. The issue became complicated in the twentieth century by socialist governments, which wanted to nationalize private businesses for ideological reasons, even when they would have been viable on their own, and later by conservative governments, which wanted to privatize out of similarly ideological convictions.[9]

Thus while the government has reduced its role, it is uncertain how quickly and how vigorously private enterprise can emerge from two centuries of subservience to the state and provide an enduring engine of growth.

A particular problem for France is the high rate of unemployment, to which the government has responded by reducing both the normal retirement age and the length of the workweek. The result of promoting early retirement is that France now has one of the highest dependency ratios (the proportion of the economically inactive to those in work) in the developed world. In addition, the average French worker puts in fewer hours of work over a lifetime than anywhere else in the world. This is shown in Table 6.3.

The burden on those in work is likely to be exacerbated in the near future by two developments. One is a policy shift—a current governmental initiative to lower

---

[9] Francis Fukuyama, *Trust: The Social Virtues and the Creation of Prosperity* (New York: The Free Press, 1995).

■ TABLE 6.4

FRANCE: DEMOGRAPHIC TRANSITION

	1995	2000	2010	2020	2030	2050
Population (thousands)	58,048	59,425	60,993	62,121	62,661	62,120
Elderly dependency ratio	22.1	23.6	24.6	32.3	39.1	43.5
Total dependency ratio	52.2	52.8	51.2	59.6	67.9	73.6

SOURCE: International Monetary Fund.

the legal workweek from 39 hours to 35. The administration expects that this will result in lowered unemployment due to "work sharing," but critics fear that it will only cause a sharp increase in costs in the manufacturing industry, lowering competitiveness and cutting growth. The other development is the aging of the French population, which is shown in Table 6.4. "Graying" is common to all European nations and is caused by falling birthrates, but it is particularly acute in France. It will inevitably cause a further increase in the dependency ratio. Despite France's natural prosperity it is hard to see how a nation can both increase the ratio of non-workers to workers and reduce the work time of those employed and still maintain average income levels commensurate with the most affluent nations.

KEY TERMS AND CONCEPTS

Colbertism

concertation

dirigisme

economie concertée

economie dirigée

indicative planning

Jean Monnet

laissez faire

normative planning

Plan de l'État

Plan de la Nation

planning contracts

warranted growth rate

QUESTIONS FOR DISCUSSION

1. What "market failure" is indicative planning designed to address?
2. Do you think that French planning is normative (prescribing what should be) rather than positive (describing what is)?
3. Why does Charles Kindleberger compare the process of French planning to a revivalist meeting?
4. What are the ways by which the actors in the French economy may be induced to committing to the targets of the plan?

5. What is *dirigisme?*

6. Why does France's membership in the European Union make the process of planning more difficult?

7. Why does "broadening" the dialogue make the practice of planning less precise?

RESOURCES

WEB SITES

Commissariat General du Plan . . . . http://www.plan.gouv.fr/
The Web site of the Planning Commission where you can find information about the CGP's current mission and projects.

Ministry of the Environment. In English: . . . . http://www.environnement.gouv.fr/

Ministry of the Economy, Finance, and Industry. In French: . . . . http://www.finances.gouv.fr/
The home page of the economics super-ministry, from here one can get to the Ministry of Economics, Finance, and Industry, the Ministry of Trade, the Ministry of Industry and Communications, and even the mint.

Ministry of Foreign Affairs. In French: . . . . http://www.france.diplomatie.fr/

Ministry of Employment and Solidarity. In French: . . . . http://www.travail.gouv.fr/
This ministry handles employment, social security, and health. A major segment is on the reduction of the workweek.

National Institute of Statistics and Economic Studies . . . . http://www.insee.fr/
In French only, but the place to look for economic statistics.

Embassy of France in Washington, D.C. . . . . http://www.infofranceusa.org/

Le Monde . . . . http://www.lemonde.fr/
A national newspaper in French.

La Liberation . . . . http://www.liberation.fr/
A national newspaper in French.

France.Com . . . . http://www.france.com/index.html

BOOKS AND ARTICLES

Adams, William J. *Restructuring the French Economy: Government and the Rise of Market Competition since World War II.* Washington, D.C.: Brookings Institution, 1989.

Adams, William J., and Christian Stoffaës, eds. *French Industrial Policy.* Washington, D.C.: Brookings Institution, 1986.

Estrin, Saul, and Peter Holmes. *French Planning in Theory and Practice.* London: George Allen & Unwin, 1983.

Hayward, Jack. *The State and the Market Economy: Industrial Patriotism and Economic Intervention in France.* New York: New York University Press, 1991.

IMF. *France: Selected Issues.* IMF Staff Country Report No. 98/1.

Javetski, Bill. "France Wants Out of Business; Balladur's Sell-off of State-Owned Companies Ends the Dirigiste Era," *Business Week*, 7 June 1993, 46–48.

Levy, Jonah D. *Tocqueville's Revenge: State, Society, and Economy in Contemporary France.* Cambridge, Mass.: Harvard University Press, 1999.

Liggins, David. *National Economic Planning in France.* Lexington, Mass.: Lexington Books, D.C. Heath & Co., 1975.

Lutz, Vera C. *Central Planning for the Market Economy: An Analysis of the French Theory and Experience.* Harlow, England: Longmans [for] the Institute of Economic Affairs, 1969.

Mayer, Colin, and Tim Jenkinson. "The Privatisation Process in France and the U.K." *European Economic Review*, March 1988, 482–491.

McCarthy, Patrick. *The French Socialists in Power, 1981–1986.* Westport, Conn.: Greenwood Publishing Group, 1987.

Muet, Pierre-Alain, Alain Fonteneau, and Malcolm Slater. *Reflation and Austerity: Economic Policy under Mitterrand.* New York: Berg Publishing, 1991.

"A Survey of France: The Grand Illusion." *The Economist*, 5 June 1999, 52.

7

SWEDEN AND SOCIAL DEMOCRACY

FUNDAMENTAL FEATURES OF THE SWEDISH MODEL

Chapter 4 discussed the operation of a market economy and some of the failures that might result. Different in type from the problems of externality and public goods was the concern that income distribution resulting from the operation of a market economy might not be equitable or "fair." In a pure market system, an individual's income is dependent on his or her ownership of factors of production. The pattern of economic well-being generated might be considered unsatisfactory from a variety of points of view, providing a motivation for government action. In fact, one of the largest activities of governments in modern market economies involves modifying the income distribution. This involves the use of transfer payments, the public provision of goods that might otherwise be supplied privately and the finance of these expenditures out of taxation. This activity is what is generally referred to as the operation of a "welfare state."

Sweden is generally regarded as the quintessence of the welfare state; everyone who is prepared to work is guaranteed a high minimum standard of living, and all the population has access to a wide range of services provided by the government. These services include free education at all levels (with stipends for students above the high school level), free health care, and a comprehensive pension scheme. Such policies have ensured a high profile for the government in many aspects of economic life. Total government expenditures in Sweden are equal to about two-thirds of total gross domestic product. Payroll taxes amount to over one-third of the total payroll, and the marginal income tax rate paid by most blue collar workers is over 40 percent.

A further feature of the "Swedish model" is the high level of government activity in the labor market. This has two aspects. In macroeconomic terms, the government has been aggressive in its use of monetary, fiscal, and exchange rate measures to maintain a high level of employment. On the microeconomic side, the government has used a comprehensive system of assisted job search and retraining programs to keep the level of frictional unemployment low.[1] These policies have ensured that the rate of unemployment in Sweden has until recently been consistently below that of most other market economies.

---

[1] Frictional unemployment is unemployment that results when a worker is engaged in some form of job search while out of work. It is compatible with a high level of demand in the labor market.

By maintaining low unemployment and high levels of social goods and social insurance, Sweden has avoided the sharp contrasts between the affluent and the poor that can characterize pure market capitalism. The Swedish model has also gone a step further by its use of highly centralized collective bargaining practices. Wages are, by and large, determined by negotiations between representatives of labor and employers on the national level, which are undertaken under the stewardship of the government. Sweden is the most heavily unionized society in the world—85 percent of workers are covered by some form of collective bargaining agreement—and such central bargaining is a key feature of the determination of the distribution of the social product in Sweden.

One objective of this collective bargaining system has been to eliminate social waste by arriving at settlements without resort to socially and economically damaging strikes and labor disputes. Another objective has been the promotion of "wage solidarity." This involves an overt attempt to keep the earnings of all workers more closely grouped than is the case in less socially conscious societies. This aspect of policy is directed at producing a high degree of social cohesion within the population, and the consequent elimination, or at least minimization, of class conflict.

Although the distribution of income and goods in kind in Sweden is strongly shaped by the government, the means of production are almost entirely owned by the private sector. Thus, many authors describe Sweden as being representative of a "middle way"—socialist in terms of its distribution policy but capitalist (relying on markets and competition) in production. Because of this, and the apparent elimination of the "market failure" of highly skewed distribution of well being, the Swedish model is, at first sight at least, highly attractive. However, critics point to the high level of taxes required to finance redistribution policies, and the consequent erosion of incentives, as the flaw that ultimately hobbled the Swedish system. Moreover, although Swedish firms are capitalist in terms of ownership, the strength of unions, powerful labor laws, and other government restrictions place constraints on Swedish managers' ability to operate. These constraints may have adverse long-term affects in terms of maintaining international competitiveness. This chapter looks at the key features of the Swedish model and asks whether other countries—developed, developing, or in transition from some form of socialism—might profitably learn from the Swedish experience.

CHARACTERISTICS OF SWEDISH SOCIETY

The first thing to note about Sweden is that it is a small country. It has a population of only nine million people, and that population is remarkably homogenous, both politically and ethnically. There is no great racial conflict, and the political debate is rather localized in terms of the ideological spectrum. Most Swedes accept the essential propositions of Swedish society, a commitment to wage solidarity and social cohesion. Whether this consensus is a product of the model or a cause of it is an open question. Government has largely been the monopoly of the Socialist party since the 1930s, with only an occasional aberration. Moreover, whoever has been in power, the political system has remained highly corporatist. Decision making is collective, but only through institutions that are sanctioned by the state and granted access to the process. Groups outside of those formally recognized by the government (and therefore made a part of policy making) have only a small voice. While the level of individual liberty is relatively high, there is an expectation of conformity to the basic objectives of society.

Sweden is also a high-income society. Although recent inflation, slow growth, and currency depreciation have cut into Sweden's international ranking, it remains among the group of most affluent societies in the world. In 1987 only Switzerland and the United States ranked ahead of Sweden in terms of purchasing power parity per head of population. More recently the World Bank placed it about 16th. In current terms, its 1994 gross domestic product (GDP) per head was about $17,000, and its real purchasing power per head is about 66 percent of the U.S. level. Sweden's income distribution is remarkably uniform when compared to most other nations. The ratio of the income share of the most affluent quintile to the least affluent is only 4.6 to 1, thus Sweden may be thought of as about twice as "equitable" as the United States. This equality owes much to the strong role of the government, which spent 66 percent of GDP in 1995. Although this is down from 71 percent in 1993, it is well above the average for the European Union (EU), which was only 50 percent, and twice the relevant U.S. figure. Social security transfer payments alone account for 19 percent of GDP, against an average of 10 percent for the industrialized world and only 7 percent for the United States. General government revenue was about 60 percent, pointing to one of the enduring problems of the Swedish welfare state—chronic government deficits that require financing.

Contrary to much popular wisdom, Sweden is not a nexus of social problems, and statistics show it does well on most measures. It has one of the highest life expectancies in the world (second only to Japan) and one of the lowest infant mortality rates. There are fewer people in prison in Sweden than the average in the industrial world; in fact, the incarceration rate is only about 11 percent of that of the United States. Suicides are about the mean for developed nations. In terms of overall "human development,"[2] as defined by the United Nations Development Programme (UNDP), Sweden ranks 10th in the world. The divorce rate is about the same as that of the United States, though births outside of matrimony are higher. Alcohol consumption is low, and (perhaps not coincidentally) injuries in traffic accidents are one-fifth of the U.S. level. Sweden has probably the oldest population in the world; 18 percent of the population is now above the age of 65, and the share is growing. This gives Sweden one of the highest dependency ratios in industrialized countries, and the necessity of providing for this growing retired population will put further strain on the public finances.

---

[2] The World Bank's Human Development Index is prepared as a weighted average of life expectancy, literacy, higher education, and income per head.

SOCIAL DEMOCRACY

Even after the reforms of the early 1990s, Sweden remains the best example of **social democracy,** which is defined by Henry Milner[3] in terms of six basic principles governing the interaction of government and citizens. They can be summarized as follows:

1. *A fair distribution of economic well-being.* The fruits of economic prosperity are to be distributed fairly, but in such a way as not to undermine that prosperity. In other words, taxes and transfer payments are to be used but care should be taken lest high tax rates or overgenerous transfers create substantial disincentives to effort.

2. *Work for all as the primary means of eliminating deprivation.* Since human beings seek to live productively, fair distribution is to be effected through decently remunerated employment rather than simply cash or services.

3. *A high degree of social solidarity to bind individuals to a common purpose.* Individuals are members of communities through ties of culture and history. Members have reciprocal rights and obligations over and above the right of all human beings to be treated with tolerance and compassion without distinction as to race, sex, disability, and so on.

4. *Rules to be made by a democratic process.* A society of justice must follow rules, without which it degenerates into a jungle in which the "fittest" prosper. Democracy entails that the rules to be obeyed—by leaders and followers alike—result from decisions made by the people themselves through free elections that fully safeguard fundamental political freedoms.

5. *Participation extends beyond electoral democracy.* Especially in modern societies with complex systems of economic coordination, democracy entails active decentralized decision making and employee participation in management.

6. *All citizens should have access to information.* Democratic participation requires open and informed discussion—that is, a free and responsible press, an informed, well-educated citizenry, full public access to information based on data reliably gathered and presented, and publicly accountable independent boards of inquiry into matters of controversy.[4]

While Sweden is perhaps the best real-world example of a social democracy, it fell short of these defining characteristics in key ways. In particular, the first principle's drive for equalitarianism has conflicted with economic efficiency, hampering the operation of the labor market, reducing saving, and leading to high rates of

---

[3] This section on the underlying principles of social democracy is taken and modified from Henry Millner's *Sweden: Social Democracy in Practice* (New York: Oxford University Press, 1989), 4–5.

[4] A final principle could be added: respect for the environment. Through creative decentralized planning, social democracy ideally protects and enhances the natural environment as vital to human existence.

absenteeism. This led to rising unemployment and a falling sense of solidarity. Although democratic in terms of its electoral policies, real power in Sweden was held by a small group of individuals within a limited set of institutions. This chapter asks whether egalitarian labor market policies and high degrees of redistribution through transfer payments are compatible with continued growth in the long run.

THE TAX AND TRANSFER SYSTEM

The cornerstone of social solidarity is Sweden's very comprehensive system of social insurance and redistribution, which ensure that a worker who is willing to work will not be unduly harmed by involuntary job loss, injury, sickness, or even family responsibilities. The Organization of Economic Cooperation and Development (OECD) calls it "[a] universal and generous system of social protection [that] has combined with progressive income taxes to achieve a high degree of poverty alleviation and equalization of incomes." Sweden outperforms most other countries in terms of relative income levels for key groups such as families with children and old-age pensioners.[5] A full 35 percent of all household income in Sweden results from transfer payments up from only 15 percent in the mid-1960s. Table 7.1 shows that today Swedish workers lose little of their take-home pay for most unwelcome circumstances, on the whole much better than the other countries illustrated, all of whom have a reputation for being something of a welfare state.

Unemployment insurance funds are government financed but administered by the powerful and omnipresent labor unions. Membership is voluntary but open to all members of the labor force, and benefits may be claimed after 12 months of membership with a replacement rate of 80 percent of gross earnings. Benefits are exhausted for younger workers after 300 days and if the worker is out of work for a year the last 65 days carry no unemployment benefit. Hence the **replacement wage** for a full year's unemployment is only 69 percent, as seen in Table 7.1, though workers over 55 can receive benefits for 450 days. The same table also shows that Sweden's sickness, injury, maternity, and retirement schemes are generous by global standards.

Households unable to reach a reasonable living standard can claim social assistance benefits, administered by local authorities, but access is subject to strong means testing, requiring recipients to sell capital assets. Housing benefits are means tested too, depending on the number of children, the income of the household, and the level of housing costs. Weekly cash payments are issued for each child in the family, with a higher amount coming into effect from the third child on. Family benefits compensate parents for staying at home to take care of their children during the period immediate after their birth. The replacement rate is 80 percent (as elsewhere in the social insurance system) for the first 12 months. Day care for

---

[5] OECD *Economic Survey of Sweden*, 1999, 16.

■ **TABLE 7.1**

INTERNATIONAL COMPARISON OF SOCIAL INSURANCE SCHEME
(PERCENTAGE CHANGE IN ANNUAL DISPOSABLE INCOME FOR THE AVERAGE PRODUCTION WORKER [APW] IN MOVING FROM EMPLOYMENT TO SOCIAL INSURANCE, 1996)

Benefit	Sweden, 1997*	Denmark	Finland	Germany	United Kingdom	Netherlands	Canada
12 months unemployment, insured	−29	−35	−38	−42	−79	−27	−44
Sickness, 1 week[†]	−0.8	0	0	0	−0.4	0	−1.5
Work injury, total incapacity	0	+26	−8	+15	−57	−27	−10
Maternity leave, common duration	−2	−3	−2	0	−3	0	−4
Old-age pension,[‡] full work record	−36	−44	−33	−25	−47	−53	−45

* Based on a general replacement rate of 75 percent in social insurance, the increase to 80 percent in unemployment insurance in the fourth quarter is taken into account.

[†] Including occupational pensions.

[‡] Maximum (and not average) benefit in public schemes but without additions from occupational schemes.

SOURCE: H. Hansen, "Elements of Social Security," *Report 98:4* from the Danish National Institute of Social Research, 1988; *ESO Report Ds 1997:73*, in OECD *Economic Survey of Sweden*, 1999, 125.

children is provided at prices below cost and dependent on parental income. Transfers are taxed on a par with labor income when they substitute for a short- or long-term earnings loss to avoid tax considerations playing into the take-up of benefits. Social insurance benefits are thus generally provided gross of taxes, the exception being social assistance. Child and housing benefits are consequently provided net of taxes.

This comprehensive system does not come cheaply and Sweden has long been notorious for its high level of personal taxation. However, concerns about the disincentive effects of high taxation brought about a comprehensive reform in the tax system. The top rates of tax on unearned income remain high since reforms only cut the effective tax rate[6] from about 63 percent in 1989 to 60 percent today, still almost twice the U.S. rate of 35 percent. Table 7.2 shows that capital taxation in Sweden is not punitive and compares favorably with the United States, although Sweden does have a wealth tax of 1½ percent per annum in principle levied on all personal wealth over about $110,000 (however, loopholes abound and evasion is common).

---

[6] Defined as employees social security contributions plus personal income taxes as a percentage of gross labor costs.

- **TABLE 7.2**

Interest, Profits, Dividends, Capital Gains, and Wealth Taxes

	Highest Tax Rate on Interest Income	Corporate Tax Rate	Total Dividend Taxation	Taxation of Capital Gains	Wealth Tax	
					Rate	Threshold
Sweden	30	28	50	30	1.5	0.9
Austria	25	34	50	0	0	
Belgium	15	40	49	0	0	
Denmark	59	34	60	0–40	0	
Finland	28	28	28	28	0.9	1.65
France	25	33	66	26	0.5–1.5	6.25
Germany	56	58	49	0	0	
Ireland	48	32	55	40	0	
Netherlands	60	35	74	0	0.7	0.77
Norway	28	28	28	28	0.7–1.1	0.13
United Kingdom	40	31	48	0–40	0	
United States	47	35	68	0–20	0	

Notes: Tax rates are in percentages and thresholds are in SKr million.

SOURCE: OECD; International Bureau of Fiscal Documentation, "European Tax Handbook 1998," United States Internal Revenue Service, in OECD *Economic Survey of Sweden*, 1999, 133.

CORPORATISM

Though ideally social democracy gives everyone a role in the decision-making process, in reality Sweden is a highly corporatist state with much of the power, especially in economic matters, being located in the government (which has been Social Democratic for most of the postwar period), the employers' federations, and the labor unions. We saw in chapter 5 that Sweden is the most highly unionized society in the world with the vast majority of workers represented by unions. However, this concentration of power by labor is matched by a similar centralization in capital. Sweden is home to a disproportionately large number of major companies, and as Table 7.3 shows it has the highest density of companies among Europe's 500 largest of any European nation. Moreover, because of a limited domestic market, those companies must be globally competitive and reach markets beyond Sweden's seven million consumers. These export-oriented industries are vital for Sweden's well-being and play a key role in wage negotiations. Government's close relationship with the few business leaders who dominate Swedish industry is one reason why rates of taxation on capital are relatively modest compared to those falling on labor income—28 percent for corporate taxes as opposed to over 60 percent for wage income under the personal income tax.

Not only is Swedish industry dominated by large firms, the corporatist structure of the country is increased by the dominance of a single holding company,

LARGE COMPANIES PER MILLION INHABITANTS, 1998:
NUMBER OF COMPANIES AMONG EUROPE'S 500 LARGEST COMPANIES

Country	Number of Companies	Country	Number of Companies
Sweden	**3.6**	Ireland	1.7
Switzerland	3.5	Denmark	1.3
United Kingdom	2.7	Portugal	1.1
Belgium/Lux.	2.3	France	1.1
Netherlands	2.1	Norway	0.9

SOURCE: *Financial Times*, 1999.

Investor AB, which holds controlling interests in many of the big companies. Firms either controlled by Investor or in which it has a dominant interest make up about 40 percent of the Stockholm stock market's capitalization. Concentration of economic power is further exacerbated by the fact that 40 percent of Investor AB is owned by members of, or trusts controlled by, the Wallenberg family. Economic power in Sweden is much more centralized than in any other major capitalist country, and this facilitates the operation of the troika of employers, unions, and the Social Democratic Party that has controlled Sweden for decades.

THE SYSTEM OF LABOR RELATIONS

THE BASIC SYSTEM

One of the most distinctive features of the Swedish economy, and the one that we wish to focus on here, is the system of collective bargaining and industrial relations. This system originated in the late 1930s in discussions motivated by the need to reduce the then high degree of industrial unrest that Sweden had experienced in the 1930s. In 1938 a basic agreement was signed between the employers' federation (the SAF) and the Swedish Trade Union Confederation (the LO) in the resort town of Saltsjöbaden, near Stockholm. This **Saltsjöbaden agreement** is the cornerstone of the system. It provides a mechanism of collective bargaining to determine the rate of wage increase across industry and places limits on the nature of industrial action by the unions.

As we have noted, Sweden is now one of the most heavily unionized societies in the world. Some 85 percent of workers are members of some union.[7] The LO represents only blue collar workers and now has about 2.2 million members. White collar workers, which have been growing as a percent of the workforce, are represented by their own confederations, the largest of which is the Swedish

---

[7] United Nations Development Programme *Human Development Report*, 1995, 201.

Confederation of Professional Associations (TCO). The SAF now represents some 42,000 firms of all sizes including all of the major employers. Government-sector employees are represented by their own agency.

Throughout the entire postwar system until the end of the 1980s, national level negotiations between the SAF and the LO provided the framework for changes in wage costs. Both sides saw benefit in this. The employers viewed the agreements as being able to deliver lower increases in labor costs, and lower prospects of strike activity, than might result from disaggregated bargaining. The unions supported the policy because it offered an avenue toward their overall political goal of **wage solidarity** (discussed later). Negotiations conducted at the national level hammered out a framework agreement that determined the overall increase in the wage bill. This was subsequently supplemented by industry agreements, which translated the total settlement with norms for the various sectors of the economy.

THE EFO MODEL

A primary constraint on the system of wage settlement was the need to maintain international competitiveness. Sweden, a small and relatively open economy, exports roughly one-quarter of its GDP, and wage cost inflation could not be allowed to jeopardize international competitiveness. To ensure this, the system of negotiation explicitly differentiated between a competitive ("exposed") sector (comprised of firms like Volvo, Saab-Scania, and Electrolux) that had to operate in world markets, the price structure of which was beyond the control of anyone within Sweden, and a domestic ("protected") sector in which prices might be endogenously determined.[8] The rate of wage increase in the competitive sector was determined first on the proposition that the rate of growth of unit labor costs (basically wage cost increases less any anticipated productivity gains) should not outpace the rate of growth of prices for Swedish exports, which were determined in world markets. This implies that

$$\dot{W}_x = \dot{P}_x + (\dot{Q}_x - \dot{L}_x)$$

where $\dot{W}$ is the rate of change of wages; $\dot{P}$ is the rate of change of prices; $\dot{Q}$ is the rate of change of output; and $\dot{L}$ is the change in the use of labor. $(\dot{Q} - \dot{L})$ is therefore the change in productivity; subscript x denotes the **exposed sector.** Any wage increase above this rate harms international competitiveness, resulting in a fall in exports, balance of payments problems, depreciation of the currency, and serious inflation in an open economy like Sweden's. An arithmetic example of the process is useful. If world prices for Swedish exports are expected to advance by 4 percent and productivity gains in Swedish industry are predicted to lower costs by 2 percent, the maximum increase in unit wages compatible with sustained export competitiveness is 6 percent. This determined the wage settlement in the exposed

---

[8]This procedure is known as the EFO model after the Gösta Edgren, Karl-Olaf Faxen, and Clas-Eric Odhner, who were the chief economists for the SAF, LO, and TCO, and who literally wrote the book on Swedish collective bargaining, *Wage Formation and the Economy.*

sector. Subsequently, the rate of wage increases in the protected (i.e., nonexport) sector would be fixed at a rate comparable to that determined for the exposed sector. Such agreements were truly national and employees in the nontradable service and government sector were able to enjoy a rate of increase of wages predicated on the rate of price increases and productivity gain in the most competitive sector.

WAGE SOLIDARITY

This model enabled the trade union movement to pursue one of its most cherished objectives—wage solidarity. The underlying idea is that the wages for all jobs requiring comparable effort and comparable skills should be the same across the industry. To put it another way, the unions were committed to equal pay for equal work and to the notion that one's wage should not depend on the profitability of the industry that one works in. This proposition conflicts with the market logic that wages are linked to the marginal value product. Critics predicted that adherence to wage solidarity would lead to a variety of problems. Growing firms would find it hard to attract labor. Work incentives would be lowered, and the workforce would be inefficiently allocated between occupations and industries. Nevertheless, the unions did have considerable success in eroding wage differentials between industries. In 1959 the spread between average wages in the highest and the lowest paid industries was 39 percent. By 1964 it had fallen to 26 percent and by 1981 was down to only 12 percent. A similar narrowing was observed in terms of wage differentials by sex. Average female wages in Sweden are 90 percent of the male level, considerably above the "60 cents on the dollar" experienced in the United States.

The sustained growth of the government's role in the Swedish economy and the extensive provision of social goods made the public sector Sweden's largest employer. The Municipal Employees' Union is now the largest union in Sweden, and the workforce actually engaged in the exposed sector has diminished as a share of total employment as the services and government sectors grew. Furthermore, because any increase in pay for government-sector workers had to be financed from taxes, a system where public-sector wages shadowed those of the most competitive sector embodied a serious problem. Simply, whenever productivity or prices rose in the export, or exposed, sector, wages for the workers in that sector would increase. The system of national wage negotiation meant that a wage increase in the service and government sectors would inevitably follow. This implied domestic inflation, as well as tax increases to pay the increased wages in the government sector, both of which had ultimately injurious consequences for competitiveness in export markets.

THE BREAKDOWN OF NATIONAL AGREEMENTS

While praiseworthy in terms of equity, attempts to ensure that equal work meant equal pay dulled the efficiency of the labor market. Wages in a market system, like other prices, are signaling devices that indicate shortages; rising wages set in motion shifts that act to eliminate shortages. Since Swedish policy explicitly tried to eliminate wage differentials, the labor market could not adjust to rectify shortages

■ TABLE 7.4

	1994	1995	1996	1997	1998
Aggregate wage growth, percent	2.4	3.3	6.0	4.5	3.6
Contribution from					
Central bargaining	1.5	2.1	4.4	3.8	2.8
Wage drift	1.0	1.2	1.7	0.7	0.8

SOURCE: Statistics Sweden; National Institute of Economic Research; Ministry of Finance, in OECD *Economic Survey of Sweden,* 1999, 68.

in particular industries or sectors. With demand for Swedish products in world markets high, employers in the exposed sector found themselves short of labor and unable to increase wages to attract new workers. Expansionary macroeconomic policies ensured that the aggregate level of employment was high, and because of the national agreements, wages in **protected sectors** were close to those in the exposed sector and workers were reluctant to change jobs.

Initially, employers in firms short of labor attempted to attract new workers while nominally living within the wages determined by the national agreement. Because nominal wage rates could not be raised at a rate above the agreed level, special "perks" and fringe benefits were introduced as inducements to retain the workforce and attract new recruits. These included productivity-related bonuses, extra premia for shift work, shorter hours, and longer vacations. This phenomenon of raising the effective wage per unit labor while leaving the basic wage unchanged is known as **wage drift.** It has been estimated that during the 1980s about 50 percent of effective wage increase was attributable to wage drift. Wage drift is still present but has fallen to a smaller share of overall wage increase; in 1998 it represented less than 25 percent of the total changes. (See Table 7.4.)

Nonetheless, the employers in firms facing high demand still felt shackled and in 1983 the Engineering Employers' Association (VF), a member unit of the SAF, decided to go alone and concluded its own set of wage agreements with the Metal Workers Union signaling the end of effective national wage determination. Since 1983 there has been no national agreement on wage increases, although in some years the LO and the SAF have recommended a nonbinding norm to their membership. The role of the union confederation has been reduced to one of coordination and oversight rather than a lead negotiator.

OTHER ASPECTS OF LABOR MARKET POLICY

Although centralized wage negotiation was the centerpiece of the labor market policies, it was not the whole of the story. Sweden also has a highly **active labor market policy** that remains in place despite the demise of centralized wage bargaining and the consequent slippage of wage solidarity. This policy embraces relocation grants, training, and retraining schemes, private-sector employment subsidies, and, where necessary, public-sector job schemes.

Active labor market policy was a necessary complement to centralized wage bargaining. In a free labor market, wage differentials between industries and occupations provides the incentives for workers to change jobs and so resolve shortages. This ensures the flow of labor between occupations and a consequent microeconomic equilibrium, while real wage flexibility maintains full employment. Because the Swedish system for many years actively discouraged the development of wage differentials, the government had to resort to active labor market schemes to solve the problem.

The first point of intervention is via the **"labor exchanges,"** government offices that assist in matching displaced workers with vacancies. In Europe active labor market policy is more important than in the United States, but in most countries labor exchanges operate with high levels of caseloads per staff worker. In Britain, for example, the ratio is 375 cases per employee; in Germany it is 370, and in the Netherlands 160. In Sweden, in contrast, it varies between 15 and 30, depending on the region and as a result the individual attention afforded to each job seeker is high. The law requires that employers must report all vacancies to the authorities and the labor exchange professionals have access to essential information concerning all job openings in the country. Consequently they can work actively with the human resource departments of firms to find the best match between job seekers and vacancies. To further decrease rigidities and frictional cost to the unemployed, funds are available for site visits and, should a job seeker accept a distant vacancy, for relocation expenses. If suitable openings are not available for a job seeker, retraining funded by the government is in order and is made available. Furthermore, in order to cope with potentially large crises, the authorities require that they be told well in advance about plant closings and downsizing, allowing forward thinking on strategies to address the problem and the institution of retraining schemes even before plant closings occur.

Unemployment benefits in Sweden are generous and the reduction of take-home incomes consequent to job loss is small. However, benefits are contingent on active job search and also have strict time limits. Should an individual's benefits run out, the government acts as an "employer of last resort" and will provide a job for at least six months. As a result of this combination of policies, unemployment rates in Sweden were until recently very low, generally between 1 and 1.5 percent.

ATTEMPTS TO SOCIALIZE CAPITAL

The policy of wage solidarity resulted in the repression of wages in the profitable, exposed sectors of industry, and although this contributed to managers' problems, lessening their ability to recruit qualified labor, it had a positive impact on profits by keeping wage costs low. Workers in these industries felt that they should have a share of the excess profits generated by their restraint. In 1976 the Congress of the LO adopted a resolution proposed by Meidner, their chief economist, to establish **wage earner funds.** The idea behind the ambitious original plan was that each year all firms that employed more than 500 workers should hand over 20 percent of their pretax profits to a union-controlled fund specific to that industry. These monies would be used by the union to purchase (at book value) shares of the firm in which the profits had been made. Consequently, the share capital of the large, profitable elements of Swedish industry (which were concentrated in the exposed, export sector) would be increasingly accumulated by the unions. In the limit the unions might control all industrial capital, with the most profitable firms passing most quickly to union control. When the union share holdings represented a majority, they would be in a position to appoint management and assume strategic control of the firm. Had the **Meidner plan** been followed the Swedish system would have come to resemble the Yugoslav system of worker management. There would, however, have been two important differences:

1. Union workers, rather than society as a whole, would have been the owners of capital.
2. Control of the firm would have passed to industry-wide unions, rather than to the workers in the specific enterprise.

The Swedish parliament balked at enacting the Meidner plan into law, despite aggressive union lobbying. It was a radical idea and would have transformed the Swedish model by progressively eliminating private capital, leading to union control of both sides of the labor process. It proved too ambitious, even for the ruling Social Democrats, and was staunchly opposed by Sweden's tight group of capitalists. As a compromise Parliament went for a watered-down version, establishing five regional funds financed by a 20 percent tax on "excess profits" which were empowered to buy shares not at book value but at the much higher market value. They are constrained not to accumulate any more than 8 percent of the capital of any one firm, and total ownership by all of the funds together must not exceed 49 percent, thus denying the possibility of union control of business.

RECENT LABOR MARKET DEVELOPMENTS

One of the most startling recent developments in Sweden has been the rise in the unemployment rate. In 1980 using OECD standardized unemployment rates joblessness in Sweden was 2.0 percent, most of it frictional, against an OECD average of 5.8 percent. By 1995 the Swedish rate had ballooned to 9.2 percent, while the OECD average had only risen to 7.5 percent. Given the commitment of Swedish social democracy to limiting unemployment to ensure general well-being, this increase was alarming. On the positive side, it must be noted that the Swedish unemployment rate is still lower than most of its partners in the European Union. Standardized unemployment in the European Union in 1995 was 11.2 percent. There is also some evidence of Sweden's success, relative to most developed countries, in eradicating long-term unemployment. Workers in Sweden have a much higher chance of ultimately finding work than in other countries, a powerful point in favor of its active labor market policies.

Table 7.5 shows some of the developments in the labor market in recent years. The unemployment rate has fallen from its highs in 1996, nevertheless 13.8 percent

■ **TABLE 7.5**

LABOR-MARKET DEVELOPMENTS

	1994	1995	1996	1997	1998
Labor force, 1,000 persons	4,268	4,319	4,310	4,264	4,255
Unemployment rate	8.0	7.7	8.1	8.0	6.5
Unemployed and covered by government programs (%)	14.2	13.2	14.3	14.8	13.8
Percentage covered by make-work programs	5.2	4.4	4.5	4.3	3.9
Percentage covered by education programs	0.9	1.2	1.7	2.4	3.4
Unemployed for more than a year	1.8	1.9	2.1	2.3	1.9

SOURCE: Statistics Sweden; National Institute of Economic Research; Ministry of Finance, in OECD *Economic Survey of Sweden*, 1999, 68.

of the total Swedish labor force is either unemployed or in a government make-work or education program, higher than the rate in 1995. More people are enrolled in education programs and fewer are actually idle or in a make-work program. In theory this should lead to a better trained and more productive workforce, though there is too little evidence to judge the effectiveness of job retraining schemes. The OECD reports that

> the authorities have launched an extensive adult education programme. This is aimed at those with inadequate qualifications and has now been running, in line with the quantified objectives set, for two years. Insofar as educational qualifications are closely linked to unemployment risk, an emphasis on human capital enhancement is a key ingredient in the long-term improvement of labour-market outcomes.[9]

LESSONS OF THE SWEDISH MODEL

Fifteen years ago it would have been tempting to draw a positive lesson from the Swedish experience. In the period from the establishment of the system of centralized wage bargaining in the late 1930s to the early 1980s, Sweden had an enviable record of labor peace and economic growth. However, since the beginning of the 1980s recurrent economic problems have made Swedish success look much more questionable in the long-term perspective.

Swedish experience in the labor market is exemplary of the problems that confront a society's attempts to suspend the role of wages in furthering an efficient allocation of labor. While the convergence of wages toward equality might be

[9]OECD *Economic Survey of Sweden*, 1999, 13–14.

regarded as a laudable social goal, without differential wages to encourage worker mobility the labor market cannot work smoothly. The conflict between the drive for equity in society at large and the needs of export-oriented industry caused the breakdown in the national system of wage bargaining. The question is, can it be put back together or is it permanently consigned to history? Both parties to the labor agreement seem to be optimistic:

Whether the social partners will be able to act in concert in order to get the economy moving again is something we cannot yet tell. . . . We can only express the hope that out of the present labor pains a new Swedish model will be born, resembling its forerunner. There are, in fact, good chances of this. Despite the adverse trends . . . there are many sound elements of the Swedish economy and industrial relations system that have survived and can be built on. . . . In their hearts the Swedes share a deep community of values. The representatives of labor and management can still mix with each other centrally and locally in a spirit of trust and are capable of working together on matters of common interest. Promising signs are the agreements that have been concluded in recent years on such collaboration and, above all, the fact that the debate on wage policy is now being conducted in the broader context of the nation's economic health.[10]

There was similar guarded optimism from the union side:

Many people in Sweden see . . . the frequent breaches of labor peace as linked to the departure from the centralized bargaining system. At the same time there is widespread agreement that prosperity must be safeguarded and equitably shared. This is why I believe that the pressures favoring the return to co-ordinated central negotiations will prevail, even if slight changes may be expected in the unions' distribution policy. The bargaining system that has come to be known as the Swedish model of industrial relations has stood the test of time and I am confident that given the opportunity it will continue to serve both sides of industry well for many years yet.

Whatever the future of national labor negotiations there seems agreement that the umbrella nature of the Swedish social welfare system has hurt macroeconomic performance. The high rates of taxation required to finance the welfare state probably had a disincentive effect on both worker effort and savings, retarding growth to a rate that was in the 1970s half the OECD average. This is perhaps the most important issue to be addressed in a comprehensive welfare state. Millner noted it in the 1980s:

The most important and difficult question raised by critics of the welfare state concern the system of rewards resulting from the combination of wages, taxes, transfers, and other sources of income on individuals and, ultimately, its effect on the workings of the economy. They are perhaps most fully explored in the work of the distinguished and increasingly critical Swedish economist Assar Lindbeck. In Lindbeck's recent work is found perhaps the most sophisticated expression of the often-made argument that somewhere in the 1970s the excessive redistributiveness of Swedish welfare policy

---

[10] Both this and the following quote were from the *International Labour Review*, 1986, cited in Milner, 225–226. The employers view is from L. G. Albåge and the union position from Harry Fjällström.

began to actually decrease the aggregate quantity of socially useful work by significantly increasing leisure through shorter work years and absenteeism and pushing activity into the "unofficial economy" in the form of barter, do-it-yourself work, and other forms of tax avoidance.[11]

Disincentive effects of high benefits and taxes are seen in a variety of ways. A 1986 report by the engineering employers' association found that blue collar Swedish workers were on the job less, putting in only 1,546 hours a year compared to 1,654 in West Germany and 1,930 in the United States in part due to increased absenteeism and "sick outs." High tax rates have forced activity into the black economy. One study found that between 12 and 25 percent of income in Sweden was unrecorded.[12]

An OECD report a decade later addressed the issue of incentive and came to the following conclusion:

> A universal and generous system of social protection has combined with progressive income taxes to achieve a high degree of poverty alleviation and equalisation of incomes. Sweden outperforms most other countries in terms of relative income levels for key target groups such as families with children and old-age pensioners. This redistribution has been accompanied by a continuous extension of transfers, from 15 per cent of household incomes in the mid-1960s to 35 per cent in the late 1990s, with the result that as much as two-thirds of transfers reflect redistribution over the life-cycle of individuals and only one-third interpersonal ("pure") redistribution.
>
> High tax rates and generous replacement rates, with a *de facto* indefinite duration of unemployment and sickness benefits, have worked to this effect. Income taxes and social security contributions combine with means-tested housing and day-care benefits to reduce substantially the return from taking a better-paid job or increasing hours worked. The added effect of the internationally high 80 per cent replacement rate in benefits actually produces a substantial penalty for many on moving from unemployment to employment. Close to 40 per cent of unemployed would see no or insignificant increases in disposable incomes from moving back into work.[13]

KEY TERMS AND CONCEPTS

active labor market policy

corporatism

EFO model

exposed sector

labor exchanges

Meidner plan

protected sector

replacement wage

---

[11] Henry Milner, *Sweden: Social Democracy in Practice* (New York: Oxford University Press, 1989). The best example of Lindbeck's views may be found in Assar Lindbeck, *Swedish Economic Policy* (Berkeley: University of California Press, 1974).

[12] Edward Feige, "Sweden's Underground Economy," in *The Economics of Institutions and Markets*, ed. Gunnar Eliason (Stockholm: UIU, 1986), 127.

[13] OECD *Economic Survey of Sweden*, 1999, 16–18.

Saltsjöbaden agreement

social democracy

wage drift

wage earner funds

wage solidarity

QUESTIONS FOR DISCUSSION

1. Why is the concept of wage solidarity central to Swedish society?
2. Why does an attempt to limit the distribution of wages lessen the effectiveness of the labor market?
3. Why is an active labor market policy a possible remedy for the absence of wage signaling?
4. In what ways does Sweden as a society differ from an "ideal" social democracy?
5. Is it appropriate to describe Sweden as corporatist? Why?
6. What were the pressures from the exposed sector that led to the breakdown of national agreements?
7. What sort of socialism would the extensive use of wage funds have led to?

RESOURCES

WEB SITES

Central Bank http://194.52.62.248/

Swedish Municipal Workers Union . . . . http://www.kommunal.se/english/english.cfm

Ministry of Finance . . . . In Swedish:http://finans.regeringen.se/

Swedish Employment Service . . . . http://www.amv.se/index_eng.html

Investor AB http://www.investor.se/lang3/m1-0/m1-0.asp

Swedish Confederation of Professional Associations . . . . http://www.tco.se/index.htm

The Swedish Trade Union Confederation, LO . . . . http://www.lo.se/

Swedish Government Offices . . . . http://www.regeringen.se/inenglish/

BOOKS AND ARTICLES

Bosworthy, Barry P., and Alice M. Rivlin, eds. *The Swedish Economy.* Washington, D.C.: Brookings, 1987.

Calmfors, Lars, ed. *Wage Formation and Macroeconomic Policy in the Nordic Countries.* Oxford: Oxford University Press, 1990.

Canova, Timothy A. "The Swedish Model Betrayed." *Challenge,* May–June 1994, 36–40.

Cohen, Peter. "Sweden: The Model That Never Was." *Monthly Review,* July–August 1994, 41–59.

European Parliament. *Social and Labour Markets Policy in Sweden.* Directorate-General for Research, Working Papers, Social Affairs Series, July 1997.

Lindbeck, Assar, Per Molander, Torsten Persson, Olof Peterson, Agnar Sandmo, Birgitta Swedenborg, and Niels Thygesen. "Options for Economic and Political Reform in Sweden." *Economic Policy,* October 1993, 219–263.

Maccoby, Michael, ed. *Sweden at the Edge: Lessons for American and Swedish Managers.* Philadelphia: University of Pennsylvania Press, 1991.

Milner, Henry. *Sweden: Social Democracy in Practice.* New York: Oxford University Press, 1989.

Palme, Marten O., and Robert E. Wright. "Gender Discrimination and Compensating Differentials in Sweden." *Applied Economics* 24 (1992): 751–759.

Persson, Inga, ed. *Generating Equality in the Welfare State: The Swedish Experience.* Oslo: Norwegian University Press, 1990.

Ramaswamy, Ramana. "Wage Bargaining Institutions, Adaptability, and Structural Change: The Swedish Experience." *Journal of Economic Issues* 26, no. 4 (December 1992): 1041–1061.

"A Survey of the Nordic Countries: Happy Family?" *The Economist,* 23 January 1999, 50.

"A Survey of Women and Work." *The Economist,* 18 July 1998, 48.

8

THE HISTORY AND INSTITUTIONS OF THE EUROPEAN UNION

THE HISTORY OF THE EUROPEAN UNION

PRECURSORS TO THE EUROPEAN UNION

While many visionaries have sought the peaceful unification of Europe, and a few dictators have looked to do the job by force, serious planning for economic and political unification in Europe did not occur until after World War II. A strong impetus for change was the damage caused by nationalism and war in the three decades between 1914 and 1945. Even after the war, tensions were raised and energy absorbed in the dispute between the conflicting and, to many eyes, largely bankrupt ideologies of nationalism, communism, and fascism. "Europeanism" offered an alternative, which could both influence domestic political agendas and provide a supranational goal to diffuse nationalist tensions. The potential economic rewards of a united Europe were appreciated from the beginning, but they were initially less important than the prospect of political gain.

A further push toward unity was given shortly after the war by the creation of the American-financed **Marshall Plan** and the institution created to administer it, the Paris-based **Organization for European Economic Cooperation (OEEC).**[1] Today the Marshall Plan is almost universally remembered and revered as a rare example of enlightened altruism on the part of the United States. Rather than extracting revenge and reparations from the defeated powers, as the Treaty of Versailles, which concluded the First World War, had done, the Marshall Plan was designed to assist the reconstruction of Europe by helping both victor and vanquished. As well as administering project aid, the OEEC was active in alleviating the dollar shortage, financing the bilateral currency imbalances, and helping to remove the trade barriers that had multiplied in the prewar periods. After three years of slow growth across the continent, the OEEC efforts began to bear fruit. American exports to and investment in Europe soared and prosperity began to return to the continent. While often credited with the revival of Western Europe, the Marshall Plan has been seen by some scholars as a decisive step in the division of postwar Europe. The Soviet bloc was invited to participate in the Marshall Plan,

---

[1] This body with a larger membership is now known as the Organization for Economic Cooperation and Development or OECD.

THE CREATION OF THE EUROPEAN UNION—A BRIEF CHRONOLOGY

DATE	EVENT	DATE	EVENT	DATE	EVENT
1947	Initiation of the Marshall Plan to promote the economic revival of a Europe devastated by war	1957	Signing of the Treaties of Rome establishing the European Economic Community (EEC) and the European Atomic Energy Community (Euratom)	1986	Portugal and Spain join the European Community
1948	Benelux Treaty creating the common economic space of Belgium, the Netherlands, and Luxembourg enters into force			1987	Signing of the treaty and entry into force of the Single European Act
		1967	Merger of the institutions of the three communities (ECSC, EEC, and Euratom)	1989	Signing of the Social Charter by all members except Britain
1948	Creation of the Organization for European Economic Cooperation (OEEC) to administer the Marshall Plan	1968	Completion of the customs union	1990	Unification of Germany
				1992	Signing of the Treaty on European Union (the Maastricht Treaty)
1949	Creation of the Council of Europe located in Strasbourg	1972	Treaties of Accession of Denmark, Ireland, Norway, and the United Kingdom	1993	Introduction of the single European market and the European Economic Area
1950	Schuman Declaration	1973	Denmark, Ireland and the United Kingdom join the European Community. Norway chooses to stay outside.	1993	Maastricht Treaty becomes effective creating the European Union
1951	The Treaty of Paris establishes the European Coal and Steel Community (ECSC)			1995	Austria, Finland, and Sweden join the European Union
1952–1954	Preparation, and failure, of plans for a European Defense Community (EDC)	1979	Signing of the Treaty of Accession of Greece	1999	Economic and Monetary Union Established: Sweden, Britain, and Denmark opt out, and Greece is denied entry
		1979	First election of the European Parliament by direct universal suffrage		
1955	Renewed vitality for the idea of European unity provided by the Messina Conference	1981	Greece joins the Community		
		1985	Signing of the Treaties of Accession of Portugal and Spain		

but Stalin rejected aid because it was conditioned on extensive information sharing. The exclusion of Eastern Europe helped draw the "iron curtain" that divided the nations of Europe until 1989.

In 1948, a conference at which all the major western European nations were represented was convened at The Hague. Originally called the Congress of Europe, this body became known as the Council of Europe and made its permanent home in Strasbourg in eastern France. It became a useful forum in which to debate and define the competing models of European integration. An important issue was

Britain's role. Britain had emerged from the war with a great deal of moral authority and might have taken the leadership role on European unity had it not favored European integration through intergovernmental cooperation rather than by creating supranational organization. In retrospect we can see that the British leadership failed to appreciate that major changes had occurred in the global political landscape and conceived of World War II as merely the latest in a series of continental conflicts requiring British intervention to restore the balance of power. At the end of the war, Britain turned to concentrate on world trade and the remnants of its empire to the neglect of its interests in Europe. Britain's position of cooperation without political integration was supported by the Scandinavians, and the Council of Europe was unable to offer a clear path toward the federal solution preferred by the other west Europeans.

The real precursor of the contemporary European Union (EU) was the **European Coal and Steel Community (ECSC),** first suggested by **Jean Monnet** and later advanced by another Frenchman, **Robert Schumann.** It was originally proposed to combat the fear that the revival of the German economy might cause German military power to rise once more. The idea of the ECSC was to create a "common market" in coal and steel, removing the basic ingredients of a war machine from national control, and placing its oversight with a "high authority," independent of national governments. Initially the ECSC consisted only of France and Germany, but the Benelux countries and Italy joined to form "the Six," signing the Treaty of Paris in 1951. The ECSC not only succeeded in reducing tensions in western Europe, but it also provided a compelling model of the value of pooling national markets.

Buoyed by the success of the ECSC, the Six tried to move toward political unity at an unrealistic pace. In 1952 a treaty establishing a European Defense Community (EDC) was drawn up, followed in 1953 by the draft of a treaty creating a European Political Community (EPC). Although five of the members of the ECSC were happy to go along with this, in 1954, the French National Assembly failed to ratify the EDC, a move that proved fatal for the EPC as well. Persuading European governments to yield sovereignty in the defense and political arenas was always to prove tougher than harmonizing economic arrangements.

THE TREATY OF ROME

The failure of the EDC and EPC initiatives set back the European movement; Europeanists shifted their emphasis from rapid political unification toward consolidating economic integration. The foreign ministers of the Six met at Messina in 1955 and began a process that culminated in the **Treaty of Rome.** This established two new bodies, the European Economic Community (the EEC, often called the European Common Market) and Euratom, the European Atomic Energy Community. Together with the ECSC these bodies constituted the European Communities (EC).

The most important move was the establishment of the EEC. The success of the ECSC demonstrated that economic gains could be made by increasing the size of the market and therefore allowing both greater competition (with a long-term impact on efficiency and dynamism) and a greater degree of specialization. Moreover, in the 1950s confidence in the power of economies of scale was high. National firms might be uncompetitive in global terms because of the limited size of the domestic market, but European firms could amass the size to compete internationally.

While it is generally accepted that economic integration offers benefits to all participants, there are different degrees of economic integration. At the lowest level, a **free trade area** allows the movement of goods between countries without the hindrance of tariffs or quotas. A **customs union** not only provides for such movement but requires that the members have a **common external tariff (CET)** applied to their imports from third-party countries. A **common market** is a customs union with the additional commitment to the free movement of factors of production within the member states. The member countries had as their ultimate goal a common market, but the first step toward this was the completion of a customs unions and the establishment of a common external tariff.

THE COMMUNITY OF SIX

The Community of Six, established by the Treaty of Rome, gave itself a 12-year adjustment period to establish a customs union. During this time internal tariffs between constituent nations were to be progressively reduced to zero and the tariffs on goods originating outside the community harmonized. By 1968 this customs union was complete, although progress toward the liberalization of factor movements, required for a true common market, was much slower and would, in fact, take another quarter of a century to effect.[2]

Outside the EC there was concern about the prospect of **fortress Europe,** a market shielded by high tariffs, which would have been against the prevailing trend of multilateral tariff liberalization. However, despite the threat to its economic interests, the United States supported the development of the EC because it offered the political reward of European stability. Fears on the economic front were eventually disarmed when it became clear that the final external tariff structure of the EC was to be more liberal than that of the original members. Trade relations between the EC and the United States have not always been harmonious, and fears of restricted access to the European market have been chronically recurrent. Nevertheless, the tariff reductions negotiated in both the Dillon and Kennedy rounds of General Agreement on Tariffs and Trade (GATT) were translated into cuts in the common external tariff.

Although economic aspects of the Europeanism thrived, progress toward a politically united Europe was limited, with both defense policy and foreign policy remaining the domain of national governments. However, the stances of Germany and France, the two most powerful nations, became increasingly coordinated as German Chancellor Konrad Adenauer and French President Charles de Gaulle cooperated closely in "the Bonn-Paris axis," and their interaction frequently determined European policy. However, despite increased cooperation such policy making was at the national and not the Community level.

---

[2] The common market was finally completed in 1993 due to the Euro-92 program.

Shortly after the Treaty of Rome, Britain had second thoughts about its failure to pursue EC membership. The remnant of its empire, the British Commonwealth, was largely going its own way and the treasured "special relationship" with the United States was becoming less close with each successive year.[3] In 1959 Britain took the lead in the creation of the **European Free Trade Area** (**EFTA,** otherwise known as the "outer seven"), consisting of Britain, three Nordic nations (Sweden, Denmark, and Norway), Austria, Switzerland, and Portugal. It was designed to capture the benefits of a free trade area without any commitment to social expenditures or to political union. From the British point of view it was unfortunate that all of its partners were small, since each of them gained much more in terms of market access than did Britain. Quickly recognizing the limitations of EFTA, Britain formally reversed its position on the EC, announcing in 1961 that it was interested in full European membership, but negotiations were unilaterally terminated by French President de Gaulle, who used the French veto to deny entry.

EXPANSIONS OF THE 1970S AND 1980S

After de Gaulle resigned in 1969, British entry became a possibility once more. In December 1969 talks began to admit not only Britain, but also Ireland, Norway, and Denmark. Britain secured entry, but paid a price in terms of budget contribution that was a higher share of gross national product (GNP) than that of any other member. Ireland and Denmark also joined, but Norway, although admitted, rejected membership in a national referendum, influenced by the fear that its valuable fisheries would be opened to wider exploitation. The short-term consequences of membership were unfavorable for Britain. Food prices soared as a result of the protectionist **common agricultural policy (CAP)** that ended cheap imports from Australia and New Zealand.[4] British industry was not competitive and lost market share at home without significant expansion of exports to continental Europe. In the early 1980s the Thatcher administration eventually negotiated a lower British budgetary contribution and even secured a modest refund, but the British population remained skeptical about the benefits of membership.

Greece joined the EC in 1981 and Spain and Portugal in 1986. The new members were noticeably poorer and less developed than the existing EC nations, increasing the population by one-fifth but its income by only one-tenth, and were therefore a net drain on EC finances. Membership for these nations involved a different calculus of gains and losses. Although they did contribute something in terms of increasing the accessible market for existing members, the main gains of these expansions were seen as political. Entry into the EC was thought to have a centralizing impact on the domestic politics of member nations, and it was hoped that

---

[3] The Suez crisis and the U.S. insistence that Britain withdraw from Egypt or face economic sanctions was, in some ways, the final straw in pursuit of the special relationship.

[4] See chapter 9 for a discussion of the CAP.

membership would put these countries, all of them recently under fascist regimes, on the road to moderate politics.

EC-1992: COMPLETING THE INTERNAL MARKET

Experience had shown that deepening the political links of the EC was a difficult operation, because it involved the sacrifice of domestic sovereignty, but liberalizing the internal economy of Europe was less contentious. In 1985, with the absorption of Spain and Portugal almost complete, the European Commission issued a White Paper containing 300 proposals for the "completion of the internal market." In 1987 the Treaty of Rome was amended by the passage of the **"Single European Act,"** the most important proviso of which was the end of any individual country's power to veto economic legislation on the grounds of national interest. This important measure cleared the way for the project known as **EC-1992,** the completion of the internal economic space to allow totally free movement of goods, persons, services, and capital.

Total liberalization of trade within the EC required the elimination of three types of trade impediment. The first were the physical barriers at national borders. Under preexisting arrangements a good deal of resources and time were wasted at borders because of customs regulation and paperwork. EC-1992 sought to eliminate these by harmonizing product standards and value-added taxation. A second set of barriers related to the procurement patterns of national and local government, which tended to favor local firms with resultant efficiency loss. The third group of barriers lay in the financial services industries, which had been slow to integrate and were characterized by inefficient national markets. The elimination of these barriers would each bring substantial gains but they would also produce so-called supply-side effects by fostering increased competition and facilitating the grasping of economies of scale.

The European Commission's official estimates of the gains of EC-1992 are summarized in Table 8.1. The elimination of border controls was estimated to yield a once and for all increase in gross domestic product (GDP) of 0.4 percent, cut consumer prices by 1 percent, and lead to the creation of an additional 200,000 jobs within the Community. Similar gains were seen to result from increased integration of financial services and a "level playing field" for public procurement. The supply-side effects of the extended market were estimated as the largest. Grasping economies of scale constrained by national market size and increased transnational competition would raise GDP by 2.1 percent, cut consumer prices by 6.1 percent, and lead to the creation of 1.8 million jobs. The single market program was also estimated to cut the budget deficits of the member countries by 2.2 percent, and improve external position of the EC vis-a-vis the world. In addition to these medium-term consequences second-order effects were predicted as the results of a virtuous circle of high investment, stable prices, and rapid growth.

Although progress was slow, by 1993 most of the legislation to complete the internal market was finished. The most serious problems were encountered in service industries where complex national rules, many ostensibly designed for consumer protection, had to be dealt with. Although public procurement was, in

▪ TABLE 8.1

MEDIUM-TERM PROSPECTIVE GAINS FROM THE COMPLETION OF THE INTERNAL MARKET, EC-1992

	Border Controls	Public Procurement	Financial Services	Supply Side Effects*	Total Average Value
GDP	0.4	0.5	1.5	2.1	4.5
Inflation	−1.0	1.4	−1.4	−2.3	−6.1
Employment	200	350	400	850	1800
Budgetary Balance	0.2	0.3	1.1	0.6	2.2
External Balance	0.2	0.1	0.3	0.4	1

* Due to economies of scale and increase in competition. GDP, Inflation, Budgetary, and External Balance as a percent of GDP. Employment in thousands of workers.

SOURCE: Cecchini Report, 1988, 98.

theory, liberalized strong indications of national bias still persist. Integrating labor markets has also proved to be difficult, but passports are no longer required within the EU for EU citizens.

The growth and success of the EU overshadowed the modest achievements of EFTA, whose members saw that the free trade area could never offer a market of the size and depth of the EU. Consensus favored a closer alliance with the EC and several EFTA members actually applied for full membership. In 1991 EFTA and the EC combined to establish a common free trade area, for manufactures but not agricultural goods, an institution that became known as the **European Economic Area (EEA).**

It is hard to gage the success of the internal market project. It has failed to deliver the promised economic gains, and EU growth since the completion of the market has been lackluster. In the period 1991–1996, GDP growth in the EU has only averaged 1.5 percent per annum, the slowest of the "triad" consisting of the EU, Japan, and the United States (see Table 8.2). Employment has actually contracted during this period, and rising unemployment has become one of Europe's largest social problems. Whether or not the position would have been even more dire without EC-1992 is hard to tell.

THE SOCIAL CHARTER

The **Social Charter** (officially the "Community Charter of Fundamental Social Rights of Workers") was a declaration adopted by the heads of state or government of 11 member states of the European Community[5] at the meeting of the European Council in Strasbourg in December 1989. It set out broad principles shared by the

---

[5]There were 12 member states at that time and the United Kingdom "opted out."

■ **TABLE 8.2**

**ECONOMIC GROWTH IN EUROPE, JAPAN, AND THE UNITED STATES
(AVERAGE ANNUAL PERCENTAGE CHANGES)**

	Real GDP Growth		
	1974–1985	**1986–1990**	**1991–1996**
European Union	2.0	3.3	1.5
United States	2.3	2.8	2.3
Japan	3.4	4.6	1.7
	Employment Growth		
	1974–1985	**1986–1990**	**1991–1996**
European Union	0.0	1.3	−0.4
United States	1.8	2.1	1.2
Japan	0.7	1.0	0.7

SOURCE: Eurostat.

signatories and constituted a first step in the harmonization and establishment of consistent labor law across the EU. The Conservative British government of that time, committed to the interests of business, felt that the clauses in the Social Charter designed to strengthen the power of labor in the workplace would both lessen the freedom of management and the mobility of labor.

The rights expressed in the Social Charter are quite general and involve shared commitment to a safe workplace and social protection. One clause asserts the right of all workers to a paying job, clearly a dead letter given the high rates of unemployment in the Community. Of particular importance are three specific sets of provisions that were obnoxious to the British Conservatives. The first protects labor unions and guarantees their right to engage in collective bargaining. This might have been palatable had not the charter gone beyond this in providing that workers must be informed about the activities and plans of the management and that workers participate in the running of the company through representation on the board. To the business-oriented Conservatives, this seemed to allow the unions to usurp management prerogatives and was styled by Margaret Thatcher as "back door socialism." A second set of provisions guarantees the absolute freedom of workers to move within the EC, and a third guarantees the equal treatment of men and women, including equal pay for comparative work. The Social Charter is a statement of general commitment but does not impose any specific action on a member country.

THE MAASTRICHT TREATY

Following the relative success of EC-1992 in completing the economic space, the EC faced new challenges in both economic and political spheres. On the political side, progress toward an ever-closer political union had been placed in abeyance while the single market project had been pursued. The economic sphere was politically the easier one, since it offered clear and sometimes quantifiable benefits. It involved less sacrifice of sovereignty than the political agenda and was supported even by "euroskeptics" like Margaret Thatcher. However, the next step toward full economic integration was more controversial. It involved the creation of a single currency, which, Europeanists argued, would tie the European economy closer together in the way that the existence of the common dollar ties together the elements of the United States.

In December of 1991 the European Council, consisting of the heads of state and of government of the member nations, met in the previously obscure Dutch town of Maastricht and drafted the **Treaty on European Union,** almost always referred to as the **Maastricht Treaty.** This document was the foundation of the next stage of the European project, even changing the name of the community to the **European Union (EU).**

In a ponderous architectural metaphor, the treaty defined the Union as resting on three "pillars." Pillar One is concerned with economic matters and covers agriculture, transportation, the environment, energy, research and development, and regional policy. Pillar Two is concerned with establishing a common foreign and security policy, a priority objective for some time, but on which progress had been halting. Joint Community policy failed to emerge in either the conflict in the former Yugoslav territories or in the response to the Gulf War. Pillar Three is concerned with cooperation in the fields of justice and home affairs and aims to achieve the free movement of persons inside the Union and to promote measures of common interest in the fields of external border control, asylum policy, immigration policy, terrorism, drug trafficking, and other serious forms of international crime. Because Britain did not sign the Social Charter, the Maastricht Treaty was forced to embody those principles in a separate protocol entitled "The Agreement on Social Policy," usually referred to as "the Social Chapter."[6] In a sense, therefore, the "social chapter" is a fourth pillar of the Union.

THE PRINCIPLE OF SUBSIDIARITY. One of the most difficult political issues facing the EU is how much sovereignty and power should be gathered in Brussels and how much should be allowed to remain with the governments of the member nations or some lower regional authority. The EU has been frequently criticized by the citizens of member nations as being remote, dictatorial, and bureaucratic, laying down directives impinging on the local culture and economy without due regard to circumstance. The Maastricht Treaty sought to meet this criticism by establishing limits to EU action. Article 3b of Title II of the treaty requires that

> [i]n areas which do not fall within its exclusive competence, the Community shall take action, in accordance with the principle of subsidiarity, only if and in so far as the objectives of the proposed action cannot be sufficiently achieved by the Member.

---

[6]The current Labour Government led by Prime Minister Tony Blair has now committed Britain to the Social Charter and the agreement on social policy.

In short, this **principle of subsidiarity** affirms that all issues are to be handled at the lowest level that can effectively deal with them. Any organ of the EU (including the European Council, the European Parliament, and the Commission) can intervene only in areas of common concern when the individual states cannot act effectively on their own. Even then, impositions from above must respect the specific characteristics of the states and regions and highlight their diversity. When any item of EU legislation is proposed in Brussels, it must therefore satisfy three key criteria: that the item acts at the all-union level, that the EU's action is not excessive, and that any legislation is clear and transparent.

The principle of subsidiarity is relevant in many areas, not all of them specifically economic. For example, one concern that has been in the news is the issue of the protection of migratory birds and in fact the EU itself has used this as an example of how the principle might work. The Commission determined that it is not for the European Union to set the dates for the opening and closing of hunting seasons in specific EU regions. Hunting seasons should be decided on according to local hunting traditions, with agreement reached on how each of the EU's member states is to comply with the overall objectives of bird protection. However, classic "externality" problems remain. France allowed generous hunting rules, extending into breeding seasons, which threatened the continent-wide bird population. Other countries demanded action by Brussels while France resisted, citing the principle of subsidiarity.

In more strictly economic matters, the principle emerges in other important ways. Two examples are worth mentioning here, though they will be dealt with in more detail in chapter 9. The first is competition and merger policy, which had traditionally been handled at the national level, but with the introduction of the single market required, for some industries at least, Union-wide treatment. The other is the expenditure of monies granted through the structural funds. The recipient nations feel that they have a better knowledge of how such monies should be spent, while the Commission as grantor feels it should maintain a say in its use.

FUTURE EXPANSION

The European Union is not expected to remain at its current membership of 15 for long. Many nations have applied to enter the EU, including 10 countries that were formerly part of the Soviet Bloc or Soviet Union. In 1997 the EU defined its strategy for future enlargement to the east. Unlike the last expansion, which admitted three nations (Austria, Finland, and Sweden), all of which were all relatively prosperous with a long market tradition, the next expansion will allow relatively poor nations with a recent tradition of socialism and central planning. The new admittants will be a drag on the budget and there is concern that the cheap labor available in the east will draw investment away from current members and aggravate the high levels of unemployment now endemic through continental western Europe. However, expansion offers clear political gains by ensuring the stability and moderation of the countries to the east.

In 1997 the European Commission conducted a comprehensive evaluation of each candidate country's political and economic readiness for EU membership.

Five central European countries (Hungary, Poland, Estonia, the Czech Republic, and Slovenia), in the words of the Commission's report, "came closest to satisfying the membership eligibility criteria of having secure democratic government, a well-functioning market economy and the ability to take on the obligations of EU membership." With the exception of Poland, these are relatively small countries that will not impose a major burden on either the agricultural or the structural funds, despite the fact that their average income per head is well below the EU average. Poland is both the largest and the poorest of the new applicants. In 1995 it had a GDP per head of only $2,790 (compared to Greece's $8,210) and will certainly be a drain on both CAP and the structural funds.[7]

However, this group of five nations is certainly better off than the subsequent group, which the European Commission has decided to groom for membership over the long term (Bulgaria, Latvia, Lithuania, Romania, and Slovakia). Their GDP per head is less than 10 percent of the EU average, and less than one-fifth even if measured in purchasing power parity terms. Their economies are performing quite badly, and institutional reform is slow. The EU will assist this group of five to improve performance and open accession negotiations as soon as possible. The Commission is prepared to beef up existing aid to the countries of central and eastern Europe by setting aside a total of ECU 45 billion for enlargement. The applicant countries are being prepared for membership under a so-called preaccession strategy adopted in December 1994. The strategy is based on agreements aimed at expanding trade links and political dialogue between the EU and individual countries in central and eastern Europe.

Turkey has waited for entry for a long time with little success. The ostensible reason is that Turkey is not primarily on the continent of Europe, while the original treaty of Rome defined the Communities as being made up of European nations. A more substantial reason is that Turkey is a large and poor country, and would therefore have a considerable say in the European institutions but would be a net receiver of funds from Brussels. Cyprus, an island currently divided between a Greek and a Turkish zone, is similarly in abeyance pending the resolution of the political problems that have divided the island.

THE INSTITUTIONS OF THE EUROPEAN UNION

The European Union is to an outsider a confusing political entity. Its powers consist of issuing directives and regulations that are binding on members to various degrees, managing a budget, and making a very limited number of agreements in the international sphere. These powers are exercised by common institutions residing in Brussels, Strasbourg, and Luxembourg whose structure is complex and unfamiliar to most non-Europeans and baffling to many Europeans as well. Therefore it is useful to outline the distribution of decision-making authority in some

---

[7]Even when assessed in terms of the more realistic purchasing power parity estimates, it has an average of only $5,400 against the current average of $20,000.

detail. This analysis is about the relationships of the nation-states to the EU, the "democratic" structure of the EU, and the direction of further integration.

THE EUROPEAN COUNCIL

The overall agenda of the European Union is determined by the **European Council,** which is composed of the political leaders ("the heads of state and government") of the 15 member nations. It sets the key policy guidelines and provides the impetus on the most important subjects. It also arbitrates disputed questions in which agreement has not been reached within the European Union Council of Ministers. Each member country presides over the European Council in turn for a six-month period: Greece and Germany in 1994, France and Spain in 1995, Italy and Ireland in 1996. During the six-month presidency, therefore, each country has the power to determine the agenda of what is discussed and to some extent what is pushed forward.

THE EUROPEAN COMMISSION

The **European Commission** is the Brussels-based permanent bureaucracy of the EU, employing some 17,000 people. The Commission draws up common projects and, after a decision has been taken by the European Union Council of Ministers, sees that it is properly implemented.

It is directed by 20 commissioners and has a permanent president, now Romano Prodi who is replacing Jacques Santer of Luxembourg. An important principle of the Commission is that it operates independently of the national governments. Each commissioner takes an oath of office by which he or she forswears consideration of national interest in favor of a European perspective. Despite this, the commissioners are not selected from the member nations strictly according to ability. Each nation gets to send at least one commissioner, and the larger nations send two, and since the commissioners are appointed by national governments, the job is frequently a reward for loyal political service. Despite the rhetoric, commissioners are likely to act to some extent in the interests of the government of their home nation.

While commissioners are politically appointed, the bureaucracies of the various directorates general that compose the Commission are long-serving permanent officials. Because of this, the bureaucrats have considerable power. Their commissioners have to rely on them as the repository of experience and knowledge and therefore they can control information flows and to some degree the agenda. The function of the Commission is to implement the common policies of the Union: agriculture, fishing, research, energy, environment, and so on. Also, when it is mandated by the member countries, it negotiates international agreements on cooperation and trade.

The Commission is not merely a passive body, but it also has the power to initiate reform. That is why the principle of subsidiarity, which places power whenever appropriate on a lower level of government, is so significant. On its own initiative or in response to a citizen's complaint it may bring an action before the European

Court of Justice should the Union's laws not be respected in member states. The Commission also manages the Union's annual budget (ECU 86 billion in 1996), which is dominated by farm spending allocated by the European Agricultural Guidance and Guarantee Fund and by the Structural Funds, designed to even out the economic disparities between the richer and poorer areas.

THE EUROPEAN PARLIAMENT

The EU does have a directly elected parliament; 626 members of the European Parliament (MEPs), who are elected for five-year terms to sit in Strasbourg, form the **European Parliament.** The powers of the Parliament are limited and, although its responsibilities have grown over time, it remains largely a symbolic and consultative group rather than an embodiment of representative democracy.

All of Europe's major political currents are represented in the Parliament, ranging from far left to far right. Close to 100 political parties have MEPs, who are organized in a limited number of groups (presently eight) along ideological, not national, lines. Much of the effective work of Parliament is conducted in its 20 committees covering all areas of the European Union's activities, ranging from agriculture to common foreign and security policy, from legal affairs and citizens' rights to overseas cooperation and development. Parliament maintains friendly relations with elected assemblies all over the world and MEPs meet regularly with representatives from the Parliaments of member states in interparliamentary committees and delegations.

POWERS OF THE PARLIAMENT. The European Parliament's powers fall into three areas:

Legislation. The original Treaty of Rome gave the European Parliament only a consultative role, and it was at best a "talking shop" on legislative matters. However, subsequent amendments (through to the Maastricht Treaty) have extended its authority and now the Parliament has the power of codecision (with the European Council) over policy areas (such as the free movement of workers, consumer protection, education, culture, health, and trans-European networks). Many legislative proposals now require an opinion from Parliament before they can be resolved by the Council. In the event of a conflict, a conciliation committee made up of equal numbers of MEPs and Council members is formed to seek a compromise. If the conflict is insoluble, Parliament can pass a motion of censure on the Commission and force it to resign.

The Budget. The Parliament approves the EU's budget each year and can propose modifications or amendments to the Commission's initial proposals. The Council has the last word on agricultural spending and costs arising from international agreements, but the Parliament decides on other expenditures in, for example, education, social programs, regional funds, and environmental and cultural projects. In exceptional circumstances, the

European Parliament can vote to reject the budget if it feels that its wishes have not been adequately respected.

Supervision of the Executive. The Parliament exercises overall political supervision over the conduct of the European Union's policies. Executive power in the EU is shared between the Commission and the Council of Ministers, and their representatives appear regularly before Parliament. Parliament is also responsible for selecting a new president of the Commission every five years.

THE EUROPEAN UNION COUNCIL OF MINISTERS

Most of the day-to-day decision-making power within the European Union lies in the **Council of Ministers** and in its permanent bureaucratic counterpart *Coreper* (the French acronym for the Council of Permanent Representatives). Each member state has a national delegation in Brussels headed by permanent representatives, normally very senior diplomats. Though nominally only an administrative adjunct of the Council of Ministers, *Coreper* has a lot of power in day-to-day matters and only the most sensitive matters are actually handled by the Council of Ministers.

Actions of the Council take several forms: First there are *regulations,* binding and directly applicable to all citizens. At a level of compulsion below the regulations are *directives,* binding on all but indirect, these must be first "transposed" into the law of each country in a way that satisfies the intent of the directive. *Decisions* are binding and directly applicable but only to the institutions, bodies, businesses, or citizens specifically named. Finally there are *recommendations, advisory opinions,* and *resolutions,* which are consultative or guidance texts addressed to the states.

OTHER EUROPEAN BODIES

The Economic and Social Committee and the Committee of the Regions are major consultative committees that relay the advice of professional groups and local bodies to the Commission, the Council, and the Parliament. All the guidance documents (which are known as White Papers and Green Papers) and all the proposed European laws are submitted for consultation to these two committees. The Economic and Social Committee is made up of representatives of the workers, large and small businesses, farmers, families, and consumers of each country. The Committee of the Regions is the voice of the municipalities, departments, and regions of the European Union.

The European Court of Justice is responsible for the proper implementation of the treaties and community legislation. It consists of judges and independent advocates general; citizens may appeal to it through the European Commission (complaint) or a national court. The European Court of Auditors is responsible for auditing the legality and regularity of EU revenues and expenditures.

The **Ombudsman** is a peculiar European institution, the name and function of which are Scandinavian in origin. The purpose of the office is to provide a clear avenue for any European citizen or resident of the EU with a complaint against a policy or institution of the EU. The Ombudsman hears grievances and has the authority to investigate and if necessary take action on them. In the United States, the function would be achieved by bringing suit against the federal government or its agency, but the Ombudsman is less formal and less expensive. The Ombudsman is named by the European Parliament after each election to the Parliament for the duration of the legislature.

MAKING DECISIONS IN THE EUROPEAN UNION

One of the most important features of the Maastricht Treaty was to reduce the power of any single member state to frustrate change within the Union. For matters within Pillar One, action generally starts with a proposal from the Commission which, after consultation with Parliament and the Economic, Social, and Regional Committees, the Council of Ministers can either adopt, amend, or ignore. In most cases (including issues that involve agriculture, fisheries, internal market, environment, and transport), the Council decides on the basis of a "qualified majority vote," with member states having the voting power shown in Table 8.3. A proposal needs the support of 62 votes (70 percent of the total of 87), which must be cast by at least 10 different member states. In practice the Council tries to reach the widest possible consensus at the committee stage before taking a vote, and only 14 percent of the legislation adopted by the Council in 1994 was the subject of any negative votes and abstentions. In general, the larger nations, while having the

▪ TABLE 8.3

REPRESENTATION IN THE EUROPEAN UNION

	Population (millions)	Members of European Parliament	Council Votes	Members of Economic and Social Committee	Population per EMP	Population per Council Vote
Germany	81.5	99	10	24	823	8,150
United Kingdom	58.4	87	10	24	671	5,840
France	57.9	87	10	24	666	5,790
Italy	57.1	87	10	24	656	5,710
Spain	39.1	64	8	21	611	4,888
Netherlands	15.4	31	5	12	497	3,080
Greece	10.4	25	5	12	416	2,080
Belgium	10.1	25	5	12	404	2,020
Portugal	9.9	25	5	12	396	1,980
Sweden	8.8	22	4	12	400	2,200
Austria	8.0	21	4	12	381	2,000
Finland	5.1	16	3	9	319	1,700
Denmark	5.2	16	3	9	325	1,733
Ireland	3.6	15	3	9	240	1,200
Luxembourg	0.4	6	2	6	67	200
European Union	370.9	62 6	87	222	592	4,263

SOURCE: Eurostat.

greatest absolute number of votes, are under-represented in terms of their population, and the system favors the smaller nations. A combination of seven relatively small nations (Greece, Belgium, Portugal, Ireland, Luxembourg, Denmark, and Finland), with a total population of only 44 million, or 12 percent of the total, might block a move, while a combination of Germany, Britain, and the Netherlands, with 42 percent of the total population, could not. Other policy areas within Pillar One (including taxation, industry, culture) remain subject to unanimity. In Pillars Two and Three unanimity (and therefore the veto) remains the rule.

Table 8.3 illustrates an important aspect of governance and democracy within the EU: citizens of small states have a disproportionately large say in the workings of the Union. In Germany there is one MEP per 823,000 citizens and only one Council vote per 8 million. In Luxembourg there is one MEP per 67,000 people and one Council vote per 200,000. In other words, the weight of a citizen of Luxembourg in EU affairs expressed through the Council is about 40 times as great as that of a German. Increasing democracy within the EU would reduce the power of smaller nation-states.

CONCLUSION

Having given an historical background to the development of the European Union and provided some analysis of how it functions, we will now turn in the next chapter to the consequences that evolution of the EU has had for the economic systems of its member states and the economic outcomes that have resulted.

KEY TERMS AND CONCEPTS

common agricultural policy (CAP)

common external tariff (CET)

common market

Coreper

Council of Ministers

customs union

EC-1992

European Coal and
Steel Community (ECSC)

European Commission

European Council

European Economic Area (EEA)

European Free Trade Area (EFTA)

European Parliament

European Union (EU)

fortress Europe

free trade area

Jean Monnet

Maastricht Treaty

Marshall Plan

Ombudsman

Organization for European
Economic Cooperation (OEEC)

principle of subsidiarity

Robert Schumann

"Single European Act"

Social Charter

Treaty of Rome

Treaty on European Union

QUESTIONS FOR DISCUSSION

1. Why did Britain perceive it gained little from EFTA and needed the larger market afforded by the EU?
2. Why was the ending of the veto by the Maastricht Treaty important for the development of the EU?
3. What is the principle of subsidiarity and how might it lessen the popular fear of Brussels bureaucrats?
4. Why will admitting the poorer nations of Eastern Europe be a challenge to the EU?
5. What are the particular problems of Turkey's application to the EU?
6. In what sense is the EU a democracy?

RESOURCES

WEB SITES

Europa . . . . http://europa.eu.int/
This is the front door to all of the official sites of the European Union. This gives access to Eurostat, the statistical agency, and the Web sites of the Commission, Parliament, the Court of Justice, the Court of Auditors, all of the secretariats, and the Economic and Social Committee.

European Central Bank: . . . . http://www.ecb.int/
Useful for statistics, policy statements, and working papers, and will grow in importance in the years ahead.

The Official French Foreign Ministry Site . . . .
. . . . http://www.france.diplomatie.fr/frmonde/euro/sommaire.gb.html
In English, this site gives good explanations of the evolution of Europe and French Policy.

Center for West European Studies, University of Pittsburgh . . . .
. . . . http://www.pitt.edu/~wwwes/social.guide.html
A useful site for research with many links.

The EC Information Society Promotion Office . . . . http://www.ispo.cec.be/topic
An English-language site in Belgium addressing issues concerning the EU and the "information society."

The European Parliament . . . . http://www.europarl.eu.int/

Europe in the United States . . . . http://www.eurunion.org/
The official site of the EU delegation in the United States. Good information and useful links.

European Parliament . . . . http://www.europarl.eu.int/dg4/wkdocs/en/default.htm#soci

European Parliament Fact Sheets . . . .
. . . . http://www.europarl.eu.int/dg4/factsheets/en/default.htm

Policies and Legislation of the European Union . . . .
. . . . http://www.eurunion.org/legislat/index.htm

European Central Bank . . . . http://www.ecb.int/

The Text of the Maastricht Treaty . . . .
. . . . ftp://uiarchive.cso.uiuc.edu/pub/etext/gutenberg/etext96/maast10.txt

BOOKS AND ARTICLES

Britton, Andrew, and David Mayes. *Achieving Monetary Union in Europe.* London: Sage Publications, 1992.

Cecchini, Paolo. *The Cost of Non-Europe.* Brussels: European Commission, 1988.

Devinney, Timothy M., and William C. Hightower. *European Markets after 1992.* Lexington, Mass.: D. C. Heath and Co., 1991.

Fossati, Amedeo, and Giorgio Panella, eds. *Fiscal Federalism in the European Union.* Vol. 9 of *Routledge Studies in the European Economy.* New York: Routledge, 1999.

Giordano, Francesco, and Sharda Persaud. *The Political Economy of Monetary Union: Towards the Euro.* New York: Routledge, 1998.

Gros, D., and Thygesen, N. *European Monetary Integration.* New York: St. Martin's Press, 1992.

Kluth, Michael F. *The Political Economy of a Social Europe: Understanding Labour Market Integration in the European Union.* New York: St. Martin's Press, 1998.

Milward, Alan S. *The Reconstruction of Western Europe: 1945–51.* London: Methuen & Co., 1984.

Nevin, Edward. *The Economics of Europe.* New York: St. Martin's Press, 1990.

Padoa-Schioppa, Tommaso. *Efficiency, Stability and Equity: A Strategy for the Evolution of the Economic System of the European Community.* Oxford: Oxford University Press, 1987.

Pinder, John. *European Community: The Building of a Union.* New York: Oxford University Press, 1991.

Pohl, Gerhard, and Piritta Sorsa. "Is European Integration Bad News for Developing Countries?: A Comment on Hughes Hallet." *World Bank Research Observer,* January 1994, 147–155.

Price, Victoria Curzon, Alice Landau, and Richard Whitman. *The Enlargement of the European Union: Issues and Strategies.* Vol. 7 of *Routledge Studies in the European Economy.* New York: Routledge, 1999.

Story, Jonathan, and Ingo Walter. *Political Economy of Financial Integration in Europe: The Battle of the Systems.* Cambridge, Mass.: MIT Press, 1997.

"A Survey of EMU: An Awfully Big Adventure." *The Economist,* 11 April 1998, 42.

"A Survey of the European Union: Europe's Mid-life Crisis," *The Economist,* 31 May 1997, 52.

United Nations. *Economic Commission for Europe Annual Reports.*

THE ECONOMIC CONSEQUENCES
OF THE EUROPEAN UNION

THE MAKEUP OF THE EU

Since its last expansion on January 1st of 1995, the European Union (EU) has consisted of 15 member states with a total population of 371 million persons. Its average gross national product (GNP) per head measured at current exchange rates is a prosperous $20,500 (Table 9.1). Calculations based on the purchasing power of domestic currencies places it as a slightly more modest $18,000 (largely because of the high cost of food within the EU). The total GNP of the EU (the sum of the national GNPs) is about $7.5 trillion at current exchange rates making it a larger economic entity than the United States and, therefore, a global force to be reckoned with. Although economic growth in Europe was strong during the early days of the European Economic Union (EEC), the pace has slackened of late and the EU has been growing more slowly than North America, although recently it has turned in a better performance than slumping Japan. Few Europeans regard the growth rate of income per head of 2.1 percent per annum, exhibited between 1980 and 1999, as creditable, especially as slow growth in output has led to an increasing unemployment. The causes of this poor performance are much debated, but most observers place some blame on inflexible labor markets and a lag in the pace of technological innovation relative to other nations.

THE WELFARE EFFECTS OF THE COMMON MARKET

The theory of the economic consequences of the creation of the EEC, and its successor the European Union, is well developed. The impact can be divided into static effects, which are examined formally next, and the longer-term dynamic effects, looked at in the following section.

STATIC EFFECTS

The static effects of a common market, or customs union, are shown in Figure 9.1. Let us start with the assumption that the same good is produced in three countries, A (the domestic economy), B (its neighbor and ultimate partner in a customs union), and C (the lowest cost producer in the world). For simplicity we assume that Country C can supply effectively unlimited quantities of the good to Country A, which is relatively small, at a constant price of P_c. Under these conditions all

SELECTED MACROECONOMIC INDICATORS FOR EU MEMBERS

	Population Millions	GNP per Head 1997 $'000	GDP per Head PPP 1997 $'000	GDP 1997 $'000	Real GDP Growth 1990–1997 % per Annum	Inflation 1990–1997 % per Annum
Germany	81.7	28.3	21.3	2,312.1	2.4	2.9
United Kingdom	58.6	20.7	20.5	1,213.0	1.9	3.1
France	58.1	26.1	21.9	1,516.4	1.3	1.9
Italy	57.3	20.1	20.1	1,151.7	1.1	4.5
Spain	39.3	14.5	15.7	569.9	1.6	4.6
Netherlands	15.6	25.8	21.3	402.5	2.3	2.0
Greece	10.7	12.0	13.1	128.4	1.8	11.3
Belgium	10.2	26.4	22.3	269.3	1.2	2.8
Portugal	10.1	10.4	13.8	105.0	1.7	6.3
Sweden	8.9	26.2	19.0	233.2	0.9	2.6
Austria	8.1	28.0	21.0	226.8	1.6	2.9
Finland	5.2	24.1	18.9	125.3	1.1	1.7
Denmark	5.4	32.5	22.7	175.5	2.3	1.8
Ireland	3.8	18.3	16.7	69.5	6.5	1.8
Luxembourg	0.4	45.3	34.5	18.1	4.5	2.4
European Union	373.4	22.8	20.0	8,516.8	1.8	3.4

SOURCE: World Development Report 1999, OECD Economic Outlook, June 1999.

of A's imports of the good (an amount shown by gh in the diagram) originate in C, and the balance of consumption Q_1. B is by and large a lower cost producer than A, selling at at P_b, but it cannot compete with C's price of P_c. Now let us consider the effect of a protective tariff of magnitude t. Because of the small country assumption, C's output remains at the same price on world markets, but within A is increased by the full amount of the tariff. Therefore the price within A's economy rises from P_c to P_t. The output of neighboring Country B is, in the presence of the tariff, priced at $P_b + t$, which is still above C's price of $P_c + t$ or P_t. Imports, therefore, come exclusively from the lowest cost producer country C, but they are now restricted by the tariff to a level of ab. The balance of domestic consumption is supplied A's own protected producers, who are able to expand production behind protective barriers. Revenue from the tariff is the rectangle $abji$—that is, the volume of imports, ab, multiplied by the tariff, t. The welfare consequences of this tariff are a fall in consumers' surplus of $P_c hbP_t$, and the protection raises producers' surplus by an amount $P_c gaP_t$. Total deadweight loss is given by the two triangles aig and bjh.

From this point we can consider the results if the neighboring countries A and B form a customs union. They agree to eliminate all tariff and quota restrictions between each other but maintain a common external tariff of size t with respect to the rest of the world. Now tariff-free goods from B are cheaper than the tariffed goods that originate in C. As a result, imports from the rest of world are eliminated, and

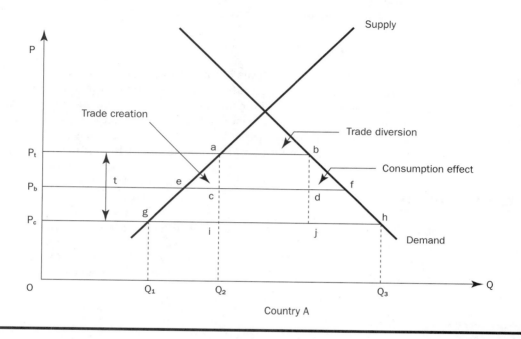

Country A

instead they originate in B. The price of the good established in A is the production cost of B, (i.e., P_b). Total imports are of a magnitude ef. Part of this total, an amount cd (= ab), replaces the imports from the C. This is called the **trade diversion effect** of a customs union. However, total imports are greater than before. An amount ec replaces a part of domestic production and is termed the **trade creation effect.** The amount ef is an increase in consumption brought about by lower prices and is termed the **consumption effect.**

Compared to the situation where A imposes a tariff on imports from all sources, the customs union does represent a welfare gain. Consumers in A have access to goods at a lower price, P_b, than would be the case if there were tariff barriers against all imports. The gain in consumers' surplus is $P_b fbP_t$ and is clearly greater than the sum of the loss of producers' surplus $P_b aeP_t$ and the foregone tariff revenue $abdc$. However, these welfare gains are smaller than those that would result under free trade. The largest gainer from A's entry into the market in this example are the producers, and workers, of B who gain access to A's market; they see their production increase by an amount ef to meet the demand from A. Compared to free trade, A's consumers are losers, and the only gainers are the producers of B.

Consequently, viewed in a strictly static way, A would only join a customs union if it felt that in some industries it was in the position of lowest cost producer of the member nations. In reality this does reflect the perceived benefits of joining the EU. The greater overall size of market allows greater specialization and division of labor. Economies become more open and trade flows increase. Some domestic industries are likely to decline as imports from other member countries cut into the market, while the output of other industries increases.

DYNAMIC EFFECTS

While the static effects of a customs union are important, long-term dynamic considerations are probably more significant in providing a rationale for the creation of a common market than the static ones. Certainly from the inception of the EEC, one driving motivation was the beneficial effect of exposure of European firms to greater competition from its partners within the common market. A second was the ability to grasp economies of scale from the larger domestic market.

THE TRADE OF THE EU

Table 9.2 indicates some of the changes in trade volumes that occurred following the formation of the EEC and its successor the EU between the 1960s and 1990s. In terms of the openness of the whole Community as a bloc of economies, little has altered in this 30-year period. Between 1960 to 1967, about 8.8 percent of the GNP

■ TABLE 9.2

OPENNESS OF EU ECONOMIES, 1960–1994 (AVERAGE OF IMPORTS AND EXPORTS OF GOODS AS A PERCENTAGE OF GDP; INTRA-EU TRADE IS GIVEN AS A PERCENTAGE OF TOTAL TRADE)

	1960–1967		1991–1994	
	World	**Intra-EU**	**World**	**Intra-EU**
Belgium and Luxembourg	37.5	64.8	53.3	70.0
Denmark	27.0	52.3	25.4	53.0
Germany	15.9	44.8	20.7	52.2
Greece	12.7	50.6	17.0	59.2
Spain	8.1	47.8	15.2	62.9
France	11.0	45.8	18.7	63.3
Ireland	33.6	72.2	50.3	68.8
Italy	11.7	42.9	15.9	56.4
Netherlands	37.7	62.7	43.9	65.9
Portugal	19.8	48.3	28.5	73.3
United Kingdom	16.0	26.7	20.2	52.1
EU-12	8.8	45.0	8.9	58.6
Austria	—	—	25.6	66.1
Finland	—	—	22.4	46.7
Sweden	—	—	23.6	54.9

Note: For the member states, these figures include intra-Union trade; for EU-12, intra-Union trade has been excluded.

SOURCE: Eurostat. [Loukas Tsoukalis, *The New European Economy Revisited*, 182.]

of the 12 nations, then part of the EEC, was traded. The comparable figure for the same group of countries between 1991 and 1994 was 8.9 percent. This stability is surprising since the average openness of most of the economies in the world increased sharply during this time, and the considered globally trade to GNP ratios rose rapidly. While trade with nations outside of the EU has only kept pace with the growth of output, trade within the EU has grown considerably more rapidly. On average the nations of the EU conducted 45 percent of their trade with other members in 1960; by 1991–1994 this had risen to 58.6 percent. The evidence therefore points to substantial trade creation and trade diversion effects

THE EXTERNAL TRADE POLICY OF THE EU

DEVELOPED NATIONS

After the end of World War II, the United States directed its energy into creating a nonpreferential system of world trade predicated on the **most favored nation principle** of the General Agreement on Tariffs and Trade (GATT). The creation of customs unions like the European Community (EC) was facilitated by a special clause in the GATT (Article XXIV), which allowed the establishment of formal free trade areas. The United States allowed and even encouraged this development because it felt a strong Europe was essential to contain an expansionist Soviet Union. Nevertheless there has always been ambivalence in the American view and a recurrent fear that Europe might choose to close itself behind high tariff or walls.

Fortunately, the trade policy of the EU has been in line with GATT policy. The fears of Fortress Europe have been soothed by successive reduction in the **common external tariff (CET).** The EU has also sought to extend the free trade area beyond its core membership. The first extension was the creation of a free trade area linking the EC and the European Free Trade Area (EFTA) called the **European Economic Area (EEA).** Subsequently the central and east European economies in transition have been afforded special status through the signing of economic agreements (EAs) committing the parties to move toward a zero tariff status over a 10-year period. After U.S. pressure, and in partial compensation for the stalling over its full membership, Turkey has been admitted into the customs union without participating in the other aspects of the EU.

TRADE WARS. Despite overall conformity with the rules of the GATT, the EU has used nontariff barriers to protect sensitive industry. This has led to frequent disputes, especially between the EU and the United States with respect to farming. These problems are often related to agricultural products, which is not surprising given that agriculture lay beyond the purview of the GATT and the highly protectionist postures of both Europe and the United States. One outburst in 1997 was over new European Union rules requiring that exporting countries comply with the EU's food hygiene standards. The EU blocked the import of American chickens and turkeys, and the Clinton administration responded by promising to block $300 million worth of meat imports annually. Like other disputes before it, it was resolved; but an undercurrent of mutual suspicion endures.

POLICY TOWARD DEVELOPING NATIONS. The EU's relationships with the "developing" world are governed by the **Lomé agreements;** the latest of these (Lomé IV) was signed in 1989 and subsequently modified in 1995. The Lomé pact is between the 15 nations of the EU and some 70 third-world countries known as the African, Caribbean, and Pacific (ACP) nations, many of which have historic colonial ties to members of the EU. The agreements allow virtually tariff-free access into the EU for most exports of the ACP nations without any reciprocal obligation. Furthermore, the Lomé arrangements were backed by the stabilization of prices of agricultural exports (Stabex) and mineral exports (Sysmin). In addition, the European Development Fund disburses about 6 percent of European Union revenue in aid to the ACP nations.

However, despite their apparent generosity, the Lomé agreements have done little to assist either development in, or exports from, the ACP group. In fact, EU imports from the ACP countries fell sharply between 1970 to 1994, from over 8 percent of total non-EU imports to about 3 percent. While the pure transfer element of the grants-in-aid and the stabilization schemes is still important, the trade concessions have become less valuable over time as the size of the common external tariff has fallen.

THE ECONOMICS OF A SINGLE CURRENCY

The biggest recent change in the European Union is the adoption of a single currency. This must surely be ranked one of the most important events of the late 20th century, both for its ramifications for the global system of finance and for its impact on the policies of the member countries of the EU. The single currency remains, however, a controversial issue. While on balance most studies have found economic gains from the creation of a single currency, there are attendant costs that must be balanced against them.

ECONOMIC AND MONETARY UNION, EMU

In March 1971, the member states of the EC expressed "their political will to establish an economic and monetary union." The first step was the adoption of the "currency snake" linking the European currencies through fixed exchange rates while the rest of the industrial world moved toward floating rates. The next step, in 1979, was the creation of the **European Monetary System (EMS)** and the **European Currency Unit (ECU).** The EMS was a fixed exchange rate scheme in which most currencies were held in a narrow band against each other (2¼ percent either side of the central parity). Rates were not totally stable, and there was considerable realignment caused by differential inflation rates. The ECU was used as a unit of valuation only.

In June 1989, the European Council adopted the proposal of Jacques Delors, president of the Commission, to embark on a three-stage program leading to a single currency. The first step beginning in 1990 consisted of closer coordination in monetary policy under the supervision of the Committee of Governors of the EC Central Banks.

In late 1992, progress to monetary union was set back by the consequences of German reunification. The need for income support and reconstruction assistance required that the German government pour some DM100 billion per year into the territories that had formerly been East Germany. This depleted federal finances and led to increased borrowing by the German government, which raised interest rates and pushed up the value of the mark, severely straining the fixed exchange rates of the EMS. The maintenance of existing parities within the EMS required other countries to increase their own interest rates. Both Britain and Italy were un-willing to surrender monetary policy to the EMS in this way and left the system. For the countries remaining, the bands around parity were widened to 15 percent, and their very width meant that although the EMS survived, it could no longer be regarded as a truly fixed parity arrangement.

Despite the disruption to the system and the threat to the EMU, the leaders of the member nations resolved to initiate the second stage at the beginning of 1994. The most visible development was the establishment of the **European Monetary Institute (EMI)** in Frankfurt. This location was the subject of some contention since Britain felt that the EMI should be located near the European Union's largest finan-cial market, London. However, the fact that the United Kingdom had removed it-self from the EMS, and the political reality that the mark dominates the EMS, favored a German site.

Proponents of the EMU felt that the key to a successful common currency lay in the economic convergence; the so-called **Maastricht criteria** were adopted to en-sure that the economies were on a similar path. No state was to be admitted into Stage 3 of monetary union unless it met the following criteria:

1. Its inflation rate did not exceed by more than 1.5 percent that of the average of the three member states with the lowest inflation.

2. Its long-term interest rate did not exceed by more than 2 percentage points that of the three best states in terms with the lowest inflation rates.

3. Its current public sector deficit was less than 3 percent of GDP.

4. Its public sector debt was less than 60 percent of GDP, or approaching 60 percent at a satisfactory pace.

5. Finally, a member state's exchange rate must have been stable over the two preceding years, showing no more than "normal variation."

As late as 1997 no EU nation (except tiny, wealthy Luxembourg) met these criteria, and a desperate drive to conform (especially to items 3 and 4) initiated a period of fiscal austerity that slowed growth of the EU economies. In March 1998 the European Monetary Institute produced an assessment of each country's per-formance in meeting the criteria, which was to be the basis for accession to the EMU. When it came to the crunch, only Greece was found to have failed to meet the criteria, although Britain, Denmark, and Sweden were skeptical about mone-tary union and opted not to enter the system at its initiation in 1999. Only three na-tions met the strictest definition of condition 4, all the other nations were found to be reducing their ratio of public debt to GDP at a "satisfactory" pace. This was some-thing of a stretch. Belgium (with a debt/GDP ratio of 122.2 percent) and Italy (121.6 percent) were on the face of it well beyond the limits, but political considerations led to their inclusion under the generous "fudge factor." Consequently, a group 11 nations (styled Euro-11) were admitted to initiate the monetary union.

THE BENEFITS OF A SINGLE CURRENCY

Currency union is expected to bring several benefits. The most obvious is the elimination of currency conversion, releasing substantial resources in the banking sector.[1] Another is from the end of exchange rate uncertainty, which should encourage trade and allow more efficient allocation of resources within the EU, through specialization and economies of scale.

A third benefit is that the participating nations can largely eliminate their holdings of international currency and bullion reserves. The combined reserves of the members of the EU in 1990 was about ECU 200 billion, while the United States with an economy similar in size had reserves of only about ECU 40 billion. Although the special position of the dollar as a reserve and intervention currency means that the United States can keep lower reserves than other economies, a substantial reduction in overall European reserves can be anticipated.[2] Finally, the creation of a common European currency unit will increase the importance of European currency in world markets. More of the world's reserves will be held in Euros and the EU will be able to benefit from *seigniorage* (the process of creating money to be held by others) and lower interest rates than would otherwise have been the case.

THE COSTS OF A SINGLE CURRENCY

Adopting a single currency, however, involves costs, the chief of which is the elimination of exchange rate policy as a means of accommodating shocks and balancing the external accounts. To understand this, consider a country that experiences a sudden fall in the demand for its exports. If it has its own currency, it can devalue, or allow it to depreciate, and can regain international competitiveness at lower real incomes without causing a fall in nominal income or a rise in unemployment at home. If it is part of a currency union, it must absorb the shock in terms of lower income and higher short-term unemployment. The size and openness of the economy determines the seriousness of losing currency flexibility. Small countries have relatively large propensities to import and therefore are able to achieve external balance through proportionately small changes in GDP. Larger countries, which are generally more closed, require a larger movement of output to rectify external imbalances. As a rule therefore small countries have lower costs of joining a fixed-rate system and especially a monetary union.

---

[1] The quantification of these benefits involves making some assumptions but the adoption of a single currency is estimated by the European Commission as providing cost savings equivalent to some ECU 15 billion per annum, capable of creating a boost to the GNP of the participant countries of about 0.4 percent if, of course, the unemployed resources are put to use.

[2] However since most of these reserves are currently held in interest-bearing assets, the actual degree of saving might well be small.

■ TABLE 9.3

EUROPEAN AND AMERICAN INDUSTRIAL STRUCTURE:
EUROPE BY NATION, UNITED STATES BY STATE

Sector	European Community		United States	
	Mean Percentage Share	Variance	Mean Percentage Share	Variance
Food, beverages, and tobacco	11.2	11.3	8.3	3.9
Textiles, clothing, and leather	8.1	25.9	4.8	15.9
Wood and wood products	3.8	1.4	4.3	3.1
Paper and paper products	7.4	5.9	8.8	8.6
Chemical and chemical products	17	5.8	17.1	33.9
Nonmetallic mineral products	4.8	1.4	2.7	0.3
Basic metals	6.2	2.4	4.1	3.7
Metal products	9.3	2.9	7.4	5
Nonelectrical machinery	10.1	12.9	19.8	27.2
Electrical machinery	10.5	8.6	10.3	9.6
Transport equipment	11.7	7.5	12.5	26.4
Totals	100.1	8.4	100.1	18.0

SOURCE: Bini Smaghi, and L. and S. Vori, "Rating the EU as an Optimum Currency Area," *Banca D'Italia Temi do Discussione,* January 1982.

A second factor is the exposure of a national economy to an asymmetric shock, one affecting it more severely than the rest of the monetary union. If all parts of the union are hit similarly by an economic shock, it can be accommodated by coordinated union-wide monetary, and possibly fiscal, policy. The relationship between the economic structure of each member country and the whole of currency union becomes key. The more a country resembles the union-wide average, the less harmful is the loss of an exchange rate flexibility. The greater the similarity between the structures of all the member countries, the more likely is it that it comprises "optimum currency area." Table 9.3 shows that though there is considerable variance in the industrial structure of the members of the Europe Union, it is actually less than that between the states of the United States, which share a common currency.

The degree of factor mobility also affects the desirability of a currency union. Highly mobile labor or capital helps adjustment to a negative shock by moving quickly from the impacted region to areas where they are in higher demand. Consider an example from the United States. The state of Maine had a high proportion of employment in footwear manufacture, much higher than the U.S. average. When cheap shoes from low labor-cost countries began to flow into the United States, unemployment mounted in Maine. If the state had had its own currency, we would have seen a depreciation of the "Maine $" and a movement toward restoring external balance. However, the shock was absorbed by lower real wages in Maine, which prompted an outflow of labor to states where wages were higher, and some investment in new industry in Maine to take advantage of the cheap

■ TABLE 9.4

ESTIMATES OF NET BENEFITS OF EMU MEMBERSHIP EU OF 12

	Benefits	Costs	Net Benefits
Belgium/Luxembourg	44.5	−1.39	43.11
Denmark	13.65	−6.47	7.18
Germany	14.35	−1.81	12.54
Greece	13.25	−14.01	−0.76
Spain	8.95	−2.07	6.88
France	12.95	−0.71	12.24
Ireland	38.85	−8.48	30.37
Italy	9.7	−2.02	7.68
Netherlands	34.2	−5.14	29.06
Portugal	24.55	−10.31	14.24
United Kingdom	10.7	−8.4	2.3

Benefits: Intra-EC trade as a percentage of GDP.

Costs: Difference between nation's economic structure and the EC average.

SOURCE: D. Gros and N. Thygesen, *European Monetary Integration* (New York: Addison Wesley, 1998), 258.

labor. Labor mobility between the EU nations is, however, much lower than inter-state mobility in the United States. Net regional migration in the EU represented only 0.2 percent of the total population in the five-year period from 1980–1985, only 25 percent of the level in the United States.

WHO GAINS AND WHO LOSES FROM A SINGLE CURRENCY?

Because of the complexity of these considerations, it is difficult to establish whether a particular group of countries does indeed constitute an **optimum currency area,** or even which countries will benefit from membership. Nevertheless, using heroic assumptions it is possible to get a quantitative handle on the issue. Table 9.4 shows one attempt to forecast the gainers and losers for the EC-12.[3] The measure of benefits consists of the proportion of GDP that is traded within the EC. The measure of cost is the degree to which the industrial structure of the member countries differs from the EC average, a gauge of the degree of susceptibility to asymmetric shocks. In general, the smaller, more open economies show the greatest gains. However, these same countries also tend to have less diversified industrial structures, differing from the community average. However, net benefits seem to be enjoyed by all potential members except Greece.

Such a two-dimensional representation of the costs and benefits is potentially misleading. In reality, the economic implications of the EMU are still shadowy, and it is probable that political factors dominated economic in its formation. Some

[3] D. Gros and N. Thygesen, *European Monetary Integration* (New York: Addison Wesley, 1998), 258.

suggest that, like a bicycle rider, the EU needs forward momentum to maintain its stability. After the completion of the internal market, a new project was needed and it was found in monetary unification. Although it maintains the momentum of EU integration, the current two-tier structure creates a rift between the fast-track members of the monetary union (the EMU-11) and the more cautious or less prepared remainder (Denmark, Sweden, the United Kingdom, and Greece).

TRYING TO COMPLY WITH THE MAASTRICHT CRITERIA

Although all the members of the EU, with the exception of Greece, were determined to have satisfied the Maastricht criteria, much was owed to the generous use of the "fudge factor." The new monetary union must find a way of ensuring that the convergence required for entry is maintained into the future. Given the rigors that some countries have undergone to meet the criteria, or at least to appear to be moving in that direction, and the high level of unemployment throughout the EU,[4] there is a temptation now for countries to indulge in expansionary fiscal policy. All members of the EMU have committed themselves to a **stability and growth pact** requiring the continued enforcement of the Maastricht criteria. To ensure compliance, the Germans favor a system of fines levied on any country that allows a fiscal deficit greater than 3 percent of GDP. It is unlikely that such a measure will become a reality, or if it does that it will be enforced, since many members feel that the lack of an independent monetary policy makes a discretionary fiscal policy the more vital.

THE INDEPENDENCE OF THE EUROPEAN CENTRAL BANK

In theory, the new **European Central Bank (ECB)** will be highly insulated from political pressure from member governments. If this proves a reality it will be an unusual European institution, since most of the major issues are decided by the European Council or the Council of Ministers, both of which are direct functions of the national governments. The rationale for independence is clear. Only in the absence of direct political pressure will the president and the members of the executive board be able to make decisions based on expertise rather than on political exigency. Therefore, both the board and the president of the ECB are appointed to eight-year nonrenewable terms. There are defined avenues by which the Council of Ministers, the Commission, and the European Parliament can make their views known to the ECB, but the bank is under no obligation to respond. However, despite its theoretical independence, the status of the ECB was undermined at the outset by the French insistence on their own candidate, the governor of the Bank of France, as president of the ECB, and their refusal to accept the consensus candidate, the president of the ECB's precursor the European Monetary Institute.

---

[4]Except, somewhat ironically, in Britain, which has the lowest EC joblessness rate and has chosen not to be a member.

A compromise was achieved by splitting the eight-year term into two four-year terms, but the prospects for independence are not good.

THE COMMUNITY BUDGET

The European Union has a surprisingly modest budget. In 1994 it amounted to 73.4 billion ECUs ($97 billion at the current exchange rates), less than 1.2 percent of total GDP of the member states. Expenditures averaged 2.4 percent of total public expenditure of member states—200 ECUs or $260 per head per year.

Finance comes from four sources, as shown in Figure 9.2. The first is the levies imposed on imported agricultural goods. These are an integral part of the **common agricultural policy (CAP)** and are designed to bring the price of imported food into line with European costs. It is a useful source of revenue, although one that is raised at considerable cost and with a high excess burden that falls on the European consumer. It will decline in the future as a result of the Uruguay accords of the World Trade Organization to bring European agricultural prices into closer alignment with world prices. The second source of revenue consists of tariffs levied on industrial goods as they enter the EU. This contributes about 15 percent of the budget. The third source of income is the proceeds of a 1.4 percent surcharge, which is levied as a part of the members countries' value-added tax (VAT). Finally an additional contribution is demanded of members to bring their budget contribution to 1.27 percent of their GDP.

The common agricultural policy is the largest element of expenditure in the EU. It currently represents almost half of the total budget expenditures, about $49 billion. The second largest component is broadly grouped as structural measures. These are primarily regional development and income transfer accounts for an additional 34 percent ($30 billion). Industry, research, the environment, and transport share 6 percent of the budget. External activities (emergency aid and cooperation) correspond to 6 percent of the budget and priority is given to the countries of Eastern Europe, the Mediterranean, Latin America, and Asia. Aid to the African countries and the island countries of the Caribbean and Pacific (ACP), signatories of the

■ **FIGURE 9.2**

SOURCES OF EU REVENUE, 1996

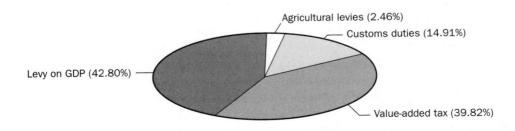

Agricultural levies (2.46%)

Customs duties (14.91%)

Levy on GDP (42.80%)

Value-added tax (39.82%)

SOURCE: Eurostat.

Lomé Convention, is handled through a specific budget (the European Development Fund, EDF) financed by contributions of the member states. Administrative expenses represent 4.95 percent of the budget. In all, 94 percent of the EU budget expenditures benefit the member countries themselves. The 1995 enlargement of the European Union from 12 to 15 members (after the accession of Austria, Sweden, and Finland) resulted in an increase of 6 percent in the budget. However, the new members are globally net contributors to the EU finances; the taxes and levies they contribute to the budget are greater than the direct expenditure received. The financial management of the European Commission is overseen internally by financial auditors and externally by the European Court of Auditors and the European Parliament. Fraud is a persistent charge in EU institutions, and both the Commission and member states have decided to step up the fight against it.

THE COMMON AGRICULTURAL POLICY

As Figure 9.3 shows, almost half of the budget goes to support agriculture. Although its share of total expenditure has fallen over recent years and will fall further in the near future, the dominance of the Common Agricultural Policy (CAP) is still obvious. The system is complex and varies from commodity to commodity, but in essence it consists of manipulating prices within the EU to produce a desired level of farm income. This is achieved by both high intervention prices (at which the EU buys excess produce) and various output restriction schemes. Excess production is stored (in "butter mountains," "oil lakes", etc.) and exported to other countries often at very low prices.[5] To keep EU prices above world levels, agricultural goods entering the EU pay a variable import levy, which bridges the difference between world and EU prices. The main beneficiaries of CAP are the producers within the EU, and to some extent foreign consumers, while the losers are consumers within the EU and foreign producers. The system certainly imposes substantial deadweight losses.

At one level, CAP transfers income from country to country. A big agricultural sector leads to an inflow of funds and since the CAP guarantees prices, nations with efficient agricultural sectors, relative to the European average, gain most. "Winners" fall into two groups. One consists of Greece, Ireland, and Spain, relatively poor countries with large, low productivity agricultural sectors. The other is made up of France and Denmark, rich countries with high productivity in agriculture. The rest of the countries are losers with the largest being Germany, Italy, and the United Kingdom. These transfers are no accident. Freeing trade in manufactured goods benefited Germany's expanding industrial machine, and CAP was a political counterweight, ensuring membership benefits for France, which had a

---

[5] At one point in the late 1980s, the then-Soviet Union was able to buy European butter at 12 cents a pound. Stocks of beef were so high in 1986 that the Commission had to hire refrigerated ships lying in Rotterdam harbor to store the surplus. See Dennis Swann, *The Economics of the Common Market*, 6th ed. (London: Penguin, 1988), 219.

EXPENDITURES OF THE EU, 1996

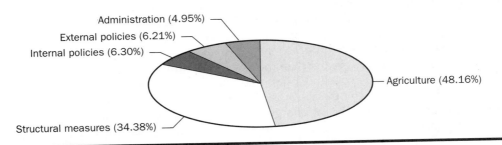

SOURCE: Eurostat.

large agricultural sector. Support is more generous for meat, dairy, and cereals than for "Mediterranean produce," which in part explains why both Italy and Portugal with large agricultural sectors are net losers.

However, viewing redistribution as a national issue alone misses much of the picture. CAP involves subsidies that enable poorer farmers in Scotland, Ireland, Norway, and the "Club Med" countries to stay in business. This has several benefits, including the maintenance of a basic level of prosperity in remote regions, contributing to one of the objectives of regional policy. However, the system also favors rich, efficient farmers, and the overall distributional effect of CAP is regressive, moving funds from relatively poor urban consumers (who spend a large proportion of their income on food) to the wealthier farmers of northern France, East Anglia, and Denmark. This pattern of transfers lowers social support or **cohesion** within the EU by taking from the poor and giving to the more affluent. Partly to rectify this, but also to meet the objectives of the Uruguay agreement and the World Trade Organization, CAP is shifting its emphasis from price support to income maintenance for poor farmers. By eliminating the subsidies to the "rich" farmers of northern Europe, the cost of CAP will be reduced, European prices will be more in line with world prices, and the expensive and inefficient system of purchasing and inventory will be eliminated.

The success of CAP as a policy is debatable, and one's conclusion depends largely on one's viewpoint. One objective was to stabilize prices with the Community, and this has been achieved. There has been less price volatility in the Community than found in world markets or even within the United States, which also has an extensive and expensive system of supports. However the cost of stability has been the most expensive food in the world, except perhaps in Japan. A second goal was certainty of supply. Since the EU is now self-sufficient, this target has been met. However, one might question the value of the objective itself. Food is easily available from a variety of producers, most of whom can reasonably be expected to remain politically friendly to Europe. Therefore it is hard to make a case for strategic self-sufficiency. (This contrasts with, say, the energy sector, which has fewer supply points, many of which are constrained with political problems.) Moreover, self-sufficiency has been more than achieved; overproduction, and the disposal of excess, has become a major preoccupation of the EU. A third objective was to raise agricultural productivity in Europe. The existence of CAP has coincided with a sharp improvement in agricultural productivity, though a cause-and-effect relationship is unclear. All developed countries have seen in the last forty years an increase in both yield per acre and labor productivity. It can be argued that by guaranteeing the incomes of marginal farmers, CAP has shielded producers from market discipline, an effect that will become stronger when CAP's emphasis shifts from price support to income guarantee.

Thus CAP's success lies in the eye of the beholder. Farmers like the policy, and consumers have in general suffered. Nevertheless it has contributed to the cohesion of the EU, by winning the support of the poorer nations at the periphery. It is no coincidence that Ireland, a significant gainer from CAP, was the first country to enthusiastically embrace the Maastricht Treaty in a popular referendum. Moreover, CAP is instrumental in preserving an economic pulse in depressed regions.

THE STRUCTURAL FUNDS

Composed of 15 nations, many of whom have wide regional differences within themselves, the EU is characterized and enriched by diversity. There are differences in language, culture, and landscape between nations and between regions of nations. While Europe celebrates these differences, concern has grown that socio-economic disparities may prove harmful to the unity of the EU, and economic and social cohesion is now regarded as a prerequisite for both political stability and economic efficiency.

In the 1960s and 1970s most member countries of the EU had aggressive "regional policies" designed to foster convergence in regional incomes and employment. Over time, these policies became discredited as expensive, achieving little of lasting consequence, and attempting to overrule the market as arbiter of efficiency. Far from producing national cohesion, regional policy often led to resentment in the territories that had been "net payers." Italy provides a significant example. Despite a battery of policies designed to encourage growth in the "Mezzogiorno," or South, regional disparities persisted and grew. The burden of the expense of redistributive transfers has now led to the emergence of a political party (the Northern League) devoted to promoting regional separatism.

However, the Single European Act brought regional policy to the fore. This act added a new title to the Treaty of Rome specifically stressing economic and social cohesion and providing specific instruments—the **structural funds**—to address it. Structural funds were not themselves new,[6] but what changed was the willingness of the EU to finance regional development. In 1993, 21 billion ECU ($25 billion) was spent on the structural funds, and this rose to ECU 30 billion ($33 billion)

---

[6] The European Social Fund (ESF) had existed since the beginnings of the Europe of Six. The European Regional Development Fund was established in 1975, in the aftermath of the expansion of the early 1970s. The third structural fund was made up of the guidance component of the CAP. A fourth structural fund was added in 1993—for fisheries.

by 1999, including ECU 2.6 billion ($3 billion) in a newly established specific cohesion fund directed to the poorest members of the EU known as the **"cohesion four"**: Greece, Ireland, Spain, and Portugal.

The structural funds have clear objectives:

1. To promote development and economic adjustment in regions whose GDP per head is less than 75 percent of the EU average[7]
2. To radically improve the economic base of regions most seriously affected by industrial decline
3. To combat long-term unemployment
4. To address the labor market problems of young people
5. To promote rural development and structural adjustment in agriculture and fisheries
6. To assist regions with an extremely low population density

Expenditure on the structural funds will necessarily rise with the accession of poorer countries into the EU, which is projected for early in the 21st century. While the Czech Republic and Slovenia are relatively prosperous, their per-head income is less than 50 percent of the EU average, even when measured in purchasing power terms. Other potential entrants have incomes as low as 20 percent of the average.

INDUSTRIAL POLICY

Although much smaller than the agricultural or the structural funds, the next largest item in the EU budget is expenditure on internal policies, embracing research and development, industrial subsidy, and transportation. Together these activities take almost 6 percent of the total budget.

GENERAL TRENDS IN EUROPEAN INDUSTRIAL POLICY

European nations have traditionally taken an interventionist stance on economic development, a feature that has distinguished a "continental school," more inclined to government intervention than the **laissez faire** Anglo-Saxon school, more dominant in Great Britain and the United States. Furthermore, since the early 1970s there has been concern that Europe lags behind the United States (and Japan), in technology, in the ability to grasp scale economies, and in finance. Finally, many Europeans feared that U.S.-based multinational corporations had established an

---

[7] This single objective absorbed three-quarters of total regional expenditure in 1999, and practically all goes to Portugal, Spain, Southern Italy, Eastern Germany, and the overseas departments of France.

almost irresistibly dominant position.[8] These concerns nurtured a series of initiatives specifically directed to putting European industry on a more competitive footing.

NATIONAL INDUSTRIAL POLICY AND THE ERA OF NATIONAL CHAMPIONS

As the single market in Europe emerged, industrial policy in member nations favored promoting "national champions" with the size and resources to compete in the European arena. National antitrust policy was jettisoned in the face of growing competition from other European firms, and governments engaged in brokered mergers trying to grasp the largest share of the European market. This "new mercantilism" ran counter to the logic of division of resources and comparative advantage that underpinned the idea of the common market. It was also a limited and expensive policy, and one doomed to failure if, as indeed seemed to be the case, the European high-tech and communications industry was losing out to rivals in North America and the Far East. The use of nontariff barriers and subsidies to promote national champions in each of the countries led to a fragmentation of the market, and the consequent reduction in competition within Europe was itself a key ingredient in the loss of global competitiveness and the failure to innovate.

THE INDUSTRIAL POLICY OF THE EU

As barriers to trade and investment came down within the EC, it became apparent that a truly European stance on industrial policy was necessary. One possibility was that the Commission should work to promote the development of "European Champions" able to compete against the giants of North America and Japan in the same way that national governments acted in the 1960s and 1970s. This approach had several potential defects. First, it favored creating great market power within the Community, to the detriment of European consumers. It also failed to give European industry access to advanced technology from Japan and the United States, and many companies looked to mergers and joint ventures with non-European firms as a more attractive avenue. Rather than risk these outcomes, the Commission has taken a facilitating, but not an active role, limiting its activities to the removal of fiscal and legal impediments to cross-border mergers.

EU industrial policy is based in the belief that public authorities can have a vital role in promoting successful competitive strategies and that comparative advantage can be created by policy initiative rather than being the result of factor endowment alone. However, in theory at least, EU industrial policy rejects outright protectionism and favors market orientation.

---

[8] This belief was articulated in a popular book authored by Jean Jacques Servan-Schreiber, *The American Challenge (Le Defi Americain)* (New York: Athenaum, 1968).

Its most important dimension is fostering collaborative research and development initiatives. These policies started in the early 1980s when the "technological gap" by which Europe lagged the United States and Japan was estimated at between one and two years. The Commission considered two broad strategies to catch up. One, strongly preferred by the French, was to erect protective barriers around the markets for sensitive products; behind these walls European firms would grow strong enough to meet potential international competition. This strategy was rejected by the majority of nations because it would have insulated Europe from the global competitive trends. Instead a policy of promoting Community-wide cooperation and collaboration in research and development was adopted. First the Commission would identify industries that were at risk of falling further behind, then a jointly funded international research effort involving all of the Europe's leading firms in the industry would be established.

Information technology was seen as the greatest risk, and in 1982 the European commissioner for industrial affairs, Viscount Davignon, succeeded in getting the heads of the 12 largest European electronics firms around one table. As a result, the **European Strategic Programme for Research in Information Technology (ESPRIT)** was born. The program's emphasis was on precompetitive basic research, and it operated on a multiyear planned basis. Its success is questionable. It initiated cross-border cooperation and established agreement on basic standards and protocols, but it has not succeeded in closing the technology gap, although it can be argued that the gap would have widened in its absence.

Despite the uncertain record, ESPRIT's promise was enough to encourage imitators, notable for the subtlety of their acronyms, if not for their results. A new program for **Basic Research in Industrial Technology (BRITE)** and another that sought to perform Research in Advance Communications for Europe (RACE) were two examples. Finally, collaborative research was sought even beyond the borders of the EC. The **European Research Coordinating Agency (EUREKA),** an agency to institute shared research throughout western Europe, was established in 1985.

In most industries, heavy-handed protectionist and national champion policies were abandoned in favor of greater market logic, augmented and rationalized by the use of collaborative research; the exceptions to this were the defense and aerospace industries. These industries have not been subject to initiatives from the European Union itself but have been organized and promoted by agreements between national governments and companies acting through consortia. The most prominent of these is the Airbus Industrie, which is a subsidized and aggressive attempt to maintain European production of civilian air transport and to seize part of the global market from Boeing, which as a result of growth and merger had a near global monopoly.

European industrial policy has been most evident not in the promotion of growth but in easing the death throes of industrial contraction. The ancestor of today's EU was the European Coal and Steel Community, largely concerned with managing a downturn in demand in those basic industries. In steel, for example, the Commission considered itself faced with a crisis. It has at times organized the cartelization of the industry, used quotas to divide output between national firms, and has adopted both price guidelines and required minimum prices to avoid "excess" competition between producers and to coordinate an orderly reduction in overall output. The EU has also interceded with foreign suppliers to initiate voluntary export restraint. However, it also acted in both steel and textiles to prevent the subsidy of output by member governments. Any government grants to industry were only allowable if they were a part of a systematic industrial restructuring designed to reduce output in the medium term.

COMPETITION POLICY

In its early years the EC lacked a centralized competition policy. Each member country had its own approach, but only Britain, France, and Germany had effective antimerger legislation. The growing integration of the European market brought with it the need for a European policy, although member countries were reluctant to relinquish their authority to Brussels. As a compromise it was agreed that only large mergers would be an issue for the EU. If the combined annual turnover of the merging firms was in excess of ECU 5 billion, and at least ECU 250 million of that turnover was in nations of the EU, Brussels could act; otherwise action would be guided by national regulations.

These rules give European regulators a reach that is well beyond Europe's borders. For example, when the world's largest aircraft manufacturer, Boeing, sought to merge with McDonnell Douglas in 1997, the joint turnover and European sales put the case within the EU purview, and the deal was saved only by an 11th-hour compromise. The merger of two large U.S. firms, Allied Signal and Honeywell, was reviewed because of fears that it might threaten global competition in avionics. Although to date the Commission has only banned eight mergers, it has attached strings to many others—usually in the form of required asset disposition as a means to dilute a strong market positions.

One of Europe's merger problems is an asymmetry in the ease of hostile takeovers between countries. Takeovers are more feasible where there is an active **market for corporate control.** When most companies are publicly traded, rather than held by large institutional or family investors, there is a good chance of rivalry for control, which can be an effective means of correcting managerial failure and ensuring that investors get full share value. Within the EU, the market for control is most active in the United Kingdom, which has a high ratio of stock capitalization to GDP (112 percent in 1994) and a very active stock market. As barriers to international mergers fall, takeovers and industrial restructuring have occurred in the United Kingdom at a rapid pace. In countries characterized by low market capitalization (34 percent of GDP in France and only 26 percent in Germany in 1994), the scope for mergers has been much more limited. Barriers to takeovers caused by low stock market activity has been augmented in many countries by other factors. These included the predominance of family holdings in Italy, the important role of banks as shareholders in Germany, and legislation against hostile takeovers in France. Thus merger policy represents another example of the clash between an Anglo-Saxon market-reliant approach and a continental model (which we also see in Japan) that puts greater emphasis on long-term relations between investors, managers, and employees.[9] There is a certain irony in that the lowered barriers to intra-European mergers made firms in the market-oriented United Kingdom easy takeover targets for German and French companies that subscribed to an approach that put much less reliance on short-term value realization. The British have lobbied for a leveling of the playing field that would make continental European firms more easy to acquire. While it is conceivable, and even likely, that specific legislation that impedes mergers will be removed, the barrier takeovers imposed by low capitalization, or bloc holding, are not easy to legislate away.

As well as being able to deny or modify mergers, the Commission has also the power to investigate any anticompetitive arrangement and levy fines for such issues as price fixing or supply constraint. For example, it charged that a cartel existed in the cement industry and imposed fines totaling 268 million ECUs on 33 producers. The Commission also tries to deny the use of subsidies for national firms and has acted several times especially against "flag" airlines—including Air France, Iberia, and Olympic.

SOCIAL POLICY

What should be apparent from much of this discussion is that the prevailing social philosophy of the European Union is concerned with the construction and maintenance of what is now referred to as cohesion, and this frequently has adverse consequences for competitiveness. In fact, it is to some extent that the debate that much occupied economists in the 1960s—the two "Es," equity versus efficiency—has within the EU become the two "Cs," cohesion versus competitiveness.

THE PROBLEM OF UNEMPLOYMENT

The most serious problem undermining the cohesion of the European Union as a whole is unemployment. For the bulk of the postwar period, unemployment within the countries that now make up the EU was very low, especially relative to the United States. As Table 9.5 shows, through the middle of the 1970s the rate was between 2 percent and 2.5 percent of the active workforce. However, global stagnation of the late 1970s and early 1980s saw a sharp rise to almost double digits, and despite a decline in the activity rate, it has failed to fall significantly since. Now almost 18 million people are registered as unemployed. The situation is possibly more serious than that simple figure indicates because a large number of people

---

[9]The clash of cultures was vividly illustrated in November 1999 when Vodafone of the United Kingdom attempted the takeover of Mannesmann. This was not only the biggest ever hostile takeover, it was also the first attempted hostile acquisition of a German company. The takeover was even opposed by German Chancellor Gerhard Schroeder, who opined, "Hostile takeovers destroy the culture of the company . . . those who launch such ventures in Germany underestimate the virtues of our joint [union-management] codirection. . . . For these reasons I am warning those who want to jump into such an adventure to be careful." Following a considerable increase in the offer price, Vodafone was ultimately successful in acquiring the German company (*The Economist*, 12 February 2000, 68).

■ TABLE 9.5

THE GROWTH OF THE EMPLOYMENT GAP*

		1960	1973	1985	1991	1995
1	Population of working age[†]	193.8	208.4	229.7	246.0	249.0
2	Activity rate, % (= 3/1)	68.9	66.9	65.7	67.7	66.6
3	Active population (4 + 6)	133.4	139.5	150.9	166.6	165.9
4	Unemployment	3.1	3.5	14.8	13.6	17.9
5	Unemployment rate (%)	2.3	2.5	9.8	8.1	10.7
6	Total employment	130.41	136.0	136.2	153.0	148.1
7	Employment rate (6/1)	67.3	65.2	59.3	62.2	59.5
8	Potential employment[‡]	128.4	138.1	152.2	163.0	165.0
9	Employment gap1 (= 6−8)	2.0	−2.1	−16.0	−10.0	−16.9
10	Potential employment[§]	135.6	145.9	160.8	172.2	174.3
11	Employment gap2 (= 6−10)	−5.3	−10.0	−24.6	−19.3	−26.2

*Includes E. Germany.

[†]15–64.

[‡]Average rate in Europe 1960–1973 (66.2%).

[§]Comparable to the average of the Scandinavian countries, the United States, and Japan.

SOURCE: European Commission.

have dropped out of the active workforce because of their inability to find a job. One way of viewing the problem is to estimate how many jobs would need to be created to get back to the kind of employment rates (numbers of employed workers per member of the adult population) that were typical in the relatively prosperous 1960s. During that time an employment rate of about 66.2 percent was typical. That would imply that some 16.9 million jobs would need to be created to get back to the conditions that prevailed then. Another more exhaustive standard is to estimate the required job creation necessary if activity rates in the European Union were to mirror those that prevail in Japan, Scandinavia, and the United States. In such a case, the unemployment gap rises to about 26 million persons.

CAUSES OF UNEMPLOYMENT IN EUROPE

Whatever measure is used, it is clear that Europe's employment performance gives considerable cause for alarm. It represents a nexus of problems for which there is no easy solution and threatens, because of its cost, the very nature of the welfare state in the EU. Europe (as a group of nations) and the European Union (as an institution) are committed to an idea of a high degree of social stability and social cohesion. This means that there is a strong preference for maintaining a substantial degree of social protection, guaranteeing incomes and services for those out of work, and to maintaining a commitment to a principle of "equal pay for equal work," rather than relying on the unfettered working of a labor market. Both of these objectives tend to lessen labor market flexibility, creating unemployment. The high degree of joblessness entails a high degree of expenditure on social protection.

Public expenditure on social protection averages 22% of GDP in EU-15 on the basis of 1990 data, approaching 35% in some Northern European countries, as opposed to 15% in the U.S. and only 12% in Japan). The difference in the amount spent by governments is also backed by different popular expectations; a very large majority of Europeans seem to expect their governments to provide a basic income for all, including income support for the unemployed. . . . Solidarity has become a key word in the political culture of European societies; is it likely to change in the new economic environment characterized by high rates of unemployment and the growing financial pressures on the welfare states? [10]

THE SYSTEM OF COLLECTIVE BARGAINING.   In Western Europe most workers are covered by national wage agreements negotiated at the industry-wide level, as opposed to being subject to more flexible plant or enterprise agreements that are more common in the U.S. context. Individual employers, therefore have remarkably little control over what they pay their workers, a source of labor market inflexibility contributing to joblessness. The rising unemployment rates in EU countries have favored the trend toward decentralization, and national and industry-wide bargaining are now losing ground. Even in countries such as Germany, where industry-wide negotiations are still the norm, there is increasing recourse to "opening clauses" that allow works councils and employers to negotiate amendments to these agreements at the enterprise level.

Despite these trends, decentralization is still limited in most western European countries. An International Labour Organization (ILO) report found that

In 1995, enterprise agreements covered only 8% of the private sector in the Netherlands (compared to 75% for industry wide agreements), 14% in Spain (compared to about 70% for industry wide agreements) and 15% in France (compared to over 80% for industrywide agreements). In Sweden, while central wage agreements are no longer the order of the day, bargaining at industry level remains a current practice. Even in Germany, considered a bastion of the European model, employers in the chemical and metal industries continue to favor industry wide bargaining. The major change that has occurred is that industry wide bargaining now offers much more scope for enterprise negotiation on day to day productivity issues. [11]

Although most bargaining is at the industry—not the firm—level, works councils are increasingly relied on to encourage dialogue and cooperation within the enterprise. The goal of these councils is, in most cases, to restructure work assignments in line with technological changes and competitive pressures and to maintain employment. The ILO report concludes that "with very few exceptions, collective bargaining in Europe focuses primarily on the issue of working time (taken here in the broadest sense: reduction, organization, job sharing, retirement, etc.) and related means of saving jobs." The same report finds that both industry-wide and enterprise-level agreements show similar preoccupations: "the most

---

[10] Tsoukalis, *The New European Economy Revisited*, 115.

[11] International Labour Organization, *World Labour Report*, 1996–1997 (access through Web page Presskit).

frequent job-related topics are wage moderation or even reduction, reduction in working time with a corresponding drop in wages, and payment of overtime at the base rate or in the form of compensatory leave." Measures to ease access to employment, including hiring at reduced rates and increasing the number of apprenticeship places, are often parts of the agreements.

HIGH RESERVATION WAGES.   The high degree of social protection in Europe means that the cost of losing a job is much less than in many other labor markets, and this has an impact on productivity. Furthermore, the generous income support for the unemployed means that a job search tends to be less pressured than in, say, the United States; this leads to workers adopting a high reservation wage, the lowest rate that will induce an unemployed person to accept a job. The "replacement" rate (the percentage of take-home pay that continues to be received after loss of employment) varies from country to country and according to family circumstance, as well as with the duration of unemployment. In France, for example, a married person with two children receives 88 percent of take-home pay when first unemployed. The Organization for Economic Cooperation and Development (OECD) average is a more modest 77 percent, largely because of low replacement levels in the United States. Even by the 60th month of unemployment, a French worker would still receive 83 percent of initial in-work take-home pay.[12] Recognizing these high levels of support as being in part responsible for unemployment, European governments have struggled to contain the costs of social protection and to lower benefit levels. Until 1993 a unemployed worker in Sweden would receive over 90 percent of in-work pay when first unemployed. Reforms in 1993 reduced that to 80 percent, and in 1996 it was further reduced to 75 percent.[13]

A case can be made for the economic efficiency of more protracted periods of unemployment, since a longer period of search should ultimately ensure a better match between the requirements of the vacancy and the skills of the applicant. Moreover, European nations tend to pay close attention to active labor market policy, using government institutions to place the unemployed and using job training schemes and public employment as a means of changing the skills of the unemployed. However, while labor exchanges might speed up the process somewhat, the high level of income protection means a loss of urgency on the part of the job seeker and leads to higher rates of unemployment and a less flexible labor market.

NONWAGE COSTS.   While maintaining social solidarity is a priority in western Europe, there is increased realization of its cost. The transfers to the unemployed, the disabled, and the elderly are generally financed by heavy payroll taxes, nominally shared by employers and workers, although the real incidence drives up the cost of labor and acts as a deterrent to taking on more workers. The actual burden

---

[12] OECD, *Economic Survey of France*, 1996/1997, 81

[13] European Parliament, Directorate General for Research, "Social and Labour Market Policy in Sweden," W-13, 39, July 1997.

TOTAL TAXES ON LABOR IN THE EU

	Implicit Tax Rate (%)		As a Percentage of Total Tax Receipts		As a Percentage of GDP	
	1970	1995	1970	1995	1970	1995
EU6	28.7	44.5	43.2	52.5	14.5	22.7
EU15	—	42.1	—	51.4	—	21.4
Belgium	31.3	45.7	43.3	51.2	15.6	23.9
Denmark	34.7	47.6	46.2	48.9	18.7	25.1
Germany	29.6	44.1	44.2	56.2	15.8	24.0
Greece	—	45.9	—	45.1	—	14.4
Spain	—	38	—	48.8	—	16.9
France	30.5	44.4	42.9	51.8	15.1	23.0
Ireland	16.1	30.1	26.6	39.5	8.3	13.6
Italy	21.6	44	38	44.3	9.8	18.1
Luxembourg	27.5	29.6	41.3	37.4	12.8	16.4
Netherlands	34.2	48.8	50.6	55.5	18.9	25.2
Austria	—	44.5	—	55.2	—	24.2
Portugal	—	36.7	—	46.9	—	17.4
Finland	—	53.7	—	59.5	—	27.7
Sweden	—	56.2	—	62.8	—	32.0
United Kingdom	21.7	27.0	34.6	42.0	12.8	14.7

SOURCE: Eurostat.

varies from nation to nation within the EU. France, for example, has a generous social protection scheme and has experienced one of the sharpest increases in the level of unemployment. This has instituted a vicious cycle: rising unemployment pushes up the total cost of social protection, causing in turn an increase in the payroll taxes. However, because payroll taxes are levied on a shrinking workforce and must support more dependents, the tax rates have to rise, discouraging employment. By the mid-1990s the combined payroll tax on the lowest paid, and least skilled, workers was about 62 percent, with employers paying social security contributions of about 40 percent of gross wages and the employees contributing a further 22 percent.[14] Thus, although increases in wages themselves were moderating, real costs for unskilled labor in France were about 40 percent higher than in the United States.

Table 9.6 shows the total taxes (payroll—both employers' and employees' shares—and income taxes) that fall on wage income in the members of the EU. While the various components of the total tax bite vary from country,[15] in every

[14] OECD, *Economic Survey of France*, 1996/1997, 71.

[15] Denmark, for example, has a generous social protection scheme but finances it almost entirely out of general tax revenue and has only a very small social insurance tax.

country there is a sizable "wedge" that distorts the labor leisure decision and raises costs to employers, creating a bias for off-shore production and capital intensity.

FRAGMENTED LABOR MARKETS. Although the European Union constitutes a single economic space, its labor market is highly fragmented because regional, national, cultural, and linguistic differences cause pockets of high unemployment to coexist with areas of tight labor demand. This is true even within a single member country. For example, unemployment in northern Italy's Alto Adige region is only 3.4 percent, a figure that would be regarded as close to full employment by most economists, whereas in Campania and Calabria in the south (barely a day's drive) the rate is more than 25 percent. Within the EU as whole there are even wider differences. Luxembourg has a jobless rate of 3.2 percent, while Andalucia, a poor region of southern Spain, experiences 32 percent unemployment, an unusually pronounced difference in the absence of legal barriers to the movement of labor. In fact labor flows among the nations of the EU have actually decreased as the barriers to movement have been removed. "The internal market programme seems to have had very little effect on Intra-EU labour flows which remain very small. Thus, labour mobility should not be expected to play a significant role as a means of economic adjustment in the context of a . . . monetary union."[16]

THE ANTIEMPLOYMENT BIAS OF GROWTH. Europe's performance was not strong during the 1990s, and certainly unemployment would be lower had the aggregate growth rate been higher. But as Table 9.7 shows, Europe's growth has been antiemployment in its character, both in the absolute and when compared to the United States and Japan. At 1.4 percent per annum, European growth rate was slower than that of the United States, which averaged 2.3 percent per annum over the same period. However, the residual growth of GDP that cannot be explained by increases in the employment of factors of production was more rapid than in the United States. Such growth, so-called total factor productivity growth (TFP), is generally ascribed to technical progress and innovation. TFP alone accounted for 1 percent of Europe's 1.4 percent average growth performance. In addition, the European economies substituted increased capital for labor, and this increase in capital accounted for a further 1.1 percent expansion per annum. Labor employed actually fell. Although growth both due to technical change and capital deepening is generally regarded as a positive long-term development for an economy, the consequence for Europe in the medium term has been growing unemployment.

In short, Europe has grown at a slow pace, and such growth as has occurred is biased toward economizing on labor, and the result has been growing joblessness. The data of Table 9.7 are merely an accounting of this process; the causes have already been itemized—the system of collective bargaining, the high reservation wage brought about by generous social protection, high nonwage costs, and fragmented labor markets. To this should probably be added another factor: the shift

---

[16]Tsoukalis, 120.

■ **TABLE 9.7**

OUTPUT, PRODUCTIVITY, AND CAPITAL LABOR SUBSTITUTION (ANNUAL PERCENTAGE RATES)

	1961–1973	1974–1985	1986–1995	1986–1990	1991–1995
1. Technical Progress = TFP Growth					
European Union	2.8	1.0	1.2	1.5	1.0
United States	0.6	0.9	0.8	0.6	0.9
Japan	6.3	1.1	0.9	2.3	−0.5
2. Macroeconomic Capital-Labor Substitution = Labor Saving Growth (2 = 3 − 1)					
European Union	1.5	1.0	0.7	0.4	1.1
United States	0.3	0.1	0.1	0.0	0.2
Japan	1.8	1.6	1.1	1.2	1.1
3. Apparent Labor Productivity Growth (3 = 1 + 2)					
European Union	4.4	2.0	1.9	1.9	1.9
United States	1.9	0.5	0.8	0.6	1.1
Japan	8.2	2.7	2.0	3.6	0.6
4. Employment Creating Growth (4 + 5 − 3)					
European Union	0.3	0.0	0.4	1.3	−0.5
United States	1.9	1.8	1.7	2.1	1.2
Japan	1.3	0.7	0.9	1.0	0.7
5. Actual GDP Growth (5 = 1 + 2 + 4)					
European Union	4.7	2.0	2.3	3.3	1.4
United States	3.9	2.3	2.5	2.8	2.3
Japan	9.7	3.4	2.9	4.6	1.3

SOURCE: European Commission.

to more restrictive fiscal policy occasioned by trying to match the Maastricht criteria, which has resulted in a contraction in government service expenditures.

THE EU PROGRAM ON UNEMPLOYMENT

The Commission and the European Council are aware that unemployment is a threat to social cohesion, despite the paradox that joblessness has been created by an attempt to promote social cohesion through highly redistributive policies. At the 1994 meeting of the European Council in Essen, an outline plan to address unemployment was presented, building on a 1990 White Paper on Employment and Growth. The plan envisaged five sets of policies to tackle the joblessness problem.[17]

Some of these are rather "old hat" and represent the repetition of long-held beliefs rather than a true change in policy. Among these are a faith in **vocational training** and **life-long education,** and aid for groups most hard hit by unemployment. There is also a commitment to "increase the **employment-intensiveness** of

---

[17]"The Presidency Conclusions" of the European Council Meeting, Essen, December 1994, can be located at http://www.europarl.eu.int/dg7/summits/en/ess1.htm#emplIn

growth." However, there are also more innovative ideas. One of these consists of a wages policy that encourages labor-intensive investment by moderating wage increases to a rate below the growth of productivity. Another is a series of initiatives, particularly at regional and local level, that create jobs in the environmental and social services spheres. The European Council also attempted to come to grips with some of the root causes of unemployment—high nonwage labor costs and income support policies that are "detrimental to readiness to work."

REDISTRIBUTION AMONG NATIONS IN THE EU

The European Union is a redistributive organization. A variety of programs redistribute income among individuals and nations. Table 9.8 gives some estimates of the extent of that redistribution. Because of administrative costs and the provision of foreign aid, the costs of the EU outweigh the allocated benefits. Some countries benefit from administrative more than others. Belgium has the benefit of the Commission being located in its capital, a considerable gain to the economy of the Brussels region. Luxembourg and France also gain from the Court of Justice and the Parliament, respectively. Given these limitations we can see that there are six

▪ TABLE 9.8

NET TRANSFERS THROUGH THE EU BUDGET, 1980–1994 (RECEIPTS MINUS CONTRIBUTIONS EXPRESSED IN MILLIONS OF ECUS AS AS PERCENTAGE OF NATIONAL GDP)

	1980		1988		1994[*]	
	ECU millions	Percentage	ECU millions	Percentage	ECU millions	Percentage
Belgium	−273.4	−0.32	−995.0	−0.79	−307.4	−0.16
Denmark	333.9	0.7	350.9	0.38	188.1	0.15
Germany	−1670.0	−0.28	−6107.1	−0.6	−13,834.1	−0.9
Greece	—	—	1491.6	3.3	3812.6	4.62
Spain	—	—	1334.3	0.46	3006.0	0.74
France	380.4	0.08	−1780.9	−0.22	−2801.0	−0.25
Ireland	687.2	5.0	1159.3	4.3	1726.9	3.94
Italy	681.2	0.21	124.2	0.02	−2805.7	−0.58
Luxembourg	−5.1	−0.15	−67.4	−1.2	249.8	2.12
Netherlands	394.5	0.32	1150.0	0.6	−1811.1	−0.64
Portugal	—	—	514.9	1.45	1880.9	2.55
United Kingdom	−1364.6	−0.35	−2070.0	−0.3	−1585.4	−0.18

Note: Approximately 10% of all expenditure is absorbed by administrative costs or is used for development aid. These outlays cannot be apportioned among the member states and consequently the aggregate of member states' contributions to the EU budget exceeds the total for receipts.

[*]For 1994 adminstrative costs have been apportioned among member states. Therefore, for those countries with European institutions, namely Belgium, Luxembourg, and to a lesser extent France, results are biased.

SOURCE: Court of Auditors, Annual Reports; and Commission (for GDP data). [Loukas Tsoukalis, *The New European Economy Revisited*, 218.]

"gainers" and six "payers." The gainers are primarily the small poor countries (Greece, Portugal, and Ireland) that are beneficiaries of the CAP, and the various forms of structural funds including the newly established cohesion funds. The gains of these three countries are considerable—close to 5 percent of GDP in the case of Greece in 1994. Spain, Denmark, and Portugal also gain. The main payee is Germany with both the largest economy and the largest net loss as a percentage of GDP.

KEY TERMS AND CONCEPTS

Basic Research in Industrial Technology (BRITE)

cohesion

Common Agricultural Policy (CAP)

Common External tariff (CET)

consumption effect

Economic and Monetary Union (EMU)

employment intensiveness

European Central Bank (ECB)

European Currency Unit (ECU)

European Economic Area (EEA)

European Monetary Institute (EMI)

European Monetary System (EMS)

European Research Coordinating Agency (EUREKA)

European Strategic Programme for Research in Information Technology (ESPRIT)

laissez faire

life-long education

Lomé agreements

Maastricht criteria

market for corporate control

most favored nation principle

optimum currency area

reservation wages

stability and growth pact

structural funds

trade creation effect

trade diversion effect

vocational training

QUESTIONS FOR DISCUSSION

1. Do you think that the creation of regional organizations like the EU will hasten or impede moves to freer global trade?

2. Why does the trade creation effect enhance welfare, while trade diversion lessens it?

3. Are you surprised that the openness of the EU with respect to the rest of the world has not changed since the 1960s? What accounts for this?

4. Why was it thought necessary to improve the Maastricht criteria on potential entrants of the EMU?

5. How is the convergence issue to be handled after the creation of the EMU?

6. Is Europe an optimum currency area?

7. Why is it important to have an independent central bank for Europe?

8. Has the common agricultural policy been a success?

9. Why is cohesion now the most important issue in the EU?

10. Discuss the evolution of competition policy in the EU. Why is the EU concerned at the merger of two U.S. firms like Allied Signal and Honeywell?

11. What have been the root causes of growing unemployment in the EU? Are they the result of the economic system?

RESOURCES

BOOKS AND ARTICLES

Britton, Andrew, and David Mayes. *Achieving Monetary Union in Europe.* London: Sage Publications, 1992.

Buiter, Willem, Giancarlo Corsetti, and Nouriel Roubini. "Excessive Deficits: Sense and Nonsense in the Treaty of Maastricht." *Economic Policy,* April 1993, 58–100.

Devinney, Timothy M., and William C. Hightower. *European Markets after 1992.* Lexington, Mass.: D.C. Heath and Co., 1991, 52.

El-Agraa, Ali M., ed. *The Economics of the European Community.* 3rd ed. New York: St. Martin's Press, 1990.

Fossati, Amedeo, and Giorgio Panella, eds. *Fiscal Federalism in the European Union.* Vol. 9 of *Routledge Studies in the European Economy.* New York: Routledge, 1999.

Frieden, Jeffrey, Daniel Gros, and Erik Jones, eds. *The New Political Economy of EMU.* London: Rowman and Littlefield, 1998.

Molle, Willem. *The Economics of European Integration (Theory, Practice, Policy).* Aldershot, England: Dartmouth Publishing, 1990.

Nevin, Edward. *The Economics of Europe.* New York: St. Martin's Press, 1990.

"A Survey of Business in Europe: Present Pupils." *The Economist,* 23 November 1996, 1–16.

Swann, Dennis. *The Economics of the Common Market,* 6th ed. London: Penguin Books, 1988.

Tsoukalis, Loukas. *The New European Economy Revisited.* Oxford: Oxford University Press, 1997.

United Nations. *Economic Commission for Europe Annual Reports.*

ASIAN ECONOMIES

10

JAPAN

INTRODUCTION

With a population of 125 million and a GDP in 1997 of roughly $4 trillion,[1] the second largest in the world, there can be little doubt that Japan remains a formidable economic power, although compared with its position a decade ago it is much diminished. In the late 1980s, prevailing opinion regarded the Japanese economic system as a juggernaut, on an inexorable course to being the world's leading economy. Western economic commentators were prone to see in Japan's interventionist policies an advantage that would lead to the eclipse of American business unless strong countermeasures were enacted or Japanese practices imitated.[2] The situation is now very different. In recent years real gross domestic product (GDP) growth in Japan has lagged behind that in the United States and much of Europe; between 1990 and 1997 it barely topped 1 percent per annum. Japan's financial system, the core of its industrial policy, is under great pressure; most banks need refinancing, and many need closing. Perhaps most important, much of Japan's self-confidence has been lost, which is reflected in indecisive policy making and a lack of consumer and investor confidence. Admired, envied, and imitated a decade ago, the Japanese system is now openly questioned, and reform at the most fundamental level is called for. This chapter provides an overview of the development and operation of the Japanese system and examines its prospects for success and reform.

A BRIEF OVERVIEW OF ECONOMIC HISTORY

EARLY DEVELOPMENT

The modern development of Japan dates from the appearance of the so-called black ships of the American Commodore Matthew Perry in Tokyo Bay in 1853. This intrusion of the world into Japan's isolationism prompted rapid social and economic change, fostered and accelerated by the restoration of the Meiji dynasty in 1868. The feudal system, which had been preserved in Japan, was brushed aside,

---

[1] Using the current official exchange rate.

[2] See, for example, Clyde Prestowitz, *Trading Places: How We Are Giving Our Future to Japan and How to Reclaim It* (New York: Basic Books, 1993).

and the warrior **Samurai** class was integrated into the civil society. Most important, the government initiated a program of state-led industrialization and modernization, which not only transformed Japan's economic base but also imbued Japanese capitalism with many of the distinctive characteristics visible today. A strong governmental role in industrial development has remained a characteristic of the Japanese model. Aggressive public investment provided the basic infrastructure for growth through spending on communication, railways, postal services, and education. The government also entered direct production in many industries including steel, engineering, and shipbuilding. The financial sector to this day is dominated by the publicly owned Bank of Japan, established in 1882.

Alongside the growth of the state-sponsored industries, social pressure was used to stimulate the growth of the private sector. The government assisted and guided development, encouraging the acquisition of foreign techniques and the imitation of western industrial and military technology. The members of the Samurai aristocracy, who were at best an anachronism in Japan and who constituted a potential deterrent to progress, were encouraged and financed to undertake industrial ventures. Although not all of the new industrial class had Samurai roots, the effect of government sponsorship of a limited number of leading families was to be one of the important features of Japanese economic development for the succeeding century.

The favored family industrial groups grew into *zaibatsu*—closely held, diversified industrial and financial combines that dominated economic activity. Each combine was composed of roughly 20 to 30 firms that generally spanned the gamut of economic activity—coal mines, steelworks, shipyards, banks, trading companies, insurance, and so forth. This system led to the substantial concentration of economic power in a relatively small number of diversified groups. Mitsui, the largest of the prewar *zaibatsu*, employed about 1.8 million workers; Mitsubishi, the second largest, employed more than a million.

Class links between the leaders of industry and the members of the government, and the great concentration of economic power, led the Japanese political system toward corporatism, a close alliance of government, finance, industry, and, importantly in the Japanese case, the military. Economic growth in Japan was rapid, shown in Figure 10.1, which depicts an index of real gross national product (GNP) from 1885 to 1930. The early part of this period might well be termed the first Japanese economic miracle, during which time Japan established itself as an industrial power. Real GNP rose by 60 percent between 1887 and 1897. Despite some setbacks between 1898 and 1904, GNP doubled once again between 1905 and 1917. Growth was spurred by the onset of World War I in 1914, which sharply raised global demand for heavy industrial goods. The Japanese metal, defense, and engineering industries all benefited, and the resultant surge in exports spilled over into all sectors of the economy. The collapse of demand after 1918 hurt output in the short run, but the economy recovered by the late 1920s.

In contrast to the rest of the world economy, Japan continued to expand throughout the global depression of the 1930s. Growth was led by the surge in military purchases required for the military occupation of Manchuria and China, and

■ **FIGURE 10.1**

JAPANESE ECONOMIC GROWTH 1887–1930

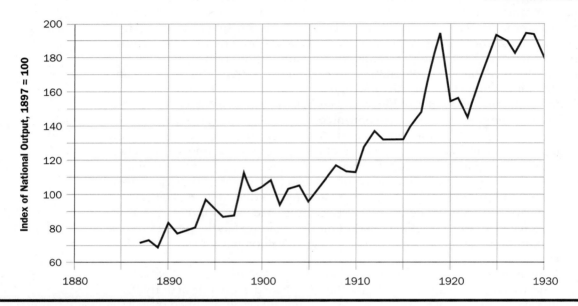

SOURCE: Data from Boulding and Gleason, 242–243.

continued until the onset of more general warfare in 1939, when the military burden began to crowd out industrial investment. The destruction and economic dislocation caused by the conclusion of World War II led to the complete collapse of the Japanese economy. Figure 10.2 shows that by 1946 output was well below the levels of 1930.

POSTWAR RECONSTRUCTION

After the war, the United States occupation authorities radically restructured the Japanese economy. The *zaibatsu* and the close relationship between industry and state were considered by the Americans to have been at least partly responsible for Japanese military adventurism in China and the Pacific.[3] Therefore the occupation authorities decided that breaking up the *zaibatsu* was essential to curbing future expansionism.

Subsidiary enterprises of parent holding companies were converted into independent entities and their share capital sold off. For example, the Mitsui *zaibatsu* was split into 180 nominally independent firms whose shares were then sold into

---

[3] In fact, later scholarship has found that the link between the traditional *zaibatsu* and the expansionist policy of the 1930s was very questionable. The highest involvement seems to have been with a collection of new firms with specific interests in Manchuria and China. See Boulding and Gleason, 253.

■ FIGURE 10.2

JAPANESE GROWTH 1930–1960

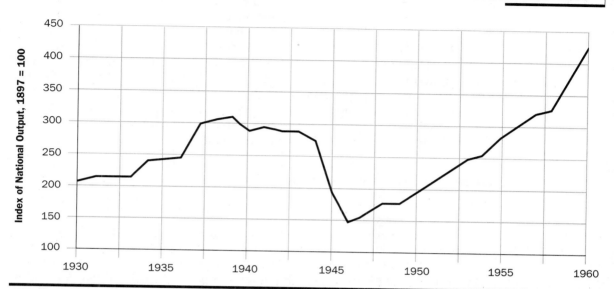

SOURCE: Data from Boulding and Gleason.

and traded on an open market. However, the destruction of the Japanese economy during the war had left little wealth in the hands of individuals. Most of the demand for shares of the newly independent enterprises had to come from other corporations, often in the form of exchange for their own shares. In fact, much of the stock in many firms was acquired by companies that were themselves former members of the same *zaibatsu*. Such "sister" companies had historical allegiances, trading links and a high degree of proprietary information that naturally gave them interest in each other. The dissolution of the *zaibatsu* was accompanied by antitrust regulation, which was modeled on American policy, but in actuality it was weakly enforced. The result was that the *zaibatsu* were not eliminated but rather were transformed into **keiretsu**—diversified industrial groups similar to the *zaibatsu* but held together by interlocking shareholding rather than being held by a single parent. (More on the structure of these *keiretsu* is presented later.)

THE EMERGENCE OF THE "IRON TRIANGLE"

The late 1940s and 1950s saw rapid and sustained economic growth, mostly attributable to the reemployment of the labor and capital idled at the end of the war. Japan exploited its comparative advantage in labor-intensive goods, and by 1955 output had once more reached the levels of the 1930s. By 1960 the "gap" created by the war and its aftermath had been largely eliminated. (See Figure 10.2.)

Although expansion was rapid in the 1950s, Japan was far from a harmonious society. Labor/management relations were contentious and strikes, frequently

quite violent, were common. The government threw its weight behind the employers and helped them break the more radical labor unions—especially in the
coal-mining industry. This period saw the modern model of Japanese economic
system evolve more clearly. Power rested on three supports—the politicians (principally those of the Liberal Party, which held a near monopoly of government
throughout the postwar period), the leadership of industry (primarily the heads of
the *keiretsu*), and the planning and financial technocracy, mainly in the **Ministry of
International Trade and Industry (MITI)** and the **Ministry of Finance (MoF).** This
constellation of power is usually called the "iron triangle." In Japan, in contrast to
most west European countries, labor took a back seat. Docile company-organized
unions emerged, and aggressive collective bargaining was abandoned in return for
the paternalistic principle of "life-time employment."

SUCCESS OF THE JAPANESE ECONOMY

Throughout most of the postwar period, Japan must be regarded as an immensely
successful economy. From the low point of 1945, Japan enjoyed rapid and sustained year-on-year economic expansion for more than 50 years. Growth slowed
over time as the potentialities for expansive growth, using under-employed factors
of production, and "catch-up," facilitated by importing more advanced technology
from abroad, became exhausted. From an average of 4.3 percent per year in the
1970s, growth of GDP slowed to 4.0 percent in the 1980s. The pace slackened further in the 1990s and had turned negative by 1998. However, Japan is today still the
second largest economy in the world and is also second in terms of GDP per head,
which in 1997 measured about $38,000 in current exchange terms.[4] Unemployment
remains low by international standards, although it has risen recently to levels that
are uncomfortable in the Japanese context. In 1998 it reached 3.7 percent, the highest since the 1950s. For the past three decades, Japan has enjoyed a balance of
payments surplus and is currently the world's largest overseas investor in terms
of annual capital flows, with its net creditor position fast becoming the world's
largest.

The distribution of income in Japan is very even in comparison to most developed market economies, close to the "social-democracies" of northern Europe. The
average income of the top 20 percent of households is only 4.3 times that of the lowest. Japan has also performed well in social terms. Conventional measures of social
dislocation (crime rates, incarceration rates, etc.) are all modest relative to other developed market economies.

There is no single causal explanation of Japan's growth and many different
policy lessons have been drawn from the country's experience. Success has been
attributed to the system of labor management, the determining role of industrial

---

[4]Data are from the *World Development Report.* Comparisons are less favorable in terms of purchasing
power parity, because of the high cost of living in Japan, particularly for food and accommodation. In
this measure Japan ranks sixth with per-head GDP of $23,400. The comparable figure for the United
States is $28,740.

policy, the system of directed credit, respect for social order, and the absence of large defense expenditures (which may have allowed for high investment rates). Nevertheless, the current slow growth of the economy has led to a critical re-assessment of the Japanese model, and a skeptical reappraisal of the lessons to be learned, particularly with regard to the financial sector.

SOCIAL CHARACTERISTICS

The Japanese economy and its performance must be viewed in the context of a broader society. Westerners, particularly those in the Anglo-Saxon tradition, value a market system, in part at least, for its impersonal rationality. This is not the case in Japan. Permeating both society and the economy is a deep sense of interpersonal responsibility. In some ways Japanese society still resembles the vertical and reciprocal personal obligations that characterized feudalism. Relations within the firm tend to be hierarchical and, by and large, respectful. This also reflects Confucian thought, which stresses personal respect for authority and mutual obligation between members of society. Consequently, while bureaucrats tend to be mistrusted in the United States, in Japan they have enjoyed great respect, because they are the immediate embodiment of authority. Strangely to western eyes, similar respect has also been afforded to politicians, despite the almost ceaseless corruption scandals that have permeated recent political life in Japan.

In Japan there is a high degree of individual identification with a variety of collective institutions, reinforcing the system of reciprocal obligation. The family is of prime importance. Children, for example, are expected to care for their parents, and they do to much higher degree than in the United States. In Japan more than half of all retired persons live with their offspring, although this tendency is declining with time. School and university affiliations tend to be long lasting. The workers of the major firms identify with their employers to a higher degree than would be found in the United States. When asked for their occupation, Japanese are prone to tell you who they work for, rather than what they do. This close identification is a result of the "lifetime employment" obligation of the employers to some workers (discussed later), but this is a relationship under some pressure as Japanese firms respond to economic problems by downsizing. Within firms, workers are organized in groups, or cliques, that again are characterized by personal obligation and mutual assistance.

INDUSTRIAL GROUPS—THE *KEIRETSU*

Since the prewar *zaibatsu* were considered by the United States to bear some responsibility for the aggressive nationalism that led to World War II, the American occupying authorities insisted on their dissolution and to prevent their reemergence, a ban against holding companies was written into antimonopoly legislation. The *keiretsu* groups that emerged are looser in structure than the *zaibatsu* and are

■ FIGURE 10.3

JAPAN'S INDUSTRIAL GROUPS: THE *KEIRETSU*

SOURCE: Nanto, 238.

■ TABLE 10.1

THE SEVEN LARGEST COMPONENTS OF THE MITSUBISHI *KEIRETSU*, 1997

	Revenues ($ millions)	Profits ($ millions)	Assets ($ millions)	Stockholder's Equity ($ millions)	Employment
1. Mitsubishi	140,204	394	77,871	8,864	35,000
2. Mitsubishi Chemical	15,379	− 106	15,981	3,883	28,933
3. Mitsubishi Electric	33,073	76	33,096	6,311	113,353
4. Mitsubishi Heavy Industries	27,899	1,097	35,161	10,862	67,117
5. Mitsubishi Materials	10,536	131	13,247	2,479	29,724
6. Mitsubishi Motors	32,601	103	26,064	3,921	27,827
7. Mitsubishi Trust & Banking	11,130	100	150,576	5,899	6,224
Total	270,822	1,795	351,996	42,219	308,178

SOURCE: *Fortune 500.*

held together by a variety of devices including cross-holding of shares, the use of a single group bank, reliance on a group trading company for sales and project coordination, consultation between CEOs in a presidential council, and the foundation of joint subsidiaries.

Figure 10.3 shows the eight largest conglomerate *keiretsu* in Japan, of which six are traditionally considered to be major. Three of these are linear descendants of the prewar *zaibatsu;* these are Mitsubishi, Mitsui, and Sumitomo. Each of these is grouped around a ***sogo sosha,*** or major **trading company** (discussed later) that creates a center for the group. An example of the operation of the various companies within a single "conglomerate" *keiretsu,* the Mitsubishi Group, is given in Table 10.1.

▪ TABLE 10.2

INTRAGROUP SHAREHOLDING OF THE SIX MAJOR *KEIRETSU*

	Average Linkage to Other Members*	Average Stake Size (percent)	Ratio to Total Capitalization
Mitsubishi	75.3	1.8	38.2
Sumitomo	94.5	1.6	28
Mitsui	57.6	1.3	19.3
Average of the prewar *zaibatsu*	75.8	1.6	28.5
Fuji	46.8	1.3	16.9
Sanwa	27.5	1.4	16.7
DKB	29.4	1	14.2
Average of the bank-centered groups	34.6	1.2	15.9
Average of the six major groups	55.2	1.4	22.2

* Average linkage is the percentage probability that any member firm of the group holds shares in another firm within the group.

SOURCE: OECD, *Economic Surveys of Japan*, 1995–1996, 156.

This table gives only figures for the largest members of the group, the ones that themselves show up in the *Fortune* 500 listings. The group, or "Community of Companies," as Mitsubishi likes to call itself, is much larger, embracing 40 major corporations in Japan and literally hundreds of overseas subsidiaries and joint ventures.

The principal way in which these groups are held together is by the cross-holding of equity capital, a practice that became prevalent immediately after the war, during the division and disposition of the *zaibatsu*. A further impetus to cross-holding of shares within a *keiretsu* was provided in the 1960s and 1970s when fears of hostile takeovers (possibly from foreign firms) arose and cross-holding presented an effective defense.

Table 10.2 shows the extent of cross-holding of shares in the major *keiretsu*, the ones that were illustrated in Figure 10.3. These data show that 38.2 percent of the capital of all the constituent members of the Mitsubishi group is held by firms that are themselves a part of the group. This is the highest rate of cross-holding of shares of any of the major *keiretsu*. The comparable figure for the Sumitomo Group, for example, is 28.0 percent, and that for Mitsui is only 19 percent. For the **bank-centered** *keiretsu* groups (Fuji, Sanwa, and DKB), the percentage is uniformly lower. The same table also shows that, on average for all the groups, there is a greater than 55 percent probability that any one firm within a major *keiretsu* will hold shares of any other firm within the group. For the economy as a whole, Hugh Patrick, a well-known authority on the Japanese economy, estimates that the cross-holdings amount to as much as 22 percent of total paid-up capital.

This cross-holding not only leads to close relationships within the group, but also creates a mutuality of interest and a reason to look to group members as both suppliers and customers. On the downside, however, the impact of cross-holding is to insulate management from an impartial "market for corporate control." Shares

SHAREHOLDING OF PUBLIC COMPANIES:
JAPAN AND THE UNITED STATES COMPARED BY CATEGORY

Category	U.S. Companies	Japanese Companies
Institutional investors	71.7	12.9
Financial institutions with business relationships	1.9	35.6
Nonfinancial institutions with business relationships	1.9	9.4
Parent companies or companies in same group (keiretsu)	1.9	30.7
Owner families	15.1	5.4
General investors	5.7	2.5
Other	1.9	3.5

SOURCE: OECD, *Economic Surveys of Japan*, 1995–1996, 153.

held within the group are rarely sold, and consequently executives are largely safe from outside takeover bids. Hence a depressed share price, the failure to realize a firm's potential, does not trigger the hostile mergers and asset stripping that occur in more aggressive capitalist markets. Table 10.3 contrasts the structure of shareholding in the United States and Japan, showing why the market for corporate control is likely to be more active in the United States.

Cross-holding is not the only means by which *keiretsu* are held together. Cohesion within the group is enhanced by the operation of "presidential councils," made up of the chief executive officers of the larger firms of the group. They generally convene once a month, and while they are not in theory policy-making bodies, they do discuss the current economic outlook, investment policies, market research, R&D, and other factors having a direct bearing on the efficient operation of the firms, as well as the potentialities of new business ventures. At a slightly lower level, *keiretsu* solidarity is further enhanced by the reciprocal representation of company officers on the boards of sister companies. Furthermore, startup companies to exploit new areas of business activity are often established as joint enterprises between group members, with equity capital put up by member companies, and a board including officers from the parent companies.

Conglomerate *keiretsu* groups (those with activities in a broad range of industries) are frequently grouped around a core company, which plays a leadership role in group management. Such a company may be a general integrated trading company or it may be a bank. Trading companies, which specialize in sales and marketing especially overseas, are, on this scale, institutions largely unique to Japan. Not only are the general trading companies themselves among the largest commercial operations in the world, but also each of the groups that are led by these companies has several major corporations that stand high in the *Fortune* 500 list. The *keiretsu* that have their origin in the prewar *zaibatsu* are also very old, tracing their history back some hundreds of years. The box titled "The Mitsui Group" traces the history of that organization from its origins in 1568.

Other conglomerate groups are best described as bank centered. (Although the *keiretsu*, of *zaibatsu* origin, include a group bank, the lead company in these cases

THE MITSUI GROUP

The Mitsui Group can be described as the largest business enterprise in the world. Its flagship company is the world's oldest general trading concern, Mitsui & Co. Ltd. The group, or *keiretsu*, consists of 842 companies, of which 333 are located outside Japan. The group has major operations in construction, investment, finance, transportation, machinery, chemicals, nonferrous metals, and foodstuffs. Japan's largest liquid propane gas transport fleet is operated by a Mitsui company, and Mitsui & Co. dominates the Japanese import market for cigarettes and sports and hobby goods. The economic slowdown in Japan and the strong yen have prompted Mitsui management to pursue a range of projects overseas, particularly around the Pacific Rim.

A BRIEF HISTORY

After they were defeated by the Japanese shogun Nobunaga, the Mitsui family fled Omi Province in 1568. Unemployed, the samurai Sokubei Mitsui opened a sake and soy sauce brewery at the urging of his wife, who eventually took over management of the business. She encouraged her sons to enter business and the youngest, Hachirobei,

went to Edo (now Tokyo) and opened a dry goods store in 1673. Breaking with Japanese retailing tradition, the store offered merchandise at fixed prices on a cash-and-carry basis.

In 1683 Hachirobei started a currency exchange that ultimately evolved into Mitsui Bank. The business received a boost in 1691 when it became the Osaka government's official money changer. The bank introduced money orders to Japan and profited by securing up to a 90-day float on funds transfers between Osaka, Edo, and Kyoto. Before he died in 1694, Hachirobei wrote a nontraditional will, by which control of the business passed to all related family members, not just to the eldest son's family.

In the mid 1800s the Japanese government ordered Mitsui to help finance its war with rebels. The family hired an outsider with government links, who managed to protect Mitsui from increasing demands for cash. The company then made a timely switch of support to the victorious rebel side and Mitsui became the bank of the Meiji government at the time of the restoration. The new government encouraged, as part of its industrialization drive, and sup-

ported Mitsui's diversification into paper and textiles, and a machinery business that was an antecedent of Toshiba. Expansion in foreign trade and banking led to the creation of Mitsui Bussan (now the Mitsui & Co. trading company) in 1876. In the late 1800s the Mitsui *zaibatsu* profited from Japanese military activity, and also moved into shipping, challenging Mitsubishi's monopoly. The Mitsui family withdrew from management of the company in 1936, following a violent campaign by nationalist, expansionist fanatics against the more liberal members of the capitalist establishment.

Prior to World War II the group benefited from the Japanese military buildup. After the war, the U.S. occupation forces split the Mitsui *zaibatsu* into more than 180 separate entities. However, in 1950, 27 leaders of former Mitsui companies began meeting and the Mitsui group became established. The group has expanded rapidly in petrochemicals and metals. In 1990 Mitsui Bank and Taiyo Kobe Bank merged to form the world's second largest bank. Its recent emphasis has been on China and by the year 2000 Mitsui plans to have 100 joint ventures operating there.

is the general trading company.) These groups are Fuyo (centered on Fuji Bank), DKB (Dai-Ichi Kangyo Bank), and Sanwa (Sanwa Bank). These banks at the core of these *keiretsu* still remain, despite their present difficulties, among the most powerful financial institutions in the world. (See Table 10.8, presented later in the chapter.)

Today both legislation and practice place limits on the role of the bank within the group. The law prohibits *keiretsu* banks from lending exclusively within the group and requires that nongroup borrowers receive equal access. Similarly, group companies have increasingly sought financing from outside the group. Both of these changes represent prudent risk diversification. Nevertheless, the role of the bank within the group continues to be important, and this may be a source of inherent weakness in the Japanese system. The group bank is likely to be more compliant in granting loans to member companies and might as a result end up with a badly performing loan portfolio, reflecting a form of "soft budget constraint." Moreover, banks are unlikely to force group members into liquidation, although it may be rational for them to do so. On the other hand, proximity offers an opportunity for close monitoring of creditworthiness and loan performance.

Distinct from the conglomerate *keiretsu* are the groups that are vertically integrated and oriented around the production of a single product. Patrick identifies 39 of these vertical *keiretsu,* the largest of which is the Toyota Group, focused on automobiles and parts, with involvement in distribution and finance. Toyota is the 10th largest company in the world in terms of turnover, and its structure differs little from other automobile firms (like General Motors, Ford, or Fiat), which are also complex groups involving all stages of manufacturing and distribution.

Despite the intent of U.S.-inspired legislation to break up the groups, tight-knit linkages reemerged in Japanese industry. Rather than a holding-company/ subsidiary structure, the case in the *zaibatsu,* linkages within a *keiretsu* are subtler and more "around a circle." Successive Japanese governments have taken a lenient view toward the reemergence of highly concentrated power in the corporate sector. This is not surprising since the government, too, was part of the "triangle" of power and saw the existence of a relatively few groups as an easy way to facilitate policy making and implementation. Moreover, recent scandals have shown that leading politicians, predominantly those of the dominant Liberal Democratic Party (LDP), were in receipt of substantial bribes and illegal political contributions. However, the effect of the reemergence of the major groups on consumer welfare and economic growth is unclear. While the trend toward concentration did lessen competition as traditionally measured in some markets, as we will discuss in more detail later, Japanese industrial policy did foster effective competition albeit between a limited number of participants in a wide range of product markets.

The *keiretsu* system implies a closer relationship than exists between purchaser and supplier in most countries. The relationships are long term and largely non-market. Mutual reliance and trust replace detailed contracts (thus economizing on the services of lawyers), and an enduring sense of dependence and obligation is key. This form of relationship also extends to the many suppliers and subcontractors who are not group members but whose businesses are tightly dependent on the group. There are many such firms in Japan. While the impression from the outside is that most employment is within the large firms, in fact, most Japanese work in firms that employ fewer than 200 employees, existing as suppliers to the big companies. Again, this proximity offers mixed blessings. Closeness enables stability, coordination, and such efficiency-enhancing systems as just-in-time (JIT) inventory control. It also is conducive to tight quality control, as the ultimate user is closely involved with the supplier. Moreover, supply contracts in Japan often call for prices to fall over time, since it is expected that the amortization of capital and a leaning curve will enable costs to be cut over the long run.

On the other hand, there are costs to the system, which proponents of market coordination see as important. First, it is very difficult for a new supplier to break into this tight circle. Even an innovation that led to an improved product, or a lower cost, might be slow to be introduced into production. Second, the close relationships necessarily involve a high degree of interdependence and the potential for one firm's failure having repercussive effects is high. In the past the strength and dynamism of the Japanese economy made such contingencies unlikely; however, today the stability of the Japanese system is more open to question, and the risk is greater.

DISTRIBUTION *KEIRETSU*

A feature of the group structure in Japan is its extension into the retail market. Major manufacturers frequently have their own network of stores that handle their own products exclusively. This is unusual; in the United States, though a system of exclusive outlets dominates in automobile retailing, this would not be acceptable in most product lines. In some industries the groups are almost totally dominant. For example, in electronics, Matsushita owns 24,000 shops, Toshiba 11,000, Hitachi 9,000, Sanyo and Sharp, 5,000 each, and Sony 3,000. Clearly this structure can be regarded as anticompetitive, and it makes changing the existing balance of market share extremely difficult. New firms and foreign imports are at a particular disadvantage because of these substantial barriers to entry.

TRADING COMPANIES

A unique and significant feature of the Japanese economic system is the existence of the "general, integrated trading companies" or *sogo shoshas*. While there are companies with similar ranges of activities in western economies, they do not have the same centrality to the overall economic system as in Japan.

There are eight major trading companies and among them some of the largest companies in the world.[5] Table 10.4 shows that in 1995 Japanese general trading companies made up 6 out of the 20 largest companies in the world when measured in terms of revenues.[6] It is important to emphasize, however, that such revenue comparisons overstate the importance of these firms. In terms of assets or employment, the companies are by no means as significant. Mitsubishi, for example, ranks 7th in revenue, 103rd in assets, and 295th in terms of employment. However, purely because of its turnover, which represents enormous buying power and selling ability, the company carries great importance. The three largest general trading companies (Mitsui, Mitsubishi, and Sumitomo) form the core of three of the largest *keiretsu*. The trading companies have played a formative role in Japanese

---

[5] The integrated Japanese trading companies are (in order of turnover in 1996): Mitsubishi, Mitsui, Itochu, Sumitomo, Marubeni, Nissho Iwai, Tomen, and Nichimen.

[6] The rankings have, in fact, been greatly altered by the "Asia crisis." In 1995 Japanese general trading companies made up five out of the six largest companies in the world measured by revenue.

■ **TABLE 10.4**

THE 20 LARGEST COMPANIES IN THE WORLD, BY REVENUE 1998

Rank	Company		Revenues ($ billion)	Profits ($ billion)	Assets ($ billion)	Stockholders' Equity ($ billion)	Employees
1	General Motors	Autos	161.3	3.0	257.4	15.0	594.0
2	Daimler Chrysler	Autos	154.6	5.7	159.7	35.6	441.5
3	Ford Motor	Autos	144.4	22.1	237.5	23.4	345.2
4	Wal-Mart Stores	Retail	139.2	4.4	49.3	21.1	910.0
5	Mitsui	Trading	109.4	0.2	56.3	5.7	33.0
6	Itochu	Trading	108.7	(0.3)	56.8	2.6	5.8
7	Mitsubishi	Trading	107.2	0.2	74.7	8.0	36.0
8	Exxon	Petroleum	100.7	6.4	92.6	43.8	79.0
9	General Electric	Machinery	100.5	9.3	355.9	38.9	293.0
10	Toyota Motor	Autos	99.7	2.8	124.6	52.1	183.9
11	Royal Dutch Shell	Petroleum	93.7	0.4	110.1	55.0	102.0
12	Marubeni	Trading	93.6	(0.9)	55.0	3.0	65.0
13	Sumitomo	Trading	89.0	(0.1)	45.5	4.8	30.7
14	IBM	Computers	81.7	6.3	86.1	19.4	291.0
15	AXA	Insurance	78.7	1.7	451.9	15.9	87.9
16	Citigroup	Banking	76.4	5.8	668.6	42.7	170.1
17	Volkswagen	Autos	76.3	1.3	70.5	10.8	298.0
18	NTT	Telecom	76.1	4.7	147.0	52.5	224.4
19	BP Amoco	Petroleum	68.3	3.3	84.5	41.8	96.7
20	Nissho Iwai	Trading	67.7	(0.8)	39.3	1.4	19.5

SOURCE: *Fortune 500*, 1999.

growth and development, and they constitute a formidable force for nonmarket-based economic coordination. First and foremost the trading companies are the eyes and ears of the *keiretsu* and the Japanese industrial base. They have been influential in identifying market demand and scour the globe for sales opportunities, inputs, and raw materials. They also bring companies together to form joint ventures to produce new products. In short, they perform market research, provide a window on the world, take a stand on the future, and provide coordination within a group.

LABOR RELATIONS

The conventional wisdom is that, compared to most of the industrialized world, the Japanese workplace is characterized by an absence of conflict. This reveals itself in a low rate of strikes, sharing of the objectives of the firm, and a generally harmonious and consensual set of on-the-job relationships. Like many of our preconceptions about Japanese life, this picture is only partly true. Moreover, harmonious industrial relations in any real sense have only been a feature of the past 35 years. The 15 years immediately after the end of World War II were characterized by deep acrimony and even violence. However, since 1960 strike incidence has been relatively low, certainly less than in the United Kingdom or the United States, but very much on a par with Germany.

Although the Japanese system of wage determination is in theory decentralized, there are strong elements of national coordination. The International Labor Organization considers that the state is a major protagonist in industrial relations, intervening both through legislative action and the conduct of industrial policy. The most prominent form of national coordination is the *shunto*, organized annual wage bargaining, the outcome of which directly affects about 25 percent of Japanese workers and which sets a benchmark for wage increases in small- and medium-sized enterprises, where unionization levels are low.

Japanese industrial relations are often referred to as having three "treasures": **lifetime employment,** known in Japanese as *sushin koyo*, which protects many of the workers from being laid off; **seniority wages *(nenko),*** which ensures that compensation increases in terms of an employee's age rather than one's responsibilities; and the widespread reliance on **company unions.** In fact, however, while these institutions are very important in some spheres of Japanese economic life, they are by no means universal. Moreover, as well as constituting advantages that have assisted Japan's remarkable growth, these so-called three treasures also have limitations and may be detrimental to the long-term development of the economy.

LIFETIME EMPLOYMENT POLICIES

Lifetime employment refers to the practice that, after a worker takes a job, the firm has an obligation to continue that employment despite downturns in business activity. In return the worker recognizes his or her responsibility to work productively and to show loyalty to and identify with the company. While lifetime employment is an important feature for those who enjoy it, it applies to only roughly 30 percent of the total workforce. This is a feature of the duality of Japanese industrial structure. While there are many large firms and groups, only 15 percent of all workers are employed in organizations of more than 1,000 persons. Only larger firms offer guaranteed lifetime employment, and they exclude from coverage part-time employees and a growing force of "contract workers." For the 40 percent of Japanese workers employed by firms of fewer than 30 workers, there is never an explicit or implicit lifetime guarantee. A second reservation relates to the worker's age of retirement from primary lifetime employment. This is expected to occur at around the age of 55, but most workers need to continue working for at least another decade. Thus even the most privileged of the workforce must find a new occupation for the last 10 years before retirement.

Table 10.5 shows that the Japanese labor market is considerably less fluid than that of other Organization for Economic Cooperation and Development (OECD) countries. A full 63 percent of workers have been with their employer for more than 5 years compared with about 50 percent for the OECD average and less than 40 percent for the United States, which is the most labor mobile economy. The same trend is confirmed by Table 10.6, which shows that in 1995 over 45 percent of Japanese workers aged 40 had only had one employer. In smaller Japanese firms,

■ **TABLE 10.5**

**AVERAGE EMPLOYMENT LONGEVITY IN SELECTED OECD COUNTRIES
(PERCENTAGE OF WORKFORCE)**

	Less Than 1 year	1–5 years	5–10 years	10–20 years	More Than 20 years
Australia	21.4	39.2	16.2	15.2	8.1
Canada	23.5	31.9	15.2	19.4	10.0
Finland	11.9	37.3	16.7	21.4	12.8
France	15.7	26.3	16.2	25.6	15.8
Germany	12.8	28.2	17.8	24.5	16.7
Japan	**9.8**	**27.6**	**19.7**	**23.7**	**19.3**
Netherlands	24.0	38.4	11.4	15.2	11.0
Norway	14.9	29	19.7	24.1	12.3
Spain	23.9	22.5	14	21.3	18.4
Switzerland	17.6	32.3	16.8	18.8	13.8
United Kingdom	18.6	36.2	16.1	19.3	9.6
United States	28.8	32.9	11.7	17.8	8.8
Unweighted average	**18.6**	**31.8**	**16**	**20.5**	**13**

SOURCE: OECD, *Economic Surveys of Japan,* 1995–1996, 98.

■ **TABLE 10.6**

PERCENTAGE OF MALE GRADUATES WITH ONLY ONE EMPLOYER

	Age			
	40	45	50	55
1980	37.6	30.9	20.2	6.3
1985	45.4	34.4	24.8	12.5
1990	42.9	42.5	29.1	16.2
1995	45.3	40.4	35.3	21.7

SOURCE: OECD, *Economic Surveys of Japan,* 1995–1996, 100.

however, those that constitute the secondary sector, there is greater mobility, and the labor market is fluid, with flexible employment and wages.

Downsizing, a common phenomenon in the United States today, is much more difficult in Japan, because a sizable proportion of employees of large firms enjoy lifetime guarantees. But that is not the only cost of *sushin koyo.* Lifetime contracts are also an impediment in getting the "right people to the right job." They present a barrier to promotion on ability and may stifle corporate innovation and progressiveness. Deadwood accumulates at the middle management level, and it is hard to reward the productivity and initiative of younger workers. This problem is in part resolved by the fact that the lifetime contract covers workers only into their early fifties, rather than their middle sixties, the normal retirement age in the United

States. Workers are expected to move on at that time to another post if they have not risen appropriately in the company. Here another feature of the Japanese system comes into play—the close relationship between a firm and its suppliers. Many larger companies try to place their senior workers and middle management with their suppliers, who often cannot refuse for fear of upsetting an important business relationship and who sometimes see it as an advantage for deepening relations.

SENIORITY WAGES

In some sectors of the Japanese economy, wages are more dependent on length of service than is the common practice in other developed economies. Managerial pay is less a function of perceived individual productivity than the number of years that an employee has spent with the firm. Like guaranteed employment, the scope of this *nenko* system is limited and generally applies only to those privileged workers who have a lifetime commitment to, and from, the firm.

The combination of lifetime employment and seniority wages presents larger Japanese firms with serious problems. Since the natural management structure in most organizations is pyramidal, the upper echelons of Japanese management tend to become very crowded, as a cohort advances. There are simply not enough productive upper management positions for those whose seniority with the company would qualify them. Moreover, a seniority wage demands that these employees be paid more than their younger colleagues, who because of their education, energy, and competence might logically be better paid and faster advancing. The net result is an overcrowded, and overpaid, management structure that is a drag on profits in good times and is dangerous to the livelihood of the company in recessions.

COMPANY UNIONS

The third of Japan's "treasures" is the institution of company unions. More than 80 percent of unionized workers are organized in unions that are unique to the organization that they work for. In other countries, occupational unions that are organized across firms are more often the rule. From the perspective of collective bargaining, the system is not altogether unique, however. Where Japanese practice does differ is in the close consultation and information flow between the unionized workers and management. This usually takes the form of a consultation meeting, held monthly, in which issues of management policy, production plans, and work practices are raised. This high degree of consultation means that unions, and their workers, operate closely in line with the company and tend to identify with it.

This system of company unions and consultation was introduced during the 1950s in an attempt to reduce militancy, lower the high degree of labor conflict, and combat the possibility of rising communist power. The government and employers confronted the unions in a series of important industrial actions in the steel and coal industries. In the aftermath of the 1970s oil shocks, many more large companies established worker/employer cooperation committees, which continue today and which many non-Japanese enterprises have sought to imitate. Trade unions would appear to be a major factor in facilitating the committees. In 1994, 56 percent of enterprises maintained such committees, but in enterprises where trade unions are present, the figure was 81 percent, versus 32 percent for nonunion enterprises.

The degree of unionization in large enterprises remains high in Japan, but this is balanced by very low levels of union representation in small firms. In 1993, trade union membership in enterprises with more than 1,000 workers stood at an average of 58.2 percent, compared to only 1.8 percent in enterprises with fewer than 100 employees. While the large company union is under no real threat, the pressure felt by the union movement worldwide is also apparent in Japan. The problem of getting a job amid mounting unemployment has made Japanese workers in second-tier labor markets increasingly individualistic. Nearly half of all small- and medium-sized enterprises have alternative forms of representation for determining conditions of employment.

ACTIVE LABOR MARKET POLICY

One consequence of the high longevity of job occupancy and the low level of unemployment is that the scope of active labor market policy (those policies designed to retrain workers, match applicants and vacancies, and provide public-sector employment) in Japan is very limited, as shown in Table 10.7. For a highly interventionist state, this is in some ways surprising. Japan spends only one-tenth of 1 percent of its GDP on active labor market policy, about the same as the United States. Germany in contrast spends more than 1.3 percent of its GDP on active labor intervention; this is still low compared to the Nordic countries, especially Sweden. This difference is in part explained by the historically low unemployment rate, but Japan also displays a low intensity of expenditure. The share of GDP expended per unemployed worker is also very low—about one-half the OECD average.

■ **TABLE 10.7**

EXPENDITURE ON ACTIVE LABOR MARKET POLICY: SELECTED OECD COUNTRIES, 1995

	Expenditure (percentage of GDP)	Unemployment Rate (percentage of labor force)	Expenditure Intensity
United States	0.2	5.6	0.04
Japan	**0.1**	**2.9**	**0.04**
Germany	1.3	9.4	0.14
France	1.2	12.3	0.1
Italy	0.9	10.5	0.09
United Kingdom	0.5	8.2	0.06
Canada	0.6	9.5	0.06
Average (unweighted)	0.7	8.3	0.07

SOURCE: OECD, *Employment Outlook.* OECD, *Economic Surveys of Japan*, 1995–1996, 125.

FINANCIAL STRUCTURE

The Japanese financial system is characterized by four essential features. First, the central bank, the Bank of Japan, has very limited independence and functions largely as an arm of government policy rather than an independent balance to the administration. Second, the highly concentrated system of commercial banks operates closely with the government and competition between them has historically been limited. Third, there is a high degree of functional separation between the various forms of financial intermediaries. The government has promised to deregulate the financial sector to lower these barriers (discussed later), but so far little has been achieved. Fourth, although there is a very high rate of household saving, there is a limited choice of investment instruments for households. Most household saving, and 20 percent of all saving in Japan, is gathered through the postal savings system, universal across Japan and the prime means of saving for the less affluent. The postal savings bank has over one trillion dollars in assets. Savings are accumulated by the postal savings system and then passed through the Bank of Japan, the central bank, to the city banks.

Unlike the Bundesbank in Germany or the U.S. federal reserve, the Bank of Japan (BoJ) has no pretensions to independence and acts in concert with the government. That it is an important tool of macroeconomic policy is not especially surprising or unique. However, unlike most other central banks, the BoJ plays an important role in microeconomic industrial policy since it enables the system of directed credit to priority industries to function.

THE BANKS

The large commercial banks of Japan are known as the city banks. Following a period of merger and consolidation, there are now 10, though if the current proposed merger between the Industrial Bank of Japan (IBJ) with Dai-Ichi Kangyo Bank (DKB) and Fuji Bank, which are both city banks, goes through there will only be 9.[7] City banks have a key role in fostering and financing the projects that are favored by the Ministry of International Trade and Industry (known as MITI). The process of industrial policy in Japan is more fully discussed later, but the essential procedure is that a dialogue between MITI and industry determines the sectors and projects that are going to receive priority treatment. MITI then determines exactly which companies are to have the central role, and the next step is to ensure that the required finance is available. At this point, MITI consults with the Bank of Japan and the Ministry of Finance, and the BoJ provides the necessary liquidity to the banks that will be responsible for providing the finance.

A strong criticism of this system is that the banks in Japan are not allowed to act as rational and profit-maximizing entities but are rather the tools of the bureaucracy.

---

[7] The three combined would produce the world's biggest bank in terms of assets, with ¥141 trillion-worth ($1,270 billion), 645 branches, and 34,000 employees.

■ **TABLE 10.8**

THE 20 LARGEST BANKS IN THE WORLD BY ASSETS, 1998

Rank	Institution	Country	Assets ($ million)	Profits ($ million)	Rate of Return on Assets (percentage)
1.	Deutsche Bank	Germany	735,808	1,879	0.3
2.	UBS	Switzerland	687,316	2,091	0.3
3.	Bank of Tokyo-Mitsubishi	Japan	663,628	−680	−0.1
4.	Bank of America Corp.	United States	617,679	5,165	0.8
5.	HypoVereinsbank	Germany	541,032	2,127	0.4
6.	ABN AMRO Holding	Netherlands	507,324	1,993	0.4
7.	Fuji Bank	Japan	489,129	(3,302)	−0.7
8.	HSBC Holdings	United Kingdom	484,735	4,316	0.9
9.	Credit Suisse	Switzerland	474,974	2,117	0.4
10.	Sumitomo Bank	Japan	464,144	(4,451)	−1.0
11.	Dai-Ichi Kangyo Bank	Japan	463,440	(3,484)	−0.8
12.	Credit Agricole	France	458,689	2,089	0.5
13.	Societe Generale	France	450,330	751	0.2
14.	Dresdner Bank	Germany	429,171	1,034	0.2
15.	Sanwa Bank	Japan	425,292	(3,681)	−0.9
16.	Westdeutsche Landesbank	Germany	416,093	377	0.1
17.	Norinchukin Bank	Japan	414,619	452	0.1
18.	Sakura Bank	Japan	413,834	(3,749)	−0.9
19.	Fortis	Belgium	396,874	1,521	0.4
20.	Industrial & Commercial Bank	China	390,916	417	0.1

SOURCE: *Fortune 500*, 1999.

This implies in turn that they cannot have the impartial role in assessing the viability of investment projects that is essential for the capital market to do its job. If the MITI officials are in error in their assessment concerning which projects to support, they might place the financial stability of the banks in jeopardy, and the banks might be left with a portfolio of nonperforming loans. As we can see from Table 10.8, Japanese banks are very large and powerful in global terms. Eight of the world's ten largest banks measured in terms of assets are Japanese. However, in recent years their profitability has been dismal. Five out of the eight biggest Japanese banks actually incurred losses in 1998, and the rate of return on assets of the other three was poor. This lack of profitability and independence in banking was a cause of financial instability in Japan and lies behind the larger Asian banking crisis. Currently it is believed that the portfolio of nonperforming loans in Japanese banking is as much as ¥80 trillion, 12 percent of GDP.[8] Clearly this raises anxiety about the stability of the banking system and curtails a bank's ability to make any form of risky loans, reducing domestic investment.

---

[8] *The Economist*, 20 June 1998, 22.

DEREGULATING THE FINANCIAL SYSTEM

The financial system in Japan has been highly regulated by a plethora of rules designed to exclude foreign competition. This protectionism is increasingly regarded as a weakness of the Japanese system and pressure has grown to initiate a comprehensive package of financial-market reforms known collectively as the **"big bang,"** similar on paper to the reforms known by the same name in the United States in the 1970s and in Britain in the 1980s. Measures are being phased in during the five-year period concluding at the end of 2000 that should, on the surface, totally transform the Japanese financial landscape. However, many fear that the commitment to reform is cosmetic rather than fundamental, and the proposals for reform are designed to appease criticism while actually affecting little.

LIBERALIZING FOREIGN EXCHANGE. Although the yen has been convertible to some extent since the 1950s, few Japanese have easy access to foreign currency. Retail banks do not supply foreign exchange, and even Japanese business has limited access. This will change in the next two years. Convertibility will be enhanced for all actors in the economy, local branch banks will sell foreign exchange, and companies will be able to conduct their overseas business in dollars, euros, or any other currency.

REDUCING FINANCIAL REPRESSION. One of the advantages enjoyed, and exploited, by Japanese businesses has been the low cost of capital. This is the result of financial repression—limiting opportunities for small savers and forcing them to put their money in low-yielding deposit accounts, generally in the postal savings banking system. These savings are recycled through the Bank of Japan and the city banks to become the source of low-interest investment funds for prioritized sectors. The "big bang" legislation proposes the end of repression, allowing small savers access to higher interest instruments. There is skepticism about how far the liberalization will be pursued. The end of repression would inevitably create a mismatch in the term structure of bank balance sheets. The assets of the banks are long term (consisting largely of industrial and housing loans); withdrawal of savings in pursuit of higher interest would almost certainly exacerbate the crisis in the banking sector, as parallel reforms in the United States crippled the savings and loan industry. Given the fragile state of banking in Japan at present, it is hard to see how this reform can proceed without the commitment of extensive government subsidies to banks in the short to medium term. Moreover, the very essence of the Japanese industrial policy lies in the use of directed credit. Opening opportunities for small savers would inevitably reduce the leverage of the bureaucrats to favor prioritized projects. While this might enhance efficiency, it would also involve a reduction in bureaucratic power that the authorities might be unwilling to allow.

CUTTING FINANCIAL MARKET SEGMENTATION. At the moment the Japanese system has "Glass-Steagall" style regulation, creating legal barriers between commercial banking, investment banking, brokerage, and insurance. Everywhere in the world market forces are tending to erode these distinctions, and changes in technology are making them out of date. In Japan, regulatory change to accommodate these shifts is likely.

INCREASED INVOLVEMENT OF FOREIGN FINANCIAL INTERMEDIARIES. The Japanese have been forced to recognize that foreign financial intermediaries have performed better than their domestic counterparts. The big bang will, in theory, allow a more level playing field and let foreign banks, brokerages, and insurance companies into the Japanese market. The problem is that the efficiency differential between "best worldwide practice" and average Japanese performance is huge, and many Japanese companies would go to the wall or would be acquired by foreign firms. Given the traditional protectionist bent of Japanese policy, reforms might be limited to preserve the essentially Japanese character of the banking sector.

INDUSTRIAL POLICY

The Japanese economy embodies a high degree of "industrial policy," the active intervention of the government to promote or change the course of industrial development. Of course, Japan is not alone, many countries have active policies to promote industrial growth, and many examples may be taken from history. However, in Japan industrial policy has assumed a comprehensiveness that has prompted some observers to use the rather biting sobriquet of "Japan Inc." It is useful to distinguish, however, between what Hugh Patrick has termed **macroeconomic industrial policy** and its microeconomic counterpart.

MACROECONOMIC INDUSTRIAL POLICY

This category embraces measures designed to increase the pace of overall industrial growth, while having only a limited impact on industrial structure. Such policies include measures to promote savings, to provide universal and accessible education, to protect industry from overseas competition, and to stimulate exports. All of these measures, as long as they provide a level playing field across industry and do not favor any particular sector or type of firm, are not particularly invasive. They have long been a part of the Japanese scene and have led to a large share of the country's savings finding its way to the industrial groups, rather than to consumer spending or investment in social projects—like housing. On the whole, such macroeconomic industrial policy has been successful in accelerating the pace of industrial growth, albeit at the expense of the consumer.

MICROECONOMIC INDUSTRIAL POLICY

However, when we talk of industrial policy we generally envisage its microeconomic form. Indeed, one prominent economist, Richard Cooper, has defined industrial policy as action "whose intended purpose is to affect the structure of output." In this sense, industrial policy is designed as a substitute for the allocative function of the market and may be justified by the existence of some form of market failure. Again there are a broad range of policy instruments available: access to investment funds, direct subsidies, differentially favorable tax treatments, tariff or quota protection, and so forth. The success of **microeconomic industrial policy** in Japan is open to question. There have been notable successes, but equally there are examples in which promotion of a specific industry or products has led to failure and wasted investment.

It is also important to bear in mind that microindustrial policy has two faces. The more glamorous aspect is the promotion of industries selected as candidates for growth; however, equally important, especially as older "rust-belt" industries lose markets, is the rationalization of industries that are inevitably in decline.

PICKING WINNERS.   If microeconomic industrial policy is to improve economic performance, there must be an economic justification as to why bureaucrats are able to outperform the market. Industrial policy in Japan originates with the Ministry of International Trade and Industry (MITI) and there are several rationales for intervention. First is a belief that the Japanese economy is characterized by substantial market failure, including the existence of significant economies of scale, the strong linkages between industries, public good effects, and capital market imperfections. In addition to these general justifications, MITI also takes the view that the *keiretsu* system actually encourages unhealthy competition because each of the major groups feels that it must have a presence in practically every product line. This concern about the wasteful duplication of investment results in the belief that restraint on competition can be socially beneficial. Hence government intervention to shape market structure can lead to a more efficient use of capital. A further rationale for industrial policy is that markets are myopic and left to themselves, they fail to assume the long-run optimal level of risk. By anticipating the direction of change, industrial policy can actually speed up the operation of the market. MITI has also taken a long-term view on the industrial mix required to raise Japan to the level of a first-class economic power and keep it there.

MITI's interventionism started in the early 1950s and initially relied on four measures—import restrictions, directed credit, tax incentives, and foreign exchange controls. The Export and Import Trading Act of 1953 legalized the formation of cartels and price fixing and limited imports. In these early years the system of directed credit consisted of funneling the savings gathered through the postal savings system and civil service pension surpluses into Japan Development Bank (JDB) and other trust funds created under the Fiscal Investment and Loan Program (FILP) that were functionally oriented toward industrial finance. Between 1952 and 1955, 28 percent of total finance to Japanese industry was through the FILP trust programs. A discretionary tax system enabled the adoption of discriminatory tax rates and depreciation codes. Finally, since foreign exchange control existed throughout the period, MITI was able to control the access to foreign technology and scarce imports, allocating the required permits only to favored firms whose projects had received approval.

As well as using material incentives and restrictions, MITI also made use of propaganda and moral suasion. Such jawboning was not always successful. In

1955, MITI put forward a plan to create a single automobile company in Japan, believing economies of scale to be so strong as to prevent multiple Japanese firms from competing in the world market. It was forced to abandon the scheme in the face of protest from the various *keiretsu*. After this, vigorous competition between the various companies ensued, and ultimately four strong, exporting motor companies resulted.

In the late 1950s, MITI was forced to modify its policies. After Japan became a signatory of the General Agreement on Tariffs and Trade (1955) and joined the OECD (1964), Japanese economic policy was subject to international regulation. Trade had to be liberalized and foreign exchange convertibility increased. This removed some weapons from MITI's arsenal, and greater reliance began to be placed on moral suasion and the establishment of consensus. The importance of the FILP trust funds began to recede, and more reliance was placed on directing credit through the private banks.

The 1960s saw MITI make another misstep in promoting the development of an oil and petrochemical industry. This effort failed as world energy prices rose sharply following the OPEC oil crises. MITI then took a hard look at the future and decided to promote "knowledge-intensive industry," especially computers and communications. The Agency for Industrial Science and Technology (AIST) was created within MITI. Its purpose was to conduct and finance basic and applied research to assist in the development of the computer, communications, ceramics, and computer-aided manufacturing systems (robotics).

PLANNING THE DECLINE OF LOSERS. Japan's success in the 1960s was to a large extent based on the development of industries that comparative advantage favored while Japan's labor costs were low—textiles, steel, rubber, shipbuilding. Now, as in the United States and Europe, these industries are in decline. An issue is whether the market should be allowed to be the arbiter of who survives and who sinks, or whether there is a constructive role for government. Japan has taken the latter tack. Using legislation that dates back to the early 1950s, MITI has frequently sponsored the cartelization of declining industries so as to see an orderly restructuring of output. This has, the Japanese believe, been more beneficial in terms of the preservation of industrial capital, social infrastructure, and healthy communities than merely allowing the market to choose the losers.

THE EFFICACY OF INDUSTRIAL POLICY. It is hard to evaluate the success of Japanese industrial policy, because it is very difficult to establish a counterfactual, a consensus on what kind of path Japan would have followed in the absence of industrial policy. Japan has indeed demonstrated impressive growth since the war, but what Hugh Patrick characterizes as "myths" have frequently been wrongly credited for the success and in his opinion the biggest myth is that of industrial policy, which he finds to be frequently the subject of facile and misleading generalizations. He considers that the macroeconomic elements of industrial policy that have created a platform for growth without favoring any particular industry or initiative have been successful, while microeconomic industrial policy ("picking winners") has had a much more mixed record. While the successes might be the ones that catch the eye, there have been several conspicuous failures. Patrick documents the ill-starred, energy-intensive industry drive in the 1950s and 1960s and MITI's aborted attempt to promote concentration in the automobile industry in the 1950s. A more recent case is the promotion of the analog system of high-definition television (HDTV), which has lost out to a digital version and may have cost as much as $10 billion. Moreover, many of Japan's most impressive achievements have been brought about without MITI's help, and in some cases over MITI's objections. The performance of the Japanese economy in the 1990s and the fragility of the banking system (caused in large part by the system of microeconomic industrial policy and directed credit) have thrown the validity of the entire system into doubt. Now the winning strategies promoted by MITI seem to be fewer and the losers more conspicuous. Popular wisdom is moving toward favoring a less prominent role for MITI and a greater reliance on market logic.

THE FUTURE OF THE JAPANESE SYSTEM

At the turn of a new millennium the successes of the Japanese system are being discounted in the light of the current failure. What were seen as the strengths of the system just a decade ago—the ability to take a long-term view of growth, the achievement of consensus among the principal actors, eschewing short-run profits for a strategic view—now seem to be a catalog of weaknesses. However, it is important to establish whether Japan's current stagnation is due to its system or to specific policies of government that hampered the performance of that system. This is vital because the answer determines whether the solution to the current problems involves a difficult and irreversible systemic change, requiring deregulation across a wide range of industry and finance, or whether the malaise can be largely cured by a resort to fiscal stimulus. Some slowing of growth had to occur since the growth of the labor force has fallen from 1 percent to less than ½ percent per year. However, another important source of growth, labor productivity in manufacturing, continues at roughly the same pace as in the 1980s, about 3 percent per annum. Thus the potential output of the Japanese economy has been growing at more than 3 percent per annum, while actual output has increased by only 1.3 percent. This suggests that there might now be a positive output gap that would allow an increase in GNP to be sustained for several years without being impeded by any substantial bottlenecks, given the appropriate boost in demand through fiscal policy.

KEY TERMS AND CONCEPTS

bank-centered *keiretsu*	lifetime employment
"big bang"	macroeconomic industrial policy
company unions	microeconomic industrial policy
keiretsu	Ministry of International Trade and Industry (MITI)

Ministry of Finance (MoF)	*sogo sosha*
nenko	*sushin koyo*
Samurai	trading company
seniority wages	*zaibatsu*
shunto	

QUESTIONS FOR DISCUSSION

1. What are the *keiretsu?* In what ways do they resemble and in what ways do they differ from the *zaibatsu?* How are *keiretsu* held together?

2. How general is the system of lifetime employment? In what ways does it help and in what way does it hurt productivity?

3. How are Japanese trade unions organized? Does this contribute to labor peace?

4. How does a system of "seniority wages" differ from the normal assumptions of microeconomic theory? Can you see any advantages?

5. How has Japan's system of directed credit harmed its financial sector?

6. What constitutes "macroeconomic" industrial policy in Japan? Has it been successful?

7. Is microeconomic industrial policy just about "picking winners"? What else is important?

RESOURCES

WEB SITES

Ministry of Finance . . . . http://www.mof.go.jp/english/index.htm

Central Bank . . . . http://www.boj.or.jp/en/index.htm

Ministry of International Trade and Industry . . . . . . http://www.miti.go.jp/indexe.html

Statistical Bureau http://www.stat.go.jp/1.htm

Economic Planning Agency . . . . http://www.epa.go.jp/ee/menu.html

Economic Research Institute . . . . http://www.epa.go.jp/ee/eri/menu.html

National Tax Administration . . . . http://www.nta.go.jp/outline/outline.htm

Tokyo Stock Exchange . . . . http://www.tse.or.jp/eindex.html

Japan Development Bank . . . . http://www.jdb.go.jp/index_e.html

Import-Export Bank of Japan .http://www.japanexim.go.jp/

Japanese External Trade Organization . . . . http://www.jetro.go.jp/top/index.html

Mitsubishi Companies . . . . http://www.mitsubishi.or.jp/e/index.html

Sumitomo Group Companies . . . . http://seusa.sumitomo.com/SEUSA/sumitomog.html

Office of Foreign Affairs . . . . http://www.mofa.go.jp/

Japan Times National Newspaper . . . . http://www.japantimes.co.jp/
Embassy of Japan in Washington, D.C. . . . . http://www.embjapan.org/
The Project Gutenberg E-text of the Constitution of Japan . . . .
. . . . ftp://sunsite.unc.edu/pub/docs/books/gutenberg/etext96/jcnst10.txt
Economic and Financial Data for Japan (updated daily) . . http://www.stat.go.jp/19.htm
An Outline of Japanese Tax Administration . . http://www.nta.go.jp/outline/outline.htm

BOOKS AND ARTICLES

Abe, Etsuo, and Robert Fitzgerald. "Japanese Economic Success: Timing, Culture, and Organisational Capability." *Business History,* April 1995, 1–31.

Alam, M. Shahid. *Governments and Markets in Economic Development Strategies: Lessons from Korea, Taiwan, and Japan.* New York: Praeger, 1989.

Aoki, Masahiko. "Toward an Economic Model of the Japanese Firm." *Journal of Economic Literature* 78, no. 1 (March 1990), 1–27.

Boulding, Kenneth, and Alan Gleason, "War as Investment: The Strange Case of Japan." In *Economic Imperialism,* ed. Kenneth Boulding and Tapan Mukherjee, 240–261. Ann Arbor: University of Michigan Press, 1972.

Calder, Kent E. *Strategic Capitalism: Private Business and Public Purpose in Japan.* Princeton, N.J.: Princeton University Press, 1993.

Callon, Scott. *Divided Sun: MITI and the Breakdown of Japanese High-Tech Industrial Policy, 1975–1993.* Stanford: Stanford University Press, 1997.

Carlile, Lonny E., and Mark Tilton, eds. *Is Japan Really Changing Its Ways?: Regulatory Reform and the Japanese Economy.* Washington, D.C.: The Brookings Institute, 1998.

Drucker, Peter F. "The End of Japan, Inc.?: An Economic Monolith Fractures." *Foreign Affairs,* spring 1993, 10–15.

Fingleton, Eamonn. "Japan's Invisible Leviathan." *Foreign Affairs,* MarchApril 1995, 69–85.

Francks, Penelope. *Japanese Economic Development: Theory and Practice.* London: Routledge, 1992.

Gerlach, Michael L. *Alliance Capitalism: The Social Organization of Japanese Business.* Berkeley: University of California Press, 1993.

Gibney, Frank. *Unlocking the Bureaucrat's Kingdom: Deregulation and the Japanese Economy.* Washington, D.C.: The Brookings Institute, 1998.

Grabowski, Richard. "The State and Economic Development." *Studies in Comparative International Development,* spring 1994, 3–17.

Hart, Jeffrey A. *Rival Capitalists: International Competitiveness in the United States, Japan and Western Europe.* Ithaca, N.Y.: Cornell University Press, 1992.

Hobday, Michael. *Innovation in East Asia: The Challenge to Japan.* Aldershot, England: Edward Elgar Publishing, 1995.

Hollerman, Leon. *Japan, Disincorporated: The Economic Liberalization Process.* Stanford: Hoover Institution Press, 1988.

Ito, Takatoshi. *The Japanese Economy.* Cambridge: MIT Press, 1992.

Japan Science Foundation. *US–Japan Comparison in National Formation and Transformation of Technology Centering around Mass Production Systems, 1900–1990.* Tokyo: Japan Science Foundation, 1992.

Johnson, Chalmers. *MITI and the Japanese Miracle: The Growth of Industrial Policy, 1925–1975.* Stanford: Stanford University Press, 1982.

Johnson, Chalmers, Laura D'Anrea Tyson, and John Zysman. *Politics and Productivity: The Real Story of Why Japan Works.* Cambridge, Mass.: Ballinger Publishing, 1989.

Katz, Richard. *Japan, The System That Soured: The Rise and Fall of the Japanese Economic Miracle.* Armonk, N.Y.: M.E. Sharpe, 1998.

Kikkawa, Takeo. "Kigyo Shuda: The Formation and Function of Enterprise Groups." *Business History,* April 1995, 44–53.

Komiya, Ryutaro, Masahiro Okumo, and Kotaro Suzumara, eds. *Industrial Policy of Japan.* Tokyo: Academic Press, 1988.

Kosai, Yutaka, and Yoshitaro Ogino. *The Contemporary Japanese Economy.* Armonk, New York: M.E. Sharpe, 1984.

Lee, Chung H., and Ippei Yamazawa, eds. *The Economic Development of Japan and Korea: A Parallel with Lessons.* New York: Praeger, 1990.

Lincoln, Edward J. *Japan: Facing Economic Maturity.* Washington, D.C.: The Brookings Institution, 1988.

Lincoln, Edward J. *Japan's Unequal Trade.* Washington, D.C.: The Brookings Institution, 1990.

Morikawa, Hidemasa. *Zaibatsu: The Rise and Fall of Family Enterprise Groups in Japan.* Tokyo: University of Tokyo Press, 1992.

Morishima, Michio. *Why Has Japan "Succeeded"?: Western Technology and the Japanese Ethos.* Cambridge: Cambridge University Press, 1982.

Mosk, Carl. *Competition and Cooperation in Japanese Labour Markets (Studies in the Modern Japanese Economy).* New York: St. Martin's Press, 1995.

Nanto, Dick K. "Japan's Industrial Groups: The *Keiretsu.*" In *Comparative Economic Systems: Models and Cases,* 7th ed., ed. Morris Bernstein. Burr Ridge, Ill.: Irwin, 1994. 236–251.

Nester, William R. *The Foundation of Japanese Power: Continuities, Changes, Challenges.* Armonk: M.E. Sharpe, 1990.

Odagiri, Hiroyuki. *Growth through Competition, Competition through Growth: Strategic Management and the Economy in Japan.* Oxford: Oxford University Press, 1992.

Okazaki, Tetsuji, "The Evolution of the Financial System in Post-War Japan." *Business History,* April 1995, 89–106.

Oppenheim, Phillip. *Japan without Blinders: Coming to Terms with Japan's Economic Success.* Tokyo: Kodansha International, 1992.

Patrick, Hugh T., and Yung Chul Park. *The Financial Development of Japan, Korea and Taiwan: Growth, Repression and Liberalization.* Oxford: Oxford University Press, 1994.

Pempel, T. J. *Regime Shift: Comparative Dynamics of the Japanese Political Economy (Cornell Studies in Political Economy).* Ithaca, N.Y.: Cornell University Press, 1998.

Shichihei, Yamamoto. *The Spirit of Japanese Capitalism and Selected Essays.* Lanham: Madison Books, 1992.

Shigeto, Tsuru. *Japan's Capitalism, Creative Defeat and Beyond.* Cambridge, England: University of Cambridge Press, 1993.

Shimotani, Masahiro. "The Formation of Distribution Keiretsu: The Case of Matsushita Electric." *Business History,* April 1995, 54–69.

"A Survey of Tomorrow's Japan." *The Economist,* 13 July 1996, 1–16.

Tai, Hung-chao, ed. *Confucianism and Economic Development: An Oriental Alternative?* Washington, D.C.: The Washington Institute Press, 1989.

Takenaka, Heizo. *Contemporary Japanese Economy and Economic Policy.* Ann Arbor, Mich.: University of Michigan Press, 1991.

Tatsuki, Mariko. "The Rise of the Mass Market and Modern Retailers in Japan." *Business History,* April 1995, 70–88.

Teranishi, Juro. "Economic Recovery, Growth and Policies: 'Gradualism' in the Japanese Context," *Economic Policy,* Issue 19 supp. (December 1994): 137–154.

Udagawa, Masaru. "The Development of Production Management at the Toyota Motor Corporation." *Business History,* April 1995, 107–119.

Whitehill, Arthur M. *Japanese Management: Tradition and Transition.* London: Routledge, 1991.

11

SOUTH KOREA

INTRODUCTION

The Republic of Korea, generally known as South Korea, has shown one of the most impressive records of economic growth over the past 35 years. In 1961 the economy was largely agrarian (65 percent of the workforce was in agriculture), the state was weak, labor unrest was frequent, and industrial growth was slow. In that year, a group of army officers seized control of the country, initiating a series of events that resulted ultimately in the elevation of General Park Chung Hee to the presidency. Park ruled as an authoritarian dictator for the next 25 years, during which Korea was transformed from an agrarian state to a modern industrial society.

Korean development has strong parallels to that of Japan, including the dominance of large diversified industrial groups (in Japan prewar *zaibatsu* and postwar *keiretsu*, in Korea **chaebol,** or **jaebul**), the powerful role of the bureaucracy, the rapid import and implementation of foreign technology, the low levels of direct foreign investment, and the export-orientation of growth. Nevertheless, it would be an oversimplification to consider Korea merely a new application of the "Japanese model." Korea offers lessons in its own right, not the least in how it will resolve the economic and political difficulties pressing on it in the early 21st century.

HISTORICAL BACKGROUND

THE COLONIAL LEGACY

For about 600 years (between the 13th and 19th centuries), Korea was ruled as a feudal state by the Yi dynasty. Power was held by an elite (the *yangban*) composed of the monarchy, the landowners, and the scholars. The conservative interests of these groups effectively blocked economic and political reform. The vast majority of the population were peasants living in subsistence conditions. Any agricultural surplus was used either to support the consumption of the elite groups, or went as tribute to Imperial China, which maintained a sleepy suzerainty over the peninsula.

In the late 19th century, this stability was disturbed by two forces. First, rapid population growth increased the demands on the fragile agricultural resources of the mountainous Korean peninsula, leading to peasant unrest. Second, following the Meiji reformation (see chapter 10), Japan embarked on an outward-oriented policy, trying to augment its limited resource base by acquiring territory in China's waning sphere of influence. The Treaty of Khangwa in 1876 established Japanese commerce through Korean ports, and by 1910 Japan's military muscle allowed the establishment of formal colonial status.

There is a lively debate about the role of Japanese colonialism on Korean development. Some authorities see it as "modernizing," because it swept away the feudal barriers to economic progress; Japanese occupation destroyed the class system, abolished slavery, broke up the great estates, and paved the way for land reform. The colonial period led to increased education for the average Korean, the transfer of managerial skills in industry and commerce to Koreans, and the creation of an urban industrial workforce.

While admitting the elimination of barriers to change, another view emphasizes the distortionary nature of Japanese colonialism and the negative effects of subsuming Korean development to Japanese needs. Certainly the Japanese occupation did not result in Korean-controlled industrialization or create a large Korean business community. The vast majority of industrial investment in Korea was Japanese. By 1938 Koreans held only 12 percent of the total capital of Korean industry, and just six Japanese *zaibatsu* accounted for fully 70 percent of Korean industrial capital. During the 1920s, after a decade of intense discrimination against Koreans, the Japanese did allow the evolution of what economist Alice Amsden calls a "wafer-thin stratum" of indigenous capitalists. Among these were some of the families that would in the postwar period develop the great Korean industrial groups,[1] but who in the interwar years were allowed only to serve Japanese interests. Korea produced food, raw materials, and semifinished goods for Japanese industry. As war approached, the Japanese created a Korean heavy industrial base using the peninsula's mineral wealth, which remained nevertheless completely under Japanese control. Table 11.1 shows some indices of Korean growth for the start of Japanese colonial rule until 1941.

THE POSTWAR PERIOD

By the end of World War II in 1945 Korea's economy had been shattered. The industrial base built in the interwar and early war years had been stripped toward the end of the war. Moreover, Korea's economy had been part of an integrated Japanese trading system involving close links with Japan, North Korea, and Manchukuo (the Japanese-controlled puppet state in Manchuria). As these links dissolved, the economy collapsed. Half of the manufacturing establishments operating under the Japanese closed during the immediate postwar period, and many others drastically reduced employment and production. In addition, the U.S. occupying forces dismantled and removed most of the Japanese facilities that had been producing war material. Industrial output fell by 85 percent in less than two years.[2]

---

[1] For a full exposition of the thesis that the Korean miracle had its roots in the Japanese occupation, see Carter J. Eckert, *Offspring of Empire: The Koch'ang Kims and the Colonial Origins of Korean Capitalism* (Seattle: University of Washington Press, 1991).

[2] Vittorio Corbo and Sang-Mok Suh, eds. *Structural Adjustment in a Newly Industrialized Country: The Korean Experience* (Baltimore: Johns Hopkins University Press, 1992), 7.

INDICES OF OUTPUT AND POPULATION, 1910–1941 (1929 = 100)

Period	Agriculture	Forestry, Fishing, and Mining	Manufacturing	Total	Population
1910–1912	67.3	33.7	17.4	54.2	66
1914–1916	86.5	45.9	31.5	69.6	—
1919–1921	88.6	46.2	59.7	76.9	84.5
1924–1926	91.2	69	97.5	89.6	—
1929–1931	100	100	100	100	100
1934–1936	98.7	161.5	194.2	127.1	—
1939–1941	117.3	227.6	255.5	165.5	115.2

SOURCE: Hwang, 17.

Agriculture was little better. Neglect during the war years, a shortage of inputs, and an inadequate distribution system put Korean agriculture in difficulty. For several years following the war there was a general shortage of food and some localized cases of famine. The food crisis was exacerbated by the repatriation to South Korea of about two million Koreans who had been working in Japan or who had fled to China to avoid Japanese occupation. On top of this, two to three million refugees had fled from the communist north as the country was partitioned. Finally, the outbreak of the Korean War not only hampered economic reconstruction but also resulted in the destruction of 40 percent of industrial capacity and 20 percent of the housing stock.

Extensive U.S. aid got Korea through the 1950s. In 1960, exports amounted to only 3 percent of Korean gross domestic product (GDP), while imports amounted to about 13 percent. However, financial inflows from the United States, consisting of "development aid" (in excess of $200 million annually) and substantial expenditure by the U.S. military, represented 10 percent of GDP. Like Japanese rule, U.S. presence in Korea had a modernizing function, but it was also highly distortionary, since U.S. military needs warped industrial growth and led to bias toward the service sector. Simultaneously, the generous economic development aid enriched a new entrepreneurial class, whose prosperity depended on close political links to the government and military.

Corruption was pervasive during the First Republic (1948–1960) and great fortunes were amassed by a new capitalist class. The gravy train started with sales of Japanese property at below-market prices to friends of the government, and subsequently favored firms were allocated hard currency to import scarce materials—grains and fertilizers—to be resold on the domestic market at monopoly prices. Some firms were also given access to loans at subsidized interest rates, granted tax exemptions, and awarded preferential contracts for large-scale government projects.[3] Despite their shady origins, these entrepreneurs had certain advantages in

---

[3] Alice Amsden, *Asia's Next Giant*, 39.

promoting economic development. First, they came without preconceptions; they were less conservative in style than Korea's older textile industry chiefs and were far more growth oriented. Second, although these businessmen came from a wide range of industries, they were not wedded to any particular sector, but were business generalists, specializing in making money by whatever means. Third, steering aid in their direction gave them substantial funds for investment and solved the problem of initial capital accumulation. Finally, their corrupt past gave the Park administration a hold over them that could be used as a lever to ensure complicit behavior. These men were the founders of many of the diversified business groups, or *chaebol*, that remain so important in Korea today.

THE POLICIES OF PARK CHUNG HEE

The First Republic ended in 1960 with the death of Syngman Rhee, and a brief experiment with democracy ended when General Park Chung Hee led an army coup, unopposed by the United States. Two years later Park resigned from the military and was elected president of the Republic, though his close military links persisted through the 25 years of his presidency. Park was an ascetic individual who expected and demanded that all Koreans should make sacrifices to further his vision of the new Korea. His views were highly influenced by South Korea's security problems and the need to develop a strong industrial base to support the military establishment. In particular, it was clear that North Korea (The People's Republic of Korea), by pursuing a program of Stalinist industrialization, was outgrowing South Korea and worsening the strategic position of the south. Park's pursuit of industrial growth was oriented to furthering the creation of military power rather than toward the economic well-being of the population. In that sense, Park's policies may be viewed as being purely mercantilist, "the pursuit of power over plenty."

Park was able to centralize power because there was little to oppose him. Japanese colonization, World War II, and the Korean War had transformed the class structure of Korean society, leveling landlord and scholar classes. The communist threat tended to solidify society, and also silenced U.S. criticism of the regime's excesses. Plentiful labor and high unemployment initially made the unions powerless. Park was also able to call on Korea's heritage of **Confucianism** to enrich his rhetoric on the relation of the individual to the state, and by extension to his or her employer.[4]

---

[4]The role of Confucianism in economic development is a much-debated topic. Max Weber argued that Confucianism, with its emphasis on the moral over the material, had been a major deterrent to the development of capitalism in China, analogous to the role of Catholicism and orthodoxy in Europe. Morishima in turn tried to distinguish between the Confucianism of Japan, which tended to support economic growth, from Chinese Confucianism, which did not. Nowadays, however, the Confucian ethic of obedience to superiors is seen as a major positive factor in the growth of Korea, Hong Kong, Taiwan, and Singapore. Lee Kuan Yew, the former prime minister of Singapore, is especially eloquent on the role of Confucian philosophy in economic growth.

In addition to these political advantages, Park had two important levers by which to control business: access to imports and access to finance. In the early 1960s Korea's international trade was governed by a complex system of licensing and tariffs. To receive a license, a firm had to show both the absence of a domestic substitute and the necessity of the imports for the production of goods that were either to be exported or vital to the domestic economy. In addition, protective tariffs averaged over 40 percent in 1962 and a complex system of multiple exchange rates put further restraint on trade. By giving favored firms import licenses, hard currency at discounted rates, and tariff wavers, the government allowed the appropriation of economic rents by selected industrial leaders.

Park further tightened control of the economy by the nationalization of the commercial banks,[5] which made about one-third of all loans in Korea and provided most industrial finance. The four specialized banks,[6] which together made about 12 percent of loans, were also taken under public control. This gave the government the ability to control credit and the power to discipline any firm that displeased it by blocking any refinancing of its debt.

PHASES OF KOREAN GROWTH

EXPORT PROMOTION, 1961–1973

The early years of the Park regime saw a heavy emphasis on exporting. Initially exports consisted mostly of textiles and light manufactured goods because Korea's cheap labor gave it comparative advantage in these industries. Policy changes in 1961, including a 50 percent devaluation of the Korean currency (the won) and the elimination of multiple exchange rates, did a lot to boost exports. The government also used more direct action. Successful exporters were assured import licenses, finance for expansion, tariff relief, and direct subsidies. The government also imposed a 1 percent surcharge on imports and used the proceeds to finance specialized institutions[7] to promote exports. Export targets were established for individual firms, and although there were no direct penalties for failing to achieve these goals, finance was more likely given to those who had succeeded in such competition, an early example of the "market-augmenting" competitions used by Asian economies to allocate credit.

The results of the export promotion campaign were staggeringly successful. Between 1963 and 1973, exports grew at an *annual* rate of 44 percent, and increased from about 1 percent of gross national product (GNP) in 1963 to over 25 percent in 1973. The commodity composition of exports also changed, from a heavy

---

[5] They had been privatized in 1957, brought back under government management in 1961, and reprivatized in 1982, but until 1993 the government appointed all bank presidents.

[6] The Industrial Bank of Korea, the Citizen's National Bank, the Korea Housing Bank, and the National Agricultural Cooperative.

[7] These were the Korean Trade Promotion Association, founded in 1964 to perform market research abroad, and the Korean Traders' Association, which was financed by a 1 percent levy on imports.

concentration in textiles in the early years, to more diversified light manufacturing in the later ones. Imports increased as well, although at a slightly lower rate. Imports also rose because of the need for raw materials and capital goods. Investment rose from 11.5 percent of GNP in 1964 to 27 percent in 1969 before moderating to 23 percent in 1973 as global economic conditions worsened.

THE HEAVY AND CHEMICAL INDUSTRIES DRIVE, 1973–1979

Despite the economic success of the late 1960s, the Park government decided that the future of the Korean economy lay in heavy industry and in 1973 inaugurated the **Heavy and Chemical Industries Development Plan (HCI).** This shift was motivated by three factors. First, the belief that military self-sufficiency, necessary in an era of a reduced U.S. presence, required the development of a heavy industrial base. Second, increased globalization of production and accelerating integration of Asian countries into the global economy was eroding Korea's comparative advantage in light industry, which was based on cheap labor. Wage costs in Indonesia, the Philippines, and Malaysia were much lower than in Korea, and higher Korean wages, and living standards, could only be sustained by higher labor productivity and that required more capital-intensive industry. Third, despite rapid export growth, the Korean balance of payments remained in deficit and a greater production of heavy industrial materials and chemicals would reduce import dependence. The HCI initiative was opposed by most of Korea's economic advisors, particularly the World Bank and the United States on the grounds that it ran counter to the established pattern of comparative advantage.

Iron and steel, nonferrous metals, shipbuilding, machinery, and chemical industries were chosen as growth sectors. The HCI drive illustrates the financial leverage wielded by the Korean government. Large firms, selected on the basis of their past performance and connections, were "invited" to expand production into specific industries. They were guaranteed generous access to finance at favorable rates from the nationalized banking sector, priority access to imports, assistance with technology and frequently direct subsidies, tax holidays, accelerated depreciation, and investment tax credits. By the end of the 1970s, the effective marginal corporate tax rate on heavy industry was 30 percent less than the comparable rate on light industry. The level of import protection in these industries also rose during this time, reversing the global trend toward freer trade.

Directed credit, however, was the most powerful tool. At the outset of the HCI drive in 1973–1974, heavy industry accounted for just one-third of total bank loans to industry; just two years later in 1975–1976, heavy industry received over 60 percent of such loans. Increased government involvement in the credit allocation process occurred at the same time. The share of "policy loans" from the commercial banks (that is, those loans made at the behest of the government) rose from less than 50 percent in 1970 to more than 60 percent in 1978.

There is still controversy about the effect of the HCI campaign. It did succeed in sustaining expansion during a period of severe global stagnation; GNP growth in the 1970s averaged 9.6 percent per year, on a pace with the 1960s. Exports, too, continued their rapid expansion at a rate of 31 percent per annum, slower than the 44 percent managed in the 1960s but still remarkable by most standards. The structure of output in Korean industry was certainly changed. In 1971 light industry represented 56 percent of the total, and heavy industry 44 percent, but by 1980 this proportion had reversed.

However, the drive also represented a distortion of the economy, and even after allowing for all of the material incentives enjoyed by firms to induce them to enter heavy industry, there was still considerable short-term economic sacrifice. Amsden presents evidence that throughout the 1970s, profitability remained highest in labor-intensive industry; was greater in light, rather than heavy, industry; and was higher in the older established industries as opposed to the new ones.[8]

The HCI drive probably went against the short-term interests of Korean industrialists, who participated because of government pressure. That in itself does not mean it was misguided, because it is possible that dynamic and short-term efficiency are not coincident. One way to view the HCI drive is as a massive infant-industry protection scheme in which firms were induced to follow long-term national interests by both the carrot and the stick. The result was technological inflow, learning-by-doing, the grasping of economies of scale, and the establishment of an entirely new basis for the Korean economy. Adherence to strictly market logic (a **market-conforming approach**) would not have led to the rapid development of a heavy industrial sector in Korea. The alternate **market-augmenting approach** forced industrialists to accept a lower rate of return on capital in the short-run, but it may well have ensured the continuation of the "miracle" into the 1990s. That said, there is also much evidence to suggest that the HCI drive was carried too far, and that the extirpation of criticism or open-thinking by the government was counterproductive.

Despite its success in sustaining the growth of both GDP and exports, by the late 1970s it was clear that the HCI was creating serious problems, particularly overheating in some sectors. Unemployment fell to an all-time low of 3.2 percent in 1978; and the real income of workers in manufacturing rose by 110 percent between 1974 and 1979, well above the rate of productivity increase; coupled with the rise in oil prices, the wage increases pushed inflation over 20 percent. International competitiveness suffered, the current account lurched into deficit raising international debt, which reached $20.3 billion in 1979, a five-fold increase over 1974. Imports surged, led by the growing need for imported energy, and the increased openness raised Korea's dependence on export markets. As a result, Korea became more vulnerable to shifts in international economic activity, and very serious consequences for the Korean economy resulted from the global downturn in 1980.

The HCI had also increased the fragility of the financial sector. The extensive use of directed credit to finance the expansion of the heavy industrial sector left the banks with a very high proportion of badly performing loans, eroding the asset base of the banking sector.

---

[8] Amsden, 85.

ECONOMIC LIBERALIZATION

The years 1979 and 1980 were bleak for a country conditioned to success. In 1979 Park was assassinated by members of his own secret service. In 1980 the global recession and falling competitiveness caused exports, and output, to fall for the first time in a quarter of a century. The incoming government of General Chun Doo Hwan moved quickly to stabilize the economy through restrictive fiscal and monetary policies, which by 1984 had cooled inflation, at the cost of domestic recession.

The new government feared that the protectionism and isolation of the Korean economy were having a detrimental effect on long-term prospects, so it outlined an ambitious liberalization program. This included partial privatization of the financial sector, lower barriers to entry for nonbank financial intermediaries, reduced use of priority loans (directed credit), and liberalization of foreign trade and capital flows. However, the pace of liberalization was disappointing, and the changes initiated in the early 1980s represented more scaling back the system of state-directed development rather than the establishment of a genuinely free market economy.

PLANNING IN KOREA

Formal economic planning dates from the beginning of the Park regime in 1961 when the Economic Planning Board (EPB), staffed largely by U.S.-trained economists, was established to prepare five-year plans. The First Plan covered the period 1962–1996. Korean planning has always been "top down," initiated by the politicians and technocracy, largely in isolation of the views of business or labor. This contrasts with the role of Ministry of Industry and Trade (MITI) in Japan, or the "concertation" of the indicative planning procedure in France, where consensus building is an important part of the process. Policy proposals are not in general open for discussion, although the process has become more transparent in recent years. This unilateralism was especially characteristic of the Second Plan, and the HCI initiative of the 1970s. The deliberate insulation of the EPB from Korean society had both good and bad points. While it minimized corruption and the possibility of "capture" of the bureaucracy by business, it encouraged bureaucratic arrogance and kept fruitful discussion between government and industry to a minimum. One U.S. advisor to the EPB reported that insulation was so great that there was actually debate within the EPB as to whether policy proposals that originated from outside the board would even be considered.

The EPB used an input/output model, supplemented by industry studies and projections of economic conditions in a wider global context, arriving at a list of products and projects to be pursued by Korean business. Then, in conjunction with the **Ministry of Finance (MoF)**, the **Ministry of Trade and Industry (MTI),** and other relevant ministries, these projects were allocated to particular firms and the necessary inputs, imports, and finances arranged.

Although it used input/output matrices, Korean planning did not establish firm production targets, as in the Soviet system. Consistent with the priority of exports in economic thinking, each firm was given an **export quota.** These quotas were not absolutely binding, but governmental support in future projects or continued access to finance was frequently contingent on success in meeting export targets. A survey of Korean firms in the 1970s found that about 37 percent of firms reported that these targets had a positive effect leading to increased production. Ten percent reported no effect, while 53 percent found that there was some negative impact for the firm—including lower quality, lower productivity, and lower profitability.[9]

In a symbolic move signaling an attempt to shift away from government direction and toward a system of market coordination, the government has recently announced the phasing out of the Economic Planning Board. Since this was the agency created by Park to implement his own personal development strategy, this does mean a shift from the past, but it will not mean an end to interventionism. Most of EPB's powers will still reside in the ministerial structure.

INDUSTRIAL STRUCTURE

THE DOMINANCE OF THE *CHAEBOL*

One of the most singular features of the Korean economy is the role played by its large, diversified industrial groups, the *chaebol*. Generally these groups had their origins in the aid-rich, rent-dominated economy of the 1950s. However, they have continued to grow largely as a result of state-sponsorship, since under the system of state-directed capitalism the government controlled entry into industry, access to raw materials and imports, and, most important, finance. The ascent to dominance by a small group of leading *chaebol* is documented in Table 11.2. In 1974 the combined sales of the top 10 *chaebol* accounted for only 15 percent of GNP, but only a decade later the comparable figure was 67.4 percent. The two largest *chaebol* (Hyundai and Samsung) each had sales equal to 12 percent of GNP.

In 1992, 78 groups were registered as *chaebol* under the Fair Trade Act.[10] These groups were composed of a total of 1,056 subsidiaries. The average number of subsidiaries was therefore 13. The *chaebol* ranged considerably in size. The two largest at the end of 1996 were Hyundai and Samsung. Both these groups had assets of about $63 billion and the groups comprised about 50 subsidiaries. They were followed by Lucky Goldstar (now renamed the LG Group), with assets of $48 billion, and Daewoo ($40 billion).

The dominance of these "big four" groups in the Korean economy is huge. Together they accounted in 1994 for 22 percent of total assets, 32 percent of total sales, 57 percent of total exports, but only 3 percent of total employment. The top 10 *chaebol* account for over 70 percent of sales and roughly one-quarter of all the value added in the economy.

---

[9] Amsden, 69.

[10] Under the old rules, all groups of companies with combined assets of more than $500 million were considered to be *chaebol*. New rules introduced in 1993 define only the largest 30 of these groups as *chaebol*.

■ TABLE 11.2

CUMULATIVE COMBINED SALES OF TOP TEN *CHAEBOL*, PERCENTAGE OF GNP, 1974–1984

Groups	1974	1976	1978	1980	1982	1984
1	4.9	4.7	6.9	8.3	10.4	12
2	7.2	8.1	12.9	16.3	19	24
3	9	11.3	16.9	23.9	27.4	35.8
4	10.3	12.9	20.7	30.1	35.6	44.3
5	11.6	14.5	22.9	35	42.2	52.4
6	12.7	16.1	24.7	38.2	46	56.2
7	13.5	17.5	26.4	41	49.2	59.4
8	14.3	18.4	27.7	43.6	52.2	62.1
9	14.7	19.3	28.9	46	55.1	64.8
10	15.1	19.8	30.1	48.1	57.6	67.4

SOURCE: Amsden, 116.

CHAEBOL AND *KEIRETSU* COMPARED

Chaebol are frequently compared to Japanese *keiretsu,* and there are clear similarities. However, there are also important differences:

1. The first, and perhaps most important difference is that the equity capital within a Korean *chaebol* is even more closely held than in a Japanese *keiretsu.* Many groups are still led by the original founders, who still hold the majority of the capital. Many of the subsidiaries within the groups are wholly owned and not publicly listed. Only 163 of the 623 subsidiaries of the largest *chaebol* are listed. High debt-to-equity ratios within the *chaebol* (Daewoo, for example, has a 9:1 ratio) allow relatively small amounts of equity capital to control large assets. In Japan the policy of the postwar occupation authorities to dissolve the close-held *zaibatsu* system led to a greater dispersion of equity holdings.

2. The family nature of *chaebol* ownership is reflected in the management structure. Many *chaebol* are still headed by their original founder and senior management is often recruited from within the family. In general, the major Japanese groups are led by professional management.[11]

3. The relationship between the groups and the government has been less cooperative in Korea than in Japan. President Park needed the *chaebol* to pursue heavy industrial growth, on which depended military security. Consequently he cajoled, bullied, and bribed them into compliance. Decision making was unilateral, flowing from government to industry. In Japan

---

[11] There are, as always, exceptions on both sides. Sony, Honda, and Toyota are all headed by founders, while Daewoo is in the hands of professional managers.

"the iron triangle" worked more cooperatively and ideas flowed in both directions. After Park's assassination business-government relations did change, but not in a healthy way. The power that Park had established over the *chaebol* became more open to manipulation, and Park's single-minded, somewhat ascetic approach became tempered by corruption. Recent court proceedings have revealed that President Roh Tae Woo received more than $650 million dollars in bribes from business during his eight-year career. While scandals have rocked the Japanese political establishment too, the stakes have not been this high.

4. A feature of most of the Japanese *keiretsu* is the group bank, which provides credit to member companies. In Korea, the government nationalized the banking system, and groups had no access to internal finance, heightening the degree of government control over the groups.

5. *Chaebol* conduct an even wider range of activities than *keiretsu*. Many *keiretsu* are vertically oriented (like Toyota) and although the group consists of many firms, all are oriented around a core activity. Even the horizontal *keiretsu*, which are diversified, tend in general to be more closely grouped around core activities than the *chaebol*.

6. *Chaebol* are even more burdened by debt than Japanese companies. The use of soft loans rather than equity fostered rapid growth in Korea, but resulted in high debt-to-equity ratios, threatening both industry and finance. It also complicates reform. At this point in time, imposing a hard budget constraint on enterprises nurtured on soft loans would produce bankruptcies, which would reduce bank assets and produce failure in the financial sector. The government would need to guarantee the debts of the firm, or else the consequences on the financial system would be serious.

THE *CHAEBOL* AND ECONOMIC EFFICIENCY

The Korean government had a leading role in establishing the dominance of the major *chaebol*, particularly during the HCI drive and the subsequent business downturn. Table 11.2 shows that in 1974, at the start of the drive, the combined sales of the top 10 groups amounted to only 15 percent of GDP; no group had sales of more than 4.9 percent of GDP. However, government policy was to nurture heavy industry by inviting the major *chaebol* to enter into new fields while providing the necessary loan capital and import licenses. Each success was rewarded by new invitations and new privileges. By 1984, the largest two groups (Hyundai and Samsung) each had sales of 12 percent of GDP, and the share of the top 10 had risen to 67.4 percent.

Most goods markets in Korea are characterized by concentration ratios that are high relative to western standards; an economy-wide analysis in 1981 showed an average three-firm concentration ratio of 62 percent, indicating even greater concentration than Japan or Taiwan. Though this did not mean the total absence of competition since *chaebol* compete with each other aggressively over market share and although competition is often nonprice in nature, it does put limits on the abuse of monopoly power and promotes efficiency.

However, the main force for efficiency comes from the need to compete in international markets. Since the early 1960s, when Park declared that exports were Korea's "economic lifeline," industry's success has been evaluated in terms of export performance and larger enterprises had to face, and succeed against, international competition in foreign markets. However, by the late 1980s doubts about the ability of an industrial structure dominated by the *chaebol* to sustain growth became widespread.

REFORMING THE CHAEBOL

The *chaebol*, and the unwavering government guidance and support that they had enjoyed, are usually credited with the rapid growth of the Korean economy, its development of a heavy industrial base, and its export performance. Although performance in export markets provided some check on competitiveness, until the late 1990s the government never allowed any of the groups, or even parts of groups, to fail. Sometimes operations were transferred from one group to another in search of better performance, but by and large a soft budget constraint operated as universally as in any socialist country. Moreover, the very high ratios of debt to equity in Korean business meant that any failure in manufacturing could have dire consequences for the banking system. Consequently, the government acted to bail out almost any failing enterprise.

Economic performance began to falter in the late 1980s, and doubts grew about whether a *chaebol*-dominated structure was adequate to sustain the economy into the next century. In 1992 the incoming administration of Kim Young Sam made a serious commitment to systematic reform of the economy, including the *chaebol*, whose influence was seen as a barrier to further economic growth due to several factors:

1. They represent an unhealthy concentration of power in product markets. As noted earlier, the *chaebol* (especially the "big four") dominate many markets, exports, and investment.

2. The demands of the *chaebol* for investment funds have tended to squeeze out nascent small enterprise and have handicapped the growth of innovative companies.

3. The *chaebol* are integrally connected with the corruption of the Korean economy.

4. Diversification within the *chaebol* creates substantial diseconomies of organization. Top management, often drawn from the founding family, does not have the expertise to operate in wide-ranging markets, yet these managers are unwilling to delegate.

5. Finally, the government is concerned that the strategy of aggressive globalization pursued by the major *chaebol* involves too many risks. This fear owes much to the costly disaster of the 1980s when Korean overseas construction operations fell victim to recession, became bankrupt, and left the government to clean up the mess. The pace and scale of globalization in

the mid-1990s was impressive. In 1994 Korean companies initiated almost 2,000 overseas investments with a total value of more than $3.5 billion; the figures for 1995 were comparable. Daewoo planned to establish 600 overseas companies by the year 2000. LG Group planned to invest $10 billion in mainland China alone between 1991 and 2008, a figure larger than Korea's total overseas investment in 1994.

The Korean government has chosen to rein in the *chaebol* by regulation rather than by allowing increased competition. Foreign economists question this, arguing that a quicker way would be to liberalize financial markets and open the door for foreign firms to market and invest in Korea. That would force *chaebol* to retrench into core areas where they hold an advantage and to sell off less productive assets to owners who can put them to higher value uses. However, such retrenchment and downsizing brings with it loss of employment and increased foreign ownership, both of which might lead to political dissatisfaction. Consequently, the government has acted to intervene rather than to liberalize, getting the chaebol to agree to reduce the number of subsidiaries and transfer assets between each other in return for continued protection and support. This has led to skepticism about both the government's commitment to a market solution and outcome. The main activity with respect to the five major *chaebol* are shown in the box titled "Restructuring the *Chaebol*" on page 261.

There are other elements to the reform agenda:

1. *Real name financial accounting.* Korean corruption has been facilitated by a system that allowed bank accounts to be opened with dummy names, which made tracing bribes difficult. Now such accounts will be outlawed and only "real name" accounts will be legal.

2. *Restriction of founding family's investments.* Only subsidiaries in which the founding family's holding is less than 8 percent will be able to raise capital and pursue new businesses.

3. *Restrictions on* **intragroup cross investment.** No company in a *chaebol* will be able to invest more than 40 percent of its capital in a company in the same group. This percent is scheduled to decline with time, reducing the within-group financial linkages.

4. *Restricting outgoing foreign investment.* To curb overseas investment by Korean firms, new regulations require that all overseas investments above $100 million require at least 20 percent domestic capital.

It is possible that much of this regulation may be unnecessary. Economics alone is forcing many *chaebol* to evaluate their structure and to question whether, in the view of the problems created by size and complexity, it is necessary to offer such a breadth of products. Since entry into many industries was the result of government intervention, lower profile government may allow market processes to initiate rationalization. Moreover, the dynastic nature of many *chaebol* is leading to division of power within the group. Just as Charlemagne's empire was split among his sons, so the need to accommodate a new generation is leading to the breakup

RESTRUCTURING THE *CHAEBOL*

The Korean government responded to the problems of the economy by sponsoring the restructuring of the *chaebol*. Although much of the activity involved shifting assets between major *chaebol*, for the first time foreign capital was actively encouraged to play a role. As of mid-1999 the following steps had been taken with respect to the five largest groups:

HYUNDAI GROUP

- Hyundai Group agreed with the South Korean government to cut its number of affiliates to 31 from the current 63 by the end of 1999 through spin-offs, sell-offs, or mergers.

- The group aims to attract $4.5 billion in foreign capital in 1999 through joint ventures, asset sell-offs, and issues of securities.

SAMSUNG GROUP

- Samsung Group made plans to reduce the number of subsidiaries to 40 from 65 by end-1999, and ultimately to 23. Plans to expand steel output have been opposed by the government because it fears competition with the government-owned POSCO works.

- The government opposed its expansion into automobiles and has brokered the transfer of troubled Samsung Motors to Daewoo Group in return for Daewoo's electronics businesses.

- Samsung Electronics sold its 45 percent share in a joint venture company with Hewlett-Packard Co.

- Samsung Heavy Industries sold its construction equipment unit for $702 million to Sweden's Volvo Group.

DAEWOO GROUP

- The Daewoo group is the most troubled of the *chaebol* and is a test of government resolve to reform. Founded in the 1960s by Kim Woo Choong, a former shipyard worker, the group's story mirrored the rise of South Korea.
  Daewoo tried to swim against the tide of austerity. When the economic crisis forced most of the *chaebol* to cut back, Daewoo added 14 new firms to its existing 275 subsidiaries, although the group lost a combined 550 billion won ($458 million) on sales of 62 trillion won ($51 billion), adding 40 percent in debt. By 1999 it was insolvent, but rather than let it fail the government has supported it and propped up the bond market to do so.
  It has now agreed to focus on 10 companies in the fields of vehicles, shipbuilding, trade, construction, and financial services.

LG GROUP

- LG Group would cut the number of its affiliates to 32 units from the current 53 by end-2000.

- The group aimed to attract $6.5 billion from overseas by the end of 1999 through sales of business lines and other foreign investments.

- LG Group sold its 23.5 percent stake in LG Telecom to British Telecommunications for $390 million.

SK GROUP

- SK Group plans to reduce the number of units to 22 from 49 by the end of 2002.

- The group sold Yukong Erastomer Co. to Sumitomo Chemical Co. Ltd.

of the tight autocratic structure that prevailed hitherto. Each of the four brothers of Chung Ju Woon, the founder of Hyundai, runs a satellite *chaebol*; the largest, Halla, is the sixteenth biggest in the country.[12] Samsung has spun off two smaller groups in the last two years—one run by the founder's sister and one by his niece.

---

[12] *The Economist*, 18 May 1996, 69.

■ **TABLE 11.3**

SAVINGS AND INVESTMENT RATES AS A PERCENTAGE OF GDP, 1961–1990

	Private Saving	Government Saving	Foreign Saving	Investment
1961–1965	6.8	0	8.1	14.8
1966–1970	10.3	5.5	9.8	25.8
1971–1975	15.5	3.7	9.1	27.6
1976–1980	18	6.2	6.4	31.3
1981–1985	18.4	6.5	4.9	30.1
1986–1990	29.2	7.5	− 4.5	31.6

SOURCE: Kuznets, 43.

INVESTMENT AND SAVINGS

Korea has maintained a high investment rate since the early 1960s. Fixed capital formation has taken at least a quarter of GDP in every time period since then. Since the outset of the HCI, private investment has averaged more than 30 percent of GDP per annum. However, the savings behavior of Koreans has changed considerably.

Table 11.3 shows the rate of gross domestic capital formation as well as the means of finance. One of the most salient features of the table is the high degree of reliance on foreign saving as a source of funds for investment during the early years. In the 1960s and early 1970s, this category (comprised largely of foreign aid transfers and net borrowing from the rest of the world) made up at least 30 percent of total capital formation. It fell sharply in the early 1980s and in fact turned negative (repayments were greater than new borrowing) by the 1990s. This extensive overseas borrowing implied a growing external debt, which peaked at the end of 1985, at a level of $47 billion.

Private domestic saving[13] has risen considerably in recent years. Studies of the Korean economy in the 1980s noted the relatively low level of personal saving in Korea, relative to Taiwan and Japan.[14] Since then, however, personal saving in Korea has increased to about one-quarter of disposal income, implying relatively high personal marginal savings rates. Korea now has a higher gross savings rate (domestic savings/GDP) than any member of the Organization for Economic Co-operation and Development (OECD), including Japan.[15] The World Bank reports

---

[13]Private saving is the saving of both businesses (through retained earnings and depreciation allowances) and private households.

[14]For example, see Tibor Scitovsky, "Economic Development in Taiwan and South Korea, 1965–1981," in *Models of Development: A Comparative Study of Korea and Taiwan*, ed. Lawrence J. Lau (San Francisco: San Francisco, Institute of Contemporary Studies, 1986), 168–178.

[15] Actually Luxembourg's is greater but this is due to small size and special circumstance.

that at 35 percent of GDP in 1993, Korea has the sixth highest gross savings rate in the world, an achievement bettered only by Thailand, Malaysia, Singapore, Gabon, and Jamaica.

THE FINANCIAL SYSTEM

BANKING

The structure of the Korean Financial System is relatively simple. At the top is the central bank, the **Bank of Korea, BoK.** Since May 1962, when the military government made the central bank subject to its political will, the BoK has enjoyed little independence. Despite the retention of a board of governors, all important matters are decided by the minister of finance, and, in cases of deep disagreement between the minister and the board of governors, by the cabinet as a whole.

There are two forms of deposit institutions: commercial banks and specialized banks. There are 14 nationwide commercial banks and 10 regional ones.[16] The commercial banks are largely funded by retail deposits, augmented by borrowing from the central bank. The military regime nationalized the commercial banks in 1962, and they remained under government control until 1982. Although nominally private, the government controls their actions and until 1993 vetted all important personnel changes. The commercial banks made about one-third of total loans in the 1990s. Six specialized deposit banks, all government controlled, represent about 12 percent of total loans made in Korea. The oldest of these is the Korean Development Bank, which finances major development projects. The Industrial Bank of Korea is oriented to small- and medium-sized business, and the Citizens' National Bank operates in household finance. There are also three banking cooperatives: for farmers, livestock producers, and fisheries.

Until recently, the conduct of banking was not based on market principles. Interest rates paid to depositors were controlled by the government and kept low. Loans to industry were directed by the government and frequently carried lower interest rates than the depositor received. Depending on inflation, it was not uncommon for depositors to receive, and for borrowers to pay, negative real interest rates. This had several undesirable effects. The supply of savings was consequently depressed, and businesses, especially those not in favor with the government, were denied access to funds.

Inevitably an unofficial street or **curb market** arose. Interest rates paid to lenders were substantially above those paid in the banks.[17] The size of this market was hard to gauge, but it has been estimated that between one-third and 40 percent[18] of all business loans originated there. In 1972 the government attempted both to

---

[16] In addition, 55 foreign banks have branches operating in Korea.
[17] In 1970 the time deposit rate was 22.8 percent where the curb rate for deposits was 50.8 percent.
[18] Song, 162; Cho, 130.

suppress the curb market and to meet industry demands for cheaper credit. Nominal bank deposit rates were cut (to 12 percent), loan rates to industry reduced, and the curb market penalized. However, with inflation hovering around 20 percent throughout the 1970s, real interest rates in the formal sector were negative, and the curb market paying positive real rates continued to prosper well into the 1980s. The cause of the curb market was **financial repression** in the formal market, but from the 1970s onward the government allowed and encouraged the growth of nonbank financial institutions. This, coupled with the higher rates paid by the commercial banks, has much reduced the scope of the curb market.

EQUITY MARKETS

The privately incorporated **Korean Stock Exchange (KSE)** is the sole official stock exchange. It is overseen by a **Securities and Exchange Commission** responsible to the Ministry of Finance. Government policy toward the stock market has been interventionist and has, through tax and other measures, encouraged its growth. In the 1960s; for example, the government required large companies to issue attractively priced shares and use the proceeds to reduce bank debt. The number of traded stocks rose sharply, from 34 in 1968 to 688 in 1992. Market capitalization was $107 billion at the end of 1993; this was about one-third of GDP and the 14th largest market in the world. Further use of the equity market is desirable since it would further reduce the debt-to-equity ratios of Korean industry, contributing to both business and financial-sector stability.

There are concerns about the stability of the stock market itself. The government, as in many other areas, has seen fit to intervene. It has actively promoted the market, encouraging the activity of small and unsophisticated participants, making the market quite volatile. The government has also manipulated stock prices ostensibly in the interest of stabilization, a policy fraught with danger since markets in which the government is known to intervene are more likely to be unstable. The market needs a more even-handed approach and more transparent supervision at this point.

FURTHER LIBERALIZATION

The development of the Korean economy has been distorted by the fact that investment capital was available in different industries at widely different rates of interest. As late as 1992 the Bank of Korea reported that, while the average cost of funds in the electricity industry was 7.6 percent, in textiles it was 12 percent and in food production 17 percent.[19] While this dispersion was considerably lower than observed a decade earlier, it still had injurious consequences for Korean economic

---

[19] The rates are lowest for heavy industry because the government usually acts to secure foreign finance at a level below Korean rates.

welfare since it biased investment in favor of heavy industry and against the consumer sector.

The five-year liberalization program for the financial sector, introduced in 1993, attempted to further reduce distortion by deregulating interest rates for both borrowing and lending. This should have the effect of reducing the implicit subsidy to heavy industry and the *chaebol*. The main beneficiary is likely to be the household sector, which will receive higher interest rates on deposits (possibly causing the household saving rate to rise further) and a reduction in the cost of credit for consumption and home construction.

PUBLIC FINANCE

SIZE OF THE GOVERNMENT SECTOR

Despite its continued heavy intervention in many areas, the government sector in Korea is small relative to most developed countries. About 25 percent of GDP is gathered by the government in taxes, the lowest of any OECD member. This is about two-thirds of the Japanese level and about half of the average level in the OECD. The main reason for this is the relatively rudimentary social security system, introduced only in 1988.

THE VALUE-ADDED TAX

The revenue system places heavy reliance on the value-added tax (VAT). It has a nominal single rate of 10 percent supplemented by additional levies on certain goods, imposed both to discourage consumption and to raise revenue. Taken together, these indirect taxes on consumption provide 46 percent of general government revenue. Property taxes raise a further 14 percent. Consumption taxes like the VAT are generally regressive, taking a larger share of the income of less well-off families. Studies have indicated that this is true in Korea, but the reliance on indirect taxation, and the regressivity of the system, may be helpful in meeting development objectives. The disincentive effects of progressive income tax rates are avoided while capital accumulation and savings by high income groups are promoted.

THE PERSONAL INCOME TAX

Income taxation (i.e., the personal income tax plus corporate income taxes) accounts for about 35 percent of tax revenue. Both corporate and personal taxes have recently been reformed to move them away from a "schedular" system, in which the rates varied sharply between sources and industry. This system was an overt tool in selective industrial development. The new "global" system seeks to provide a more level playing field.

Most Koreans pay no income tax at all; only about 5 percent of the total population files a tax return, against about 45 percent in the United States. Even among those who file, most pay only an effective rate of 3.8 percent of income. Rates are progressive and rise to a maximum of 50 percent, but this is paid at the margin only by those whose income is more than 6.5 times the average. To encourage saving, and as a hangover of the schedular system, there is a ceiling tax rate on interest and dividend income of 20 percent.[20]

THE CORPORATE INCOME TAX

Corporate taxes once varied between industry and between source. Profits from exports, for example, were once tax exempt. Now, however, the corporate tax is flat: 20 percent for small companies and 34 percent for large. Incentives are retained in the form of tax credits for exports (2 percent of total sales) and a 10 percent credit for investment in research and development.

LABOR MARKETS

THE ROLE OF ABUNDANT LABOR

Korea's success in penetrating export markets relied on plentiful cheap labor, which was the result of three factors:

1. The existence of a large subsistence agricultural sector, with low marginal productivity, from which labor could be drawn at low wages and with little impact on agricultural output.

2. The failure of an active and radical union movement to emerge during the first 25 years of rapid growth. Amsden considers this to be a common feature of late industrializers and attributes it to the absence of a cadre of skilled workers, "a labor aristocracy," which provided the model for unionization in Europe and the United States.

3. The policy of the successive governments (especially Park and Chun) to repress worker activity and intervene with force in labor disputes. A general feature of regime changes in Korea has been a great deal of strike activity immediately after a change of president.[21] Strong government action usually restored a "law-and-order" antiunion policy.

---

[20] To encourage "going public," dividends of unlisted companies are taxed at a higher rate of 25 percent.

[21] Peaks of strike activity occurred in 1960–1961 after the death of Syngman Rhee, 1979–1980 after the death of Park, and in 1987–1989 after the replacement of Chun with Roh Tae Woo. See Rodgers in Lawrence B. Krause and Fun-koo Park, *Social Issues in Korea: Korean and American Perspectives* (Seoul, Korea: Korean Development Institute, 1993) 78.

THE RISE OF UNIONISM

In the late 1980s, however, the situation was permanently changed. Incoming President Roh was confronted by worker and student activism. Loathe to use force lest world reaction led to a cancellation of the 1988 Seoul Olympics, Roh changed legislation to allow more union activity. Union membership doubled to 1.9 million between 1986 and 1990 and the density of membership among eligible workers rose to 23.7 percent. Union militancy in pursuit of higher wages has increased, due in part to the growth of new unions, which were technically illegal, outside the moderate structure of the Korean Federation of Trade Unions (KFTU). Wage increases accelerated, averaging 17 percent per annum between 1987 and 1996; real increases after inflation were considerably less, around 10 percent, but still substantial and greater than the gain in labor productivity, implying increasing labor costs.

BARGAINING PROCEDURES

Wages are negotiated at the plant level, between the employers and the representative unions. However, national negotiations between the KFTU and its employers' counterpart, the Korean Employers Federation (KEF), supervised and guided by the government, provide the context. The government would like to strengthen collective bargaining at the national level and is promoting a "national wages board," which would determine a fixed aggregate pace of settlements. To date, it has failed to induce the unions to accept the wages board. Nevertheless, the government does promote specific guidelines for wage increases and indulges in considerable "jawboning" to see it is followed.

The outcome of collective bargaining at the plant level has generally exceeded the figure negotiated between the unions and the employers at the national level as well as the government's suggested guidelines. For example, in 1991, after a demand for an increase of 17.5 percent by the KFTU and an offer of 7.0 by the KEF, the national bargain process settled at 10.5 percent, close to the government guideline of 10 percent. However, the actual outcome of the plant agreements led to an increase of 17.2 percent. Wages at larger firms have increased most rapidly in recent years, widening the gap with those who work in smaller establishments. If labor markets were competitive this differential should disappear over time, but the growing power of the unions might create a dualistic labor market.

MANAGING LABOR IN THE WORKPLACE

Labor management in Korea has been criticized for its rigidity. While generalizations are dangerous and exceptions may be found, emphasis in Korean factories seems to be placed on discipline rather than on worker initiative. Deference is paid to the conception of workplace efficiency, Taylorism, rather than to modern methods. This is in contrast to the policies in Japan's large corporations. These repressive practices might become a greater problem as the economy develops because they stifle individual initiative.

■ **TABLE 11.4**

EDUCATION ATTENDANCE IN KOREA AS A PERCENTAGE OF RELEVANT AGE GROUP

	1970	1980	1990
Kindergarten	1.8	4.1	55.4
Elementary school	100	100	100
Middle school	51	95.1	96.3
High school	28.1	63.5	86.8
Tertiary Education	8.8	16	37.6

SOURCE: Korean Educational Development Institute, *Education Indicators in Korea.*

EDUCATION AND HUMAN CAPITAL

Korea has made a very large social investment in the education of its young people. In 1990, 3.6 percent of GDP was devoted to expenditure on education, up from just 2 percent in 1960, which represented a huge increase in real terms because of the growth of the economy. Education ranks high in the government's priorities and 22.5 percent of total government outlays was devoted to educational expenditures in 1990. Today, school attendance is on a par with almost all of the developed market economies. This can be seen in Table 11.4. Particularly noteworthy is universal primary school attendance and the gains in middle and high school and tertiary education. Moreover, unlike in many developing or recently developed countries, there is little bias in the education system between male and female children. Female enrollment ratios in primary school are 100 percent, and this slips to 85 percent in high school, much the same as the overall figure. Female attendance in tertiary is lower than male attendance. However, statistics show substantial bias in the workplace against women. Women make up only 3 percent of the managerial and administrative workforce. This might in part be a generational problem. Female educational attainment has increased rapidly, but if Korea follows the Japanese experience, women will have a hard time reaching the upper echelons of management.

The gain in education has not only been in terms of numbers attending school. The educational achievement of Korean children has also been very high. Standardized international tests (see Table 11.5) show Korean students with extraordinary attainment in math and science-related areas of the curriculum.

SOURCES OF GROWTH

Until the mid-1990s Korean growth was remarkable not only for its rapidity, but also for its consistency. Real GDP grew at 9 percent between 1963–1973, accelerated slightly during 1973–1979 (the period of HCI), and pulled back slightly to

▪ TABLE 11.5

EDUCATIONAL PERFORMANCE: ATTAINMENT ON STANDARDIZED TEST, AGE 13, 1997

	Math	Science
Korea	73.4	77.7
Switzerland	70.8	73.7
France	64.2	68.6
Italy	64.0	69.9
Canada	62.0	68.8
Scotland	60.6	67.9
England	60.6	68.7
Ireland	60.5	63.3
Spain	55.4	67.2
US	55.3	67.0

SOURCE: OECD.

8.2 percent between 1979 and 1990 (see Table 11.6). Later figures (not included in the table because they have no accompanying breakdown on the sources of growth) indicate that the rate recovered to over 9 percent during 1990 and 1991, slipped to around 5 percent in 1992 and 1993, but was trending upward again in 1994, before falling during the Asian crisis of 1997–1998.

However, the bulk of that growth has been the result of an increase in factor inputs, rather than an improvement in **total factor productivity (TFP)**.[22] In other words, most of Korean growth is attributable to the increase in the number of hours worked, an increase in the amount of capital per worker, and the movement of workers from the low productivity rural and self-employed sector into the industrialized urban sector. Only in the early period of growth did advances in knowledge have a distinct effect on the increase in output. TFP grew at a rate of about only 2.4 percent across the whole period, falling between the earlier and the later years. In the export-oriented period of 1963–1973, total growth of 9 percent could be decomposed into 5.6 percent due to factor inputs and 3.4 percent TFP. Labor inputs grew at 3.2 percent, largely due to an increased labor force participation rate. Capital inputs (residential and nonresidential) grew at 2.4 percent. In terms of increase in efficiency, the biggest free lunch was the movement of workers from the agricultural sector into higher productivity manufacturing and service sector jobs, and a substantial increase due to increased applied technology.

During the HCI period, both labor and capital inputs increased more rapidly; the movement of labor from the rural to the industrial sector increased its role,

[22]Recall that TFP is defined as the increase in output per factor input, and is usually measured as a residual after controlling for the increase in inputs. It represents mostly the growth that results from an improvement in allocative efficiency, the grasping of scale economies, and the effect of increases in technical expertise.

■ **TABLE 11.6**

GROWTH OF GDP AND ITS SOURCES (BY SUBPERIOD, PERCENT PER ANNUM)

	1963–1973	1973–1979	1979–1990	1963–1990
GDP growth rate (annual average)	9.00	9.26	8.21	8.74
Contributions to Growth				
Factor inputs	5.64	7.01	6.66	6.36
Business labor input	3.18	3.49	2.66	3.04
Employment	2.28	2.13	1.64	1.99
Hours worked	0.5	0.52	−0.07	0.27
Age-sex composition	−0.06	0.3	0.14	0.1
Education	0.47	0.55	0.94	0.68
Nonresidential capital input	1.19	1.79	2.66	1.92
Residential capital input	1.24	1.67	1.26	1.35
Land	0.03	0.06	0.08	0.06
Output per unit of input (TFP)	3.37	2.25	1.55	2.38
Improved resource allocation	1.23	1.76	0.96	1.24
Effect of weather on farming	0.23	0.18	−0.11	0.08
Economies of scale	0.26	0.34	0.21	0.26
Advances in knowledge	1.64	−0.02	0.50	0.80

SOURCE: Organization of Economic Cooperation and Development. *Economic Survey: Korea.* Paris: OECD, 1996.

but advances in knowledge and other residual factors had no positive impact on growth, confirming the suspicions that the distortions of the HCI drive had a negative effect on overall efficiency. In the final period of the table capital increased its role once more, and reallocation of labor had a smaller effect as the reserve of labor in agriculture had been largely used up.

This profile has led to a reexamination of the nature of the "Korean miracle." In an influential article published in *Foreign Affairs* in 1994, Paul Krugman drew attention to a large and growing literature that indicated that the "miracle" owed far more to increased participation rates, the movement of labor, and rapid accumulation of capital than it did to increases in efficiency per se. He compared the industrialization of South Korea with that of Stalin's Soviet Union: it was due much more to increase in factors of production (labor and capital) than to the more efficient use of those factors. We will return to this in a fuller discussion of the Asian miracle.[23]

UNIFYING NORTH AND SOUTH KOREA?

In our discussion of Asian economies we have concentrated on capitalist systems and have said little about North Korea, which remains one of the most closed and

---

[23] See more on this issue in chapter 14.

■ **TABLE 11.7**

THE KOREAS AND THE GERMANYS: SOCIAL AND ECONOMIC INDICATORS

	(1) South Korea	(2) North Korea	(3) (2) as a percent of (1)	(4) West Germany	(5) East Germany	(6) (5) as a Percent of (6)
Population	44.9	23.3	51.9	62.1	16.6	26.7
GDP per head, $ PPP	10,067	957	9.5	19,283	5,840	30.3
Exports, % of GDP	27.7	3.3	11.9	28.3	24.5	86.6
Imports, % of GDP	29.9	5.9	19.7	22.4	24.3	108.5
Infant mortality per 1,000 births	12.8	31.3	244.5	7.4	7.7	101.4
Farm population, % of total	13.1	37.6	287	3.7	10.8	291.9
Radios per 1,000 population	1003	207	20.6	830	990	119.3

Data for the Koreas is 1995 and that for Germany is 1989.

SOURCE: Dresdner Bank, reproduced in *The Economist*, 10 May 1997, 78.

isolationist states in the world. Although information is scarce, it seems that currently the economy is in crisis and faces possible collapse. In these circumstances the military standoff that has dominated Korean political life (and has had a sizable impact on economic development) might soon be a thing of the past.[24] Moreover, it seems increasingly likely that we shall see the reunification of the two Korean states, as we witnessed in Vietnam in the 1970s and in Germany in the late 1980s. Therefore it is logical to inquire as to what the economic impact of such a reunification would be.

In the long run, the reunification might give South Korean industry access to substantial additional natural resources, but the economic benefit of this alone will be slight. Despite the optimistic prediction of many economists in 1989, the unification of Germany was a very traumatic episode. We will review some of that history in chapter 20. The main cause of this was the low level of productivity in East German industry coupled with the political necessity of unifying the currency system at a rate that would give something like comparable standards of living. The impact of that unification is now well known. After unification, East German labor was very highly paid relative to its productivity, and therefore the region could not compete with manufacturing industry in the European Community. The result was a massive loss of jobs, considerable out-migration, the commitment of 5 percent of West Germany's GDP to Eastern reconstruction, and considerable ill will. The task in the Korean peninsula would be even more formidable. The data provided in Table 11.7 give some indication of this. Unification led to an increase of the West German population of about 23 percent. In Korea the addition would be almost 52 percent. On average, East Germans were about 30 percent as well off as West Germans. GDP per head in North Korea is less than 10 percent of that in

---

[24] Despite its economic difficulties, North Korea continues to prioritize the military and add technologically advanced weaponry to its arsenal.

the south. Equal distribution of the joint GDP in Korea would involve a transfer of about one-third of the total product of the south. Even the much more modest goal of raising average income in the north to 50 percent of that in the south would involve a transfer of about $60 billion annually, over 13 percent of South Korean GDP. In Germany the level of transfers was close to 5 percent of West German GDP. Although there would be very significant savings in terms of military expenditure on the forces now ranged across the 50th parallel, the short-term consequences of that would be deflationary and the "peace dividend" would be secured only after substantial changes in the structure of production. In short, as an economic proposition, reuniting the North with South Korea would be very costly to South Korea in the near term.

THE PROSPECTS FOR KOREA

At the time of writing, the prospects for the Korean economy are somewhat mixed. Although attempts have been made to force reform and curb the power of the large *chaebol*, the success of this drive has so far been limited. The largest five groups account for 37 percent of output and 44 percent of national exports, and their share might grow as other groups look in greater difficulty. Many subsidiaries of large *chaebol* are in financial difficulties, but the government is unwilling to let them go bankrupt for fear of provoking a widespread domino effect.

The government has taken an active approach to restructuring the groups. It tried to require that the ratio of debt to equity be reduced to 200 percent by the end of 1999, involving a considerable amount of debt-equity swapping, whereby the banks receive shares in payment for loans. In mid-1997 the *average* debt-to-equity ratio for the top 10 *chaebol* was over 800 percent. Also the government is attempting, through the Financial Supervisory Commission (FSC), to rationalize the groups by swapping subsidiaries to reduce the horizontal spread of the groups and foster greater specialization, allowing concentration of management expertise. However, this program is running with difficulty, and groups fight over who should get control of particular sectors of industry. To encourage the growth of small and medium-sized industry, the government has created a special fund of $1.2 billion for development loans. The top 5 *chaebol* are banned from access to this fund altogether and the next 25 largest are limited to only 30 percent of the total capital available. While the intent is good, the implementation is still interventionist and supplants the "level playing field" of the market with a new form of directed credit.[25]

A major test of the government's resolve occurred in August of 1999 when Daewoo, then the second largest *chaebol*, was unable to meet its obligations on its $50 billion of debt.[26] The group had continued to expand and pick up companies at cheap prices throughout the Asian financial crisis, and as a result its debt became unmanageable. Although the government of Kim Dae Jung has been emphatic that

---

[25] See "The Chaebol That Ate Korea," *The Economist,* 14 November 1998, 67.

[26] "The Death of Daewoo," *The Economist,* 21 August 1999, 55.

it will not bail out the group, neither government nor the banks have moved to liquidate a single Daewoo company. A financial restructuring will give bondholders a title to 80 percent of the value of the debt they hold, but the group will continue to be under the direction of Kim Woo Chang, who founded the firm in 1967. While government policy is overtly directed to destroying the hold of the major *chaebol*, it is unwilling to let any die through bankruptcy.

Restructuring on an economy-wide basis will be very difficult until there is tightening of Korea's rather toothless bankruptcy law. As *The Economist* has reported:

> To reform a country's economy, weak firms must be weeded out so that the strong have more room to grow. Yet South Korean bankruptcy does not work like that. In the United States, under Chapter 11, a court typically appoints new managers to restructure the firm or to liquidate it in an orderly fashion; in Korea, most bankrupt firms simply carry on as before. Managers stay at their desks and rarely shut business. The most popular bankruptcy route, chosen by more than 80 percent of the firms that filed for court protection last year, leaves the existing management untouched. Called *Hwaeui*, it allows firms to defer their existing debts and interest payments, and even to take out new loans, without relinquishing day-to-day control.[27]

Perhaps even more worrisome is that government is allowing bankrupt firms a more lenient path if it considers their core-business to be sound. Under this arrangement government sponsorship gives some firms preferential access to bank loans and hence once more sets the bureaucrats above the market. Until such policies are abandoned, it is hard to see Korea flourishing in a true market economy.

KEY TERMS AND CONCEPTS

Bank of Korea (BoK)

chaebol

Confucianism

curb market

export promotion

export quota

financial repression

Heavy and Chemical Industries Development Plan (HCI)

intragroup cross investment

Korean Stock Exchange (KSE)

market-augmenting approach

market-conforming approach

Ministry of Finance (MoF)

Ministry of Trade and Industry (MTI)

Security and Exchange Commission

total factor productivity (TFP)

QUESTIONS FOR DISCUSSION

1. In what ways may the Japanese colonial period be said to have assisted Korean development? How did it hurt it?

2. Why was the Korean economy "distorted" in the 1950s?

---

[27] "Death Where Is Thy Sting," *The Economist*, 17 July 1999, 59.

3. Did the export promotion drive follow comparative advantage?

4. In what ways can it be said that the Chemical Industries Drive was an exercise in creating comparative advantage?

5. What tools did Korean planners use to favor particular *chaebol?*

6. Why is the concentration of power in *chaebol* alarming? Does it hasten or retard growth?

7. What are the chief differences between the *keiretsu* and the *chaebol?*

8. Is government reform of the *chaebol* likely to be successful?

9. How will increased union activity change the Korean economy?

10. Has Korean growth been extensive or intensive in nature?

11. Why would Korean unification be different from the reunification of Germany?

RESOURCES

WEB SITES

Central Bank . . . . http://www.bok.or.kr/

Korea Herald—**National Newspaper** . . . . http://www.koreaherald.co.kr/

South Korea Subject Guide . . . .
. . . . http://darkwing.uoregon.edu/~felsing/kstuff/kshelf.html

Embassy of Korea in Washington, D.C. . . . . http://koreaemb.org/

BOOKS AND ARTICLES

Alam, M. Shahid. *Governments and Markets in Economic Development Strategies: Lessons from Korea, Taiwan, and Japan.* New York: Praeger, 1989.

Amsden, Alice H. *Asia's Next Giant: South Korea and Late Industrialization.* New York: Oxford University Press, 1989.

Bedeski, Robert E. *The Transformation of South Korea: Reform and Reconstruction in the Sixth Republic under Roh Tae Woo, 1987–1992.* New York: Routledge, 1994.

Chang, Ha-Joon. "The Political Economy of Industrial Policy in Korea." *Cambridge Journal of Economics* 17 (1993): 131–157.

Cho, Lee-Jay, and Yoon Hyung Kim, eds. *Economic Development in the Republic of Korea: A Policy Perspective.* Honolulu: University of Hawaii Press, 1991.

Clifford, Mark L. *Troubled Tiger: Businessmen, Bureaucrats, and Generals in South Korea.* Armonk: M.E. Sharpe, 1994 (rev. by William McGurn in *The American Spectator,* March 1995: 59–61)

Corbo, Vittorio, and Sang-Mok Suh, eds. *Structural Adjustment in a Newly Industrialized Country: The Korean Experience.* Baltimore: Johns Hopkins University Press, 1992.

Eckert, Carter J. *Offspring of Empire: The Koch'ang Kims and the Colonial Origins of Korean Capitalism, 1876–1945.* Seattle: University of Washington Press, 1991.

Hamilton, Clive. *Capitalist Industrialization in Korea.* Boulder: Westview Press, 1986.

Hwang, Eui-Gak. *The Korean Economies: A Comparison of North and South.* Oxford: Clarendon Press, 1993.

Jacobs, Norman. *The Korean Road to Modernization and Development.* Urbana: University of Chicago Press, 1985.

Kim, Eun Mee, ed. *The Four Asian Tigers: Economic Development and the Global Political Economy.* London: Academic Press, 1998.

Kim, June Dong. "Incidence of Protection: The Case of Korea." *Economic Development and Cultural Change,* April 1994, 617–629.

Kuznets, Paul W. *Korean Economic Development: An Interpretive Model.* Westport, Conn.: Praeger, 1994.

Kwon, Jene K., ed. *Korean Economic Development.* New York: Greenwood Press, 1990.

Lee, Chung H., and Ippei Yamazawa, eds. *The Economic Development of Japan and Korea: A Parallel with Lessons.* New York: Praeger, 1990.

Leightner, Jonathan Edward. "The Compatibility of Growth and Increased Equality: Korea." *The Journal of Development Studies,* October 1992, 49–71.

Lie, John. *Han Unbound: The Political Economy of South Korea.* Stanford: Stanford University Press, 1998.

Mo, Jongryn, and Chung-In Moon, eds. *Democracy and the Korean Economy.* Stanford: Hoover Institution Press, 1998.

Park, Hans S. *North Korea: Ideology, Politics, Economy.* Saddle River, N.J.: Prentice Hall, 1995.

Patrick, Hugh T., and Yung Chul Park. *The Financial Development of Japan, Korea and Taiwan: Growth, Repression and Liberalization.* Oxford: Oxford University Press, 1994.

Pettman, Ralph. "Labor, Gender and the Balance of Productivity: South Korea and Singapore." *Journal of Contemporary Asia,* no. 1 (1992): 45–56.

Song, Byung-Nak. *The Rise of the Korean Economy.* Oxford: Oxford University Press.

"A Survey of the Koreas: Yesterday's War, Tomorrow's Peace." *The Economist,* 10 July 1999, 52.

Wornoff, Jon. *Korea's Economy: Man-made Miracle.* Seoul: Si-sa-yong-o-sa, 1983.

12

THE PEOPLE'S REPUBLIC OF CHINA

INTRODUCTION

With a population of more than 1.2 billion persons, the Chinese economy casts a very long shadow over the world. If the current rate of economic growth, which has already transformed much of the country, is maintained, China will be one of the world's largest economies in the 21st century. With a long history as a unified state, its huge population, and a considerable resource base, China should indeed be a major player. However, for the past century and a half, invasion, imperialism, civil wars, instability, and poor management have all played a role in keeping that vast potential unrealized.

Nevertheless, the growth of the economy in recent years has been quite spectacular, averaging close to 10 percent per annum during the 1980s and 1990s, and never less than 4 percent per annum, even during a slow spell in the late 1980s. This rate of growth has resulted in a more than fourfold rise in gross national product between 1980 and 1995, and if it can be sustained national income will double about every seven years. The world's largest economy in population will rapidly become highly significant in terms of both production and investment. In 1996 Borensztein and Ostry calculated that if the 8 to 9 percent annual real growth (envisaged in the five-year plan covering 1996 to 2000) were sustained until 2013, Chinese gross national product (GNP), corrected for purchasing power parity, will surpass that of the United States.[1] In fact, Chinese growth slowed in the years 1997 to 1999 while that of the United States accelerated; nevertheless it is likely that sheer size and numbers will put China on a par with the United States sometime in the next 50 years. The living standards of the average Chinese, reflected by both growing incomes and increased consumer durable ownership have already risen sharply.

Recent Chinese growth has its roots in substantial productivity gains per worker (particularly in agriculture and light industry), a more efficient deployment of the workforce, and an increase in employment. Employment has risen at an annual rate of about 3 percent and has been sufficient to more than absorb the considerable population "bubble" caused by the high birthrates of the 1960s. Despite immigration from the rural areas to urban conurbations, the urban unemployment rate, which was over 5 percent in the 1960s, fell to about 2 percent by the late 1980s.

---

[1] Borensztein and Ostry. "Accounting for China's Growth," *American Economic Review,* May 1996, 224.

Of course, China started from a very low base. Income measured at current exchange rates was only about $250 per person in the mid-1970s. Purchasing power comparisons generally give a better picture of overall living standards, but even these show consumption on average of roughly $1,000 per person, one-sixth of the figure in the Soviet Union and only 6 percent of that for the United States. Moreover, China has low levels of national wealth. World Bank estimates put wealth per head (including natural resources and human capital) at about $6,600, about one-fiftieth of that of Germany and among the lowest in the world.

CENTRAL PLANNING, 1952–1959

The triumph of the Communists over the Nationalists in the civil war that closely followed the end of World War II led, in October 1949, to the creation of the People's Republic of China. The Nationalists withdrew to the offshore island of Taiwan and created there a very successful state and economy, which we will examine in chapter 13. The communist Chinese leadership set out to imitate the economic system developed in the Soviet Union over the previous 25 years. Private industry and commerce were nationalized and sweeping agricultural reform took the land from the landlords and wealthier farmers and placed it under peasant control in communes. As in the Soviet Union, a great deal of investment was poured into heavy industry, with faith in the power of capital-intensive technology and economies of scale to produce high rates of economic growth.

The Soviet model was followed by reliance on five-year plans. Soviet planners and technicians were imported and a formal planning apparatus put into place. However, in the early 1950s the Chinese economy was by no means in a parallel position to that of the Soviet Union, leading to problems in the application of a centrally planned model. One fact was that China's population was much larger (by a factor of 4), and its communications and transportation systems were much less well developed. In any system of centralized planning, the availability of reliable information at the center is crucial.[2] In the Chinese case, problems impeding the flow of information to the center and back to the enterprises proved to be even worse than in the Soviet Union, and this had a fundamental impact on the success of the planning experiment.

Moreover, the Chinese economy was not as highly unified and integrated as that of the Soviet Union. Poor transportation and the historically high degree of regional self-sufficiency (exacerbated during the period of "warlordism" in the 1920s and the struggle with the Japanese) meant that gains from centralizing the economy were much more difficult to grasp. A greater degree of power remained in the hands of municipalities and provinces, and even the prefectures and townships, than had been the case in the Soviet Union.

---

[2] See part 5 for a fuller discussion of information and central planning.

One measure of the difficulty of implementing centralized planning is how few goods were brought under formal control. Even at the height of planning in China, only 500 commodities fell under mandatory central control, in contrast to the more than 20,000 commodities that were part of the Soviet material balance plans.

THE GREAT LEAP FORWARD, 1958–1961

The end of the first five-year plan in 1958 coincided with reforms to the planning system that recognized the impracticability of "taut"[3] central planning in the Chinese economy, allowing the necessity, and even the desirability, of a high degree of provincial initiative. However, the potential for success of the revised system will never be known because the development path of the economy was disturbed by the intrusion of political rhetoric, in the form of Mao's **Great Leap Forward,** a political initiative to harness the ideological fervor of the Chinese population to the task of raising industrial output. At the same time as China continued to pour investment into capital-intensive heavy industry, Mao and the leadership exhorted the population to increase the output of basic industrial goods through labor-intensive enterprises in rural areas. This approach of using both capital- and labor-intensive technologies to produce the same goods was characterized as "walking on two legs."

Although labor-intensive enterprises were found in many industries, including building materials, mining, food-processing, and machine-building, the political leadership defined the key industry as steel. Mao Tse Tung urged a sharp increase in steel production through the development of small-scale furnaces, and it is estimated that some two million small furnaces were established during the first two years of the Great Leap Forward, employing some 80 million people on a full or part-time basis. Official statistics show that industrial output grew sharply at the outset of the Great Leap Forward; net material product was up by 22 percent in 1959 alone, but it soon became apparent that this was being achieved at great cost, and much of the growth was actually an illusion. For example, the steel produced in rural furnaces was, in general, of poor quality and expensive in terms of factor cost. Moreover, much of the "new" output consisted merely of the melting down and recycling of steel and iron that had already been produced; ornamental and structural steelwork was pulled down and fed to the furnaces. Woods and forests were cut down, and even buildings were cannibalized, to provide charcoal and fuel.

After an initial period of feverish activity, the incentives of revolutionary fervor and rhetoric cooled. The recycling of previously produced material slowed as stocks became exhausted, and the depletion of woodland made charcoal increasingly short in supply. The countryside became scarred and the environment adversely affected. China's Soviet advisors were frustrated by what seemed a per-

---

[3] *Taut* in this context refers to a "lack of slack" in the planning system, provided by keeping inventories to a minimum.

verse rejection of socialist rationality, and in an atmosphere of growing antago-nism between the two nations, technical assistance was suspended in 1960.

Net material product in China fell sharply in 1961 and 1962, but greater stabil-ity was reestablished in 1963 and a period of relative calm saw a rise in industrial output. Continuing investment in heavy industry helped the rebound, and indus-trial output rose sharply between 1963 and 1966. Chinese technocrats filled the void left by the departing Soviets, pursuing central planning once more, though with a greater degree of pragmatism. The high degree of provincial autonomy left local governments free to use their flexibility to increase output in whatever way they chose.

THE CULTURAL REVOLUTION, 1966–1970

In 1966, however, political furor again swamped the economic system due to the inception of Mao's **Proletarian Cultural Revolution.** Exactly what prompted the Chinese leader to embark on that course at that moment in history is still open to dispute. In part he seemed convinced that only complete rejection of western influence would enable Asia, including China, to be economically self-reliant. He was also genuinely convinced that Stalinist economic management had resulted in a new structure of class and privilege as obnoxious to him as the old. Finally, and perhaps decisively, he felt a need to strengthen his own political position vis-à-vis the technocrats and bureaucrats. The Cultural Revolution resulted in Chinese society being turned upside down. Bureaucrats, planners, and technocrats were stripped of authority and sent off to the countryside for "political reeducation," while power shifted to radical political cadres. There were considerable economic costs to the turmoil. Again the economy lurched into a sharp recession with mate-rial output falling by about 15 percent in both 1966 and 1967; it rebounded again in the last years of the decade as some form of normality returned.

By the beginning of the 1970s it was clear that the era of Mao and Chou En Lai was nearing its close, so political factions began maneuvering for power. On the left, the **gang of four,** led by Mao's wife, tried to sustain the Cultural Revolution. On the right, a moderate and technocratic leadership sought the restoration of rule by bureaucracy and party. Both Mao and Chou died in 1976 and nominal power passed to Mao's chosen successor Hua Qua Feng. However, by this time the mod-erates were in ascendance and Deng Xiaoping, a highly capable administrator, was rehabilitated from the indignities inflicted on him during the Cultural Revolution and restored as party leader.

THE FIRST PHASE OF REFORM, 1978–1993

Because the economy had stagnated, and in some areas declined, during the period of the Cultural Revolution and the rule of the gang of four, Deng resolved to find new approaches to promote growth. December 1978 saw a profound shift in the direction of the Chinese economy as the Central Committee of the Communist

Party of China (CCP) issued a communiqué that, in effect, launched the modern period of reform, moving the Chinese economy away from a planned economy and toward a market one.

AGRICULTURAL REFORM

The first reforms were aimed at revitalizing the rural sector, whose fortunes had flagged during the previous three decades. The high percentage of the population engaged in agriculture and the necessity of creating an agrarian surplus to fuel industrial growth and feed a growing population made agricultural reform essential. While heavy industrial output had experienced sustained high growth during the previous 15 years, agriculture had remained dormant. Grain output per person employed had risen by less than 10 percent during a 25-year period, despite considerable expenditures on infrastructure, informational outreach, and factor inputs, especially fertilizers. The key to raising output lay in radical reform of the collectivized agricultural system so painfully created in the 1950s and 1960s.

Under collectivization, agricultural production had been organized into *communes* (typically with a population of about 40,000 people). These were further subdivided into *brigades* and *production teams.* Decisions about what to grow and how to grow it were passed to the communes from superior political units (the prefecture and provincial governments) and were as a result quite often inflexible to local conditions. Worker remuneration was generally through sharing the net production of the brigade on a per worker basis taking little account of individual or family productivity. This resulted in a chronic absence of incentives and a pervasive "free rider" problem. Households were allowed small plots for the own cultivation, from which the surplus could be sold in the local markets, and productivity was in general much higher in these small niches in the system.

The reforms that began in 1979 were largely the result of local initiative and were, in fact, opposed at the outset by the State Council in Beijing. Motivation for reform was the belief that productivity in the agricultural sector could be greatly increased simply by raising the economic incentives to family units. Initially this took the form of enlarging the size of the private plots and increasing the procurement price that the state paid for crops that were produced privately. Local officials were encouraged by the success of this limited action, and the reforms evolved into the **household responsibility system (HRS),** which became the dominant arrangement in agriculture after 1982.

Under HRS quite large plots of collectively held land were leased to households for a fixed period of time, initially 15 years for annual crops and up to 40 years for tree crops. In return for tenure, each household was responsible for providing a share of the production team's output quota based on plot size. Production in excess of this "contract" could be sold either on the free market for what it would fetch or to the state at negotiated prices. By 1984, 93 percent of China's cultivated land was contracted to households, but, and this is highly illustrative of the progress of China's reforms, it was not until 1985 that the state passed legislation formally sanctioning it.

Agricultural production rose sharply after the reforms. Annual growth of output was twice the rate experienced in the 1960s and 1970s, illustrating the importance of individual incentive in agriculture. Labor productivity in agriculture rose at an even higher rate, producing a labor surplus in most of the rural collectives, which ultimately provided the workforce for the rapid expansion of rural light industry. Higher food prices moved the terms of trade (defined as food prices divided by manufactured goods prices) sharply in favor of the farmers and resulted in a substantial increase in real income in the rural sector. However, the authorities in Beijing were concerned about political unrest among urban workers and were unwilling to allow the burden of increased farm incomes to be passed directly to urban consumers in the form of higher food prices. The government provided substantial subsidies, which resulted in a growing fiscal deficit.

The state next tried to reduce the size of the subsidy by cutting the procurement prices for grains, but farmers responded by shifting resources out of grain production and into more profitable, less regulated commodities like vegetables and meat. Grain output fell as a result in the mid-1980s. The government's response was to raise the procurement prices of grain once more, but this time it tried to avoid the fiscal consequences by increasing the prices paid by urban consumers. This step toward price liberalization led to the ultimate deregulation of the grain market; by May 1993 grain prices were decontrolled in about 80 percent of the country and prices determined by the interplay of supply and demand.

THE RISE OF RURAL ENTERPRISE

The rapid rise in agricultural output, labor productivity, and incomes set in train a further development in the rural areas: the emergence of **township and village enterprises (TVEs)** as the most dynamic sector in the Chinese economy. TVEs are industrial activities that are collectively owned by the communes. They were made possible by a progressive rollback of restrictions on the nonagricultural activities of collectives, culminating in 1984 when local authorities were given the power to sanction communal industrial activity. The new enterprises absorbed much of the excess labor created by high birthrates and rising labor productivity in agriculture, while increased rural incomes provided the seed money for the initial investments.

Although they are collectively owned, TVEs are much more akin to western firms than **state-owned enterprises (SOEs)** for several reasons:

1. They face a **hard budget constraint** and are seldom bailed out by government subsidy. Moreover, in the absence of government support, banks are inclined to extend credit only on strictly economic terms.[4]

---

[4] Although initially they had access to credit from the rural credit cooperatives, the financial sector cut the SOEs off from credit almost completely between 1988 and 1991, resulting in a lot of failures and employment loss.

2. As new enterprises, TVEs fell outside the scope of the rather rigid planning system and were from the beginning unfettered by mandatory controls. They enjoy, therefore, considerable freedom of initiative over what to produce and how. Moreover, since the Chinese planners had concentrated on the growth of heavy industrial output, there was a large pent-up demand for light industrial products both for the domestic market and overseas. TVEs were able to exploit this vacuum.

3. Unlike SOEs, TVEs had no captive market for their products and from the start success depended on identifying demand and meeting it with quality products. In both domestic and overseas markets strong forces of consumer sovereignty were at work, which encouraged an emphasis on quality and product development that was absent in the state sector.

4. TVEs were allowed to sell their products at market prices, and given the fact that they were operating largely in competitive markets, this implied a continuing pressure to contain costs and advance productivity.

5. TVEs were not encumbered by the social expenditures required of state enterprises. In common with many socialist countries, SOEs in China were responsible for a range of social services including child care, education, and health care that raised labor costs.

6. TVEs were also able to be much more nimble in their employment practices (hiring and firing) and were able to establish performance-based compensation systems, which maximized individual incentives and raised productivity.

7. TVEs are allowed to retain profits and keep them within the enterprise as investment. Initially the TVEs were assisted by concessional tax treatment that was helpful in building capital in the "infancy" stage.

Growth of TVEs was also favored by particular features of the Chinese economy in the previous three decades:

1. The concentration on heavy industrial growth had led the state to neglect the light industrial sector. This left a wide window of opportunity in light industry through which the relatively nimble TVEs could quickly, and profitably, move.

2. The rise in agricultural productivity and the high birthrates of the 1960s had left large reserves of labor in the rural communes. The extension of educational opportunities, especially for women, under communism had created substantial human capital.

3. The high degree of provincial autonomy and the concern of local governments to promote economic development (in part motivated by the need to absorb surplus labor) meant that few impediments were placed on TVE growth, and many incentives were offered at the local level.

Starting from a very low base at the beginning of the 1980s, the emergence of TVEs has had a rapid impact on China's economy. By 1993, there were some 19 million TVEs within China, employing more than 100 million workers, or about

25 percent of the rural labor force. The collective sector as a whole accounted for only 19.2 percent of industrial output in 1978, but this had doubled to 38.8 percent by 1992.

REFORMING STATE-OWNED ENTERPRISE

Although the TVEs are the bright star of the Chinese economy, sustained economic development depends on successful reform of the state-owned enterprises (SOEs). Once seen as the key to China's industrial future as well as representing employment security to the masses, a job with an SOE was by and large guaranteed for life, usually carried housing benefits, and was often referred to as an "iron rice bowl." In 1993, there were some 100,000 state-owned enterprises, of which some 11,000 were classed as "medium" or "large." Of these almost one-quarter were recording losses, despite the fact that price controls, mandatory planning controls, and captive markets provide a hidden subsidy. In 1978 SOEs accounted for over 80 percent of industrial output; this had shrunk to 48 percent by 1992 as collectives, private enterprise, and foreign-owned corporations all grew at a much faster rate.

Initiative in the SOE sector had been stifled throughout the postrevolutionary period until the onset of enterprise reform, which started in 1986, slightly later than in the rural sector. Early reform efforts tried to replicate in the state-owned industrial sector the responsibility system that had been successful in the rural areas. This resulted in a scheme, known as the **contract responsibility system (CRS),** by which SOEs contracted for a four-year period to a production quota to be delivered to the state, and to specified financial payments it would make to the state in lieu of the profit remittances that the enterprises had formerly paid. Any output above the quota level could be disposed of by the enterprise at market prices. By 1988, 90 percent of all SOEs were operating under such contracts.

In parallel with these arrangements, and introduced during the same period of 1986–1988, a third responsibility system was introduced—the **fiscal contract responsibility system (FCRS).** This supplanted the enterprise income tax, which had been levied at a standard rate of 55 percent, with an individually negotiated contract that fixed the total size of tax payments over several years and specified the division of the total between central, provincial, and local governments. The combination of the two contract systems meant that payments to the government were invariant to the level of profit of the organization. In short, tax elasticity was zero, and while this was to prove a problem, of greater significance were the FCRS's distortionary features. Because tax payments were all negotiated and the outcome depended to a large extent on political "pull," effective rates varied greatly from enterprise to enterprise, with little pursuit of any underlying economic objective.

These arrangements, however, did provide great incentives for the enterprise. Exceeding a quota was highly desirable as excess output could be sold for whatever the market would bear. Moreover, since the marginal tax rate on profits was zero, and the dividends payable to government fixed, all the profit above predetermined fixed levels could be retained in the enterprise. The industrial output of the SOEs rose sharply in response. However, the reforms also had features with negative consequences for long-term economic development. First, each contractual arrangement was individually negotiated, and enterprises had an incentive to fight for high levels of inputs and low quotas to acquire the resources for a surplus to sell on the private market. Given the asymmetry of information between the bureaucracy and the enterprise, this had significant negative consequences.

The second disadvantage was the abandonment of all pretense of a "level playing field" in the tax system in favor of what should more accurately be called a "revenue" system. In developed market economies, tax systems are expected to have defined rules including "horizontal equity," which requires that equivalent units should be treated equally. Because of the discretionary element, the fiscal contract responsibility system resulted in widely disparate average tax rates between enterprises, as well as falling average rates over time.

Third, although the boom in the industrial sector should have increased government revenue from taxes on enterprises, revenues proved highly inelastic with respect to growing income. In fact, real revenues tended to fall as income and output rose because the contracts fixed tax payment in nominal terms, with no inflation escalator. A buoyant economy and the progressive decontrol of prices led to inflation and reduced the real value of the contracted nominal tax payments.

A fourth, and very important, problem was that the CRS resulted in a two-tier price system—the procurement price set by the responsibility contract, and paid on the contracted quota, and the market price. The procurement price was in general lower than the market price. There were, therefore, large potential gains from arbitrage between the state and private sectors and from the deliberate understatement of quota outputs. This led to a sharp increase in corruption.

Finally, it should be emphasized that although the incentives provided by the reforms were considerable, a soft-budget constraint continued to apply to many enterprises. Over 30 percent of SOEs made losses in 1988 and direct state subsidies (not including foregone or forgiven taxes) amounted to some 60 billion yuan. Taxes paid by SOEs amounted to only 120 billion yuan, or to put it more simply—half of the taxes paid by SOEs went straight back out as subsidy. A bankruptcy law applying to SOEs was introduced in 1986 but has been seldom used. By 1992, subsidies had fallen to 44.5 billion yuan, and taxes had risen to 155.5 billion yuan, although much of this was a nominal gain caused by inflation and did not represent a real increase in tax yield. Taxes on SOEs in 1992 represented about 2.6 percent of GNP.

These problems are well known to the authorities and are on the agenda for further reform. In 1995, Chen Jinghua, minister in charge of the State Planning Commission wrote:

> The overall structure [of industrial production] is irrational, the variety and quality of the products do not meet the needs of the market, economic performance is poor, and some enterprises are manufacturing and stockpiling unmarketable products, wasting resources that could be better used elsewhere.[5]

---

[5] From the *Annual Report to the National People's Congress* (6 March 1995), cited in Borensztein and Ostry.

CREATING A MODERN ENTERPRISE SECTOR

Recognizing the problems emanating from the responsibility system in the SOE sector, the Chinese government embarked on a new series of reforms to change the structure of ownership, governance, and accounting in the SOEs and also reform the fiscal relationship between the enterprises and the various levels of government. However, progress has not been easy because of the need to control rising unemployment and the implicit lifetime employment guarantee associated with most state employment.

While content to let private firms, **foreign-financed enterprises (FFEs),** and the collectivized sectors prosper, Chinese authorities have little current intention to embark on the mass privatization of most state assets. The cornerstone of the economy in the foreseeable future will continue to be the predominance of SOEs in strategic sectors. The strategy is to develop a "socialist market economy," in which the assets of much of the industrial sector are owned by the state, but in which the primary functions of coordination are performed by the market, subject to guidance from the center. In some sense this model is not dramatically different from that of certain European economies, like the French or British in their preprivatization period when much of heavy industry was held in public ownership.

The first step in the creation of this "modern enterprise sector" has to be the corporatization of the SOEs; the foundation to achieve this was laid down in the *company law,* which became effective in July 1994. The most salient thrust of the company law is to clearly separate "ownership" (which for the time being lies with the state) from management. It clarifies the rights of enterprises as legal entities, establishes the rights and responsibilities of management, and limits the power of ministries to interfere directly in enterprise management. The law also relieves SOEs from many of their responsibilities for the social security of their workers and families. Ultimately, it is planned that responsibility for the oversight of enterprises will pass from the ministries into the hands of state holding companies. The government does not intend to rush into this without some experimentation. Some 10,000 medium- and large-scale enterprises (10 percent of the total) are part of a project that involves comprehensive asset valuation, financial autonomy, and the adoption of a new accounting system. In 1,000 of these firms the steps will be larger, and the management of their assets will be handed over to newly established state holding companies.

REFORMING THE TAX FINANCE SYSTEM

A successful transition from a centrally planned economy to one that is market oriented must involve the creation of certain institutions that are essential for the long-term stability of the economy. One of the most important of these is the fiscal system, which plays two important roles. First, it provides the resources for government expenditures. In the absence of an effective tax-gathering system the government usually is financed by money creation an "inflation tax," which transfers resources from creditors to debtors (the largest of which is the government) in a capricious and inefficient way.

Second, the fiscal system provides the government with an important policy tool meant to promote macroeconomic stability and control the direction of economic development. China today does not have a well-functioning tax system, but rather a *revenue system,* which can provide fiscal resources for various levels of government but, because of a lack of consistency and equity, creates perverse incentives. The Chinese authorities are aware of the need to overhaul the tax system and the complex fiscal contract responsibility system will be replaced by a standard rate of tax of 33 percent on all business profits.

THE PERSONAL INCOME TAX

Other parts of the tax system are also being reformed. The direct taxation system in China comprises the enterprise tax and the personal income tax. At present, the role of the personal income tax in both revenue raising and fiscal policy is negligible. Its nominal incidence is primarily private business owners and foreigners (who pay on a higher schedule than domestic Chinese). The high rates encourage both evasion and avoidance; compliance is consequently low, revenue is small, and deadweight burdens quite high.

The new personal income tax will have as its base all personal income from wages, salaries, rents, and business sources, less a standard deduction of about $90 per month for Chinese citizens. This excludes a large part of the domestic population from paying tax at all, especially rural residents. For everyone above the threshold, income will be subject to sharply rising progressive rates starting at 5 percent. In the case of wage income the maximum marginal rate is 45 percent, and for "unearned" income the top rate is 35 percent. This is an unusual configuration. In most societies with multiple rates, unearned income is taxed at a higher rate than earned income, complying with a widely held view that individuals are more entitled to money that they have labored for. Moreover, the disincentive impact of high taxes on labor are usually thought to be greater than on capital. The Chinese authorities hope that the lower rate on capital income will increase the tax base by fostering compliance in the private business sector.

INDIRECT TAXES

In China, indirect taxes provide the greater part of tax revenues. They fall into three categories: excise taxes, value-added taxes (VAT), and turnover taxes on business, each of which supplies a little less than 3 percent of GNP in revenue. The objective of reform is to simplify the system by enlarging the coverage of VAT and standardizing the rates. Under the new system, VAT will have close to universal coverage with a 17 percent rate applied to most goods and a 13 percent rate on food, farm supplies, and utilities. In addition, a consumption tax will replace the excise tax and will be levied only on the sale of tobacco, alcohol, gasoline, and luxury goods (including cars). A special business tax will apply to services not covered by VAT.

Customs and Tariffs

China's growing participation in world trade, and in the international agencies that oversee trade, requires a rationalization of a complex tariff structure that has been constructed piecemeal with both revenue raising and protectionism in mind. Customs duties have historically provided about 8 percent of tax revenue. The average tariff rate is about 40 percent, but rates rise with the degree to which the goods are "finished." Raw materials are subject to rates in the 0 to 20 percent range, intermediate and capital goods fit into the 20 to 40 percent category, and finished may be subject to duties as high as 80 percent. The effective rate of protection for the Chinese manufacturing industry provided by this structure is very high.

Reforms presently being implemented will reduce the maximum tariff on all goods to less than 40 percent, and many categories of goods will be placed in the zero bracket. The impact of this on revenue is not clear and depends on the elasticity of imports to tariff changes; it is conceivable that revenues will rise if imports increase in response to lower rates of protection.

THE FINANCIAL SYSTEM

As in the case of the tax system, the effective reform of the financial sector can do double duty. First, a stable and rationally developed system allows for greater allocative efficiency through the improved channeling of resources from savers to investors. Second, a coherent financial system is essential for the implementation of effective monetary policy.

The Banking Sector

Prior to 1978 the banking system in China had a very limited role. Its main purpose was akin to the role of the monobank in any centrally planned system. Through the management of the accounts of the various SOEs, it provided a financial counterpart to the movement of goods, and therefore a check on the satisfactory fulfillment of the plan, and it also made available to state-owned enterprises the credits for investment and subsidy approved in the plan.

The People's Bank of China (PBC) was the dominant agency and served as a commercial, investment, and central bank. In 1984 the PBC became a central bank, responsible for supervision of the financial system and the conduct of monetary policy. Its other functions were devolved to four specialized banks whose assets are shown in Table 12.1. Together these five institutions represent over 90 percent of the assets in the banking system and almost 70 percent of the branches. The only other elements of the banking system are the credit cooperatives, which collect deposits and supply loans at the grassroots level. There are 53,000 rural credit cooperatives and 4,000 urban ones—though total cooperative assets represent less than 6 percent of the assets of the entire banking system. There are three development banks (one national and two provincial ones in Guandong and Shenzhen), but their assets are small.

■ **TABLE 12.1**

ASSETS OF THE MAIN CHINESE BANKS, 1992 (BILLIONS OF YUAN)

Bank	1992 Assets
The Bank of China (BOC)	1,430
The Industrial and Commercial Bank of China (ICBC)	789
The People's Construction Bank of China (PCBC)	1,422
Agricultural Bank of China (ABC)	816

SOURCE: International Monetary Fund.

The creation of the PBC and the specialized banks was, somewhat optimistically, seen at the time as a strong forward step toward creation of a market-oriented financial system. In the interests of efficiency, the greater freedom afforded to enterprises to identify and pursue their own avenues of investment had to be accompanied by changes in the banking system to allow the competitive rationing of credit between firms.

In reality, however, the authorities have been slow to relinquish power over credit allocation and actually acted in 1988 to tighten control. The main vehicle for credit allocation remains the **credit plan,** which is controlled from the center and determines the activity of the central bank, the specialized banks, and the six universal banks. The banks are subject to credit ceilings and are required to provide the finance for approved projects. Interest rates are largely administered by the government although the banks are allowed a small degree of latitude around the administered rate. In 1988 the government also moved to increase its control over the cooperatives and the growing number of nonbank financial intermediaries (NBFIs) and actually cut off the growing TVE sector from access to the credit cooperatives for a short time.

Continued reliance on a directed credit through the credit plan has been criticized[6] as being at odds with the principles of decentralization, competition, and marketization, which have been the primary elements of the reforms in other areas. However, Chinese planners can point not only to their own experience but also to the prevalent use of directed credit by both the Japanese and the South Koreans during the periods of greatest growth in their countries. The planners have been reluctant to relinquish their last lever of control, and their nearest northeast Asian neighbors are advertisements for its efficacy.

More damaging than the mere principle of directed credit is the criticism that the credit plan adopted by the authorities is based on flawed principles. Japanese and Korean directed credit was based on the principle of identifying growth areas and financing export-oriented development in the most dynamic sectors. Chinese

---

[6]See International Monetary Fund, *Economic Reform in China: A New Phase,* 1617.

credit, on the other hand, is more defensively dispositioned and frequently seeks to guard the interests of the existing SOE sector. Moreover, the credit plan itself has proved ultimately ineffective. There are frequent breaches, on an ad hoc basis, of the planned limit on credit expansion and allocation. Furthermore, the specialized banks are required to make a large number of **policy loans** that run against good banking practice but are part of the overall plan. The result of this is that the recently created specialized banks already have a portfolio of nonperforming loans. The PBC has conceded that one in five of the loans owed to the specialist banks are in arrears on payments. *The Economist* reports that a former central bank employee estimates that more than 30 percent of the loans due to the specialized banks have no hope of repayment.[7] This sum is sufficient to destroy the entire asset base of the banking system. Even if such a catastrophe were averted, this evidence suggests a high degree of "softness" in the budget constraints that the authorities attempt to impose on the SOEs, resulting in the type of inefficiency described by Janos Kornai, the Hungarian economist, in his article "The Soft Budget Constraint."

Further reform of the banking system is being implemented to put the specialized banks on a better commercial footing. This is to be done by routing the policy lending through stronger development banks. The Agricultural Bank of China (ABC) will become the Agricultural Development Bank; an Export Import bank will make subsidized loans for trade finance, and an augmented State Development bank will assume broader domestic responsibilities. This will, in theory, leave the Bank of China (BOC), the Industrial and Commercial Bank of China (ICBC), and the People's Construction Bank of China (PCBC) to pursue purely commercial objectives.

INTERNATIONAL TRADE

Before the onset of reform, all of China's foreign trade was handled through a few foreign trade corporations that acted as import and export agencies. Since reforms began in 1993, trade has been liberalized, both in terms of the agencies who can enter into international trade and in terms of the tariffs and licensing restrictions that constrained it. Enterprises, whether in the state, the collective, or the private sectors, have become more able and more anxious to seek out and export to markets of their own choosing.

The impact of this export boom on China's trade position has been huge. In 1978 the trade to GNP ratio for China was about 5 percent; by 1993 this had risen to 35 percent, making China a highly open economy by world standards.[8] The Chi-

---

[7] *The Economist,* 9 September 1995, 74.

[8] Some care should be taken with this statistic; although trade is valued in dollars, GNP is understated since it is not in PPP terms. In reality, the denominator should be larger. Moreover, at this time trade with Hong Kong was accounted as a foreign trade transaction.

■ TABLE 12.2

HIGHLIGHTS OF CHINESE OVERSEAS TRANSACTION, 1989–1995
(MILLIONS OF U.S. DOLLARS)

	1989	1991	1993	1995
Exports	43,220	58,919	75,659	128,110
Imports	48,840	50,176	86,113	110,060
Trade balance	−5,620	8,743	−10,454	18,050
Current account balance	−4,317	13,272	−11,609	1,618
Outgoing direct investment	780	913	4,400	2,000
Incoming direct investment	3,393	4,366	27,515	35,849

SOURCE: International Monetary Fund.

nese share of world trade doubled between 1978 and 1993, from 1 percent to 2 percent of the total.

Table 12.2 shows the highlights of China's overseas transactions in the first half of the 1990s. Exports showed remarkable growth and tripled in dollar terms in a six-year period, making China one of the world's largest traders. The commodity composition of trade also underwent a dramatic shift. In 1978 agricultural products dominated exports, comprising 63 percent of the total. Outgoing direct foreign investment was more than $4 billion in 1993.

SPECIAL ECONOMIC ZONES

China has made extensive use of various forms of **special economic zones (SEZs)** in its reform push. The first SEZs were established by the State Council in 1979. They were all located in south coastal China, near the overseas Chinese communities in Macao, Hong Kong, and Taiwan. Three SEZs were placed in Guandong Province (Shenzhen, Zhuhai, and Shantou) and one (Xiamen) in Fujian. Subsequently Pudong near Shanghai was added in 1990. The State Council also sanctioned the creation of 15 **economic and technological development zones (ETDZs)** and 34 **high-technology development zones (HTDZS).** The common feature of all of these zones is that they all enjoy considerable relief from central government taxation. The rate of tax on profits of enterprises located in the zones is 15 percent as opposed to the 55 percent prevailing in non-SEZs at the time of their inception. The four original SEZs plus Pudong also offer two-year tax holidays. Local governments, anxious to raise the pace of economic development, have introduced their own zones with varying levels of relief from local taxes. It was estimated that by the end of 1992 there were 9,000 such zones.

Many economists are skeptical about the role of tax concessions applied to limited geographical areas. It can be argued that such provisions make for additional distortions in an economy that is already far from providing a level playing field. Unless there are known market failures that such provisions are intended to correct, the effect may be counterproductive in terms of aggregate welfare. There is, therefore, concern that the incentives granted in such zones only serve to move activity from one place to another, and the elasticity of aggregate investment and employment with respect to the tax reductions is low. If this is the case, then the government is certain to experience a loss of tax revenue, which may be uncompensated by positive economic effects.

There may, however, be economic logic in the provision of such zones:

1. In the case of a region dependent on a declining industry, concessional treatment might attract investment that would secure employment and prevent the waste of already committed social investment.

2. There may be economies of scale in the provision of infrastructure and services, and incentives designed to increase the density of industrial activity may be rational.

3. There may be external economies of agglomeration in the form of spillover and pool effects. For example, one of the frequently cited reasons for technology parks is the high degree of knowledge spillover; in other industries labor pool effects may be important.

4. The government may wish to restrict some activities and policies to a limited geographical area. This may be done for environmental reasons or, in the special case of China, it might be desirable to limit the impact in order to analyze the effects before generalizing the policies.

The first reason is not relevant in the case of the Chinese special economic zones. Both the second and third statements have been cited as rationales and may indeed have played a role. However, it is probable that the most important reason is the fourth. The State Council and national planning authorities have used the economic zones as laboratories in which the efficacy and consequences of certain policy shifts can be gauged. All of the important reforms concerning foreign exchange, foreign direct investment, state-owned enterprise organization, labor markets, and the use of joint-stock companies with tradable equity capital have been pioneered in the enterprise zones.

Only those that have been successful, and that the decision-making apparatus of the state believes it can manage and control, have been allowed to mature and spread. This experimentation and groping forward has been an essential part of the Chinese reform strategy discussed later.

THE IMPORTANCE OF A "KINDRED MODEL"

Despite the poverty of the country and the limitations of its resource base, China has enjoyed in its transformation an asset that most countries can only experience in a much lesser degree: assistance and example from "kindred" populations abroad. The *tongbao* (which literally means "same womb") populations of Hong Kong, Macao, and increasingly (at least until the decline in relations in early 1996) Taiwan have played a very important role in Chinese growth. Singapore, geographically and culturally more remote but with an affluent population, expensive labor, and surplus capital, also has had an increasing part to play.

Although these communities have in total a very small population in relation to the People's Republic (about one-fortieth), they have had an important role in several dimensions:

1. *A demonstration effect.* These communities have provided a demonstration that Chinese people can transform their economic circumstances in a relatively short period of time, given favorable policies. The standard of living enjoyed in Taiwan and Hong Kong is an assurance to many Chinese that economic transformation is feasible. This tends to promote both personal saving and investment as a response to confidence in the future.

2. *Trading partner.* The overseas communities have provided an important trading partner for China. This is especially true of Hong Kong, whose prime function is to serve as an entrepôt for the mainland. Over 40 percent of China's exports are routed through Hong Kong, and although the opening of other city ports will reduce this share, the proximity of Hong Kong to the rapidly growing areas is highly significant.

3. *Investor.* Overseas Chinese communities account for the larger part of incoming direct foreign investment into China. Hong Kong alone accounts for over 50 percent, and Taiwan is growing as a source as its economy experiences rapidly increasing labor costs.

4. *Sources of information.* In the early stages of transformation of a socialist economy, information about technologies and markets is at a premium. Residents of the overseas communities do much to provide China with a window on the world: over 95 percent of visitors to China are people of Chinese ethnicity.

THE CHARACTER OF CHINESE REFORM

Chinese reform has differed in form and in consequence from the approach taken in the Central and Eastern European Economies (CEEEs). At the moment, many observers see the Chinese model as superior. The most obvious point in China's favor is that it has avoided the sharp contraction of output, surging inflation, and elevated unemployment that characterized transition in all of the CEEEs.[9] In sharp contrast to Eastern Europe, Chinese growth accelerated with the onset of reform. Employment grew and unemployment fell despite the fact that China had a much higher population growth rate than that of Russia or the other CEEEs.

Certainly much of the difference in macroeconomic performance was due to the fact that reforms were less sweeping in China than in the CEEEs, but some is also a function of differing states of development. The Central and Eastern European

---

[9]See Blanchard, "Theoretical Aspects of Transition," *American Economic Review,* May 1996, 117, for evidence on the similarity of the post-Soviet transitions.

Economies are industrial economies. Markets that had been guaranteed under domestic planning, or trade arrangements overseen by the Council for Mutual Economic Assistance (CMEA, otherwise known as COMECON), disappeared. Suppliers became reluctant to sell at old prices and demanded hard currency payments. This created a disarticulation in the system; a macroeconomic contraction and unemployment resulted. Prices were adjusted to world levels and inflation was a consequence. Since planned international trade was less important to China than to the Eastern European countries, this disruption resulted in fewer macroeconomic consequences.

Agriculture was in China a much more dominant part of the economy in the pre-reform period. The economy was less dependent on a complex set of markets and suppliers. Moreover, the Chinese had experienced and adjusted to great disorganization in both the Great Leap Forward and the Proletarian Cultural Revolution. That said, we turn now to examine some of the distinctive characteristics of the Chinese reform experience.

GRADUALISM

One difference in reform strategy can be highlighted by the use of a metaphor. Vaclav Havel, the playwright who became president of the Czech Republic during its transition to a market economy, once characterized the CEEE approach to reform by stating that it is impossible to "cross a chasm in two leaps." The Chinese approach, on the other hand, can be summarized by stating that China is "touching stones to cross a river." In other words, China proceeded on its own path by a process of experimentation, moving forward slowly only in areas where policies had been tested and seen to work. So far, it must be said, this has proved a more successful policy than revolutionary reform, or an economic "big bang."

PARTIAL REFORM

China has not been averse to creating situations in which reform is incomplete. The clearest of these areas lies in the contract responsibility systems, which resulted in a two-tier price system for agricultural and industrial goods. Such systems have the advantage of keeping with the gradualist approach to reform, and they also provide substantial incentives to the relevant economic actors. Marginal economic allocation decisions are made in response to market prices, and this fact has a beneficial impact on overall economic efficiency. However, as noted earlier, two-tier prices provide considerable returns to arbitrage from the state to the market system, and that engenders corruption.

DECENTRALIZATION

Chinese reform has been accompanied by a weakening of central control over the constituent parts of the economy. This is not an uncommon feature; a parallel can be seen in the breakup of the Soviet Union and in the fissiparous tendencies currently in evidence in Russia. In China the outcome of devolution has been positive, in that it has allowed the provincial authorities to be flexible and pragmatic. Some observers are concerned that this trend will end in the demise of China as a centralized state, torn apart by growing income inequality, increased provincial chauvinism, and a weakened center inadequately supported by a national fiscal system.

ACCOMMODATING SPONTANEOUS REFORM

While from the outside it might appear that the entire process has been one of rational experimentation, in reality Chinese reform has been characterized by a willingness to allow spontaneous reform. In part this is because the weakening control of the State Council, discussed earlier, leaves it with little alternative but to acquiesce, and reform legislation has the character of making virtue of necessity.

ECONOMIC LIBERALIZATION WITHOUT POLITICAL DEMOCRATIZATION

The main point of difference between change in Central and Eastern Europe and China has been the relative pace of political and economic reform. In the former Soviet Union and Eastern Europe, political reform was rapid and ran ahead of economic reform. This tended to feed the raising of expectations with respect to economic progress, which were disappointed. In China the reverse has been the case. Economic freedom has evolved much more rapidly than the political variant. Social stability has been correspondingly greater, dissent has been suppressed, and this, it can be argued, has provided a solid platform for growth and incoming direct foreign investments. Western nations might like the idea of democracy, but their entrepreneurs are more prone to invest in predictable authoritarian states.

HAVE REFORMS ACCELERATED GROWTH?

In most people's minds, the rapid growth of the Chinese economy during the 1980s and 1990s was caused by the reforms that began in 1978 and have continued since. However, in evaluating the success of any change in economic policy it is important to establish a counterfactual: What would have occurred in the absence of the policy shift? It is certainly true that since 1978 we have witnessed substantial improvement in just about every economic indicator. It is also true that the rates of improvement of these indicators are better than in the pre-reform period from 1953–1978. This can be clearly seen from comparing the first and second columns in Table 12.3. Output rose faster in both aggregate and per capita terms, and labor productivity grew more quickly. While the labor force grew at about the same rate, capital growth was actually marginally slower than in the pre-reform era.

However, some authors have drawn attention to the fact that a comparison of these periods may be biased; included in the 1953–1978 period were the major disturbances caused by the Great Leap Forward and the Cultural Revolution. These were not periods in which the socialist-planned Chinese economy operated normally, but were rather periods of great political upheaval akin almost to a civil war.

DECOMPOSITION OF CHINESE ECONOMIC GROWTH, 1953–1990: AVERAGE ANNUAL GROWTH RATES

	1953–1978	1979–1994	1953–1978 (excl. 1959–1970)
Output	5.9	9.2	7.6
Output per head of population	3.8	7.5	5.4
Output per worker	3.1	6.3	4.5
Ratio of investment to net material product	19.9	24.8	21.7
Capital	10.2	9.9	13.2
Labor	2.6	2.7	3
Total factor productivity	−0.7	3.8	−0.8

SOURCE: Eduardo Borensztein and Jonathan Ostry, "Accounting for China's Growth Performance," *American Economic Review,* May 1996, 225.

The appropriate comparison might well be to view the performance post-1978 against the "normal" years of socialist planning. By excluding the period 1959–1970, the substantial dips in output occasioned by the two political convulsions are eliminated. Now, a comparison can be made of the post-reform era with the "normal" period of socialist economics—the third column in Table 12.3 versus the second column. The contrast is by no means as pronounced, although growth of output and labor productivity growth were superior after the reform.

From the table we can see evidence of a difference in the type of economic growth between the two periods. The pre-reform period was characterized by the extensive growth that we often see in socialist systems. The labor force increased rapidly (by 3 percent per annum) and capital accumulation was very high (13.2 percent per annum). The growth of output is wholly accounted for by the growth of inputs; in this case we note that total factor productivity is negative, indicating a loss of aggregate efficiency.

In the post-reform era, labor force and capital growth are slower than in the pre-reform era, yet output grows more quickly. The key to this is the growth in total factor productivity, which moves ahead at a respectable 3.8 percent per annum in the post-reform period. Total factor productivity (TFP) is calculated as a residual and its main components are static efficiency gains from moving workers from low marginal product occupations to higher ones and dynamic gains due to ongoing technical progress. By the rapid growth of TFP we can see that reforms did achieve something, but the unanswered question is whether the gains were static or dynamic.

CAN GROWTH BE SUSTAINED?

It is tempting to believe that the Chinese economy has made the transition into a "take-off into self-sustaining growth," momentous though such an assumption would be. As we noted at the beginning of this chapter, extrapolation of current growth trends of the 1990s implies that the Chinese economy would be larger in terms of GDP than that of the United States early in the 21st century.

The sustainability of the growth rate depends to a large extent on whether or not total factor productivity will continue to improve and to what extent this may be attributable to an increase in technical efficiency. To this point it is probable that the greatest contribution to TFP change has been the result of

1. an increase in productivity in the agricultural sector due to the introduction of greater material incentives,
2. the movement of workers from low productivity (perhaps even zero marginal productivity) agricultural occupation to work in industry and services, and
3. an increase in the human capital invested in the workforce.

In addition to these factors, there are statistical irregularities that need to be accounted for. The main one is "underdeflation" of industrial output—that is to say using a price index for industrial output that increases less quickly than the "true" rate of inflation, leading to an overstatement of real industrial output. A second area is the inclusion of essentially unsalable inventories in the SOE sector as part of output at inflated prices. When these factors are corrected for, the rate of growth of TFP seems to be much smaller, and may even be negative, as it was during the socialist planned period. As the potential for increasing output by redeploying agricultural labor becomes exhausted, the rate of growth of GDP will slow, and unless the rate of growth due to technical innovation increases, it will be largely dependent on the rate of growth of the capital stock.

CHINA AND THE WORLD TRADE ORGANIZATION (WTO)

In November 1999 China took a remarkable step forward, one that will put severe strains on the economy in the short run but will lead to a much truer market system in the long run. As a precursor to applying for membership in the World Trade Organization, China concluded a bilateral deal with the United States establishing a timetable for the dismantling of much of China's tariff and quota walls. With the task of reforming the inefficient state-owned enterprises barely begun, and with China already experiencing the socially divisive consequences of rising unemployment, this is certainly a gamble.

Agriculture will be sharply affected. Tariffs on wheat and maize will fall by the year 2004 to just 14.5 percent, not enough to protect most of China's farmers from more efficient U.S. producers. Manufacturing tariffs are set to tumble as well. In automobiles, for example, the tariff will fall from 100 percent to 25 percent, a shift that will put most of China's many vehicle makers at risk, although foreign manufacturers are likely to be fast in establishing or expanding production in China.

Joint ventures are to be sanctioned in telecommunications, which will expose the state-owned telephone dinosaurs to the best of foreign technology.

However, the biggest sectoral impact may well be in banking and finance. Foreign banks will be largely freed of restrictions and will be able to operate throughout China. The inefficient and poorly financed state banks will be forced to compete for funds and loans, and a banking crisis is likely. The most probable result will be an extensive failure of Chinese banks and their takeover by foreign, mostly American, concerns.

KEY TERMS AND CONCEPTS

contract responsibility system (CRS)

credit plan

decentralization

economic and technology development zones (ETDZs)

fiscal contract responsibility system (FCRS)

foreign-financed enterprises (FFEs)

gang of four

gradualism

Great Leap Forward

hard budget constraint

high technology development zones (HTDZs)

household responsibility system (HRS)

"kindred model"

partial reform

policy loans

Proletarian Cultural Revolution

special economic zones (SEZs)

spontaneous reform

state-owned enterprises (SOEs)

township and village enterprises (TVEs)

QUESTIONS FOR DISCUSSION

1. Why was Soviet-style planning hard to apply in China?

2. How did the Great Leap Forward and the Cultural Revolution harm economic development?

3. How did allowing agricultural reform lead to the rapid expansion of light industry?

4. Why have township and village enterprises been so successful?

5. What attempts have been made to reform state enterprise, and how successful has it been?

6. What has been the role of the special economic zone in Chinese development?

7. What has been the role of Chinese overseas communities in the development of China?

8. Discuss the metaphor of "crossing the river by feeling the stones" with respect to reform in China.

9. Why is opening the financial sector to competition, agreed to in the deal with the United States in November 1999, so important for the development of a market economy in China?

RESOURCES

WEB SITES

Central Bank . . . . http://www.cbc.gov.tw/

Ministry of Foreign Trade and Economic Cooperation . . . . . http://www.moftec.gov.cn/

Ministry of Economic Affairs . . . http://www.moea.gov.tw/~meco/Intro_e/xmoe0.htm

China News Services and China News Agency . . . . http://www.chinanews.com/

China Online . . . . http://www.gcinfo.com/

Banking Institute of the Republic of China . . . . http://www.biroc.org.tw/english/Welcome.htm

BOOKS AND ARTICLES

Bell, Michael W., Hoe Ee Khor, and Kalpana Kochhar. *China at the Threshold of a Market Economy.* International Monetary Fund Occasional Paper 107. Washington, D.C.: International Monetary Fund, September 1993.

Borensztein, Eduardo, and Jonathan D. Ostry. "Accounting for China's Growth." *American Economic Review,* May 1996, 224.

Blejer, Mario. "China: Prolonged Reforms and the Weakening of Fiscal Control." In *Transition to Market,* ed. Mario Tanzi. Washington, D.C.: International Monetary Fund,1993. 253–269.

Blejer, Mario, David Burton, Steven Dunaway, and Gyorgy Szapary. *China: Economic Reform and Macroeconomic Management.* Washington, D.C.: International Monetary Fund, January 1991.

Cardoso, Eliana and Shahid Yusuf. "Red Capitalism: Growth and Inflation in China." *Challenge,* MayJune 1994, 49–57.

Chen, Aimin. "Chinese Industrial Structure in Transition: The Emergence of Stock-Offering Firms." *Comparative Economic Studies,* winter 1994, 1–19.

Chen, Kang, Gary H. Jefferson, and Inderjit Singh. "Lessons from China's Economic Reform." In *Comparative Economic Systems,* 7th ed., ed. Morris Bornstein. Burr Ridge, Ill.: Irwin, 1994.

"China's Coastal Development (The Great International Cycle) and Decentralized Management of the Economy." *Chinese Economic Studies,* fall 1991 and winter 1991–1992.

Chow, Gregory C. *Chinese Economy.* 2d ed. River Edge, N.J.: World Scientific Publishing, 1987.

Fulton, Trish, Jinyan Li, and Dianqing Xu, eds. *China's Tax Reform Options*. River Edge, N.J.: World Scientific Publishing, 1998.

Gao, Shangquan. *Two Decades of Reform in China*. Washington, D.C.: World Bank, 1999.

Ge, Wei. *Special Economic Zones and the Economic Transition in China*. River Edge, N.J.: World Scientific Publishing, 1999.

Hsu, Dave Y. C. "Experience and Lessons of China's Agricultural Development." *Journal of Contemporary Asia* 20, no. 2 (1990), 212–223.

Hu, Yaoxing. "Market-Oriented Reforms in China." *Development Policy Review* 11, no. 2 (June 1993): 195–204.

Huang, Yasheng. "Information, Bureaucracy, and Economic Reforms in China and the Soviet Union." *World Politics*, October 1994, 102–34.

Itoh, Fumio. *China in the Twenty-First Century: Politics, Economy, and Society*. New York: United Nations Publications, 1997.

Jefferson, Gary, and Inderjit Singh, eds. *Enterprise Reform in China: Ownership, Transition, and Performance*. Oxford: Oxford University Press, 1998.

Koo, Anthony Y. C. "The Contract Responsibility System: Transition from a Planned to a Market Economy: Government and Enterprise in the Reform Process." *Economic Development and Cultural Change*, July 1990, 797–820.

Kung, James Kaising. "Egalitarianism, Subsistence Provision, and Work Incentives in China's Agricultural Collectives." *World Development* 1994: 175–187.

Lieberthal, Kenneth G., and David M. Lampton, eds. *Bureaucracy, Politics, and Decision Making in Post-Mao China*. Berkeley: California University Press, 1992.

Lichenstein, Peter M. *China at the Brink: The Political Economy of Reform and Retrenchment in the Post-Mao Era*. New York: Praeger, 1991. Reviewed in *Studies in Comparative International Development* 28, no. 3 (fall 1993): 98–10.

Liren, Shen, and Dai Yuanchen. "Formation of 'Dukedom Economies' and Their Causes and Defects." *Chinese Economic Studies*, summer 1992, 6–34.

Mei, Zhu. "Non-agricultural Industrial Development in Chinese Rural Areas." *Development Policy Review* 11, no. 4. (December 1993): 383–392.

Naughton, Barry, ed. *The China Circle: Economics and Electronics in the PRC, Taiwan, and Hong Kong*. Washington, D.C.: Brookings Institution Press, 1997.

Nolan, Peter. "The China Puzzle: Touching Stones to Cross the River." *Challenge*, January–February 1994, 25–31.

Pomponio C. J. "A Tiger by the Tail: Chinese Agrarian Reform." *Journal of Contemporary Asia* 21, no. 3 (1991): 379–395.

Sachs, Jeffrey D., and Wing Thye Woo. *Understanding China's Economic Performance*, Working Paper Series, Working Paper 5935. Cambridge, Mass.: National Bureau of Economic Research., 1997.

"Survey: China: When China Wakes." *The Economist*, 28 November 1992, 1–18.

"Survey: China: Ready to Face the World?" *The Economist*, 8 March 1997, 62.

Tseng, Wanda, Hoe Ee Khor, Kalpana Kochhar, Dubravko Mihaljek, and David Burton. *Economic Reform in China: A New Phase*. Washington, D.C.: International Monetary Fund, November 1994.

Wall, David. "China's Economic Reform and Opening-Up Process: The Role of the Special Economic Zones." *Development Policy Review* 11, no. 3 (September 1993): 243–260.

Wang, Gungwu, and John Wong, eds. *China's Political Economy*. River Edge, N.J.: World Scientific Publications, 1998.

Wang, Hsiao-Chiang. *China's Price and Enterprise Reform (Studies on the Chinese Economy)*. New York: St. Martin's Press, 1998.

Weidenbaum, Murray, and Samuel Hughes (Contributor). *The Bamboo Network: How Expatriate Chinese Entrepreneurs Are Creating a New Economic Superpower in Asia*. New York: Martin Kessler Books, 1996.

Wen, G., and D. Xu. *The Reformability of China's State Sector*. River Edge, N.J.: World Scientific Publishing, 1997.

Woetzel, Jonathan R. *China's Economic Opening to the Outside World: The Politics of Empowerment*. New York: Praeger, 1989.

World Bank. "Chinese Economic Reform Experience." In *Comparative Economic Systems*, 7th ed., ed. Morris Bornstein. Burr Ridge, Illinois: Irwin, 1994.

Xiaoqiang, Wang, and Bai Nanfeng. *The Poverty of Plenty*. New York: St. Martin's Press, 1991. Reviewed in *Studies in Comparative International Development* 28, no. 3. (fall 1993): 98–104.

13

Taiwan, Singapore, and Indonesia

Taiwan

Understanding the development of the Taiwanese economy from the 1950s onward requires a little history. The island was a colonial possession of the Japanese for almost half a century and its economy was well integrated into the Japanese imperial system. This colonial association was by and large economically positive. Taiwan's gross domestic product (GDP) had grown at a rate of about 3.8 percent per year between 1911 to 1938, faster than that of Japan itself. At the start of World War II, the island had a productive agricultural sector and a growing industrial base.

At the end of World War II, Taiwan became part of China once more, but the nation was divided by civil war. After defeat by the Communists, the Nationalist **Kuomintang (KMT)** government, with the remnants of its army evacuated to the island, ostensibly pending the reestablishment of control over all of China. The indigenous Taiwanese population of about six million was confronted by the influx of almost two million soldiers, politicians, and their families. The incoming regime took up the reins of economic control left by the Japanese colonial administration, and assumed ownership of much of the property on the island, including agricultural land and manufacturing plants. Because of its claim to rule all of China, the KMT depended very little on local approval, since as the nominal government of one billion Chinese, it had little reason to cede influence to ethnic Taiwanese, who represented in theory only a single, small province of the whole. Today the population of Taiwan is about 21½ million people, 84 percent of Taiwanese descent (they or their parents had lived on the island prior to 1948) and 14 percent of mainland Chinese stock whose families immigrated after the communist revolution. They are among the most prosperous people in Asia, with a GDP per head of about $13,500 per year, quite equitably distributed across the population.

Agricultural Development and Land Reform

Embarrassed by the victory of the Communists in 1948, and dissatisfied with the quality of nationalist leadership, the United States initially tried to terminate its

■ **TABLE 13.1**

THE STRUCTURE OF MANUFACTURING ENTERPRISE IN TAIWAN, 1984
(NUMBER, EMPLOYMENT, AND PRODUCTION AS A PERCENTAGE OF THE TOTAL)

	1–19	20–99	100–499	500–999	1,000+
Number	82.1	13.8	3.5	0.4	0.2
Employment	17.4	24.1	28.8	10.3	19.6
Production	8.9	17.6	26.0	10.6	36.8

SOURCE: Provisional Data from Sixth Census (February 1984), Wade, *Governing the Market*, 67.

relationship with the KMT. However, the outbreak of the Korean War made the preservation of "free China" in Taiwan an important strategic objective. U.S. aid and advice flowed toward the island, playing an important role in the development of the economy.

The first priority for the Americans was land reform, and they persuaded the Nationalists to pursue this goal aggressively. In the early 1950s, ownership of 37 percent of the island's cultivable land passed from landlord to tenant,[1] making agriculture a dynamic and export-oriented sector. Output grew at 4.4 percent per annum, and crop yields were the highest in Asia outside Japan, providing the surplus needed as preconditions for industrial growth. Restrictions on agricultural exports kept food cheap, to the benefit of the industrialists since it enabled wages to be kept down.

INDUSTRIAL GROWTH

With a rapidly rising population and limited resources and land area, Taiwan's comparative advantage lay in a labor-intensive, relatively small-scale manufacturing industry, although a disproportionate volume of output was in large enterprise (see Table 13.1). Manufacturing output doubled between 1952 and 1958 (a rate of 12 percent per annum). To market-oriented economists,[2] Taiwan was a clear example of the power of competitive capitalism and a lesson for other developing nations. However, more recently "revisionists"[3] have stressed the central role of the government in the management of the development effort.

---

[1] Robert Wade, *Governing the Market* (Princeton, Princeton University Press 1970), 10.

[2] See W. Galensen, *Economic Growth and Structural Change in Taiwan: The Postwar Experience of the Republic of China* (Cornell: Cornell University Press, 1979).

[3] *The East Asian Miracle: A World Bank Policy Research Report* (New York: Oxford University Press, 1993), 9.

THE NEOCLASSICAL INTERPRETATION OF TAIWANESE GROWTH

Neoclassical economists[4] have emphasized the lack of government intervention in the Taiwanese economy especially after trade liberalization in 1958, which established a single realistic exchange rate, low tariffs, and easy access for foreign capital. In addition, Taiwan enjoyed free and fluid labor markets, with an increasingly well-trained labor force. The industrial structure was highly competitive compared to other East Asian economies, with a relative absence of large companies and monopoly. Although Taiwan does have "business groups," they are less central to the economy than the *keiretsu* in Japan, the *chaebol* in Korea, or even the family holding companies that have emerged in Indonesia. For example, while Korea's Hyundai *chaebol* employs hundreds of thousands, Taiwan's largest group, The Formosa Plastics Group, employs only 30,000 people.

Perhaps one of the strongest indices of the laissez faire nature of Taiwanese capitalism is the very rapid turnover of firms on the island. Recent research[5] indicates that it is easy both to go bankrupt and to start a business in Taiwan. Competition drives a lot of companies to the wall, and, more important, the government does not intervene with soft money to save them but rather lets them die. This Schumpeterian process of creative destruction requires efficiency for survival and might be one source of Taiwan's impressive growth of total factor productivity. In 1991, for example, 40 percent of Taiwan's chemical output came from firms that had not existed five years before; from another perspective, the firms that had contributed 58 percent of the output in 1981 had gone out of the business by 1991. Competitive pressures ensure constant attention to efficiency, and there is little evidence of a "soft budget constraint."

THE FINANCIAL SYSTEM

Critics often characterize the Taiwanese financial system as rigid, slow-footed, and antiquated. However, whatever its shortcomings, the system was remarkably effective in financing much of the sustained economic development that occurred from the 1950s through the 1980s and proved much more robust than other Asian banking systems when financial markets came under pressure in the mid-1990s. Consequently, some reevaluation of the Taiwanese system and its slow pace of change is in order.

Historically, the government dominated banking and owned virtually all banks until the mid-1990s.[6] Direction of credit was less overt than in Korea or Japan.

---

[4]The most prominent with respect to Taiwan are Ian Little and Gustav Ranis.

[5] Bee An Aw, M. Roberts, and X. Chen, "Firm-level evidence of productivity differentials." *National Bureau for Economic Research working paper #6235*, October 1997.

[6]In fact, one major bank was privatized in 1971, following the "derecognition" of Taiwan by the United Nations and many countries, in order to have a nongovernmental entity that could operate overseas.

Periodically the Council for Economic Planning and Development, with the cooperation of the Ministry of Finance and Economic Affairs, issued a list of "preferred industries." Inclusion on the list indicated a priority borrower to the bank and generally ensured access to credit. The system favored larger enterprises; smaller firms were often forced to a semilegal and unregulated **curb market** charging rates 50 to 100 percent higher than the banks. The curb system relied on the **postdated check.** On receiving the loan a borrower gave the lender a check for the value of the loan plus interest, dated for the day that the loan is due. If the check bounced the issuer was subject to criminal penalties.

At the commercial level, Taiwanese banking has been very conservative. Loan maturities tend to be short, with up to 75 percent of all bank loans having a maturity of one year or less. On top of that Taiwanese bankers have been almost obsessive about collateral and lend only against assets that are liquid and easily fungible. These two tendencies have made the banking system unresponsive to industry's demands, but has kept bank balance sheets solid and well-protected against financial crises.

The stability of the commercial banks was not reflected in **local Community Financial Institutions,** roughly equivalent to U.S. savings and loans (S&Ls), which were frequently under the control of local agricultural or fishermen's associations. Loans were often made to acquaintances or political connections, and are therefore "soft," leaving the institutions vulnerable. They suffered much more than the commercial banks in the recent Asian banking crisis. Out of the roughly 300 institutions, 24 suffered from crippling runs in 1996, and many had bad loan ratios of more than 50 percent.

Liberalization of the banking sector began in the early 1980s when foreign banks were first allowed to establish branches on the island. Change accelerated in 1985 with a push to privatize state-controlled commercial banks, a move motivated in part by a desire to modernize banking and in part by the need to raise revenue to close a growing government budget deficit. Two large banks (Farmers' Bank and Chiao Tung Bank) are now fully privatized, and the big three commercial banks (Chang Hwo, First Commercial, and Hua Nan) have been partially sold with the government retaining between 30 percent and 40 percent of capital in each case.

INDUSTRIAL STRUCTURE

The economic philosophy of the Taiwanese government owes much to the doctrines of Sun Yat Sen, the founding nationalist leader. He emphasized that the state not only had a strong role in economic affairs, but could also demand obedience from a population that should value the well-being of the whole nation above their own. In this respect, the philosophy of the Nationalists may be thought of as a type of **Confucianism.** In practical economic development terms, although private property was protected and entrepreneurship encouraged, the state was central. The government in Taiwan invested in and developed large-scale upstream facilities that provided raw material for downstream privately owned manufacturing establishments. Thus the government dominated such industries as petroleum,

■ TABLE 13.2

CHARACTERISTICS OF MANUFACTURING ENTERPRISES IN TAIWAN BY FORM OF OWNERSHIP, 1986

	Private Corporations	Family Firms	State-Owned Enterprises	State-Owned Enterprise Share of Total (%)
Number of firms	57,477	61,224	221	0.19
Employment (thousands)	2,299	337	93	3.41
Fixed capital (millions NT$*)	1,013	101	294	20.88
Value added (millions NT$)	2,835	170	325	9.76
Employment per firm (thousands)	40	5.5	420	—
Capital per employee (thousands NT$)	440	300	3,161.2	—
Value-added per employee (thousands NT$)	1,233	504.4	3,161.3	—
Output-capital ratio	2.8	1.6	1.1	—

*New Taiwanese dollars.

SOURCE: *The Report on the 1986 Industrial and Commercial Census,* Taiwan-Fukien Area, Republic of China (1988), 178; Wing Thye Woo, Stephen Parker, and Jeffrey Sachs, eds., *Economies in Transition Comparing Asia and Europe* (Cambridge, Mass.: MIT Press, 1996), 211.

plastic feedstock, and steel, as well as more traditional areas of state activity like utilities, finance, and communications.

Table 13.2 shows the Taiwanese industrial structure of the mid-1980s. There were, at that time, 221 state-owned manufacturing enterprises. Although they represented only 3.5 percent of the workforce, the state-owned enterprises (SOEs) were highly productive and capital intensive, constituting almost 10 percent of the economy's value added and over 20 percent of its fixed capital stock. The average state-owned firm was 10 times larger in employment terms than a private-sector corporation and employed about 8 times as much capital per employee.

In addition to its medium- and large-sized private corporations (of which there were about 60,000 in 1986), Taiwan has many family firms, which employ on average about five persons. These highly labor-intensive firms (about 61,000 in 1986) accounted for about 11 percent of employment in 1986.

INDUSTRIAL POLICY

Ownership of upstream enterprise gave the government one of the keys in a comprehensive system of industrial policy. The other controls were over (1) credit direction via the banking system, (2) tax incentives and subsidies, and (3) tariff and nontariff barriers to influence trade. Taiwan has had a formal system of planning since the early 1950s, producing four- or five-year development plans. These are prepared by the Council for Economic Planning and Development (CEPD), an advisory body attached to the cabinet. The plans are not command, but are broadly indicative in nature and express the desired direction of the economy rather than specific targets.

The emphasis of these plans has shifted over time. In the 1950s the focus was on agricultural development and strengthening the balance of payments via import substitution. In the 1960s the priority shifted to export-oriented growth concentrated on light manufacturing industry. The 1970s saw an emphasis on large-scale basic manufacturing, while in the 1980s high-technology exports were given prominence. The task in the 1990s was seen as reducing the role of government, streamlining regulation, and privatizing much of the state-owned sector. At the same time, a new emphasis on social welfare, quality of life, and sustainable development has emerged in the plans. Government expenditure on social welfare and transfer programs has increased rapidly, creating fiscal problems.

Implementation of the guidelines drawn up by the CEPD is the responsibility of the Ministry of Finance (MOF) and the Ministry of Economic Affairs (MOEA). Since a lot of power resides directly in the central bank, the MOF is less influential than in other Asian economies. Most planning of industrial production is done by the Industrial Development Bureau (IDB), an agency within the MOEA, which turns the CEPD's broad plans into specific action. Since it has responsibility for foreign trade and foreign investment, as well as industrial development, it has a wide range of policy levers, including the issuance of import licenses and control over fiscal incentives.

SAVING AND INVESTMENT

Taiwan has always had a high savings rate, limiting the need for foreign borrowing. Table 13.3 shows that even in the 1950s, savings exceeded investment, creating

■ **TABLE 13.3**

TAIWAN: SAVING BY SECTOR AND INVESTMENT AS A PERCENTAGE OF GNP

	Gross Domestic Savings					Gross Domestic Investment	Net Foreign Flow
	Private		Government				
Year	Households	Enterprises	General	Enterprises	Total		
1955	2.7	4.5	5.1	2.3	14.6	13.3	−1.2
1960	4.8	4.9	4.0	4.1	17.8	20.2	2.4
1965	8.2	6.2	2.6	3.7	20.7	22.7	2.0
1970	11.0	6.4	3.6	4.6	25.6	25.6	0.0
1975	11.0	4.6	7.1	4.0	26.7	30.5	3.8
1980	11.5	8.0	7.9	4.9	32.3	33.8	1.6
1985	16.3	6.5	5.2	5.5	33.5	18.7	−14.8
1990	14.1	5.7	5.8	3.6	29.2	21.9	−7.3

SOURCE: Hugh Patrick and Yung Chul Park, eds., *The Financial Development of Japan, Korea and Taiwan* (New York: Oxford University Press, 1996), 276.

a net capital outflow.[7] During the 1960s and 1970s all sources of savings increased sharply and financed an investment boom. As incomes rose, household savings grew particularly quickly, ballooning to 16 percent of GDP. However, in the mid-1980s investment in Taiwan fell, for two main reasons. One was a fall in confidence in the economy's growth prospects. The other, more positive, was the opening up of mainland China to foreign investment. In 1985 net capital outflows totaled 15 percent of GDP, a trend which rapidly established a large overseas investment position. Although net flows have moderated in the 1990s, Taiwanese investment in mainland China now totals over $60 billion, with at least an equal amount invested elsewhere in Southeast Asia.

THE BUDGET

Table 13.4 provides data on the structure of government revenue and expenses in Taiwan. One obvious feature is the high level of defense expenditure, which drains over 20 percent of the budget. Another large item is education, accounting for 16 percent of expenditures but important in nurturing the development of human capital that is the island's strength. Welfare and pensions are rapidly growing functions of the aging population; because the budget has run in deficit for some years, the interest cost of the accumulated debt is a hefty 16 percent. Revenues come largely from two sources: taxes and the profits of state-controlled monopolies, an item which will shrink as these enterprises are privatized (see next section). The strategy is to use the proceeds of the sale of these enterprises to pay off part of the national debt and hence reduce interest costs.

PRIVATIZATION

In line with global trends, Taiwan is examining ways to reduce government's role in the economy and to move from **state-managed capitalism** to a clearer market model. In 1989 the cabinet set up a committee specifically charged with developing a program of privatization. After initial study, the committee's work was suspended in 1991, to be reactivated in 1996 when a timetable to privatize some 47 state-owned enterprises was produced.

The renewed commitment to privatization has several sources. One is pressure from both home and abroad to improve allocative efficiency by allowing fuller scope to the market. Another is a desire to broaden the base of Taiwanese capitalism by increasing equity ownership. A third is the need to raise revenue and relieve the pressures on the budget. Public production's share of total output is small, and there is no pressing immediacy, therefore a variety of techniques of

---

[7]Because of the large inflow of U.S. aid in the 1950s, the export of capital by Taiwanese residents was much greater than the 1.2 percent of GDP shown in Table 13.3.

THE TAIWANESE BUDGET, 1998

(Amounts in billions of New Taiwan $)	1998		1998–1999: Change	
	Amount	Percent	Amount	Percent
Real income revenues	**1176.0**	**93.8**	**41.6**	**3.7**
Taxes and monopoly revenues	834.4	66.6	−12.6	−1.5
Enterprise profits	217.1	17.3	32.6	17.7
Fines	27.1	2.1	−6.6	−19.6
Property revenue	88.8	7.1	34.7	64.3
Other receipts	8.4	0.7	−6.5	−43.5
Total expenditures	**1253.4**	**100**	**28.1**	**2.3**
Normal government expenditures	133.7	10.7	23.3	21.2
National defense	265.4	21.2	7.9	3.1
Education, science, and culture	197.9	15.8	10.7	5.8
Economic development	123.4	9.8	−4.9	−3.8
Social welfare	160.3	12.8	2.6	1.7
Community development/environmental protection	17.3	1.4	0.7	4.5
Pensions	137.3	10.9	−15.5	−10.2
Debt	203.0	16.2	27.6	15.7
Regular subsidies/other expenses	14.7	1.2	−24.4	−62.4
Deficit	**77.3**	**6.2**	**−13.5**	**−14.9**
Public debt	68.0	5.4	−2.0	−2.9
Leftover revenue	9.3	0.8	−11.5	−55.2

SOURCE: Presidential Office, *Taiwan: Past Year in Review* (1998).

privatization can be used.[8] The majority of sales are scheduled to be initial public offerings (IPOs), with a special "citizens' preferred offering program" to broaden share ownership. However, open tender auctions, private placement, and at least one employee stock ownership plan (ESOP)—designed to encourage greater worker involvement—have been used.

THE FUTURE OF TAIWAN

The greatest cloud over the future of Taiwan is political. The government of the People's Republic of China (PRC) still claims it is an integral part of the mainland. In 1971 the island's government lost the recognition of the world community, and it is excluded from the major multilateral forums and agencies. Doubt about its continued independence has negative economic consequences, and in an attempt to redress this uncertainty, the six-year development plan introduced in 1997 focuses on four goals:

---

[8] Unlike, for example, the mass privatizations that were the rule in Eastern Europe and the former Soviet Union.

1. The strengthening of Taiwan's international competitive position, especially the continued development of high-tech industry.

2. The improvement of the overall quality of life for the Taiwanese people; this new explicit goal is a contrast from the traditional objective of fast growth of GDP.

3. Promoting sustainable development; again a new goal recognizing the stress that high rates of industrial growth and population growth have placed on Taiwan's environment.

4. Developing the island into a center for corporate operations throughout East Asia. The government refers to this goal as making the island an **Asia-Pacific Regional Operation Center (APROC).** This will be hard to achieve, simply because of political uncertainty. The island's appeal would be greatest if, like Singapore, there were few doubts about its continuing stability and independence. The Taiwanese workforce has the skills and education to provide a center for regional corporate operations and is overqualified and becoming overpaid to sustain Taiwan as manufacturing center. But Taiwan's relationship to China, and the ability of Chinese authorities to place sanctions on firms based on the island, is a disincentive for multinationals to locate there.

In the meantime, however, the Taiwanese economy seems to prosper. It avoided the worst of the Asian crisis, and has become one of the world's largest producer of "no-name" components for high-tech assembly. We can expect that the government's role in economic life will continue to shrink, although banking liberalization must be high on the reform agenda.

SINGAPORE

INTRODUCTION

By almost any standard Singapore has been a spectacularly successful economy. Table 13.5 gives basic data on the performance of the economy between 1973 and 1993. Except for a period of moderate growth in the mid-1980s following the "wage correction" policy (discussed later), growth has always averaged more than 7 percent, and GDP per resident has grown by over 5 percent per annum. This momentum has been maintained during the 1990s. In the 30 years from independence[9] to 1995, real GDP has grown at an average rate of 8¼ percent per annum, or 6¼ percent per head. Most of the growth can be attributed to the very rapid increase of the capital stock; fixed capital accumulation has represented 35 percent of GDP annually, the highest rate in the world. Singapore's savings rate has also been the

---

[9] Singapore received self-rule status in 1959 and independence within the Federation of Malaysia in 1963. It was expelled from the federation in 1965.

■ **TABLE 13.5**

**SINGAPORE: OUTPUT, PRICES, AND LABOR MARKET DEVELOPMENTS
(AVERAGE ANNUAL GROWTH RATE AS A PERCENTAGE)**

	1973–1975	1976–1978	1979–1984	1985–1987	1988–1993
Real GDP	7.3	7.9	8.7	3.1	8.5
Employment	4.0	4.8	3.4	—	3.9
Unemployment rate	4.3	4.0	3.1	5.1	2.5
Earnings	13.5	5.8	11.5	3.9	8.5
Consumer prices	14.5	2.0	4.7	−0.1	2.6
Real earnings	−1.0	3.8	6.8	4.0	5.9
Productivity	5.2	3.5	4.6	4.7	3.9

SOURCE: *Singapore, A Case Study in Rapid Development*, International Monetary Fund, ed. Kenneth Bercuson (Washington, D.C.: February 1995), 30.

highest in the world, and this has been supplemented by substantial inflows of direct foreign investment. The labor supply is limited and increased employment has made little contribution to the expansion of GDP. Significantly, 1¼ percent of annual growth can be attributed to the increase in total factor productivity; that is above and beyond that accounted for by the increase of factor inputs, representing therefore the increase in efficiency and technology.

POSTINDEPENDENCE REFORM

From the start of autonomous rule, the People's Action Party (PAP), founded and presided over by Lee Kuan Yew, has controlled the island. Immediately after independence, Singapore was a part of Federation of Malaysia, but was forced out because its presence exacerbated ethnic conflict between Chinese (the dominant group in Singapore) and Malays. Since Singapore's primary role was as the port and entrepôt for the Malay Peninsula, expulsion from Malaysia cut Singapore from its hinterland, temporarily at least, and a depression resulted. To make matters worse, in 1965 the British closed their naval dockyard throwing some 40,000 people (13 percent of the total workforce) out of work.

Unemployment was the greatest but not the only problem. Union militancy was high and labor unrest frequent. Four official languages were used among a population of barely 2.5 million. Most important, there existed a very high potential for ethnic discord. The Chinese, who represented about 76 percent of the population in 1965, were the dominant group, both politically and economically. Malays constituted only about 15 percent of the population, but they had a higher birthrate and their share of the population was growing. The other substantial group consisted of Indians (predominantly Tamils) who made up about 6 percent. The remaining 4 percent were mainly Europeans.

Singapore's development is to a large degree the product of Lee's vision, dominance, and political astuteness. In his youth Lee had been a socialist, and he carried a strong faith in the centrality of the state in the economy. However, as a leader he has been eclectic and has used the market when it suited his purposes. Recently he has emphasized the importance of Confucian philosophy in Asia, particularly the subsidiarity of the individual to the state, useful in justifying his near-dictatorial rule.

From the start Lee made sweeping social and economic changes, some strongly criticized as intrusive on individual liberties. The 1968 Industrial Relations Act curtailed union power. Strikes against public utilities were made illegal and the scope of issues subject to collective bargaining was reduced, lessening the area of potential confrontation. Management was given full discretionary power over hiring, firing, and the use of labor in the workplace. The 1969 Employment Act set statutory limits on the kind and level of fringe benefits that firms might pay to workers, hence curbing "wage drift" and keeping labor costs down.

English was established as the predominant language for education and business, restricting dispute between the ethnic communities and making Singapore an attractive destination for foreign capital, which was often looking for employees who spoke the *lingua franca* of the business world. An emphasis on social order made Singapore even more appealing to foreign investors. Heavy penalties were imposed for almost every class of crime, with especial attention being paid to vandalism, drugs, and prostitution. Failure to pay the fare on public transportation could bring a $3,000 fine, and even neglecting to flush a public toilet would incur a fine of $150. Long hair is still disapproved of, and any male with hair over the ears is automatically at the back of any service line. The government controls all broadcast media, and strict censorship is used to control the press.

THE PILLARS OF SINGAPORE'S DEVELOPMENT

Singapore's growth may be thought of as resting on three pillars. The first consists of the government-controlled **statutory boards,** which implement the development plans formulated by the **Ministry of Finance and Trade and Industry.** There are seven boards in total. Their functions include promoting investment, providing infrastructure and public housing, and operating the communications, transportation, and harbor systems. The most important, and oldest, is the Economic Development Board (or EDB), established in 1961, with an initial objective of reducing unemployment. It attracted direct foreign investment through grants, loans, and the provision of factory sites and infrastructural services, although subsequently it has delegated a great many of its functions to the other six, more specialized boards.

The second pillar consists of the government-controlled industries. The Ministry of Finance Incorporation Act of 1959 enabled the government to actively participate and hold shares in private companies, either directly or through the statutory boards, or para-statal entities such as the Development Bank of Singapore.

■ TABLE 13.6

CONTRIBUTION OF FOREIGN ESTABLISHMENTS TO MANUFACTURING IN SINGAPORE (PERCENTAGE OF CATEGORY TOTAL)

Category	Year	Ownership Structure		
		Wholly Foreign Owned	Majority Foreign Owned	Wholly Locally Owned
Value added	1962	24.6	—	47.5
	1970	37.0	49.4	35.6
	1975	47.4	62.7	24.3
	1980	54.1	67.4	19.1
	1988	61.9	71.7	14.9
Gross output	1962	31.4	—	45.6
	1970	43.4	55.8	31.0
	1975	56.2	71.3	18.1
	1980	58.7	73.0	15.6
	1988	61.1	75.0	14.1
	1991	62.1	75.3	16.0
Employment	1962	14.1	—	66.4
	1970	17.7	34.7	45.3
	1975	31.5	52.0	32.8
	1980	39.9	58.4	28.1
	1988	49.0	59.5	27.6
Direct exports	1962	26.3	—	44.7
	1970	56.7	—	16.5
	1975	66.1	84.1	8.9
	1980	71.5	84.7	7.1
	1988	72.6	86.1	6.5

SOURCE: *Singapore, A Case Study in Rapid Development,* International Monetary Fund, ed. Kenneth Bercuson (Washington, D.C.: February 1995), 16.

In this way the government holds a controlling interest in about 160 manufacturing and service companies ranging from petrochemicals to tourism.

The third pillar of the economy is foreign capital, which is more dominant in Singapore's economy than any other in the world. Under the **Economic Expansion Act of 1967** the government can offer foreign firms many incentives, even seeming to favor foreign firms over domestic ones. The growing dominance of foreign capital in output, employment, and especially exports is illustrated in Table 13.6. It shows that by the mid-1980s foreign firms dominated manufacturing, producing 70 percent of output, employing half of the workforce, making more than 80 percent of new capital investment, and accounting for over 90 percent of exports. Domestic capitalists claimed that policies favored foreign firms, but in reality any bias was the result of larger firms being better able to meet the export targets, which open the doors to government-subsidized credit. While such pecuniary incentives are attractive, foreign capital is drawn by the streamlined bureaucracy and the political stability offered by Singapore when other South East Asia nations were unpredictable.

CHANGE OF DIRECTION

The policy of promoting light manufacturing industry to feed export-oriented growth proved successful in the short run. The unemployment problem, serious at independence, was solved and by the early 1980s Singapore was short of labor. More women, especially married women, entered the workforce, raising the participation rate (see Table 13.7). Ultimately domestic sources of labor proved inadequate to meet the needs of industry and, to alleviate the shortage, "guest workers" from Malaysia and Indonesia were allowed in. However, the government was unwilling to liberalize immigration drastically because it might disturb the ethnic balance, threatening the political dominance of the Chinese.

During the 1960s and 1970s, Singapore was host to a large number of foreign light manufacturing firms attracted by low wages, location, and political stability. However, the government came to realize that in the long run Singapore could not compete in labor cost terms with neighbors like Malaysia, Indonesia, and the Philippines, who had much larger and more rapidly growing populations. Moreover, semiskilled employment in light industry could never be compatible with long run affluence. Income per head in Singapore would never grow to the level of Western industrial nations unless human capital and productivity were raised and the work force became more predominantly white collar.

The government adopted a two-tiered program to raise average incomes. One approach was to increase the level of skill of the population, especially in the area of vocational training. Government expenditure on education jumped by over

■ TABLE 13.7

SINGAPORE: POPULATION, LABOR FORCE, AND EMPLOYMENT (AS A PERCENTAGE)

| | Growth Rates Percentage per annum | | | Labor Force Participation Rate** | |
	Population*	Labor Force*	Employment*	Total	Female
1957	—	—	—	57.0	21.6
1970	2.8	2.5	2.5	56.5	29.5
1980	1.0	4.2	5.2	63.2	44.3
1990	1.7	3.1	3.3	63.1	48.8
1992	2.0	4.2	3.4	64.5	50.6

*Average annual intercensus percentage change for 1970–1990.

**Participation rate for years shown; prior to 1990 as proportion of population over 10; from 1990, over 15.

SOURCES: *Singapore, A Case Study in Rapid Development,* International Monetary Fund, ed. Kenneth Bercuson (Washington, D.C.: February 1995), 57.

50 percent between 1977 and 1984. A supplementary payroll tax was levied on all firms and the proceeds were used to finance government-approved in-house training programs within private firms.

The other, more controversial, aspect of the program involved deliberately raising the cost of Singaporean labor to the point where it was simply too expensive to be used for unskilled and semiskilled work in manufacturing industry. Labor negotiations in Singapore are coordinated by the **National Wages Council (NWC),** a tripartite body on which employers, unions, and the government were represented. In the 1970s, instead of restraining the pace of wage settlement (which had been its policy in the 1960s), the NWC actually tried to increase the pace of wage inflation. In 1979 its guidelines advocated a 20 percent across-the-board wage increase. This was followed by additional substantial increases in both 1981 and 1982. The wisdom of this policy, referred to as **wage correction,** was called into question in the middle 1980s. Slow growth throughout South East Asia was compounded in Singapore by the closure of manufacturing facilities by several large direct investors. Unemployment rose and the "wage correction" took the blame. Nevertheless, when growth returned in the late 1980s and 1990s, Singapore's economy had been structurally changed: the share of manufacturing employment was down, and today the high wage service and financial sectors dominate. Singapore currently serves as the regional headquarters of European, Japanese, and American companies. It is actively searching for cheap labor sites in Malaysia, Indonesia, and even as far away as India as centers of manufacturing activity that would report to headquarters in Singapore. The nearby Indonesian island of Batan, for example, serves as a satellite tariff-free processing zone.

SAVING AND INVESTMENT

Although the government intervenes in many aspects of life, Singapore is by no means a welfare state or social market economy. There is no system of unemployment insurance on the island, and retirement has to be funded from personal savings or by compulsory contributions to individually vested accounts in a government agency, the **Central Provident Fund (CPF),** founded in 1955. Its funding originally consisted of a payroll levy of 5 percent on both employer and employee, which was credited to an account specific for the individual. These rates of contribution have increased over time and now employees must contribute 21.5 percent and employers 18.5 percent to the fund. Thus 40 percent of the total wage bill must now go to the CPF, which accounts for about one-third of total national savings (see Table 13.8). Although the main purpose of CPF accounts is to finance retirement, funds can be withdrawn to pay for housing, education, health emergencies, and, recently, specified investment projects. The bulk of CPF funds are invested in government bonds and thus finance much of the development activity at quite low rates.

CPF contribution rates are high relative to social security taxes in other countries, and the effect on aggregate saving levels is controversial. The International Monetary Fund (IMF) has concluded that compulsory savings have been offset by

■ **TABLE 13.8**

SINGAPORE'S GROSS NATIONAL SAVING RATE (AS A PERCENTAGE OF GNP)

	1970–1974	1975–1979	1980–1984	1985–1989	1990–1992
Gross national saving rate	24.4	31.2	42.2	39.7	43.6
Private saving	17.9	23.4	32.2	30.3	33.0
Central Provident Fund (CPF)	4.8	8.9	14.2	14.4	13.8
Other	13.2	14.5	17.9	15.9	19.1
Public Saving	6.5	7.8	10.0	9.4	10.7

SOURCES: *Singapore, A Case Study in Rapid Development,* International Monetary Fund, ed. Kenneth Bercuson (Washington, D.C.: February 1995), 43.

reductions in private saving. Though the savings rate is high, its roots lie in rapidly growing incomes, low demographic dependency ratios and high levels of public saving.[10]

SOCIAL ENGINEERING

Singapore's government is unapologetically interventionist in social matters. It believes that "good" behavior should be promoted by the government and has little tolerance for antisocial behavior. Individual liberty is often a casualty, but this is regarded by the government and by much of the population as acceptable in the drive for prosperity and stability.

One example of aggressive interventionism is Singapore's population policy. Immediately after independence there were worries about overpopulation and a Family Planning Board was formed to promulgate birth control. Extensive use was made of media propaganda, but economic incentives were also used. Maternity hospital costs were raised for 3rd or 4th children, and families with more than two children were given lower priority in selection of the schools. By the early 1980s the fertility rate had fallen to 1.44 per woman, and depopulation (and more immediately reduction in the Chinese dominance) was feared. Population control was scrapped, replaced by a selective **pro-natalist movement.** Less well-educated women were still encouraged to undergo sterilization after the second child by a cash grant of $5,300. However, to address the concerns that ethnic Chinese women, in general well educated, were marrying too late (if at all) and having too few children, a Social Development Unit to encourage marriage was established. Again extensive use was made of propaganda to encourage a more practical bent in mate selection ("Dreams can take a lifetime—choose reality"), and the government even sponsored "singles' cruises." Maternity leave was made more easily available for

[10] Aasin Husai, "Determinants of Private Saving in Singapore," in *Singapore a Case Study in Rapid Development* (Washington, D.C.: International Monetary Fund, 1995).

women, especially graduates. Financial teeth were added in 1989 when the government announced a $10,000 tax *rebate* for fourth children, a benefit only useful for those with high taxes. The policies of the pro-natalist movement have been criticized as racist. The subsidies for child rearing go primarily to the educated and wealthy Chinese, while cash bonuses for sterilization still restrict the growth of the Indian and Malay minorities.

Lee Kuan Yew himself has said:

> I am often accused of interfering in the private lives of citizens. Yet if I had not done that we would not be here today. And I say without the slightest remorse that we wouldn't be here, we would not have made economic progress, if we had not intervened on very personal matters—who your neighbor is, how you live, the noise you make, how you spit, or what language you use. We decide what is right. Never mind what people think. That's another problem.[11]

RECENT DEVELOPMENTS

Lee Kuan Yew retired as prime minister in 1990 but he retains control over the People's Action Party and through it the direction of Singapore. The progress of the island-state in becoming an almost entirely "white collar enclave" is illustrated by Table 13.9. Total employment increased between 1991 and 1996 by 223,825. The most rapid growth was in financial and business services (where employment grew at 8.9 percent per annum), closely followed by transport and communication. The move to "professional status" is illustrated even more clearly in the lower panel of the same table. The growth rate of employment in management and professional occupations was 10 percent per annum, while that of production workers was only 2.5 percent per annum.

Singapore, in its position as a financial, management, and communications center, was rocked by the financial crises that affected Asia in 1997 and 1998. However, although the stock market took a beating,[12] no fundamental flaw emerged in Singapore's economic structure. Bank failures were few; the number of banks operating in Singapore remained constant at about 150 throughout the crisis. The rapid and repeated currency devaluation, a common feature elsewhere in the region, was avoided.

Monetary and exchange stability during the crisis was enhanced by the very conservative nature of the monetary system. From 1899 to 1982 Singapore had a **currency board** system, which required both a fixed exchange rate and the complete backing of all domestic currency issue by hard currency reserves. This completely limited credit creation, assured convertibility, and instilled economic discipline. Singapore abandoned that system in 1982, but remains very

---

[11] Lee Kuan Yew's speech on National Day, 1986, cited in Christopher Tremewan *The Political Economy of Social Control in Singapore* (London: MacMillan, 1986), 2.

[12] The leading *Straits Times* Index, which stood at over 2,000 in February 1997, fell to a low of 856 in August 1998. Over the same period, market capitalization fell from S$375 billion to S$261 billion.

■ **TABLE 13.9**

EMPLOYMENT GAINS BY INDUSTRY AND OCCUPATION, SINGAPORE, 1991–1996

Industry and Occupation	Employment Gain		
	Number	Share (%)	Growth (% p.a.)
Industry			
Total*	223,825	100.0	2.8
Financial and business services	82,699	36.9	8.9
Social, community, and personal services	45,648	20.4	2.7
Transport and communications	42,404	18.9	5.0
Construction*	15,992	7.1	3.1
Commerce	60,568	27.1	3.6
Manufacturing	(23,294)	−10.4	−1.1
Occupation			
Total*	223,825	100.0	2.8
Legislators, administrators, and managers	77,907	34.8	9.7
Technicians and associate professionals	121,862	54.4	10.7
Professionals	51,316	22.9	10.9
Clerical workers	37,811	16.9	3.6
Production and related workers	(75,063)	−33.5	−2.5
Service workers	14,590	6.5	1.4

*Figures include foreign workers, except those staying at construction sites.

SOURCE: Monetary Authority of Singapore, Occasional Paper no. 5 (May 1998).

conservative in approach, and the Singapore dollar has remained extremely stable—an attractive feature to overseas investors.

Singapore's long-term problem is whether or not it can exist as a "head without a body." As the financial capital of a region dedicated to low-wage manufacturing, its income differs dramatically from that of its neighbors. The biggest risk to Singapore is that political turmoil in the adjacent economies will detach Singapore from them and leave it without a hinterland to provide financial services to.

SINGAPORE AS A MODEL

Because of its size, location, and special circumstances, it is hard to view Singapore as a useful model for its Southeast Asian neighbors or other developing nations, despite its success. It has surpassed almost all of the developed industrial nations in terms of income per head. In 1995 it had an estimated purchasing power parity income of $22,770—ahead of every nation except the United States, Switzerland, Hong Kong, and Kuwait—but its experience is not generalizable, although there are lessons to be learned:

1. *The importance of political stability.* Despite its small size and relatively expensive labor force, Singapore developed first as a manufacturing locale and

then a financial services center, because it offered political stability in a region where it was in scarce supply. It does not matter to foreign investors that this stability relies to some degree on questionable claims of Confucian authority; what matters is that uncertainty is reduced.

2. *Transparency in regulation attracts foreign capital.* Singapore's tax codes and regulatory framework are clearly written and by and large evenly applied, up to the point where domestic capitalists complain that foreigners are preferentially treated.

3. *A docile labor force is an asset in development.* The government has ensured an environment of almost total labor peace. Strikes have been virtually nonexistent for the past 20 years.

4. *Rising living standards and sustained development require investment in human capital.* Education has been a vital key to Singapore's ability to move "up market" from manufacturing to services.

5. *A competent civil service is an asset, but it must be rewarded.* Singapore's civil service is well paid and efficient. The World Bank found that only in Singapore were civil servants paid more (about a 15 percent premium) than their counterparts in private industry.

INDONESIA

INTRODUCTION

Indonesia is a vast nation with a diverse ethnic structure. With almost 200 million inhabitants it is the world's fourth most populous nation. It occupies about 13,677 islands, within which about 300 recognizable languages and dialects are spoken. The dominant ethnic group is Javanese, constituting about 46 percent of the population. About half of the Indonesian population live on Java itself, so the government encourages through its "transmigration program" movement from Java to the less populated islands.

Indonesia attained its independence in 1949. A three-year Japanese occupation was followed by a brief struggle with the Dutch, who tried to reimpose their colonial rule in 1945. From independence until 1965 the nation was led by Sukarno,[13] who attempted to articulate a **nonaligned movement** that adhered to neither of the Cold War superpowers. In 1958 Sukarno abandoned both free elections and the market system, adopting the twin policies of **guided democracy** and **guided economy.** All of the residual Dutch interests were nationalized and 40,000 Dutch were expelled, a loss of expertise that, in the short term at least, the economy could ill afford.

Between 1958 and 1965 the performance of the economy worsened. Per-head income fell by 15 percent, foreign exchange reserves were depleted, and inflation

---

[13] Javanese usually use only one name.

accelerated. Despite its inherent fertility and large agricultural workforce, the country could not feed itself. By 1965 it had become one of the poorest economies in the world with an average per-head income of about $70, lower at that time than either India or Bangladesh. Also, 60 percent of the population lived in the direst poverty, with a daily dietary intake of less than 2,150 calories per day. Life expectancy at birth was a mere 41 years, and the infant mortality rate was 225 per 1,000.

THE NEW ORDER

By the mid-1960s there was further evidence of the destructiveness of Sukarno's policies; inflation reached 600 percent per annum. In October 1965 a series of coups and counter-coups occurred, the origin of which remains uncertain to this day. The official version was that Communists, alarmed by Sukarno's declining health and influence, struck to seize power, and the coup had been rebuffed by senior army officers. An anticommunist and anti-Chinese *pogrom* resulted, during which many people died. In the chaos old scores were settled and practically all debts eliminated as creditors were disposed of.

When the smoke cleared, it was apparent that the army was in power. One general, Suharto, emerged as president and declared a **New Order.** Nominally he had been elected by the People's Consultative Congress (PCC), but there was little democracy in his elevation. The PCC consisted of 360 directly elected representatives, along with 207 presidential appointees and 276 officers of the armed forces. Consequently the army, in conjunction with the president's appointees, were able to outvote the elected representatives. Suhartos's first steps sought to restore order to the economy, relying on a group of western-trained economists, known collectively as the "Berkeley mafia," who stressed monetary restraint, a realistic exchange rate, and a greater role for market economics.

AGRICULTURAL DEVELOPMENT

Faced with widespread malnutrition, the New Order government was acutely aware of the need for agricultural reform. Despite the engagement of 70 percent of the workforce in agriculture, the nation was the world's largest food importer, a major burden on the balance of payments. Increasing rice production was given the highest priority—an effort encouraged and assisted by the multilateral agencies and the United States. Extensive land reform was not required, since most land was already held in communal village arrangements, but new strains of rice were acquired from the International Rice Research Institute in the Philippines. These strains had to be indigenized and also required a great deal of fertilizer, which had to be subsidized by the government. Education in the new techniques was made a priority, and 12 percent of Indonesia's development budget was directed to improving local infrastructure. Price supports were adopted to strengthen the incentives to increase production and bring it to market. While purists regarded the use of subsidies and price supports as distortionary, the policies produced dramatic results. Output rose almost 70 percent from 12 million metric tons in 1970 to over 20 million in 1980, and self-sufficiency was achieved in 1984.

■ TABLE 13.10

INDONESIA: TRENDS IN KEY ECONOMIC AGGREGATES

	Annual Rates of Growth				
	1960–1967	1967–1973	1973–1981	1982–1988	1988–1991
GDP	1.7	7.9	7.5	3.3	7.1
Nonoil GDP	1.7	7.3	8.0	4.3	7.7
Agriculture	1.6	4.1	3.4	2.9	3.0
Manufacturing	1.0	9.5	14.1	5.2	11.0
Services	2.0	9.0	10.0	5.0	7.8
Fixed investment	1.1	23.5	11.7	−0.5	13.5
Public	—	—	11.0	−2.0	8.2
Private	—	—	12.3	0.7	16.9
Nonoil Exports	2.1	25.6	0.0	7.6	16.5
Per capita GDP	−0.5	5.5	5.2	1.3	5.3
Per capita income	−0.4	5.6	9.1	−0.2	5.1
Per capita consumption	−0.6	3.0	5.5	1.4	5.0

SOURCE: Amar Bhattacharya and Mari Pangestu, "Indonesia, Development Transformation since 1965 and the Role of Public Policy" (Washington, D.C.: The World Bank, 1993).

RENT-SEEKING CAPITALISM

By 1995 even the most critical observers of the Indonesian economic and political system were forced to admit that very substantial positive changes had been made. Per-head income at current exchange rates had risen to $980, and in purchasing power parity terms was closer to $3,800 per year. Annual real growth of GDP had averaged more than 6 percent throughout the 1980s and accelerated to 7.6 percent in the 1990s. Growth of the industrial sector was even faster. Infant mortality had fallen to 51 per 1,000 live births and mean life expectancy at birth had risen to 64. Although about 30 million still lived on less than $1 a day (measured in purchasing power parity terms), the overall incidence of poverty was much reduced. The sharp contrast between growth experiences in the 1970s and 1980s and the stagnation of the Sukarno era is shown in Table 13.10.

However, this economic progress was accompanied by considerable social stress and growing protest. At the heart of this discontent was the fact that Indonesia represented a form of economic organization that can best be called "bureaucratic capitalism."[14] Prominent figures were granted or seized control in particular sectors of industry and used their power to extract monopoly rents. Furthermore, the army is a prominent actor in the economy. This unusual phenomenon has its roots in the Sukarno era of the 1960s, when, in the face of budgetary chaos, the army was unable to meet its payroll. It used its assets to build "for-profit" businesses, mainly in transportation. When, with the army's backing,

[14]Richard Robison, "Toward a Class Analysis of the Indonesian Military." *Indonesia,* no. 25 (April 1978): 17–39.

Suharto came to power, his uniformed supporters were able to appropriate control of large enterprises and in many cases the revenues that streamed from them. The Sukarno era had also seen the forging of strong links with the mainly Chinese businessmen who supplied the army, which carried over into the New Order economy.

The most famous case of **khaki capitalism** is that of Pertamina—the national oil and gas monopoly. Since the discovery of extensive oil fields off Sumatra in the early 1970s, the rise in Indonesia's known oil reserves, its oil exports and oil revenues, produced a major windfall for the Indonesian state. Revenues rose from less than $1 billion in 1970 to more than $13 billion in 1980. Pertamina, under the guidance of General Sutowo, diversified into banking, steel, and even hotels, borrowing more than $10 billion to finance expansion. In the mid-1970s, Pertamina started losing money (a surprising development in view of the continued high price of oil), could not meet its debts, failed, and as a result a scandal erupted.

However, the Pertamina affair is only one example of the systemic extraction and appropriation of rent in the Indonesian economy. The market is frequently restricted and not permitted to coordinate activity simply because there are rents to be earned if licensing, subsidy, and favoritism are pursued the liberalizing policies of the "Berkeley mafia" have been in constant conflict with the interests of economic nationalists, who favor building up domestic industry behind protective tariff barriers and subsidies. Despite the lip service paid by the Indonesian government and the multilateral organizations to market principles, entrepreneurial activity became increasingly dominated by a few major groups, usually controlled by Chinese Indonesians, who relied for patronage and protection on the government. The largest were the Astra Group, the Salim Group, and the Lippo Group (which recently achieved notoriety through illegal U.S. election campaign contributions). Suharto's own family also greatly enriched themselves by appropriating certain monopoly privileges. While family interests tend to be important throughout Asia, Table 13.11 shows that Indonesia's economic structure is dominated by

■ **TABLE 13.11**

CONTROL OF PUBLICLY TRADED COMPANIES IN EAST ASIA

Country	Number of Corporations Studied	Widely Held	One Family Holds More Than 30 Percent	State Holds More than 30 Percent
Hong Kong	330	50.3%	34.4%	0.9%
Indonesia	178	24.7	58.7	6.7
Japan	1240	94.8	2.8	0.4
Korea	345	76.2	20.1	1.2
Malaysia	238	41.2	45.6	8.2
Philippines	120	58.3	22.1	2.1
Singapore	221	45.2	32.6	11.3
Taiwan	141	73.0	18.4	2.8
Thailand	167	24.6	54.8	7.5

SOURCE: Claessens, Stjin, Simeon Djankov, and Larry H. P. Lang, "Who Controls East Asian Corporations," World Bank Working Paper, no. 2054 (February 1999).

family groups to a higher degree than elsewhere. Taking the 30 percent of share capital as the measure of control, the data show fewer "widely held corporations" and more family-dominated ones than elsewhere in Asia (with the exception of Thailand).

Support for economic nationalism has not been without counter-currents favoring a more liberalized market, but whenever the economic nationalists were in the ascendancy, import substitution became a priority. They offered the business groups privileges such as import licenses or protection for their own firms to induce them to undertake projects that were valued by the government as development objectives. One example is the relationship of the Salim Group to the steel industry. The government wanted to expand the basic capacity of the economy and wished to double the size of the Krakatau steel mill, originally built by Pertamina. The Salim Group agreed to invest $800 million in the project and, as *quid pro quo*, received a short-term monopoly over the import of cold-rolled steel. This enabled it to inflate the price in Indonesia by 25 to 45 percent and creamed off monopoly rent. This price distortion caused considerable damage to other nascent firms in Indonesia, who were faced with high raw-material costs. In a similar case, plastic imports were monopolized by a company controlled by Suharto's son, Bambang.[15]

PLANNING IN INDONESIA

Formal planning of the Indonesian economy had its origins during the Sukarno period. The first five-year plan covered 1956–1960. It was interrupted by the nationalization of Dutch capital in 1957 and the inception of the "guided economy." It was replaced by an eight-year plan, which, because of the downward spiral of the economy, failed to meet any of its targets.

Following the coup in 1965, the New Order government established a national planning agency (BAPPENAS) under the control of foreign-trained technocrats. This group was responsible for the drafting of a series of five-year development plans, known by the acronym **Repelita.** The first of these, Repelita I, covered the period 1969–1973 and focused on raising the output of staple foods (primarily rice) and developing the infrastructure for growth. The second plan, Repelita II (1979–1983) continued the push in agriculture but also attempted to achieve greater growth outside of Java. The third plan (1984–1988) shifted the focus toward industrial development, and the fourth plan chose to emphasize the buildup of basic industry, steel, plastics, and petrochemicals. Repelita V (1989–1993) sought to upgrade transportation and communications.

As noted earlier, planning has throughout been a struggle between market-oriented reformers on the one hand and economic nationalists on the other, from time to time each group achieving ascendancy. In the 1980s the economic nationalists, who favored a strong push for basic industry and the use of tariff and non-tariff barriers for protection, gained influence.

---

[15] William Frederick and Robert Worden, *Indonesia: A Country Study.*

The chief proponent of economic nationalism was B. J. Habibie, who went on to replace Suharto as president after the riots in mid-1998. Habibie's background was as an airplane designer with Messerschmidt-Bohn-Bolkow in Germany. While minister of state for research and development he espoused a policy of leapfrogging Indonesian industrial development by "creating comparative advantage" rather than by following it. Accordingly, he attempted to create from nothing an aerospace industry in Indonesia, establishing the Archipelago Aircraft Industry (IPTN). This venture required a great deal of government subsidy, and perhaps more damaging to the economy, it also absorbed a great deal of the nation's scarce reserves of skilled labor. IPTN employed more than 2,000 graduates. Its sales were entirely within Indonesia, and it failed to penetrate investment markets.[16] This prioritized pattern of development was criticized for raising costs for the majority of firms in Indonesia. As a response, during the late 1980s the market reformers were relatively successful in reducing both the complexity of the import control structure and the effective rate of protection. Between 1985 and 1991 the average rate of tariff fell from 37 percent to 20 percent, and the average rate weighted by import value fell from 22 percent to 10 percent.[17]

FINANCIAL MARKETS

At the beginning of the New Order period the state dominated the banking system. It controlled not only the central bank, but also the five main commercial banks, and several specialized banks for import-export finance and development funding. State banks held in total 74 percent of assets of deposit-taking banks. Although there were many private banks (both domestic and foreign), they accounted for only 25 percent of the assets and made only 6.3 percent of the loans. The banking sector was used for directed and subsidized credits toward the priority sector of the economy. This control of the economy through directed credit was common to most developing economies and had been a part of the "East Asian Model."

Indonesia followed an unusual approach by liberalizing the financial sector at a faster pace than the manufacturing and industrial sectors. In the 1970s the government took an unusual step for a country at its stage of development in allowing the free movement of capital in and out of the country. However, the banking system remained highly regulated throughout the decade. Directed, subsidized credit was used to foster a specific pattern of development, and tight credit ceilings were imposed in a bid to limit inflation. In 1983 the government abolished credit ceilings and interest rate controls and in 1988 reduced barriers to entry, encouraged greater

---

[16] One wit has referred to it as a *"bonsai* industry"—it is expensive, it requires constant attention, and it never grows.

[17] Nominal tariff rates are not an accurate gage of the real extent of protection. Effective rates of protection, however, remain quite high; the average rate for the import competing sector is still over 35 percent.

branch banking, and lowered the reserve requirement. As a result, prior to the Asian financial crisis, Indonesia had the least regulated banking sector in all of East Asia.

The outcome of deregulation was a sharp upsurge in banking activity. Between 1983 to 1990 the number of domestic banks nearly doubled to 119. Credit became available at competitive interest rates throughout the economy, and there was every sign that the overall effect on growth would be positive. In particular the small- and medium-sized industries, those outside the big groups, finally had access to credit. This tendency was reinforced by a government decree that required all banks to make at least 20 percent of their loans to small businesses. While popular in some quarters, this requirement was inefficient because it forced many banks to move away from the competitive advantages. In this liberal environment, credit was dramatically extended, often without adequate credit checks.

The World Bank's view at the time was approving:

> The reforms were immensely successful. . . . While credit had been readily available only to producers and traditional services, it now became available to a wide range of borrowers, including consumers and investors in the real estate and stock markets.[18]

However, the long-term result was a deterioration of bank balance sheets and progressive weakness throughout the system—a real estate and stock market bubble was fueled by easy credit. Banks began to fail, and the government was forced to reregulate, raising liquidity requirements and belatedly imposing more adequate supervision into the banking sector. It became clear that there were, in fact, too many banks in Indonesia for the available capital, qualified labor, and regulatory capacity. Despite the bullish sentiment expressed by the World Bank and the impact of financial deregulation, the overextended banking system became a liability. Depositors withdrew their money, putting more pressure on banks, who were unable to recover unsecured loans that they had lent to the private sector. A domino effect resulted and by 1997 the banking system was in chaos. The government resorted to dramatic surgery, liquidating 16 banks but guaranteeing the deposits of the remainder.

JAVANESE IMPERIALISM

Although Indonesia is a multiethnic and polyglot society, Java is by far the most populous of the islands and Javanese represent the largest and most powerful ethnic group. There are about 70 million Javanese, about 36 percent of the population. The population density on Java is about 2,070 persons per square mile, almost 10 times the average for the nation as a whole and over 200 times the density on Irian Jaya.

This imbalance has led the government to promote the movement of population from densely populated Java (also Bali and Madura) to the "out islands." A

---

[18] *The East Asian Miracle: A World Bank Policy Research Report* (New York: Oxford University Press, 1993), 239.

transmigration program moved almost 1½ million families (6.4 million persons), and there was also significant private movement.[19] The population of the out islands was 6 percent Javanese by 1980. Subsequently statistics have not been published because of the political context of the issue. The movement of the population has created some disturbances in the out islands and has invited accusations of Javanese imperialism, although the population relocated has been predominantly working class. The exploitation of the natural resource wealth in the out islands has also been a contentious issue. Much of the gathering of timber is done by foreign concerns, little permanent wealth is generated, and most of the rents and fees accrue to the center. In addition, industrial development is concentrated on Java, particularly Jakarta and the port city of Surabaya. The geographical extent of Indonesia and the wide ethnic mix present a constant challenge to the unity of the country. As a response, the government maintains a very close control on all activity and the vast preponderance of decisions have to be made in Jakarta. As a result, Jakarta has grown very rapidly and has a recorded population of almost 17 million. While the government has paid lip service to the idea of devolution of power, little real progress has been made.

INDONESIA'S PROSPECTS

With extensive natural resource wealth and a large and cheap labor force whose literacy and skill level was greatly increased by investment in primary education, Indonesia should be capable of resuming a path of economic growth. In the short run, however, a series of tasks must be accomplished before the foreign capital that is essential for Indonesia's growth will be confident enough to return.

The first must be the reconstruction of the financial system. The rapid and unregulated expansion of the banking system inevitably led to chaos and failure when the Asia crisis struck. Even those banks that have survived to this point are in need of extensive recapitalization. There are probably two effective ways of achieving this: (1) by nationalizing the banks and restructuring them, and subsequently reprivatizing them under a much tighter regulatory regime, or (2) by allowing the banking system to be taken over by foreign capital. Second, the country has to achieve some form of exchange rate stability. Indonesia for a while considered adopting a currency board, which requires fixed exchange rates and a currency backed completely by foreign exchange reserves. This option no longer seems as likely, but some form of currency stabilization to facilitate the regrowth of trade and investment is necessary.

An attack must be made on the **crony capitalism** and family groups that currently dominate and are a problem for the economy. In May 1998 after street demonstration, Suharto was succeeded by Habibie, who withdrew from consideration as president in the election of 1999, leaving the field clear for a Muslim

---

[19] Department of Foreign Affairs, Republic of Indonesia

cleric, Abdurrahman Wahid. The new government has stressed privatization, decentralization, and the promotion of small industry as priorities, but Wahid has many links to members of the Suharto administration and it is doubtful if the assault on interest groups will be rapid or sustained.

KEY TERMS AND CONCEPTS

Asia-Pacific Regional Operation Center (APROC)

Central Provident Fund (CPF)

Community Financial Institutions

Confucianism

Council for Economic Planning and Development (CEPD)

crony capitalism

curb market

currency board

Economic Expansion Act of 1967

guided democracy

guided economy

Javanese imperialism

khaki capitalism

Kuomintang (KMT)

Ministry of Finance and Trade and Industry

National Wages Council (NWC)

New Order

nonaligned movement

postdated check

pro-natalist movement

rent seeking

Repelita

state-managed capitalism

statutory boards

transparency in regulation

wage correction

QUESTIONS FOR DISCUSSION

1. What is the basis of the Confucian content of Taiwanese economic management?

2. What has been the role of household saving in Taiwanese growth?

3. How has the conservatism of the Taiwanese financial system proved a long-term asset?

4. What were Singapore's biggest problems at independence, and how did the PAP government address them?

5. Why was the "wage correction" of 1979–1982 so unusual? Has it proved successful?

6. Why might the requests of the Central Provident Fund not have increased aggregate saving?

7. Does Singapore provide a generaliszable development model for other less developed countries? Why or why not?

8. What were the achievements of the "New Order" economic reforms?

9. Why did the army play such a central role in Indonesian development?

10. What kind of planning was practiced in Indonesia?

11. Why did the World Bank consider Indonesia's financial reforms to have been successful and what were their long-term consequences?

RESOURCES

WEB SITES

TAIWAN

Central Bank	http://www.cbc.gov.tw/
Taiwan Research Institute	http://www.taiwaninformation.org/
Taiwan Institute of Economic Research	http://www.tier.org.tw/
Ministry of Economic Affairs	http://www.moea.gov.tw/
Central News Agency	http://www.cna.com.tw/indexe.html
Taiwan Online	http://www.asiadragons.com/taiwan/
Banking Institute of the Republic of China	http://www.biroc.org.tw/english/Welcome.htm

SINGAPORE

Ministry of National Development	http://www.gov.sg/mnd/ndhq/index.html
Ministry of Finance	http://www.gov.sg/mof/
Stock Exchange	http://www.gov.sg/mof/
Economic Development Board	http://www.sedb.com.sg/index1.html
Monetary Development Board	http://www.mas.gov.sg/publications/index.html
Department of Statistics	http://www.singstat.gov.sg/
The Singapore Government	http://www.gov.sg/
Singapore Online	http://www.asiadragons.com/singapore/
The Business Times—National Newspaper	http://businesstimes.asia1.com.sg/
The Financial Services Interaction Hub	http://www.infront.com.sg/
Singapore infomap: country profile	http://www.sg/flavour/profile/proeconomy2.html#A

INDONESIA

Central Bank	http://www.bi.go.id/intl/
Stock Exchange	http://www.IndoExchange.com/
Department of Foreign Affairs	http://www.dfadeplu.go.id/
Suara Merdeka—National Newspaper	http://www.suaramerdeka.com/harian/9908/27/x_english.html
Embassy of Indonesia in Ottawa Canada	http://www.prica.org/
Indosite	http://www.indosite.com/

Books and Articles

Taiwan

Alam, M. Shahid. *Governments and Markets in Economic Development Strategies: Lessons from Korea, Taiwan, and Japan.* New York: Praeger, 1989.

Chen, John-Ren. "The Effects of Land Reform on the Rice Sector and Economic Development in Taiwan." *World Development,* November 1994, 1759–1770.

Chen, Tain-Jy. "Determinants of Taiwan's Direct Foreign Investment: the Case of a Newly Industrializing Country." *Journal of Development Economics,* October 1992, 397–407.

Chou, Tein-Chen. *Industrial Organization in a Dichotomous Economy: The Case of Taiwan.* Aldershot: Avebury, 1995.

Deyo, Frederic C., (Ed.). *The Political Economy of the New Asian Industrialism.* Ithaca, N.Y.: Cornell University Press, 1987.

Fields, Karl J. *Enterprise and the State in Korea and Taiwan.* Ithaca, N.Y.: Cornell University Press, 1995.

Hong, Sung Gul. *The Political Economy of Industrial Policy in East Asia: The Semiconductor Industry in Taiwan and South Korea.* Northampton, Mass.: Edward Elgar Publishing, 1997.

Ku, Yeun-Wen. *Welfare Capitalism in Taiwan: State, Economy and Social Policy.* New York: St. Martin's Press, 1997.

Liu, Chien and J. Michael Armer. "Education's Effect on Economic Growth in Taiwan." *Comparative Education Review,* August 1993, 304–321.

McBeath, Gerald A. *Wealth and Freedom: Taiwan's New Political Economy.* Brookfield, Vt.: Ashgate Publishing, 1998.

Naughton, Barry, ed. *The China Circle: Economics and Electronics in the PRC, Taiwan, and Hong Kong.* Washington, D.C.: Brookings Institute Press, 1997.

Patrick, Hugh T., and Yung Chul Park. *The Financial Development of Japan, Korea and Taiwan: Growth, Repression and Liberalization.* Oxford: Oxford University Press, 1994.

Qi, Luo. *Economic Interests vs. Political Interventions: The Case of Economic Relations between Mainland China and Taiwan.* River Edge, N.J.: World Scientific Publishing, 1998.

"A Survey of Taiwan: A Change of Face." *The Economist,* 10 October 1992, 1–18.

"A Survey of Taiwan: In Praise of Paranoia." *The Economist,* 7 November 1998, 58.

Wade, Robert. *Governing the Market: Economic Theory and the Role of Government in East Asian Industrialization.* Princeton: Princeton University Press, 1990.

Wade, Robert. "Managing Trade: Taiwan and South Korea as Challenges to Economics and Political Science." *Comparative Politics,* January 1993, 147–167.

Wang, N. T., ed. *Taiwan in the Modern World: Taiwan's Enterprises in Global Perspective.* Armonk, N.Y.: M.E. Sharpe, 1992.

Singapore

Crawford, Robert. "An Industrial Policy for Singapore." *Technology Review* 5 (May–June 1992): 24–25.

Heng, Toh Mun, and Tan Kong Yam, eds. *Competitiveness of the Singapore Economy: A Strategic Perspective.* Singapore: Singapore University Press, 1998.

Hobday, Mike. "Technological Learning in Singapore: A Test Case of Leapfrogging." *Journal of Development Studies*, July 1994, 831–859.

Hon, Wong Seng. "Exploiting Information Technology: A Case Study of Singapore." *World Development*, December 1992, 1817–1829.

Huff, W. G. *The Economic Growth of Singapore: Trade and Development in the Twentieth Century.* Cambridge: Cambridge University Press, 1994.

LePoer, Barbara Leitch, ed. *Singapore: A Country Study*, 2d ed. Washington, D.C.: Federal Research Division, Library of Congress, 1991.

Peebles, Gavin, and Peter Wilson. *The Singapore Economy.* Northampton, Mass.: Edward Elgar Publishing, 1996.

Perry, Martin. "Promoting Corporate Control in Singapore." *Regional Studies*, June 1992, 289–294.

Ramesh, M. "Social Security in Singapore: Redrawing the Public-Private Boundary." *Asian Survey*, December 1992, 1093–1109.

Sisodia, Rajendra S. "Singapore Invests in the Nation-Corporation." *Harvard Business Review*, May–June 1992, 40–48.

Tremewan, Christopher. *The Political Economy of Social Control in Singapore (St. Anthony's Series).* New York: St. Martin's Press, 1996.

INDONESIA

Booth, Anne, ed. *The Oil Boom and After: Indonesian Economic Policy and Performance in the Soeharto Era.* Oxford: Oxford University Press, 1992.

Emmerson, Donald K., ed. *Indonesia Beyond Soeharto: Polity, Economy, Society, Transition.* Armonk, New York: M.E. Sharpe, 1999.

Evers, Hans-Dieter, and Ozay Mehmet. "The Management of Risk: Informal Trade in Indonesia." *World Development*, no. 1 (1994): 1–9.

Frederick, William H., and Robert L. Worden. *Indonesia: A Country Study*, 5th ed. Washington, D.C.: Federal Research Division, Library of Congress, 1993.

Hill, Hal. *The Indonesian Economy Since 1966: Southeast Asia's Emerging Giant.* Cambridge, England: Cambridge University Press, 1995.

Kim, John T., Gerrit Knaap, and Iwan J. Azis, eds. *Spatial Development in Indonesia: Review and Prospects.* Aldershot: Avebury, 1992. Reviewed in *The Journal of Development Studies*, October 1993, 246–248.

"A Survey of Indonesia: Suharto's End-Game." *The Economist*, 26 July 1997, 46.

14

THE ASIAN MIRACLE

INTRODUCTION

Development economists have paid a lot of attention to the extraordinary growth performance of East Asian economies. The widely used and authoritative Summers and Heston data set shows that in the 25-year period from 1960 to 1985, no fewer than six East Asian countries placed in the top seven economies of the world in terms of growth of gross domestic product per head of population. The region of East Asia as a whole sustained growth of over 5.5 percent per annum for this same period. This record was significantly better than both that of the industrialized West and that of developing nations located in other parts of the world, even including the petroleum-rich countries of the Middle East and North Africa, which had experienced rapid resource-driven growth in the 1970s and early 1980s.

Other measures also show the strength of East Asia's record: exports have grown even faster than gross domestic product (GDP). Moreover, economic expansion in East Asia has been accompanied by a more equitable pattern of wealth and income distribution than has been the case in rapidly growing economies elsewhere. The financial crisis of 1997 and 1998 has tended to take some of the gloss from this spectacular performance, but it would take many years of declining GDP to erase the gains of the past quarter century.

Because of this speedy expansion, a lot has been written on "The Asian Miracle," a catchphrase that taken literally implies that the path of economic development in these countries cannot be explained by the action of human agency or the normal laws of economics, but rather must be attributed to some extra-normal factor, even divine intervention.[1] Paradoxically, many of the authors who favor the "miraculous" description also seek to draw lessons from the East Asian experience and recommend the same policies and institutional structure to other countries pursuing growth.[2]

Hyperbole aside, analysts, policy makers, and politicians share the perception of the Asian experience as being out of the ordinary. If growth records for 1960

---

[1] The World Bank has been particularly fond of the miracle analogy. See, for example, the World Bank Policy Report, *The East Asian Miracle: Economic Growth and Public Policy,* and Joseph Stiglitz and Arilou Uy, "Financial Markets, Public Policy and the East Asian Miracle," *World Bank Research Observer* (1996).

[2] See Joseph Stiglitz, "Some Lessons from the Asian Miracle," *The World Bank Research Observer* 11, no. 2 (August 1996): 151–177.

to 1985 were randomly distributed across the countries of the world, there would be a less than 1 chance in 10,000 that the East Asian Group would have enjoyed such high and similar growth trajectories. The World Bank has devoted considerable attention to the performance of eight **high-performing East Asian economies (HPAEs):** Japan, Hong Kong, South Korea, Singapore, Taiwan, Indonesia, Malaysia, and Thailand. Also performing remarkably well, although mostly outside of the purview of the World Bank study (because of its different starting point as an economy in transition from planned socialism), has been the People's Republic of China.

This chapter examines four closely related issues. First it describes the characteristics of the Asian Miracle—what has been achieved in terms of economic change and higher levels of economic welfare. Next we look at the economic factors associated with such growth. In some analyses these are termed causes, but as we shall see the relationships are often complex and reciprocal. In the third section we look at two aspects of a current and lively debate. One is the extent to which credit for growth should be given to market forces, rather than interventionist government policy. The other is whether the outcomes in Asia are explicable by looking at changes in the quantities of factors of production (primarily labor and capital) that are used. The fourth section examines the sustainability of recent growth performance.

THE CHARACTERISTICS OF THE MIRACLE

Economic variables are often highly correlated and a difficult problem is to identify cause and effect. To one observer, for example, high savings cause high investment and therefore rising incomes, while to another rising incomes have been the consequence rather than the cause of rapid growth. Standard statistical tests provide some help but will not give unambiguous answers. In this section we will identify the characteristics of the "miracle" and leave until later an examination of the extent to which this is attributable to policy and institutional factors.

HIGH AND PERSISTENT ECONOMIC GROWTH

The most obvious change in East Asia has been the growth of gross domestic product. The nine East Asian economies[3] all placed in the top 20 economies in terms of growth of GDP over a 25-year period. Growth has in almost every case been sustained and steady. Until the recession of 1998 each year built on the last and saw a record GDP. This pattern of continuing growth contrasts with the experience of

---

[3] The eight World Bank HPAEs plus the People's Republic of China.

other countries in the same time period—for example, Brazil or Mexico—and the experience of the East Asian group at other times. It is common for a nation to experience rapid growth for a limited period of time, when it is "bouncing back" to a level of income—or even to a growth trajectory—from which it had fallen as a result of war, disasters, or inept economic management. Economists generally view this as a return to the production possibility frontier, bringing unused capacity back into production after a shock. Such was the case, for example, of Japan in the 1950s, when it struggled to reach the levels attained in the 1930s after a fall due to war and its aftermath. Similarly, many economists expect a period of sustained growth in the Eastern European and former Soviet countries, which saw dramatic contractions in output from late 1980s to mid-1990s, largely as a result of the disarticulation of the former Soviet system.[4] However, in East Asia the growth has largely been toward new high ground. The production possibility envelope has been pushed consistently outward.[5]

GROWTH WITH INCREASING EQUALITY

The relationship between the distribution of income and economic growth is a complex one. There are at least two causalities at work. One is the extent to which inequality in income distribution favors economic growth, while the other is the effect that growth has on the distribution of income. East Asian economies have combined high growth performance with increasing equality in distribution. This is illustrated in Figure 14.1, which shows that in the East Asian countries high rates of growth have been associated with a falling Gini coefficient.[6] In contrast, in Latin America growth rates have been lower and accompanied by increasing inequality.

In conventional analysis the increasing inequality of income that often accompanies rapid growth is brought about by rising incomes in a dynamic sector, while traditional sectors lag behind. Such dispersion can assist the process of economic growth because the affluence is biased toward wealthier families who have a higher propensity to save, and increased savings can generate funds for investment. Nevertheless, East Asia has shown rapid growth and high propensities to save, despite a narrowing of the dispersion of income.

Another way of looking at the issue of economic inequality is to see what has happened to the percentage of the population, and the numbers of individuals, who are subsisting on incomes less than *the poverty level*. Poverty is a relative measure defined by the World Bank as an inability to maintain a minimal standard of living. In all of the East Asian countries, rapid economic growth has been accompanied by sharp falls in both the poverty rate and the absolute numbers living below the poverty level. In most other countries of the developing world, the poverty

---

[4] So far, however, as we shall see later on, only Poland is currently living up to this expectation.

[5] The exception is the crisis of 1998, which put many Asian economies into contraction.

[6] We discussed the Gini coefficient in chapter 1. In technical terms, it measures the area between an observed Lorenz curve and the line represented by absolute equality. Consequently, a high Gini coefficient indicates greater inequality.

■ **FIGURE 14.1**

INCOME DISTRIBUTION AND GROWTH

This figure plots the relationship between the average per-head change in income and the change in the Gini coefficient for each of the economies. A fall in the Gini coefficient indicates increasing equality.

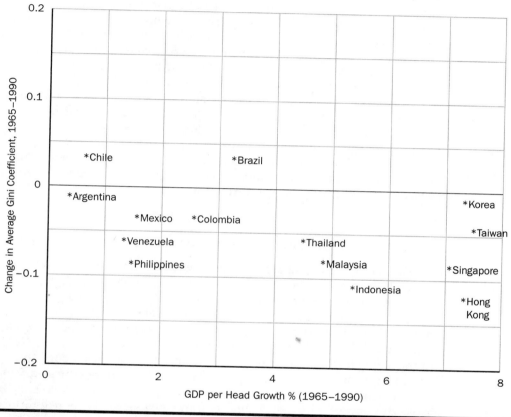

SOURCE: The World Bank.

rate has fallen (Africa provides frequent exceptions), but a high population growth rate has kept the numbers in poverty growing.

ECONOMIC FEATURES OF THE MIRACLE

A RAPID DEMOGRAPHIC TRANSITION

Traditional societies are characterized by high and quite stable birthrates and high, though fluctuating, death rates. Industrialized societies, in contrast, are typified by low and relatively stable death rates, accompanied by low and occasionally fluctuating birthrates. The shift in these parameters from the traditional to the developed pattern is known as the **demographic transition.** Generally speaking, improved public health measures that eradicate catastrophic epidemics lead the death rate to fall first, followed later by a fall of the birthrate as the cultural norms that favored larger families adjust to a changing environment. The lag between the two shifts is commonly called the "demographic gap" and results in a rapid increase in population as a low death rate is accompanied by a high birthrate for a generation or so. The longer the transition, the greater the population increase, and the greater the strain on the economy as population growth makes it hard to raise living standards. Gains in aggregate output fail to yield higher average welfare since the growing pie must be shared by a rapidly growing population.

The demographic transition in East Asia has been unusually rapid, and the fall of death rates has been almost coincidental with the drop in birth rates. Average birth and death rates both fell by about 50 percent between 1965 and 1980. This contrasts sharply with sub-Saharan Africa, where a fall in the death rate comparable to East Asia was accompanied by a drop in the birth rate of less than 10 percent, resulting in rapid population expansion. Similar rapid population increases occurred in South Asia and Latin America.

A RAPID ACCUMULATION OF HUMAN CAPITAL

One cause of rapid demographic transition has been the sharp increase in human capital through education and the swift erosion of differential educational achievement between girls and boys. The success of HPAEs in narrowing this gender gap, especially in primary education, had two consequences. First, it led to an increase in the available workforce equipped with basic tools of literacy, paving the way for a speedy increase in the female activity rates. Second, it is one factor responsible for the falling birthrate, an effect confirmed by many studies though the causation is not simple and takes several paths. For example, more educated women are likely to marry later, are more likely to be engaged in paid employment (which increases the opportunity cost of children), and are likely to be more informed about contraceptive technologies. Moreover, as rising educational levels speed the demographic transition, falling birthrates themselves allow for rapid increases in human capital per individual. In countries where the birthrate remains high, the growth of the school age population absorbs more educational resources slowing the growth of enrollment rates and years of schooling per pupil. In East Asian countries there has been a virtuous cycle: sharply lowered population growth fostered higher average educational attainment, and this in turn results in further lowered birthrates. Enrollment rates in both primary and secondary education in East Asian countries have exceeded the global average, even when income levels are controlled for. Not only have more public resources been expended on education in East Asia than in other countries of similar affluence, but the education itself has been more effective than elsewhere. In all of the reliable international comparisons of educational achievement, East Asian children tend to perform better, perhaps explained by strong support for education in the family and the culture as a whole.

SHARP AND SUSTAINED INCREASES IN SAVINGS RATES

Another feature of East Asian economic performance has been the rapid increase in savings rates, now the highest in the world. In 1965 average saving in East Asian economies was about 17 percent of GDP, a point or two less than in Latin America. During the following 25 years, savings rates have more than doubled in East Asia, while they have remained unchanged in Latin America. It is tempting to attribute the sustained increase in investment and the consequent increase in income to this high savings rate, but what caused this shift in savings behavior? One explanation is the government's role in creating and maintaining stable and accessible financial institutions. These gave savers confidence that their money would be safe in financial intermediaries and raised the expected rate of return by eliminating risk associated with possible bankruptcy.

However, whether the rapid increase in savings has been the cause or the consequence of rapid income growth is still an important issue. Considerable evidence suggests that where income grows unexpectedly rapidly, consumption lags behind, creating increased savings that are in a sense unplanned. Another explanation lies in demographic factors. Falling birthrates and rapid increases in economic participation have reduced the **dependency ratio**—the ratio of the nonworking population (who must be supported) to those who work. Life cycle savings theories[7] support the idea that middle-aged workers save more in order to maintain a relatively stable consumption stream into retirement and old age. This becomes an ultimate reason for a fall in the savings rates. The greater the percentage of the population in retirement, everything else being equal, the lower the savings rate will be: a powerful reason for falling savings rates in the aging societies of North America, Europe, and Japan.

Although both rapid income growth and demographic factors played a part in increased savings, public policy and institutional change have also had an effect. The most important macroeconomic factor in encouraging savings is the maintenance of positive real interest rates. If inflation outpaces the nominal interest rate, the real return to savings is negative, and incentives to save, rather than to consume or invest in goods and real estate, are reduced. Taming inflation, through fiscal and monetary conservatism, can be important. By and large (although not universally) the HPAEs have been successful in restraining inflation and maintaining positive real interest rates. The average real rate in the HPAEs for the late 1970s and 1980s was 1.59 percent.[8] Most other regions of the less developed world

---

[7] Ando, Albert, and Franco Modigliani, "The Life Cycle Hypothesis of Saving: Aggregate Implications and Tests," *American Economic Review* 53, no. 1 (1963): 55–84.

[8] Of the HPAEs, only Hong Kong and Japan showed negative real rates during this period.

showed negative real interest rates and lower savings rates. Moreover, real interest rates in all HPAEs showed a low standard deviation, giving an element of predictability important for savings behavior.[9]

East Asian governments have also created a system that favors savings by reducing the risk to bank depositors and ensuring that they share in the increased demand for funds. One approach has been bank regulation and relatively successful supervision of the problem banks. Such regulation has reduced the probability of bankruptcy and loss of deposits, the high incidence of which is a strong disincentive to savings in the formal sector. Banking crises have been seen in all of the HPAEs, and they are probably inevitable in rapidly growing economies, but their severity and duration have been curtailed by timely intervention.

Most East Asia nations have regulations that limit competition and keep banking the preserve of a few correspondingly larger banks. Hong Kong, Indonesia, and Singapore are notable exceptions and welcome new financial institutions. (Indeed the livelihood and development strategy of both Hong Kong and Singapore depend in large part on the attraction of financial intermediaries, while Indonesia is notable for the rapid—and, in some eyes, premature—liberalization of its capital markets.)[10] The success of a restrictive policy depends on a trade-off between the beneficial effects of greater stability (which tends to increase savers' confidence in the safety of their assets and, therefore, raises the savings rate) and the potential for inefficiency and higher costs because of monopolistic practices (tending to reduce the return to savers and thus lower savings). The evidence is ambiguous though it is probable that there is enough oligopolistic competition to limit inefficiency and protect the saver.[11]

As an additional guarantee for the saver, the governments of the HPAEs (with the exception of Hong Kong and Singapore) have resorted to a policy of regulating interest spreads from time to time. Such a policy limits the amount of economic rent that the banks earn from the monopoly power created by regulatory limitations on entry. Margins, when regulated, have generally been set at levels comparable to those in developed nations and have been lower than those commonly found in developing countries.

Savings by small savers were generally encouraged by the existence of state-owned **postal savings institutions.** Before this institutional innovation (which was a common feature of virtually all Western European economies) was applied to Asia, high transaction costs, poor access, and minimum deposit requirements had

[9] The exception that should be noted is Latin America, which, largely because of strongly positive real rates in Bolivia and Chile, showed regional positive averages. However, the standard deviations in the economies of Latin America were very large, indicating a low level of predictability in the real return and a consequent disincentive for saving by the risk averse.

[10] See World Bank, *The East Asian Miracle* (New York: Oxford University Press, 1993), 238–239.

[11] In fact, the concentration ratio in the banking sector in East Asia is similar to that of developed countries, where we assume that there is adequate competition. However, the paths taken to arrive at that point are quite different. In most developed countries, high concentration ratios were arrived at through merger and consolidation, not barriers to entry.

prevented many rural savers from access to top financial intermediaries at all. The postal savings institutions gathered and aggregated small savings and used them to finance development and private bank loan activity.

Finally, it should be noted that three of the HPAEs (Malaysia, Japan, and Singapore) have required forced savings through comprehensive and mandatory pension plans or provident funds. The evidence on whether the existence of these plans increased total saving is mixed, and, to some extent at least, they have substituted for private saving. One study of Japanese savings patterns concluded that total savings were reduced by the mandatory pension scheme.

A High Rate of Private Investment

East Asian economies have maintained the investment share of GDP at a level 7 percent higher than that of other low- and middle-income economies, and saving takes some of the credit. In a world of mobile capital, domestic savings are not the only source of investment finance, nor need all domestic savings necessarily be used for capital formation at home; some may be invested or lent abroad. However, it is a fact that refraining from consumption provides a source of funds that can be channeled for domestic investment.

High investment has other causes. First, credit must go to credible and defensible property rights. Experience from other parts of the world (especially the transition economies of Eastern Europe) [12] indicates that one of the largest deterrents to investment is uncertainty about whether the property will be secure from expropriation by the government or others in the future. Second, the East Asian governments generally have been successful in providing the physical infrastructure and human capital to make investment both possible and attractive. Transportation facilities and access to electrical power are particularly important aspects of economic infrastructure and the available evidence suggests that large strides have been made in these areas. An adequate supply of appropriately skilled labor is also complementary to investment, and the efforts and results of the aggressive increase in primary school education provides East Asia with an attractive labor force, which increases the efficiency of domestic capital and is a lure for foreign capital.

PROVIDING ACCESS TO CAPITAL. These government policies all have played a role in increasing the level of domestic activity and are relatively uncontroversial as to their effect. More contentious has been the active intervention in credit markets, which has been a feature of East Asian governmental policy. In general, economic efficiency is fostered by reliance on market mechanisms to allocate factors of production among competing uses. Intervention in the operation of markets is justified only by market failure, or when it can be clearly demonstrated that the social rate of return on investment differs substantially from the

---

[12] Boycko, Maxim, Andrei Shleifer, and Robert Vishny, *Privatizing Russia* (Cambridge: MIT Press, 1996).

perceived private rate. With respect to the credit markets, in the HPAEs the two causes of market failure most generally adduced are information failures and co-ordination problems.

DIRECTED CREDIT.   One feature of the East Asian system has been the presence of government policies to direct credit, frequently at below-market interest rates, to industries that are deemed vital and have been selected by the authorities as being strategically important for growth. The specific mechanisms to achieve this have differed from country to country. In Korea, where the banking sector was almost totally nationalized during the period of the most rapid growth, this was achieved very directly. In other countries the government has "leant" on the banking sector to provide the loans to the targeted sectors. If a directed credit policy is to result in a higher aggregate rate of investment rather than merely to affect the distribution among industries, the government action must correct some imperfection in the capital market, perhaps the reluctance of the banking sector to shoulder loans in long-term industrial projects rather than real estate or commerce.

DEVELOPMENT BANKS.   In addition to directing the credit policy of private banks, some HPAEs (particularly Japan, Korea, and Taiwan) have created specialist publicly owned development banking institutions whose exclusive purpose is to make long-term loans to industry. Frequently these institutions have focused on small and medium-sized industry because this sector is often neglected by the private banking sector as too risky or too costly to operate in. In these countries the development banks played an important role, especially in the early stages of development, tending to be less vital as later development produced financial deepening.

THE LIMITED ROLE OF STOCK AND BOND MARKETS.   The role of equity and bond markets in providing investment capital to industry in the East Asian economies has been modest, though it has increased with economic and financial maturity. In the Asian context, the expansion of both bond and stock markets should be seen as a result of growth rather than the cause of it. In part this is due to a policy decision; government control of the financial sector repressed all the forms of financial deepening, including debt and equity markets. In Japan, for example, the government gave the banks a monopoly in the issuance of long-term debentures, which suppressed the growth of corporate bond trading. Stock markets provided only limited capital in the early stages of industrialization in Japan and have grown to some degree subsequently. Joseph Stiglitz, formerly chief economist at the World Bank, finds the evidence suggests that equity markets play only a small role anywhere in Asia.[13]

---

[13]See Stiglitz, "Some Lessons from the Asian Miracle," *The World Bank Research Observer* 11, no. 2 (August 1966): 151–177.

TAX POLICIES.   Taxation affects the attractiveness of private investment by changing the after-tax, or net return. High rates of corporate or profits taxes reduce the net return to investment and tend therefore to lower investment rates. Lower business taxes, or preferential personal tax rates for business-related income, increase investment rates by raising the after-tax yield. Two broad alternative strategies are open to governments in determining the appropriate taxation on investment income. On the one hand, they may pursue a policy of generally low and nonselective rates. This will tend to make investment relatively attractive, but it will leave the composition of investment between the different sectors to be determined by private market forces. The alternative strategy is to use the tax system to discriminate between sectors and hence encourage those activities that the government, rather than the market, prizes most highly.

In general, East Asian governments have opted for the latter approach, adopting quite high basic corporate tax rates and using a complex system of investment credits, tax holidays, and discriminatory rates to encourage particular industries. In the eyes of most economists such discriminatory policy is *a priori* dangerous and can be justified only in the case of market failure. This may occur, for example, when the government has more information than is available to the actors in the financial market or when social returns deviate substantially from private returns. Even when there is convincing evidence of market failure and discrimination is seen to be justified, the tax scheme has to be well designed and efficiently managed to achieve the intended results. Japan, South Korea, Taiwan, Malaysia, Thailand, and Singapore all offer examples of highly interventionist tax policy, and there is a good deal of evidence to suggest that in many cases it has been counterproductive. One study of South Korea suggested that only about 6 percent of total Korean growth between 1962 and 1982 could be attributed to interventionist tax policy. Such a yield probably does not justify the uncertainty introduced into the system, nor the resources that the constantly changing system absorbs. Hong Kong, with very low overall rates, stands as an exception to the tinkering of most other Asian governments and may be a preferred model.

LOW CAPITAL GOODS PRICES.   The real level of investment is determined both by the nominal resources committed to capital formation and the price of investment goods. East Asian countries have been successful relative to other nations in keeping down the domestic price of imported investment goods. During the 1960s most low- and middle-income countries saw more rapid inflation in the price of investment goods than in GDP as a whole. This was achieved through the management of tariff policies and exchange rate movements. Most important was the policy of allowing investment goods to enter virtually tariff free. A cost of this was that a protective strategy for the domestic investment goods sector was impossible, but cheaper access to capital goods benefited a broader range of industries.[14]

---

[14] World Bank, *The Asian Miracle*, 232.

BOUNDING RISKS.   The rate of investment is largely determined by the expected rate of return, which is itself a composite of upside and downside risk. Government programs placed limits on the downside risk for many industries by granting subsidies to those firms that undertook risky projects and by allowing firms to combine into cartels to resist the impacts of downturns in demand.

CONTROLS ON THE EXPORT OF CAPITAL.   One way of encouraging domestic investment is to place controls on the outflow of capital. The governments of Japan, Korea, and Taiwan all had policies that deterred or prevented private capital from leaving, tying the hands of domestic investors and forcing them to choose between investing at home or not investing at all. In the long run such **capital controls** might lower the rate of return on capital and hinder the growth of gross national product, but in the short term it does have positive effects on domestic capital formation and therefore employment and labor productivity.

REPRESSION OF INTEREST RATES.   A feature of East Asian growth has been the moderate **repression of interest rates.** This means that the rate of interest that has been paid to the saver has been kept low and consequently funds have been available for capital investment at correspondingly lower rates. Repression is most common when inflation rises without a corresponding adjustment in government-regulated interest rates. This could lead to very low and possibly negative interest rates for savers, which might have a serious and depressing impact on savings. The key therefore is "moderation." Several Asian economies have been successful in keeping the real rate for savers relatively low, and, arguably, thereby increasing the rate of investment and growth.

EXPORT GROWTH

No discussion of the characteristics of East Asian growth can omit the extraordinary emphasis that has been placed on the export sector. As we noted earlier, the rate of growth of exports in the Asian economies as a group has been remarkable, and a case can be made for overall success originating in the export sector. However, while exporting has been important, it is essential to understand that export growth owed much to domestic reform.

HIGH LABOR PRODUCTIVITY GROWTH

The rate of labor productivity growth in the HPAEs has been consistently high, and this can be attributed to several factors. Some of the growth is due to high rates of investment increasing capital per worker, and some may be owed to increased human capital as a result of schooling. However, some is the result of more efficient practices and the adoption of new technology; this is called **total factor productivity (TFP)** growth and is conventionally measured as a residual, after allowing for the effects of increased physical and human capital. The World Bank finds that about two-thirds of HPAE productivity growth is due to capital accumulation and therefore about one-third is due to TFP growth, in its view, a high rate. However, this view has its critics who note that much of the increase of TFP has resulted from movement of workers from sector to sector, and though this is a gain in allocative efficiency, it is a general and predictable consequence of industrialization. We turn to this debate in the following section.

THE DEBATE OVER THE MIRACLE

THE MARKET, OR NEOCLASSICAL, EXPLANATION

In the 1980s much of the literature concerned with East Asia's high levels of growth focused on reliance on market fundamentals and limited government intervention. This neoclassical view stressed the importance of markets in establishing prices that reflect scarcity and therefore lead to efficient resource allocation. The role of the state was crucial but largely limited to establishing macroeconomic stability and the framework (including the legal structure, property rights, and the provision of public goods) within which markets and businesses could operate.

In this view intersectoral distortions were limited:

> East Asia's success is due to the similar rewards for selling in the domestic and foreign markets. Because variation of incentives across sectors, as measured by the effective rate of protection of value added, has been limited, inputs have flowed to sectors roughly on the basis of static comparative advantage, and international competition has provided an impetus for cost discipline and technological upgrading. Traded inputs have been made available to exporters at international prices, and exporters have faced an international price regime in making their decisions. Finally, factor markets have been roughly competitive, so positive real rates of interest have prevailed, and there has been an absence of duality in the wage structure by size of firm or sector of production.[15]

THE REVISIONIST CRITIQUE

In the late 1980s a series of criticisms of this neoclassical explanation began to be articulated stemming from detailed research on the operation of the Japanese, Korean, and Taiwanese economies, especially in the work of Howard Pack and Larry Westphal, Amsden, and Wade. These authors carefully documented that at least in Japan, South Korea, and Taiwan, the governments had targeted particular sectors

---

[15]See World Bank, *The Asian Miracle*, 82.

for growth, had afforded these sectors protection from foreign competition, and had granted subsidized access to capital, frequently on the basis of export performance. Far from providing only a level playing field, the revisionists argued, government intervention had favored specific sectors and these had been coincident with high-growth sectors that effectively powered the economy.

The revisionists stressed the high level of incidence of market failure in developing economies. Information is lacking; there are many spillovers into other industries from the development of one and the market is incomplete and therefore unable to fulfill the task of coordination. Thus the government has acted to lead the market and has attempted to correct for these imperfections by manipulating key prices(especially in capital markets) in order to promote growth, presenting the vision of the government outperforming the market. This is in some eyes troublesome, particularly as there are in the recent economic history of Korea, Japan, and Taiwan many instances of the bureaucracy leading industry into socially unproductive blind alleys. These range from the petrochemical drive in Japan to highdefinition TV and the current financial chaos in Korea.

THE "MARKET FRIENDLY" APPROACH

To accommodate the idea that the market is in the long run efficient, yet there may be gains from selective government intervention, the World Bank changed slightly to stress that the East Asian approach is not market oriented or wholly interventionist but is, in a phrase, **"market friendly."**

In the World Bank's view:

> The market friendly approach captures important aspects of East Asia's success. These economies are stable macroeconomically, have high shares of international trade in GDP, invest heavily in people, and have strong competition among firms. But the characteristics are the outcome of many different policy instruments. And the instruments chosen particularly in the north-east HPAEs, Japan, Korea, Taiwan, China, sometimes included extensive government intervention in markets to guide private sector resource allocation.[16]

AUGMENTING THE MARKET THROUGH COMPETITION. One of the principal problems of government interventionism is that it leads to a soft budget constraint. The virtue of the market is that it is unsentimental and winnows out the weaker firms, forces firms to minimize costs, and focuses attention on producing goods that are in demand. In contrast, government subsidies become politicized, and therefore under-performing firms are able to remain in business because of their access to forms of subsidy. As we have seen, one of the chief tools of government interventionism in East Asia is directed credit, accessed by firms at below-market

---

[16]See World Bank, *The Asian Miracle*, 85.

rates. A key to successful intervention is to develop a system that performs the same job as the market—picks winners—and therefore determines the direction of subsidy.

One way to do this is to promote the development of several firms in an industry and conduct a form of contest among them to see who will enjoy further government support. In East Asia the goal of the contest, for which the prize of renewed subsidy is awarded, has frequently been export success. This serves two purposes. It provides the necessary foreign exchange to pay for imports of necessary raw materials, defense equipment, and capital goods. It also offers a more objective test of efficiency than the domestic market. Although exports might be helped by undervalued exchange rates, such an advantage would be common to all domestic firms and therefore relative export performance is a good index of relative competitiveness. In the World Bank's opinion using exports as a performance yardstick generated substantial benefits because export success is a better indicator of economic efficiency than performance success in a protected domestic market.

INSULATING THE BUREAUCRACY. The usefulness of any competition depends on a clear definition of the rules and effective arbitration of any disputes. In matters of trade policy it is largely up to the economic bureaucracy to articulate the rules, and, until very recently, the conventional wisdom was that the East Asian bureaucracies were both competent and insulated from the pressures of politics and business. In most of East Asia civil service posts are well paid and enjoy respect. However, the recent plethora of corruption has led to questioning of bureaucratic honesty. Given the massive payments from business to politicians, something must have gone in return, and that presumably was preferential access to some form of subsidy. Despite the World Bank's glowing comments about the insulated bureaucracy, the evidence suggests that in Japan and Korea substantial influence peddling was at work by both bureaucrats and politicians.

THE ROLE OF TRADE. We noted earlier that export growth has been a persistent feature of the East Asian success, and it is very tempting to regard this as being fundamental to economic growth in the region. Certainly in the World Bank's eyes export success had provided a yardstick of efficiency, a source of funds to purchase capital equipment and technology, as well as to provide substantial employment.

However, several critics have taken the World Bank to task for overrating the role of trade. Alwyn Young has asserted that the criterion to judge "miracles" is not the growth rate *per se*, because that is largely a function of the accumulation of factors of production. The proper criterion for a miracle is an unusually rapid rate of growth of total factor productivity, the residual left in the growth rate where the contributions of increased quantities of capital and labor are all accounted for. Young shows in a series of articles that TFP growth in Asia has not been especially rapid despite surging exports; indeed, it has been lower than that in several economies in which export growth has been slower. Consequently he finds that exporting in itself is no guarantor of growth. Indeed, it has been argued that restricting access to the domestic market (the opposite of openness) has been more crucial than export penetration of foreign markets.

Dani Rodrik has argued with respect to Japan that it was this closure to the world, coupled with a high degree of domestic competition that contributed most to Japanese success. He cites Hiroyuki Odagiri and Akiri Goto:

> The restriction on imports and foreign direct investment [into] Japan was probably the most important policy until the early 1970s (as regards innovation). Restricting the growing Japanese market, already the second largest in the capitalist world in the late 1960s, to the Japanese firms who were competing intensively among themselves gave a strong incentive to invest in plants, equipment and R&D.[17]

THE SUSTAINABILITY OF THE MIRACLE

Despite the astonishing speed of growth in many Asian economies, there is an on-going and vital dispute about the nature of the growth process. One school has declared that it is no "miracle" at all: the rapid observed growth is explicable in terms of conventional economics. That is to say that most of the increase in output could be attributed to increases of factor inputs (labor and capital), the securing of economies of scale, and the redeployment of workers from sectors with low marginal products per worker (largely small-holding agriculture) to those with higher marginal products (the manufacturing sector). In our analysis of Korea, for example, we saw that most economic growth could be readily accounted for by the increase of factor inputs. The population has been mobilized, participation rates have increased, and the capital input per worker has been raised. In the case of Korea, roughly 75 percent of the growth between 1963 and 1990 was accounted for by changes in factor inputs. The gain in the productivity of those factor inputs represented only a residual 25 percent. Moreover, most of the gain in output per unit of input was accounted for by the relocation of labor from low productivity agriculture to industry and well-documented, though limited, economies of scale. That leaves less than 1 percent of growth to be accounted for by improvement of technique, gains in skill, higher productivity due to supervision, and other factors not included elsewhere. This has led Paul Krugman to claim that, relying on increased factory production, East Asian growth is like the growth of Stalin's Russia, impressive but extensive, and therefore not sustainable.

In response to such objections, supporters of the view that Asian growth is a miracle have argued that the conventional way of measuring total factor productivity systematically understates the real role of technology and technical change.

Moreover, there are other considerations that suggest that what happened in Asia was a profound and unusual change. First, there is the very real achievement

---

[17] Rodrik, Dani, "King Kong Meets Godzilla: The World Bank and the East Asian Miracle," in *Miracle or Design? Lessons from the East Asian Experience*, ed. Albert Fishlow et al. (Washington, D.C.: Overseas Development Council).

of breaking the cycle of inward-looking underdevelopment. Second, the elevation of savings rates from about 6 percent of household income to over 30 percent is a kind of miracle in itself, particularly when it has been associated with a consistent ability to match saving with productive investments.

THE LESSONS OF THE MIRACLE

The "lessons" of the miracle are complex, and the applicability of the East Asian experience to other countries (for example, in South Asia or in the successor states to the Soviet Union) must be in doubt; but some useful generalities about the role of systems and policy in establishing sustained development may be drawn out here:

1. Macroeconomic stability is an important prerequisite for sustained economic expansion. Growth is not possible in a hyperinflationary situation, or for that matter in one of widely fluctuating demand. However, single-digit inflation is not a necessity; moderately high inflation rates have been associated with rapid growth in South Korea and elsewhere.

2. Government action is essential in establishing the preconditions of growth, especially in transportation, communication, and education. As Patrick found in Japan, macroindustrial policy creating infrastructure and human capital does work.

3. The record of microeconomic industrial policy has been mixed. Some apparent successes have been counterweighed by some very notable failures. Problems are more likely the closer the economy gets to the cutting edge of new technology. In the early stages of industrialization it is easier to predict the most appropriate sectors to favor, since changes in the industrial structure can follow an established pattern of comparative advantage. In later phases of growth it becomes harder to "pick winners," as the Japanese experience with *inter alia* HDTV shows.

4. Reliance on directed credit may have adverse consequences for the banking sector, which can be left with a portfolio of losers. If they are not guided by bureaucrats, bankers will pay care to assess the risks associated with a loan. The direction of credit by planning agencies distorts the allocative efficiency of financial markets and removes discretion from the bankers. Being forced to lend to politicians' favorites, rather than the most potentially productive firms, can upset the stability of the financial sector, as experiences in South Korea and Japan showed in the Asian financial crisis.

5. Education expenditure is generally worthwhile, but is most effective when it is directed toward elementary education. Raising the literacy rate is cheap relative to producing a university graduate, and the greatest gains in workforce productivity are provided by a literate workforce.

6. The probity of financial markets is important. Individuals are less likely to save if they lack faith in financial intermediaries. The implications of the East Asian financial crisis of 1997–1998 might be long lasting because confidence in the financial institutions of Korea, Japan, and Indonesia has certainly been reduced.

7. Stock markets have not been an important element in the initial growth and development of Asian economies. Equity markets in early stages of development have tended to be shallow, rather volatile, and more significant in the redistribution of wealth than in the creation of it. Even in the most developed of the Asian economies, Japan, the stock market has been manipulated and has been a potential source of economic instability.

8. Foreign direct investment has not been a dominant factor in Asian growth. Japan's success was financed to a very large degree out of domestic saving; in Korea loans from multilateral agencies were a substantial factor. In Indonesia and Singapore foreign investment has been more vital.

9. Competitions—for example, those predicated on export performance—can be useful ways to augment the market, but only if they are well designed and disinterestedly administered. Recent problems in Korea concerning the dominance of few major groups calls into question how well Korean "competitions" helped the long-run growth of the economy.

10. Well-paid and respected civil servants lower the probability of corruption. For a long time the image of incorruptible and very competent civil servants was a vaunted characteristic of the Asian model. American businesspeople, deeply mistrustful of government officials at home, attributed farseeing powers to those of Japan and Korea. However, more systematic studies of the Asian experience have revealed a much higher degree of corruption and a lower degree of competence, than once thought the case.

KEY TERMS AND CONCEPTS

augmenting the market

bounding risks

capital controls

demographic transition

dependency ratio

directed credit

high performing East Asian economies (HPAEs)

insulating the bureaucracy

"market friendly" approach

postal savings institutions

repression of interest rates

total factor productivity (TFP)

QUESTIONS FOR DISCUSSION

1. How did a rapid demographic transition help growth in most East Asian economies?

2. How have high rates of investment been maintained in East Asian economies?

3. Have stock markets and foreign capital been important in Asian growth?

4. How has financial repression assisted growth?

5. What led to East Asian growth being described as "market friendly"?

6. Is insulating the bureaucracy from political pressure a good thing? How is it done?

7. How can competitions for credit be said to be "market-augmenting"?

RESOURCES

WEB SITES

East Asian Growth Before and After the Crisis (International Monetary Fund) . . . .
. . . . http://www.imf.org/external/pubs/CAT/longres.cfm?sk=2749.0
The Asian Economic Crisis: Policy Choices, Social Consequences, and the Philippine Case . . . . http://www.asiasociety.org/publications/update_crisis.html

BOOKS AND ARTICLES

Adams, Gerard F., and Shinichi Ichimura, eds. *East Asian Development: Will the East Asian Growth Miracle Survive?* New York: Praeger, 1998.

Amsden, Alice H. "Why Isn't the Whole World Experimenting with the East Asian Model to Develop?: Review of *The East Asian Miracle.*" *World Development* 22 (1994): 626–633.

Arogyaswamy, Bernard. *The Asian Miracle, Myth, and Mirage.* Westport, Conn.: Quorum Books, 1998.

Bello, Walden, and Stephanie Rosenfeld. *Dragon's in Distress: Asia's Miracle Economies in Crisis.* San Francisco: Institute for Food and Development Policy, 1990. Reviewed in *Journal of Contemporary Asia* 22 (1992): 546–551.

Campos, Jose Edgardo, and Hilton L. Root (Contributor). *The Key to the Asian Miracle: Making Shared Growth Credible.* Washington, D.C.: Brookings Institute, 1996.

Chen, Xiangming. "The Changing Roles of Free Economic Zones in Development: A Comparative Analysis of Capitalist and Socialist Cases in East Asia." *Studies in Comparative International Development,* fall 1994, 3–25.

Claessens, Stjin, Simeon Djankov, and Leora Klapper. "Resolution of Corporate Distress: Evidence from East Asia's Financial Crisis," World Bank Working Paper, 1998.

Claessens, Stjin, Simeon Djankov, and Larry H. P. Lang. "Who Controls East Asian Corporations?" World Bank Working Paper, 1998.

Deyo, Frederic C., ed. *The Political Economy of the New Asian Industrialism.* Ithaca, New York: Cornell University Press, 1987.

Fishlow, Albert, ed. *Miracle or Design? Lessons from the East Asian Experience.* Washington, D.C.: Overseas Development Council, 1994.

Garran, Robert. *Tigers Tamed: The End of the Asian Miracle.* Honolulu: University of Hawaii Press, 1998.

Goldstein, Steven M. *Mini Dragons: Fragile Economic Miracles in the Pacific.* New York, Ambrose Video Publishing, 1991.

International Monetary Fund. *East Asian Growth before and after the Crisis,* IMF Working Paper, International Monetary Fund, 1998.

Jomo, K. S., ed. *Tigers in Trouble: Financial Governance, Liberalisation and Crises in East Asia.* London: Zed Books, 1999.

Kwon, Jene. "The East Asia Challenge to Neoclassical Orthodoxy." *World Development,* 1994, 635–644.

Lall, Sanjaya. "*The East Asian Miracle:* Does the Bell Toll for Industrial Strategy?" *World Development,* 1994, 645–654.

Litonjua, M. D. "Outside the Den of Dragons: The Philippines and the NICs of Asia." *Studies in Comparative International Development,* winter 1994, 3–30.

McVey, Ruth. *Southeast Asian Capitalists.* Ithaca: Cornell University Press, 1992. N. Reviewed in *The Journal of Development Studies* by Mick Moore, April 1994, 724–725.

Perkins, Dwight H. "There Are at Least Three Models of East Asian Development." *World Development,* 1994, 655–661.

Rodrik, Dani. "King Kong Meets Godzilla: The World Bank and the East Asian Miracle." In *Miracle or Design? Lessons from the East Asian Experience,* ed. Albert Fishlow Washington, D.C.: Overseas Development Council, 1994.

Sengupta, Jati K. "Growth in NICs in Asia: Some Tests of New Growth Theory." *Journal of Development Studies,* January 1993, 342–358.

Stiglitz, Joseph E. "Some Lessons from the East Asian Miracle" *The World Bank Research Observer* 11, no. 2 (August 1996): 151–177.

Stiglitz, Joseph E., and Arilou Uy. "Financial Markets, Public Policy and the East Asian Miracle," *World Bank Research Observer,* 1996, 249–276.

"A Survey of Business in Asia: The Search for the Asian Manager." *The Economist,* 9 March 1996, 1–26.

"A Survey of East Asian Economies: Frozen Miracle," *The Economist,* 7 March 1998, 58.

Tai, Hung-chao, ed. *Confucianism and Economic Development: An Oriental Alternative?* Washington, D.C.: Washington Institute Press, 1989.

Tan, Gerald. *The End of the Asian Miracle?: Tracing Asia's Economic Transformation.* Singapore: Times Academic Press, 1999.

Terry, Edith Buchanan. *The Rise and Fall of the Asian Miracle.* Armonk, N.Y.: M.E. Sharpe, 1999.

Wade, Robert, ed. *Miracle or Design? Lessons from the East Asian Experience.* Washington, D.C.: Overseas Development Council, 1994.

Woo, Wing Thye, Stephen Parker and Jeffrey D. Sachs. *Economies in Transition: Comparing Asia and Europe.* Cambridge, Mass.: MIT Press, 1997.

World Bank. *East Asian: The Road to Recovery.* Washington, D.C.: World Bank, 1998.

World Bank. *The East Asian Miracle: Economic Growth and Public Policy.* New York: Oxford University Press, 1993.

World Bank Policy Research Reports. *The East Asian Miracle: Economic Growth and Public Policy.* New York: Oxford University Press, 1993.

Young, Alwyn. "Lessons from the East Asian NICs: A Contrarian View." *European Economic Review,* April 1994, 964–974.

SOCIALIST ECONOMIES

15

THE COMMAND ECONOMY

WHY STUDY PLANNED ECONOMIES?

At this juncture of history it is tempting to view both the theory and the experience of central planning as an irrelevant footnote. Both popular and academic opinion now consider command planning as a dead end, a mistake into which many nations were dragged for a few decades and from which they have now largely emerged. Today about 30 of the world's nations,[1] with an aggregate population of about 1.6 billion people, who were previously committed to some form of central planning are now regarded as **economies in transition**—converting from a socialist system to a capitalist one. However, it would be premature merely to salute "the triumph of capitalism" and turn away from any consideration of the achievements and the shortcomings of socialism and central planning, since there is a lot to learn from the careful examination of their history.

CENTRAL PLANNING IS NOT EXTINCT AS A SYSTEM

Mark Twain once observed that "reports of my death have been greatly exaggerated," and the same may be the case for central planning. Despite current appearances and political trends, it is conceivable that some form of centralized planning will be reestablished, possibly emerging once more within the group of former socialist nations. Indeed, several of the largest nations are by no means so well advanced in the transition process that the situation is irreversible. China, for example, still retains the strong political control required to revert back to centralized planning if the social problems of greater liberalization continue to grow. Vietnam, despite some liberalization and a lot of incoming foreign investment, is committed only to an experiment in what its leadership calls **market Leninism.** Even within the nations of Central and Eastern Europe, former Communists have made strong showings at the polls, and though nominally committed to maintaining a path toward a full market economy, they still have an ideological bias toward central control. In Western Europe a recent tilt in electoral sentiment has put left-wing parties back into power. Finally, the chaos in Asian

---

[1] Of these, 15 were formerly republics that constituted the Soviet Union and four were part of Yugoslavia, which pursued a market socialist path that differed in some fundamentals from that of the Soviet Union.

markets during 1998 leaves some to wonder whether market capitalism is the most efficient system of economic organization.

COMPREHENSION OF THE PLANNED PAST IS THE KEY TO A SUCCESSFUL TRANSITION TO A MARKET FUTURE

An effective transition to a market economy depends on a full understanding of the constraints imposed by the legacy of the prior system. Although many economists advising the nations in transition seem to conceive of the task as building a system "from the ground up," in reality the culture, mores, institutions, and much of the distribution of power of the old system are very much alive. The direction of transition is contingent on the legacy of the socialist period in most countries and change requires the acquiescence of the more privileged elite established by the prior order.

MOST ECONOMIES MAKE USE OF SOME FORM OF PLANNING

As we have noted, none of the world's economic systems is purely private. All nations pursue some mixture of both private and public systems. Studying the consequences of generalized planning in command economies can help inform our discussion of mixed systems, point to the limitations of government, highlight the need for incentives, and indicate when planning can be the best approach for meeting social needs.

THERE ARE LESSONS TO BE LEARNED FROM EXAMINING FAILURE

Finally, we should have a clear idea of why centrally planned systems failed. That those who fail to understand history are doomed to repeat it is an over-used expression, but in terms of choosing an economic system, this perspective may well be valid. Central planning was attractive because it offered a rational alternative to the repeated recessions and skewed income distribution that characterized capitalism. When, in the 1950s, Nikita Khrushchev declared that "we will bury you," he was talking in terms of systems, and at that time many in the capitalist world feared that he might be right. However, having watched the stagnation and relative decline of the socialist nations, we now know that socialism's apparent advantages are bought at a high cost.

A BRIEF OVERVIEW OF RUSSIAN ECONOMIC HISTORY[2]

For our example of central planning, we turn to the experience of the Soviet Union. This was the earliest example of comprehensive planning, and efforts in other

---

[2]This overview is indeed brief, and any interested student is referred initially to Paul Gregory and Robert Stuart, *Soviet and Post Soviet Economic Structure and Performance,* 5th ed. (Reading, Mass.: Addison-Wesley, 1999), for a much richer exposition.

countries, notably in Eastern Europe after World War II and in China, drew their expertise and inspiration from the Soviet model.

THE CZARIST ECONOMY

No system develops independently of historical influence, and the emergence of the planned Soviet state was no exception. The development of modern Russia, including the Soviet period, owes much to Peter the Great. He was the first great modernizer, aggressively importing Western technology and science, while simultaneously resisting the liberalizing influence of Western political thought. He began the process of Russian industrialization, founding a variety of state industries. He revolutionized public finance and increased the income of the treasury fivefold. However, he did little to reform serfdom, which was the basic institution of the labor market, and relied heavily on forced labor for his projects, the most enduring of which was the construction of his "European" capital, St. Petersburg. Consequently, the dualism of Russian society increased: a more affluent and westward-looking aristocracy contrasted increasingly with a backward and exploited peasantry.

The repressions of an absolutist monarchy, an elitist aristocracy, and a highly conservative Orthodox Church were formidable barriers to economic change, and Russia, despite its great potential, remained relatively poor. Failure to defeat a rather small Anglo-French force in the Crimean war of 1853–1856 underlined Russian backwardness and in 1861 led Czar Alexander II to take the immense step of liberating the serfs, who then represented about three-quarters of the population. Emancipation was accompanied by land reform and after their manumission the peasants held, through communal organizations, about half of the country's agricultural land. Predictably the aristocracy retained ownership of the best land,[3] and the poorer acreage transferred to the serfs was not given but sold on mortgage, so from the start of their liberty the peasantry was encumbered by heavy debts.

The government set about modernizing the Russian infrastructure, with special emphasis on the transportation needs of the vast empire. More than 20,000 miles of railway track were built between 1861 and 1894, opening up the interior for export-oriented agriculture. The supply of grain for export was stimulated by the need of the peasants to sell much of their output for cash to meet their heavy debt obligations and taxes. By the 1890s Russia had emerged as the world's largest grain exporter, and the hard-currency revenues were used to finance the import of capital goods required for the aggressive industrialization scheme of the finance minister, Sergius von Witte. Industrial output tripled between 1880 and 1900 and after a brief dip due to the global recession in the first years of the 20th century, industrial growth accelerated again, making Russia the world's fifth largest industrial power in 1913.

---

[3] Marx noted in the Communist Manifesto in 1882 that this form of "primeval communism" might make it possible for the Russian peasantry to pass more easily to a higher form of communist ownership.

Living conditions remained grim for both agrarian and industrial workers. The peasants, "held in a vise of ruinous aggregate taxation,"[4] were forced to sell the bulk of their output to raise cash for taxes and debt service payments. The conditions of industrial workers were little better, and labor discontent led to political organization. Support grew among the industrial workers for the Russian Social Democratic Party, which held its first convention in 1903, but the party was from the first divided into two factions. The more moderate **Menshevik** wing consisted of social reformers, committed to piecemeal liberalization along the lines of Western Europe. The other wing, Lenin's followers—somewhat inaccurately termed the **Bolsheviks,** or majority—favored radical revolutionary change. The two factions of the party became increasingly alienated and formally split in 1912.

The Russo-Japanese war of 1904–1905 proved another rude shock to the czarist system. Russia was rapidly defeated by an Asian nation that had, only 35 years previously, been isolated in a state of feudalism. The losing war effort led to privation at home, accompanied by rioting and strikes. A peaceful protest in front of the Winter Palace in St. Petersburg was fired on by the military, and sympathy for the regime fell, forcing the czar into a series of political reforms, among them the formation of a permanent parliament, the Duma. On the economic front, the **Stolypin reforms** (named for the finance minister) accelerated the rate of industrial growth, freed the peasants from the communes, and alleviated their crushing debt burden.

It is possible that in the aftermath of the Stolypin reforms Russian economic development might have followed the path of peaceful evolution taken in Western Europe, where feudalism had given way to industrial capitalism in a relatively leisurely and peaceful fashion. However, a look at the sources of Russian industrial growth provides a reason to doubt a thesis of a gradually evolving market capitalism. Although expansion had been rapid, and as a result Russia had emerged as one of the world's major industrial powers, the growth of output owed most to the increase of the industrial labor force and sustained growth in the volume of capital employed. Expansion was therefore highly extensive in character, the result of an increased use of factors of production, not of rising factor productivity. Total factor productivity growth (the residual increase in output, after allowing for the increase in labor and capital employed) was negligible. Industrial expansion could not in these conditions be accompanied by rising wages or living standards, and one likely scenario is that prolonged capitalism in Russia would have seen only the continued increase of a badly paid, and consequently angry, workforce, which might have provided revolutionary material at any time.

WAR COMMUNISM

Because of the turn of world events, we will never know whether the mold of extensive growth would have been broken or whether increasing labor demand

---

[4] A. Gershenkron, "Russian Agrarian Policies and Industrialization," *The Cambridge Economic History of Europe,* vol. 6 (Cambridge: Cambridge, University Press, 1965), 744.

would have ultimately resulted in burgeoning labor productivity and rising wages. In 1914 Russia became involved in a dispute with Austria and its ally Germany over the Balkans, and in August 1914 Russia was propelled into war along with its own allies, France and Britain. World War I was immensely costly to Russia as its massive but badly equipped and poorly led army absorbed enormous casualties—two million dead in less than three years. At home even the barest essentials of life became unavailable for both the peasants and the urban poor, leading to food riots. In May 1917 the czar abdicated, and power passed to the Mensheviks, led by Alexander Kerensky. Menshevik policy was to continue the unpopular war, despite persistent failure on the battlefield and growing deprivation at home. Germany contrived to return the exiled Lenin from Switzerland to St. Petersburg where he led the Bolsheviks to power in the revolution of October 1917. Initially Bolshevik control was largely limited to the capital, with most of the countryside in dispute, and reunification of the country took three years of civil war.

The first decisive act of the new Bolshevik government was to end the war with Germany by the treaty of Brest-Litovsk signed in 1918 on terms close to capitulation. It consigned a large part of the czarist empire to German control, including much of Poland and the Ukraine, the industrial heart and breadbasket of the Empire. France, Britain, and the United States intervened in an attempt to restore the czar and bring Russia back into the war with Germany. However, their somewhat half-hearted efforts were fruitless and the Red Army slowly won control of Russia and ultimately of most of the former czarist territory.

The system of economic organization instituted by the Bolshevik administration during this period is known as **war communism.** Economic management was almost totally by command; food was "requisitioned" in the countryside by police and party officials and distributed in the cities. Thirty-seven thousand enterprises were taken into state hands, including every firm that employed more than 10 workers (5 in establishments where artificial power was used). The coordination of economic activity was ostensibly the preserve of the Supreme Council of National Economy *(VSNKh)* but effective action was fatally hampered by an almost total lack of meaningful information. Workers were conscripted and organized by military methods, and economic incentives for the industrial and agricultural labor forces alike were replaced by dictum and force.

Market economic relations were replaced by what the political leaders termed "natural" ones; housing, electricity, food, postal services and transportation were all supplied to the public without charge. Inter-enterprise relations between the state-owned production units were of bookkeeping significance only. Obviously the system of war communism had many shortcomings, as without doubt efficiency suffered and corruption was rife. However, a dispassionate evaluation of this period as an economic system is not very meaningful. The country was in a state of civil war, struggling to recover from a disastrous defeat in war with Germany, the food and material shortage was acute, and desperate needs justified the desperate measures adopted. Moreover, from the Bolshevik viewpoint the near-term objective was merely survival and the economic system of war communism enabled them to gather enough resources to defeat both White Russians and foreign interventionists.

THE NEW ECONOMIC POLICY

By 1920 the civil war was more or less over and the Bolsheviks had established their rule not only within Russia itself but also on almost all of the former czarist empire, including areas that had been conceded to Germany in the treaty of Brest-Litovsk. The economy fashioned by von Witte and Stolypin was reunited, and the Bolshevik leadership had an opportunity to develop a new economic system in relative peace.

The blueprint for development was the **New Economic Policy (NEP)** articulated by Lenin in 1921, which attracted recent attention because it has common features with the Soviet (and subsequently) Russian reforms of the late-1980s and early 1990s. It is important to understand that the early leaders of the Bolshevik state were working in a vacuum. To legitimize their revolution they had to create an alternative to capitalism that was not only superior in its theoretical rationale but also in its concrete results, at least in terms of the distribution of income and the avoidance of mass unemployment. Moreover, this system had to be in some sense Marxian, although Marx's writings gave the Bolshevik leadership little guidance. An astute observer of capitalist societies and economies, Marx had little to say on the socialist future. Moreover, he had predicted that the first socialist revolutions would occur in the most advanced capitalist societies (Britain and Germany were the most likely candidates), and so revolution in Russia was somewhat anathematic to his theories. Lenin was careful to establish the orthodoxy of his revolution by a subtle reinterpretation of Marx, whose thought, he asserted, was really that revolution would occur in "the weakest link in the capitalist chain," rather than necessarily in the most advanced capitalist economy. Despite his care in establishing the Marxian pedigree of the Bolshevik Revolution, Lenin was surprisingly liberal in his design of the economic institutions embodied in the NEP. Although he allowed considerable economic freedom, he regarded the NEP as a pragmatic step backward to establish stability before the creation of socialism could proceed.

During its brief life, the NEP was a form of market socialism. The "natural" economic relations of war communism were terminated in favor of price mechanisms. Control of food production was returned to the peasantry, and market relations were reinstituted to regulate the flow of food to the cities. Small enterprises (defined as those employing fewer than 20 persons) were reprivatized, some were restituted to their former owners and others leased to new entrepreneurs. Most of large-scale industry remained in state hands. Sectors seen as strategically essential—the **commanding heights of the economy,** including fuels, metals, banking, transportation, and foreign trade—became an integral part of the state, dependent on budget allocations and controlled in all important dimensions by the government. The rest of industry was granted substantial subsidies by the state but had no production quotas to meet and was otherwise encouraged to act in a profit-maximizing fashion.

The NEP was not a planned economy. The state had considerable financial control, but enterprises were able to enter into contracts, fix their own prices, determine output levels, and decide on production techniques. Although **Gosplan,** the state planning agency, was founded in 1921, its functions in the early years of the NEP were limited to forecasting. Coordination in the economy relied increasingly on the concentration of economic power in the industrial sector, as individual enterprises combined to form "trusts," integrated production units promoted by the government. By 1923, 75 percent of all industrial workers were employed by the 478 government-chartered trusts. Subsequently, these trusts themselves combined into even larger units, known as syndicates, involving higher degrees of horizontal integration. By the late NEP period, the production by the syndicates accounted for more than 80 percent of industrial output.

In terms of its primary goal—promoting stability—the NEP was a success. By 1926, output had climbed back to and exceeded 1913 levels in most commodities. Agricultural output was the exception; it remained well below prewar levels, an ominous precursor of the problems in food production that would haunt the entire Soviet experience. Another sharp difference from the prewar world was the diminished role of trade. The Soviet economy was much less open to world trade than the czarist economy had been, in part because of the disappearance of the agricultural surplus that had been the czarist state's largest overseas earner. However, by the mid-1920s the days of the NEP were numbered, its demise resulting from three factors:

1. *Dissent within the Communist Party.* Most Bolsheviks believed that the NEP was a temporary concession, and the expectation grew within the party that, since stability had been restored and the economy was stronger, the task of creating a truly socialist economy could be commenced in earnest.

2. *The "terms of trade" between the urban and the rural sectors.* The reform issue was brought to a head by the so-called **scissors crisis,** which occurred during 1922 and 1923 when the price of agricultural goods fell sharply while the prices of industrial goods rose.[5] When these indices were plotted graphically, they resembled the two blades of an open scissors (see Figure 15.1), hence the name. The Bolshevik leadership assumed that this fall in the real price of grain would cause the peasants to sharply reduce supply to urban markets and create famine in the cities. This presumption, based on little evidence, led the authorities to consider a return to a command economy entailing the forced requisition of agricultural goods. After intense debate, the government tried regulation and attempted to move real prices in agriculture's favor by imposing price ceilings on consumer goods. At the lower real prices consumer goods were in short supply, especially in rural markets. Since there was no rationing, this "goods famine" led to a black market, with intermediaries from the cities reaping the rents from arbitrage

---

[5] This was due to the fact that agricultural output had risen to about 60 percent of its prewar level, while industrial goods output had recovered to only 35 percent.

■ FIGURE 15.1

THE SCISSORS CRISIS

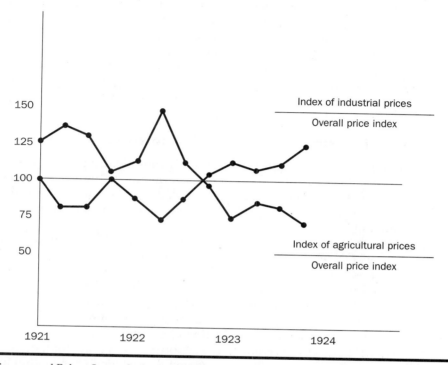

Index of industrial prices
Overall price index

Index of agricultural prices
Overall price index

SOURCE: Paul Gregory and Robert Stuart, *Soviet Economic Structure and Performance*, 4th ed. (Reading, Mass.: Addison-Wesley, 1997), 65.

between the official and the black market prices. This exploitation created resentment among the peasants, who at this point withheld much of their corn for their own consumption and shifted production to higher-value crops and livestock. Net sales of grain to the urban sector fell to close to 50 percent of the prewar level, creating famine in industrial areas and jeopardizing the whole development effort.

3. *The industrialization debate.* The scissors crisis brought home the difficulty of controlling the rate of industrial growth within the prevailing market framework of the NEP. The party leadership came to recognize that industrialization depended on an adequate and sustained flow of food and material from the rural sector and was a potential hostage to the *kulaks*, more prosperous peasants regarded by the party as a counterrevolutionary threat. The two sides of the debate were defined by the radical left views espoused by E. **Preobrazhensky** and the more moderate agenda of Nikolai **Bukharin.** Preobrazhensky favored unbalanced development and saw a "big push" in

heavy industry as necessary to close the gap with the West. This would be facilitated by forcing savings in the agrarian sector and transferring them to the industrial sector by "nonequivalent exchange," a program incompatible with the market mechanism of the NEP. Bukharin, while recognizing the need for rapid capital accumulation, especially in industry, feared that the divisiveness of discriminating against the agricultural sector would shatter the fragile alliance of peasants and industrial workers (the *smychka*). His predilection was for balanced growth, which would not only avoid discrimination against one sector or another, but also the bottlenecks that rapid expansion of one sector of the economy could produce.

STALIN AND THE COMMAND ECONOMY

After Lenin's death in 1924, **Stalin** rapidly consolidated power and by 1927 was unopposed. Stalin favored the rapid transformation of the economy by sustained expansion of the heavy industrial sector. Although initially allied with centrists like Bukharin, as soon as he had secured his rule Stalin shifted to Preobrazhensky's more radical position.

His economic strategy embraced two "reforms." One instituted command planning over the entire economy. The first **five-year plan** was formulated in 1928 and from this point forward the state would control the production and movement of all finished and intermediate goods. A debate arose within the leadership as to the degree of attention that any plan should pay to the demands of the general public. Some adopted what was termed the "geneticist" approach and saw the plan as an instrument to rationalize production along lines ultimately dictated by the consumer.[6] Stalin, however, envisaged a more proactive role for the state. Rather than responding to demand, the plan would be a tool for shaping individual tastes and behavior according to goals determined by the political authorities. This "teleological" approach dominated politics and planning throughout the history of the Soviet Union.

The second reform involved agriculture. Rapid industrialization depended on the availability of agricultural surpluses to the industrial sector to provide the raw material of investment, but the prospect of disruption in future scissors crises, caused by movements in agricultural prices, remained real. Consequently Stalin terminated market relations between the industrial and agricultural sectors by collectivizing agriculture, a move designed both to increase the level of central control over the agricultural sector and to eliminate the counterrevolutionary potential of the rich peasants, the *kulaks.* Individual land holdings were confiscated and the peasants forced into communes. Since the Communist Party lacked a rural power base, this was effected by the dispatch of about 25,000 political operatives

---

[6]Such planning is generally called "geneticist" and was advocated by, among others, N. D. Kondratiev, the founder of business cycle theory.

from the cities who imposed collectivization by force. *Kulaks* (and the definition was loose enough to include any peasant who had fallen foul of the political authorities) were dispossessed, but rather than becoming part of the communes, they were internally deported, usually to Siberia, or placed in penal labor camps. The collectivization program was rapidly instituted; in 1928 less than 2 percent of Soviet farm households were collectivized, but by 1931 this had risen to 52 percent, and by 1938 it had reached 94 percent. Many *kulaks* lost their lives as well as their livelihoods; precise figures are unavailable, but deaths were certainly in the millions.

THE GROWTH OF PLANNING

Initially planning in the Soviet Union was little more than indicative. Gosplan started issuing **control figures,** which were basically tentative output targets, in 1925, and during successive years these figures assumed a greater importance. In the first five-year plan in 1928, they had a more compulsive character and were increasingly supported by detailed production and financial plans *(promfinplans)* at the sectoral level. At the same time as the system of materials balance planning, a response to shortages of key materials emerged. Early work by Russian economists on the precursors of input-output analysis gave Gosplan the technical basis for its work. Material balances for iron and steel were first compiled in 1925; energy products and building materials soon followed. By 1928 Gosplan was the primary coordinating agency for the whole process, preparing control figures that gave general direction to the economy while controlling a growing list of strategic materials by materials balance planning.

In the 1930s Stalin increased his power over the planning process and extended control into every aspect of the economy. Centralized price determination became an essential part of the overall procedure, and the manipulation of prices became a tool in the achievement of the overall goals. The emphasis was on heavy industrial growth, the First Plan calling for a 400 percent increase in investment in state industry.

PLANNING AND THE WAR

Despite the alliance of Germany and the Soviet Union, forged in the notorious Hitler-Stalin pact, the Nazis invaded the USSR in 1941, making rapid inroads into the western industrial belt. The war's impact on the Soviet economy was profound and enduring. First, it prompted an extensive relocation of economic activity deep into the country beyond the Urals and into Central Asia. Economist Susan Linz has estimated that six million persons were relocated along with some 1,500 large enterprises. Although this led to widespread disruption and dislocation of output, much of the core of the Soviet industrial base was salvaged by this remarkable operation. Second, war led to a tightening of the system of planning, and by 1945 materials balance plans were drawn up for some 30,000 commodities.

THE POSTWAR PERIOD AND KHRUSHCHEV

By the end of the war, the Soviet Union had lost between 10 and 15 percent of its population to military action, starvation, or exile to the *gulag*. Thirty percent of the prewar capital stock was destroyed and most of the gains achieved during the industrialization program of the 1930s had been erased. Despite these heavy losses, postwar recovery was rapid, and by 1950 most indices of production were above their 1940 levels, a dramatic effort in difficult circumstances. Agriculture proved the most difficult area, due in part to the low priority assigned to it in the planning process, but also because of the lack of incentives on the collective farms. Lack of attention and investment led to generally depressed conditions throughout the rural sector. Heavy industry, on the other hand, which enjoyed a high priority in the investment allocation process, continued a strong performance, and light industry performed well too, doubling its 1940 output by 1950. Consistent with Stalinist orthodoxy, total capital investment grew at a double-digit rate throughout the 1950s. Stalin's last major initiative before his death was institution of the so-called transformation of nature, which called for massive projects of irrigation and engineering.

Stalin died in 1953 and, after a couple of years of joint rule, the party leadership was assumed by Nikita Khrushchev, who attempted fundamental change in economic and political life in the following ways:

1. Making the leadership aware of dissent, denouncing in 1955 Stalin's cult of personality, and drawing attention to Stalinist abuse of human rights.

2. Regionalizing the planning system, reversing the centralization that had made the Moscow ministries not only centers of power but also sources of bureaucratic delay, and putting more authority into the hands of **regional economic councils** *(sovnarkhozy)*.

3. Opening a debate on the management of the economic system. The most publicized reform proposals were those of Evsei Liberman, whose central idea was to replace physical targets for managers with an incentive system incorporating bonuses based on the enterprise's rate of profit. The central planning authority itself would have continued largely unchanged except that greater flexibility would be given to enterprises in the hopes of economizing on material. Though these proposals received front page treatment in *Pravda*, their importance, both in theoretical terms and in practical significance, may have been overstated.

4. Making a concerted effort to reform the agricultural sector. One aspect was the conversion of depressed and stagnant collective farms **(kolkhoz)**, nominally operated by the peasants, to state farms *(sovkhoz)*, which functioned like other enterprises, employing a workforce paid by weekly wages plus bonuses rather than a share of the profit. He also put more investment into agriculture, increased inputs of fertilizers, and raised the prices received by the collective farms as an incentive to increase output.

■ **TABLE 15.1**

PERCENTAGE ACHIEVEMENT OF PLAN IN THE SOVIET UNION

	Plan V, 1951–1955	Plan VI, 1956–1960	Plan VII, 1959–1965
National income	107	97	97
Investment	103	101	106
Private consumption	104	95	98
Industrial production	109	99	102
Agricultural production	na	89	68
Steel	91	96	103
Coal	105	86	95
Oil	101	110	104
Electricity	104	91	99
Gas	94	118	86
Machine tools	66	78	95
Motor vehicles	99	80	80
Textiles	94	88	91
Meat	70	67	63
Milk	83	74	71

SOURCE: Vera Lutz, *Central Planning for the Market Economy: An Analysis of the French Theory and Experience* (Harlow, England: Longmans, Green and Co., 1969).

As Table 15.1 shows, while the planners managed to achieve targets in basic industries (steel, electricity, coal), both sophisticated manufacturing (motor vehicles and machine tools) and especially agriculture were serious problems. The inability of the Soviet Union to feed itself began to manifest during this time, and in the Seventh Plan, Khrushchev's ambitious plans for agriculture were under-fulfilled by 32 percent, and meat output was 37 percent off target.

Table 15.2 shows some relevant growth rates. Growth of gross national product (GNP) and agricultural output accelerated during the Fifth Plan (1955–1960), but progress was not sustained. The service sector expanded quite rapidly, while the falling rate of industrial growth mirrored slippage in the growth of investment.

BREZHNEV AND THE "PERIOD OF STAGNATION"

Much of the communist leadership found Khrushchev's policies too liberal, and in 1964 he was ousted by other members of the Central Committee, power passing to the more conservative Leonid Brezhnev. Nevertheless, at the start of Brezhnev's regime some parts of the reform initiated under Khrushchev continued and even yielded results. In 1965 Alexei Kosygin, the chief economic official, announced reforms to the system of targets given to enterprises by which managers were no longer to be held to physical targets established by the planners but were to be free to focus on maximizing what was called "realized output" (in western terms

■ TABLE 15.2

AGGREGATE ECONOMIC PERFORMANCE, 1951–1970: ANNUAL PERCENTAGE CHANGE

	Plan V, 1951–1955	Plan VI, 1955–1960	Plan VII, 1961–1965	Plan VIII, 1966–1970
GNP	5.4	5.9	5.0	5.2
Industry	10.2	8.3	6.6	6.3
Agriculture	3.5	4.2	2.8	3.5
Services	1.9	3.5	4.4	4.2
Consumption	4.9	5.7	3.7	5.3
Investment	12.4	10.5	7.6	6

SOURCE: Gregory and Stuart, 128–130

equivalent to the value of sales). Management was allowed to retain a large slice of the difference between the value of sales and the cost of materials (profit) to use to provide material incentives for themselves and their workers.

Greater freedom of initiative produced promising results, productivity in many enterprises and sharply rising profits, but unfortunately the very success of the measures alarmed the leadership. By allowing a substantial part of the profit to accrue to the enterprises, and to workers in the form of bonuses, reform led to increased disparity in inter-enterprise wage differentials, a potentially disruptive development. Moreover, rising labor productivity would be followed by reductions in employment at the firm level and might lead to widespread unemployment. These fears led the leadership to be more tentative about reform, and the size of incentive funds and bonuses was limited. Although the initial intent of reform had been to reduce the scope of planning and give initiative to managers, the tide soon ran in the opposite direction. Despite reformist rhetoric, the bureaucracy was expanded and its powers strengthened. Khrushchev's reforms to devolve power to regional councils were reversed, and the Moscow ministries assumed the management of the enterprise on a union-wide scale. Despite a clear reluctance to enact serious reform, every year of the 1970s saw some new strategy to alter the performance of the system, always amounting to nothing. The fundamental problems lay in the structure of incentives embodied in the system of central planning, and this remained unaddressed.

Hesitancy over reform led to the lackluster economic performance shown in Table 15.3. The growth rate of GNP, already down from more than 5 percent per year in the Khrushchev years, fell from 3.7 percent to 2.3 percent by the first half of the 1980s. During the 1970s the true state of the Soviet economy was disguised by the dramatic rise of oil prices, which benefited the Soviet Union as the world's largest energy producer, financing the import of needed technology and capital equipment, as well as consumption goods as basic as grain. However, bountiful energy, and the failure of the Soviet price system to value it appropriately, made Soviet industry wasteful in its use and ultimately uncompetitive in global terms. Labor productivity, which might have risen had proposed reforms in incentives

▪ TABLE 15.3

AGGREGATE ECONOMIC PERFORMANCE, 1971–1987: ANNUAL PERCENTAGE CHANGE

	1971–1975	1976–1980	1981–1983	1984–1987
GNP	3.7	2.7	2.3	1.6
Industry	5.9	3.4	1.5	2.1
Agriculture	−2.3	0.3	4.2	0.8
Services	3.4	2.8	2.1	—
Consumption	3.6	2.6	1.7	2.4
Investment	5.4	4.3	4.2	3

SOURCE: Gregory and Stuart, 133

▪ TABLE 15.4

PLAN FULFILLMENT: PLANNED VERSUS ACTUAL GROWTH

	Average Annual Growth			
	1966–1970	1971–1975	1976–1980	1981–1985
GNP				
Plan	6.5–7	5.8	5	4
Actual	5	3.1	2.2	1.8
Industry				
Plan	8.2	8	6.5	4.9
Actual	6.3	5.4	2.6	1.8
Agriculture				
Plan	5.5	3.7	5	5
Actual	3.7	−0.6	0.8	2.1

SOURCE: Gregory and Stuart, 135

been followed up, remained very low. After the collapse of the Soviet Union, studies estimated that output per labor hour in the 1980s was only about 25 percent of the average in Western Europe, although Soviet planners were convinced that they were experiencing labor shortage and guest workers were brought in from North Korea and Vietnam.

Although the poor performance of the economy clearly indicated serious structural problems, the planners initially remained optimistic that growth could be maintained and even accelerated. Table 15.4 gives a comparison of the planned targets and the actual outcomes for the four five-year plans between 1965 and 1985. What is interesting is that as the planners reluctantly factored in the underperformance of the early plans and lowered their sights, plan fulfillment slipped further. Agricultural performance was especially dismal and, compounded by severe shortcomings in distribution, led to serious food shortages in many areas. Famine was avoided only by substantial grain imports from the United States and Canada, financed by energy exports. Considering that Russia led the world in grain exports in 1913, 50 years of socialism had yielded poor results.

GORBACHEV

After Leonid Brezhnev died in 1982, he was briefly succeeded by two long-serving senior members of the party. However, neither Yuri Andropov nor Constantine Chernenko had either enough time in office or the resolve to take on the entrenched system of the Soviet privileged elite *(nomenklatura)* or to articulate a cohesive reform package. Andropov, a former head of the KGB, was convinced that the failures of the Soviet system were attributable to a lack of order and discipline. During his 16-month reign (from November 1982 to February 1984), he initiated campaigns against absenteeism, corruption, and excessive alcohol consumption, all with little effect. He also attempted to correct the deficiency of the Soviet quality control and product improvement by allowing enterprises to apply for price increases of up to 30 percent for "product improvement." Chernenko, an aging *apparatchik*, led the Soviet Union for only 13 months (February 1984 to March 1985) and followed the cautious Andropov line of exhorting greater efficiency and attempting to fine-tune the system of managerial incentives. By March of 1985 both men were dead and power was assumed by the relatively young and active Mikhail S. Gorbachev, an Andropov protégé.

Gorbachev, aware of the shortcomings of the Soviet economy, was resolved to change its direction. He will always be remembered for his introduction of twin reform tracks: *glasnost,* usually translated as openness and signifying democratization and the tolerance of dissent, and *perestroika,* or restructuring in the economic sphere. Although at the time Gorbachev's reforms were thought far-reaching, in reality they were timid, faltering, and based on inaccurate premises. Despite being highly critical of the reform efforts of the Brezhnev era (which he dismissed as an attempt "to improve things without changing anything"), his own reforms were similarly tentative, believing that substantial economic gains, in terms of increased output and efficiency, could be grasped by relatively modest changes in the economic system.

Gorbachev was, until his downfall, a member of the Communist Party. He sought reform of the system of central planning, selectively using prices and market incentives to iron out "bottlenecks," rather than trying to overthrow it. He was especially sanguine about the potential of imported technology to raise productivity and restore competitiveness. Although his program has been compared to the NEP of the 1920s, it was really the intellectual child of the piecemeal Kosygin reforms of the 1960s. His first steps moved to cut the power of the economic bureaucracy and give enterprise managers freedom and incentive to pursue their own initiatives; this resulted in the demolition of the old command system of allocating resources, but it did not allow enough freedom to permit a genuine market system to replace it, leading to a dislocation of the economy and a sharp fall in output, which made subsequent progress toward reform more difficult.

THE LAW ON ENTERPRISE REFORM.   A second-phase of reform was initiated in 1987 with the **law on state enterprises,** which tried to put firms on a corporatized and accountable basis. The key concepts were **self-management** and **self-finance.** Under self-management, workers would take a more active role in the direction of the enterprise and would have a role in the selection of management. Under self-finance, capital was no longer allocated by the planners at subsidized interest rates, but rather each firm would have to finance investment either from retained profits or credit from banks by loans with "hard" interest payments. Investment funds from the government were to be used only for infrastructural improvements or the startup of new business sectors.

Gorbachev was also bent on the reform of the inflexible system of wage payments, which allowed little variation for worker productivity and, therefore, tended to reward indolence as much as effort. The reforms gave enterprises control over a **wages fund,** enabling them to reduce their workforces (though they could avoid unemployment only by attrition) and to use any money saved to increase the wages of remaining workers in line with productivity growth. By 1990, 75 percent of all industrial personnel were working under these new wage arrangements.

Although much was commendable in Gorbachev's reform plan, it was a gradualist agenda that attempted to increase enterprise freedom within the planned system of output quotas. This tinkering, short of radical reform, produced dislocation. While conditions improved for some, the Gorbachev era saw the start of a 10-year contraction of Soviet industrial output. Although modest growth in output was achieved during 1986–1988, in 1989 and 1990 the economy entered a phase of sharp contraction that continued until 1997. Even more dispiriting, despite the enterprise reforms, both labor and capital productivity fell throughout the period. During 1989 and 1990, the economic crisis became more intense. There were acute shortages of basic consumer goods and growing popular discontent with the reform effort.

FOREIGN TRADE REFORM.   Under central planning, foreign trade, as well as the domestic resource allocation, was controlled by planners. Within the area known in the West as the Soviet bloc, the procedures for international trade were broadly similar to those that governed the planning of domestic production. Trade within the bloc was conducted under the auspices of the **Council on Mutual Economic Assistance (CMEA)** (often referred to as COMECON, an acronym for Communist Common Market). Trade planning was made on the basis of physical units and prices were adjusted so that trade flows were roughly equalized in currency terms. No member of the CMEA, therefore, experienced a balance of payments problem because prices were soft and manipulated to equilibrate payments. Just as in domestic planning, the idea of economies of scale was very important in structuring COMECON trade. Each nation within the CMEA was required to specialize in the production of certain goods, and the other members were expected to import all of their needs from them. Because trade was planned, comparative advantage, the basic underlying principle assumed to govern the direction and volume of trade between market economies, played a negligible role. Because the Soviet Union was rich in natural resources, especially energy, and the satellites were not, it supplied them with primary commodities at prices highly subsidized in terms of world levels and received manufactured goods in return. While world energy prices shot up during the 1970s, the prices charged within the CMEA system of trade adjusted only a little, and the terms of trade shifted sharply in favor of the satellite nations.

Trade outside the CMEA bloc was based on different principles, though they were no more rational in terms of basic economics. A decision was made at the central level about the amount of foreign exchange that was required to be generated. This was generally a function of the amount of imports that had to come from the non-CMEA world. Special **foreign trade organizations (FTOs)** would purchase the export goods from domestic suppliers and would sell them at agreed upon, usually world, prices. The existence of FTOs insulated domestic producers from world markets. Because of the intercession of the FTO, the domestic producers had no opportunity to profit from foreign trade, nor were they exposed to the competition in foreign markets.

This highly indirect system contributed to the inability of Soviet bloc enterprises to pursue international competitiveness through innovation and efficiency. Unlike the trading companies of Japan, which sought out foreign markets, educated domestic producers, and facilitated the import of ideas and technology, the FTOs were passive and formed a barrier between Soviet management and the world. Because no individual firm in the Soviet Union could benefit to any great degree from foreign trade, enterprise management had little interest. There was no global market research or attempt to conform to international norms and standards.

In January of 1987, the FTO monopoly of foreign trade was broken when 20 ministries and 76 large enterprises were allowed to initiate direct trade and to retain a substantial proportion of any hard currency earnings. The scheme was rapidly expanded and by the middle of 1990 more than 14,000 enterprises had the right to trade abroad on their own behalf. This liberalization was well intentioned and should have borne economic fruit, but it led instead to considerable corruption and personal enrichment. Soviet manufactured goods were of uncertain quality, poor design, and were much less likely to find markets than primary commodities like petroleum and forest products. These tended to be diverted from their planned use and sold abroad with the receipts frequently accruing to individual accounts offshore. The result was a lack of resources at home and problems for plan fulfillment.

THE FAILURE OF PERESTROIKA. Gorbachev's *perestroika* program fell between two stools. The reforms were too creeping for a rapid transformation to a market economy based on prices that reflected shortage and opportunity cost. However, they were enough to disrupt and create serious problems for the old system to which they were appended, leading to a fall in output. More fatally for Gorbachev, they alarmed the old guard of the Communist Party.

THE COUP OF AUGUST 1991. Throughout 1990 and early 1991, the economic and political system of the Soviet Union teetered on the brink of reform. In August of 1991 a coup by the old guard of the Communist Party pushed out Gorbachev, but the so-called *putsch* rapidly unraveled largely because it failed to neutralize Boris Yeltsin, the elected (and therefore legitimate) president of the Russian Federation. Yeltsin remained within the "White House," the Russian Parliament building, defying the authority of the Communist Party of the Soviet Union and communicating freely with other leaders, both in other republics of the Soviet Union and the West. The failure of the *putsch* led to the death of the Soviet Union as the constituent republics refused to recognize the Soviet Union authority. Within Russia, Yeltsin inherited power.

KEY TERMS AND CONCEPTS

Bolsheviks

Bukharin

commanding heights of the economy

control figures

Council on Mutual Economic Assistance (CMEA)

economies in transition

five-year plan

foreign trade organizations (FTOs)

glasnost

Gosplan

gulag

kolkhoz

kulaks

Law on state enterprises

market Leninism

Menshevik

New Economic Policy (NEP)

nomenklatura

perestroika

Preobrazhensky

promfinplans

regional economic councils

scissors crisis

self-finance

self-management

Stalin

Stolypin reforms

wages fund

war communism

QUESTIONS FOR DISCUSSION

1. Why did the economic situation of serfs liberated in 1861 lead to the rise of Russia as an agriculture exporter?

2. Why is Lenin's New Economic Policy often referred to as a kind of market socialism?

3. What was the importance of the scissors crisis? Why are the terms of trade between the rural and urban sectors so important in industrialization? Can you think of a similar set of problems in China? How was the situation resolved in each case?

4. How did World War II affect the planning system and structure of the Soviet economy?

5. What was the thrust of Khrushchev's reforms? Were they successful?

6. How did the Soviet Union remain in the arms race and the space race despite faltering technology and slow growth?

7. How was trade conducted under the Soviet system?

8. Why did Gorbachev's policy of perestroika fail?

RESOURCES

BOOKS AND ARTICLES

Bergson, Abram. *Welfare, Planning and Employment.* Cambridge, Mass.: MIT Press, 1982.

Carr. E. H. *The Russian Revolution: From Lenin to Stalin.* New York: Free Press, 1979.

Dunmore, Timothy. *The Stalinist Command Economy: The Soviet State Apparatus and Economic Policy, 1945–53.* New York: St. Martin's Press, 1980.

Goldman, Marshall I. *Gorbachev's Challenge: Economic Reform in the Age of High Technology.* New York: W. W. Norton, 1987.

Goldman, Marshall I. *U.S.S.R. in Crisis: The Failure of an Economic System.* New York: W. W. Norton, 1983.

Gregory, Paul R. *Before Command: An Economic History of Russia from Emancipation to the First Five-Year Plan.* Princeton, N.J.: Princeton University Press, 1994.

Gregory, Paul R., and Robert C. Stuart. *Russian and Soviet Economic Performance and Structure (Addison-Wesley Series in Economics).* Reading, Mass.: Addison-Wesley, 1997.

Guroff, Gregory, and Fred Castensen, eds. *Entrepreneurship in Imperial Russia and the Soviet Union.* Princeton, N.J.: Princeton University Press, 1983.

Hewett, Ed A. *Reforming the Soviet Economy: Equality versus Efficiency.* Washington, D.C.: Brookings Institute, 1990.

Hewett, Ed A., and Victor H. Winston, eds. *Milestones in Glasnost and Perestroyka: The Economy.* Washington, D.C.: Brookings Institute, 1991.

Hochschild, Adam. *The Unquiet Ghost: Russians Remember Stalin.* New York: Penguin, 1995.

International Monetary Fund. *A Study of the Soviet Economy.* Washington, D.C.: International Monetary Fund, 1991.

Jones, Anthony, and William Moskoff, eds. *Perestroika and the Economy: New Thinking in Soviet Economics.* Armonk, N.Y.: M.E. Sharpe, 1989.

Lavigne, Marie. *Financing the Transition: The Shatalin Plan and the Soviet Economy.* New York: Institute for East-West Security Studies, 1990.

Nove, Alec. *The Soviet Economy, an Introduction.* 2d ed. New York: Praeger, 1968.

Remnick, David. *Lenin's Tomb: The Last Days of the Soviet Empire.* New York: Random House, 1993.

Stuart, Robert C., ed. *The Soviet Rural Economy.* Totowa, N.J.: Rowman and Allanheld, 1984.

Ulam, Adam Bruno. *The Bolsheviks: The Intellectual and Political History of the Triumph of Communism in Russia.* Cambridge, Mass.: Harvard University Press, 1998.

16

THE OPERATION OF THE SOVIET PLANNED ECONOMY

THE INSTITUTIONS OF THE SOVIET STATE

Because the economic and political systems of the Soviet Union were so closely interwoven, understanding the operation of the economy and the planning system requires some knowledge of the institutional makeup of the Soviet state.

THE COMMUNIST PARTY OF THE SOVIET UNION

The dominant force in Soviet society was the Communist Party of the Soviet Union (CPSU). All important strategic decisions relevant to the operation of the economy were ultimately made by the party. The most powerful figure in the country was therefore the general secretary of the Communist Party, the post occupied by Stalin, Khrushchev, Brezhnev, and Gorbachev. The general secretary of the CPSU was *ex officio* leader of the **politburo,** the governing body of the party, whose other members represented the major regional party organizations, the officials responsible for foreign affairs, the organs of state security, and the major ministries. Although to the outside world the Soviet Union seemed to be a one-man dictatorship, in reality, at least for most of the post-Stalin period, a great deal of power resided with the other members of the politburo. They had the power to remove the general secretary from his post when his personal policy preferences deviated from those of the party; in the case of Khrushchev that was exactly what they did.

THE LEGISLATURE

Viewed through Western eyes, the legislature of the Soviet Union seemed very weak. It was composed of two chambers: the Supreme Soviet and the Praesidium. The 370 members of the Supreme Soviet were nominally elected by popular vote, but in effect they were appointed by the party, which retained tight control over the slate of candidates. The Supreme Soviet met twice a year, when its members, who served part-time and had other jobs, would assemble in Moscow essentially to rubber-stamp the legislative changes and the appointment of officials determined by the party bureaucracy. The Praesidium, which might be regarded as the upper house, was more compact and enjoyed more responsibility. Its members were mainly government officials, and it met twice monthly under the leadership of a chairman, who performed the function of head of state.

THE JUDICIARY

The judicial branch in the Soviet state was even weaker than the legislature. It had little independence from the political process, a fact reflected by Nikita Khrushchev's now infamous remark "who is the Boss, us or the Law: we are the masters over the Law, not the Law over us."[1] This was true at two levels. In most developed market economies, particularly in the United States, a constitution, guarded by an independent judiciary, has ultimate authority over the political system and constrains the type of laws that the legislature might pass. This was not the practice in the Soviet Union. Although a written constitution existed in the Soviet Union (in fact, it closely resembled that of the United States), in effect it was inoperative, because there was no independent judiciary to enforce it. Moreover, the structure of power led to capricious and politically determined implementation of whatever laws were on the books. Thus the Soviet Union was characterized by what John Litwack has called an absence of **legality,** in which "*Legality* is associated with *rule by law* as opposed to the discretion of leaders."[2]

This absence of legality was especially important in economic matters, as Litwack points out:

> Recent research in economic history has emphasized the importance of the replacement of legal for discretionary rule in explaining the rapid economic development of the western world, as well as the disparities in wealth between the advanced capitalist and underdeveloped countries. . . . [The Soviet system] contains particular mechanisms of coordination, incentives, and distribution that function in the virtual absence of economic legality. The fundamental features that explain how the system actually works are the discretionary power of bureaucrats over subordinates, enforced by the political dictatorship of the Communist Party, and the reputation effects from personal, often informal, long-run ties.

THE MECHANISM OF PLANNING

The politburo and the party determined the basic direction in which the economy was to move and the policies to be followed. Thus the fundamental economic questions of what, how, and for whom were all answered by the political leadership. The broad directives of the party were embodied in the plan by the bureaucrats of the State Planning Commission, **Gosplan,** which although only one of more than 20 state committees, had the preeminent role in economic planning. Other committees with an economic function were **Gosbank** (the state bank), Gosstroi (the state committee for construction), Gosten (the state committee on prices), Gossnab (the state committee for material and technical supply), Goskomstat (the statistical service), and MinFin (the Ministry of Finance).

---

[1] Quoted in K. Simis, *The USSR: The Corrupt Society* (New York: Simon and Schuster, 1982).

[2] J. Litwack, "Legality and Market Reform in Soviet Type Economies," *Journal of Economic Perspectives* 5, no. 4 (fall 1991).

THE TIME FRAME OF THE PLANNING PROCESS

Early in the planning year, Gosplan collected information on the performance in the previous year from the various actors in the economic system, with most information coming from the production side of the economy since Soviet planners gave little weight to the opinions of consumers.[3] Even if there were a desire to cater to consumers' demands to a greater degree, there was very little that could be done about quantifying consumers' concerns. In a supply-deficit economy with fixed prices like that of the Soviet Union, most goods found some buyer, even if it were an unhappy one. Goods in high demand were actively sought through bribery or queuing, symptoms that could not be expressed quantitatively to Gosplan. Thus at best any estimation of demand from consumers was likely to be highly anecdotal.

After analyzing this information, Gosplan reported to its political masters in the Praesidium of the party's central committee, which studied both the achievements and the problems experienced in the previous year and then set down broad directives for the following year. These were general statements like "raise housing construction" or "increase the quantity of clothing available." For example, in April 1985 the plenary meeting of the CPSU central committee determined that

> it is planned to increase the national income used for consumption and accumulation by 19–22 percent. Ensure that the entire increase in the national income is reached by enhancing social labor productivity. Reduce its inputs of materials by 4–5 percent, power by 7–9 percent and metals by 13–15 percent.[4]

Gosplan took note of such party directives and during the summer drafted a preliminary planning balance for the economy, a first attempt at accounting for all sources and uses of the principal products produced or required in the economy. This was an exhaustive and time-consuming operation covering at the height of central planning some 30,000 different commodities; for each one, production sources and users were identified and quantified. This tabulation constituted the material balances for the economy. As an illustrative tool, Table 16.1 shows this kind of initial tabulation giving a hypothetical listing of the sources and uses of steel. It is highly simplified; in reality many different types of steel (construction, sheet, pipe, etc.) had to be planned for. Such a table had to be prepared for each major commodity, and it was vital that the supply and use must balance. The need of all the other industrial sectors for any commodity had to match its production, net import, and inventory change.

Demands and uses of commodities are interdependent, and the next task for the planners was reconciliation of the tables. If it was found that the projected needs for steel were greater than planned supply, the output of the steel had to be raised

---

[3] This policy goes back to the triumph of the "teleologists" over the "geneticists" in the late 1920s, which was discussed in chapter 15.

[4] *Guidelines for the Economic and Social Development of the USSR for the period 1986–1990, and for the Period Ending in 2000* (Moscow: Novosti Press, 1985), 21–22.

■ TABLE 16.1

**SCHEMATIC REPRESENTATION OF MATERIALS BALANCE FOR STEEL
(MILLIONS OF METRIC TONS)**

Sources		Uses		
Production	150	Industry		165
Imports	20	(a) Mining	20	
Starting inventory	20	(b) Machinery	80	
		(c) Railways	10	
		(d) Steel	10	
		(e) Agriculture	5	
		(f) Construction	20	
		(g) Shipbuilding	20	
		Households		0
		Government		5
		Export		10
		Year-end inventory		10
Total sources	190	Total uses		190

■ TABLE 16.2

REPRESENTATION OF INPUT-OUTPUT ANALYSIS

Sources	Intermediate Uses	Final Uses
1. $X_1 - S_1 + M_1$ =	$a_{11}X_1 + a_{21}X_2 + a_{31}X_3 + a_{41}X_4 + \ldots\ldots a_{1n}X_n$	$+ C_1 + I_1 + Ex_1$
2. $X_2 - S_2 + M_2$ =	$a_{21}X_1 + a_{22}X_2 + a_{32}X_3 + a_{42}X_4 + \ldots\ldots a_{2n}X_n$	$+ C_2 + I_2 + Ex_2$
3. $X_3 - S_3 + M_3$ =	$a_{31}X_1 + a_{23}X_2 + a_{33}X_3 + a_{43}X_4 + \ldots\ldots a_{3n}X_n$	$+ C_3 + I_3 + Ex_3$
4. $X_4 - S_4 + M_4$ =	$a_{34}X_1 + a_{24}X_2 + a_{34}X_3 + a_{44}X_4 + \ldots\ldots a_{4n}X_n$	$+ C_4 + I_4 + Ex_4$
n. $X_n - S_n + M_n$ =	$a_{n1}X_1 + a_{2n}X_2 + a_{3n}X_3 + a_{4n}X_4 + \ldots\ldots a_{nn}X_n$	$+ C_n + I_n + Ex_n$

Where X_i is the output of the ith industry, a_{ij} is the requirement for input X_i per unit of output in the jth industry, S is the change in the stocks, M represents planned imports, C is consumers' use, I is investment use, and Ex is planned exports.

accordingly. This required the increased use of other inputs—steel itself, iron ore, coal, limestone, and so forth—so the output in all these other industries had to be raised, requiring yet a further adjustment in steel output.

Soviet planners were helped in this iterative reconciliation by input/output tables, which required the preparation of a matrix of the general form illustrated by Table 16.2. Resolving this system requires the solution of a system of simultaneous equations. Each product group is represented by a row, with the possible sources represented on the left-hand side and the uses on the right. The right-hand side can be separated into intermediate uses (where the product is an input for the production of some other good) and final uses (where it is destined for consumption, use in investment, or for export). The columns represent the demands for intermediate goods that must be supplied by other industries to achieve the indicated level of production, according to the norms of the planners. For example, if product 1 is steel and products 2 and 3 are coal and electricity, then the attainment of an output level of X_1 of steel requires $a_{11}X_1$ of steel, $a_{21}X_2$ of coal, $a_{31}X_3$ of electricity, and so forth.

The coefficients used to estimate the amount of input required are calculated by the planners using fixed-proportion production functions, based on the average "good practice" needs of industry. A matrix of this kind was maintained by the Soviet planners for about 250 of the most important product groups, which potentially required establishing 6,250 coefficients. In actuality, a substantial proportion of the coefficients would be zero, since many goods are not demanded as inputs by other industries. For example, fertilizers are not directly required by the mining industry, nor cereals by aluminum smelters. Thus the matrices can be solved in many cases by separating them into subsystems. Nevertheless, the task of compilation was huge, and many of the problems of the planners were technical. Data management and computer systems in the Soviet Union during this period were not highly advanced, and this handicapped the operation of the planning system. However, the bigger problem was getting reliable information to the center, a topic to which we will return.

At the height of its coverage and complexity, Soviet planning embraced some 30,000 commodities and thus a complete **input-output matrix** would have some 900 *million* cells, clearly an impossible task. Industrial groups were planned using the materials balance sheets like that in Table 16.1. These could be less aggregated than the I-O matrices and did not have to rely on assumptions of fixed input proportions and the absence of economies of scale.

THE DRAFT PLAN

These preliminary estimates of both target outputs and planned inputs were called **control figures,** and in the next step Gosplan disseminated them to the lower levels of the planning bureaucracies: the ministries and the regional planning centers. From there they were further disaggregated, and these tentative targets were passed down to the enterprise level—the units that were actually responsible for the work—in the form of a **draft plan.** The breakdown among enterprises was, by and large, based on past performance, the **level previously achieved.**

This introduces an important feature of central planning. Senior enterprise management in the Soviet system received a large part of their total remuneration in the form of bonuses paid to reward the achievement of plan targets. Senior management could receive bonuses of as much as 50 percent of their basic salary for meeting their plan target and up to 4 percent more for each percentage point by which the plan was overachieved. Thus any effort expended by managers in lobbying the planners to hold the output targets low, while receiving a high allocation of inputs, was probably well spent in terms of the likely outcome on managerial salaries. However, although the bonuses paid for overfulfillment of plan targets were substantial, management in many cases chose to be cautious in determining by just how much to exceed their targets. This is because if output is exceeded by a large margin in the current year, planners would likely raise output targets for successive years, because they based targets "from the level previously achieved." Overperformance with respect to one year's target might be praised at the time, and might lead to a big bonus in that year, but it is likely to lead to problems for the enterprise managers in the succeeding year because the output target will be ratcheted up. Thus the incentive to overachieve was limited. David Dyker, an authority on Soviet planning, called this the Micawber principle, after the Dickens character whose maxim was "Income one pound, expenses nineteen shillings and sixpence, result happiness. Income one pound, expenditure twenty shillings and sixpence, result misery." There is considerable evidence that a wise manager tried to meet the target and overachieve a little, but did not exert himself to achieve dramatic growth because of the consequences of having to achieve an elevated target the year after.

After the enterprises received their targets for the following year and their allotment of inputs, the direction of planning reversed. Enterprises turned to their immediate bureaucratic superiors and disputed their ability to meet the targets with the inputs that they had been allotted, arguing with all of the influence at their disposal for lower output targets and greater inputs. It is important to recognize that this part of the planning exercise was very personal and was really an intense bargaining exercise. One way of describing this is as "struggle," but it was generally a polite affair in which the participants sought to capitalize on their contacts, influence, and reserve of favors.

When some form of resolution was arrived at, the *draft plan* was then passed back up the hierarchy and was appropriately modified until it arrived at Gosplan again. At every point, the planners attempted to reach a reconciliation, or compromise, between the higher authorities (who tried to preserve compliance to the original draft plan, which represented conformity with Gosplan's control figures) and the lower authorities, who had the responsibility for meeting the targets. This process of reconciliation coincided with the "tightening" of the plan as production responsibilities became more and more precisely defined. On occasion, of course, all the loose ends could not be tied up and Gosplan had to resolve the basic structure of the plan in order to take account of the problems.

MAKING THE PLAN INTO LAW

Those at the lower levels of the planning process knew that during this period they had to make their own production targets as realistic (in fact, as minimal) as possible. Once the final balance was struck, the politburo approved the plan and the **Praesidium** turned it into law. It was a punishable offense to fail to meet the plan target, while substantial bonuses were paid to enterprise management for plan achievement and overachievement. After enactment into law, the plan was then passed down the hierarchy of ministries and regional councils with the degree of detail being increased at each level. Ultimately each enterprise entered into contractual arrangements with suppliers and major customers.

THE DETERMINATION OF PRICES

Up to this point the planning process was concerned exclusively with physical units of commodities, whether outputs or inputs. Prices were determined quite separately and fulfilled a different function from the role that they serve in a market economy. They were set primarily by the bureaucracy, were altered as infrequently as possible, and did not aspire to reflect either resource cost or demand. Price changes are a nuisance, incur "menu costs," and have little point if the base levels do not reflect scarcity to begin with. Moreover, it was a point of ideological pride that socialism was immune from capitalism's worst diseases, inflation and unemployment. Under Soviet central planning there were three main types of prices for goods: wholesale industrial prices, agricultural prices, and retail prices.[5]

WHOLESALE INDUSTRIAL PRICES

These were the prices at which firms sold goods to each other and were determined by a combination of pragmatism, opportunism, and ideology. The underlying principle was that prices should represent the average cost of production of a good across all the enterprises in the relevant industry group. Recall from chapter 3 that it is marginal cost, not average cost, that reflects scarcity, and therefore the role that prices played in the efficient rationing of scarce resources within the Soviet system was slight. Moreover, cost to the Soviet planners conformed to a Marxian conception and was defined as consisting of labor costs, raw material costs, and depreciation, with no allowance made for the opportunity cost of capital (interest) or land (rent). After arriving at an estimate of average cost for each firm, the planners would exclude obvious outliers in the calculation of the industry average; any enterprises with abnormally high costs were not considered, although they remained in production and therefore required subsidy.

Adjusted average costs of production were then modified to yield the prices for the plan year, a small amount being deducted to reflect lower costs due to technological change or productivity increase, and a small margin added for profit. Prices arrived at in such a way could never, except by the most unlikely coincidence, reflect relative scarcities and were not a crucial factor in determining enterprise behavior. In a market economy, a firm's revenue is determined by the product of volume and sales price, and that represents a **hard budget constraint** to the firm. In the long run the firm cannot spend more than its revenues. Under centrally planned socialism, if revenue is less than cost, some way would frequently be found to raise revenues through price changes or subsidies or to reduce costs by lowering administered input prices or taxes. These **soft budget constraints** had a profound effect on Soviet performance, an important fact that we will return to later.

---

[5] In addition, we will discuss the price of labor and the functioning of the labor market.

One of the more shocking consequences of this system of administered prices was discovered during liberalization in the 1990s. There were a substantial number of **negative value-added enterprises**—firms for whom the sum of the value of outputs evaluated at world prices were, in fact, less than the value of inputs assessed in the same way. This was the result of the subsidies implicit in low input costs (especially those related to energy where Soviet prices and world prices were in stark disagreement) and the low quality of output. In the supply-deficit Soviet economy, this output could generally find a buyer, but not in free world markets. How many true negative value-added enterprises there were is hard to know, but a larger class of industry operated at a profit under Soviet accounting and would have shown a loss when rent, capital cost, and concessionary tax policy was accounted for.

AGRICULTURAL PRICES

In chapter 15 we discussed the scissors crisis of the early 1920s and the young Bolshevik government's determination to control the terms of trade between the agricultural and industrial sectors. Until the final collapse of the Soviet planned economy, agricultural procurement prices were set to establish the terms of trade for the peasants on the **collective farms** *(kolkhozy)* and thus control their purchasing power over goods from the larger economy. Both the unit costs of the inputs of collective farming and the physical volumes of inputs required under the plan were determined by the planners. The planners also fixed the total cost (and hence the average cost) of the production dictated by the plan. If, as was generally the case in the supply-constrained Soviet economy, consumer goods were in short supply, one way to alleviate the shortage was by cutting the purchasing power of the peasants. The price of farm output could be set at the level that would just cover costs. Then each peasant's share of net farm income would be small, allowing for few purchases of consumer goods. In some cases an even greater squeeze was applied by making farm incomes less than necessary planned expenditures, forcing peasants to draw down "idle" monetary balances that had accumulated in the farm sector from prior years. The same set of agricultural prices applying to collective farms also applied to the state farms *(sovkhozy).* These were socially owned and operated in the same fashion as industrial firms, with managers appointed by the state and employing workers for money wages rather than as share of the surplus. Thus they could operate at a profit or were positioned to receive subsidies.

RETAIL PRICES

A third type of price were the *retail prices* charged in the socially owned state retail stores and consumer cooperatives (which, like the collective farms, were jointly owned by groups of individuals). These prices were dependent on the industrial wholesale and agricultural procurement prices, but they differed by the imposition of a differentiated turnover tax. This tax had two purposes. One was to attempt to bring supply and demand at the consumer level into line by taxing the goods in short supply at a heavier rate than those that were more plentiful. The tax also provided a substantial part of the state's revenue.

LABOR MARKETS

We have already discussed how the Soviet system determined disposable income and purchasing power for agricultural workers on the collective farms. In contrast, the income of industrial and service sector workers (as well as the wages of laborers on state farms) were contractual rather than residual. The labor markets in the Soviet Union were by and large much freer than was the popular conception in the West. Workers were not assigned occupations and workplaces by the state, except in the case of the first job of university graduates. However, locating in Moscow (the perpetually attractive "center") was subject to a residency permit, and a chronic shortage of housing put tight constraints on geographical mobility. The choice of occupation was largely up to the worker, though the educational system was highly manipulated and influential in replicating the skill mix of the population that the planners considered appropriate in the long run. In the short run, wages were set by the state to equilibrate the supply with the demand for labor in each use. A crude form of wage adjustment was used with percentage markups to a basic wage applied for such factors as location (the less attractive the higher the wage), unpleasant working conditions, the degree of physical effort, and so forth. In addition, many enterprises resorted to systems of piecework where workers received most of their income as a function of individual or group output.

MARKET CLEARING

The income received by workers, as well as by farmers, could be freely spent on whatever commodity (though not productive asset) that could be found. There were, therefore, elements of consumer *choice*. This should not be confused with the consumer *sovereignty* fostered by the operation of the free market. Consumer sovereignty implies that the consumers' demands are impartially met through the market via the incentives that it provides. In the centrally planned system the politicians and planners are sovereign; the plan determines what kinds and quantities of consumer goods are produced, and each consumer decides which of these he or she wants. If a surplus or shortage for any good should develop, production is *not* automatically shifted by the action of self-oriented economic agents but is changed only by the will of the political leadership.

The planners determined (1) the volume of production of the various goods, (2) the prices that were charged for them, (3) the money incomes of the workers, and (4) the real income of the collective farmers; it was therefore, in theory, possible that aggregate supply and demand might be balanced. Although there are an infinite number of sets of prices that would satisfy this aggregate condition, in general the prices failed to equilibrate supply and demand in the markets for individual goods. In a market economy such disequilibria are met first by a change in price and subsequently by a change in quantities, but in the centrally planned system neither response occurred. Output plans were seldom realized, especially for consumer goods, and therefore general shortages, as well as unsatisfied demand for particular products, resulted. One consequence was that centrally planned economies were often characterized by high levels of household savings, forced because goods were not available to spend money on. Because of a lack of goods, the end of the Soviet era saw substantial money balances in consumers' bank accounts, known as the **monetary overhang,** and this was one engine of inflation in the early months of liberalization. However, for our assessment of the planning system the most important point is that the prices set by planners neither reflected the relative scarcity of goods in the short term nor provided an accurate measure of the resource costs of production.

PRIVATE AGRICULTURE

One area of free market activity was provided by granting workers in collective farms, state farms, and other enterprises plots on which to raise their own crops, which could be sold at uncontrolled prices. These plots averaged about two-thirds of an acre and were slightly larger on the collective farms than on the state farms, and, as might be expected, the productivity per acre of these plots was well above that seen on either the state or collective farms themselves. Although private plots represented only 3 percent of total arable area in the Soviet Union, they accounted for about 25 percent of output and for some crops were a very significant source of supply. In 1984 they accounted for 58 percent of potato production; about 30 percent of the production of eggs, meat, vegetables, and milk; and 24 percent of wool production. Private plots fulfilled two important functions: ameliorating otherwise desperate conditions on collective farms and providing an outlet for the reluctant savings of industrial workers. However, the irrationality of the pricing structure in the planned sector and the profit incentives of the small-holder plots did make for some very distortionary outcomes. A small holder from the republic of Georgia, in the Transcaucasus, was able to fly on the highly subsidized state airline, Aeroflot, to Moscow with a couple of suitcases of tomatoes and make enough on the sidewalk market in the capital to pay for his flight, room, and board—not the most efficient way of getting the produce to market!

MONITORING PLAN FULFILLMENT

We now turn to the question of verifying the plan. How did the planners see to it that the physical performance specified in the plan was conformed to? It would be an onerous task to certify at each stage that the planned volume of goods had physically passed from one concern to another. In fact, the physical plan was monitored through financial flows that mirrored the movement of goods and commodities as recorded by the monopoly state bank, Gosbank. This was known as **control by the ruble.**

To illustrate, let us take a simple example of the movement of a commodity from its point of initial production to its final use. A state farm produced cotton, which was sent to a textile factory that processed it into cloth for a clothing factory, which in turn shipped its output to a retail store. When the farm delivered its cotton output to the factory, it would obtain a document, an acceptance, from the textile factory verifying that the latter had received its raw cotton. This document was then turned over to Gosbank, which credited the farm's account with the value of the cotton delivered, using the plan's industrial prices, and debited the textile factory's account by the same amount. Similarly, after the finished cloth was produced and shipped to the clothing factory, the textile factory obtained a document verifying its delivery of cloth. Again, the document was turned over to Gosbank, which this time credited the textile factory's account and debited the clothing factory's account. Likewise, the clothing factory made the garments and shipped them to the store, again receiving an acceptance. Gosbank credited its account and debited that of the store. Finally, when households purchased the clothing with cash, the state store deposited its cash receipts with Gosbank and was given a credit of equal value.

With this simple example, we can see how every transfer of *physical* output from one location to another, and every bit of value added in production, was mirrored by an associated *financial* transfer through Gosbank. Monitoring by Gosbank of these financial transfers would, in theory at least, show whether the physical movements of goods had been performed. If less than the planned amount was delivered in any specified time period, Gosbank would be alerted. If inputs or outputs were stolen and diverted to the black market, Gosbank would know, and the failure to perform could be investigated and rectified. To discipline the system, the state bank had at its disposal a range of sanctions, from the expropriation of a firm's deposits to a full-scale party investigation into enterprise affairs. However, the information needs of full oversight were enormous, and often the system would be perfunctory rather than exhaustive. Sanctions were used sparingly and oversight was ineffective. As a result, failure to perform was frequent and unpunished, and corruption was extensive.[6]

Control by the ruble required restrictions on the use of money and credit, which lowered the degree of initiative that managers could show. Enterprise accounts with Gosbank could only be used to pay for the type and quantities of inputs that

---

[6]One of the most famous abuses came to light in the late 1970s in the cotton industry. Large quantities of fictitious cotton were shipped from state farms in Central Asia. The appropriate acceptances were issued but concealed by a web of corruption that extended up to and included Yurii Churbanov, Brezhnev's son-in-law. It took years for the scheme to be uncovered, and billions of rubles were diverted. Ultimately several people were put to death for "economic crimes."

were specified in the plan. No enterprise could grant credit to another enterprise.[7] Enterprises were virtually forbidden to hold cash for any purpose other than payment of wages. Even the cash receipts of state stores had to be first deposited with Gosbank and subsequently withdrawn to meet the payroll.

While planning was performed in terms of physical units, the financial sector of the centrally planned economy allowed the state bank to monitor the execution of the plan.

INCENTIVES IN SOVIET-TYPE SYSTEMS

In chapter 1 we discussed in general terms the issues of incentives in economic systems, and the unraveling of the centrally planned economies is a case study in their importance. The successes and failures of Soviet planning can be largely attributed to the set of incentives provided, and it is worthwhile to discuss these incentives as they fell on each group.

COLLECTIVE FARMS

Agriculture is generally regarded as one of the greatest failures of Soviet economics, and the dismal performance of collective agriculture has to shoulder a great deal of the blame for the ultimate demise of the system. We saw that income on collective farms was the residual between the revenue received by the farms and their expenses on material factors of production. Revenue itself was a function of the volume of output and the prices determined by the planners, whose objective was frequently to limit the real income, and therefore the demand for consumers' goods by the peasants on the farms. Expenditure on material inputs was, as well, determined in Moscow. Thus the incentive to raise output on the farms was dulled by the knowledge that prices could be reduced as a response.

Moreover, there was little incentive to raise the effort and diligence of individual peasants on the farms. The income of the farm was divided among the workers on the basis of work points. In theory this might mean that harder work was rewarded with higher income, but in reality work points did little to reflect effort. A serious free rider problem resulted, because aggregate output of the farm changed little on the basis of one person's contribution as any gain in output was spread among the members of the collective or work brigade. To counter this, the authorities attempted to reduce the size of the work teams from their original conception of 100 plus down to much smaller groups, in some cases as small as the family. However, in terms of living standards it was better to spend time on one's own

---

[7]This is in sharp distinction with the post-liberalization system in Russia and other newly independent states in which an extensive net of inter-enterprise credit has grown up with the tacit support of the government. Many suppliers of raw materials, especially in the energy sector, are owed huge sums of money by their customers, who cannot pay often because they are owed by customers further down the production chain.

personal plot than to work hard for the collective enterprise; it is not surprising that productivity remained low and output stagnated for long periods of time. At the very end of the Soviet period, contract systems began to be favored; a group, or family, agreed to supply part of the collective farm's target at fixed prices with the knowledge that any excess could be sold to the farm at "market" prices or sold directly on the farmers' markets.[8]

WORKERS

Workers, whether on state farms or within manufacturing or extractive industry, had much the same set of incentives as workers in the capitalist West. Pay was largely by the hour and the incentives for high performance were in part coercive, enforced by management supervision, and part pecuniary, in that good job performance might lead to promotion and betterment. Alienation, which Marx identified as one of the key weaknesses of capitalism, was as prevalent as in the industrialized West.[9] Despite the urging of the state and management, working for the glory of the country became a less significant motivating factor, while advancement into the higher echelons of management had as much to do with political connection as with job performance. To link job performance more closely with pay, much of the socialist world turned to "piece working," where workers are paid as far as possible in proportion to individual output. There is an irony here since this is traditionally regarded by the left as being the most exploitative labor management practice and also one that stifles both individual initiative and group cooperation. In advanced capitalist systems it remains only in "sweat shop" situations.

Ultimately a worker toils for goods rather than for money. Because centrally planned economies were chronically inept in providing consumer goods, the incentive to work hard was correspondingly reduced. Goals that have proved powerful motivators to workers in capitalist countries—such as buying a house, acquiring financial assets, or traveling abroad—were simply not options. A select group of workers were chosen to travel to vacation spots within the socialist world, but again this was largely the result of political connections rather than work performance. The high rate of forced household savings and the monetary overhang were testaments to the failure of monetary incentives in a demand surplus economy.

MANAGERS

Enterprise managers in the Soviet system operated under a strong material incentive system with a substantial portion of income dependent on meeting the plan targets, and this could be further increased by overfulfillment. This was reinforced

---

[8] Such "household responsibility systems" were very successful in China because they provided a much higher degree of incentive than do collective farms.

[9] In fact, the stock remark about Soviet work was that "We pretend to work, and they pretend to pay us," or sometimes "They pretend to pay us, and we pretend to work."

by coercive negative incentives; failure to meet targets might lead to loss of job, disciplinary action, or, in the rare limit, prosecution and incarceration. The combination of incentives proved less than optimal in a variety of ways. First, the incentives did little to increase the efficiency of industry in terms of the optimal use of factors of production. Second, the system did little to encourage either product or process innovation. Third, quality control was a serious problem, and there was little motivation for the production of consumer goods whose design and quality might be most appreciated by the ultimate user. Finally, and perhaps most crucially, the incentives encouraged the relaying of misleading data from the enterprise units to the center.

EFFICIENCY. The system of incentives did very little to encourage optimum use of factors of production. Capital was largely allocated by the planners and generally came without cost, or with a high subsidy, to the enterprise. When capital charges were used, they did not reflect the opportunity cost of capital. Consequently, there was no systematic device to encourage optimal use of capital; each manager would attempt to lay his hands on as much equipment as possible and stockpile it against some future exigency.

A similar situation applied in the use of labor. Any gains resulting from a reduction in the workforce were not retained within the enterprise but were remitted to the center. Rather than promoting economy of labor, incentives encouraged managers to retain as much labor as possible. In a capitalist system, a profit maximizing entrepreneur will tend to hire workers up to the point where the wage is equal to the product of the marginal worker, but in the Soviet system it was worthwhile to have any worker around as long as the marginal product was positive.

Output targets were defined in annual terms, and it would have been optimal to produce smoothly throughout the year. However, in Soviet enterprise the same human factors applied as in, say, a student's work habits. Production proved to be slow early in the year, far from the deadline, but as the end of the planning period approached, meeting the target became a matter of greater urgency. The last few months were characterized by what became known as **storming,** a fevered attempt to raise output to meet the target. At this point the excess labor and machinery became especially valuable, but hoarding spread beyond capital and labor. Intermediate goods and inputs required by other productive units in the system were frequently in short supply early in the year and became available only as the storming behavior in supplying enterprises kicked in, so keeping high inventories was quite rational.

INNOVATION. Innovation in any system is a relatively risky business, whether it entails the development of new products or the introduction of a new technique for production. However, in market systems successful innovation is often rewarded by greater efficiency and lower costs, or in tapping new sources of consumer demand and increased sales; each possibility yields higher profits. The Soviet system did little to encourage such innovation.

Consider first new techniques of production. These generally entail some teething period during which glitches are ironed out and output necessarily falls. If these problems are prolonged, then it might prove impossible to recover during the fixed horizon of the planning year. Output targets would then not be met and the enterprise manager's income would suffer, or some more dire consequence (loss of job or even criminal sanction) might result. Consequently, innovation was often not attractive. Managers generally found it easier and more comfortable to produce by tried and tested methods in which the outcome was predictable.

Similarly, there was not much incentive at the enterprise level to develop new products. The plan did not usually require them, since the planning process consisted largely of revamping the previous period's output figures. New products took management time and other resources away from current production and opened the possibility of falling short of targets, inviting the same loss of income or worse.

QUALITY CONTROL. Planning targets were usually laid out in terms of physical units. Although in theory all the output was meant to be of "acceptable" quality, and retail stores or users of intermediate goods could reject the products that were substandard, in reality quality control was poor. In market systems the real cost of poor quality is a loss of reputation and repeat business; in the planned system the customers had no choice. Their suppliers were defined by the plan, and those suppliers simply could not lose sales as a result.

INFORMATION. A planning system in which decisions are taken centrally can only function well if the data received at the center are accurate. However, in the Soviet system there were powerful incentives for enterprise managers to keep the planners in the dark. It was not good for them to reveal the real potential of their enterprises. That would result in an upward adjustment in output targets in the next planning round and make the job of reaching those targets more difficult. It was in the enterprise managers' interest to mislead the planners by overstating their real needs for labor, machinery, and material inputs. If successful, that produced a cushion that could be called on in times of emergency.

THE BUREAUCRATS

Finally, we turn to the incentives that operated on the planners themselves. Why should they work to produce a good plan and ensure compliance to it? As we have noted, the basic outline of the plan was determined by the political masters. It was the function of the bureaucrats to turn these ideas into a working document, and, like other members of the entire Soviet hierarchy, it was best to achieve this in as painless a way as possible.

The planners put a lot of energy into improving the techniques of planning, but when it came to actually coming up with ideas to reform the incentive structures there was little to motivate them. From time to time planners went out on a limb to proclaim the importance of, say, increasing the role of prices to reflect costs, but a wise planner would only do that with the clear approval of the political leadership. Furthermore, he or she might be aware that shifts in the preferences of the leaders are not permanent. Khrushchev encouraged unorthodox thinking to a degree that his predecessor Stalin had not, and those who displaced him were alarmed by this. The kind of ideas that were rewarded under one first secretary could lead to trouble under another. The safest behavior was to move slowly and conventionally.

CONCLUSION

There was little in the Soviet system to encourage either fresh thinking, high quality, new ideas, or new products. Overwhelmingly the incentives encouraged a repetition of the status quo, and consequently the economy ran out of sources of extensive growth—there was no new land, the participation rate of workers had been raised to the maximum, and the marginal productivity of capital was so low as to make new investment almost valueless—in all, there were no sources of total factor productivity growth. Relative decline was inevitable and reform of the economy vital. Whether this reform and transition will be successful is discussed more thoroughly in part 6 of this book.

KEY TERMS AND CONCEPTS

collective farms	legality
control by the ruble	level previously achieved
control figures	monetary overhang
draft plan	negative value-added enterprises
Gosplan	politburo
Gosbank	Praesidium
hard budget constraint	soft budget constraints
input-output matrices	*sovkhozy*
kolkhozy	storming

QUESTIONS FOR DISCUSSION

1. In what ways did the planning in the Soviet Union hinge on interpersonal relations and influence?
2. What is the significance of the plan "from the level previously achieved" for the functioning of the planning process?
3. Discuss the function and the role of prices in the Soviet Union under planning.
4. How was plan fulfillment monitored in the Soviet system?
5. Why was the yield on private agriculture plots so much greater than on state and collective farms?
6. What incentives did management have to give misleading information to planners?

7. Why did Soviet firms have a tendency toward high degrees of vertical integration?

8. Why was the Soviet system so deficient in producing goods for consumers?

9. Did Soviet management have a strong incentive to pay attention to quality control?

10. Which of capitalism and Soviet socialism had the strongest incentives for innovation? Why?

RESOURCES

BOOKS AND ARTICLES

Flakierski, Henryk. *Income Inequalities in the Former Soviet Union and Its Republics.* Armonk, N.Y.: M.E. Sharpe, 1993. Reviewed in the *Journal of Comparative Economics,* October 1994, 260–271.

Goldman, Marshall I. *What Went Wrong with Perestroika,* chapter 15. New York: W.W. Norton, 1991.

Gray, Kenneth R., ed. *Soviet Agriculture: Comparative Perspectives.* Ames, Iowa: Iowa University Press, 1990.

Gregory, Paul R., and Robert C. Stuart. *Soviet and Post-Soviet Economic Structure and Performance,* 5th ed. New York: HarperCollins, 1994.

Hare, Paul G. *Central Planning.* Chur, Switzerland: Harwood, 1991.

Huang, Yasheng. "Information, Bureaucracy, and Economic Reforms in China and the Soviet Union." *World Politics,* October 1994, 102–134.

International Monetary Fund, The World Bank, Organization for Economic Co-operation and Development, and European Bank for Reconstruction and Development. *A Study of the Soviet Economy.* 3 vols. Paris: Organization for Economic Cooperation and Development, 1991.

Kornai, János. *The Socialist System: The Political Economy of Communism.* Princeton, N.J.: Princeton University Press, 1991.

Litwack, John. "Legality and Market Reform in Soviet Type Economies," *Journal of Economic Perspectives* 5, no. 4 (fall 1991).

Malle, Silvana. *Employment Planning in the Soviet Union.* New York: St. Martin's Press, 1990.

Pryor, Frederic L. *The Rise and Fall of Collectivized Agriculture in Marxist Regimes.* Princeton, N.J.: Princeton University Press, 1992.

Simis, Kostantin M. *The USSR—The Corrupt Society: The Secret World of Soviet Capitalism.* New York: Simon and Schuster, 1982.

Standing, Guy, ed. *In Search of Flexibility: The New Soviet Labor Market.* Geneva: International Labor Office, 1991.

Wolf, Thomas. *A Foreign Trade in the Centrally Planned Economy.* Chur, Switzerland: Harwood, 1988.

17

THE PARTICIPATORY ECONOMY: THE CASE OF YUGOSLAVIA

We turn now to consider a type of market socialism that prevailed in the Republic of Yugoslavia between the 1960s and the break up of the Yugoslav state in the 1990s and still exists today within Serbia. The term **market socialism** is revealing and appropriate because the Yugoslavian system involved elements of both these polar extremes. The socialist aspect is ownership of the means of production by the state rather than by individuals. However, while in the other socialist states of Eastern Europe and the former Soviet Union coordination of the economy was brought about by a plan, in Yugoslavia coordination was left largely to market forces.

Another common term to describe the Yugoslav system was **labor management,** reflecting that enterprises, while using capital owned by society as a whole, were managed by the workers, or more precisely by management appointed or elected by the workers. The theory of labor-managed economies was largely developed by Jaroslav Vanek,[1] who used the term **participatory economies** because workers were involved in the decisions of the firms in which they were employed and workers' income was a function of profits.

THE PARTICIPATORY ECONOMY

VANEK'S PRINCIPLES

Although Yugoslavia was his model, Vanek's theory of the participatory economy was a normative ideal, rather than a positive description of a specific state, that conformed to five basic underlying principles:

1. *Participation in management.* Every worker should participate in the management of the enterprise in which he or she worked on an equal footing. In most cases this implies a representative democracy in which workers delegate their day-to-day responsibility to an elected chief executive, a board of directors, and a workers' council who make most decisions on behalf of the workers.

---

[1] See Jaroslav Vanek, *The Participatory Economy: An Evolutionary Hypothesis and a Strategy for Development* (Ithaca: Cornell University Press, 1971).

2. *Income sharing.* In a participatory economy, rather than being paid a fixed wage, the workers in each firm receive their income by dividing the profits among them in an equitable fashion, usually dictated by a formula democratically determined by the workers themselves. Differences in the size of workers' shares should reflect work of different intensity, skill level, or quality.

3. *Capital to be owned by society as a whole.* Socialism is defined by society, rather than individuals, owning the means of production, and Vanek's participatory economy is socialist in that sense. The capital employed by any enterprise is not owned by that enterprise or indeed by the workers of that enterprise, but rather by the state, which rents out the capital for a contractual fee. This fee should not be merely nominal but should reflect the scarcity, or opportunity cost.

4. *Coordination via the market not the plan.* In Vanek's conception, the participatory economy should be fully decentralized. All of the actors in the system—consumers, enterprises, associations, and the various levels of government—should be free to make decisions without interference from the government (or the party). While there should be no command planning, some form of indicative planning to allow better coordination is appropriate. Vanek does call for government intervention to resolve abuse of monopoly power and, by implication, other instances of market failure, but the important principle is the sovereignty of individuals operating through the market, rather than the preferences of planners or politicians.

5. *Freedom of employment.* The final characteristic of the ideal participatory state is that each individual is at total liberty to choose his occupation and his particular place of employment. A necessary counterpart to this is that each enterprise is at full liberty to hire, or not hire, any person. The problem of establishing appropriate grounds for dismissal is more difficult and enterprises should be free to create their own rules for limiting the ability to dismiss workers, even when strictly economic criteria might call for it.

THE OBJECTIVE OF THE ENTERPRISE

From this list of characteristics it is clear that the objective of the labor-managed firm in a participatory economy will be quite different from that of either the capitalist firm or a typical enterprise in a centrally planned economy. Under capitalism profit maximization is assumed to be the objective of the firm,[2] whereas under centralized planning the enterprise's goal is less clear, but it derives from the preferences of planners, politicians, and party members rather than the workers. In the labor-managed firm, the objective is to maximize the income (or perhaps a more

---

[2] The various behavioral theories of the firm deal with issues concerning the practicability of profit maximization and the "real world" constraints on this objective.

OPTIMUM EMPLOYMENT IN A LABOR-MANAGED FIRM

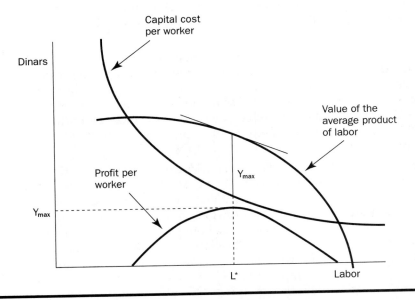

abstract notion of well-being) of the workers of the firm. Generally this is taken to be equivalent to maximizing the amount of profit per worker. The simple analytics are shown in Figure 17.1.

Because the firm rents its capital from the state, for any contract period the rental fee constitutes a fixed cost. Therefore the cost of capital per worker falls as the number of workers increases. (In fact, this curve will take the form of a rectangular hyperbola, asymptotic to both axes.) Let us assume that labor is the only variable input. The value of the product produced by the average worker is shown as the "value of the average product of labor" VAP_L schedule in Figure 17.1. It is constructed by multiplying the average physical product curve, which will be downward sloping,[3] by the price of the product, which will be a constant in competitive markets, because the firm faces a horizontal demand curve.

The point of greatest profit per worker **(income maximization)** occurs at the output where the capital cost per worker curve and the value of the average product

---

[3] There is no reason why the principle of diminishing marginal returns will not hold in such economies, since it is at base a technical consideration. The amount of capital is fixed and as the number of workers increases, beyond some point, the marginal product of labor will decline, ultimately bringing down the average product with it.

RESPONSE TO PRICE INCREASE IN A TWO-FACTOR LABOR-MANAGED FIRM

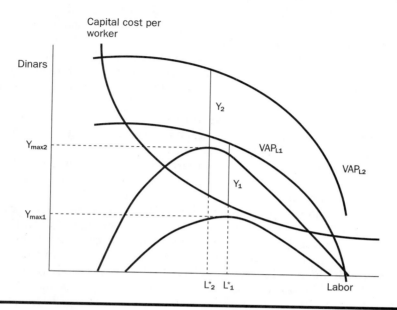

of labor curve are at the greatest distance from each other. This is when they have equal slopes, and therefore the optimal amount of labor is shown by L* in Figure 17.1. Note that this is not the same as the profit maximizing position, which would occur where the marginal revenue product curve intersects the wage schedule. Generally the income-maximizing level will occur at a level of employment (and output) less than the profit-maximizing level of employment.

Under these assumptions, a somewhat strange result occurs, one that brings attention to the potential differences between the performance of labor-managed and the profit-maximizing firms. Consider a change in the price of the product due, for example, to an exogenous increase in demand. Such a move would shift the VAP_L curve vertically upward and would increase its (negative) slope at all levels of labor input (Figure 17.2). If the capital cost remains the same, the point of greatest divergence between the two curves (where the slopes are the same) actually occurs at a lower level of labor input, and therefore a lower level of output— as product prices rise. Thus, under these assumptions, we obtain the rather strange result that an increase in product prices leads the labor-managed firm to operate at a lower level of output and employ fewer workers, $L*_2$ rather than $L*_1$. The reverse is true if product prices fall—output and employment are increased if income per worker is to be maximized. Thus an increase in price results in reduced supply, and a fall in price brings about increased supply. Under these assumptions the individual firm's supply curve is actually downward sloping, raising questions about market stability. An analogous result follows with respect to capital cost. If the state reduces the contract price of capital, the capital cost per worker curve shifts vertically downward, and the optimal amount of employment again shifts to the left and fewer workers are employed. An increase in the cost of capital leads to greater employment. These two results were pointed out in 1958 by Benjamin Ward[4] and, at the time, created something of a controversy. Although theoretically valid, these unexpected results are particularly sensitive to specific assumptions. If we generalize to consider more variable inputs than labor alone, the results can be shown to be different.

For example, if the numbers of workers employed is held constant, any action that increases profit raises average income. In such a case a labor-managed firm will follow the general rule that inputs are used up to the point where their marginal value product is equal to marginal factor cost, the same rule that elementary textbooks ascribe to capitalist firms. Moreover, if we assume that more than one output is produced by the firm, if the increase in the price of a good does result in a reduction of labor employed, the fall in output may be in a good other than the one whose price has risen. Thus, in a more complex "real world," the downward sloping supply curve is less likely to occur than on paper. However, it is generally accepted that in a labor-managed environment the firm's response to increased prices in the product market is likely to be less elastic than in a capitalist one; output would be slower to increase in response to increase in demand.

BENEFITS OF THE PARTICIPATORY ECONOMY

Vanek was an unashamed promoter of the idea of the participatory economy and saw in it a logical "evolutionary" solution to some of the detriments of capitalism. Indeed, some authors have argued that through the growing tendency to pay workers at least in part with shares or attractively priced options, participation has in fact come to capitalism. Vanek offered several advantages for labor management, which are discussed as follows with some of the limitations brought out:

1. *A participatory economy will show reduced tendency to monopolization, and hence increased consumer welfare, relative to a capitalist economy.* This conclusion stems from several assumptions, some of which are problematic. First, it is assumed the structure of enterprise governance will tend to keep productive units small, which results in a market structure of many small firms that are in broad terms competitive with each other. There will be no tendency to create a gigantic entity, because worker management in such a firm would be clumsy. Second, the fact that the objective maximand of the firm is earnings per worker rather than aggregate profits per se makes the labor-managed firm less prone to attempt to dominate through size. Under capitalism doubling output by doubling all inputs may lead to doubling

---

[4]Benjamin Ward, "The Firm in Illyria," *American Economic Review* 48 (1958): 566–589.

of profits. In the labor-managed context such action results again in the doubling of profits, but since the number of workers is doubled too, the net result is only a constant profit per worker. Therefore increasing size is not particularly attractive to the workers who ultimately control the firm. However, it must be admitted that if a larger size creates more market power and therefore leads to increased product prices, then it can result in higher earnings per worker, and that monopoly, with the consequent ability to manipulate prices, can be attractive to a socialist manager as well as capitalist one.

2. *Nonproductive expenditure in the participatory economy would be less than under capitalism.* Since the advantage of size is limited under labor management, expenses on advertising and marketing designed to win larger market share are less remunerative than in the capitalist environment. Thus a participatory economy wastes less on nonproductive expenses than a capitalist one. However, it must be conceded that if the promotional expenditure does result in product differentiation, it would allow higher prices and therefore generate increased income per head.

3. *Participatory firms will show reduced workplace friction, and a smaller incidence of strikes relative to capitalist firms.* This would seem to be a common-sense consequence of labor management. Strikes are usually the result of a dispute over the relative returns to capital and labor. When the owners of capital and the workers are nominally the same, the potential for disagreement should be much reduced. Viewed from a slightly different perspective, labor management gets around the principal-agent problem because the owners are the workers. These features are, of course, the logic behind the use of equity as a substitute for wages to reward workers, an increasingly common feature of capitalism in developed market economies.

4. *A participatory economy will have a greater tendency to full employment compared to capitalism.* This claim of macroeconomic stability is important to Vanek, but it is one of the most difficult to substantiate. It is true that there will be an inherent tendency of worker-managed firms to retain labor during downswings in the economic cycle, because these employees are part of the "democracy" of the plant. They are enfranchised and help to choose management, and they therefore have both rights and power. It follows that there will be a tendency to maintain the output of the firm during recessions because workers will be kept in employment, a feature with obvious counter-cyclical implications. Because short-term shifts in demand variations are not followed by adjustments of quantity, either up or down, the size of short-term price movement in response to demand shocks is likely to be greater than under capitalism and quantity movements correspondingly smaller.

   However, there is another reason why the participatory economy is more resistant to unemployment. The state owns the capital and, for political reasons, it might be slow in enforcing repossession when capital payments are in arrears. Thus the participatory firm might face a "soft budget constraint," cushioning against unemployment in the short run but fostering inefficiency in the longer term by tying up capital in unproductive enterprises. Moreover, if substantial unemployment does come into being, there is no mechanism to eliminate it in a more rapid fashion in a participatory economy than under capitalism. With conventional labor markets, unemployed workers offer themselves for employment at lower wages; this drives down the wages that the capitalists pay and hence increases employment. Under labor management and profit sharing, each additional worker hired will tend to drive down the average profit per worker (see Figure 17.1), and therefore adding new workers will not be appealing to the existing worker managers, except in cases in which the impact on average capital costs outweighs the impact on average value product.

5. *A participatory economy will have a lower long-run tendency toward inflation.* It is possible that in the long run (as opposed to the short-run discussed earlier) the participatory form of organization has a lower tendency to inflation than conventional capitalism. This stems from two factors. One is the resistance to size and monopolization that is inherent in this kind of organization; this was discussed earlier. The other is the absence of labor unions. With no unions to bargain for increased wages, an inflationary cycle cannot start with "wage push."

6. *Firms in the participatory economy will be more socially responsible than a capitalist firm.* Finally, there is the claim that a worker-managed firm is likely to be more socially responsible than a capitalist firm, especially with respect to the environment. Consider the case of pollution, which tends to be "oversupplied" under capitalism because real costs of production are imposed on third parties, with no compensation. Since the owners of the capital live far away from the factories, their lives are not adversely affected by a decline in environmental quality, nor are their children likely to suffer poor health as a result. However, since the workers who control a participatory firm live locally, they are more likely to "internalize" the externality of pollution and trade lower monetary rewards for a better environment.

NEGATIVE FEATURES OF THE PARTICIPATORY ECONOMY

Some of the potential detriments resulting from labor management were introduced contextually in the preceding section, but it is useful to underscore a couple of them.

1. *Firms in the participatory economy are likely to be less responsive than the capitalist firm.* There will be more resistance to changing the size of the workforce in either direction than under capitalism, and therefore quantity responses are likely to be slower. In some circumstances this might be a fatal flaw since resistance to downsizing might cause the firm to operate inefficiently and put itself into bankruptcy rather than fire workers. In the ideal case, as profits per worker fall, some workers will be motivated to move to firms where they can make a greater positive contribution to average profits, but

in reality this process is likely to be highly frictional and take a long time to complete.

2. *Firms in the participatory economy offer limited capability for innovation.* Research and development require substantial resources, and it is frequently argued that the smaller firms encountered in a participatory economy can afford it less well than the larger ones we see under capitalism. Certainly, research is largely a fixed cost, and a firm with a high volume of sales is in a position to spread the cost across a greater number of units of output.

DEVELOPMENT OF THE YUGOSLAV STATE

The state that most closely embodied Vanek's ideas of participation, and from which he gained inspiration, was Yugoslavia. Today the Yugoslav state is split into several republics, some in conflict with each other, and it is hard now to envisage it as a laboratory for evolutionary socialist principles. Nevertheless for most of the post–World War II period, the Yugoslav economy represented an intriguing third way that tried to balance the efficiency and coordination of the market with the egalitarian principles of socialism.

THE INSTITUTIONAL HISTORY OF YUGOSLAVIA

Yugoslavia was created at the end of World War I and owed its existence to the Wilsonian principle of national self-determination. However, the architects of the peace treaty feared that the ethnic nationalities of the Balkans might be too small and too quarrelsome to survive as independent states. Consequently, they created the Kingdom of the Serbs, Croats, and Slovenes, which in time became the Kingdom of Yugoslavia, literally the land of the south Slavs. The new country was made up of part of the former Austro-Hungarian empire (Croatia and Slovenia), the Kingdom of Serbia, and parts of the Ottoman empire. From the first, issues of ethnic heterogeneity and economic divergence dominated the new country. It was overrun by the Germans in 1941, and the German occupation increased ethnic rivalry because of the cynical application of divide and rule.

At the end of the war, the Communists established their rule and the leader, Josef Brosz Tito, was a firm admirer of both Stalin and central planning. Initially he tried to implement the Soviet model in Yugoslavia but was unwilling to see domination by the Nazis being replaced by that of the Soviets. He insisted from the first on Yugoslavia's total independence as a nation, outraging Stalin, who expelled Yugoslavia from international communist organizations (*Cominterm*) in 1948. Under Tito's firm rule, ethnic divisions, troublesome before and during the World War II, and which were to result in the ultimate breakup of the Yugoslav state, were put on a back burner. Expulsion from *Cominterm* allowed Yugoslavia to experiment in economic policy. For a brief period, Soviet-style planning was intensified, but from 1950 onward Tito led the country toward a system in which individual firms had much greater freedom in determining output level, technical choice, and prices.

■ TABLE 17.1

THE REGIONAL DISTRIBUTION OF INCOME: 1947–1986 PER HEAD INCOME AS A PERCENTAGE OF AVERAGE

Republic or Autonomous Region	1947	1953	1979	1986	Population (millions) 1986
Kosmet	58	53	31	30	1.8
Bosnia-Herzegovina	72	79	70	72	4.3
Macedonia	71	69	68	66	2
Montenegro	43	58	64	78	0.6
Serbia	100	91	96	94	5.8
Vojvodina	125	96	120	121	2
Croatia	105	111	125	123	4.7
Slovenia	157	182	200	211	1.9
All Yugoslavia	100	100	100	100	23.2
Highest / Lowest	3.65	3.43	6.45	7.03	

SOURCE: Richard Carson, *Comparative Economic Systems* (Amonk, N.Y.: M. E. Sharpe, 1990), 365.

THE REGIONAL PROBLEM

One of the problems confronting Yugoslavia was very unequal income levels between the constituent republics. In 1947 the northernmost republic, Slovenia, enjoyed a per-head income about 57 percent above the average for Yugoslavia as a whole, while the poorest republic, Montenegro, was 57 percent below the average. One would expect that under market coordination arrangements this differential would have narrowed over time, and in a socialist state where the government has a role not only in directing infrastructural investment but also in allocating investment capital and technology between regions, convergence should have been even faster.

Table 17.1 shows this was not the case and far from narrowing, the differential widened over time. Slovenia became relatively wealthier while other provinces and regions, particularly in the south, remained less developed. By the middle 1980s the poorest area was Kosmet (the acronym for the Autonomous Region of Kosovo and Metohija, an area populated predominantly by ethnic Albanians), despite its special status granted by Tito.

There are several reasons for the failure to converge. Although language was not a major difficulty, deep ethnic, cultural, and religious differences kept labor mobility between republics low. The system of worker management limited the extent to which new workers would be brought into an organization since in most cases new workers did not increase average profit. Hiring might be tolerable if the marginal worker were a relative, a neighbor, or a local political appointee, but not a migrant worker from another republic.

Federal policy transferred resources from the more prosperous north to the south, but the extent was limited by the need to minimize political conflict between the republics; transfers were a cause of grievance and unrest within the richer areas. In addition, despite the availability of cheap labor, capital had a lower marginal product in the south, and though investment rates were higher in poorer regions, income disparities remained large. Toward the end of federal Yugoslavia, the average worker in the south was equipped with as much capital as his or her counterpart in the north—but labor productivity was still inferior in the south. The failure to grow was largely explained by lower average education and the scarcity of management skills in the poorer regions, while productivity in the northern republics was helped by proximity to Austria and the European Union (EU), which kept demand high and led to technological spillovers. Low labor cost suppliers on the periphery of prosperous Western Europe, Croatia, and especially Slovenia prospered.

At the onset of communist rule, income in Slovenia was three times as great as that in Kosovo-Metohija; by 1986 the ratio was 7:1 This worsening situation fanned Kosovar separatism and escalated ethnic and religious tensions. However, of more importance to the breakup of the Yugoslav state was the fact that Slovenian income was 140 percent higher than in the ethnically Serb areas of Montenegro and Serbia proper. Remaining within a federation would imply continued transfers from the Slovenes to the Serbs. It is not, therefore, surprising that the Slovenes were the first to leave federal Yugoslavia and the first to apply for EU membership, where they would be recipients of transfer funds, rather than payees.

YUGOSLAV MARKET SOCIALISM

THE YUGOSLAV SYSTEM

The Yugoslav system differed in key respects from the conditions that Vanek thought essential for a participatory economy.

1. *Capital was socially owned and enterprises did "rent" the capital from the state,* but the **capital charge** was well below an equilibrium interest rate. As a result, capital was always in short supply, and there was excess demand for investment funds. Consequently rationing these scarce resources had to be a political decision.

2. *There was a theoretical reliance on the market to coordinate the system, with each firm pursuing its income-maximizing objective,* but there were also many price controls and administered prices, not merely in the capital market.

3. *Although in theory the workplace operated as a form of representative democracy, with free elections for management, the list of eligible managers was tightly controlled by the Communist Party,* and instead of being free to elect the best man or woman for the job, the workers had to choose from a list constrained by politics.

4. *Nominally there was total freedom of employment, and each worker could choose where to work,* but in reality firms tended to hire from within family and neighborhood groups, and movement between regions or ethnic areas was especially difficult.

5. *Although the social sector firms did practice income sharing, it was limited on the downside,* and wages could not, by law, fall by more than 30 percent in any

year, whatever the profit situation of the firm. This required a form of soft-budget constraint.

THE OPERATING STRUCTURE OF A YUGOSLAV FIRM

The shift from command planning to worker management in Yugoslavia occurred in the early 1950s. In 1953, the workers' councils assumed the authority to manage enterprises, although their capital still belonged to the state. Councils were elected by the workers of the firm (with the exception of the management) and they had the responsibility of choosing management, as well as providing broad direction over all financial and policy matters.

The organization closest to the Western concept of a firm was known as an **organization of associated labor (OAL).** However, the OAL was not the smallest unit. Large enterprises were subdivided into units known as **basic organization of associated labor** (or **BOAL**s). Each BOAL (which may be thought of in terms of their analogue in Western firms—the profit center) produced an identifiable and salable good or service. Importantly, profit was calculated at the level of the BOAL, and the incomes of workers are a function of the profitability of the smaller unit—not the larger firm. Strictly speaking a complex OAL was no more than a voluntary association of its constituent basic organizations of labor. The BOALs had to ratify all important pricing, production, and finance decisions, and could, in theory, secede if it would not disrupt the parent OAL. In 1985 the Yugoslav social sector consisted of some 14,280 undivided enterprises (OALs), and a further 4,062 major OALs, subdivided into 18,927 basic organizations of labor.

This conception of the firm proved problematic. Although the products of the basic organizations could be identified, in reality the effectiveness of each of the units within the firm is a function of management's ability to elicit cooperation between the various parts. As in any multidivisional firm, there is likely to be a turf war over who is responsible for profits and who is liable for costs, but the whole is generally interdependent. Service functions within the firm (accountancy, maintenance, security, etc.) are handled by "work communities," where incomes derive from a pro rata sharing of the profits of all the BOALs. The general flow of funds within a basic organization of associated labor is shown in Figure 17.3.

Within the "profit center" incomes are determined by the division of residual profits between the workers, not on a simple per-head basis, but rather on the basis of **work points** determined by workers' councils on the basis of the skills, training, and effort required in various occupations. Table 17.2 gives an example of work points system of a Zagreb textile factory in the early 1960s. The categories include education, skill, physical effort, and working conditions. In addition, total wages may be amended by the granting of individual performance bonuses (or penalties), and total compensation reflects a considerable in-kind component that is available to all workers, including housing, health care, and child care. While we might dispute the relative importance of all these factors, they did provide a basis for income determination. However, it was necessarily arbitrary in nature, and, because it paid little account to supply and demand in the labor market, it did not guarantee that all positions would be filled by qualified people. The differential

THE FLOW OF FUNDS OF A YUGOSLAV SOCIAL SECTOR BOAL

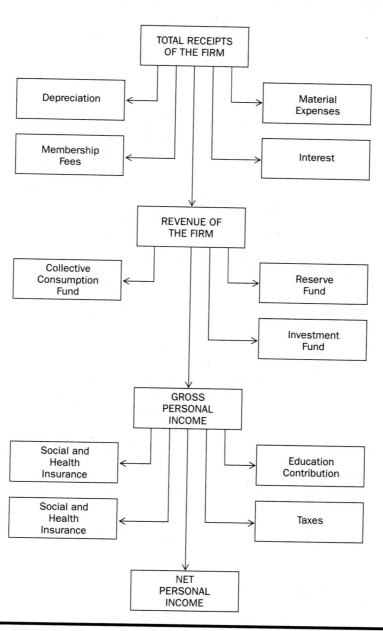

SOURCE: Carson, 377.

■ **TABLE 17.2**

AN EXAMPLE OF WORK POINTS ASSIGNMENTS: ZAGREB TEXTILE FACTORY, 1961

	Education	Skill and Experience	Authority	Respon-sibility	Physical Effort	Mental Effort	Working Conditions	Total
Managing director	100	170	150	190	10	100	10	730
Technical director	130	140	140	160	10	90	10	680
Works manager	100	130	100	120	10	90	30	580
Foreman	80	60	40	50	10	40	40	320
Skilled weaver	50	40	0	40	35	30	40	235
Skilled spinner	30	20	0	20	30	10	40	150
Sales manager	100	130	100	140	10	90	10	580
Accountant	100	100	50	90	10	80	10	440
Truck driver	80	60	0	70	30	40	40	320
Female cleaner	20	10	0	10	40	10	40	130

SOURCE: Bicanich, Rudolf, "La Politique des revenue Ouvriers en Yougoslavie," *Economie Appliquée,* October–December, 1963, 587, cited in Carson, 381.

between the senior management and the workforce was particularly crucial, and top management in Yugoslavia was relatively badly paid (as a multiple of average earnings) compared to other socialist and capitalist countries. In the example here, the managing director (CEO) receives only about five times the income of a cleaner and only a little more than twice that of a factory foreman.

The theory of worker management holds that the relatively small work groups discourage alienation and maintain peer discipline. Division of profits among responsible workers maximizes effort and reduces to a minimum agency problems. The selection of management by the workers' councils ensures that the best candidate for the overall well-being of the firm is chosen and that conflicts between management and workers are kept to a minimum. Unfortunately, experience revealed a more problematic side to each of these assumptions. Profit sharing and small organization did not solve all the problems of work effort; "free riding" was still common and was exhibited in problems of labor productivity. Supervision was still required. The system of management selection did not guarantee that the best person got the job. In the first place, the slate of candidates was politically determined. Local party officials had considerable say over who constituted "qualified" candidates. Beyond this, workers had an incentive to choose a candidate for other reasons than the long-run health of the firm—perhaps, for example, to maximize job security.

PROBLEMS OF THE YUGOSLAV ECONOMY

INVESTMENT

One of the most important negative characteristics of the Yugoslav economy was the absence of capital markets with any real role in the rationing of investment funds among competing uses. One of the important tenets of Vanek's system was that capital should be owned publicly and rented out to the enterprises at realistic charges, but in reality interest rates were never allowed to play a significant role. Real interest rates were always low and frequently were negative. The demand for investment capital by the enterprises at these rates was practically limitless, and therefore allocation among competing uses had to be on the basis of political decisions rather than economic ones.

An additional potential source of investment funds in the labor-managed firm was retained earnings, an excess of revenue over costs not distributed to the workers in income. To some extent profit retention was a legal requirement because by law each firm had to maintain the value of its capital, accounting for depreciation of capital equipment and amortizing it in a "business fund." Workers could in theory vote to distribute even less of earnings as income, increase the business fund, and hence contribute to the purchase of new capital equipment. However, workers do not have full ownership rights in the firm, and no individual worker is secure in knowing that his or her share of the principal invested will be recovered in full at the end of his or her time horizon. Unlike a worker in a capitalist enterprise, who is sure that any money he or she puts into shares in the company is to some degree liquid (although there is risk of capital loss, as well as the prospect of capital gain), any investment made by the Yugoslav worker is highly illiquid. In contrast, if the money is received as income and deposited in individual savings accounts, the worker has security over both principal and interest. Moreover, the fact that financial repression kept interest rates below market clearing values ensured a black market for funds that paid even higher rates than the savings accounts. Consequently, workers would be motivated to invest in the firm only if the expected rate of return were considerably above that offered in savings accounts or black-market loans.

UNEMPLOYMENT

One of Vanek's predictions for the participatory economy was a high level of employment, going so far as to write:

> the participatory economy does guarantee full employment. It does so in the sense that the economy will normally operate at, or very near, full employment, and if as the result of some drastic disturbance, unemployment were to arise, there are forces, inherent in the system, that will tend to restore full employment. In this respect the participatory economy has a definite edge over capitalist economies.

While one of the enduring problems of capitalism has been unemployment, it is not clear that the participatory economy has the edge over flexible labor markets. It is true that worker-managed firms will be less willing to shed labor in downturns, but once it is established unemployment can prove very stubborn. The same factors that militate against the growth of worker-managed firms act to prevent surplus labor being absorbed by existing enterprises. Only if the marginal revenue product of an additional worker is above the average revenue product of existing workers will new hires be made. Otherwise the income of existing workers will fall.

The data show that Yugoslavia suffered from acute unemployment. In the mid-1980s about 1,000,000 workers were registered as unemployed. Part of this total was frictional, comprised of workers who were between jobs or receiving education; however, it is probable that about 700,000 of the total were properly described as unemployed and seeking work. In addition, some 350,000 Yugoslavs were working abroad, mostly in Germany[5] as *Gastarbeiter,* (guest workers). Finally, it should be noted that Yugoslavia retained a "reserve" of potential industrial workers employed in low-productivity agriculture. On the whole, the participatory Yugoslav economy did not do an excellent job at eliminating unemployment.

During the 1980s, most of the unemployed were young people. Layoffs were rare in Yugoslav industry (a feature Vanek had accurately predicted), but startups of new firms were few and job creation sluggish. Much of the responsibility lay with the highly imperfect capital market, which tended to allocate funds to existing large and politically powerful enterprises. Unemployment, like income, was distributed very unevenly between the republics. In relatively wealthy Slovenia, next to the Austrian border, the unemployment rate was less than 1.8 percent, while in impoverished Kosovo, largely inhabited by ethnic Albanians, it was close to one-third. Cultural and religious barriers prevented labor mobility and allowed disequilibrium in the federal labor market.

STRIKE ACTIVITY

Vanek's assertion that a labor-managed firm would be largely immune from labor disputes and strike activity would seem on the face of it likely to be borne out in fact. Surely workers who could elect their own management, and who could have a powerful say in the operation of the enterprise, could have little to complain about and would be unlikely to indulge in such self-destructive behavior.

However, the social sector of the Yugoslav economy was by no means insulated from labor unrest, especially as real incomes fell in the late 1970s and early 1980s. Despite the fact that they had elected them, workers mistrusted management, especially over layoffs in the face of falling demand. Moreover, the complex structure of Yugoslavia's OALs allowed areas of dispute among the various BOALs that made up the enterprise, particularly about contributions toward the overhead (management, maintenance, sales, etc.) of the firm as a whole. It is not wholly surprising that there were more than 1,000 strikes in the first nine months of 1987.

INDUSTRIAL CONCENTRATION

Another of Vanek's predictions was confounded by Yugoslav experience. He argued that the participatory economy would tend to a low degree of product

---

[5]This figure was down from a peak of about 535,000 in the mid-1970s and the returning workers had exacerbated the problem at home.

■ **TABLE 17.3**

INCIDENCE OF MONOPOLY AND OLIGOPOLY IN CONSUMER-ORIENTED INDUSTRIES, 1985

	Number of Divisions		
Industry	Total	Single Producer	< 8 Producers
Final wood products	112	4	38
Finished leather products	101	7	36
Footwear and accessories	40	2	14
Food products	221	22	90
Beverages	24	2	10
Final tobacco products	4	1	3

SOURCE: John P. Burkett, "Self-Managed Market Socialism and the Yugoslave Economy, 1950–1991," in Morris Bornstein, *Comparative Economic Systems* (Homewood, Ill.: Richard Irwin, 1994), 333.

market concentration compared to capitalist countries. He based this on the idea that while capitalist profits would rise with market share, income per worker would be largely unchanged (except when monopoly power might be exploited or substantial economies of scale exist).

In fact, Yugoslav industry showed a remarkable concentration in many markets. Table 17.3 gives some evidence from 1985. In food products, for example, 10 percent of the subdivisions of the industry were completely monopolized, and over half had less than eight producers. Moreover, barriers to inter-republic trade meant that the *de facto* monopoly power of many enterprises was even greater than the data indicate. Often there was a single producer in each republic, protected by substantial barriers to entry.

We can speculate about the causes of such concentration, but much of the responsibility lay with the system of allocating investment funds. Because the interest rate on investment capital was below its opportunity cost, every firm was interested in attracting as much funds as possible. In general, the larger firms had a greater voice and political influence and were able to attract more capital for expansion and modernization, and so they progressively squeezed smaller firms out of the market.

INFLATION

The Yugoslav economy did not exhibit the low inflation that Vanek expected. Part of his case rested on the absence of union power, which in capitalist economies was a powerful factor for "cost push" inflation through high wage settlements. He also argued that a socialist economy was less prone to unemployment than a capitalist one, and therefore there would be less need for expansionary fiscal and monetary policy, a frequent policy response of capitalist governments and one that accelerates the rate of inflation.[6] Despite these theoretical conclusions, Yugoslav inflation was brisk relative to other European countries, and both federal and the republic governments tried to use price controls to fight it. The effect of these controls was to create series of shortages, excess demand, and black markets for key commodities.

ENVIRONMENTAL QUALITY

Finally, Vanek believed that a labor-managed economy would be more respectful of the environment and lead to a lower level of pollution than would occur under capitalism. He argued that workers who lived near the factory would be resistant to the emission of pollutants because of the negative effect on their own quality of life. Managers in capitalist firms, responsible only to distant shareholders, would be more inclined to pillage the environment for an increase in profit. Again Vanek's prediction proved wide of the mark. Capitalist economies in the postwar period have been "cleaner" than socialist ones, Yugoslavia included. The reason for this is that environmental regulation is more advanced in the wealthier economies of Western Europe, perhaps because environmental concern is a "luxury" better afforded in wealthier nations. Also the widespread environmental chaos throughout socialist Eastern Europe reflects the "problem of the commons"—that which belongs to everyone in fact belongs to no one.

CONCLUSION

Despite the promise of labor-management, its overall performance in Yugoslavia must be regarded as disappointing. Vanek's predictions proved wrong on almost every score, in part because his expectations for participation were overly optimistic and in part because Yugoslavia adopted only three out of the five basic institutions of the ideal participatory economy. It is impossible to do more than speculate on the development of Yugoslavia if truly free markets for goods, and realistic charges for capital services that would have equated supply and demand, had been adopted.

KEY TERMS AND CONCEPTS

basic organization of associated
   labor (BOAL)
capital charge

income maximization
labor management
market socialism

---

[6] Indeed, modern literature in this "trade-off" suggests that any attempt to reduce unemployment below the natural rate is necessarily reflected in increased prices rather than in expanded output and reduced unemployment.

nonproductive expenditure

organization of associated
    labor (OAL)

participatory economies

work points

QUESTIONS FOR DISCUSSION

1. What were Vanek's five principles for a participatory economy? To what degree were they fulfilled in the Yugoslav system?

2. Why is it that the supply curve may be negatively sloped in a labor-managed economy? Is this a general result?

3. Why should a labor-managed economy enjoy greater workplace peace than under capitalism? Was this the reality in Yugoslavia?

4. To what degree did we observe greater macroeconomic stability in Yugoslavia than in Western capitalist economies?

5. Why did Vanek argue that a labor-managed firm would pay greater attention to environmental concerns than a capitalist firm?

6. Why did the Yugoslav economy show so little tendency toward convergence and maintain high regional income differentials?

7. How well did the labor market function in Yugoslavia? Did the system of income sharing and work points ensure a fluid and efficient labor market?

8. Did the inability to reduce the interregional productivity gaps contribute to the break up of the Yugoslav state?

RESOURCES

BOOKS AND ARTICLES

Dyker, David A. *Yugoslavia: Socialism, Development, and Debt.* London: Routledge, 1990.

Flakierski, Henryk. *The Economic System and Income Distribution in Yugoslavia.* Armonk, N.Y.: M.E. Sharpe, 1989.

Ireland, Norman J. *The Economics of the Labor-Managed Enterprises.* London: Croom Helm, 1982.

Jackall, Robert, and Henry M. Levin, eds. *Worker Cooperatives in America.* Berkeley, Calif.: University of California Press, 1984.

Mellor, Mary. *Worker Cooperatives in Theory and Practice.* Milton Keynes, England, and Philadelphia: Open University Press, 1988.

Miller, David. *Market, State, and Community: Theoretical Foundations of Market Socialism.* Oxford: Oxford University Press., 1989.

Stephen, Frank H. *The Economic Analysis of Producers' Cooperatives.* London: Macmillan, 1984.

Vanek, Jaroslav. *The General Theory of Labor-Managed Market Economies.* Ithaca, N.Y.: Cornell University Press, 1970.

Vanek, Jaroslav. *The Participatory Economy: An Evolutionary Hypothesis and a Strategy for Development,* Ithaca, N.Y.: Cornell University Press, 1971.

Wachtel, Howard. "Workers' Management and Inter-Industry Wage Differentials in Yugoslavia." *Journal of Political Economy,* May–June 1972.

Wachtel, Howard. *Workers' Management and Workers' Wages in Yugoslavia.* Ithaca, N.Y.: Cornell University Press, 1973.

Ward, Ben. "The Firm in Illyria: Market Syndicalism," *American Economic Review,* September 1958.

18

The Possibilities of a Third Way

Central planning has many appealing features. A plan enables tasks to be prioritized rather than relying on what seem at times to be the whims and myopia of the market. A plan can also facilitate the mobilization of resources to achieve specific aims, such as the creation of infrastructure or the creation of a new industrial sector. Because income from property accrues to the state, public ownership of the means of production, which is a usual but not a necessary feature of centrally planned economies, avoids extreme bias in the distribution of income. Despite the recent dismal economic history of centrally planned states, planning retains an appeal. It is still considered a rational activity within a firm or a household, and this lends some justification for planning in the management of the national economy.

However, from its earliest applications the deficiencies of centralized planning have been apparent. Effective command planning requires the centralization of a vast amount of information, so much in fact that it is almost impossible to process and to reconcile. This very need for data often creates perverse incentives that encourage enterprise managers to mislead the center for their advantage. Planning has no mechanism whereby consumer preferences are rapidly transmitted to the center, and so the preferences of individuals must be guessed at or ignored. Finally, of particular importance is the fact that only in the rarest of circumstances will prices in a planned system reflect relative scarcities or resource costs.

MARKET SOCIALISM AND SOCIAL MARKETS

Because the polar conceptions, market capitalism and socialist command planning, have defects, a middle way that grasps the market's advantages in allocative efficiency and marries it to the distributional equity of socialism is very attractive.

There are two main approaches to a third way. A system in which capital is owned by the state but the prices of final products and inputs are determined in the marketplace is generally referred to as **market socialism,** and we observed this system in our review of the Yugoslav economy. Such a system enables the market to allocate factors of production, while coordination of the system is achieved through price signaling. Usually the one price not market determined is that of capital, because it is owned by the state and is lent or rented out at prices determined by the planners or the politicians.

A second approach is to allow a more completely operative market system, in which capital may be privately owned and rationed by the market but the government puts constraints on the ultimate outcome of the system, and prescribes how the economy will perform in terms of income distribution, access to basic goods and services, and sometimes price determination. This kind of economy is properly referred to as a **social market economy,** and we studied this in the Swedish case, although sometimes the distinction between the two is blurred.

MARKET SOCIALISM

We turn first to market socialism. While this system appeals because it represents the best of two worlds, providing both allocative efficiency and equity, both recent experience and current scholarship have tended to emphasize the vital importance of an impartial capital market for the functioning of any market system. Any attempt to maintain a competitive system of prices in the goods and labor markets alone will fail because it divorces the functioning of those markets from the market for capital, to which they are inescapably related.

THE FUNCTION OF THE CAPITAL MARKET

The foremost function of a capital market is to disinterestedly evaluate the performance and potential of each firm. Those firms that are traded in equity markets have their share values determined by an impersonal stock market, which adjusts values to reflect prospects. Those firms that borrow by issuing bonds and paper are subject to the judgment of the bond market, again with many authors pursuing self-interest, on the value of its credit. Those firms that borrow directly from banks have to compete with other borrowers for capital and have to demonstrate the soundness of the business plans and pay premiums according to the riskiness of their ventures. The Israeli economist Michael Keren has summed up the essential function of the capital market:

> The basic service the capital market supplies is the evaluation of each traded firm's net worth. This signals to its management and its owners how the market judges its future prospects. If this value declines relative to that of similar firms, this may be taken as an indication that the market considers the firm's policies inferior to those of its competitors. In severe situations, this may convey a recommendation to change the top management team of the firm, possibly through a takeover by an alternative team. In extreme cases, when the market believes that the expected present value of the firm's cash flow is negative or significantly below the breakup value of the firm, the capital market may apply direct sanctions by bankrupting the firm.[1]

The most important point here is that the verdict of the market is the collective judgment of a large number of people, all of whom have an interest in being well informed, but none of whom is by him or herself decisive. In this way the market

---

[1] Michael Keren, "On the (Im)Possibility of Market Socialism," in *The Road to Capitalism*, ed. Kennett and Lieberman, 45–52.

not only provides capital to firms in order to grow, but it also provides information about the relative performance of current management that is transparent and available to all.

MAKING CAPITAL DECISIONS UNDER SOCIALISM

In the absence of an objective capital market, decisions about which firms are to be given funds for capital investment and which denied must be made by a political process. We can conceive of two broad institutional approaches to addressing this problem. On the one hand, we can allow allocation of capital among competing investment projects to be in the hands of a state hierarchy, consisting of the political leaders and the bureaucrats, the approach followed under central planning in the Soviet Union and Soviet bloc. The politicians laid down guidelines, while the planners complied by crafting them into the plan, and any perceived deviation by the planners from the interest of the politicians would likely be met by their discipline or removal. The system produced, as we have seen, very mixed results: the growth of heavy industry was both rapid and sustained, but enterprise managers had little incentive to innovate and new enterprises were few. Bankruptcies were even rarer as the political process often acted to preserve the status quo. These tendencies impeded the development and adoption of new technology by the planned economies and may account for their ultimate failure in the face of the technological revolution of the 1980s.

An alternative approach might be to establish "investment boards," made up of impartial "experts" who could take a dispassionate view of the prospects of various potential enterprises. Unless specific arrangements were made to protect their tenure and hence to insulate the board members, this only pushes the problem one step away. The performance of the boards would not be subject to an independent evaluation, but the board members would serve at the pleasure of the politicians and would themselves be political appointees. Safeguards (such as long-term tenure) could be designed to insulate such boards from political pressure, but they are not likely to be perfect. Under such political uncertainty, it is hard to see how the action of any planning agency or board can effectively simulate the performance of a financial market. In the market it is not one individual or group that decides the fate of firms, but the weighted opinion of many market participants. The best that can be done in its place is a considered judgment by a narrower group that can never be impersonal.

It can, however, be argued with some justification that the behavior of investment boards or planners might in some cases be better than the behavior of the market. Markets might be short-sighted in their evaluation of prospects, and deny capital to enterprises that, though worthy, will be slow to pay back principal. Planners or investment boards might be more capable of taking a longer view. It is also possible that planning might facilitate a more comprehensive view of the costs and gains of a project than the market does. Market decisions frequently fail to take into account significant positive and negative externalities, and, in theory at least, planners can take a more holistic view of the cost-benefit matrix of an investment. Consider, for example, constructing a railway line. A private firm would consider only the costs and revenues of the venture itself. A planning or investment board would want to take in consideration a much broader set of effects: the effect of alleviating road congestion in transport, the impact on the environment, and so forth. With respect to investments with infrastructural and spillover consequences, the board might well arrive at a more socially optimal decision than the market.

Ludwig von Mises, the promarket Austrian economist, argued trenchantly that a socialist state would be unable to handle the question of a railway investment very well:

> Suppose, for instance, that the socialist commonwealth was contemplating a new railway line. Would a new railway line be a good thing? If so, which of many possible routes should it cover? Under a system of private ownership we could use money calculations to decide these questions. The new line would cheapen the transportation of certain articles, and, on this basis, we could estimate whether the reduction in transport charges would be great enough to counterweigh the expenditure which the building and running of the line would involve. Such a calculation could be made only in money. We could not do it by comparing various classes of expenditure and savings in kind. If it is out of the question to reduce to a common unit the quantities of various kinds of skilled and unskilled labor, iron, coal, building materials of different kinds, machinery, and the other things which the building and upkeep of railways necessitate, then it is impossible to make them the subject of economic calculation. We can make systematic economic plans only when all the commodities which we have to take into account can be assimilated to money. True, money calculations are incomplete. True, they have profound deficiencies. But we have nothing better to put in their place. And, under sound monetary conditions, they suffice for practical purposes. If we abandon them, economic calculation becomes absolutely impossible.[2]

While von Mises's point that rational planning requires valuation in terms of some comparable unit is quite valid, it is by no means clear that his example is a good one. A government may be much more qualified to calculate the complete benefits over space and time of a major infrastructural improvement. For example, the establishment of a railway line will involve inevitable consequences for other means of transportation. Roads will be less congested, pollution will be lowered, time will be saved, and other spillovers experienced. Quite contrary to von Mises's assertion, the planner is better able to consider the social benefit of large-scale infrastructural change.

THE SOFT BUDGET CONSTRAINT

The political control of investment credit is a facet of a general problem articulated by the Hungarian economist Janos Kornai.[3] He had worked his entire career within

---

[2] Ludwig von Mises, "Economic Calculation in Socialism," in *The Road to Capitalism*, ed. David Kennett and Marc Lieberman (Fort Worth, Tex.: Harcourt Brace, 1993), 38–39.

[3] Janos Kornai, "The Soft Budget Constraint," *Kyklos* 39 (1986), 3–30.

the Hungarian planning system and well understood the way that such a system operated. The "soft" budget constraint refers to a situation in which the firm or enterprise is unconstrained by the basic maxim that long-run revenues must exceed long-run costs. A "hard" budget constraint is experienced by firms in competitive markets. They cannot expect to receive a subsidy toward the operation in the long run, and they therefore must earn enough revenue to meet their costs of materials and factors of production including capital. Although they might go into debt in the short run, in the long run the debt must be amortized.

In socialist economies, because both capital costs and operating costs are frequently subsidized by the state, the soft-budget constraint is the norm, not the exception. There are subtle ways of introducing "softness" into the system through direct subsidies, discriminatory taxation, or the manipulation of administered prices to ensure the appearance of financial viability. In this chapter, however, what concerns us is the existence of "soft credit," a phenomenon that embraces two related features. The first is the provision of credit at an interest rate that fails to reflect the opportunity cost of capital, implying that the demand for investment funds will generally speaking exceed its supply and that it has to be allocated or rationed by a nonprice system, opening the door to political or personal favoritism. By itself, however, a nonprice allocation system does not necessarily represent soft credit: if payment reschedules are required to be adhered to, then even loans at subsidized interest rates can be "hard." If debt service payments are not met, then the firm can be forced into bankruptcy, merger, or takeover. What makes the system truly "soft" is a second feature, the knowledge that the political process will ensure the continued existence and even the growth of the firm despite continued failure to meet the prescribed repayment schedule. The **soft budget constraint** enables the firm to continue to exist although its long-term obligations are not met. To put it a different way, its long-term expenditures are greater than its long-term revenue and credit continues to be granted by the authorities, although there is little prospect of repayment.

THE IMPACT ON THE CONDUCT OF THE ENTERPRISE

If the firm believes that its budget constraint is indeed soft, incentives exist for it to behave in ways that will lower the efficiency of the economy. The firm's elasticity of demand for inputs will become markedly reduced. If increases in costs are compensated by external assistance, there is little reason for an enterprise manager to economize on the use of the newly expensive factor. Under a soft budget constraint, a rise in input prices does not lead a decision maker to change input mix or alter output level but rather to get on the phone to persuade the planners to change prices or to grant additional credits.

While the short-term consequences may be grave, the longer term is of greater consequence. Kornai has summarized this situation:

> The most important issue is dynamic adjustment. If the budget constraint is hard, the firm has no other option but to adjust to unfavorable circumstances by improving quality, cutting costs, introducing new products or processes, i.e. it must behave in

an entrepreneurial manner. If, however, the budget constraint is soft, such productive efforts are no longer imperative. Instead, the firm is likely to seek external assistance, asking for compensation for unfavorable external circumstances. The State is acting like an overall insurance company taking over all the moral hazards with the usual well-known consequences; the insured will be less careful in protecting his wealth. [Joseph] Schumpeter [the Austrian economist] emphasized the significance of "creative destruction": the elimination of old products, technologies, organizations which were surpassed by the more efficient new ones. The soft budget constraint protects the old production line, the inefficient firm against constructive destruction and thus impedes innovation and development.[4]

THE POSSIBILITY OF MARKET SOCIALISM

The foregoing argument suggests that the problems of capital allocation are fatal to any attempt at market socialism. Whenever investment funds are controlled by the government, or by boards appointed by the government, there will be some inevitable softness in capital allocation. Enterprise managers knowing that projects are ultimately supported on political rather than economic grounds will not adopt the behavior that results in allocative efficiency.

In Keren's terms the vital aims of market socialism are equality and decentralized decision making. The former requires the public ownership of productive assets. The latter requires hard budget constraints and an absence of state intervention. However, these two aims are in conflict. The exclusion of private market and the bureaucratic process cannot serve as an adequate proxy. Enterprises become aware that survival and growth are politically, not economically, determined, and their behavior changes as a result.

While it is hard to pick holes in this logic, its flaw is that it sets straw men against each other. Financial markets, because they are disinterested, are assumed to be superior to the political process in allocating investment. However, the lessons of recent history are that private markets are capable of enormous errors in getting funds to projects that have failed—America's savings and loans crisis and the Asian banking debacle are two examples that stand out.[5] Similarly, socially owned banking systems—for example, in Taiwan or in France during "les trentes glorieuses"—have done an adequate job in credit allocation. A pure market can offer advantages in allocative efficiency over politically controlled investment processes, but myopia, panic, a narrow definition of the "bottom line" are all problems that can afflict a market system and can lead to social consequences that are hard to predict and expensive to correct.

---

[4] Kornai, "The Soft Budget Constraint," 10–11.

[5] The indigenous financial systems of most East Asian countries relied on directed credit; however, much of the blame for the crisis must be placed on the inflow and outflow of "hot" monies from competitive financial systems.

THE SOCIAL MARKET ECONOMY

THE GERMAN MODEL

While market socialism seems to be largely out of favor, the search for a middle way is nevertheless active. European nations, which had swung to the right in the 1980s, had moved back to the left by the mid-1990s, and their economies embody high degrees of regulation and redistribution. The alternative to nationalizing the means of production (which denies private ownership of most capital and hence the appropriation of its income stream by individuals) is to allow a market to operate for all goods and factors of production, including capital, but to use the power of the state to modify, to regulate, and to guarantee the distribution of income and to ensure access to basic services and opportunities. A good example of this kind of economy is the system of the Federal Republic of Germany, at least as it existed between 1949, when the postwar constitution became operative, and 1989, when the Berlin Wall fell. We will examine in more detail the economic consequences of reunification in chapter 20, but here we will look briefly at the institutions that comprise the social market.

Germany is unusual in that its constitution lays out the economic and social goals that any government of the republic is required to pursue. While to a degree symbolic, it makes explicit the shared values embodied in the constitution and contributes to the low degree of partisanship in the determination of domestic social and economic policies since all major parties are required to accept the basic goals. In the economic realm these are price stability, a stable currency, full employment, and steady growth. On the social side the goals to be pursued include social equity, social security, and social progress, vague principles but expressing a common purpose.

The German model is in a sense an extreme case but it has common features with other nations of the European Union. The economy is organized on market principles, but it is subject to extensive social regulation. The purpose of social regulation "is intended to ensure that the impersonal workings of markets do not interfere with or undermine basic needs ranging from adequate income and health care to organized representation in the workplace."[6] In other words the impersonality or disinterested quality of the marketplace is relied on to produce the wealth, but it is recognized that this might have distributional consequences or implications for individuals that are intolerable.

CODETERMINATION BETWEEN WORKERS AND MANAGEMENT

At the heart of the social market economy is the idea that society's various groups are partners rather than competitors or rivals. In the workplace this

---

[6]Lowell Turner, *Negotiating the New Germany: Can Social Partnership Survive?* (Ithaca, N.Y.: ILR Press, 1997), 3.

manifests itself as a system of *Mitbestimmung*, or **codetermination,** that gives workers a guaranteed say in the operation of companies and full access to most data on their operation. By law, workers must occupy at least half of the seats on the **supervisory boards** of companies, which are responsible for the broad direction of the enterprise and for hiring and firing of senior management.[7] The German system also guarantees a role for a works council *(Betriebsrat)* for all except the smallest firms. Representation on the works councils is determined by general ballot, and a strong union presence is normal but not guaranteed. The works councils have specific rights, including the right to veto management decisions in matters of employment classification, overtime, and to some degree recruitment and dismissal.

Codetermination extends beyond the workplace, and embraces the wage determination process that consists of collective bargaining between the unions and the employer organizations on an industry-wide basis under government supervision. Generally speaking, the process is cooperative and results in an annual wage settlement common across the industry, although it can erupt into conflict.

THE STAKEHOLDER AND THE STOCKHOLDER

The German model of worker participation and involvement in decision making (sometimes called the **Rhine model**) calls into question the conception of the **Anglo-Saxon model** that a firm's sole responsibility is to its stockholders. In Germany the system of codetermination, with labor involved in management decision making, establishes the principle that others besides the "owners" of the corporation have a stake in its future and therefore a voice in its management. This brings us to a discussion of what is now referred to as the stakeholder economy.

A **stakeholder** is defined as someone who, while not a titular owner of a business, has legitimate interest in its performance and success. The stakeholders of a corporation may include not only the shareholders but also labor, management, customers, suppliers, lenders, and the community in which the corporation is located. Consequently, if stakeholders have any legitimacy, they have a voice that influences the performance of the corporation.

It is difficult to draw strong conclusions about what the legitimation of a wide range of interests in the decisions of firms does to economic performance. If the behavior of the corporation is indeed meaningfully modified by recognizing stakeholder preferences, and if that behavior is not consistent with profit maximization, it should follow that the "stakeholder corporation" might be in difficulty because it will underperform its "profit-oriented" competitors. Less profitable

---

[7] This was the result of the Code Termination Act of 1976. In the event of a tie, the chair, always a representative of capital, has a deciding vote.

than a profit-maximizing corporation unconstrained by stakeholder preferences, a stakeholder corporation would therefore be vulnerable to, and ultimately eliminated, by market forces.

If, however, pleasing the stakeholders contributes to the maximization of long-term profits, then there is no conflict. *The Economist,* in reviewing a recent book by John Kay, a prominent British economist, that favored the view that the corporation is a "social institution" beholden to a range of stakeholders, rather than a private one beholden only to its owners, declared such a view to be ". . . either trivial or meaningless. Few companies, bar perhaps monopoly utilities, can afford to have a miserable workforce or disgruntled customers. If, that is, they want to be successful. Presumably that means making money for their customers."[8]

However, there are other interpretations to be considered. For example, take the issue of labor's "stake" in its employer. Clearly in Japan where the institution of lifetime employment covers at least some of the workforce of the major employers, workers have a greater recognized stake than in, say, the United States. This relationship has hampered the ability of Japanese corporations to deal with the downturn in demand that has afflicted the economy since 1990. Productivity and profitability in Japanese firms has been adversely affected by this inability to restructure the workforce. In the United States, in contrast, downturns in demand, or profitability, can be met by trimming the workforce, as in the well-documented downsizing of the early 1990s. Similarly, if a company takes seriously its obligations to a community, should that commitment to its neighbor/stakeholders be at the expense of shareholders?

Within the German model the most important stakeholders in the firm are, on the one hand, the employees and, on the other, the bankers, who lend the enterprise most of its capital. Often the same banks also own some of the shares of the firm, which is allowed under German law, but this is generally quite a small part of total equity.[9] However, the banks have considerable influence in the firm because they were often represented on the supervisory boards and also control the voting power of the shares they hold for clients in their role as stockbrokers and mutual fund managers. A growing criticism in Germany has been that the interest of the banks as lenders may be in conflict with the interest of the shareholders, and recent years have seen rising activism by shareholders about maximizing the return to their capital. Table 18.1 shows the dominance of banks in decision making in major German corporations; this power originates not primarily from bank ownership of stock but its ability to vote by proxy the shares that are held in investment funds and in customer accounts.

---

[8] *The Economist,* "Money Making," a review of *The Business of Economics* by John Kay (Oxford: Oxford University Press, 1996). Review of Books and Media, 16 November 1996, 12.

[9] In 1994 private banks directly held about 0.4 percent of German industrial capital, down from 1.3 percent in 1976. *The Economist,* 3 January 1995.

■ **TABLE 18.1**

BANKS' SHARE OF VOTING RIGHTS AT AGMS OF LARGE GERMAN COMPANIES, 1992

		Shares Owned By:		
Company	Banks	Subsidiary Investment Funds	Proxy Votes	Total Bank Votes
Siemens	—	9.87	85.61	95.48
Volkswagen	—	8.89	35.16	44.05
Hoechst	—	10.74	87.72	98.46
BASF	0.09	13.61	81.01	94.71
Bayer	—	11.23	80.09	91.32
Thyssen	6.77	3.62	34.98	45.37
VEBA	—	12.62	78.23	90.85
Mannesmann	—	7.76	90.35	98.11
Deutsche Bank	—	12.41	82.32	94.73
MAN	8.67	12.69	26.84	48.2

SOURCE: *The Economist,* 3 June 1995, 66.

RECOGNIZING STAKEHOLDERS

Curiously, however, there are conflicting trends at work. In Britain, there is a movement toward a broader involvement of interested parties and recognition of the legitimacy of stakeholders' interests. This was a feature of the electoral platform of Tony Blair's New Labour, in which the stakeholder economy was promoted without rigorous definition, serving as a rather loose collectivist concept. In concrete terms the most obvious trend has been the increased ownership of firms by their workers through **employee stock ownership plans (ESOPs).**

Running directly against a trend toward increased stakeholder, particularly employee, ownership has been the attack mounted on some of the older forms of stakeholder involvement in recent years. In Britain the same criticisms that had been leveled against publicly owned industry were turned against a large mutual sector composed of **retail cooperatives** and building societies **(mutual thrift institutions).** These institutions were accused of being badly managed and having low productivity. Most decisively, in a world where the principal-agent dilemma of giving incentives to top management in private industry has been tackled by the use of stock options, in the mutual sector there was no comparable way to offer rewards for management performance. In a very short space of time many of Britain's large building societies were converted into joint stock companies, distributing the shares among management, depositors, and borrowers. This might suggest that mutuals—which are comprehensive stakeholder organizations where customers (both depositors and borrowers) and potential future customers have an interest—are less efficient organizations than conventionally organized corporations. Mutuals not only lack the ability to offer stock option remuneration schemes, but also they cannot raise capital on the stock market, and these factors might lead to relative inefficiency. However, an alternative explanation is that the building societies have been systematically pillaged by management and "carpetbaggers" to the detriment of other present and future stakeholders. Explanations focusing on efficiency do not answer the question of why the mutual thrifts were so successful for such a long time and grew to have such power.[10] In the retail sector, the cooperative societies that were founded in the 19th century to give customer/stakeholders a share in the management and profit of retailing have fallen of late on hard times. Again, this is frequently attributed to the absence of incentives for management because of an inability to use stock option schemes.

In the United States the rapid downsizing that occurred in the early 1990s brought forth criticism, notably from Robert Reich, then labor secretary, that firms must be forced to live up to their obligations to stakeholders and accept this role in and responsibility to a broader community. In contrast to the United Kingdom, the fastest growing elements of the retail financial industry in the United States are the credit unions and mutual societies where both borrower and lender have an interest. Germany has a very large mutual sector, especially in finance where 2,500 mutual banking institutions have more than 14 million members and 20,000 branches. There have been few signs that these will be converted into joint stock companies as in the United Kingdom, since mutuals conform well to the German philosophy of codetermination, although interest in the British experience has grown recently.[11]

STAKEHOLDERS AS SHAREHOLDERS

One way in which the potential conflict between the rights of shareholders and the claims of other stakeholders might be resolved is by extension of share ownership to stakeholders. This arrangement could be used to resolve to some degree the principal-agent issues that have traditionally affected the labor-capital relationship. A growing number of firms are providing incentives for workers in the form of preferential employee ownership schemes, which tend to bring interests of capital and labor into much closer alignment. A similar solution might also be possible in the case of a local government, which could take an equity holding in a major local employer. Such an arrangement would, however, raise complexities of the

---

[10] In July 1999 the British Treasury issued a report on *Demutualisation,* Ninth Report of the Select Committee of the Treasury, HMSO (22 July 1999). It examined the case for and against mutual societies, but in general saw no reason to oppose demutualization.

[11] See "Demutualization in Germany. Inconceivable?" *The Economist,* 3 January 1998

■ TABLE 18.2

10 LARGEST FIRMS IN THE UNITED STATES WITH EMPLOYEE HOLDINGS ABOVE 30 PERCENT OF TOTAL EQUITY

Company	Plan	Business	Percent Owned	Number of Employees
United Parcel Service*	401(k)	Package delivery	Minority	315,000
Publix Supermarkets	ESOP	Supermarkets	Majority	103,000
United Airlines	ESOP	Airline	Majority	77,900
Tandy Corp.	ESOP	electronics	Minority	40,000
Hy-Vee Stores	ESOP	Supermarkets	Minority	35,000
Hallmark Cards Inc.	Profit-sharing plan	Greeting cards	Minority	28,500
TTC Inc.	ESOP	Employee leasing	Minority	25,000
The Freeman Companies	ESOP	Convention planning	Minority	25,000
Science Applications International	ESOP and other plans	R&D, computer systems	Majority	25,000
Ruddick Corporation	ESOP	Holding company	Minority	20,150

* UPS made a substantial move to becoming a shareholder-held company with the largest IPO offering in U.S. history in November 1999.

SOURCE: National Center for Employee Ownership.

municipalities' attitude to new entrants and competitors and might bias the level playing field.

The government in the United States has actively favored the extension of employee ownership and offers considerable tax advantages to firms that institute employee stock ownership programs, the result of which has been a rise in worker ownership of firms.

Table 18.2 shows the 10 largest majority employee-owned corporations in the United States. Although some are quite large, they are clearly only a tiny fraction of the total economy and tend to be concentrated in service industries.

CONCLUSION

The prospect of some kind of third way will continue to intrigue many people, and interest in it is likely to be fed in the future by several trends. One is the widening economic disparity that has been a feature of the economic expansion of the 1990s. A second is growing concern for the environment in its broadest sense, involving not only pollution but also the demise and decay of traditional patterns of settlement and interaction. Together these trends have focused attention on what its proponents call the social economy that attempts to define as stakeholders a much broader spectrum of interests than capital, labor, and government. A quite different theme has been toward a greater ownership of firms by the workers, a trend that owes much to the success of those firms who have increased the role and ownership of the workers and hence made them not just stakeholders but also shareholders.

KEY TERMS AND CONCEPTS

Anglo-Saxon model

codetermination

employee stock ownership plans (ESOPs)

market socialism

mutual thrift institutions

retail cooperatives

Rhine model

social market economy

soft budget constraint

stakeholder

supervising board

QUESTIONS FOR DISCUSSION

1. Distinguish between market socialism and a social market economy. Give examples of each.
2. Why is the absence of a capital market potentially fatal to market socialism?
3. Distinguish between hard and soft budget constraints.
4. Which, in your view, is better to determine the social value of a major change in the transportation system—the market or a government? Why?
5. Discuss the idea of codetermination within a firm.
6. Should stakeholders who are not owners have a say in a firm's decision making? Will a firm who recognizes its stakeholders' interests be competed out of business?
7. Why does the trend to employee stock option plans offer a way out of the principal-agent problem?
8. Why are so many traditional "mutual" firms being converted into stockholder firms? Is this good in the long run?

RESOURCES

WEB SITES

The National Center for Employee Ownership .... http://www.nceo.org/

The Association for Social Economics .... http://www.socialeconomics.org/

The U.K. Social Economy Forum . . . . http://www.social-economy.org.uk/

Aries, Social Economy online . . . . http://www.aries.eu.int/
Aries is a Euro Info Center (EIC) for the Social Economy. ARIES provides an online information, news, and networking service designed to help social economy organizations to work together and take action at the European level.

European Confederation of Workers' Cooperatives, Social Cooperatives, and Participative Enterprises . . . . http://www.cecop.org/

Coordinating Committee of European Cooperative Associations . . . .
. . . . http://www.ccace.org/uk/indexuk.htm

The Netherlands Participation Institute (NPI) . . . . http://www.snpi.nl/frameuk.htm

The Center for Economic and Social Justice . . . . http://www.cesj.org/

The ESOP Association (United States) . . . . http://www.esopassociation.org/

Integra Review . . . . http://www.iol.ie/EMPLOYMENT/integra/sepp.html

Treasury Select Committee Report on Demutualisation . . . .
. . . . http://www.parliament.the-stationery-office.co.uk/pa/cm199899/
cmselect/cmtreasy/605/60502.htm

BOOKS AND ARTICLES

Ackerman, Bruce, and Ann Alstott. *The Stakeholder Society.* New Haven: Yale University Press, 1999.

Bamberger, Bill, and Cathy Davidson. *Closing: The Life and Death of an American Factory.* New York: W.W. Norton, 1998.

Carroll, Archie B. *Business and Society: Ethics and Stakeholder Management.* Cincinnati, Ohio: South-Western Publishers, 1996.

Hutton, Bill, and David Goldblatt, eds. *The Stakeholding Society: Writings on Politics and Economics.* New York: Blackwell, 1999.

Kay, John. *The Business of Economics.* Oxford: Oxford University Press, 1996.

Kelly, Gavin, Dominic Kelly, and Andrew Gamble. *Stakeholder Capitalism.* New York: St. Martin's Press, 1997.

Keren, Michael. "On the (Im)Possibility of Market Socialism," In *The Road to Capitalism,* ed. David Kennett and Marc Lieberman. Fort Worth, Tex.: Harcourt Brace, 1993. 45–52.

Le Grand, Julian, and Saul Estrin, eds. *Market Socialism.* Oxford: Clarendon Press, 1989.

Minford, Patrick. *Markets Not Stakes: The Triumph of Capitalism and the Stakeholder Fallacy.* London: Trafalgar Square, 1998.

Plender, John. *A Stake in the Future: The Stakeholding Society.* London: Nicholas Brealey, 1997.

Turner, Lowell. *Negotiating the New Germany: Can Social Partnership Survive?* Ithaca, N.Y.: ILR Press, 1997.

Yunker, James A. *Socialism Revised and Modernized: The Case for Pragmatic Market Socialism.* New York: Praeger, 1992.

PART SIX | **THE ECONOMICS OF TRANSITION**

19

PRIVATIZATION IN BRITAIN

In 1979, when Margaret Thatcher took office as prime minister of a Conservative government, Britain was at the end of a dispiriting decade. The 1970s had proved difficult for most of the world economy, but in Britain **stagflation,** the combination of high inflation, low growth, and rising unemployment, had been particularly severe and marked the end of a century of decline relative to the rest of the developed world. After a fast start as the world's first industrial power, most economic historians pick the period between 1870 and 1913 as the time when Britain's industrial supremacy was challenged and ultimately overturned by the United States and Germany.

Between 1913 and 1945 the underlying trends in the global economy were obscured by two world wars (1914–1918 and 1939–1945) and the Great Depression, which lasted from the end of 1929 until roughly 1938. In Britain the decades between the wars saw social friction and labor unrest, while each of the conflicts had cost it dearly in terms of domestic investment foregone and foreign assets liquidated. However, Britain emerged from World War II with an aggressive plan to socialize industry and construct a welfare state. The postwar Labour government nationalized much of industry, including steel; coal; road, rail, and air transportation; and electricity and gas supply. The financial sector remained in private hands, though subject to considerable regulation. Extensive planning controls inherited from the war period, including the rationing of consumer goods, were extended into land-use planning by the 1948 Town and Country Planning Act.

On the social side, the government moved to construct a comprehensive welfare state, with free socialized medicine, increased publicly provided higher education, and extensive income support for the old, the unemployed, the young, and the sick.[1] While government's share of the economy failed to shrink from war-time levels, highly progressive taxation fell heavily on so-called unearned income originating from capital and land.

In retrospect the two decades after World War II present a conundrum. On one hand, they can be remembered as a golden age of strong and consistent growth, low inflation, and low levels of unemployment, almost living up to their billing as the "new Elizabethan era." As Table 19.1 shows, between 1950 and 1973

---

[1] The income support policy was modeled on the recommendations of a 1942 report authored by Sir William Beveridge, which outlined a blueprint for universal social insurance.

▪ TABLE 19.1

AVERAGE ANNUAL PERCENTAGE GROWTH RATES OF GDP IN FIVE ECONOMIES

	United Kingdom	France	Germany	Japan	United States
GDP					
1870–1913	1.9	1.5	2.8	2.3	3.9
1913–1950	1.3	1.1	1.3	2.2	2.8
1950–1973	3	5	5.9	9.3	3.6
GDP per Capita					
1870–1913	1	1.3	1.6	1.4	1.8
1913–1950	0.8	1.1	0.7	0.9	1.6
1950–1973	2.5	4	4.9	8	2.2
GDP per Hour Worked					
1870–1913	1.2	1.6	1.9	1.9	1.9
1913–1950	1.6	1.9	1	1.8	2.4
1950–1973	3.2	5	5.9	7.6	2.5

SOURCE: Angus Maddison, *Dynamic Forces in Capitalist Development* (Oxford: Oxford University Press, 1991).

Britain enjoyed real growth of 3.0 percent per annum, with the output doubling in 23 years. Per-head income rose by 2.5 percent per annum, more than 76 percent over the period, while unemployment was both low and stable by historic standards, particularly those of the disastrous 1930s. In terms of overall macroeconomic performance, the period 1950–1973 was probably about as good as Britain ever got, even when compared to the middle decades of the 19th century, which had laid the foundation of British prosperity. Were it not for the performance of continental Europe and Japan, the 1950s and 1960s might have been remembered for economic growth and expansion. However, though strong, Britain's growth fell dismally short of that of Germany, France, and Japan. Per-head income in Germany, defeated and humiliated in two world wars, passed that of Britain in 1961, and France followed in 1969. Of most concern, British labor productivity only increased at two-thirds the pace of the average of the 12 most developed nations. While growing in absolute terms, Britain was drifting to the back of the pack.

Although the whole world experienced a worsening macroeconomic environment in the 1970s, Britain's performance became even more noticeably below par, managing barely half the average growth rate of the rest of the developed world. Both unemployment and inflation were above those in the average industrialized country, and as labor unrest worsened, Britain became generally regarded as the "sick man" of Europe and indeed of the whole of the Organization for Economic Cooperation and Development (OECD).

Failure provoked a determined inquiry into the roots of Britain's economic performance. Some saw a cultural malaise of over-satisfaction and laziness, but there were several economic candidates for blame:

1. High and steeply progressive rates of taxation reduced the incentive to work, particularly among the more productive members of society, by lowering the take-home wage. Heavy taxes on capital income deterred saving and investment and led to the outflow of capital from Britain to offshore havens and to a consequent underinvestment in domestic industry.

2. The comprehensive social safety net provided by the postwar welfare state reduced work incentive at the lower end of the income scale, reducing the cost of job loss to workers. High taxes and income guarantees together had a suffocating effect on effort at both ends of the income distribution.

3. In industrial relations, conservative management confronted a highly unionized and militant workforce. To make matters worse, British union organization was along craft or occupation lines, rather than by place of work, and each employer was forced to negotiate with many unions, while each union had the potential to disrupt output by using its power to maximize the short-term income of its membership. The introduction of new work practices to raise productivity was consequently extremely difficult, and attempts to rationalize the use of labor often led to "demarcation disputes" between different unions. The command structure within many unions was undemocratic, requiring neither regular elections for leadership nor ballots of the membership to ratify strike decisions. Individual union leaders often held unchecked power and personally had little to lose in industrial disputes. As a result, strikes were common, driving away foreign investment and leading British capital to look for more profitable locations overseas.

4. The large public sector was perceived as wasting investment resources in industries characterized by poor productivity. A study by Richard Pryke published in 1971[2] found that on the whole the performance of the public sector was comparable to that of private industry during the 1950s and 1960s. However, a later study[3] by the same author found that the performance of the nationalized industries had deteriorated during the 1970s and that the overall record of the nationalized industry was "third rate" in comparison to the record of the private sector.

As economic conditions worsened in the 1970s, the popularity of the Labour government waned. A Conservative government under Margaret Thatcher was surprisingly elected in 1979, initiating the policies that bore her name and earned

---

[2] Richard Pryke, *Public Enterprise in Practice* (London: MacGibbon and Kee, 1971).

[3] Richard Pryke, *Nationalized Industries: Policy and Performance Since 1968* (Oxford: Robert Martin, 1981).

an immortality shared by few.[4] The main elements of **Thatcherism** consisted of curtailing public services, reducing both the level and the progressivity of taxation (on both income and real estate), coupled with a comprehensive program of "privatization." Privatization is not a very precise term, and it has been used to describe a variety of actions, ranging from the sale of state assets to the increased reliance on private suppliers for activity that had traditionally been within the government sector.[5]

KINDS OF PRIVATIZATION

Four main dimensions of privatization are relevant in economic transition.

A TRANSFER OF OWNERSHIP

Privatization's most frequent meaning is the transfer of ownership from the public to the private sector. Such a transfer can be achieved in several ways: shares can be given away—to workers, management, or the general public—or they can be sold by several means. In Britain almost all of the assets were sold, although some were disposed of at less than the fair market value of the assets employed. The choice of technique for share transfer has been of particular importance in the transformation of the former socialist systems in Central and Eastern Europe, the institutional arrangements for which are discussed more fully later.

THE PROCESS OF DEREGULATION

The term *privatization* has also been used to denote the process of deregulation, the paring back of government intervention in determination of industrial structure and prices. This process involves no formal change in the nominal ownership of assets, but it entails a shift in property rights—generally the right to determine prices or the right to enter an industry.

FRANCHISING

Franchising "involves conferring rights in the supply or distribution of goods or services to a sole producer or operator for a specific period."[6] By allowing

---

[4] Marx, Keynes, Colbert, and Ricardo are members of the same elite club who have economic doctrines named for them.

[5] Theo Thiemeyer actually identified some 12 different meanings of the word. See Theo Thiemeyer, "Privatization: On the Many Senses in Which This Word is Used in an International Discussion of Economic Theory," *Annals of Public and Cooperative Economy* 57, no. 2 (April–June 1986), 147–152.

[6] Simon Domberger and John Piggott, "Privatization Policies and Public Enterprise: A Survey," in *Privatization and Economic Performance*, ed. Matthew Bishop, John Kay, and Colin Mayer (Oxford: Oxford University Press, 1994), 51.

competition for the franchise, some element of market discipline can be introduced into an area that might be regarded as a natural monopoly. The grantor of the franchise, in this case the government, must have some device to determine who receives it. There are two main candidates. The first is to grant the right to the potential supplier who offers to charge the lowest price. Under competitive bidding, this so-called **Chadwick-Demsetz**[7] **auction** would result in "normal" expected profits (i.e., the monopoly rent would be bid away). A second possibility is a more standard auction, where the contestants offer an up-front sum for the right to the monopoly. This scheme does provide revenue for the government, but unlike the Chadwick-Demsetz auction, it allows monopoly pricing and therefore harms allocative efficiency.

REPLACEMENT OF PUBLIC PRODUCTION BY PRIVATE PRODUCTION

The final relevant meaning of privatization is the replacement of public production of goods by private industry under contract to the government. Privatization in this context generally involves the use of private firms to collect refuse, supply health services, or even, in some cases, to operate prisons.

BRITAIN'S PUBLIC SECTOR: STRUCTURE AND PERFORMANCE

Although in 1979 Britain had by many measures a large public sector, it was not out of line with most European countries. Public ownership in Britain embraced the whole of the public utility sector—electricity and gas supply, telephones, water supply, rail transportation—and also included a considerable part of manufacturing. Some industries had been taken into public ownership as part of the Labour Party's policies of controlling key economic sectors, but others had been acquired for other reasons; often the government had been the buyer of last resort, and nationalization was an alternative to bankruptcy and the consequent loss of output and employment. As a result, the British taxpayer was also the nominal owner of the coal industry, the steel industry, much of the automobile manufacturing industry, ship-building, and a great deal of aerospace and defense-related production, a collection of lame ducks saved from the extinction that the market had dictated.

The industries still under public ownership in 1981 are shown in Table 19.2. A few firms had already been sold, but they were anomalies—companies for which there was no real rationale for public ownership, but which had "accidentally" ended up in the state sector; they included Amersham International, Cable and

---

[7]These ideas were first put forward by the British economist Edwin Chadwick in 1859 and were subsequently promoted as an alternative to regulation by Harold Demsetz in 1968.

BRITISH NATIONALIZED INDUSTRIES, 1981

	Turnover (£m.)	Capital Employed (£m.)	Employment ('000s)	Percentage Change in Employment since 1979
Electricity industry	8,057	32,605	147	−8
British Telecom	5,708	16,099	246	2
British Gas	5,235	10,955	105	0
National Coal Board	4,727	5,891	279	−5
British Steel	3,443	2,502	104	−38
British Leyland	3,072	1,521	83	−31
British Rail	2,899	2,746	277	−7
Post Office	2,636	1,347	183	0
British Airways	2,241	1,338	43	−24
Rolls-Royce	1,493	992	45	−23
British Shipbuilders	1,026	655	67	−18
S. Scotland Electricity	716	2,817	13	−5
National Bus Company	618	508	53	−16
British Airports Authority	277	852	7	−7
N. Scotland Hydro-Electric	270	1,981	4	−3
Civil Aviation Authority	206	162	7	−2
Scottish Transport Group	152	157	11	−17
British Waterways Board	16	50	3	−2
Total	42,792	83,178	1,627	

SOURCE: Bishop, Kay, and Mayer, 23.

Wireless, and Thomas Cook (the tour operator). Even those remaining were a mixed bag. Some represented obvious "natural monopolies," defined by falling long-run average costs and homogeneous product, for which economists generally accept the case for nationalization, or at least regulation. Among these were the post office, British Gas, British Telecom, British Rail, and electricity supply. Some others were not in strict terms natural monopolies, but were taken into public ownership after World War II as part of the Labour Party's policy to dominate, in Lenin's phrase, the "commanding heights" of the economy. The most important of these were the National Coal Board and British Steel. The political necessity of maintaining employment in the depressed regions where mining dominated prevented successive Conservative governments from even attempting to denationalize coal at any time. Steel, on the other hand, passed in and out of the public sector but was renationalized in the 1960s when the largest firms began to fail. The remaining firms in the publicly owned sector were lame ducks, which had little reason to be either socially owned or regulated; bad management or market logic had, however, brought them to the brink of bankruptcy and the government had acted as buyer of last resort to save employment or preserve a strategic industry in being. Among these were British Leyland (automobiles), British Shipbuilders, and Rolls Royce, the airplane engine maker.

THE RATIONALES FOR PRIVATIZATION

In its pursuit of privatization, the British government sought to satisfy simultaneously a series of objectives.

RAISING PRODUCTIVITY

One goal was to raise the level of performance and productivity in the industries then in public hands. There was some evidence to suggest that the efficiency of nationalized industry was below that of the private sector, but this was by no means unambiguous; public enterprise began to show a sharp improvement in performance from 1978, well before the start of privatization. Moreover, the publicly owned firms in manufacturing had been acquired as lame ducks to save them from bankruptcy, and therefore a straight comparison of the two sectors is not really fair. In general, productivity gains were expected to result from clearer corporate governance and defining profits as the unequivocal measure of performance. Put in theoretical terms, management can be a better agent for a defined group of shareholders/owners than it can be for the nation as a whole, which is composed of individuals with different demands and expectations.

CREATING POPULAR CAPITALISM

The second objective was to broaden the base of capitalism in the United Kingdom, a move that would certainly strengthen the Conservative Party's hold on power. Share ownership had historically been narrow, at least compared to the United States; in 1979 only three million Britons (5 percent of the population) owned shares either directly or through mutual funds. Selling shares in nationalized industry offered an opportunity to create what was euphemistically called **popular capitalism,** by targeting sales to middle- and low-income households and offering shares at discount prices. The 1980s saw a dramatic change in share ownership. By 1991 an additional eight million Britons owned shares, some induced by preferential prices in the privatization and some by the advantages of tax-sheltered personal equity plans (PEPs), similar to individual retirement accounts (IRAs) and 401Ks in the United States.

REDUCING THE PUBLIC-SECTOR BORROWING REQUIREMENT

The third objective was to raise revenue, and proceeds from privatization did remove the budget constraint from the government for a decade. Asset sales also provided the resources for a thoroughgoing overhaul of the tax system, sharply reducing marginal income tax rates especially on "unearned" income for upper income groups. Supply-side proponents claimed this provided incentives for savings, investment, and the work effort of the most productive members of society. Critics saw the tax reforms as regressive and targeted to the wealthier, traditional supporters of the Conservative Party.

REDUCING THE PROBLEMS OF PUBLIC-SECTOR PAY DETERMINATION

Understanding the last objective of the privatization program requires more familiarity with British politics. Setting wage rates in the public sector was a persistent problem for successive governments. In the private sector, wage negotiations might be contentious, but ultimately the existence of a "hard" budget constraint forced compromise. Management could not allow a settlement that would drive the company into bankruptcy, and union militancy was curtailed by the knowledge that excessive demands might lead to closure and job loss. Such constraints are absent from the public sector. Subsidies from tax revenues can be used to pay increased wages, and this "soft" budget constraint makes each round of wage negotiation a test of political will. Even if the public industries were constrained to break even, monopoly power often meant that prices could be adjusted to provide the extra revenue. Attempts to base pay settlements on "comparability" with the private sector proved problematic, just as in the Swedish case.[8] Privatization offered a chance for government to get out of this politically treacherous and potentially inflationary business.

TECHNIQUES OF PRIVATIZATION

The sharp change brought about by Thatcherism meant that 1979 was the high water of Britain as a social market economy. The pace of asset sale, however, was relatively slow. The publicly owned sector represented a limited share of productive capacity (at least compared to the former planned economies), and the volume of assets disposed of in any given year was but a small percentage of the total. Moreover, because of the sophistication and depth of British financial markets, a variety of privatization techniques could be used without overburdening, and depressing, the markets.

INITIAL PUBLIC OFFERINGS

The most widely used technique was the **initial public offering (IPO),** by which the enterprise is first valued by underwriters, who have access to financial statements, and shares are offered at a price calculated to ensure their complete disposal. The communications giant British Telecom was sold off in this way, and, as in several other of the major privatizations, the government introduced special incentives allowing small buyers access at preferential rates. This policy was

---

[8] See chapter 7 and the discussion of Sweden for more on the problems that can result from a comparability wage policy.

intended to raise public participation in the ownership of industry and to make a reversal more difficult. For example, any future Labour government would have trouble renationalizing British Telecom because among its owners were Labour voters who had benefited from share ownership.[9] Most Britons who bought shares at the offer price made money as the average price rose by 40 percent on the day of issue, leading to criticism that the nation's assets were sold too cheaply.

IPOS WITH GOLDEN SHARES. A variation of an initial public offering is to sell only part of the share capital, keeping a substantial portion either in public hands or placing it with a single private buyer in return for certain undertakings. This device, known as a **golden share,** retains some control over management and prevents it from having full freedom in the disposition of the assets. The golden share is often used to prevent management from stripping out the assets and liquidating the firm, and it can also be used to prevent foreign buyers from purchasing "national champions."

NEGOTIATED SALE. Some firms have been sold entirely to a single buyer at a negotiated price, as was the case in the remnants of British car industry—British Rover, sold to British Aerospace. Such sales have been widely criticized because they are necessarily discretionary and can favor friends or supporters who acquire the assets at low prices.[10]

EMPLOYEE OR MANAGEMENT BUYOUT. In a few cases the nationalized enterprises were sold off to insiders, the management and employees. Usually this was done at extremely cheap prices, because the financial resources of the potential purchasers were small. The most celebrated case in the British context was the National Freight Corporation (NFC), a publicly owned road transportation company that had existed since 1947 and for the most part had experienced significant losses. The assets of the company had a book value of £93 million, and the government sold it to employees for £53 million, of which £46 million was earmarked to fund the pensions owed to employees themselves. Consequently, the sale netted the government only £7 million.

The subsequent history of the NFC is a case study beloved by advocates of privatization and is powerful evidence of the role of incentives. Productivity soared, profits mounted, and the value of the company increased. After only seven years under private management, profits were £90 million. In 1989 the company was taken public at a market capitalization of £890 million. The average employee stake of £600 had risen 100 fold to £60,000, certainly strong anecdotal evidence that efficiency, productivity, and incentives can all grow under private ownership.

---

[9] In almost all cases, the initial prices of shares of privatized firms were low, and a rapid appreciation of share prices followed privatization. In most cases, the price rose by 40 percent on the day of issue.

[10] This is a criticism that was frequently heard in Germany over the negotiated sale policy of the post-unification privatization agency, the Treuhandanstalt. See chapter 20 for more on this subject.

THE EFFECTS OF PRIVATIZATION ON EFFICIENCY

Such anecdotes aside, it is not easy to show that privatization has a strong effect on productivity. Certainly most of the industries showed much stronger productivity growth in the 1980s than they did in the 1970s, but many concerns were showing rapid improvement *before* they actually passed into the private sector. Steel, for example, which had seen productivity fall in the 1970s, experienced a rapid surge immediately prior to privatization. In large part this was due to the closure of smaller and more obsolete steel mills as part of the process of preparing for privatization. Because the plants with low labor productivity were closed, the average inevitably rose.

There was a strong upward trend in labor productivity in the British utilities when they were in public ownership in the 1970s,[11] but the movement started well before they were privatized, possibly as early as 1978, predating Thatcher's surprise electoral victory. Consequently, Bishop and Thompson argue that it was the result of a change in **corporate culture,** not a change of ownership. Clarity of objectives, management reorganization, incentive pay structure, as well as an increase in capital and a shift in the external environment (all of which are in principle compatible with public ownership) contributed to increased efficiency.

POST-PRIVATIZATION REFORM AND REGULATION

One immediate effect of British asset sales was to create privately owned monopolies in place of publicly owned ones. While some increase in productivity might result from better incentives and managerial organization, the presence of private monopolies constitutes a threat to the allocative efficiency of the economy, because monopoly prices are unlikely to reflect resource cost. In this respect, the privatized situation was potentially worse than when the utilities were in public hands, because private monopolists with clear profit-maximizing goals might be more damaging to consumer welfare than a publicly owned monopoly with less aggressive policies and a vague mandate to contribute to general welfare.

Consumers would clearly be better served by competition, but since many of the enterprises were "natural" monopolies, introducing a competitive element required creative attention to industrial structure.[12] Reorganization in some industries has allowed greater competition. In the case of the railways, the management and ownership of the track has been separated from the operating companies, and different firms can ply the same route competing on the basis of price and service.

---

[11] This strictly covers nine enterprises: British Airways, British Airports Authority, British Gas, British Telecom, British Steel, and Electricity Supply, all of which were privatized, and British Coal, British Rail, and the post office, which were still in public hands at the time of this study.

[12] New technologies have allowed competition in traditional natural monopolies. The best example is telephones, where satellite technology did away with need for expensive fixed lines for long-distance traffic, and now cell phones are making inroads into local phone monopolies.

Similarly, the ownership of the electricity supply grid was alienated from the producers of power, and so competition was furthered.

If there is no effective way to introduce competition into a monopolized sector of the economy, regulation is necessary to protect public interest. In the United States, regulated utilities are generally subject to a cap on the rate of return on capital. In the United Kingdom, regulation now frequently takes the form known as **RPI-X.** Under such a regime, a regulated utility is allowed to increase its prices by the rate of increase in the retail price index (RPI),[13] less the amount of increase in productivity that the regulators deem to be expected on average within the industry because of technological change. For example, if retail prices were rising at 3 percent and regulators anticipated that unit costs in the industry should be falling at 2 percent, then the allowable annual pace of price increase would be (3 percent minus 2 percent) or 1 percent. RPI-X regulation can be more efficient than rate of return regulation because it provides greater incentives. If a firm can cut costs faster than the regulators anticipate, profit margins will increase and managers and shareholders will receive the advantage of greater efficiency by being free to increase prices.

PRIVATIZATION AND THE LABOR MARKET

One of the problems of a large public sector is that the wages of a considerable part of the economy are determined by politics rather than the market. One cause of this is that public corporations are generally on a "soft" rather than a "hard" budget constraint. Unions can push for higher wages, secure in the knowledge that if the enterprise goes into the red they can use political pressure to increase the size of the public subsidy. Historically, the same principles affected the ability of management in the nationalized sector to reduce the size of the workforce or introduce productivity-augmenting work practices against union opposition. As these enterprises were put on the track to privatization, the budget constraint was hardened, management's strength increased, and the unions' power was reduced.

Table 19.3 shows how steeply employment fell in almost all the nationalized firms between 1980 and 1988. The exceptions to this downward shift were the ever-expanding British Airports Authority and the post office, which remained in public ownership. Also shown are wage increases in each industry for the same period. Consumers' prices in the United Kingdom rose by about 65 percent between 1980 and 1988,[14] so in most cases real gains were modest and in some cases they were negative. The largest increase in wages occurred in the steel industry, but this was more than outweighed by, and possibly driven by, a very sharp increase in labor productivity.

Although workers did not fare especially well in the period after privatization, management treated itself more kindly. Table 19.4 illustrates another aspect of the

---

[13] The retail price index is similar to the U.S. consumers' price index.

[14] *International Financial Statistics* (Washington, D.C.: International Monetary Fund, 1989).

■ TABLE 19.3

CHANGES IN WAGES AND EMPLOYMENT:
NATIONALIZED SECTOR, 1980–1988 (PERCENTAGE)

Company	Employment	Wages
British Airports Authority	15.9	68.6
British Airways	−4.5	79
British Coal	−61.7	82.1
British Gas	−23.2	62.3
British Rail	−27.8	85.4
British Steel	−62.4	120.1
British Telecom	−0.9	114.4
Electricity Supply Industry	−16.1	89.5
North of Scotland Hydro-Electric Board	−6.3	71
South of Scotland Hydro-Electric Board	−14	87.2
London Regional Transport	−31.2	101.6
Post Office: posts	10.7	42.9
Regional Water Authority	−23.6	81
Scottish Transport Group	−16.9	64.8
Totals	−25.6	81.5

SOURCE: Jonathan Haskel and Stefan Szymanski, "Privatization and the Labor Market," in Bishop, Kay, and Mayer, 347.

■ TABLE 19.4

TOP EXECUTIVE REMUNERATION PRIVATIZED AND PUBLIC SECTOR (1988 PRICES)

	1979 (pounds)	1988 (pounds)	Percentage Change
Privatized			
Amersham	31,000	90,000	190.3
BAA	37,000	151,000	308.1
British Airways	45,000	253,000	462.2
British Gas	49,000	184,000	257.5
Cable and Wireless	31,000	208,000	571.0
National Freight Consortium	44,000	143,000	225.0
Rolls-Royce	95,000	130,000	36.8
Average	47,400	164,300	246.6
Public Sector (1979)			
British Coal	49,000	145,000	196.0
British Rail	54,000	90,000	66.7
British Steel	58,000	134,000	131.0
Electricity Supply	45,000	82,000	82.2
Post Office	48,000	84,000	75.0
Average	50,800	107,000	110.6
Average private sector*	115,000	213,000	85.2

* Private-sector average is based on a sample of leading industrial companies, equivalent to those in the 1979 public sector.

SOURCE: Matthew Bishop, John Kay, and Colin Mayer, *Privatization and Economic Performance* (Oxford: Oxford University Press, 1994), 349, Table 17.2.

privatization program—the sharp increase in executive remuneration that occurred during the 1980s. The causes are subject to debate. One reason might be that the heads of nationalized enterprises were underpaid since it was politically difficult to pay very high salaries to corporations requiring public subsidies to stay afloat. It was also problematic to pay the chiefs of public enterprise much more than their political bosses. In this light the increases merely brought management into line with the private market. The more skeptical explanation that once free of restraint enterprise managers chose to reward themselves at the expense of consumers is countered by the fact that even after increases the average executive pay in these industries remained below the average for all private industry.

OTHER ASPECTS OF THATCHERISM

SHRINKING THE WELFARE STATE

While the Thatcher administration followed through on its plans to privatize industry, little progress was made on another agenda item, slashing expenditure on the **welfare state.** In 1979, the start of Thatcher's government, welfare spending [15] was about £122 billion (at 1995 prices), or about 23 percent of GDP. It fell marginally during the 1980s, but by 1995 it had risen to just over 25 percent of GNP, to £183 billion.

Although spending remained high, there were attempts to raise quality by introducing **quasi-markets** into both education and the health service. The 1988 Educational Reform Act established a national curriculum, allowed for open school enrollment, and enabled public schools [16] to compete with each other for students. In the same year a review board examined the operation of the national health service. Again, the basic principle of free provision was not questioned, but both hospitals and doctors were allowed more control over their budgets and could compete for patients. While in theory such competition should lead to cost saving, the evidence is scanty so far. A 1994 Audit Commission investigating the consequences of reorganization in the delivery of doctors' services found that costs had increased by £232 million, while efficiency savings amounted to only £206 million.

Reform of the social services encountered considerable skepticism among the British population. Although free provision had not been challenged, there were fears that the introduction of quasi-markets was a first step toward a pay-for-service market system. The sentiment that the values of the marketplace were corrosive to the traditional view of the welfare state hardened and the public is lukewarm at best in the issue of further reform, which has been halted following the election of a Labour government in 1997.

---

[15] Defined as the sum of spending on housing, social security, health, education, and personal social services (counseling, home help, etc.).

[16] "Public school" is used here in the American sense and should not be confused with the elite British "Public Schools," which are exclusive private establishments.

■ TABLE 19.5

INCOME TAX RATES ON EARNED INCOME, 1979–1997

	79	80	81 to 86	87	88	89	90	91	92	93 to 96	97
Lower rate	25	25	—	—	—	—	—	20	—	20	20
Basic rate	33	30	30	29	27	25	25	25	25	25	24
Top rate	83	60	60	60	60	40	40	40	40	40	40

SOURCE: Institute for Fiscal Studies.

TAX REFORM

In the area of tax reform, Thatcherism had a much more decisive effect. During the "iron lady's" years in office the top rates of income taxation fell very sharply, while those at the bottom of the scale remained largely unchanged and at times increased. Table 19.5 shows the change in tax rates on earned income over an 18-year period. Earned income is defined as income from labor activities and this table does not show the rates levied on unearned income, consisting of dividends, interest, and capital gains. Before Thatcher came to power, rates rose progressively to a top rate on earned income of 83 percent, and the rate on unearned income was as high as 98 percent. By 1989, there were only two applicable rates, 25 percent and 40 percent, and the distinction between earned and unearned income had been eliminated. Subsequently in 1992 a new lower rate of 20 percent was introduced. The shortfall in revenue caused by lower rates was bridged by the revenue from the sale of nationalized corporations.

Equally sweeping were Thatcher's reforms of local government finance. Local government revenues in Britain had originated largely from the "rates," taxes on real property, which were moderately progressive since wealthier families had larger and more valuable homes. Thatcher substituted a more regressive system, officially called the community charge, but universally referred to as the poll tax, the base of which was the number of adults resident within a dwelling. In the eyes of the Conservative government this reflected the pattern of expenditures by local government and changed the foundation of the system from one of redistribution to one of payment for benefit. Popular resistance to the poll tax was extremely strong, and it was abandoned in 1993 in favor of the less regressive "council tax."

REFORM OF TRADE UNIONS

Until 1979 trade unions were a major force in the labor markets and British politics. As many as 13.2 million workers belonged to unions, which were regarded as bargaining agents by two-thirds of employees. Moreover, the unions had very close links to the Labour Party, which had held power for 10 of the previous 15 years. The 1970s had been particularly turbulent with a great deal of strike activity. Thatcher's philosophy deviated from normal European consensus politics

■ TABLE 19.6

DAYS LOST PER 1,000 EMPLOYEES: SELECTED INDUSTRIAL NATIONS, 1970–1993

	1970–1979	1980–1984	1985–1989	1989–1993
United Kingdom	570	480	180	70
United States	na	160	90	200
France	210	90	60	90
Germany	40	50	na	30
Italy	1,310	950	300	360

Note: na = Less than five days per 1,000 employees.

SOURCE: *Employment Gazette* (December 1990, 1994).

because she did not consider the trade unions to be **social partners** on the model of Sweden or Germany, to be cooperated with and given a legitimate voice in economic policy. Rather she regarded unions as an enemy to be confronted and, where possible, smashed. She enjoyed considerable success in this crusade and fundamentally changed the nature of British labor markets.

A series of laws on industrial relations progressively encroached on union power. The right of unions to automatic recognition by employers was curbed. Secondary picketing (demonstrations by workers not directly involved in a dispute) was outlawed. Secret ballots were required before strike action could be taken, and union leadership was limited to finite lengths of service. In 1984 the government emerged victorious in a confrontation over pay and mine closures with the once-powerful National Union of Mineworkers, a decisive victory that shaped future British workplace relations.

Not all of the decline in union power could be directly traced to Conservative legislation. Britain was experiencing the same economic changes that eroded the power of unions elsewhere, and traditional bastions of union power were in decline because of falling demand and competition from abroad. The power of the mineworkers' union once came from the fact that coal had a near monopoly on energy supply in the United Kingdom. Growing use of oil and gas, much of it from the North Sea fields, cut into coal's traditional role. Road travel overtook rail and diminished the power of the railway workers. The British auto industry was in rapid decline in the face of competition from Europe and Japan, and once militant autoworkers had to fear for their jobs. Furthermore, the growing smaller high-tech enterprises were less unionized than the older factory environment, and service trades were less fertile breeding grounds of union organization than the old factories. Only in the civil service was unionization on the rise.

For this variety of causes, the climate of British industrial relations became more placid under Margaret Thatcher. As Table 19.6 shows, in the 1970s and early 1980s British strike activity was very high relative to other economies. By the beginning of the 1990s the British record is close to that of its West European partners and considerably better than that of the United States.

■ **TABLE 19.7**

REAL GDP GROWTH

	Average 1970–1980	Average 1980–1990	Average 1990–1998
United States	3.1	2.90	2.35
Japan	4.4	4.00	1.45
Germany	2.7	2.24	2.09
France	3.3	2.36	1.54
United Kingdom	1.9	2.67	1.71
G7 average	3.3	2.93	1.96
OECD average	3.6	3.02	2.18

SOURCE: *OECD Economic Outlook* (June 1998), Annex-225.

THE LESSONS OF THATCHERISM

The 1980s certainly represented a sea change in the performance of the British economy. From being the perennial underperformer among G7 nations, Britain now comes close to the top of the tree in terms of economic growth (see Table 19.7). The same improvement may be seen in the change of other measures. Labor productivity in manufacturing, for example, has shown the sharpest growth. Britain went from the bottom of the league in the 1970s to the top in the 1980s and 1990s. So it is fair to say that "something" happened. In the words of *The Economist*:

> [The] figures accord with the voluminous, albeit unsystematic, testimony of factory floor anecdote. Almost anybody who works in one will say that Britain's factories and offices are very much better run and very much more productive than they were in the late 1970s—and many will say that the change since then has been revolutionary rather than evolutionary.[17]

To some extent the rapid increase in manufacturing productivity is a statistical artifact. Many factories closed in the 1980s, and they were in general ones with a poor productivity record, and their closure necessarily raised the average among the remainder. However, Britain has subsequently grown to take up some of the slack. Her unemployment rate is now among the lowest in Europe, implying that displaced low-productivity workers have managed to find new jobs. Even the broadest economic aggregate, the rate of growth of real gross domestic product (Table 19.7), shows a distinct shift between the 1970s and the 1980s. In the 1970s, Britain experienced the lowest growth among the G7 countries, barely 58 percent of the average. Across the 1980s and 1990s the country has managed almost 90 percent of the average, although much of this has been due to slower growth among the other industrial countries rather than accelerated growth in Britain.

---

[17] "Britain's New Politics" *The Economist*, 21 September 1996, 7.

GROWTH IN GDP AND CHANGE IN GINI COEFFICIENT, G6 ECONOMIES 1980–1991

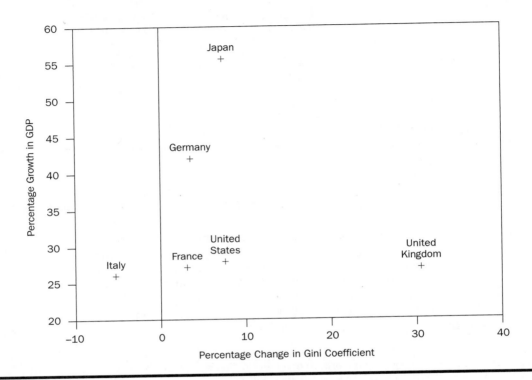

SOURCE: OECD.

Accelerating growth in Britain has been accompanied by rising inequality. Figure 19.1 plots the relationship of growth of GDP and the change in the Gini coefficient for household income between 1980 and 1991 and shows that inequality in Britain increased much more than in comparable countries. In fact, within the OECD only New Zealand showed a similar increase in the growth of inequality. The rise in inequality in Britain was much greater than in the United States, although the growth rates of the two economies were very close and the Reagan years are usually thought of as a time when income distribution became more polarized in the United States.

The question remains whether the British experience of privatization offers important lessons for economies in transition, both those that are reforming a European-style social democracy and those that are attempting to move from a command planning system to a market-based economy.

1. The British experience suggests that it is managerial culture, rather than the issue of ownership that is important in determining productivity, and gains can be achieved without privatization. A counterargument suggests that

industries that remain in public hands will inevitably be burdened with nonmarket objectives and nurtured on public subsidy—and the soft-budget constraint would ultimately have resurfaced. One measurable aspect of the Thatcher program is that prior to privatization an average citizen of the United Kingdom paid some £300 to subsidize state-owned industry; today the net taxes paid by the recently privatized firms amount to £100 per person.

2. Legislation curbing the power of the labor unions, coupled with sectoral shifts and changes in technology, has resulted in a much more flexible labor market. One consequence of this is lower unemployment, but another is rising inequality in the distribution of income.

3. When privatized industries are natural monopolies, regulation will be required to protect the public interest. Therefore some of the benefits of increased productive efficiency that could result from privatization might be countervailed by a decrease in allocative efficiency and by the administrative costs of regulation.

4. In the British case, privatization resulted in substantial short-term gains to public revenues that facilitated tax reform. Nevertheless, revenues from sales in most of the former centrally planned economies have been very small.

KEY TERMS AND CONCEPTS

Chadwick-Demsetz auction

corporate culture

franchising

golden share

initial public offering (IPO)

management buyout

popular capitalism

quasi-markets

RPI-X

social partners

stagflation

Thatcherism

welfare state

QUESTIONS FOR DISCUSSION

1. What were the possible economic causes of Britain's malaise in the 1970s?

2. What were the objectives of the privatization drive of Margaret Thatcher's government?

3. Did privatization have a demonstrable effect on efficiency? What was the role of corporate culture?

4. What was the impact of privatization on workers' and executive pay?

5. How was the trade union movement reformed under Thatcher?

6. Was perceptible progress made on either reducing government expenditure or changing the tax code?

RESOURCES

WEB SITES

All British Government Sites Homepage (searchable) ...... http://www.open.gov.uk /

Bank of England .... http://www.bankofengland.co.uk/

Competition Commission .... http://www.mmc.gov.uk/

Department of Trade and Industry .... http://www.dti.gov.uk/

Her Majesty's Treasury .... http://www.hm-treasury.gov.uk/

The Stationery Office .... http://www.tso-online.co.uk/

Office of Telecommunications Regulation .... http://www.oftel.org/

Office of the Rail Regulator .... http://www.rail-reg.gov.uk/

Office of Gas and Electricity Regulation ...... http://www.open.gov.uk/offer/offer.htm

BOOKS AND ARTICLES

Ball, James. *The British Economy at the Crossroads*. London: Financial Times–Pitman Publishing, 1998.

Bishop, Matthew, John Kay, and Colin Mayer, eds. *Privatization and Economic Performance*. Oxford: Oxford University Press, 1994.

Bos, Dieter. *Privatization: A Theoretical Treatment*. Oxford: Oxford University Press, 1991. Reviewed in *Journal of Comparative Economics*, October 1994, 281.

Buxton, Tony, Paul Chapman, and Paul Temple, eds. *Britain's Economic Performance*. 2d ed. New York: Routledge, 1998.

Cairncross, Alec. *The British Economy Since 1945: Economic Policy and Performance, 1945–1995 (Making Contemporary Britain Series)*. Cambridge, Mass.: Blackwell, 1995.

Collier, Irwin, Herwig Roggemann, Oliver Scholz, and Horst Tomann. *Welfare States in Transition: East and West (Studies in Economic Transition)*. New York: St. Martin's Press, 1999.

Cook, Paul, ed., and Colin Kirkpatrick. *Privatisation Policy and Performance: International Perspectives*. London: Harvester Wheatsheaf, 1996.

Crafts, N.F.R., and Nicholas Woodward, eds. *The British Economy Since 1945*. New York: Oxford University Press, 1991.

Foster, Christopher D. *Privatization, Public Ownership and the Regulation of Natural Monopoly*. Oxford: Blackwell, 1992.

Hetzner, Candace. *The Unfinished Business of Thatcherism : The Values of the Enterprise Culture*. Vol. 46, *American University Studies X: Political Science*. Bern Switzerland: Peter Lang, 1999.

"How to Privatize: What the Rest of the World Can Learn from the Unpopularity of Privatisation in Britain." *The Economist*, 11 March 1995, 16–17.

Kiekeri, Sunita, John Nellis, and Mary Shirley. "Privatization: Lessons from Market Economies." *The World Bank Research Observer,* July 1994, 241–272.

Kramnick, Isaac, ed. *Is Britain Dying? Perspectives on the Current Crisis.* Ithaca, N.Y.: Cornell University Press, 1979.

Marsh, David. *The New Politics of British Trade Unionism: Union Power and the Thatcher Legacy.* Ithaca, N.Y.: ILR Press, 1992.

Martin, Stephen, and David Parker. *The Impact of Privatisation: Ownership and Corporate Performance in the UK (Industrial Economic Strategies for Europe).* London: Routledge, 1997.

Mayer, Colin, and Tim Jenkinson. "The Privatisation Process in France and the U.K." *European Economic Review,* March 1988, 382–391.

"The Mother of Privatisation: Sell-off of Britain's State Industries." (editorial). *The Economist,* 16 September 1989, 15–16.

Pryke, Richard. *Nationalized Industries: Policy and Performance since 1968.* Oxford: Robert Martin, 1981.

Pryke, Richard. *Public Enterprise in Practice.* London: MacGibbon and Kee, 1971.

Pulkingham, Jane. "From Public Provisions to Privatisation: The Crisis in Welfare Reassessed." *Sociology,* August 1989, 387–407.

Swann, Dennis. *The Retreat of the State: Deregulation and Privatization in the UK and US.* Ann Arbor: University of Michigan Press, 1988.

Turner, Royce Logan, ed. *The British Economy in Transition: From the Old to the New?* New York: Routledge, 1995.

Vickers, John, and George Yarrow. *Privatization: An Economic Analysis.* Cambridge, Mass.: MIT Press.

20

THE REUNIFICATION OF GERMANY

THE GERMAN TRANSFORMATION

The last years of the 1980s saw the collapse of Soviet-style planning throughout Eastern Europe and movement toward a market economy. From the outset it was clear that most socialist economies faced considerable difficulty in moving to a market system and integrating into the world economy,[1] but East Germany was seen by most as having the best chance of a smooth transition. However, more than a decade after the fall of the Berlin Wall, the economy of eastern Germany remains in the doldrums. In the spring of 1998, unemployment in the 'New Federal States' amounted to 1,405,000, and a further 305,000 were only working as a result of federally financed job creation schemes. (Another 350,000 commuted daily to work in the former Federal Republic of Germany [FRG].) Conventional measures of unemployment put the eastern German rate at about 19 percent, more than twice the 9.1 percent of western Germany. If adjustment is made for the make-work programs, the rate was closer to 23 percent.

A **catching-up process** had been anticipated at the fall of the Wall, and there was some evidence of this for the first five years after reunification, when output in the east rose and unemployment actually fell from the level immediately after reunification. In 1995, however, the process began to stall, and by 1998 a working party of the German Economic Research Institutes concluded that

> the 'catching up' process in East Germany rapidly ground to a halt [after 1995]. In 1996 the rate of growth of the new federal states was, at just under 2 percent, still marginally higher than in West Germany; already by 1997 it was lagging behind the West German result at just 1.6 percent, and no fundamental change can be expected either in the current or the coming year. In per capita terms, nominal value added in East Germany remains at less than 57 percent of the West German level. Productivity has so far risen to only 60 percent of the West German level. Labor costs per employee in the current year represent just under 75 percent of the average figure paid in West Germany.[2]

Given the high hopes for the East German economy at the outset of reunification, these developments raise fundamental issues about the process of economic

---

[1] However, in many quarters there was a great deal of optimism about the speed and completeness of transition. For example, in Russia a well-known report by academician S. Shatalin was titled '500 Days to a Market Economy.'

[2] German Economic Research Institute, 'The German Economy in the Spring of 1998.' Accessible at http://Smith.diw.de/

transformation and lessons learned from the German experience be applied to other nations further to the east.

THE EAST GERMAN PERFORMANCE UNDER COMMUNISM

In the context of the Soviet bloc, the German Democratic Republic (GDR) was a very successful economy. Living standards were above any other centrally planned state, and productivity in industry and agriculture was believed to be the highest in the Soviet bloc. Estimates of income per head are generally unreliable for centrally planned economies, but, as shown by Table 20.1, in 1989 the United Nations put real purchasing power parity income per head in the GDR at about $8,000 per annum. This was some 25 percent above that of the Soviet Union, roughly comparable to Ireland and Spain, and higher than either Portugal or Greece, though considerably below the $14,730 recorded for West Germany. The GDR also stood up very well on many other measures, particularly basic indicators of social well-being. In educational attainment, life expectancy, and infant mortality, East Germany performed as well as many of the Western industrialized economies. In addition, its distribution of income was considerably more uniform than that in the West,[3] usually considered a positive feature of an economic system.

These achievements are especially impressive in the light of East Germany's late start on postwar recovery relative to the West. As early as 1948 the Marshall plan led to a sharp injection of funds into the Federal Republic, with a salutary impact on growth, but at the same time in the East the Soviet Union was hindering recovery in the GDR by removing plant and equipment as part of a scheme of war reparation. The strong performance in the face of handicaps led supporters of central planning to see the East German experience as a positive model of the potential of socialism, but it was hard to discount the persistently unfavorable comparison of material standards between East and West Germany. The physical division of Berlin by the Wall (built to prevent population from escaping to the West) and the obviously greater prosperity of the FRG were persistent problems. Moreover, the accessibility of information from the West was a factor in maintaining discontent in the East.

POLITICAL AND ECONOMIC UNIFICATION

After the fall of the Wall, the reunification of Germany took place in two steps. On July 1, 1990, a **monetary, economic, and social union** took effect, followed on October 3 by a political union. The decisive features of the economic and social union were the following:

---

[3] Andrew Zimbalist, Howard Sherman, and Stuart Brown, *Comparing Economic Systems: A Political Economic Approach* (Orlando, Fla.: Academic Press, 1984), 469.

■ TABLE 20.1

GNP PER HEAD FOR SELECTED SOCIALIST COUNTRIES, 1987 $PPP

GDR	8,000
Czech Republic	7,750
Soviet Union	6,000
Yugoslavia	5,000
Bulgaria	4,750
Hungary	4,500
Poland	4,000

SOURCE: *Human Development Report,* United Nations Development Programme (New York: Oxford University Press, 1990).

- The adoption of a 1:1 exchange rate between the East German mark (the Ostmark) and the Deutschmark for all wages, prices, pensions, and so on
- The conversion of most monetary assets at a rate of 2:1, except for a quota of personal savings, which was converted at 1:1
- The creation of a common legal and regulatory environment based on West German laws
- The introduction of the main features of the West German social market economy, including collective wage negotiation, extensive social insurance, and active worker involvement in company management

EAST GERMANY'S ADVANTAGES

Hopes for a seamless and rapid transition were high and rested mainly on two factors. The first was the apparent strength of the East German economy, with higher productivity and greater efficiency than any other centrally planned state, while the second was the belief that a 'merger' with an existing, strong, developed economy would be easier than 'going it alone,' which would have to be the case in Russia and the other former socialist states. In fact *The Economist* trumpeted reunification as 'the largest leveraged buyout in history.' That the East German transition was far from smooth despite these advantages gives a perspective on the immense difficulties faced by other nations in transition.[4]

LEGAL STRUCTURE AND ACCOUNTING PRACTICE

From the moment the economic and monetary unification pact was signed, eastern Germany had in place a legal and regulatory structure covering most aspects of

---

[4]Total and immediate integration with the former West Germany did present some problems to East Germany as we will see. Other states were able to protect industries in transition with trade barriers and to use currency valuation changes to absorb external shocks.

business and commerce. While the absence of enforceable contracts and a consistent code of bankruptcy law presented enormous problems for business development and deterred investment in other formerly planned states, in Germany there was a universal commercial code. In addition, the new federal states of Germany had the advantage of a regulatory system designed to tackle market failure due to monopoly and environmental degradation. A further advantage lay in the existence of an established accounting system; admittedly it would take time for the East German enterprises to adopt different accounting standards, but the model was in place with a pool of skilled workers speaking the same language available to apply it.

FINANCE

Considerable advantages were also present in finance. While other transition countries had to grow a modern banking sector from the bottom up, in Germany the sophisticated system of the federal republic simply expanded eastward as banks opened branches in the new federal states. Moreover, newly privatized or startup companies in the east had access to the financial institutions and the savings of the west.

SUPPLY OF ENTREPRENEURSHIP

In the transition from a socialized system to a market structure, entrepreneurship and management skills are often the factors in shortest supply. This constraint was less binding on East Germany since an inflow of qualified personnel from the west could fill almost any gap, a process encouraged by the techniques chosen by the privatization agency, as we shall see later.

ACCESS TO MARKETS

The fall of communism brought with it the end of the Soviet-sponsored international trade organization, the Council for Mutual Economic Assistance (CMEA), and this resulted in the loss of traditional export markets as managed trade between the socialist nations collapsed. While other transitional economies had to fight for access to markets in developed countries, firms in East Germany had immediate and unimpeded entry not only into the West German market of 80 million consumers, but also the larger European Union (EU) market of 350 million of the world's richest customers.

INFRASTRUCTURE

Not the least of East Germany's advantages was the willingness of the federal government to pour resources into eastern Germany's social and economic fabric. As in other planned economies, infastructure had suffered under socialism. Roads, a prime example, were both underprovided and badly maintained; communications

TRANSFERS FROM WEST TO EAST GERMANY, 1992–1995 (DM MILLION)

	1992	1993	1994	1995
Financial transfers to state and local government	121.9	138.5	132.4	163.5
German Unity Fund	36.1	36.4	35.8	—
Central government spending arising out of unification (net)	74.4	90.7	85.7	114.5
Redistribution of VAT-receipts among federal states	11.5	11.4	10.8	—
New system of inter-state financial compensation	—	—	—	49
Transfers to the social insurance institutions	29.1	23.9	33.2	32
Transfers from West to East German unemployment insurance	24.6	15.1	19.3	18
Transfers from west to east pension insurance	4.5	8.8	13.9	14
Total financial transfers	**151**	**162.4**	**165.6**	**195.5**
Memo item				
Borrowing by the Treuhandanstalt	29.6	38.1	37.1	—

SOURCE: Deutsches Institut für Wirtschaftsforschung, 'The German Economy in the Spring of 1995.' Accessible at the DIW Web page: http://Smith.diw.de/

technology was out of date; the environment had been badly abused; and housing was in short supply. Eastern Germany was fortunate that the federal German government was prepared to close the gap and provide the basis for sustained growth. In addition, rising infrastructural investment had a strong and positive macro-economic impact that partially compensated for the fall of demand caused by the dislocation of trade.

A SOCIAL SAFETY NET

The provisions of the monetary and economic union extended West Germany's comprehensive **social safety net** to East Germany. A common feature of the economies of all former socialist nations in the early stages of transition was a collapse of output in the manufacturing and industrial sectors. Fear of the social unrest that might result put pressure on governments to maintain employment in existing enterprises through subsidies and delayed industrial restructuring. East Germany had the luxury of being able to support high unemployment and early retirement, without real fear of either extreme poverty or social unrest.

The willingness and ability of the West German government to finance the social expenses associated with transition should not be underestimated. As Table 20.2 shows, transfers to East Germany amounted, in 1993, to some 162 billion DM,[5] roughly $100 billion at current values. This total does not include monies paid out by the EU under the social fund, nor does it make allowance for the

[5] Heiner Flassbeck and Gustav Horn put the figure at DM 170 billion. See 'German Unification: An Example for Korea?' (Brookfield, UE: Dartmouth, 1996), 192.

subsidized interest rates for investment in the new federal states. Total annual transfers have increased steadily, and by 1998 the cumulative value of the transfers from West to East Germany amounted to more than $1 trillion. Compared to this total, the amounts lent by the multilateral funding agencies to other nations are tiny, and no other economy in transition can anticipate the level of fiscal support received by East Germany.

CHOICE OF EXCHANGE RATES

One of the most heated controversies concerning the union of East and West Germany concerned the choice of exchange rate, a decision that involved both economic and political considerations. Clearly the West German D-mark was much stronger than the East German Ostmark, but by precisely how much was difficult to determine because of the Ostmark's controlled convertibility. One index was the price of the D-mark on the black market, about 12 Ostmarks per D-mark. Another measure was the rate implicit in the pricing of East German goods on world markets. The rate implied by the price structure of GDR exports to West Germany averaged 4.4 Ostmarks per D-mark. On this evidence an appropriate policy should have been to value the Ostmark well below the D-mark, perhaps 4 or 5 Ostmarks per D-mark. However, political pressures favored parity, largely because wages were lower in the east than the west even when expressed in terms of their respective currencies. The onset of economic reunification would immediately lead to West German prices being common to both economies, and if the Ostmark was valued at a fraction of the D-mark, living standards in the east would fall at a stroke, not an auspicious start for a political union.

Ultimately a compromise was adopted in which all current payments were converted at a 1:1 rate, while a higher rate was used for capital accounts. For example, if a pensioner was receiving a monthly pension of 1,000 Ostmarks, then she or he would receive in the future 1,000 D-marks. The same was true for wages, stipends, and rental agreements. However, financial assets were converted at the more realistic rate of 2:1, with the exception of a limited amount of savings per individual, which was allowed as a concession at a 1:1 rate. The overall average for the consolidated balance sheet of financial institutions was roughly 1.8:1.

THE CONSEQUENCES OF PARITY

While the political considerations mandated the 1:1 current rate, the economic consequences of its adoption were close to catastrophic. As we can see from Table 20.3, the 1:1 rate made labor in East Germany very expensive. Wages in East German industry were about 47 percent of those in western Germany, while productivity was only around 31 percent of the West German level. Hence unit labor costs were

■ **TABLE 20.3**

**LABOR PRODUCTIVITY AND WAGE COST: EAST GERMAN STATISTICS
AS A PERCENTAGE OF WEST GERMAN TOTALS**

	Gross Wage and Salary Income per Employee	Labor Productivity	Unit Labor Costs
1991	46.7	31.0	150.6
1992	60.7	43.5	139.4
1993	67.9	53.1	128.0
1994	70.5	56.0	126.0
1995	72.5	57.8	125.6
1996	73.6	59.4	123.9
1997	74.3	60.4	123.1
1998	74.8	61.0	122.7
1999	74.7	61.2	122.2

SOURCE: Deutsches Institut für Wirtschaftsforschung, 'The German Economy in the Spring of 1998.' Accessible at the DIW Web page: http://Smith.diw.de/

about 50 percent higher than in the west.[6] The immediate consequence was that goods made in the east were too expensive to find a market, either in Western Europe, or in eastern Germany itself.

Prior to the collapse of the planned Soviet-bloc trading system, the economy of the GDR was highly export oriented, sending relatively sophisticated goods throughout Eastern Europe. These markets evaporated with the dissolution of planned trade, while the high unit cost of East German labor made the capture of markets in the west an impossibility. Meanwhile, West German goods flooded into the east, and the domestic demand for goods produced in eastern Germany itself collapsed. A second effect of the exchange-rate compromise was on the balance sheets of enterprises and banks, with financial institutions being hit very hard. A substantial part of their assets was converted at the 2:1 rate, while the bulk of liabilities were converted at 1:1, meaning that, expressed in D-marks, liabilities were greater than assets. The choice of the 1:1 exchange rate for current transaction bore much of the blame for the initial output collapse in eastern Germany. No doubt a lower rate for the East German mark might have maintained the competitiveness of some of eastern Germany's production, in the short term at least; however, much of the problem stemmed from a failure to appreciate at the time of unification the size of the productivity differential between east and west. It was expected that some 70 percent of eastern German companies would make losses as a result of the 1:1 exchange rate and that 30 percent would actually be in acute danger of going

[6]Unit labor costs are computed by dividing wages by productivity.

bankrupt. In reality, some 90 percent of all of eastern Germany's enterprises were threatened with bankruptcy.[7]

THE STRUCTURE OF INDUSTRY IN THE GDR

In common with their colleagues in other planned economies, the planners and technocrats of the GDR had placed a lot of faith in economies of scale, and East German enterprises were large as a result. About two-thirds of the workforce was employed in firms of more than 1,000 workers, a much higher proportion than in western industrial economies. Furthermore, more than 50 percent worked in firms having a payroll of more than 2,500. On top of this, East German firms were organized into groups known as combines **(Kombinate),** which integrated and controlled their activities. Immediately before reunification East German industry was divided among a total of 221 combines, which together accounted for almost all output. While the intent of the combines was to coordinate production and avoid duplication, in time many came to resemble diversified holding companies. They had considerable monopoly power and, although subject to some planning control, tended to impose high prices and pay inadequate attention to efficiency and quality.

In June of 1990, immediately prior to the economic and social union, all of East Germany's industrial assets were put into the hands of a 'trust agency,' the **Treuhandanstalt (THA).** The task of the THA was to oversee the disposition of some 8,500 state enterprises, a broad swath of retail activity, as well as extensive holdings of agricultural land and forest. Though based in Berlin, the THA was staffed predominantly by West Germans and had 15 regional offices in eastern Germany empowered to dispose of enterprises of fewer than 1,500 persons.

The mandate given to the THA was to reduce the commercial activity of the state, restructure state-owned industrial enterprises, and pass those enterprises into the private sector. The main issues for the THA were how fast it should dispose of its massive portfolio of assets and how much reorganization to attempt before sale. One possible model was to undertake a comprehensive restructuring of the entire economy prior to privatization and to rationalize enterprises to conform to that structure while holding them in public ownership. However, the THA considered that such a policy was beyond its powers, resources, and expertise. A second, more modest approach was to keep the firms under THA ownership long enough to achieve substantial restructuring on a firm-by-firm basis. Again, that would have required a great deal of management time, considerable investment,

---

[7]Martin Myant et alia, *Successful Transformations?: The Creation of Market Economies in Eastern Germany and the Czech Republic* (Brookfield, Vt.: Edward Elgar, 1996), 50.

and the THA would have had to endure accusations from firms in the west of unfair competition from East German enterprises operating under state subsidy.

Ultimately the THA chose to go with a strategy of speedy privatization. It adopted a slogan best translated as 'rapid privatization, resolute restructuring, and cautious closure' but gave primacy to speedy divestment. This was largely because it had more confidence in the market's power than its own expertise to restructure enterprises. Although the expenses of maintaining an enterprise while it was within the portfolio of the THA were regarded as a necessary evil, investment in firms during THA stewardship was kept to a minimum.

The policy precluding substantial investment in new plant or equipment was of particular importance as it became clearer that the existing capital stock in East Germany was physically rundown. The Federal Statistical Office estimated that in 1991 roughly 55 percent of fixed assets in manufacturing inherited from the GDR (and 75 percent of the plant and equipment) were no longer useful. Because of its condition and because much equipment had been used to produce goods for Eastern Europe that were not in demand in the west, the assets of the firms to be privatized were worth much less than had originally been thought. Each firm held by the THA had to make strategic choices for the future, pare back its operations, and position itself for restructuring. However, the THA policy was hands off in terms of management, and the THA would only make limited investments that were investor neutral. As Martin Myant put it:

> In other words decisions on basic changes in production profiles and technology were to be left to the future owners. Thus, for a long time these companies were not allowed to invest in technological changes, even though reorientation in the market demanded just this. This was a particularly severe handicap when set in the context of the collapse of exports to the east, the shrinking domestic sales and the rapidly rising wage levels.[8]

THE STRATEGY OF PRIVATIZATION

The agency decided that 'the best way of achieving urgently needed rehabilitation in most companies [was] by gaining a new, business-oriented owner, able to bring management skills, technology, markets, and new product.'[9] This ruled out voucher privatization, which though it would involve a change of ownership, would not result in a change in management or inflow of capital. Initial public offerings (IPOs) used as the primary vehicle in the United Kingdom were not possible either; they provide no injection of cash for the firm (the revenues go to the government) and management is initially unchanged. Before IPOs are presented, potential buyers need time to appropriately evaluate the firm, and this would slow the process. Moreover, the sale of all or even a substantial part of the East German capital stock would have put a great deal of pressure on Germany's capital markets. After eliminating voucher auctions and IPOs, the remaining potential strategies were auction

---

[8]Myant, 55.
[9]Myant, 55.

sales for cash among competing bidders and negotiated sales to specific purchasers, which was the means actually chosen. Generally speaking, the buyers were companies or investment groups from outside of eastern Germany, although in some cases a sale to management was possible if appropriate assurances about finance and technological capability were forthcoming.

Its reliance on negotiated sales gave the THA a high degree of discretion, which became a source of considerable criticism. Political interests came to play a large part in the disposition of assets, but since the economic well-being of whole regions often depended on the fate of single enterprises, political lobbying was inevitable and to some extent desirable. Of more concern were accusations that West German competitors of East German firms influenced the disposal of assets and that THA employees and associates profited through corruption.

Despite the degree of latitude granted to the agency, privatization of large East German ventures proved difficult. In many cases the aging capital stock, poor product line, and low labor productivity demanded the immediate closure of the firm. Better quality and lower cost substitutes for East German products were freely available from West Germany very shortly after the start of the reunification process, and consequently demand for East German goods fell precipitously. In some cases, the THA did grasp the nettle and make immediate closures, including Trabant, the leading automobile manufacturer. Analysis of the real costs of production indicated that each underpowered two-stroke vehicle cost roughly $11,000 to produce and at best might sell for $7,000 after extensive modifications to meet environmental standards. Consequently, the Trabant factory in Zwickau was closed, though generous subsidies from the state government induced the establishment of a Volkswagen factory to employ many of the Trabant workforce.

Table 20.4 gives some statistics on the record of the THA. By September of 1993 it had processed some 13,241 firms and had fully or partially privatized about 12,000 of them.[10] In revenue terms the privatization program was a great disappointment; close to the end of the program in 1993 only some DM 44.7 billion had been raised through asset sales, about one-fourth of the annual transfer payments to East Germany. The idea of the union as a profitable leveraged buyout suggested by *The Economist* is discredited. Moreover, disappointingly few purchases involved foreign buyers, with only DM 5.3 billion coming from purchasers outside of Germany.

Table 20.4 also shows the rapid fall of industrial employment in eastern Germany. At the outset of the privatization process, 2,937,000 employees worked in companies controlled by the Treuhandanstalt. By September of 1993 this group of companies employed only 1,177,000 persons (40 percent of the original). More than 1¾ million workers lost their jobs in closures and restructuring orchestrated by the THA. As part of its negotiations the THA tried to get commitments from new management about investments to be made in the enterprises and the levels of

---

[10] The number of firms in its portfolio continued to grow throughout the period of privatization because enterprises were divided in order to dispense of them.

■ **TABLE 20.4**

CHANGE OF STATUS IN STOCK OF COMPANIES HELD BY THE TREUHANDANSTALT, 1991–1993

	January 1991		December 1991		December 1992		September 1993	
	Absolute	%	Absolute	%	Absolute	%	Absolute	%
Total portfolio of TH companies	**8489**	100	10,970	100	12,599	100	13,241	100
Dissolutions/liquidations	120	1.4	1,014	9.2	2,534	20.1	3,374	25.5
Fully/partially privatized	574	6.8	2,996	27.3	5,456	43.4	5,998	45.3
Memo item:								
operating units privatized			(1,895)		(5,258)		(6,823)	
Fully reprivatized	107	1.3	527	4.8	1,188	9.4	1,511	11.4
Fully municipalized	40	0.5	145	1.3	253	2	259	2
Others			160	1.5	593	4.7	854	6.4
Awaiting privatization (net holdings)	7648	90	6,128	55.9	2,575	20.4	1,254	9.4
Sales revenue in billion DM					40.1		44.7	
From foreigners							5.3	
Investment commitments in billion DM	44.5		114.2		169.5		182.4	
From foreigners					17		19.9	
Employment commitments in units of 1,000	255		930		1,401		1,493	
From foreigners					121		145	
Employees in units of 1,000								
In TH companies	2,937		1,372		408		213	
In ex-TH companies			285		1,047		964	
Total employees	2,937		1,657		1,455		1,177	

SOURCE: Heiner Flassbeck and Gustav Horn, *German Unification: An Example for Korea?* (Brookfield: Dartmouth, 1996), 121

employment to be achieved. Table 20.4 gives total commitments for employment of 1,493,000, but this proved too optimistic and was well above the level actually employed in 1993, which was 1,122,000. The THA had little power to hold a purchaser to its pledges on either labor use or capital injection.

The THA's problems were magnified by a recession that gripped Western Europe. Spare capacity in the west, a reluctance of management to move east, and opposition from West German unions to the 'export' of jobs to the new federal states limited interest in East German industry, and the THA strategy of finding western buyers to modernize East German industry stalled. Meanwhile, resistance to seek the views of existing management and the preference given to sales to western buyers over potential management 'buyouts' led to resentment in the east. As time went on the problems the THA was having in disposing rapidly of its assets allowed potential buyers to become increasingly selective. Since interest was scarce, they felt they could improve the terms of purchase by delaying. The THA, anxious to complete its task and sensitive about criticism of growing unemployment, felt obliged to dispose of its assets on terms increasingly favorable to the buyers.

THE IMPACT OF REUNIFICATION ON SOCIAL CONSENSUS WITHIN GERMANY

Despite the high expectations that greeted the fall of the Berlin Wall, by the mid-1990s both West and East Germans were disenchanted by the outcome. Westerners (Wessis) resented the increase in taxes and interest rates required to keep the East German economy afloat, while Easterners (Ossis) bemoaned the collapse of the indigenous economy, the reduction of benefits (which had included free day care and subsidized vacation), and the movement into East Germany of West German officials and 'carpet-bagging' businesspeople.

The catching-up process has now been stalled for over five years. By 1995 productivity in the east had risen to about 60 percent of the level in the west, an impressive achievement, but one due mostly to the collapse of the enterprises with lowest productivity. Removing those workers from the totals raised the average quite quickly, but at the cost of massive unemployment. To further raise productivity to the western levels is much more difficult from this point since it involves increasing the efficiency of workers now on the job. If West German labor productivity increases at an annual rate of 2 percent (quite modest by historical standards), productivity in East Germany will have to grow at over 7 percent per annum if it is to catch up even by 2010, a date that seems impossibly far into the future. One of the difficulties in transition states has been the expectation that living standards can adjust to western levels in short periods of time. These hopes are inevitably disappointed, and social and political pressures increase.

The changes following the fall of the Wall irreversibly altered the East German economic system but also raised the possibility that the strains of unification could destroy the West German system too. West Germany is regarded by its citizens as a **social market economy**.[11] Most of the capital is privately owned and coordination relies primarily on market principles. The 'social' aspect, however, involves subjecting the market to regulation to ensure that the 'impersonal working of the market does not interfere with or undermine basic social needs, ranging from adequate income and health care, to organized representation in the workplace, to comprehensive vocational training.'[12]

The inclusion of eastern Germany has put pressure on a 'German model' already somewhat beleaguered by global competition, recession, and rising unemployment. Whereas convergence seemed a likely outcome in 1989, today many think in terms of a **mezzogiorno scenario,** a reference to the income and productivity

[11] See chapter 18.

[12] Lowell Turner, ed., *Negotiating the New Germany* (Ithaca: ILR Press, 1997), 3.

differential between northern and southern Italy.[13] In that case wide regional differences have persisted despite relatively easy labor and capital mobility and persistent government policy aimed at closing the gap.

LESSONS FROM THE GERMAN UNIFICATION

Although Germany was a special case, there are lessons to be learned from its experience that might inform policy in other transition economies.

(1) Currency Valuation

Some of East Germany's problems were caused by an overvalued currency since political considerations forced parity between the D-mark and the Ostmark. Other economies have more latitude and should balance carefully the role of a low currency value in assisting export- and import-substituting industries against the benefits of a highly valued currency in keeping inflation in check.

(2) Privatization

One of the desirable features of any privatization scheme should be the establishment of a sense of equity. East Germans saw most of their capital stock given away or sold to West Germans at what seemed to be very low prices. In return they got access to the federal social safety net, but this did not fully assuage the feeling of dispossession. Some greater involvement of the citizens in the share capital of the privatized enterprises might have strengthened social solidarity.

(3) Market Restructuring versus Planned Restructuring

In Germany reliance was put on the market as the agent of change, and neither the privatization agency nor the government developed a clear blueprint of industrial structure after liberalization. Moreover, internal restructuring of firms was performed only on the very limited basis necessary to facilitate a sale. In the disorderly conditions of an economic and political transition, markets may not perform optimally and a more active governmental role in both macro- and micro-restructuring might ease the process.

(4) The Time Frame

German unification represented the ultimate in 'Big Bangs,' since almost in an instant discretionary tools of economic policy were swept away. The exchange rate

---

[13]See Andrea Boltho and Carlin Wendy, 'Will East Germany Become a New Mezzogiorno?,' *Journal of Comparative Economics* 24, no. 3 (1997): 249

was determined by the value of the D-mark. Tariff or quota barriers and capital controls were not feasible; imports flooded in from the west, and prices assumed world market values. While this might be desirable in the longer term, no authority in East Germany had any control over timing. Only the vast financial reserves of the West German state prevented the eruption of a social crisis.

KEY TERMS AND CONCEPTS

catching-up process

Kombinat

mezzogiorno scenario

monetary, economic and social union

social safety net

Treuhandanstalt (THA)

social market economy

QUESTIONS FOR DISCUSSION

1. How was East Germany's economic performance relative to the rest of the Eastern bloc prior to reunification?

2. What were East Germany's advantages over other potential transition states?

3. What was the strategy of privatization adopted by the Treuhandanstalt?

4. What were the issues surrounding the choice of the conversion rate for the Ostmark to the D-mark?

5. How successful was the THA in attracting foreign capital? Why?

RESOURCES

WEB SITES

Central Bank . . . . http://www.bundesbank.de/index_e.html

Ministry of Labor and Social Affairs . . . . http://www.bma.de/index_gb.htm

Ministry of Finance, In German . . . . http://www.bundesfinanzministerium.de/

Ministry of Economics and Technology . . . . http://www.bmwi.de/

Federal Statistical Office . . . . http://www.statistik-bund.de/e_home.htm

German Institute for Economic Research . . . . http://smith.diw.de/

The German Embassy and Information Center . . . .
. . . . http://www.germany-info.org/f_gic/index.html

Handelsblatt—National Business Newspaper . . . .
. . . . http://www.handelsblatt.de/englishsum/index.html

Berliner Morgenpost International . . . .
. . . . http://www.berliner-morgenpost.de/bm/international/index.html

The German Institute for Economic Research ....
.... http://smith.diw.de/diwnew/english/DIWe.html

Business Opportunities in Germany ....
.... http://www.business-in-germany.de/Engl/index1.htm

BOOKS AND ARTICLES

Boltho, Andrea, and Wendy Carlin. 'Will East Germany Become a New Mezzogiorno?' *Journal of Comparative Economics* 24, no. 3 (1997): 241–264.

Bos, Dieter. 'Privatization in East Germany.' In *The Transition to Market*, ed. Vito Tanzi, 202–223. Washington, D.C.: International Monetary Fund, 1993.

Collier, Irwin L., Jr., and Horst Siebert. 'The Economic Integration of Post-Wall Germany,' *Economic Developments and Prospects* 81, no. 2 (May 1991).

Hall, John, and Udo Ludwig. 'East Germany's Transitional Economy.' *Challenge,* September–October 1994, 26–32.

Heilemann, Ullrich, and Reimut Jochimsen. *Christmas in July? The Political Economy of the German Unification Reconsidered.* Washington, D.C.: Brookings Occasional Papers, 1993.

Jones, Alun. *The New Germany: A Human Geography.* Chichester, West Sussex, England: John Wiley and Sons, 1994.

Myant, Martin et alia. *Successful Transformations?: The Creation of Market Economies in Eastern Germany and the Czech Republic.* Brookfield, Vt.: Edward Elgar, 1996.

Owen, Robert F. 'The Challenges of German Unification for EC Policymaking and Performance,' *American Economic Association Papers and Proceedings* 81, no. 2 (May 1991).

Siebert, Horst. 'The Integration of Germany: Real Economic Adjustment.' *European Economic Review* 35 (1991): 591–602.

Sinn, Hans-Werner. *International Implications of the German Unification*, Working Paper Series, Working Paper 5839. Cambridge, Mass.: National Bureau of Economic Research, 1996.

'Survey: Germany.' *The Economist,* 21 May 1994, 1–10.

'Survey: Germany.' *The Economist,* 9 November 1996, 1–22.

'Survey: Germany: The Berlin Republic.' *The Economist,* 6 February 1999, 56.

Turner, Lowell, ed. *Negotiating the New Germany: Can Social Partnership Survive?* Ithaca: ILR Press, 1997.

21

THE PROCESS OF TRANSITION TO A MARKET ECONOMY

At the high point of the "socialist revolution," almost one-third of the world's population lived in nations using command planning to coordinate their economies. This process had started with the Bolshevik revolution in 1917, leading by the end of the 1920s to the institution of centralized planning throughout almost all of the former Tsarist empire. In the aftermath of World War II, the Baltic nations became an integrated part of the Soviet economy, and Eastern Europe fell under the economic dominance of the Soviet Union. In Asia, the communist Chinese Revolution saw planning introduced in the world's most populous nation and ultimately into the economies of neighboring North Korea and Vietnam. In the western hemisphere in the 1960s, Fidel Castro's Cuba began the same experiment and it looked as if Marxism would gain a foothold on the South American mainland. At that point it was easy to believe that central planning was indeed to be the way of the future and Nikita Khrushchev's boast that "we will bury you" did not seem at all empty.

By the late 1980s most of these economies were faltering. The exception was China, which, as shown in chapter 12, had embarked precociously, and somewhat serendipitously, on an early reform program, by allowing market forces considerable freedom in agriculture and small enterprise. The Soviet economy, on the other hand, was experiencing serious problems. Industrial output had been stagnant for over a decade, the consumer goods sector was proving woefully inadequate to meet the growing aspirations of its people, and a faltering parity in the military race with the United States was maintained only at the expense of prioritization, drawing as much as 35 percent of gross domestic product (GDP) into the military sector. The impressive Soviet growth record of the early years of command planning was now seen to have been almost entirely extensive in nature, with output rising only because of an increase in the quantities of labor and capital employed, rather than a growth of total factor productivity. Diminishing returns to fixed capital had been experienced since the 1970s, and by the mid 1990s the marginal rate of return on new investment capital was close to zero.

In 1985 Russia embarked on a gradualist economic reform program under Gorbachev's program of *perestroika* (restructuring), which was simultaneous with sweeping political change under the label of *glasnost* (usually translated as openness). The emergence of *glasnost*, and the relative decline in the Soviet Union's military muscle, allowed the nations of Central and Eastern Europe to seize their independence and take their own paths away from centralized planning. Meanwhile at home, the failure of *perestroika* to revive the economy contributed directly to the breakup of the Soviet Union. In 1980 centralized command planning was practiced in every country east of Austria and north of the Himalayas as far east as the Pacific Ocean. By 1999 only a few governments were even theoretically committed to planning principles (North Korea and Cuba, for example), and the durability of these regimes is questionable.

DIFFERENCES IN INITIAL CONDITIONS

Today there are about 30 countries in the world engaged in the process of *transition* from a centrally planned to a market economy.[1] All have the common feature of their planned past, but their starting points at the outset of transition were quite different. Some of this diversity is shown in Table 21.1, which gives selected figures for most economies in transition. These data show that at the outset of the move to market the countries exhibited wide differences in income per head, which in 1981 ranged from about $9,200 a year in Slovenia, the most northerly of the former Yugoslav republics, to only $1,400 in impoverished Albania, the most isolated of the communist economies.[2] Even within the successor states of the Soviet Union there are wide variations. The Baltic Republics were, at the start of transition, relatively rich; Latvia had a per-head income (measured in terms of purchasing power parity) of about $8,590 in 1989. The central Asian republics, on the other hand, were poor, the worst off being Uzbekistan, at less than one-third of Latvia's level. It should be emphasized that even the most affluent of the transition economies was a long way from the living standards seen in developed market economies. Average income in Western Europe in 1989, measured in terms of purchasing power, was about twice the level in Latvia. As we shall discuss later, the first years of transition resulted in sharply lower incomes for most formerly planned economies, and the gap has widened considerably.

There were also sharp differences between the transition states in terms of the level of economic development. This is a concept hard to encapsulate with simple statistics, but the percentage of the labor force engaged in agriculture is a useful index. As Table 21.1 shows, the percent of the population engaged in agriculture ranged from 56 percent in Albania, a largely peasant economy, to a low of 9 percent in the urbanized Baltic states. Again, we should note that even the most developed of transition nations were well behind the developed market economies,

---

[1] Of these, 15 once constituted part of the Soviet Union, and 3—Slovenia, Croatia, and Macedonia FYR—were part of Yugoslavia. Serbia and Bosnia may also be considered to be in transition, but they do not make the World Bank tables for political reasons.

[2] In actual fact, the highest purchasing power income probably lay in East Germany, but that former economy is not considered transitional in the sense that it merged with the Federal Republic of Germany.

■ **TABLE 21.1**

SELECTED INDICATORS FOR ECONOMIES IN TRANSITION, 1989

	Population, Millions	PPP GDP per Head 1989	Percentage of Labor Force in Agriculture	Telephones per 100 People	Average Years of Schooling, Population 25+	Population Growth Rate	Monetary Overhang as Percentage of GDP
Eastern Europe							
Albania	3.3	1,400	56	2	6.2	1	4.3
Bulgaria	8.9	5,000	17	32	7.0	−0.1	18.0
Croatia	—	6,171	—	—	—	—	12.0
Czechoslovakia	15.7	6,280	11	29	9.2	0.4	−7.1
Hungary	10.5	6,810	15	19	9.8	0	−7.7
Macedonia FYR	—	3,394	—	—	—	—	12.0
Poland	38.4	5,150	27	15	8.2	0.4	13.6
Romania	23.3	3,470	29	13	7.1	0.4	16.8
Slovenia	—	9,200	—	—	—	—	12.0
Former Soviet Union							
Armenia	3.5	5,530	11	18	5.0	0.4	25.7
Azerbaijan	7.3	4,620	15	10	5.0	1.2	25.7
Belarus	10.3	7,010		16	7.0	0.6	25.7
Estonia	1.6	8,900	9	21	9.0	0.0	25.7
Georgia	5.5	5,590	14	10	5.0	0.7	25.7
Kazakstan	17.0	5,130	20	11	5.0	0.9	25.7
Kyrgyz Rep.	4.5	3,180	16	7	5.0	1.8	25.7
Latvia	2.7	8,590	9	24	9.0	−0.1	25.7
Lithuania	3.8	6,430	10	22	9.0	0.1	25.7
Moldova	4.4	4,670	21	11	6.0	0.7	25.7
Russian Fed.	149.0	7,720	20	15	9.0	0.5	25.7
Tajikistan	5.6	3,010	14	5	5.0	2.7	25.7
Turkmenistan	3.9	4,230		6	5.0	1.9	25.7
Ukraine	52.2	5,680		16	6.0	0.4	25.7
Uzbekistan	21.5	2,740	17	7	5.0	2.0	25.7
Mongolia		2,100	40	3	7.2	2.6	7.6

SOURCE: Martha de Melo, Cevder Denizer, and Alan Gelb, "Patterns of Transition from Plan to Market," *World Bank Economic Review* 10, no. 3 (September 1996), 400, and UNDP Human Development Report, 1997.

which as a rule have less than 5 percent, and as few as 2 percent, of the workforce employed in agriculture.

The relevance of the other statistics given in Table 21.1 is fairly self-evident. The rate of population growth tells us more about the state of overall development, although there is also a great deal of "noise" created by religious factors, culture, and even housing availability. The Baltic and Slav states show low rates of population growth, while the Islamic populations of central Asia are still growing as fast as 2 percent per annum. Similarly, there are wide differences between the countries in the quantity of human capital, which is crudely measured by the average years of schooling of the adult (25 years old and more) population.

The final column in Table 21.1, the **monetary overhang,** is an important index of macroeconomic imbalance, to which we will return later. At this point it suffices to say that it is one measure of the degree to which consumer goods were under-supplied during the last years of the planning regimes. We should recall from our earlier discussion that in many cases the wage payments made to workers in centrally planned economies were greater than the amount that the consumers were able, or willing, to spend on the available (often poor-quality) consumer goods. This led to the buildup of the monetary overhang, which consists of cash and savings bank deposits that represented latent purchasing power. As long as prices were centrally controlled by fiat, this potential excess buying power could have little effect on the overall price level.[3] However, once the process of price liberalization started, the monetary overhang manifested itself as an inflationary pressure. The only alternative to allowing inflation to work itself through was neutralization by appropriate and aggressive contractionary policy measures, which would have had a highly depressing effect on output and welfare.

The figures in Table 21.1 show that the monetary overhang in the Soviet Union in 1989 was the most serious encountered in any of the transition nations. It is statistically impossible to disaggregate this all-union figure among the successor states, and so all show an identical figure of more than 25 percent, symptomatic of a potentially serious problem of repressed inflation. As it happened, the monetary overhang did provide an initial stimulus to inflation, but it could not be held responsible for the continuing price spiral, which lasted for several years, precisely because the purchasing power of the overhang was rapidly depleted to insignificance by inflation itself. In the countries of Eastern Europe, the monetary overhang was by no means as great as in the Soviet Union, and the negative figures in the Czech Republic and Hungary indicate a growing use of consumer credit and the greater availability of consumer goods, which allowed consumers to incur household debt.

COMMON FEATURES

However, despite these differences, all of the transition economies shared at the outset several important points of commonality:

1. In all of these economies, macroeconomic balance was achieved by direct control of the planning agencies rather than by a reliance on the market or the more conventional tools of macroeconomic demand management used in the developed economies. (It was the failure to keep the purchasing power of total wage payments equilibrated with the available supply of

---

[3]Of course, prices could be bid up on the black market, and were. Also, the monetary overhang found its way into the illegal currency markets. Rubles, of limited use because of the shortage of consumer goods, were exchanged for "hard" currency at exchange rates wildly different from the official ones. The hard currency so obtained could be expatriated or used to buy goods in hard currency stores (called *berioskas* in Russia).

goods to be purchased by consumers that led to the existence of the monetary overhang.)

2. The plan, not market forces, was the primary coordination mechanism of the economy.

3. There was no adequate institutional framework within which a market economy could operate. This deficiency was clearest in terms of intertemporal coordination, where the absence of defined property rights and enforceable contracts was most limiting.

4. The relative prices of goods and factors of production reflected neither relative costs nor relative scarcities.

5. Entry into most economic activity was controlled by the government, and many activities that would be regarded as socially beneficial in a market economy were illegal during, and in the immediate aftermath, of central planning.

6. The extent of private property was limited. Although in some countries (e.g., the former Yugoslavia) there was an attempt to combine socially owned capital with market coordination, such experiments had not in general been fruitful. The rapid extension of private property is valuable in two ways. First, it makes the market function better, largely by reducing principal-agent problems, and second, it gives the citizens a stake in preserving the permanence of the new arrangements.

7. Foreign trade was controlled by the state and therefore the efficiency-enhancing impact of foreign competition was largely absent.

THE STEPS OF TRANSITION

Transition from a planned to a market economy is not a single step but a series of moves that must be made in sequence, and some countries have advanced with greater speed than others. Table 21.2 gives statistics for the performance of 26 economies in transition, divided into subgroups according to their performance on a liberalization index,[4] prepared by economists from the World Bank. This index is compounded from three sets of considerations: the liberalization of the domestic economy, external transactions, and the private sector entry. **Domestic liberalization** is defined as consisting of the easing of price controls as well as the termination of the monopoly privileges of state enterprises and has a weight of .3 in the construction of the index. **External transactions liberalization** consists of ending

---

[4]For more detail on the construction of the liberalization index, see *From Plan to Market: World Development Report 1996* and "Patterns of Transition from Plan to Market," by Martha de Melo, Cevder Denizer, and Alan Gelb: *World Bank Economic Review* 10, no. 3 (September 1996), 397 ff.

■ **TABLE 21.2**

LIBERALIZATION, GROWTH, AND INFLATION IN 26 COUNTRIES IN TRANSITION, 1989–1994

	Cumulative Liberalization Index 1994	Average Liberalization 1993–1994	Average Inflation Rate 1993–1994 (percent)	Average Annual GDP Growth 1993–1994	Average GDP in 1993–1994 as a Percentage of 1989 GDP	Lowest Level of GDP as a Percentage of 1989 GDP
Advanced Reformers						
Slovenia	4.16	0.82	26	3.0	84	81
Poland	4.14	0.84	34	4.2	88	82
Hungary	4.11	0.84	21	0.0	81	80
Czech Republic	3.61	0.90	16	0.8	81	80
Slovak Republic	3.47	0.86	19	0.4	79	77
Average	3.90	0.85	23	1.7	83	80
High Intermediate Reformers						
Estonia	2.93	0.85	69	0.9	69	67
Bulgaria	2.90	0.68	81	−1.4	73	73
Lithuania	2.72	0.79	231	−7.3	44	44
Latvia	2.45	0.71	73	−4.4	60	59
Albania	2.30	0.70	57	9.5	74	65
Romania	2.29	0.66	194	2.2	69	67
Mongolia	2.27	0.64	164	0.6	84	83
Average	2.55	0.72	124	0.0	67	65
Low Intermediate Reformers						
Russian Federation	1.92	0.63	558	−13.5	57	52
Kyrgyz Republic	1.81	0.68	744	−13.2	61	57
Moldova	1.62	0.53	558	−17.0	53	46
Kazakstan	1.31	0.37	1,870	−18.5	57	49
Average	1.67	0.55	933	−15.6	57	51
Slow Reformers						
Uzbekistan	1.11	0.37	640	−2.5	89	88
Belarus	1.07	0.35	1,694	−16.6	73	64
Ukraine	0.80	0.20	2,789	−18.6	56	48
Turkmenistan	0.63	0.19	2,751	−15.0	69	62
Average	0.90	0.27	1,968	−13.2	72	66
Affected by Regional Tensions						
Croatia	3.98	0.83	807	−0.7	69	68
Macedonia FYR	3.92	0.78	157	−10.7	57	55
Armenia	1.44	0.42	4,595	−7.4	38	38
Georgia	1.32	0.35	10,563	−24.6	24	23
Azerbaijan	1.03	0.33	1,167	−17.7	50	44
Tajikistan	0.95	0.28	1,324	−26.3	35	30
Average	2.11	0.50	3,102	−14.5	45	43

SOURCE: de Melo, Denizer, and Gelb, 405.

of export controls and export taxes, the establishment of current account convertibility, and the substitution of a moderate tariff regime for quantitative import controls. It also has a weight of .3. The final component, **private sector entry liberalization,** is measured by the extent of progress in the privatization of state assets and the entry of new firms. It has a weight in the overall index of .4.

The **advanced reformers** are the five states in Central and Eastern Europe: Slovenia, Poland, Hungary, and the two parts of former Czechoslovakia—the Czech Republic and the Slovak Republic. High intermediate reformers are the Baltic states and the southern countries of the Balkan Peninsula, and Mongolia, although relatively less developed, is a somewhat surprising member of this group. The most important of the low intermediate reformers is Russia; among the slow reformers are the Ukraine, after Russia the most populous of the European transition nations, and the Islamic states of central Asia. Several countries of the former Yugoslavia and the Caucasus have been too much affected by civil and international warfare to be successful in maintaining a coherent liberalization plan.

STABILIZATION

The common experience of almost all transition economies[5] has been macroeconomic disturbances of a magnitude and endurance that have surprised almost all observers, consisting of rapid and sustained inflation and a sharp reduction of real output. The accompanying rise in unemployment has been smaller than expected, largely due to extensive subsidies to industry.

INFLATION

Inflation has been a universal problem for East European and former Soviet reformers. Even those states most advanced in the process of reform have experienced an average rate of inflation between 1989 and 1994 of over 100 percent per annum. However, as Table 21.2 shows, this price explosion has abated in the most advanced reformers. Nevertheless, in slower reforming economies, the average inflation rate for 1989–1994 was close to 1,000 percent per annum and, in fact, accelerated as reform progressed.

The causes of inflation in the transition economies are complex, but the most important are the following:

---

[5]The main exception is, of course, the People's Republic of China, which has maintained extremely strong economic growth throughout its liberalization effort. Growth in China was 11 percent between 1989 and 1995, and inflation a modest 8.4 percent. Vietnam combined liberalization with growth—roughly 8 percent between 1989 and 1995—although inflation was in excess of 100 percent per annum.

1. The monetary overhang created by supply and demand imbalances in the planned regime. Relaxation of price controls released pent-up demand and drove prices higher.

2. The absence of an adequate taxation system and the inability of governments to borrow on financial markets forced *reliance on the creation of money and credit to finance government activity.*

3. The *continuation of soft budget constraints* in much of industry, increasing the fiscal deficit. To prevent the failure of state-owned and privatized enterprises during transition, governments frequently extended credit to industry. This is a politically necessary move in many cases, since widespread failure would lead to unemployment, political unrest, and a failure of any reforming regime to complete its program. In many cases, government support to industry had to increase sharply as implicit subsidies in the pricing system under central planning were eliminated.[6]

4. *Flight from the domestic currency* to foreign currencies (generally speaking the dollar) because of an absence of confidence in the domestic currency.

The greatest impetus to continued inflation was the creation of excessive credit by the government, and the solution to the inflationary spiral therefore lay in greater monetary discipline by central banks. However, while effective against inflation, repressive monetary policy has the effect of reducing demand for goods and services, and therefore has an adverse effect on the growth of emergent firms. A tight monetary strategy carries the political risk of rising unemployment and the economic risk of depressing long-run growth. The World Bank considers that there are clear gains to getting inflation down below 40 percent per annum, since below such a level the danger of a hyperinflationary spiral is largely eliminated, but the World Bank is more cautious about appropriate policy beyond that. In cutting inflation further, the cost in terms of lost output may be greater than the gain that results from more stable prices. Domestic output started rebounding in Poland and Estonia with the inflation rate around 40 percent, and Korea, several Latin American nations, and Israel have all combined impressive real growth with relative high rates of price increase.

High rates of inflation have profound distributional consequences in the transition economies because they act like a tax on financial assets. The losers are predominantly households and firms that held positive cash balances, who see their savings wiped out by hyperinflation. The winners are the government sector, which reaps the gains of seigniorage, and any households or firms with net debts. In general, the **inflation tax** is regressive and falls more heavily on small savers who have difficulty converting their financial assets into real property or dollars (or other foreign currencies) where it is safe from inflationary ravages.

---

[6]Consider, for example, the case of energy, which was supplied at well below world prices throughout the Soviet bloc. The elimination of the implicit energy subsidy squeezed many firms that had been conditioned to operate in a relatively energy-intensive fashion. To avoid the failure of these firms, the government had to grant generous credits.

THE COLLAPSE OF GDP

The second macroeconomic phenomenon common to the transition economies is the sharp contraction of output. As Table 21.2 shows, in all of the Central and Eastern European nations (CEEs) and successor states of the Soviet Union, GDP has bottomed out at around 80 percent of its 1989 level. The fast-reforming economies resumed growth during 1993–1994, though all are still well below the level of GDP achieved in 1989. Slow-reforming countries have seen their output levels fall further and have been longer in returning to an expansionary path. High intermediate reformers saw a contraction of about 33 percent in five years, and the low intermediate reformers, among them Russia itself, lost about half of output.

By any measure, these are very significant dips in output. Some sense of their magnitude can be seen by comparison to the Great Depression of the 1930s, when the United States, the most heavily affected of the major industrial economies, saw a fall in GDP of about one-third.[7] The contraction in other advanced capitalist economies was less drastic—about 28 percent in Germany, 9 percent in France, and only about 5 percent in the United Kingdom. The fall in output in transition economies has been proportionately greater than in the West during the Great Depression, still regarded as one of capitalism's great failures that led directly to massive political change and perhaps World War II. The only experience of capitalism that most of the 410 million people who live in transition economies (other than China and Vietnam) has been an acute and painful contraction.

It should be noted, however, that official statistics overstate the size of the economic contraction in two ways. First, much of the recorded output in 1989 consisted of official estimates of production valued at official plan prices. The immediate impact of transition was to reduce both production volumes and prices of many of the overvalued, substandard goods produced under the planned regimes. Second, a feature of the transition period has been the substantial growth of the private, small business economy. This sector of production, while not necessarily criminal, is likely to underreport its activities to minimize taxes, and thus this burgeoning activity is not fully reflected in the official statistics.

CAUSES OF THE CONTRACTION. While in reality the contractions might not have been as great as official statistics seemed to indicate, in all transition economies there were significant macroeconomic downturns, the primary cause of which was the disintegration of the coordinating structure. Planners had determined both suppliers and purchasers and, after the collapse of planning, enterprises found themselves both without secure, uncontested markets for their output and in difficulty getting the raw materials that had under the former system been at least nominally guaranteed.

Other factors were also important. After price liberalization, even when materials were available, enterprises often had to pay more than the "soft" prices that had been charged under the plan. This was a particularly acute problem with respect

---

[7]John Kenneth Galbraith, *The Great Crash*, 3d ed. (Boston: Houghton Mifflin, 1972), 172.

to energy inputs, which had been consistently underpriced under socialist planning; Soviet oil and gas had been supplied throughout the Soviet Union and the Soviet bloc at much less than the world price. Analysis after liberalization indicated that a substantial part of industry in centrally planned economies produced *zero or* **negative value added.** When both inputs and outputs were valued at the appropriate world prices, the final product was worth less than the materials from which it was made, and all of the labor, capital, and other factor services were actually directed toward reducing the value of raw materials.

Third, dislocation had domino effects because enterprises that had lost buyers suffered a shortfall of revenues and therefore had no resources to pay for raw materials. The suppliers of materials, in turn, had no money to pay their workers, to buy investment goods, or even to pay taxes. While governments in most transition economies stepped in with credits to help enterprises bridge the gap between revenues and expenses, it was seldom adequate. Out of necessity interfirm credit began to proliferate as firms, having no alternative ways to dispose of their products, continued to supply them to customers who were increasingly delinquent in payments. The entire structure of industry became very fragile, presenting the possibility of repercussive enterprise failures, which could further cut output and massively increase unemployment. Governments in most transition states responded by increasing credits to industry, therefore feeding the inflationary cycle.

A fourth problem was that trade (for example, between the Baltic Republics and Russia itself), which had been "domestic" in terms of the Soviet Union, became "international" and required convertible currency after the collapse of the Soviet Union. From the beginning of central planning in the Soviet Union, Soviet technocrats had relied on economies of scale, generally regarding bigger as better. As a result, single plants were often expected to supply the entire national consumption of certain commodities and many goods, both final and intermediary, were produced almost exclusively within a single republic. The break-up of the Soviet Union meant that suppliers and their markets were now located in different countries, and transactions across these new borders frequently became hard currency transactions.[8] The problems of currency availability and border restrictions resulted in a contraction of economic activity as trade between the republics of the former Soviet Union shrank by 70 percent almost overnight.

This dislocation was not limited to the republics spawned by the dissolution of the Soviet Union. While trade within the Council on Mutual Economic Assistance (CMEA or COMECON) had always notionally been "international" in character, it had been an artifact of planning rather than resulting from the pursuit of comparative advantage. The end of the planned system of the CMEA caused a sharp reduction in the volume of trade between former partners, again of the order of 70 percent. Imports from another former socialist country were displaced by goods from more competitive producers outside the Soviet bloc, particularly in the case of consumer goods, electronics, and capital goods. Lost markets meant lost

---

[8]This was not always the immediate case; a "ruble area," within which the ruble was the common medium of exchange, existed for some time.

■ TABLE 21.3

TOTAL LABOR PRODUCTIVITY: SELECTED ECONOMIES IN TRANSITION

	1991	1992	1993	1994	1995
Bulgaria	1.5	0.9	0.1	1.2	−0.5
Czech Republic	−9.2	−3.9	0.7	1.8	1.9
Hungary	−2.5	6.9	4.4	5.2	2.9
Poland	−1.2	7.1	6.4	4.2	6.3
Romania	−12.5	−7.2	5.3	4.1	6.9
Slovak Republic	−2.3	−8.0	−1.5	5.2	4.2
Russia	−11.0	−12.4	−7.1	−9.6	−1.9
Tajikistan	−9.9	−28.8	−14.7	−19.1	−10.1
Ukraine	−10.2	−12.0	−12.1	−20.0	−5.0
Uzbekistan	−5.1	−10.6	−2.3	−2.2	−0.8
Estonia	−10.4	0.7	3.7	−2.0	2.3
Latvia	−9.7	−32.4	−8.1	3.9	−1.3
Lithuania	−15.1	−37.9	−27.3	7.1	2.3

SOURCE: United Nations Economic Commission for Europe, 1997.

revenue and so had multiplier effects on the macroeconomies. In effect, the dislocation of the trade network established under the CMEA was akin to cutting off each economy from part of its economic hinterland.

Finally, in many countries the dislocation was aggravated by the deterioration of the internal distribution system. In Russia the internal transportation system had been close to collapse for decades and the only viable mode of moving most goods was by rail, which also suffered from inadequate investment and maintenance. Furthermore, at the collapse of the Soviet Union, rolling stock and equipment was divided between the republics largely on the basis of each country assuming possession of what lay within its borders in August 1991, resulting in a misallocation of resources and serious disruption.

LABOR PRODUCTIVITY. While output fell sharply in most transition economies, employment dipped by a much smaller amount, and therefore the initial impact of economic reform was to actually lower labor productivity. Before the onset of reform, productivity in Eastern Europe was between 20 percent and 33 percent of the level in Western Europe, and the first effect of liberalization was to widen this gap. Raising living standards depends on an increase in labor productivity and the decline was a demoralizing setback. While most countries experienced a fall, Table 21.3 shows that the faster reforms are implemented, the more sharply labor productivity initially declines, but the more rapidly it returns to the positive. Fast reformers like the Czech Republic, Poland, and Hungary saw productivity rising by 1993, while Russia and the Central Asian Republics continued to experience productivity decline.

Reform was accompanied by a shift in the composition of output. Basic "rust belt" industries contracted, compensated for in part by rises in services, consumer goods, and, where relevant, the primary energy sector, which benefited

■ **FIGURE 21.1**

INDICES OF INDUSTRIAL LABOR PRODUCTIVITY IN FOUR TRANSITION ECONOMIES

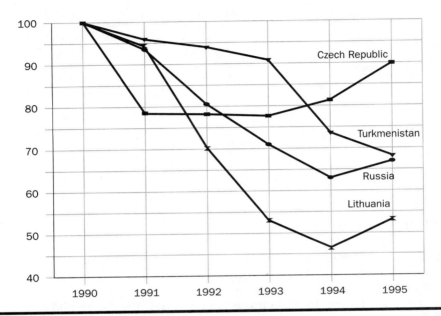

SOURCE: United Nations Economic Commission for Europe, 1997.

from increased product prices. Figure 21.1 shows the trends in purely industrial productivity for four countries: the Czech Republic (an advanced reformer), Lithuania (high intermediate), Russia (low intermediate), and Turkmenistan (slow).

The relationship between the speed of reform and the subsequent movements in labor productivity is complex. Although Lithuania's reforms are more advanced than those of its larger neighbor Russia, both economies show similar movements of industrial labor productivity. Lithuania's fall largely parallels that of Russia, but it has been deeper, due mostly to the fact that the barriers to trade created by the breakup of the Soviet Union had a more severe impact on smaller economies. The specialization built into the planned trading system meant that smaller economies were disproportionately geared to export goods throughout the Soviet Bloc and therefore lost a proportionately greater share of their markets at the breakup.[9]

There is evidence to suggest, at least among the faster reforming nations, that privatization has had a positive effect on labor productivity. In a survey of some 6,000 firms in Eastern Europe, Gerhard Pöhl and his colleagues found that privatized firms had, on average, a rapid 7.2 percent annual increase in productivity

[9] Alastair McAuley found that the share of "exports" of the Baltic States to other republics in the Soviet Union accounted for about two-thirds of the net material product.

LABOR PRODUCTIVITY GROWTH: CHANGE, 1992–1995 (PERCENTAGE)

	Privatized Firms	State-Owned Firms
Bulgaria	12.4	−1.4
Czech Republic	8.6	−2.6
Hungary	6	3.2
Poland	7.5	1.4
Romania	1	−0.5
Slovak Republic	7.8	−4.1
Slovenia	7.2	1.8
Average	7.2	−0.3

SOURCE: Gerhard Pöhl, Robert E. Anderson, Stijn Claessens, and Simeon Djankov, "Privatization and Restructuring in Central and Eastern Europe," *World Bank Technical Paper* (1997), 368.

between 1992 and 1995.[10] In contrast, the fact that labor productivity in firms remaining in the state sector continued to fall (some of these results are shown in Table 21.4) supports privatization, though some caveats should be considered. First, the results in Table 21.4 reflect in part the relative ease with which fundamentally sound enterprises may be divested from state ownership: the other side of this phenomenon is the necessity of retaining the "lame ducks" under state ownership when no private buyer is forthcoming and the political authorities fear a rise in unemployment. Consequently, the private sector is self-selected and more dynamic than the social sector. Increased productivity also results from the greater freedom of privatized industry to get rid of unproductive workers and those concerned with the noncore aspects of the typical planned enterprise (for example, health- and child-care workers).

PRICE LIBERALIZATION

Price liberalization is essential for a market economy. Central planning failed to allocate resources efficiently because prices failed to reflect either cost of production or their value to consumers. Freeing up prices is the first step to grasping the benefits of a market economy and can occur without any steps being taken toward privatization of industry or indeed reform of **enterprise governance.** Under market socialism in the Yugoslav model, free prices were compatible with socially owned means of production and with the collective governance of the enterprise. However, in most analyses building a market system in the formerly centrally

---

[10]Gerhard Pöhl, Robert E. Anderson, Stijn Claessens, and Simeon Djankov, "Privatization and Restructuring in Central and Eastern Europe," World Bank Technical Paper, 1997.

planned economies goes hand in hand with the privatization of property and the free entry of firms into the market place. Private enterprise and private ownership are more likely than social ownership to be compatible with the efficient operation of markets.

Price liberalization can produce dramatic results. In Poland, for example, shops that were empty of goods and beleaguered by queues of would-be shoppers while under central planning became well stocked in the aftermath of reform. Such a change is the product of both demand- and supply-side responses. Higher prices may bring forth a larger output, but much of the apparent increased availability of goods is due to a movement along the demand curve. In the short run, the price elasticity of demand of most produced goods is likely to be greater than the price elasticity of supply. The elimination of excess demand owes more to reduced consumption by the less well off, who can no longer afford the goods that had been cheap under central planning. In the longer run, supply responses may dominate, exhibiting the solid, welfare-augmenting growth that is the objective of price reform.

A further benefit of price reform is the reduction of the socially wasteful activity caused by price controls. Under planning, goods in demand attracted many buyers and much of the homemakers' day was spent queuing for necessities. The alternative to queuing was to resort to the black market, and illegal fortunes were made in arbitrage between the state sector, where access was controlled but prices cheap, and the black market.

In general, price liberalization hurts the less affluent since under administered prices, they had access to goods on the same basis as everyone else, and because the marginal value of their time was low, the queuing system worked to their benefit. Liberalized prices confront them with a hard monetary budget constraint and cause a fall in living standards, a case of the efficiency of the market conflicting with the greater equity of nonprice allocation.

As prices are decontrolled, the highly concentrated structure of industry promoted under central planning becomes a problem. Because of the planners' faith in scale economies, production of many goods was concentrated within a few large enterprises, which under planning had little market power because both production targets and prices were centrally determined. However, price liberalization gives these enterprises a high degree of market power and they will respond to their new freedom by raising prices and reducing output. Any gains in welfare from price reform must be set against the loss of consumers' surplus caused by enterprises exercising monopoly power. Losses can be mitigated by antimonopoly regulation, freeing market entry for domestic competitors and opening up international trade. In cases of natural monopoly or substantial barriers to entry, regulation may be the only resort.

Liberalized prices will produce fewer benefits if reform is not accompanied by the introduction of contract law with some measure of enforceability. Price liberalization alone creates the conditions for, in the words of one Russian economist, "a bazaar but not a market." The creation of a modern productive economy requires performance, and to some degree, prices to be intertemporally consistent.

REGULATION OF MONOPOLY

Soviet-style planning's love affair with size led to high levels of concentration in many product areas. To measure monopoly power, western economists have in recent years tended to turn from measures of current concentration of output to focus on the **contestability of markets** and the size of barriers to entry, since potential competition can be a significantly moderating influence on monopoly practices. In a Soviet-style economy, markets were uncontested because of the planning system and the incentives embedded in it. Enterprise managers had little to gain by broadening their production and moving into new lines—it was complicated, risky, required both management time and materials, and could therefore jeopardize the achievement of output targets. Once the planning system was abandoned, barriers to entry were low in many industries and market share could be quickly eroded by new market entrants and imported goods.

In some industries, competition can be created merely by reorganizing the administration of the enterprises. This has been achieved with some success in the service industries. Prior to the collapse of the Soviet Union, *Aeroflot* was the largest airline in the world. It has been replaced by regional and republic airlines, and the degree of competition between these successor firms, as well as new entrants, has increased. *Intourist* was a monopoly supplier of tourist services, and it has now been replaced by several competitive organizations. In both of these cases the monopoly had been artificial, and the capital stock was either small or easily divisible.

This is not the case, however, among the giants of Soviet-heavy industry, where the size of the enterprise is embodied in a single large plant and organization is around core products. Fully one-fifth of the Soviet workforce was employed in organizations of more than 10,000 workers. As Nikolay Petrakov, a Russian economist, observed:

> This is our notorious gigantomania. We always thought that a larger plant is bound to be better than a small one. We artificially propagated monopolists. An industrial giant that has already been built is impossible to break up into parts. This means that it will long remain a technological monopoly. . . . Fortunately there are not so many of them in the light and food industries. But heavy industry is full of these monsters. To speak of competition here is impossible. We will have to introduce price controls and antimonopoly legislation.

THE ROLE OF TRADE

Price controls on goods as differentiated and changing as machinery and machine tools are anathematic to most economists who would rather liberalize the trade regime to limit monopoly power. For such tradable goods, opening the economy to international competition can be an important check on the pricing behavior of domestic producers. It may be particularly effective in the case of machinery, where embodied technological change, as well as a moderating influence on prices, can result. However, there are dangers for domestic producers who are forced to confront the high quality, superior design, and low prices of goods from abroad.

Rapid attention has to be given to price and quality control or domestic producers may lose customers and go bankrupt. Competition is bound to be unpopular with domestic producers, who are likely to petition for protective tariffs or quotas on "infant industry" grounds. However, once protective tariffs or quotas are adopted, they will be hard to remove, and they should be avoided where possible.

THE REFORM OF ENTERPRISES

THE ENTERPRISE UNDER CENTRAL PLANNING

Enterprises in the centrally planned economies were quite different in structure, goals, and culture from their counterparts in developed market economies. These differences have been mentioned earlier, but a review is worthwhile:

1. *Size of enterprises.* Enterprises under central planning were larger on average than those in market economies, because of the planners' faith in scale economies and a desire to eliminate "socially wasteful reproduction" of capacity. Studies of the structure of Soviet enterprise in the 1960s revealed that the average firm had a workforce about three times larger than would have been the case for a similar market size in the West. This emphasis on size intensified during the 1970s and 1980s, as scale economies were pursued as a remedy for the economic failure. The Brezhnev reforms of 1973 resulted in the combination of smaller enterprises into larger industrial associations. By the late 1980s, almost three-quarters of the Soviet labor force was employed in enterprises of more than 1,000 persons and over 20 percent worked for enterprises with more than 10,000 workers.

2. *Objectives of management.* Under central planning the objective of management was to meet the plan targets and incentives offered to management were oriented toward this goal. In many countries a concept close to profit was eventually introduced as one of multiple targets, but the lack of clear accounting and the high degree of implicit subsidy obscured this objective. While profit maximization is not the unswerving objective of western firms, there is without doubt more attention to a defined bottom line.

3. *Marketing and sales effort.* Centrally planned economies were characterized by excess demand and each firm's customers were defined by the planners. Little attention was paid to sales effort, market research, product improvement, or customer satisfaction. In developed market economies, sales and marketing are an essential feature of corporate operation and the absence of this capacity in a newly privatized enterprise will present difficulties in securing a solid customer base.

4. *Lack of export orientation.* Export markets were of little importance for centrally planned firms. Rather than a key source of sales and revenue for the enterprise, exports were a means of raising hard currency for necessary national purchases of material and equipment. Enterprises themselves were

insulated from export markets until the late 1980s by the monopoly of the foreign trade organizations.

5. *Extent of vertical integration.* Centrally planned firms tended to be more vertically integrated than their developed market counterparts, due in large part to the failures of the distribution system and the neglect of quality control. If an enterprise were to have guaranteed access to intermediate goods of reliable quality, in a fashion timely enough to meet its own output targets, the safest way was to produce it within the organization. This led to a paradox. Although one emphasis of the centrally planned system was grasping economies of scale, in order to meet internal demand large organizations frequently produced intermediate goods in inefficiently small quantities. "Outsourcing" and precise inventory control, noticeable developments in the evolution of large enterprises in Europe, the United States, and Japan, were neglected in the Soviet-style economies.

6. *Provision of ancillary services.* Part of the reason that centrally planned firms were so large was that they were responsible for a wide range of services for workers that lay beyond the scope of operations of even the most paternalistic firms in the West. Firms were frequently responsible for housing, health services, child care, and even education, overlapping functions that in market economies are reserved for government.

CORPORATIZATION

The first step of enterprise reform is **corporatization,** placing the firm onto an organizational and accounting footing to allow management the freedom to pursue clearly defined objectives without political intervention. This is distinct from privatization, which involves placing the ownership of the enterprise outside the public sector, but it is a step in that direction.

1. *Creating independent management.* Under centralized planning not only is management appointed by the politicians but also it is directly accountable to them. This is logical since the enterprise is an extension of the state and therefore is required to pursue objectives of the state. As long as enterprises remain subject to direct political control, their purpose will be defined largely in political terms and enterprise management will not be afforded the freedom to exercise initiative to increase efficiency and promote innovation. Moreover, managers will be appointed on political criteria rather than on ability in purely economic matters. Consequently, reform of industry must start with the alienation of the enterprises from the direct control of politicians.

2. *Defining the goals of the enterprise.* Next the objective of the enterprise must be clearly defined. If private ownership is an objective, the only consistent goal will be the maximization of profit—that is, the definition of and attention to a "bottom line." It is possible to corporatize an enterprise and assign to it objectives other than profit maximization, as long as it remains in the

public sector or receives a subsidy from the state. In most developed market economies, for example, rail transportation is run by a publicly owned corporation, with an independent management structure but, because of a high level of externalities, such bodies often have broader goals than the maximization of profit.

3. *Separating ancillary services from the productive enterprise.* One of the most important aspects of enterprise restructuring is separating the provision of social services from the function of producing goods. When the means of production are socially owned, it can be convenient, even efficient, for productive enterprises to deliver social services. However, if the goals of the organization are more clearly defined as maximizing profits, any social activity that is not cost-effective in raising labor productivity must be closed down, or the firm should be compensated for this activity by some level of government. If firms that had responsibilities for housing, health, and education are allowed to shed them, then the government must assume them, or deterioration in social welfare will result, at least in the short run. As firms abandon their traditional social function, a pressing task in transition economies is the establishment of a social safety net to protect those "downsized" from state enterprise or those whose well-being is no longer the concern of their immediate employer.

4. *Establishing a realistic accounting system.* Accounting practices under central planning were neither universal nor impartial. The pervasiveness of the "soft budget constraint" and the arbitrary nature of fiat prices made firms' accounts all but meaningless in the evaluation of performance. Preparation for privatization involves the establishment of an accepted accounting system that will enable potential investors to judge the financial viability and prospects of the firm.

5. *Providing incentives to management and workers.* A final desirable step in the process of corporatization is to look to the structure of incentives within the enterprise. Under planning, incentives were frequently perverse, and revising them to encourage hard work, managerial diligence, and innovation will better enable the firm to present the value of the enterprise to potential buyers.

PRIVATIZATION

Privatization should begin after these preliminary steps have been taken, although, in fact, the privatization programs of most former socialist states have proceeded before all of these preconditions have been met.

PRINCIPLES OF PRIVATIZATION

THE PROBLEM OF THE COMMONS.   Let us pause at this point to reconsider the economic and philosophical issues that bear on privatization. The primary rationale for private ownership lies in the "problem of the commons" or, to put it differently, what belongs to everyone belongs to no one. If resources are collectively owned, no individual has a strong incentive to look after them, and since the effect of an action of an individual on the overall condition of jointly held resources is minimal, each person can be considered a "free-rider." However, the overall result is that resources held in common are abused while resources that are individually owned are likely to be better maintained because someone has a material incentive for their preservation.

PRINCIPAL-AGENT ISSUES.   The commons issue addresses the resource problem of social ownership, but the difficulties in the manufacturing and service sectors are somewhat different. Principal-agent problems occur within both socialism and capitalism. In a socialist state, politicians and the planners use positive incentives or punishments to induce enterprise managers to act in the way that the plan requires. In turn, the enterprise managers need strategies to induce workers to work in their interests. Under capitalism there are parallel issues. The owners of capital hire managers; making them behave in the interests of shareholders is a problem, and, as under socialism, these managers have to induce workers to perform optimally. In fact, these problems have been addressed in quite similar ways in socialist and capitalist systems. Managers are offered bonuses (or in capitalist firms they are frequently offered stock options) for meeting or exceeding targets, and workers are proffered a range of positive and negative incentives to raise their output— piece rates and bonuses on the positive side and tight supervision and output quotas on the negative.

Privatization of industry offers the potential of dealing with principal-agent issues more effectively than under social ownership. In some small businesses, agency problems will disappear as owner-operators emerge (for example, in retailing and the small-scale service sector). In larger enterprises, the owners of capital have a much more focused interest in the outcome in a particular enterprise and therefore provide more rigorous oversight of management's performance than would occur under planning. Corporate governance is a key to effective transition, and close attention should be given in the privatization process to establishing an effective system.

THE RESTITUTION ISSUE.   Both the "commons" and the "principal-agent" arguments suggest that privatization can foster efficiency by ensuring that resources will be dedicated to their highest value use and that appropriate oversight will be given to maximize efficiency. However, this does not tell us much about who the owners of the privatized property should be, nor about how the transfer of ownership should be addressed. Some guidance may be given by examining how the property held in the state sector originated.[11] In some cases the property was

---

[11] Such a policy ignores, of course, the thorny issue of whether the owner prior to nationalization obtained the property by a just process in the first place. Imagine, perhaps, a wealthy aristocrat who gained his estates by the gift of a tyrant.

seized without compensation (or without *adequate* compensation) from its owners, and if they or their heirs can be identified (and if the property is largely unimproved from the condition in which it was seized), restitution of the property to them may be both equitable and efficient. Such restitution has been applied to residences and (for example, in Bulgaria) to small-scale agriculture. However, socialist rule in many states has been long enough that most property cannot be associated with a presocialist owner. Moreover, much of it is new or greatly changed, especially in the industrial sector, and is not the subject of any preexisting title.

HOLDING THE NATION'S ASSETS IN TRUST. Many transition economies had been operating under a socialist system for at least 40 years, usually from the immediate aftermath of World War II. Most of the states that emerged as a result of the breakdown of the Soviet Union had been operating under planning for about 65 years. The majority of the capital stock in these economies is the result of investment made during the socialist period and the enterprises could be said to belong to all of the population that had sacrificed by deferring consumption to create investment capital—whether that sacrifice had been willing or not. The capital stock can be thought of as having been collectively financed and held, as if in trust, by the state, and this suggests that the title to the newly privatized firms should be widely, and therefore equitably, distributed across the population. However, such a policy would not resolve the nexus of "commons" and "principal-agent" issues that led to the inefficient incentive and oversight structure in socially owned enterprises. A wide distribution of shares of newly privatized firms across the whole population though equitable, would lead to weak oversight of management and poor corporate governance.

DESIRABLE CHARACTERISTICS
OF A PRIVATIZATION PROGRAM

If we list the characteristics that are desirable in a privatization program, we quickly recognize that some may be in conflict.[12] Features that we might want to see include the following:

1. *Rapidity.* The stock of assets to be transferred to the private sector in former socialist economies is large. The creation of a market economy requests tangible progress, and the process must be complete within a foreseeable period of time. The pace at which government assets were disposed of in mixed capitalist economies, like the United Kingdom or France, is not acceptable when the vast bulk of the capital stock of a nation is to be disposed of.

---

[12]Cheryl W. Gray, "In Search of Owners: Privatization and Corporate Governance in Transition Economies," *The World Bank Research Observer* 11, no. 2 (August 1996): 179–197.

2. *Improved enterprise governance.* The change in property rights must improve the governance of the enterprises. New owners must have an effective means of oversight and way of tackling principal-agent problems.

3. *Fairness.* The process of privatization should be seen as fair and leading to the betterment of those who contributed to capital accumulation. A widespread perception of inequity may threaten political stability.

4. *Gaining the support of powerful interests.* The process must be able to placate the interests of the existing elite and the present "stakeholders" in the economy because without the support of powerful interests both political and economic reform may be aborted.

5. *Facilitating the inflow of new capital, technology, and management skills.* Enterprises have been hampered by a shortage of capital as well as limited access to foreign technology and "best-practice" techniques; privatization should help overcome these difficulties.

6. *Sustaining and supporting the liberalization program.* Finally, it is always desirable that any steps taken in the privatization program should be supportive of the overall program of liberalization and the institutions that have been created.

TECHNIQUES OF PRIVATIZATION

RESTITUTION. The simplest privatization is the restitution of property to identifiable previous owners, who might have been uncompensated or only partially compensated when the assets were seized. Property rights can be swiftly transferred (as long as the title can be established), and the resultant ownership structure would be fair and lead to better governance. However, restitution is not useful in the majority of circumstances, especially in the case of medium- and large-scale enterprises, since the current firms have no identifiable prior owner.

SMALL-SCALE MASS PRIVATIZATION. The logical owners of much of the retail and service sectors (which consists of small bakeries, groceries, restaurants, small hotels, service stations, and so forth) are the state employees who operated the facilities under the planned system. It is desirable for continuity that these people stay in their jobs, and creating owner-operators can benefit efficiency and quality of service by eliminating principal-agent problems. Furthermore, these individuals probably have the best chance of being able to effectively value the business. The drawback is that, typically, such individuals have little capital, and loans to small businesses are seldom available in transition economies. Consequently, the enterprises have to be sold at very low prices, and the state receives little revenue. This is generally acceptable (except in cases where real estate or valuable inventory is involved), since employment is maintained and a potential tax stream is established with long-run positive revenues. Small-scale privatization also scores high for both speed and equity.

SALE TO INSIDERS.   If operators of small businesses are allowed to assume ownership at favorable prices, the analogy in the industrial sector is sale to workers and management. Selling to such "insiders" has two obvious advantages: it increases support for the transition process, and by making workers shareholders in the firm it helps to eliminate some of the incentive problems that lowered efficiency and productivity.[13]

There are, however, substantial drawbacks. First, neither workers nor management have access to finance and cannot pay realistic prices for the enterprises, so little revenue is generated for the state. Second, the process is inequitable when viewed from a national perspective. Workers in the best firms, with the brightest prospects and newest capital, gain the most, although this may be due to luck rather than their own hard work. Since investment in most socialist countries was determined at the national level and capital charges were unrealistically low, workers in enterprises most favored by the planners gain at the expense of the broad segment of society that made the sacrifices to provide the investment.

There is likely to be further inequity within the enterprise. Managers, though fewer in number than workers, have greater opportunities to disrupt the privatization process and therefore are able to negotiate, or to seize, a larger share of the assets. Many management-employee buyouts have resulted in the assumption of the assets by senior management at low prices. Although this is satisfactory in terms of speed, it scores badly from the point of view of equity.

Finally, sale to insiders does very little to attract new capital, new technology, or new management into the business, and therefore a prime economic objective of privatization—placing assets in the hands of those who will be able to maximize value—is not fulfilled.

DIRECT SALE TO OUTSIDERS.   One way of avoiding the problems of sale to insiders is to seek a group of investors, or a company, to purchase an enterprise as a going concern. An immediate difficulty is the shortage of capital and the underdeveloped capital markets, which make a leveraged buyout to a citizen or group of citizens unlikely. When deals are made with outsiders, prices often seem arbitrary, and there can be the appearance (and frequently the reality) of corruption.[14] Valuation techniques, even when applied by Western advisors, are rudimentary and close to useless when accounting information is poor and economic uncertainty is high.

The only groups that can afford to buy industrial enterprises "in being" are foreign investors who can pay more realistic prices for assets and are capable of

---

[13] This, of course, is the logic that offers options of shares to workers in developed market economies. There is also evidence of a very substantial impact on productivity in some privatizations. The case of road goods transportation in the United Kingdom is very revealing.

[14] This suspicion of favoritism is not limited to transition economies. Sales of this kind were an important part of Thatcher's privatizations in Britain, and they attracted criticism whenever valuable assets were transferred without an open-bidding process.

infusing capital, technology, and modern management into their acquisitions. However, there is a political price to pay in handing over prominent large enterprises to foreign control. In any case foreign buyers have been slow to buy large enterprises in transition economies. Frequently the existing plant is inappropriately designed, obsolete, and too large. Buying an existing enterprise means retaining a workforce with low productivity and bad work habits and one that has usually been granted long-term job tenure prior to privatization.

PRIVATIZATION THROUGH INITIAL PUBLIC OFFERINGS. IPOs have distinct attractions. Enterprises can be sold for realistic sums of money, thereby raising substantial revenues for the government, and widespread shareholding (and therefore support for capitalism) can be encouraged. However, success depends on some essential preconditions. First, company accounts must be accurate and accessible to allow realistic valuation. Even if this is the case, IPOs are a slow path to privatization since each enterprise must be individually prepared and the public informed and educated about the company. Capital and equity markets must be developed and deep, since even stock markets with a high capitalization can absorb only a few IPOs each year. If too much is offered in a short space of time, the whole market may be depressed.[15] Consequently, IPOs are not very useful in an economy moving from socialism to capitalism. Although they score high in terms of equity and in increasing the long-term stability of reform, poor information and shallow capital markets limit their applicability.

VOUCHER PRIVATIZATION. If the correct way to view the socialist state is that it holds productive capital in trust for its citizens, then the process of privatization should transfer some part of the capital stock to each citizen. That, in essence, is the idea behind the schemes of voucher privatization by which the government gives away, or sells at very low prices, vouchers that can then be used to claim shares in companies that are to be transferred from state ownership. This approach circumvents the problems resultant from the shortage of wealth that limits the applicability of all other approaches to privatization that involve sale, and it carries with it obvious advantages of fairness and equity. Voucher programs have been used in many of the transition economies and may be the approach that best satisfies the five desirable characteristics itemized earlier.

Cheryl Gray has summarized this:

> Well-designed voucher privatization can overcome many of the problems encountered with the various sales techniques, notably the perceived unfairness, the shortage of domestic capital, and the difficulty of placing a value on assets. Because the voucher approach can proceed rapidly, it can simultaneously stimulate the development of market institutions, create new owners, and reorient the interests of existing ones toward

---

[15] Care had to be taken in the recent French privatization lest the Paris markets were depressed by too many new shares.

further reform. Furthermore, it can speedily cut the links between enterprises and the state that both inhibit restructuring and put fiscal pressures on the state.[16]

The main problem with voucher privatization is that ownership of the enterprise becomes widely disbursed, diminishing effective governance. When a firm is divided among many owners, no single one has a strong incentive to invest time and resources in supervising management. Even if one was highly motivated, he or she would have little power (as one shareholder among many) to change management's behavior. Consequently, management is often free to act in its own interest rather than in that of the owners, and there is less incentive to maximize the return to capital and inefficiency results.

To avoid this problem, several countries have encouraged or institutionalized the development of holding companies, very much like mutual funds, that concentrate ownership and have the knowledge, incentive, and power to effectively supervise management. In Poland, for example, the government set up several investment intermediaries staffed by managers appointed by the government. Each of these intermediaries was given a number of the enterprises to be privatized to manage, and the shares of the intermediaries were distributed among the citizenry. It was hoped that by active management the investment intermediaries would reorganize the enterprises under their control to maximize value and eventually sell them off to core investors. The danger of this approach is that holding companies will not follow through on restructuring or on the active pursuit of new owners. Consequently, rather than becoming a dynamic force for change they became state-protected institutions to manage lame-duck enterprises that have no willing buyers.

In the Czech Republic intermediaries have grown as a result of market initiative rather than being created by the government. The original intent of the Czech privatization scheme was to auction shares directly to individuals using vouchers. However, investment funds arose (many of which were connected to banks), which acquired and pooled the vouchers of many individuals. These funds (420 in number) eventually acquired some 72 percent of the vouchers. The funds have proved powerful in exerting managerial oversight of the firms, and in some cases their control might have been too great. Funds managed by the banks often had a conflict of interest because the bank was both an owner of and a lender to a specific firm. In Russia, while the voucher auction scheme scheme sanctioned the development of investment intermediaries, they have not grown to the degree seen in the Czech Republic.

FINANCIAL SECTOR REFORM

The purpose of the financial sector in a market economy is quite different from that under central planning. In a modern market economy, financial institutions are

---

[16]Gray, "In Search of Owners," 90.

responsible for accumulating and rationing investment resources. The savings of small households are aggregated and commingled in financial institutions and loaned out to business enterprises looking for investment capital. The financial sector is also responsible for evaluating the risk of these loans and fixing appropriate risk-compensated interest rates. Importantly, the financial sector grants credit to those industries that are likely to grow and denies finance to moribund firms.

As we discussed earlier, the purpose of the financial system in a centrally planned economy is quite different. Under central planning a single state bank (monobank) served two purposes. First, it would passively allocate credit to enterprises in accordance with the plan. Second, it served as a system of checking plan performance, since all movements of material through the economy had their counterpart as a paper trail of credit in the banking system. If market reforms are to be successful, a functional financial system, which will perform the tasks of pooling savings, disinterestedly assessing risk, and making loans, is essential.

THE CENTRAL BANK

One of the first priorities must be the creation of a central bank, usually achieved by divesting the monobank of its other responsibilities and focusing it on functions traditionally reserved for the central bank.

These include the following:

1. Acting as a clearing bank for the commercial banks
2. Acting as the promulgator and enforcer of regulation to enhance the stability and efficiency of the financial system
3. Functioning as a lender of last resort to banks
4. Controlling the stock of money in the economy, and hence the interest rate
5. Monitoring the foreign exchange value of the currency

The degree of independence of the central bank is an important issue. Developed market economies offer little in the way of guidance to economies in transition; the United States Federal Reserve System is highly independent, and the German Bundesbank is regarded as even more so, but on the other hand, the Bank of Japan and the Bank of France are subject to tight government control. The Bank of England, for most of the postwar period an arm of the British government, has now been granted a much higher degree of autonomy.

Proponents of independence argue that central bankers have the expertise to make impartial decisions and will perform well if politicians are prevented from influencing them. The prime job of the central bank is to preserve the value of the currency, and it must frequently take a restrictive and conservative line on credit creation. When politicians are given control over the central bank, monetary policy tends to be too relaxed, and the unpleasant but necessary task of squeezing credit, and watching enterprises fail as unemployment mounts, would be avoided. The opposing view is that a totally independent central bank is answerable to no one. Since in a market economy it is an institution of great significance,[17] it is odd that in a representative democracy the people have no say in this vital dimension of policy making. In this analysis, the central bank is responsive only to the narrow financial community from which the board of governors are likely to spring. As such, an independent central bank might be unduly austere and hence jeopardize political stability by pursuing its own brand of financial rectitude. There is no right and wrong answer to this debate. Politicians are adept at judging the public will, and if they controlled the central bank we could say that a form of democracy prevailed. On the other hand, politicians have a short-term outlook and are prone to shallow compromise, whereas the financial experts insulated from pressure might effect more viable long-term policies.

COMMERCIAL BANKS/INVESTMENT BANKS

After creating the central bank, priority must be given to developing a commercial and investment banking system, which can be effective in mobilizing savings and allocating investment capital among potential borrowers. This is unlikely to be a rapid process. Some banks can be created by assuming the deposit and lending functions of the monobank, holding them for a while in the public sector, and then privatizing when conditions are appropriate. It will also probably be worthwhile to create a "post office" or "giro" savings bank in most of the transition economies; these institutions are almost universally found in Western Europe and Asia[18] and provide a means of aggregating small savings as well as providing a high degree of convenience, security, and liquidity to the less affluent households. Although these institutions have been criticized for paying only low rates of interest, in general they have proved popular with small savers.

The biggest banking problem for transition economies is controlling the growth and behavior of new financial intermediaries that spring up. In Russia, for example, at the outset of reform between 1989 and 1992 some 1,600 "banks" were created, but most did not meet the definition of banks as applied in the West. Many were created by industrial enterprises and exist largely to finance their parent companies by borrowing on the interbank market. As such, they perform little in the way of impartially assessing risk or allocating scarce capital resources to their highest value functions. It is vital for long-term development that a stable, disinterested private banking sector be established, and the first step is defining and requiring capital adequacy standards, accountancy norms, and regular audits to guarantee security to the depositor.

Banking regulations vary from country to country and as long as they are visible and enforced, a range of policy can be highly functional. In the United States and the United Kingdom commercial banking, savings institutions, and investment

---

[17] If confirmation of this were required, we have only to take note of the army of "Fed watchers" in the United States, who are concerned with predicting the Fed's behavior.

[18] Deposits in the Japanese postal savings system amount to well over $2 trillion, almost as much as the rest of the banking system together.

banks have been separated by practice and law, although these divisions are eroding over time. In continental Europe no such functional division applies and universal banks (sometimes referred to as U-banks) are the norm. U-banks are large and perform savings, lending, and underwriting functions. At the end of the day what matters most is not the specific institutional form of the banking system, but rather the degree of public confidence that it is able to inspire. With a high degree of confidence the public will entrust its savings to the banking sector; if there is little confidence in financial institutions, savings rates will be low and speculation in real assets unhealthily high.

STOCK MARKETS

Stock markets are a feature of all developed market economies and it is tempting to think that the rapid establishment of a stock exchange is an important prerequisite for growth. However, historically this has seldom proved to be the case. The reliable evidence we have suggests that the growth of the stock markets tends to follow, rather than cause, rapid economic growth. In East Asia, for example, little industrial finance originated from the equity market and only in Korea and Taiwan did it represent even as much as 10 percent. Further back into history, most of the finance for Britain's industrial revolution was generated by interfirm credit, while continental Europe and the United States relied heavily on bank lending. So although the development of an equities market is positive, it is not essential for a market economy.

The process of maturation of a stock market is a slow one and depends on the accretion of public trust, a growing number of investors, and intermediaries, and an increased number of issues and capitalization. Antoine van Agtmael,[19] in a paper published in 1982, identified five stages in the development of stock markets that have been quite general across time and economies.

1. *The dormant stage.* During the first, dormant stage, most people are not actively aware of the existence of the stock market. Trading volume is low, only a few companies are listed, and prices remain close to their issuance values. As time goes by, shares tend to become undervalued, especially in a dynamic economic environment. Inevitably, brokers or individuals discover that dividend yield alone—even excluding potential capital gains—exceeds the yield on other investment alternatives. This stage was largely absent or short lived in transition economies where expectations for equity growth were high from the outset.

2. *Manipulation.* Manipulation begins when some market participants discover that the small supply of stocks, and thus limited liquidity, makes it possible to move prices up with relatively small purchases. Rising prices

---

[19] From *Emerging Securities Markets,* 1982. Material first published by Euromoney Publications, London.

encouraged new market entrants, enabling the manipulators to get out with quick profits.

3. *Speculation.* As soon as some people begin to make substantial capital gains and boast of their profits, a wider group of investors is attracted. A speculative stage begins during which trading soars and prices are driven up well beyond appropriate values.

4. *Consolidation or crash.* At some point the speculative bubble is questioned, and stock prices begin to waver and drop. Depending on the extent of the boom during the speculative stage, prices either decline gradually or tumble deeply. The consolidation stage or crash has set in. It may take investors months or even years to regain confidence in the stock market after such a price decline. Much depends on the extent of the price drop as well as on interest rates, economic growth, corporate profitability, inflation yields on other investment alternatives, new incentives to restimulate buying, and the behavior of institutional investors. During this consolidation stage, many speculators become, out of necessity, investors. Unwilling to sell their shares at a loss, they hold on to them for long-term investment in the hope that prices will improve in the future.

5. *Maturity.* The mature stage begins when the initial investors regain confidence and are joined by new groups of investors unhurt by previous failures. Trading volume is likely to be more consistent, investment more sophisticated, the supply of shares broader, and, thus, liquidity greater. Recent experience in Southeast Asia, Latin America, and the transition economies seems to justify van Agtmael's overall conclusions.

REFORM OF INTERNATIONAL TRADE

Prior to the late 1980s the international trade of socialist nations was the concern of the state, not individual firms. The direction of trade with other socialist countries, its volume, and the prices of traded goods were subject to the plan. All trade with the nonsocialist world was conducted by specialized state-controlled foreign trade organizations (FTOs). Exports were sanctioned in order to raise the foreign exchange to finance the imports required by the plan. Individual firms had little contact with their customers and could only buy imported machinery, technology, and materials if they could make a convincing case with the planners, which usually required political influence. Under Gorbachev this system was reformed, and enterprises were allowed to trade directly with overseas counterparts, but a complex system of tariffs and licenses prevailed.

Most economists favor the elimination of licensing and the removal or moderation of tariffs in order to allow substantially free trade. In the short term, some tariff protection may be necessary because during restructuring virtually all enterprises can be regarded as "infant." While it might seem strange to regard the former Soviet Union's industrial giants as infants, in terms of efficiency, pricing, client relations, and technical innovation they have much to learn. Free trade would lead to loss of domestic market share that would be hard to recoup and would cause further macroeconomic contraction. However, protection for inefficient producers has costs, not least of which is that it denies other enterprises access to inputs and technology at world prices. Consequently, the drive to modernize within these firms may be hindered by the inflated cost of inputs. While limited protection is important in the short term, the long term growth of the economy requires that protective measures be phased out quickly or else the industry nurtured behind tariff walls can never become globally competitive.

Trade liberalization also requires currency reform. Under planning, currency convertibility was limited and often subject to multiple exchange rates—with different uses requiring conversion at different rates. This situation was inefficient, distortionary, and led to the development of black markets. Full currency convertibility is not absolutely necessary for a functioning market economy. Convertibility was not generally restored in Western Europe until the late 1950s, and many countries today limit capital convertibility and the access of residents or citizens to foreign exchange. What is essential is the establishment of a realistic exchange rate and relatively unrestricted access to foreign exchange for those firms involved in trade.

Trade liberalization often goes hand in hand with a greater role for foreign direct investment (FDI), although again it is possible to conceive of primarily market-coordinated economies in which the part played by the FDI is limited; Korea provides such an example. However, for most transition economies FDI helps to solve a series of problems since it provides capital for investment, a source of foreign exchange, technological know-how, management techniques, and links to export markets. Defined property rights, a civil legal code, consistent tax laws, and guarantees on the convertibility and repatriation of profits are important in attracting direct investment. A good deal of discretion may be retained within a general policy to encourage FDI. As a policy matter, a foreign presence can be discouraged in those sectors that are sensitive (e.g., resources) or those areas that the government feels can be adequately met by domestic enterprises (retailing, for example).

THE SOCIAL SAFETY NET

Under socialism and centralized planning, the most important form of "safety net" was the guarantee of work for everyone. In fact, being employed was a legal requirement for most people. Having a job provided workers with income and access to nonwage benefits, irrespective of their productivity in employment or the fundamental profitability of the enterprise for which they worked. Long-term success in the transition economies depends on both closing the enterprises that are unable to compete when subject to a hard budget constraint and raising the productivity (therefore cutting the workforce) of those that survive. Consequently, unemployment, which existed only in a disguised form during the socialist period, will necessarily rise during the transition. Some form of social safety net is required to protect the unemployed and to guarantee some minimum living standard for all.

The alternative to providing an effective social safety net is the alienation and marginalization of a large part of the workforce, creating an underclass and courting a high degree of political risk. Other social problems may develop including a high degree of migrancy, waste of social infrastructure, and a plethora of social pathologies including rising crime, prostitution, mounting suicide, and so forth. Furthermore, a social safety net has an economic as well as a political function by assisting the development and operation of the labor market. If there is no public support for the unemployed, displaced workers are forced to accept the first job available without being able to undertake any off-the-job search. Mismatches of skill between job and employee are inevitable.

BIG BANG VERSUS GRADUALISM

A remaining important question about transition is its speed. If market arrangements are substantially more efficient than the plan, then it can be argued that economic reform should proceed as quickly as possible. Rapid changes in ownership and property rights should bring about correspondingly rapid increases in factor productivity, output, and the general level of welfare.

However, a contrary case can be made. The existing capital stock and associated institutions were fashioned for a particular economic system involving a high degree of command and central planning. New institutions and laws will take time to draft, and the economic actors will be on a learning curve to assimilate the parameters of the new order. The existing capital stock and infrastructure have to be modified for the new conditions in which the economy must operate. Thus a "big bang" approach, in which prices are liberalized at a stroke and in which privatization is pursued vigorously, will take time to bear fruit, and in the meantime some disruption will be inevitable. Slower change (allowing economic actors to absorb lessons) and institutional experimentation might be preferable.

A drawback of a gradualist approach is the reversibility of reform. A big bang creates powerful interests committed to reform, while gradualism allows the old guard a continued lease on life and protracts the unsettling political debate about the ultimate direction of the economy. Such uncertainty might have a substantial effect on real investment, since entrepreneurs might be unwilling to commit resources to long-term projects if they foresee a strong chance of reversal. Time alone will tell which approach leads to the better outcome. Table 21.2 suggests that the rapid reformers of Central and Eastern Europe have already passed through their darkest period and are moving into a situation where sustained growth seems to be likely. However, if we look at other parts of the world, especially to the People's Republic of China (see chapter 12), gradualism and experimentation seem to have produced a more successful pattern of transition.

POLITICAL REFORM AND ECONOMIC REFORM

Table 21.5 shows the progress that had been made in economies in transition through 1997, ranking both political and economic progress. These figures were

■ **TABLE 21.5**

**PROGRESS TO POLITICAL AND ECONOMIC REFORM IN TRANSITION ECONOMIES:
FREEDOM HOUSE RANKINGS**

	Economy	Democracy
Hungary	1.63	1.44
Czech Republic	1.88	1.38
Poland	2	1.44
Estonia	2.13	2.06
Slovenia	2.38	1.88
Lithuania	2.5	2.06
Latvia	2.5	2.06
Slovak Republic	3.38	3.81
Russia	3.5	3.75
Kyrgystan	3.75	4.75
Croatia	3.88	4.25
Moldova	4	3.81
Albania	4	4.5
Armenia	4	4.75
Georgia	4.13	4.75
Ukraine	4.25	3.88
Kazakstan	4.38	5.25
Macedonia FYR	4.5	3.88
Romania	4.63	3.88
Azerbaijan	5.13	5.44
Bulgaria	5.38	3.81
Belarus	6	5.88
Tajikstan	6.13	6
Uzbekistan	6.25	6.44
Turkmenistan	6.38	6.34

SOURCE: Freedom House, *Nations in Transition*, 1997.

produced by Freedom House, a U.S. group concerned with political and economic liberalization in Europe. The figures are largely subjective, but they echo to some extent the estimates of Table 21.2. They show that political and economic reform have been closely linked. The correlation between the two indices is high, and consequently we seldom encounter either a democratic state with a highly controlled economy or a liberal economy accompanied by a totally authoritarian political structure. In general, the former Soviet satellite states of central Europe have been fastest in both political and economic reform, followed by the Baltic States of the former Soviet Union. The new nations that made up the former Yugoslavia (Croatia, Slovenia, and Macedonia)[20] are hard to classify. Slovenia is advanced in political and economic reform, while Macedonia, despite being part of the Yugoslav "participatory economy," is backward both economically and politically. As far as

---

[20] Neither Serbia (still called Yugoslavia) nor Bosnia are included in the survey, presumably because of political problems.

the European states go, the outliers are Belarus, backward in both dimensions, and Bulgaria, where economic progress lags behind political change.

KEY TERMS AND CONCEPTS

advanced reformers
Big Bang
collapse of GDP
contestability of markets
corporatization
domestic liberalization
enterprise governance
external transactions liberalization

inflation tax
monetary overhang
negative value added
principal-agent issues
private sector entry liberalization
restitution
voucher privatization

QUESTIONS FOR DISCUSSION

1. How did the "monetary overhang" arise in socialist states, and what is its significance in the transition process?
2. Why was inflation a common feature of transitional states?
3. What led to the phenomenon of a collapse of GDP being a general concomitant of liberalization?
4. What happened in most countries to labor productivity during the transition? Why?
5. Why is the problem of monopoly so pressing in transition countries? How can abuse of monopoly power be limited?
6. What is meant by corporatization?
7. How are the issues of privatization and enterprise governance linked?
8. Do you think that the central bank in a post-socialist state should be independent and insulated from political pressure?
9. Why are stock markets not likely to be important as providers of capital in the transition process?
10. What is a "big bang" approach to transition?

RESOURCES

WEB SITES

Stockholm Institute for Transition Economics and East European Economies, Stockholm School of Economics . . . . http://www.hhs.se/

International Center for Policy Studies, Kiev, Ukraine . . . . http://www.icps.kiev.ua/

Transition . . . . http://www.worldbank.org/html/prddr/trans/WEB/trans.htm
The *Transition* newsletter is a regular publication of the World Bank's Development Economic Research Group [DECRG].

REESWeb: Russian and East European Studies, University of Pittsburgh . . . .
. . . . http://www.ucis.pitt.edu/reesweb/

The Slavic Research Center, Hokkaido University . . . .
. . . . http://src-home.slav.hokudai.ac.jp/index-e.html#resource

World Bank Research on Poverty During the Transition . . . .
. . . . http://www.worldbank.org/research/transition/

The Vienna Institute for International Economic Studies . . . . . . http://www.wiiw.ac.at/

European Bank for Reconstruction and Development . . . . www.ebrd.com/

The European Union's Main Transition Initiative: The Phare Programme . . . .
. . . . http://europa.eu.int/comm/dg1a/phare/index.htm

United Nations Economic Commission for Europe . . . . http://www.unece.org/

Freedom House . . . . http://www.freedomhouse.org/

Soros Foundation . . . . http://www.soros.org/

The Corporate Governance Net http://www.corpgov.net/library/articles/abarticles.html

Sigma—The Good Governance Initiative of the Organization for Economic Cooperation and Development (OECD) . . . . http://www.oecd.org/puma/sigmaweb/

Cato Institute: Project on Global Economic Liberty . . . .
. . . . http://www.cato.org/research/glob-st.html

BOOKS AND ARTICLES

Berg, Andrew; Eduardo R. Borensztein, Ratna Sahay, Jeromin Zettelmeyer. "The Evolution of Output in Transition Economies—Explaining the Differences." International Monetary Fund Working Paper WP/99/73.

Blanchard, Olivier. *The Economics of Post-Communist Transition. Clarendon Lectures in Economics.* Oxford: Clarendon Press, 1997.

Carlin, W., and M. Landesmann. *From Theory into Practice? Corporate Restructuring and Economic Dynamism in Transition Economies.* Vienna: Vienna Institute for International Economic Studies, August 1997.

Claassen, Emil-Maria. *Exchange Rate Policies in Developing and Post-Socialist Countries.* San Francisco: OCS Press, 1992. N. Reviewed in *Studies in Comparative International Development.*

De Melo, Martha, Cevder Denizer, and Alan Gelb. "Patterns of Transition from Plan to Market." *World Bank Economic Review* 10, no. 3 (September 1996): 397 ff.

Earle, John S., Roman Frydman, Andrzej Rapaczynski, and Joel Turkewitz. *Small Privatization: The Transformation of Retail Trade and Consumer Services in the Czech Republic, Hungary, and Poland. Ceu Privatization Reports.* New York: Central European University Press, 1994.

Frydman, Roman, and Andrzej Rapaczynski. *Privatization in Eastern Europe: Is the State Withering Away?* New York: Central European University Press, 1994.

Frydman, Roman, Cheryl W. Gray, and Andrzej Rapaczynski, eds. *Corporate Governance in Central Europe and Russia: Banks, Funds and Foreign Investors. World Bank/Ceu Privatization Project.* New York: Central European University Press, 1996.

Frydman, Roman, Kenneth Murphy, and Andrzej Rapaczynski. *Capitalism with a Comrade's Face.* New York: Central European University Press, 1998.

Gray, Cheryl W. "In Search of Owners: Privatization and Corporate Governance in Transition Economies." *World Bank Research Observer* 11, no. 2 (August 1996): 179–197.

Hardt, John P., and Richard F. Kaufman, eds. *East-Central European Economies in Transition.* Armonk, N.Y.: M. E. Sharpe, 1995.

Havrylyshyn, Oleh, and Donal McGettigan. "Privatization in Transition Countries— A Sampling of the Literature." International Monetary Fund Working Paper WP/99/6.

Henderson, Jeffrey, ed., with Karoly Balaton and Gyorgy Lengyel. *Industrial Transformation in Eastern Europe in the Light of the East Asian Experience.* New York: St. Martin's Press, 1998.

Hernández-Catá, Ernesto. "Liberalization and the Behavior of Output during the Transition from Plan to Market." *International Monetary Fund Staff Papers* 44, no. 4 (December 1997).

Kennett, David, and Marc Lieberman, eds. *The Road to Capitalism: Economic Transformation in Eastern Europe and the Former Soviet Union.* Fort Worth, Tex.: The Dryden Press, 1992.

Lavigne, Marie. *The Economics of Transition: From Socialist Economy to Market Economy.* New York: St. Martin's Press, 1999.

Mann, Catherine L. *Industry Restructuring in East-Central Europe: The Challenge and the Role of Foreign Investment.* American Economic Association Papers and Proceedings, May 1991.

Milanovic, Branko. *Income, Inequality, and Poverty during the Transition from Planned to Market Economy.* Washington, D.C.: World Bank.

Pöhl, Gerhard, Robert E. Anderson, Stijn Claessens, and Simeon Djankov. "Privatization and Restructuring in Central and Eastern Europe." World Bank Technical Paper, 1997.

Rother, Philipp. "Explaining the Behavior of Financial Intermediation—Evidence from Transition Economies." International Monetary Fund Working Paper WP/99/36.

Sachs, Jeffrey D. *Reforms in Eastern Europe and the Former Soviet Union in Light of the East Asian Experiences.* Working Paper Series, Working Paper 5404. Cambridge, Mass.: National Bureau of Economic Research, 1996.

Sachs, Jeffrey D., and Katharina Pistor, eds. *The Rule of Law and Economic Reform in Russia.* John M. Olin Critical Issues Series (paper). Boulder, Colo.: Westview Press, 1997.

"A Survey of Central Asia: A Caspian Gamble." *The Economist,* 7 February 1998, 56.

White, William, *Evolving International Financial Markets: Some Implications for Central Banks.* BIS Working Paper no. 66 (April 1999).

World Bank. *From Plan to Market: World Development Report 1996.* New York: Oxford University Press, 1996.

REFORM OF THE RUSSIAN ECONOMY

THE LEGACY OF THE "ERA OF STAGNATION"

By the early 1980s the crisis of the Soviet economy had become acute, and while no sector was doing well, agriculture and consumer goods were faring particularly poorly. The system was sustained only by the hard currency proceeds of oil and gas exports used to buy food and advanced capital goods. Despite exhortation to improve economic performance, the leadership seemed determined to change nothing, and stagnation resulted.

Poor economic performance meant that the Soviet Union's relative position in the world was slowly sinking, and with it the capacity to maintain superpower status. Slippage was accelerated by emerging payments problems in the 1980s; hard-currency exports (mainly energy) peaked in the early 1980s, while imports, including food, continued to rise throughout the decade. The result was a growing external deficit and increased international indebtedness. The gross debt (i.e., what the Soviet Union owed the Western nations before making allowance for Soviet holdings of hard currency) rose from $11.5 billion in 1975 to $22 billion in 1980 and $38 billion in 1985. A measure of the scale and severity of this indebtedness is the debt service ratio (the amount of hard currency payments required annually as a proportion of normal hard currency earnings); it rose from 10 percent in 1975 to about 23 percent in the mid-1980s. Almost a quarter of the value of the Soviet exports was committed ahead of time to repaying previously incurred debts. Market economies faced with such a crisis could finance part of their balance of payments deficit through incoming foreign direct investment, but despite a lukewarm commitment to joint ventures, the reality of Soviet politics made such inflows all but impossible.

PERESTROIKA AND GLASNOST

Gorbachev's reform efforts will forever be associated with the catchwords *"perestroika"* and *"glasnost,"* usually translated as restructuring and openness. His original intentions were modest, but the political change initiated by his *glasnost* policy far outstripped his plans for the economy, and Gorbachev was swept further toward liberalization as he attempted to appease both domestic and international critics. While *perestroika* seemed to offer much at the time, in retrospect this meandering attempt at reform must be judged a failure. The six years of the program may be divided into four phases, which may be summarized as follows:[1]

Phase	Date	Description
I	1985–early 1986	Rhetorical period. A lot of talk about reform but few specifics.
II	1986–early 1988	Legislative period. Creation of superministries, new laws on self-employment, state enterprise, cooperatives, and property.
III	1988–1989	Attempted implementation of reform.
IV	1989–1991	Failure, abandonment of the *perestroika* model in favor of more radical reform.

While these stages were not totally distinct, this partition gives an overview of the history of the Gorbachev years. Immediately after he came to power, Gorbachev talked a great deal about the necessity of reform and the gains to be made, but his rhetoric obscured the vague nature of his program. What was clear, and remained the case throughout his administration, was that he aimed to modify a socialist economy rather than to shift toward a true market economy.

During 1986, decrees and laws designed to reform the economy began to dribble through. In some ways the legislation was schizophrenic. While it laid the groundwork for private property and market signaling, it increased government control by heaping new powers on the center and creating "superministries." The most notorious of these was Gosagroprom, designed to coordinate all agricultural and food distribution activity, but it only increased mismanagement and confusion. Gorbachev's agenda for industrialization hinged on three important laws and one decree:

1. The **Law on Individual Economic Activity** (November 1986) allowed the establishment of small businesses in the service sector as individual proprietorships under license from the state.

2. The **Law on State Enterprise,** passed in mid-1987 and effective as of January 1, 1988, gave much greater freedom to the management of state-owned industry. Hard planning targets were replaced by "state orders" and greater latitude was permitted in staffing, price, and choice of technique. Theoretically, enterprises were to become financially independent and accountable, initiating a "hard-budget constraint."

3. The **Law on Cooperatives** (May 1988) sanctioned the formation of larger private businesses. For ideological reasons they initially had to take the legal structure of cooperatives, but in reality this law facilitated the eventual creation of joint stock companies.

---

[1]See, for example, Gregory and Stuart, *Soviet and Post-Soviet Economic Structure and Performance*, 5th ed. (New York: HarperCollins, 1994), 324.

4. The **Decree on Property** (December 1988) allowed the sale of state-owned housing to individuals, creating a housing market and leading to the privatization of 12 million homes by 1995.

Although these reforms seemed far-reaching, their effect on the economy was mostly negative. The Law on State Enterprise gave firms both the incentive and opportunity to sell their goods in the market place for the highest prices that they could command, rather than continue to supply their traditional buyers at the prescribed plan prices. As a result, "downstream" firms frequently found themselves short of necessary inputs or unable to pay the higher prices and had to curtail production. Some enterprises even found themselves without the cash flow required to pay their workers. Coal miners, for example, were not paid for long periods in the later years of the Gorbachev administration, although the mines continued to operate and produce coal. Viewed from almost any perspective within the economy, *perestroika* was not a success.

500 DAYS TO A MARKET ECONOMY

The failure of Gorbachev's conception of *perestroika* and the protracted decline of the Soviet economy pointed to the need for more radical reform. The experience of the previous four years showed once again the ineffectiveness of tampering with the basic system of command planning, and consequently more attention was paid to moving the economy of the Soviet Union directly to a market system. In early 1990 a committee established under the leadership of Stanislav Shatalin, a respected economist and academician, produced a document known as the Shatalin report, titled *500 Days: Transition to Market*. It was deeply critical of the foundations of the Soviet system of centralized planning and sought to replace it with private property and liberalized market prices.

> The long rule of the totalitarian socio-political system dragged our society into profound crisis. Indecisiveness of the government and the mistakes it made in economic policy brought the country to the brink of collapse. . . . For a long time economic policy did not consider the people's interests. The state was wealthy while the people were poor. The state accumulated under its control almost all of the resources for production. Such resources were squandered on giant and ineffective projects, for increasing military power, and for certain ideologically flavored practices overseas even though the times have long passed since we could afford this.[2]

After attacking the leadership, the system, and Gorbachev's halting and ineffectual reforms, the report provided a rationale for a new order based on market relations. In retrospect, and given the disappointments of the decade since the

---

[2] "Man, Freedom and Market" excerpted from "On the Program Developed by Academician S. S. Shatalin from: *500 Days: Transition to Market*," in *Road to Capitalism*, ed. David Kennett and Marc Lieberman (Fort Worth, Tex.: Dryden Press, 1992), 88.

report, the idea that the Soviet economy could be put on a market footing in only a year and a half seems naive, but it did represent fresh and open thinking on the causes of and the potential solutions for the Soviet malaise.

As the economy spiraled downward Gorbachev's popularity sank with it. His authority became threatened by the emergence of a rival power center in the form of the government of the Russian Federation, led by Boris Yeltsin, the chairman of the Russian Supreme Soviet, who had in July 1990 taken the decisive step of resigning from the Communist Party. While Yeltsin unequivocally advocated a rapid shift to a market economy along the lines of the Shatalin report, Gorbachev still tended to gradualism. Consequently, although the Supreme Soviet of Russia voted to approve the Shatalin plan by a margin of 213 to 1, Gorbachev as leader of the Soviet Union rejected it, proposing a much slower and less complete transition agenda. In November 1990 the Russian Congress of Deputies took the politically charged step of legalizing private family farming, outraging the Communists, and provoking an irredeemable division.

Events of the following year, 1991, continued this conflict as the Russian government legislated an ever more liberal agenda, while Gorbachev attempted to slow the process of reform. Although Gorbachev avoided committing his administration to a radical transformation, his failure to stop Yeltsin's program allowed reform to proceed at a pace that alarmed the leadership of the Communist Party. As Gorbachev's position weakened and the failure of piecemeal reform became more apparent, Western nations, whose financial support was vital to the Soviet Union's reform effort, increased pressure on Gorbachev to adopt a more liberal stance. During the summer of 1991 a group of Soviet reformers and Western academics gathered and drafted what became known as the **Grand Bargain,** under which the Soviet Union would commit to rapid economic and political reform, while in return the West would provide very substantial economic aid. Gorbachev rejected the plan and tried to negotiate less conditional terms in a meeting with the leaders of the G7 nations, held in London in July. This was almost his last act as leader of the Soviet Union, but he came away empty-handed. While vacationing in the Crimea in August, he was the target of a coup led by Communist Party leaders, which because of an inability to neutralize Yeltsin, unraveled after a few days of chaos. This led directly to the breakup of the Soviet Union; during September most of the constituent republics declared their independence, and by March only the Ukraine and Belarus remained. On December 25 Gorbachev resigned, and over the Kremlin the red flag of the Soviet Union was replaced by the red, white, and blue banner of the Russian Federation.

THE GAIDAR REFORMS

Dramatic economic reform immediately followed. On January 2, 1992, just eight days after Gorbachev's resignation, Yeltsin, as president of the Russian Federation, launched a new phase of liberalization of the Russian economy. The chief architect of this new plan was Yegor Gaidar, a young liberal economist whose voice had become increasingly influential. The Gaidar/Yeltsin plan was spurred by Western

criticism and resembled the Sachs/Balcerowicz plan initiated in Poland the previous year with some success[3] and rested on five "pillars."[4]

(1) REHABILITATION OF THE RUBLE

The Gaidar team's primary premise was that the rehabilitation of the ruble had to
lie at the heart of any reform program. The Soviet population had lost faith in the
ruble as a store of value and opted where possible for dollars or D-marks. Without a currency in which the population had confidence, and which could serve as
vehicle for international exchange, they believed that the reform process would
stall.

(2) MARKET LIBERALIZATION

The second pillar was the creation of a functioning market economy. This involved
decontrolling prices, allowing free entry into almost all economic activity, cutting
back on the share of output absorbed by state orders, and establishing the necessary legal system required to underpin market activity. The January 2 pronounce-
ment ended central coordination of the economy, and almost all prices were
immediately liberalized.[5] Later that month, Yeltsin made a presidential decree that
declared all economic activity to be legal unless it was expressly prohibited, reversing the situation that had existed under Soviet planning, by which all private
economic activity was proscribed unless expressly permitted.[6]

The upshot was a massive rise in prices and the considerable monetary overhang came into play as idle savings pursued scarce goods. Inflation during the
first month of "shock therapy" was over 250 percent, and the prices of many key
consumer goods rose by much more. The force of inflationary pressure surprised
many observers, including the International Monetary Fund (IMF), which had
held the opinion that a rise in prices of only 45 percent would be enough to neutralize the monetary overhang. Opening the Russian economy to foreign trade also
had dramatic consequences as consumers who had been required to buy Soviet
goods now had greater choice. Imports flowed in, and the demand for domestic
output fell; for the first time Russian producers faced serious competition in markets that had been guaranteed to them under planning, and decades of neglecting

---

[3]See chapter 23 for a fuller description of the conception and achievements of Polish shock therapy.

[4]David Lipton and Jeffrey Sachs, "Prospects for Russia's Economic Reforms," *Brooking Papers on Economic Activity* 2 (1992): 213–276.

[5]The sole exception was the energy sector that remained under administrative prices. Energy prices
were raised at the outset of the reforms and were partially liberalized later in 1992, but remained at
a fraction of world prices. The government's fear was that a rapid increase of energy prices to world
levels would cause a massive contraction in industrial output since the Soviet economy was based on
cheap energy.

[6]One observer of the Soviet system had declared: "In the Soviet Union almost everything was forbidden . . . and those few things that were permitted were compulsory."

WINNERS AND LOSERS IN RUSSIA'S INFLATION 1992–1993,
PERCENTAGE OF GDP, 1993

	Losses	Gains	Net Gain
Households	12	0	−12
Enterprises	18	16	−2
Financial sector	0	8	+8
Government	0	4	+4
Other	0	2	+2
Total	30	30	0

SOURCE: William Easterly and Paula Vieira da Cunha, "Financing the Storm: Russia's Macroeconomic Crisis," *Economics of Transition* 2, no. 4 (1994).

design and quality showed. Meanwhile, because many raw materials could be now exported for hard cash, prices soared[7] from the artificially low levels administered under Soviet planning, pushing inflation and hurting domestic production.

Price liberalization had some positive effects: the monetary overhang disappeared as savings were eradicated; the black market was curtailed; and lines for goods, a great source of inefficiency and welfare loss, were much reduced. However, the distributional consequences were large. Savings in rubles were wiped out by the plunging value of the Russian currency. Table 22.1 gives some data on the extent of this redistribution. The biggest losers were the households, who saw their savings eradicated and their real wages fall, and any enterprises who held ruble-denominated balances. The gainers were largely the government and the financial sector.

The inter-enterprise payments system began to break down. Many firms were unable to pay the higher input prices since they were not receiving payment for the goods they sold and delivered. Not out of choice but out of necessity, enterprises began to extend credit to each other, creating a precarious pyramid of inter-enterprise debt. Insolvent firms ceased to pay their workers; as personal incomes fell, so did demand, creating more insolvencies. Although the linchpin of the Gaidar plan had been monetary restraint, the worsening economic situation raised pressures to liberalize credit. Lobbying from the enterprises was intense, and the growth of inter-enterprise credit led to the justifiable fear that the collapse of a few firms could lead to catastrophic domino consequences. So reluntantly the government, through the Central Bank, loosened credit and provided cheap loans (often at negative real interest rates) to bail out the industrial sector, causing excessive growth of the money supply.

---

[7]The increase in raw material prices occurred largely because the Russian economy became increasingly integrated into the world market. Input prices, especially those for energy, had been highly controlled under central planning and rose sharply toward world levels.

(3) PRIVATIZATION

The third pillar of the Gaidar program was mass privatization, deemed imperative for three main reasons. First, policy makers felt that the burden of subsidizing state enterprises could be sharply reduced, or even eliminated, once these firms had passed in private hands.[8] This would help to put public finance on a more stable footing and reduce the reliance on credit creation to keep enterprises solvent, thereby eliminating a source of inflation. Second, for reasons discussed earlier, it was expected that private management of resources would lead to greater efficiency. Third, large-scale privatization would be hard to reverse and would therefore reinforce political change because the new owners would oppose retrogression thereby "locking in" the gains of economic and political liberalization.

(4) CONSTRUCTING A SOCIAL SECURITY SYSTEM

The Soviet Union lacked an adequate system of unemployment compensation, which had been regarded as unnecessary in a society where unemployment notionally did not exist, and was, in fact, illegal. However, if the efficiency of industry was to be increased, sweeping changes in employment practices would be required, and raising labor productivity had to involve, at least in the short term, the shedding of excess labor. Without a "social safety net" to catch the unemployed there was a distinct possibility of increasing social unrest.[9]

(5) CONVERTING THE DEFENSE SECTOR

The great paradox of the Soviet economy was the coexistence of a world-class defense and aerospace sector with consumer goods and housing sectors that simply failed to deliver the goods. The key had been the high degree of **prioritization** that had locked up over 30 percent of Soviet gross domestic product (GDP) in defense, and with it most of the nation's able engineers and managers. It was hoped that "defense conversion" deploying the skilled labor and sophisticated apparatus to peaceful purpose could provide a dynamic sector around which to focus Russia's development effort.

OUTPUT COLLAPSE

The crisis accompanying the breakup of the Soviet Union led to a sharp fall in economic activity. Table 22.2 shows the sectoral impact on manufacturing and

---

[8] As we shall see, this was something of a vain hope. Privatization has not ended subsidy of the productive sector.

[9] Unemployment statistics are not reliable for the early period of reform. By mid-year 1993 the European Bank for Reconstruction and Development reported that the rate was 5.3 percent, although there is no good measure since the incidence of disguised unemployment (workers retained but not fully employed) was high.

■ **TABLE 22.2**

PRODUCTION IN SELECTED SECTORS (1992 PRICES, BILLIONS OF RUBLES)

	1990	1994	Change
Steel and metals	4,004	2,132	−47%
Light industry	1,926	512	−73%
Other industry	12,153	5,592	−54%
Agriculture	3,908	2,910	−26%
Total	22,087	10,368	−53%

Notes: Derived from Goskomstat data reported in *World Bank Statistical Handbook 1995,* "States of the Former USSR"; "Studies of Economies in Transition," paper 19 (Washington D.C., 1995).

agriculture. Overall industrial output fell by almost 60 percent in four years, and the contraction was not limited to industry. Agricultural output fell in the same period by 26 percent, due largely to the inability of collective farms to obtain or afford fertilizers and pesticides as well as the continued failure of the distribution system.

As the situation worsened during 1992, Gaidar's position eroded and in December 1992 he was ditched in favor of Viktor Chernomyrdin, a seasoned insider with a background in Russia's rich, and corrupt, energy industry. Though Chernomyrdin had a less reformist bent than Gaidar and despite Yeltsin's face-off with the Duma, liberalization and privatization continued.

THE PRIVATIZATION PROGRAM

The privatization of state-owned enterprises in Russia can be divided into three distinct programs. The first handled the transfer of property in the small-scale sector, generally conferring property rights on the operators of existing enterprises and the inhabitants of rental property. The second was the **voucher auction program** responsible for the privatization of 60 percent of the industrial sector between 1992 and 1994, and was designed to provide the basis of a market economy. Together these two programs constituted **mass privatization.** Finally there is **privatization for cash** that started in 1995 and has continued until today.

SMALL-SCALE PRIVATIZATION

In Russia shops and small service establishments were handed over to local municipalities who arranged for their transfer, usually to their current managers. Agricultural land was "decollectivized" with members of the collectives able to lease land and equipment. Apartments were sold by local authorities generally to their occupants. Those processes started during 1992, and by the end of the year about 50,000 shops, 182,000 family farms, and 3 million apartments had been sold. In addition, some 500,000 new small businesses had been registered.

VOUCHER PRIVATIZATION PROGRAM

Large-scale industrial enterprise was privatized under the aegis of the State Committee for Management of State Property, also known as GKI, or the Privatization Ministry. It was headed by Anatoly Chubais, who chose voucher auction as the primary means of transferring ownership. The voucher program, which was immense in scope and rapid in execution, was adopted during 1992, and the program officially began in December of that year, ending in June of 1994. During these 21 months some 15,779 enterprises, employing about 18 million people, were disposed of.

The very magnitude of the task and the shallowness of Russian financial markets made Chubais's choice of voucher privatization all but inevitable. In Russia 25,000 firms had to be placed in private hands and initial public offerings (IPOs) used in countries with deeper financial markets and a smaller task at hand were not capable of doing the whole job, since the detailed valuation and the offering process was simply beyond Russia's means.

Boycko, Shleifer, and Vishny put the issue this way:

> The case for privatization through cash sales falls apart on both efficiency and especially political grounds. From the point of view of efficiency, privatization through cash sales is just too slow. It requires valuation, information collection, preparation of auctions and public offerings and a variety of other services which investment banks gladly supply given ample time and generous fees. It is important to remember in this regard that West European countries typically privatize a few firms a year, and even such rapid privatizers as Mexico and Chile could handle at best a couple of hundred of firms per year. In contrast, Russia needed to privatize 25,000 medium- and large-scale firms. If these firms were properly valued, prepared for auctions, or, as some investment bankers wanted, restructured prior to sale, odds are privatization would have never gotten off the ground. Even if it did, at the rate of 200 per year, Russian privatization would have taken over a century! In the meantime, the economy would continue to stagnate. From the political viewpoint, privatization through sales is even more problematic. To be politically feasible in Russia, this approach would have required the allocation of significant stakes to insiders at large discounts and only the remaining shares could be sold. Even such sales would probably have been resented, and certainly not supported, by the public at large. First, the highest bidders in cash privatizations often turn out to be illegitimate businessmen, former party and state security officials, and foreigners. Selling off the national patrimony to these investors generates public outrage rather than support.[10]

The GKI drew up a list of which firms were to be privatized in the first phase. It covered the bulk of the industrial sector, but kept defense-related firms and much of the energy sector under public ownership. Once the list for privatization was published, the management of each firm could choose between three schemes of

---

[10]Maxim Boycko, Andrei Shleifer, and Robert Vishny, *Privatizing Russia* (Cambridge, Mass.: MIT Press, 1996), 71.

privatization. Each of the available options gave considerable benefits to insiders, to secure their support for the privatization process, because without insider support privatization could have been derailed as other economic reforms had been sabotaged in the past. Expansion of private ownership takes away some of the property rights over the firm that the management and, to a lesser extent, the workers have had in the past. It was therefore essential to compensate for the loss of these informal rights with a generous share of the ownership of the newly privatized enterprise.

Under Option I workers would be given 25 percent of the shares for free, but these shares would be nonvoting. In addition, workers could buy 10 percent of the voting shares at a 30 percent discount from book value. Book values, based on the historic cost of capital before the massive inflation of the early 1990s, were very low. Consequently, any price based on book value was close to zero. Management had access to up to 5 percent of the voting shares at a similar price. Thus "insiders" were offered 40 percent of the income of the enterprise and 15 percent of the voting power for next to nothing.

Although Option I seemed generous to many observers, it apparently offered inadequate reward for some insiders, who lobbied Chubais for better compensation for management. They succeeded in establishing an alternative, Option II, which allowed workers and management to buy 51 percent of the capital for a price of 1.7 times book value—again close to zero.[11] The rest of the share capital was to be distributed to the population at large by way of a voucher scheme. All citizens (including children) could purchase for 25 rubles a voucher with a face denomination of 10,000 rubles. This voucher could be turned over to an investment company, exercised personally at an auction, or sold. The total number of shares of each firm to be offered at auction were divided in proportion to the number of vouchers tendered for the firm. Popular firms attracted a lot of attention, and therefore the shares would be divided among many claimants. More obscure firms or those believed to have few assets or prospects attracted little attention, and a few vouchers could garner a sizable part of the share capital. Boycko, Shleifer, and Vishny summarized as follows:

> To save small investors from the need to make complicated bids, one strategy is to ask each investor to submit his voucher as a bid for the company. The equilibrium number of shares each voucher buys is then inversely proportional to the number of vouchers rendered. Thus, if the company offers 1,000 shares for auction, and 40 vouchers are submitted, each voucher buys 25 shares. If, on the other hand, 4,000 vouchers are submitted, each voucher buys only a quarter of a share. Each investor submitting vouchers is assured of getting some shares, but gets fewer shares of desirable companies.[12]

---

[11] There was also available an Option III, which allowed management to acquire 100 percent of the shares if they "promised" not to take the firm into bankruptcy and "strip" its assets. Less than 2 percent of privatization followed Option III.

[12] Boycko, Shleifer, and Vishny, 91.

THE DOMINANCE OF INSIDERS. Although one of the objectives of voucher privatization was to gain wide popular support, individual citizens were disadvantaged in buying shares because they had little information about both the intrinsic value of an enterprise and the number of potential bidders. Most of the valuable knowledge about enterprises lay with insiders and investment intermediaries. The mass privatization project created some 22,000 joint stock companies in Russia, of which 73 percent were privatized under Option II, and therefore the insiders automatically gained control; 25 percent of the privatization followed Option I, and Option III was seldom used.

The trend to insider ownership was reinforced by the free market in vouchers.[13] Both investment intermediaries and management interested in acquiring a greater part of a firm were able to buy the voucher books from the public for prices ranging from $20 to as little as $4. A large part of the population of Russia sold off their share in the country's infrastructure for an average of about $10.[14] A 1993 survey conducted by the Privatization Ministry found that management and workers owned an average of 65 percent of share capital of 143 surveyed middle sized-enterprises. Top management held about 8.6 percent, outside investors owned 21.5 percent, and the government retained an average of 13 percent of shares. While these figures are averages, in some firms the management stake was much higher.

Table 22.3 gives a slightly different perspective on this phenomena. It shows who has a majority share holding in the newly created corporations (i.e., who holds more than 50 percent of the stock). In almost two-thirds of the firms, insider employees and management have control; outsiders control only 20 percent. In over 4 percent of firms, management alone holds the controlling interest.

An active market for vouchers became established, and because the number of vouchers that were tendered for offered shares in specific companies is a matter of record, it is possible to make estimates of the implicit price for which publicly owned firms were sold. Take, for example, the automaker Zil, 30 percent of whose shares were offered in a voucher auction. The implied market value of the whole firm—which employed 103,000 persons—was a mere $16 million. Even more startling, 28 percent of the shares on offer were bought by just seven investment groups, more than one of which was affiliated to a single parent company. While the Russian voucher auction program achieved an enormous transfer of assets from the public sector to the private, the greatest beneficiaries were a narrow group who used insider information (and in many cases manipulated the auction process) in order to gain control of the enterprises. Moreover the high degree of worker and management ownership suggests that meaningful and rapid reform

---

[13] On the largest exchange, The Russian Commodity and Raw Materials Exchange, volume was about 60–100,000 vouchers per day, and this was augmented by regional exchanges and a vigorous street market.

[14] Most people did initially claim their vouchers, or someone claimed them on their behalf. 144 million vouchers were issued, and the Russian population was estimated at 148.2 million.

MAJORITY OWNERS OF PRIVATE-SECTOR CORPORATIONS,
1995 AND 1996 (PERCENT)

Majority Owners	1995	1996
Employees	59	64.7
Rank and file	26.7	30.5
Managers	2.3	4.2
Top managers	0.4	0.4
General director	0.4	0.8
No majority insider	29.4	28.8
Nonstate outsiders	17.3	19.8
State	3.1	2.6
None	20.3	12.8

Note: Numbers do not add to 100% because of rounding.

SOURCE: Joseph R. Blasi, Maya Kroumova, and Douglas Kruse, *Kremlin Capitalism: Privatizing the Russian Economy* (Ithaca, N.Y.: ILR Press, 1997).

postprivatization will be difficult, since job preservation rather than profit maximization will be an important objective.

The entire program has been criticized for giving away too much to insiders to get the process moving.[15] Certainly the result was a dramatic skewing of the distribution of wealth and control, earning for the Russian Federation and other successor states to the Soviet Union the title of **kleptocracies.**[16] While it is true that as a result of voucher privatization as many as 40 million Russians became shareholders, at least for a time, there is no doubt that the process has created hundreds of millionaires, while robbing millions of ordinary Russians of their share of state assets.

Proponents of voucher privatization defend it on the grounds of expediency, arguing that it represented the only politically feasible way forward. Although the dissolution of socialism could have been followed by an equitable parceling out of the assets among the people, perhaps in terms of equal shares, one fact to be reckoned with was that much of Russia's state-owned enterprises did not wholly belong to the state. Workers, local bureaucrats, and especially the management of firms already owned a stake in these firms, and while such a property right might have been informal, it was nevertheless real. Even more to the point, these important actors in the economic scene had the power to disrupt any potential reform if it were not in their interest to go along with it.

---

[15] These criticisms apply even more to the so-called spontaneous privatizations in which the management of some companies, along with part or all of the workforce, assumed control and ownership of an enterprise or established a cooperative that assumed the assets.

[16] Literally "States ruled by thieves," from Greek roots.

Before the fall of the Soviet system, Jan Winiecki analyzed the failure of previous economic reform efforts in centrally planned systems.[17] His work developed the view that Soviet-style economies operated to maximize the rents flowing to the ruling classes, or *nomenklatura.* On top of this primary system of rent extraction, kickbacks or side payments could be appropriated by anyone with some power over scarce resources. Those who gained from the status quo had an incentive to resist any change of the system. For example, replacement of the *nomenklatura*[18] with a more overtly merit system would be opposed because rent extractable by the Communist Party membership would be reduced. Similarly, any plans to increase the size of the private sector were objected to, nominally on ideological grounds, while the real reason was fear of the loss of economic rents:

> There are no well-paid posts to be had in small private enterprises, nor is there a "soft" budget constraint, so permissive to a variety of rent-maximizing kick backs even under reform. A shift of activity from the state to the private reduces therefore the possibilities for party apparatchiks and economic bureaucrats to extract rent. Hostility towards the private sector is therefore based not on ideology or even actual rent losses, but on gains foregone when the expansion of the state sector is curbed in favor of the private sector.[19]

A large class of people who see their well-being decline with onset of reform (even though the economy as a whole might do better) are capable of concerted action to bring down any reform plan. Hence the Russian mass privatization program had to confer considerable benefits on economic bureaucrats, politicians, and insiders in order to ensure its survival.

PRIVATIZATION FOR CASH

The voucher auction program concluded in the summer of 1994 and was assumed to have created the basis of a market economy. As Table 22.4 shows, almost 16,000 medium and large enterprises, employing about 18 million people, had passed into majority private ownership. In 1995 the Russian government shifted its emphasis to cash privatization to dispose of the assets of the enterprises still in the state sector, mostly utilities and natural resource or high-tech defense enterprises.

Lacking an adequate system of public finance, the government looked for revenue from the sale of the resource sector to close the federal government deficit, but there was limited interest in the asset sales and the government resorted to a highly controversial scheme to raise cash. At the initial suggestion of Oneximbank, one of

---

[17] Jan Winiecki, "Why Economic Reforms Fail in Soviet-Type System, A Property Rights-Based Approach," *Economic Inquiry.* 28, no.2 (1990).

[18] Winiecki defines *nomenklatura* in terms of the right of the Communist Party apparatus, from the Central Committee on down to the enterprise committee, to "recommend" or "approve" all appointments for all managerial positions in the economic administration and all managerial positions in enterprises.

[19] Winiecki, 300.

■ **TABLE 22.4**

VOUCHER AUCTIONS IN RUSSIA: DECEMBER 1992–JUNE 1994

	Dec. 1992– June 1993	July 1993– Dec. 1993	Jan. 1994– June 1994	Total
Number of enterprises sold by calendar month	2,871	5,632	7,276	15,779
Employment (thousands)	3,243	5,278	9,249	17,770
Total vouchers accepted (thousands)	16,054	27,724	69,830	113,608

SOURCE: GKI/RPC Performance Database; MaximBoycko, Andrei Shleifer, and Robert Vishny, *Privatizing Russia* (Cambridge, Mass.: MIT Press, 1996), 106–107.

the most powerful and well-connected banks in Russia, the government agreed to offer shares in publicly owned companies as collateral for loans from the private sector. For only $170 million, Oneximbank received over 50 percent of the voting shares of Norilsk Nickel, the producer of over 20 percent of the world's nickel and 50 percent of global platinum output. In theory the bank was acting like a pawnbroker; the government could redeem the shares if it came up with the cash by September 1996, but it was clear from the beginning that the government had made no budgetary provision for that eventuality. Consequently, the bank got the shares in available enterprise very cheaply. Although their worth is hard to determine, a figure of 10 times what Oneximbank paid seems reasonable. The Norilsk deal was followed by similar insider deals favoring other banks, and the government was able to meet its revenue targets for 1995 at the expense of squandering a great deal of support for the privatization program.

Despite public outcry against these **loans-for-shares deals,** no transactions were reversed, perhaps because 1996 was a poor year for revenue from share sales, and less than 15 percent of anticipated and budgeted revenues were realized. In 1997 the Russian stock market took off, and the government was able to dispose of a lot of the shares that it had retained in the oil and mineral sectors for high revenues, realizing about three times the forecast revenues and closing the budget gap considerably. However, 1998 saw a stock market fall of about 85 percent measured in local currency and 95 percent in terms of dollars, and predictably privatization revenues also fell very sharply. By late 1998 only $1 billion of revenue from privatization had been realized while the budget called for $8 billion. However, the government still owns about 40 percent of the natural resource sector, and it can raise a great deal of capital through privatization sales if the market recovers.

THE FINANCIAL AND INDUSTRIAL GROUPS

A striking feature of Russian capitalism has been the rapid emergence of the financial and industrial groups or FIGs, officially established by a law in 1995. The legislation offered tax and other privileges to groups that registered with the authorities, though in fact such advantages have been slow to emerge. There are now more than 100 officially registered groups, but a substantial part of the economic and political power in Russia lies with just seven large bank-led groups—Alfa Group, Inkombank Group, LogoVAZ, Menatep, Most, Oneximbank, and SBS-Agro.[20] These groups are closely held, highly diversified, and the larger ones are generally grouped around a bank. In some ways they resemble the *chaebol* of Korea and *keiretsu* of Japan, but they are potentially more powerful than either. They incorporate banks, where *chaebol* do not, and are controlled by a single individual to a much greater degree than contemporary *keiretsu*. As well as the bank-centered FIGs, there are also industry-centered groups. On the whole they are less powerful and less diversified than the bank-centered groups.

The consequences of the emergence of these groups are uncertain. On the positive side, they can represent a source of rapid change in Russian industry; firms acquired by these groups can be subject to tight oversight and given clear performance objectives, as well as advice and capital for restructuring. On the other hand, FIGs constitute an alarming concentration of political, as well as economic power, both in Moscow and in the regions. The leaders of the large groups are politically well connected and in several cases have held high government office. They are known as **oligarchs** and clearly influence governmental policy. To some degree the position in Russia today resembles the structure of **finance capitalism** **(*Finanzkapitalism*)** articulated by Rudolf Hilferding in the early years of this century. A coalescence of financial and industrial capital exercises a controlling influence on the policies of the state. There is an irony in that what was thought by Hilferding to be the penultimate stage of capitalism should be the first step for a socialist economy in transition.

In the summer of 1998, there were reports that the Central Bank of Russia drew up a list of 12 banks that were to be bailed out under any circumstances, because the instability of the financial system was so great; included were the lead banks of all the seven major FIGs. This brought to the forefront the twin issues of moral hazard in the banking sector and the political influence of the major banks. However, in a surprising move, the Central Bank withdrew its license from Inkombank, the country's second largest bank and lead-bank of the Inkombank FIG.

INSTITUTIONAL REFORM

THE BANKING SYSTEM

Under central planning, the state bank, Gosbank, had had a virtual monopoly of the banking sector, although specialist banks existed to finance construction and foreign trade, and a thrift bank served to facilitate small saving. The Gorbachev reforms included a reorganization of banking and introduced three new state banks.[21] More important for the longer-term structure of Russian finance, the 1988

---

[20] It is not possible to say exactly what proportion, but Boris Berezovsky, head of LogoVAZ, estimated in 1996 that it represented half of Russia's economy.

[21] The Agricultural Bank, the Industrial and Construction Bank, and the Social Investment Bank.

■ TABLE 22.5

GROUPING BANKS BY CAPITAL, 1998*

	Number	Share of Total (percentage)
Up to 100 thousand rubles	8	0.5
From 100 thousand rubles to 500 thousand rubles	113	7.3
From 500 thousand rubles to 1 million rubles	71	4.6
From 1 million rubles to 5 million rubles	405	26
From 5 million rubles to 20 million rubles	587	37.7
From 20 million rubles to 30 million rubles	98	6.3
From 30 million rubles and more	274	17.6
Total	1,556	

* Paid in authorized capital as per articles of association and registered by the Bank of Russia.

SOURCE: Central Bank of Russia.

Law on Cooperatives allowed the emergence of private banks. In 1988, 80 such banks were founded, and by the end of the Soviet era the total had risen to more than 400.

At the breakup of the Soviet Union, the assets and functions of Gosbank were assumed by the newly created Central Bank of Russia (CBR) under its first chairman Viktor Geraschenko. The CBR was established as an orthodox institution, very like the central banks in many West European countries. It is responsible for issuing currency and supervising and regulating the financial sector, as well as being the lender of last resort and the manager of foreign exchange operations. It is not an independent institution, as according to its rules of operation laid out in the constitution, "*in collaboration* with the government of the Russian Federation it [the Central Bank] elaborates and implements a uniform national monetary policy designed to protect the ruble and ensure its stability."

The Central Bank has been a pliable tool used to channel credit to keep potentially bankrupt enterprises afloat. The soft-budget constraint, meant to end with privatization, is in fact alive and well and will continue to be until a stable financial system and workable public finance system is in place. The early 1990s saw the continued growth of private banking, reaching a high of about 2,500 banks in 1995. There has been a subsequent contraction as successive financial crises have weeded out the weaker elements, and the Central Bank of Russia has withdrawn licenses from banks at the rate of roughly 250 per annum.

However, as Table 22.5 shows, many banks remain weak. Almost 40 percent of all registered banks have a capital base of less than 5 million rubles, and many are highly vulnerable to runs or falls in the value of assets held. In April 1998 Sergei Dubinin, then governor of the Central Bank of Russia, estimated that at least 25 percent of Russia's banks had "serious problems" and he expected an additional 300 to 400 to close during 1998–1999. The financial crisis of 1998 probably increased the vulnerability of many more. Without a stable banking sector it will be hard for the Russian economy to grow and especially difficult for small and medium-sized companies to get access to capital.

POVERTY AND SOCIAL ASSISTANCE

Shock therapy and its aftermath had a profound effect on the incidence of poverty in Russia. The negative growth rates of the past decade have shrunk the pie, while liberalization, privatization, and high rates of inflation have tended to skew the distribution of income. Today the highest earners receive 47.4 percent of total personal income, while the worst-off 20 percent receive only 6.3 percent of income, much less than at the beginning of privatization.

Gorbachev's reforms had little effect on income distribution, and although income contracted during the 1980s, its distribution actually became more egalitarian as Table 22.6 shows. The change since the **Big Bang,** the start of the Yeltsin administration, has been dramatic. In 1991 the income of the average "wealthy" person (in the top quintile) was only 2.8 times that of the average poor person (in the lowest quintile); by 1998 the figure had risen to about 7.5. The decline in living standards for the poorest quintile of society was sharpest between 1991 and 1993, due largely to the failure of the pension system to adjust to rapid price rises. The introduction of indexation in 1995, prompted largely by electoral considerations, stopped further decline. The working class was not favored under liberalization; in 1991 the third and fourth quintiles enjoyed almost 35 percent of personal income, by 1998 that had fallen to about 25 percent.

The regional impact of income redistribution has been even greater than for the nation as a whole. Central planning provided interregional transfers, but these largely ceased under the reforms. In 1992 the ratio of average income in the richest *oblast* (county) to the poorest was 8:1. By 1994 this had widened to 42:1.[22] Table 22.7 shows how hard poverty has hit in some of the regions. Worst affected are those that specialize in agriculture, while those with extensive mineral resources have fared the best. Nevertheless, for a region to have 30 percent of its population below the poverty level (unable to buy a standard minimum basket of goods) is commonplace, and in many regions one-fifth of the population is unable even to buy adequate food.

Of particular concern is the emergence of poverty among relatively well-educated and skilled segments of society. Human capital has been justifiably regarded as one of Russia's strengths, but protracted unemployment and poverty will cause a loss of human capital (to emigration, neglect, and despair) and create a dual labor market, trapping the poor.

THE TAX SYSTEM

Under central planning a sophisticated tax system was unnecessary. Revenues accrued to the state largely through markups on the costs of goods and by a variable tax on consumer goods. Since the start of transition there has been a constant struggle to put public finance on a stable and economically efficient footing with

---

[22] World Bank, *Poverty in Russia: An Assessment* (Washington, D.C.: 1995), 31.

■ **TABLE 22.6**

**INCOME DISTRIBUTION: PERCENTAGE SHARE OF EACH QUINTILE
(1980 AND 1991 TO 1997)**

	1980	1991	1992	1993	1994	1995	1996	1997
Top	33.4	30.7	38.3	41.6	46.3	46.9	47.1	47.4
Second	23.1	22.8	26.5	24.8	23.0	22.4	21.3	21.1
Third	18.6	18.8	17.6	16.7	15.2	15.0	14.9	14.8
Fourth	14.8	15.8	11.6	11.1	10.2	10.2	10.5	10.4
Bottom	10.1	11.9	6.0	5.8	5.3	5.5	6.2	6.3
Total	100	100	100	100	100	100	100	100

Notes: Data are for total money income.

SOURCE: Goskomstat, *Russia in Figures* (Moscow: State Committee on Statistics of the Russian Federation).

■ **TABLE 22.7**

THE INCIDENCE OF POVERTY IN SELECTED REGIONS, 1994

	Percent Poor	Percent Very Poor
Rich in Mineral Resources		
Magnitogorsk City	17.0	4.8
Yakutiya Republic (Sakha)	28.8	5.8
Intensive Agriculture and Food Industry		
Astrakhan Oblast	72.4	44.3
Oryol Oblast	58.7	32.6
Industrial or Mixture		
Adygeya Republic	51.9	19.4
Chuvash Republic	42.5	22.7
Khanty-Mansiysky District	28.8	13.2
Krasnoyarsky Krai	43.5	20.1
Moscow Oblast	41.0	19.7
Tver Oblast	39.1	18.1
Voronezh Oblast	20.4	10.2

Notes: The "poor" do not have enough income to purchase the subsistence minimum consumer basket as defined in Goskomstat poverty measures; the very poor are unable to purchase the food component of the subsistence minimum. Moscow Oblast excludes the city of Moscow.

SOURCES: G. N. Volkova and L. A. Migranova, *The Living Standards of the Russian Population by Region,* Bulletin no. 12 (Moscow: Center for Living Standards Study, Ministry of Labor, 1994).

little result. This failure has led to sustained federal budget deficits. The structure of the budget is shown in Table 22.8. One important feature is that tax revenues are only about 9.1 percent of GDP, while expenditures on current items (not even including loans and debt service) are 14.6 percent, a primary structural deficit of 5.5 percent. This, in turn, has meant that financing the accumulated debt has become a major item in the budget itself.

■ TABLE 22.8

OUTCOME OF FEDERAL BUDGET, 1997

	Absolute (billions of rubles)	Percentage of Total Revenues	Percentage of GDP
Revenue			
Profits tax	33.17	10.27	1.24
Personal income tax	1.87	0.58	0.07
VAT and excises	171.47	53.11	6.41
Taxes on trade	27.82	8.62	1.04
Other	9.10	2.82	0.34
Tax revenues	243.43	75.39	9.10
Nontax revenues	79.45	24.61	2.97
Total revenues	322.87		12.07
Expenditure			
State administration	9.63	2.98	0.36
International activity	8.29	2.57	0.31
Defense and law enforcement	123.32	38.19	4.61
Fundamental research	9.63	2.98	0.36
Services to the national economy	52.43	16.24	1.96
Social services	48.42	15.00	1.81
Debt service	41.46	12.84	1.55
Other expenditure	97.91	30.32	3.66
Overall expenditure	391.09	121.13	14.62
Net loans	18.19	5.63	0.68
Expenditure and net loans	409.28	126.76	15.30
Budget deficit	86.40	26.76	3.23
Total financing	86.40	26.76	3.23
Domestic	32.90	10.19	1.23
Foreign	53.50	16.57	2.00
GDP (billions of rubles)	2,675		

SOURCE: Institute for the Economy in Transition, *Russian Economy: Trends and Perspectives*. Available at: http://win.www.online.ru/sp/iet/trends/index.html

Regional and local authorities represent a large part of the consolidated budget, almost 50 percent of expenditures, but they manage to stay closer in balance than the federal authorities. The deficit on the consolidated budget amounted to about 3¾ percent of GDP. (Table 22.9).

Revenues at the federal level depend heavily on indirect taxation, especially the value-added tax (VAT). The personal income tax gathers little revenue for the central government (less than 1 percent of the total) because tax evasion is high and most of the revenue that is gathered goes to regional authorities.[23] The tax rate on an annual income of individuals in the 0 to 5 thousand ruble range (roughly

---

[23] A tax reform plan authored by the Yeltsin government seeks to guarantee the federal government 20 percent of income tax revenue.

OUTCOME OF CONSOLIDATED BUDGET, 1997 (PERCENTAGE OF GDP)

Taxes and payments	21.31
Nontax revenues	4.40
Overall revenue	25.71
Overall expenditure and loans minus repayments	29.49
Budget deficit	3.78

SOURCE: Institute for the Economy in Transition, http://win.www.online.ru/sp/iet/trends/apr98/2.html

from 0 to $200) is 12 percent, rising to a maximum of 30 percent above 10 thousand ($400), and wage income is also subject to very high social security contributions totaling 39 percent of salary income. Consequently, the top combined rate on labor income could reach 69 percent, clearly a level at which there may be considerable disincentives to effort and strong rewards for tax evasion.

The ineffectiveness of the tax regime is compounded by its complexity, with federal, regional, and city governments imposing a wide range of taxes, with little or no coordination.[24] There is also a great deal of discretion in the application of tax exemptions, increasing the potential for corruption and tending to discourage investment, especially from abroad.

Many Russian firms and individuals simply fail to pay their taxes, a phenomenon so widespread that it meets with social approval. The Organization for Economic Cooperation and Development (OECD) reports that "identified arrears on taxes and social contributions reached 10 percent of GDP in 1996."[25] The failure to meet tax targets means that the government cannot fund its expenditures: workers go unpaid, pensioners do not get their stipends, and essential services are curtailed. Moreover, government borrowing is increased, pushing up interest rates and thereby the cost of financing the national debt, presenting the specter of worsening debt spiral. The structure of tax arrears is shown in Figure 22.1. Although it is the large-scale corporate sector (usually the energy extracting companies) that is most often blamed for tax delinquency, in fact the bulk of the arrears lies in the failure to collect the value-added tax, a failure largely at the retail level.

Tax reform is essential for economic growth. However, tax legislation that promised to simplify the system, lower the discretionary power of government, unify the VAT rates, and clarify the responsibilities of tax payers and the powers of the tax collectors has been stalled since 1995 because of disagreement between the administration and the Duma. Lower rates and a simpler code offer the only way out of the trap of insufficient revenue, poor incentives for tax compliance and legal economic activity, and widespread evasion.

---

[24] There have been cases where aggregate rates on certain kinds of activities have exceeded 100 percent.

[25] Organization for Economic Cooperation and Development, *1996/97 Survey of Russia* (Paris: OECD, 1997), 4.

■ **FIGURE 22.1**

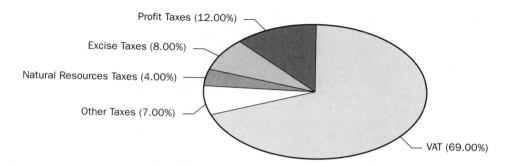

STRUCTURE OF TAX ARREARS, APRIL 1998

Profit Taxes (12.00%)

Excise Taxes (8.00%)

Natural Resources Taxes (4.00%)

Other Taxes (7.00%)

VAT (69.00%)

■ **TABLE 22.10**

CONCENTRATION IN THE FORMER SOVIET UNION

Type of Product	Percentage of Production by Largest Producer
Sewing machines	100
Washing machines	90
Freezers	100
Concrete mixers	93
Road-building cranes	75
Hydraulic turbines	100
Steam turbines	95
Polypropylene	73
Electrolytic tin plate	100
Stainless steel pipes	96
Color photographic paper	100

SOURCE: *The Economist*, 11 August 1990, 67, from Goskomstat.

COMPETITION POLICY

The legacy of planning and its obsession with scale economies has left the Russian industrial structure highly concentrated. Table 22.10 provides data on the degree of concentration in the Soviet Union. The collapse of the Soviet Union increased the degree of concentration in Russia, because competitive goods from other republics now constituted hard currency purchases, often subject to tariff or quota, and therefore, the table probably understates the degree of concentration.

International trade has provided healthy competition in some of these areas. In fact, the influx of imported "white goods" (freezers, washers, etc.) has created a serious balance of payments problem and heavy tariffs were imposed on them in 1998.

INTER-ENTERPRISE PAYMENTS PROBLEMS IN RUSSIA

A pervasive problem in many transition economies has been delinquent payments between firms. This problem has been particularly severe in the energy sector in Russia. Customers have failed to pay the energy companies, which have considerable monopoly power. In turn, these firms have failed to pay their own suppliers and the government, to which they owe both profits taxes and payments into the social security funds. Thus the problems of interfirm payments disrupt both the functioning of the economy and the system of public finance. The following two stories from a Russian news agency illustrate this problem.

TRANS-SIBERIAN RAILROAD TRAFFIC HALTED

Traffic along a 650-kilometer stretch of the Trans-Siberian railroad stopped for six hours on 10 July, 1997, after a regional power company cut off electricity supplies. The Chitaenergo company said the railroad owes it more than 30 billion rubles ($5.3 million). Railroad officials say the Trans-Siberian line is owed much more by government ministries and coal-mining companies. Service was resumed after a railroad official warned that coal shipments to heating and power stations in Chita Oblast would be imperiled by the cut.

GAZPROM SAYS ITS DEBTORS OWE $12 BILLION

Representatives of the gas monopoly Gazprom say the company is owed 69.5 trillion rubles ($12.1 billion) by delinquent domestic clients. Among the main debtors are Moscow's power stations, which owe the company a total of 6.8 trillion rubles ($1.2 billion). The figures released yesterday did not provide revenue or debt figures from Gazprom's large exports. The gas monopoly has increasingly come under pressure to pay its $2.5 billion debt to the government. Chairman Rem Vyakhirev promised that the company will pay $1.2 billion to the federal budget.

SOURCE: Itar-Tass news agency as reported on the RFE/RL Newsline, no. 71, part I, 11 July 1997.

Although patchy in coverage, Table 22.10 shows monopoly to be an acute problem in durable consumer goods and machinery. This perception is reinforced by other studies by the state statistical agency (Goskomstat), which found that 166 enterprises were absolute monopolies. Another Soviet government study found that 80 percent of output of the machine-building industry was produced by monopolists.

Russia needs an effective way to encourage competition and facilitate entry into the monopolized industries, perhaps by breaking up some of the larger concerns. The problem is not legislation, but enforcement. Competition law is both modern and well conceived, but implementation by the Anti-Monopoly Committee has been weak. Action by regional and local governments to protect local producers has aggravated the situation.

Another problem is the extent of the "natural" monopolies in gas, electricity supply, and communication. These concerns have great influence, exert considerable monopoly power, and have—especially in the case of Gazprom, the natural gas producer—been major tax delinquents. (The government has been slow to act against them because of their political influence.)

■ **TABLE 22.11**

	1992	1993	1994	1995	1996	1997
						KEY MACROECONOMIC INDICATORS (PERCENTAGE CHANGE)
GDP	−14	−9	−13	−4	−5	0.4
Fixed investment	−40	−12	−20	−10	−18	−5.0
Inflation	2,510	840	220	130	21.8	11.0
Monetary base		646	189	115	26.2	25.7
M2	605	407	192	127	33.7	28.6

SOURCE: Goskomstat of the Russian Federation.

A good example of this kind of problem is electricity supply, which is dominated by the giant electricity monopoly United Energy Systems (UES), now headed by Anatoly Chubais, the former chief of the Privatization Ministry. Before liberalization, energy was cheap in Russia, priced at about 32 percent of the world average. Prices tripled between 1993 and 1995, to levels above the then world average prices. Price regulation was ineffective although the government claimed that in its absence prices would have risen by a further 12 to 23 percent.[26] Currently, 53 percent of UES is still owned by the state, and it lies at the heart of a nexus of economic problems. It is owed very large sums of money by regional energy companies who are functionally bankrupt but unwilling to cut off nonpaying customers from the grid. The customers claim that they are in desperate straits themselves, are striving to stay in business, and cannot afford the excessive monopoly prices charged by the UES. In turn, UES claims it is owed so much money it both needs to raise rates and cannot afford to pay its taxes, while paying its workers between three and four times the average for the economy.

Clearly there is a role for more effective regulation, and restructuring of the industry to facilitate competition would pay dividends. Vertical disaggregation of the industry to allow competing suppliers and retailers to use a common regulated grid, as in the United Kingdom and Australia, would give a market a solution of greater efficiency and lower prices. Further examples of the kind of payment problems that persist in Russia are shown in the box "Inter-Enterprise Payments Problems in Russia."

PROSPECTS FOR THE RUSSIAN ECONOMY

During 1997 there was considerable optimism about the future of the Russian economy. Preliminary data (see Table 22.11) seemed to indicate that a corner had been turned, and after a long period of falling GDP, positive growth was in prospect. Although modest, the estimated .4 percent growth was welcome as a

---

[26] *Izvestiya* (13 January 1996), "Natural Monopolies: Comparing Russian and Australian Experience"; Gennadi Kazakevitch, *Russian and Euro-Asian Economics Bulletin* 5, no. 4 (April 1996).

harbinger of future expansion. Inflation was in hand, roughly at less than 1 percent per month, and the monetary growth rate level had been contained. Unfortunately events conspired to destroy this relatively rosy scenario.

The subsequent revelation that not only were the statistics unreliable, but they had also been deliberately manipulated by Goskomstat, the state statistical agency was a serious blow. It suggests that the government will resort to deliberate deception to achieve its aims, a fact that once revealed has a negative effect on incoming investment and international lenders. The next disappointment came from the Russian stock market, which after booming during 1996 and 1997, fell during 1998 and collapsed in a dramatic fashion in August, conforming largely to the analysis of the growth and consolidation of markets offered by van Agtmael (see chapter 21). This was followed by a 50 percent devaluation of the ruble (after a $4 billion IMF loan had been wasted in its defense), an indefinite default on domestic government debt, and a 90-day moratorium on payments on foreign debt. This was followed by a shift in policy as the reformist Prime Minister Sergei Kiryenko was pushed aside. His replacement was to have been Viktor Chernomyrdin, but he proved particularly unpalatable and Yevgeny Primakov was brought instead. Among Primakov's first moves was to restore the state's Vodka monopoly.

A decade after the inception of shock therapy and twelve years after the start of Gorbachev's reforms, Russia has not really made the transition to a market economy and runs the risk of retrogression.

1. The tax system still needs extensive reform, and attention needs to be paid both to revenue potential and incentive structure.

2. The privatized enterprises remain to some degree on a "soft-budget constraint." Billions of dollars have been channeled into them through "soft loans," 90 percent of which have not been repaid, even though they are ruble-denominated and inflation has made them practically worthless.

3. Competition policy needs to be enforced.

4. Foreign investment seems to be necessary if Russia is to grow, but the capriciousness of the tax system, political uncertainty, and corruption keep it low.

The unreliability of official statistics increases the value of microeconomic studies by outside agencies. A study by McKinsey and Company reported in *The Economist* makes particularly disturbing reading:

> The study compares Russian-based companies (whether foreign or locally owned) with their American counterparts, sector by sector. It shows that Russian productivity is, on average, only 19% of American levels. Before the post-Soviet slump in output, it was only 30%. Depressingly, the 10% of the workforce that works on industrial capacity installed after 1992—presumably the best—is still producing at only 30% of American levels.[27]

---

[27] "Russia's Economy: Surprise, Surprise," *The Economist,* 23 October 1999, 88.

The McKinsey report concludes that the absence of gains in productivity stems from the failure to cut back on workers (despite the fact that wages are generally in arrears) and "antiquated organizational structure." The solution would seem to be an infusion of management skills and increased capital investment. The most logical sources of both are via direct foreign investment, but political uncertainty and pervasive corruption are keeping that at bay. Moreover, capital continues to leave Russia. July and August of 1999 saw a current account surplus of over $5 billion. Some $2.5 billion was absorbed by debt service but Roland Nash, chief economist at Renaissance Capital, an investment bank quoted by *The Economist*, thought that "the other $2.5 billion just disappeared somewhere."[28]

Lack of incoming investment, political uncertainty, corruption, and capital flight all contribute to hinder the transition of the economy. Only with stability and a level playing field will economic growth accelerate and the promise of Russia's resources and human capital be realized. Whether the economy's great potential can be unleashed under the new president, Vladimer Putin, elected in early 2000, remains to be seen. Putin has pledged a program of reform, but he has both strong links to the FIGs and a tendency toward centralizing power that might be incompatible with the continued development of a competitive market.

KEY TERMS AND CONCEPTS

Big Bang	Law on Cooperatives
Decree on Property	Law on Individual Economic Activity
"Era of Stagnation"	Law on State Enterprise
finance capitalism (*Finanzkapitalism*)	loans-for-shares
financial and industrial groups	mass privatization
500 days to a market economy	*nomenklatura*
Gaidar reforms	oligarchs
Grand Bargain	privatization for cash
inter-enterprise payments problems	small-scale privatization
kleptocracy	voucher auction program

QUESTIONS FOR DISCUSSION

1. Why did Gorbachev's economic reforms fail?
2. What were the essential strategies of the Yeltsin/Gaidar reforms of January 1992?

---

[28] *The Economist,* 23 October 1999, 89.

3. How did inflation transfer wealth in Russia?

4. What were the three options by which enterprises might choose to privatize?

5. Why have "insiders" taken possession of so much of Russia's industry?

6. What are the FIGs? How might they aid growth and change and what dangers do they embody?

7. How has transition changed the distribution of income and the incidence of poverty?

RESOURCES

WEB SITES

Central Bank . . . . http://www.cbr.ru/eng/

Institute for the Economy in Transition . . http://mac.www.online.ru/sp/iet/toc-iet.html

Russian Government Online—In Russian . . . . http://gosorgan.amursk.ru/

St. Petersburg Times, **National Newspaper** . . . . http://www.sptimes.ru/

Vladivostok News, National Newspaper http://vlad.tribnet.com/1999/current/front.html

Russia Online . . . . http://mac.www.online.ru/

Russia Net . . . . http://www.russianet.ru/~oldrn/index.html

Russia Com . . . . http://www.russia.com/

Palms and Company, Inc. . . . . http://members.aa.net/~russia/palloby.html

IET-IRIS Project—Social Services Provision under the transition (health care, education, culture) . . . . http://mac.www.online.ru/sp/iet/shish.html

Russia Online: Business and Finance . . . . http://mac.www.online.ru/emain/ebiz/

BOOKS AND ARTICLES

Ash, Timothy, and Paul G. Hare. "Privatisation in the Russian Federation: Changing Enterprise Behaviour in the Transition Period." *Cambridge Journal of Economics,* December 1994, 619–634.

Åslund, Anders. *How Russia Became a Market Economy.* Washington, D.C.: The Brookings Institution, 1995.

Åslund, Anders, ed. *The Post-Soviet Economy: Soviet and Western Perspectives.* New York: St. Martin's Press, 1992.

Åslund, Anders, and Richard Layard, eds. *Changing the Economic System in Russia.* New York: St. Martin's Press, 1993. N. reviewed in the *Journal of Comparative Economics,* October 1994, 281. (Collection of papers from conference at Stockholm School of Economics, June 1992, assessment of early reform).

Bergson, Abram. "Russia's Economic Reform Muddle." *Challenge,* September–October 1994, 56–59.

Blasi, Joseph R., Maya Kroumova, and Douglas Kruse. *Kremlin Capitalism: Privatizing the Russian Economy.* Ithaca: ILR Press, 1997.

Boycko, Maxim, Andrei Shleifer, and Robert Vishny. *Privatizing Russia.* Cambridge, Mass.: MIT Press, 1995.

Buck, Trevor, Igor Filatotchev, and Mike Wright. "Employee Buyouts and the Transformation of Russian Industry." *Comparative Economic Studies,* summer 1994, 115.

Dyker, David. *Restructuring the Soviet Economy.* New York: Routledge, Chapman and Hall, 1992.

Easterly, William, and Paula Vieira da Cunha. "Financing the Storm: Russia's Macroeconomic Crisis." *Economics of Transition* 2, no. 4 (1994). 433–66.

Gregory, Paul R., and Robert C. Stuart. *Soviet and Post-Soviet Economic Structure and Performance,* 5th ed. New York: HarperCollins College Publishers, 1994.

Islam, Shafiqul. "Russia's Rough Road to Capitalism." *Foreign Affairs,* spring 1993, 57–66.

Joskow, Paul L., Richard Shmalensee, and Natalia Tsukanova. "Competition Policy in Russia during and after Privatization." *Brookings Papers on Economic Activity* (1994): 301–380.

Lipton, David, and Jeffrey Sachs. "Prospects for Russia's Economic Reforms." *Brooking Papers on Economic Activity* 2 (1992): 213–276.

Monetary and Exchange Affairs Department, International Monetary Fund. "Central Bank Autonomy, and Inflation and Output Performance in the Baltic States, Russia, and Other Countries of the Former Soviet Union." (1995–1997). IMF Working Paper, WP/99/4

Nelson, Lynn D., and Irina Y. Kuzes. "Evaluating the Russian Voucher Privatization Program." *Comparative Economic Studies,* spring 1994, 55–67.

Shlapentokh, Vladimir. "Privatization Debates in Russia: 1989–1992." *Comparative Economic Studies,* summer 1993, 19–32.

Slider, Darrell. "Privatization in Russia's Regions." *Post-Soviet Affairs,* October–December 1994, 367–396.

"A Survey of Russia: In Search of Spring." *The Economist,* 12 July 1997, 48.

Van Atta, Don. "Agrarian Reform in Post-Soviet Russia." *Post-Soviet Affairs,* April–June 1994, 159–190.

23

REFORM IN POLAND
AND THE CZECH REPUBLIC

The verdict on the reform program in Russia is, at best, mixed, and many Russians would, given the choice, revert to the *status quo ante*. Other countries have had a more successful recent history and now enjoy higher living standards than before the onset of liberalization, and we turn now to discuss two of them, Poland and the Czech Republic. Both nations have had a happier transformation than those further east, and this is due in some degree to their location and their initial condition. Both countries lie in direct contact with relatively prosperous Germany and the European Union (EU), and both also had only a 45-year exposure to communism and retained a vestigial remnant of capitalist institutions. However, it is essential to ask to what extent policy determined the relatively successful outcome of transition in these countries, since this can teach important lessons for other nations.

POLAND

A great deal has been written about the transformation in Poland, in part because of the very visible role of Western economists in advising on issues of structural change and in part because this was the first application of a so-called **Big Bang** policy.

BACKGROUND

To fully understand the Polish experience, we must review its history. Much of the credit, or blame, for the collapse of the communist state in Poland lies with the workers' movement known as **Solidarity,** which emerged in August 1980, coordinating the famous strike at the Lenin shipyard in Gdansk. Solidarity was briefly legalized by the communist government in December 1980 but was banned once more in October 1981; throughout the 1980s it was a fundamental source of both moral and material opposition to the communist regime. As a genuine and spontaneous working class movement in opposition to a government that claimed to represent the working class, Solidarity undermined the authority of the communist regime in Poland and, in a sense, all communist regimes throughout Eastern Europe. The fragility of the old order was exacerbated by the faltering economy. According to CIA estimates, the growth of the gross domestic product (GDP) in the

POLAND ■ REFORMS OF THE 1980S

period 1975–1980 was only 0.7 percent per annum, and this failure to advance living standards in an age of internationally free-flowing information became a source of popular dissatisfaction.

REFORMS OF THE 1980S

Both socialist economic orthodoxy and the need to provide domestic substitutes to reduce hard currency imports kept Poland throughout the 1970s on a path of investment in heavy industry such as shipbuilding, automobiles, and petrochemicals. Nevertheless, Poland's external account deteriorated badly as the service on a hard-currency debt of more than $25 billion was a growing burden on the economy.

From 1978 to 1982 the Polish economy faced an acute crisis during which output fell for four successive years, with a particularly sharp contraction in 1981, and hard-currency exports to noncommunist states declined while imports continued to rise, further increasing international indebtedness. The government's immediate response was to impose austerity, including a period of martial law; food and consumer goods were rationed and key industries were put under military administration. While actually increasing control in the short-term, the government prepared a reform program that was designed to move the economy away from Soviet-style central planning and toward a market socialist economy with a strong element of worker management modeled on the Yugoslav system. Under regulations unveiled in 1982, enterprises were freed of most planning targets[1] and were able to act as income-maximizing entities governed by elected workers' councils. As in the Yugoslav case, large enterprises were divided into "basic organizations of labor," akin to profit centers, and a hard budget constraint was in theory imposed since firms were to be self-financing, and free to determine wage levels and choice of technique, as well as sources of supply. The prices of roughly 50 percent of consumer goods and about three-quarters of industrial input were decontrolled (see Table 23.1). The remainder were covered either by fixed administered prices (the case in energy and basic foodstuffs) or by regulated prices, based on a conventional "cost plus" formula.[2] The 1982 reforms also broke the foreign trade monopoly of specialist foreign trade organizations and allowed individual firms more access to export markets.

The private economy had never been totally extinguished in Poland despite 40 years of communist rule. Agriculture had not been collectivized or socialized to any significant extent, remaining largely in private hands though inefficient and

---

[1] Exceptions were military goods, basic consumer goods, and export orders that had already been committed to by contract, all of which retained their planning targets.

[2] In the succeeding five years, regulation became less frequent, and more prices became subject once more to central administration.

■ **TABLE 23.1**

PRICE REGIMES IN POLAND, 1982 AND 1987 (PERCENTAGE OF TOTAL)

	1982		1987	
Type of Control	Consumer Goods	Industrial Inputs	Consumer Goods	Industrial Inputs
Administered	35	45	20	29
Regulated	15	2	5	3
Free	50	53	75	68

SOURCE: Balcerowicz, cited in Jeffries, 297.

starved of investment. Private handicrafts and some service trades had remained legitimate and as a result a commercial legal code had survived. The scope of the private sector was increased in the late 1980s when, through the **Law on Economic Activity,** the communist government allowed the expansion of small business activity, facilitated incoming foreign investment, and encouraged joint ventures between Polish and foreign enterprises. The same legislation also enabled limited privatization of state-owned enterprises (SOEs), but due either to neglect or design the rules were unclear. While some property did pass into private hands, it was mainly seized by powerful members of the Polish Communist Party, earning it the title of *nomenklatura* **privatization.**

As Poland approached transformation to a market economy, it enjoyed several distinct advantages over other socialist states:

- It had a higher share of its economic activity coordinated by the market.
- Its agricultural sector was predominantly private, and though in need of rationalization, no major land reform was required.
- It had an existing system of commercial regulations and legalized private property.
- Its state enterprises already achieved a high degree of independence from the ministries.
- Reforms had already encouraged the expansion of private entrepreneurial activity.
- It had developed strong trade links with the West, facilitating information and investment flows.

Against those pluses, however, there was an almost equal array of relative disadvantages when compared to other reformist states:

- Poland had a very large monetary overhang, amounting to about 17 percent of GDP, the result of wage increases in the 1980s outpacing the availability of goods—an inflationary time bomb that would explode with the liberalization of prices and trade.

- Repeated deficits on current account had been financed by foreign borrowing, resulting in hard currency debt, whose service preempted a large part of export earnings.

- Because of the leading role of Solidarity in the revolution, union militancy was high, and labor movements were well-organized.

- Political compromise had resulted in promises to workers that could not be kept in the context of economic restructuring.

SHOCK THERAPY

In June of 1989 limited representative democracy came to Poland. Elections were held for about half the seats in Parliament, while others were filled by the nominees of the government. The Solidarity movement swept the contestable seats and ultimately emerged as the lead party in a coalition government. Leszek Balcerowicz, the new finance minister, initiated a program of **shock therapy** designed in close consultation with the Harvard economist Jeffrey Sachs, intended by its austerity to jump-start the economy from lethargy.

In January 1990, after approval by the International Monetary Fund (IMF), Parliament passed the basic elements of this Stabilization and Liberalization Program (SLP). Balcerowicz himself had set the tenor of the plan when in September 1989 he had declared to Parliament that "it is time to shut our eyes and jump into the hole, without checking either the state of the water or the depth of the drop"—the first of many dramatic metaphors used to describe his program, which had five principal features:

1. Restrictive monetary policy, including higher interest rates and the end of "preferential credit" to favored enterprises

2. Elimination of the budget deficit, largely through the abandonment of subsidies for food, consumer goods, and energy

3. Continuation of the price liberalization that had occurred in the 1980s

4. The establishment of a convertible currency, and trade liberalization through reduction and the elimination of import quotas

5. A tax-based policy to curb wage inflation by penalizing firms through a 20 to 50 percent levy (the *popiwek*) on wage increases above the government's guidelines

The net effect of these measures was, at a stroke, to rationalize prices, but also to raise them to international levels.

THE IMPACT OF SHOCK THERAPY

Shock therapy led directly to high interest rates, declining output, and soaring levels of unemployment. The real extent of the dip in output that followed the initiation of shock therapy is open to debate. The statistical system inherited from the

POLAND: KEY INDICATORS OF REFORM IN THE 1990S

	1990	1991	1992	1993	1994	1995	1996	1997
GDP per capita at purchasing power parity ($)	4221.0	4018.0	4371.0	4668.0	5017.0	5417.0	5876.0	6406.0
GDP (% change)	−11.6	−7.0	2.6	3.8	5.2	7.0	6.1	6.9
Industrial production (% change)	−24.2	−8.0	2.8	6.4	12.1	9.7	8.3	10.8
Budget balance (% of GDP)	3.1	−6.7	−6.6	−3.4	−2.8	−3.6	−2.5	−1.4
Unemployment (%)	6.3	11.8	13.6	16.4	16.0	14.9	13.2	10.5
Average monthly wage ($)	na	na	213.0	215.7	231.3	285.5	323.0	352.7
Inflation (%)	585.8	70.3	43.0	35.3	32.2	22.0	18.7	13.2
Exports ($bn)	15.8	12.8	14.0	13.6	17.0	22.9	24.4	27.2
Imports ($bn)	12.3	12.7	13.5	15.9	17.8	24.7	32.6	38.5
Trade balance ($bn)	3.6	0.1	0.5	−2.3	−0.8	−1.8	−8.2	−11.3
Current−account balance ($bn)	3.1	−2.0	0.9	−0.6	2.3	5.5	−1.3	−4.3
Foreign direct investment flow ($bn)	.89	.1	.3	.6	.5	1.1	2.7	3.0
Foreign exchange reserves ($bn)	4.5	3.6	4.3	4.3	6.0	15.0	18.0	20.7
Foreign debt ($bn)	49.4	48.0	47.6	47.2	42.2	43.9	40.4	38.0
Discount rate (%)	48.0	36.0	32.0	29.0	28.0	25.0	22.0	24.5
Exchange rate (Zloty/$)	1.0	1.1	1.4	1.8	2.3	2.4	2.7	3.3

SOURCE: Business Central Europe from European Bank for Reconstruction and Development (EBRD), International Monetary Fund (IMF), World Bank.

planners was at best misleading and failed to provide an adequate benchmark by which to judge the progress of the economy under reform. Most series published at the time showed deep cuts in output, with GDP falling by about 12 percent in 1990 and a further 7 percent in 1991, while industrial output tumbled by twice as much. Subsequent research has reevaluated these figures and found that much of the fall in the output of large-scale enterprises was due to the elimination of low-quality, overpriced output, which was in excess supply. On the other side of the ledger, most of the output of the growing small-scale private sector[3] was omitted from official statistics, in part because it was underreported to avoid paying tax on it.

Unemployment did rise sharply. At the end of 1989 the official rate was 0.3 percent of the workforce, though of course there was extensive "disguised unemployment" and overstaffing. By mid-1992 the figure had risen to 13.6 percent, with over 2.5 million persons registered as jobless[4] (see Table 23.2). Again there are grounds to be skeptical about the statistics, because some authorities believe that up to half of the total unemployed were moonlighting in paid employment while being registered as looking for work. As the zloty fell, domestic prices adjusted to world levels; but inflation fell, inching away from the hyperinflation of 1990 and reaching

---

[3] Some 516,000 new enterprises were registered in Poland in 1990 alone.

[4] According to International Monetary Fund (IMF) figures, unemployment peaked in 1994 at 16.5 percent of the workforce with some three million persons unemployed.

more manageable levels (about 30 percent) by 1994–1995. Despite the fall in the currency imports surged, producing a trade and current account deficit that a rapid rise in direct foreign investment only partially filled.

In the assessment of one of its authors, the greatest achievement of Polish shock therapy was that shortages in the economy were eliminated virtually overnight.

> The most immediate consequence of the new environment has been the sharp reduction of shortages in the economy. Apart from those goods still subjected to administered prices, queues have all but disappeared. Meat is freely available at all times in the official shops. The notorious gas station lines are gone. Foreign consumer goods such as bananas and strawberries and consumer electronic products are now widely available. Durable goods, many of which used to require months or years for delivery, can now be purchased in department stores.[5]

While the appearance of food in previously empty stores seemed a miracle, it did not represent sudden affluence for all of the population. Part of the cause of apparent plenty lay in the fact that fewer people could afford consumer goods and food at the higher prices that were experienced after price controls were terminated and rising unemployment cut into effective demand. Domestic supply was slow to respond in the short run although imports increased sharply and reduction of demand played the larger role in achieving balance in the goods market.

INSTITUTIONAL CHANGE

With relative stability established in the macroeconomy, the way was cleared for institutional change.

PRIVATIZATION

The most important feature of institutional change in the Polish case was the privatization of industry. Agriculture was already primarily within the private sector, and the basics of property and commercial law had survived the 40 years of communist rule, minimizing the need for legal reform. The logic of shock therapy as seen by its authors depended on a rapid disposal of state assets:

> Poland must begin a rapid process of privatization of state firms, not only to ensure efficient resource utilization, but also to prevent the collapse of the stabilization itself in the medium term. Experience around the world, plus the logic of the soft budget constraint, strongly suggests that it will be difficult to maintain the financial discipline of the state enterprises beyond the short run, especially if the state enterprise sector remains the dominant part of the economy. Eventually wage pressures and lax investment decisions are likely to undermine the financial health of the state firms.[6]

---

[5] David Lipton and Jeffrey Sachs, "Creating a Market in Eastern Europe: The Case of Poland," *Brookings paper on Economic Activity* 1 (1990): 127.

[6] Lipton and Sachs, 127.

NUMBER OF ECONOMIC UNITS IN PUBLIC AND PRIVATE SECTORS ON DECEMBER 31, 1989, AND DECEMBER 1, 1995

Ownership Form	1989	1995
State enterprises	7,337	4,357
Municipal enterprises	—	482
Commercial code companies with state majority	1,224	2,023
Domestic commercial code companies (private)	15,252	90,843
Joint ventures	429	24,086
Businesses owned by individuals	813,145	1,693,427
Cooperatives (with cooperative banks)	16,691	19,822

SOURCE: Leszek Bakerowitz, Barbara Blaszczyk, and Mark Dombrowski, "The Polish Way to a Market Economy," in *Economies in Transition—Comparing Asia and Europe*, ed. Wing Thye Woo, Stephen Parker, and Jeffrey D. Sachs (Cambridge, Mass.: The MIT Press, 1997).

Thus **marketization** required on theoretical grounds the rapid sale of the bulk of the state sector. However, this was a huge task, and piecemeal reform under the communist leadership had in many cases made the task more difficult; by introducing a high degree of worker governance into the enterprises, preservation of the existing level of employment often became the objective of the enterprise, rather than the efficient use of resources or profit maximization.

In 1990 when a four-year timetable for privatization was announced, there were 8,441 state-owned enterprises in Poland. By the end of 1995 only 1,610 enterprises had been fully privatized, about 20 percent of the total and these were mostly small to medium-sized firms; only about 10 percent were large concerns employing more than 500 persons. The majority (about two-thirds) were privatized by a process of liquidating the existing state enterprise and leasing the capital stock to new companies formed by management and workers. These were insider deals, with terms subject to negotiation on a case-by-case basis. Larger enterprises were also privatized in an eclectic fashion. Of the 160 large enterprises that were successfully privatized, 22 percent were sold through initial public offerings. Most of the rest were sold directly to a single buyer or leased to management and employees. Some infusion of capital and technology was ensured by a search by the Privatization Ministry for foreign partners to be actively involved.

Table 23.3 shows the progress of privatization between 1989 and 1995. It was not slow in absolute terms, but it was in relation to the size of the task in hand. At the end of 1989 there were 8,561 enterprises that were either fully owned by the state or in which the state held a controlling interest. By the end of 1995, 4,357 were still completely owned by the state, 482 had been handed over to municipalities, and 2,023 were "commercial code companies" still controlled by the state, although with some private equity holding. In almost five years only 1,715 enterprises had been fully privatized, less than 25 percent of the total required. The slow pace of privatization did not mean that activity in the private sector was sluggish. The number of private limited-liability companies had increased sixfold to more than

■ TABLE 23.4

EMPLOYMENT IN POLAND BY SECTOR: DECEMBER 1989 AND
DECEMBER 1994 (IN BILLIONS)

Sectors	1989	1994
Private sector		
Agricultural	4.0	3.9
Nonagricultural	1.8	4.5
Total private sector	5.8	8.4
Cooperatives	2.2	0.7
Other socialized entities	0.2	—
Total nonpublic sector	8.2	9.1
Public sector	9.3	5.8
Total employment in the national economy	17.5	14.9

SOURCES: Leszek Bakerowitz, Barbara Blaszczyk, and Mark Dombrowski, "The Polish Way to a Market Economy," in *Economies in Transition—Comparing Asia and Europe,* ed. Wing Thye Woo, Stephen Parker, and Jeffrey D. Sachs (Cambridge, Mass.: The MIT Press, 1997).

90,000, and almost one million proprietorships and partnerships had been established. However, the employment situation gave cause for concern. Despite this upsurge of small business activity and the privatization process, recorded private employment rose by only 2.6 million persons between 1989 and 1994 as shown in Table 23.4. Employment in cooperatives and other socialized firms fell by 1.7 million, while the public sector shed 3½ million jobs, leading to a fall in net employment of 2.6 million persons.

MASS PRIVATIZATION

Mass privatization was finally embarked on in 1995 after a delay of more than three years. The Polish method is unique in that it seeks to solve the problem of corporate governance through the creation of government-sponsored financial intermediaries. Fifteen such **national investment funds (NIFs)** were created under the aegis of the Treasury Ministry, with Polish managers assisted by Western advisers.[7]

Title to the equity of the 512 largest state-owned enterprises was transferred to the funds with each enterprise's share capital being allocated on the lines of Table 23.5. This strucure ensured that one of the funds would have at least one-third of the voting equity of every large firm and would therefore have a strong interest in the performance of the firm, as well as be in a position to offer advice and assistance to further its growth and restructuring. Incentives were given a key role and any payments to the funds, or to any employees and consultants, are performance

[7] Western firms retained include Barclays PLC, Dresdner Bank, Chase Manhattan, and Creditanstalt.

■ TABLE 23.5

STRUCTURE OF EQUITY OF LARGE PRIVATIZED ENTERPRISES

Lead shareholding fund	33
Other 14 funds (1.93% each)	27
Employees	15
State	25

related. For a small fee of 20 zlotys, each of Poland's 27 million adult citizens could receive a certificate convertible to a share in one of the NIFs. The greater the demand for the shares of any one NIF, the less stock an individual certificate would ultimately buy. Over 96 percent of the eligible population took advantage of the offer, and now the Polish public owns the former state enterprises indirectly through ownership of the NIFs.

The NIFs are active, not passive holders of the shares. Their job is to restructure the companies by changing management, improving marketing, obtaining finance, and disposing of the unproductive parts of an enterprise in order to maximize its value. They can dispose of their share holdings in any firm or buy more. Since 1997 the NIFs have been listed on the Warsaw stock exchange and citizens can sell their shares in turn for cash, or invest more. It is too soon to tell whether the NIF approach produces superior results to other privatization techniques. Certainly there is the capacity for closer and more active governance, which in theory should improve enterprise performance.

DIRECT FOREIGN INVESTMENT (DFI)

Poland has been particularly well served by incoming direct foreign investment, which has added buoyancy to the private sector and created employment. Between 1990 and 1997 about $8.5 billion of DFI entered Poland, over 80 percent of that during 1996–1997.[8] It is currently the most popular destination in any of the formerly planned East European economies. The motivation of these flows included special factors (like the proximity of cheap labor to the German market, the associate status with the EU, and the large and influential Polish diaspora), as well as policy measures such as the liberalization of prices, the absence of capital controls, and political stability.

PROSPECTS FOR THE POLISH ECONOMY

In many ways Poland is a paradox. Its performance after the start of shock therapy policy has been the strongest of any of the Eastern European nations. Since 1992,

[8] See Table 23.2.

growth has been positive for every year, with especially strong performances in 1995 through 1997. Unemployment peaked at 16.4 percent in 1993 and has since fallen steadily to 10.5 percent in 1997, reducing the number of jobless from close to three million to only two million. The rate of consumer price increase, which verged on hyperinflation in 1990, is now down to a manageable 13 percent. The trade deficit continues to give cause for concern, but the strong inflow of direct foreign investment has kept the overall balance of payments out of difficulty. The high debt service ratios of the late 1980s have been gradually reduced.

However, at the outset the key to Polish reform was intended to be rapid privatization. In fact, Poland has been one of the slowest privatizers in terms of the progress of handing over state-owned enterprise. Despite this, growth has been very strong, and a buoyant private sector has led the way forward. The Polish experience calls into question the necessity for a rapid disposal of state assets for growth and a market transformation, but it suggests that slow privatization (although unintended in the Polish case) is compatible with marketization and private-sector expansion.

THE CZECH REPUBLIC

HISTORICAL BACKGROUND

In the period between the two world wars, the Czech lands (Bohemia and Moravia) were among the most prosperous areas of Europe. For a long time this region in the heart of Europe had served as the manufacturing center for the Austro-Hungarian Empire, enjoying an average income higher than that of Austria itself. After the empire's dissolution in 1918, the Czech lands retained some of this affluence as part of the Czechoslovak Republic, continuing to be a center of precision engineering and armament manufacture.

However, following the communist takeover in 1948, the Czech lands fell sharply in terms of productivity and income. Investment was poured into basic industries like steel and cement, in line with conventional Stalinist guidelines, but these were located mostly in the east of the country, in the province of Slovakia. The nonagricultural private sector was, in Ian Jeffries's words, "savagely repressed even by East European standards."[9] Alice Teichova estimates that there were 383,000 small companies in Czechoslovakia in 1948, and this bouyant sector was reduced to only 2,000 self-employed craftsmen by 1972.[10]

The state sector dominated agriculture as well as industry. Unlike Poland, where private farming largely survived the communist period, Czechoslovak farmers were forced into collectivization in the 1950s and 1960s. From the 1970s onward, emphasis was placed on investment in state farms, mirroring the shift from *kholkhoz* to *sovkhoz* that had occurred in Soviet Russia. By the mid-1980s, state farms

---

[9] Ian Jeffries, *Socialist Economies and the Transition to the Market* (New York: Routledge, 1993), 253.

[10] Alice Teichova, *The Czechoslovak Economy, 1918–1980* (London: Routledge, 1988), 104.

occupied 30 percent of total land area, collective farms 65 percent, and only 5 percent was left in private hands. Private production occupied an even lower percentage of arable land, 3 percent, but nevertheless managed to produce about 40 percent of the vegetables, 60 percent of the fruit, and 40 percent of the eggs.

THE PRAGUE SPRING

In the mid-1960s Prime Minister Alexander Dubcek tried to lead the Czech economy away from central planning by allowing enterprises free rein in determining both outputs and inputs, establishing workers' councils, and liberalizing prices. As a result the Czechoslovak economy might have moved toward the variety of market socialism practiced in Yugoslavia, but the assault on conventional ideology was too abrupt to be tolerated by the Soviet Union. In August 1968 Warsaw Pact forces occupied Czechoslovakia, restoring to power hardliners who were adamantly opposed to any further attempt at reform.

The net result of this history was that the Czech lands found themselves, on the eve of liberalization, in a very unreformed state, even relative to their socialist neighbors, since investment in the period 1948–1968 had been predominantly in Slovakia and in many areas the prewar infrastructure was still in place. After 1968 Czechoslovakia had been a repository of planning orthodoxy, while other nations in the Council for Mutual Economic Assistance (CMEA) experimented with economic reform. In a perverse way, the unchallenged power of the Czech state and absence of enterprise reform, gave greater opportunity to the new leaders to entirely restructure the economy. The nation enjoyed, in Gershenkron's phrase, "the advantage of backwardness," but the necessary corollary of this is that "the future development of the Czech economy depends in part—a greater part than one might wish—on the likelihood that the government will continue to be led by individuals with an ideological commitment to removing the state from day-to-day economic decision making."[11]

STABILIZATION

The **velvet revolution,** as the beginning of the transition in the Czech Republic is known, occurred during the fall and early winter of 1989 with the collapse of the Communist Party and its will to rule. Vaclav Havel, a playwright, was elected interim president, a post made permanent after the election in June 1990. Economic policy was steered largely by Vaclav Klaus, finance minister of the Czech and Slovak Federated Republic until the dissolution of the country into the Czech Republic and Slovakia in 1992, when he became prime minister of the Czech Republic.

---

[11]Roman Frydman, Andrzej Rapaczinski, and Joel Turkowitz, "Transition to a Private Property Regime in the Czech Republic and Hungary," in *Economies in Transition—Comparing Asia and Eastern Europe,* ed. Wing Thye Woo, Stephen Parker, and Jeffrey Sachs (Cambridge, Mass.: MIT Press, 1997), 101.

■ TABLE 23.6

GDP PER CAPITA IN CEFTA COUNTRIES IN 1994

	Purchasing Power Parity	Official Exchange Rate	Purchasing Power Parity	Official Exchange Rate
	In U.S. Dollars		Czech Republic = 100	
Czech Republic	9,490	4,419	100	100
Hungary	6,537	4,403	69	100
Poland	5,477	3,124	58	71
Slovakia	6,749	3,240	71	73

SOURCE: Martin Myant et alia. *Successful Transformations?: The Creation of Market Economies in Eastern Germany and the Czech Republic,* 100.

■ TABLE 23.7

GROSS EXTERNAL DEBT IN CEFTA COUNTRIES IN 1989

	Gross Debt in $Billion	Gross Debt as Percentage of GDP	Gross Debt as Percentage of Exports	Debt Service as Percentage of Exports
Czechoslovakia	7.9	14.9	108.7	18.8
Hungary	20.4	71.3	239.8	40.6
Poland	41.5	58.8	475.8	44.5

SOURCE: Organization for Economic Cooperation and Development (OECD), 1994. Cited in Martin Myant et alia. *Successful Transformations?: The Creation of Market Economies in Eastern Germany and the Czech Republic,* 100.

Despite the neglect of the communist years, the Czechs were among the most prosperous of the Eastern European nations. Table 23.6 shows that in terms of purchasing power, the citizens of the Czech Republic were considerably better off than those in the other economies of the **Central European Free Trade Area (CEFTA)** founded in 1992. Moreover, inflation did not erode prosperity to the same degree as in other reforming nations. Czechoslovakia, in its pre–World War II days and in its communist period, had a reputation for fiscal and monetary stringency. As noted in chapter 21 and illustrated in Table 21.1, most of the nations in transition had a large "monetary overhang" caused by raising wages without supplying adequate goods to the consumer market. In Czechoslovakia this was not the case and consumers had actually gone into debt to finance purchases. The significance of this was that price liberalization did not immediately lead to an inflationary surge, as shock therapy had in Poland.

The same conservatism had limited the tendency to borrow abroad, and as shown in Table 23.7, gross external debt was lower than in other reforming nations. While Poland had debts amounting to 58.8 percent of GDP, and Hungary 71.3 percent, the Czech Republic only owed $8 billion abroad (less than 15 percent of GDP).

Debt service obligations were similarly modest—only 18.8 percent of export revenue was required to finance the foreign debt and, of course, even less if substantial capital inflows from abroad in terms of direct or portfolio investment could be attracted.

On September 1, 1990, the Czechoslovak government submitted to Parliament a scenario for economic reform. On the macroeconomic front it emphasized a strict anti-inflationary policy, with all other macroeconomic goals (growth, employment, and balance of payments) "within reasonable limits subordinate" to the objective of restraining inflation. This goal justified a very severe restriction of monetary growth (a target of zero) and the development of a fiscal surplus.

On the microeconomic side, the institutional changes included the following:

■ Reform of the tax system, including the introduction of the value added tax

■ Corporatizing state-owned enterprises, making them financially independent, self-sufficient and free of subsidy

■ Privatization of property

■ Achieving full convertibility of the currency

■ Controlling inflation by the imposition of a heavy tax on any wage increases above norms prescribed by the government, while fostering collective bargaining for wage determination

In common with all transition economies, industrial output fell and unemployment rose (from its nominal zero level under socialism) and GDP fell. The loss of export markets within the CMEA hit the Czechoslovak economy especially hard since it had been the supplier of highly processed manufactured goods throughout the communist bloc, and the dislocation of the trading system created a sharp fall in output. The tight austerity that resulted from suppressing domestic demand did not help matters, nor did the scope of imports that followed trade liberalization.

However, the reforms and the austerity policy affected the two parts of the country differently. The Czech lands saw an increase in trade with the West, especially Germany, and a rise in service activity and foreign investment, while in Slovakia the large-scale industrial plants built in the 1950s and 1960s fell on particularly hard times. By the spring of 1992, unemployment in the Czech lands was 3.7 percent, while in Slovakia it had risen to 12.3 percent,[12] and the country became unglued as economic problems exacerbated ethnic difficulties. Slovakia saw itself the victim of Czech austerity, and the newly liberated Czechs, sensing real prosperity around the corner, were unwilling to countenance sustained income transfers to the Slovaks. In the summer of 1992 the two halves of the Federated Republic went their separate ways. Klaus became prime minister in Prague, and Meciar, an orthodox leftist, ruled Slovakia in Bratislava. Klaus's objective was, as he frequently remarked, the creation of a "market economy without adjectives," and he

---

[12] Karel Dyba and Jan Svejnar, "Stabilization and Transition in Czechoslovakia," in *The Transition in Eastern Europe, Vol. I,* ed. Olivier Jean Blanchard, Kenneth A. Froot, and Jeffrey D. Sachs (Chicago: University of Chicago Press, 1994), 107.

■ **TABLE 23.8**

THE CZECH REPUBLIC: KEY INDICATORS OF THE TRANSITION

	1990	1991	1992	1993	1994	1995	1996	1997
Nominal GDP ($bn)	32.3	25.4	29.9	34.3	39.7	50.3	56.6	52.9
GDP per capita PPP ($)	9526.0	8721.0	8951.0	9273.0	9794.0	10531.0	11211.0	11566.0
GDP (% change)	−1.2	−11.5	−3.3	0.6	3.2	6.4	3.9	1.0
Industrial production (% change)	−3.3	−21.2	−7.9	−5.3	2.1	8.7	2.0	4.5
Budget balance (% of GDP)	na	−1.9	−3.1	0.5	−1.2	−1.8	−1.2	−0.5
Unemployment (%)	0.8	4.1	2.6	3.5	3.2	2.9	3.5	5.2
Average monthly wage ($)	182.6	128.5	164.3	199.6	239.5	307.8	356.4	333.4
Inflation (%)	9.7	56.6	11.1	20.8	10.0	7.9	8.7	9.9
Exports ($bn)	5.9	8.3	8.4	14.2	16.0	21.4	21.7	22.4
Imports ($bn)	6.5	8.8	10.4	14.6	17.4	25.1	27.6	27.1
Trade balance ($bn)	−0.7	−0.5	−1.9	−0.4	−1.4	−3.7	−5.9	−4.6
Current-account balance ($bn)	−1.0	0.3	−0.3	0.1	0.0	−1.4	−4.3	−3.2
Foreign direct investment flow ($bn)	na	na	.1	.6	.7	2.5	1.4	1.3
Foreign exchange reserves ($bn)	1.1	3.9	0.8	3.9	6.2	14.0	16.1	15.0
Foreign debt ($bn)	6.4	6.7	7.1	8.5	10.7	16.5	20.8	22.0
Discount rate (%)	na	9.5	9.5	8.0	8.5	9.5	10.5	13.0
Exchange rate ($)	18.0	29.5	28.3	29.2	28.8	26.6	27.1	31.7

SOURCE: Business Central Europe from EBRD, IMF, and IBRD.

had no sympathy for, or interest in, the pursuit of any kind of "third way," directing policy to align the Czech economy as closely and as quickly to Western Europe as possible.

Table 23.8 gives summary statistics for the development of the Czech economy during the 1990s. The postliberalization contraction ended in 1993, and solid growth recommenced in 1994, while monetary austerity kept the inflation rate under control. The most worrying features continue to be the widening trade and current account imbalances and the relatively small flows of incoming foreign direct investment, which have led to growing foreign indebtedness.

THE PRIVATIZATION PROGRAM

Part of any drive to a market economy clearly involves the privatization of state assets, which in the Czech context can be regarded as falling into three categories:

(1) RESTITUTION. In contrast to Poland, Czechoslovakia had not been devastated by World War II, and its borders had remained largely unchanged at the end of the conflict. Immediately after the war a democratic government was briefly installed and to a large extent normality returned, including a fairly orderly system of property rights. As a result, after liberalization many owners from that period could trace title to their property despite seizure by the state during communism. Consequently the Czech Republic had the most active restitution program of any

■ **TABLE 23.9**

CZECH SMALL-SCALE PRIVATIZATION TO DECEMBER 1993

Type	Number	Average Increase over Starting Price
Shops	13,042	75%
Restaurants	1,861	54%
Hotels	430	64%
Services	3,577	14%
Other	3,435	22%
Total	22,345	49

SOURCE: J. S. Earle, R. Frydman, A. Rapaczynski, and J. Turkewitz, *Small Privatization: The Transformation of Retail Trade and Consumer Services in the Czech Republic, Hungary, and Poland* (New York: Central European Press, 1994).

of the Eastern European nations.[13] Applicants who could trace their ownership and who sought restitution of their property were required to submit their claims during a six-month period of 1991. It is hard to know exactly the extent of the program, but Tomas Jezek, head of the National Property Fund, estimated that more than 100,000 properties were restored to their former owners, the majority of which were residential properties. Other sources estimated that some 20,000 retail outlets were also reprivatized in this way.[14]

(2) SMALL PRIVATIZATION. Small privatization (primarily of shops, restaurants, hotels, and very small factories) was achieved by public auction. All Czech citizens had potential access to the auctions and insiders, either the bureaucrats of the ministries that had controlled the property or the current operators, had no special privileges beyond the advantage of having a clearer understanding of the financial potential of the businesses than would be available to an outsider.

The properties were initially valued by the privatization agency, and free bidding was to proceed upward from a designated starting price, with the property awarded to the highest bidder. If no one matched the initial starting price, it was lowered by increments of 10 percent until bidding started. The small privatization program was a success, and most properties were sold at a considerable markup to their starting price, as shown in Table 23.9. Only 3,720 properties, or 20 percent of the total, were sold at a discount to the starting price. There were accusations of ministry officials and enterprise managers attempting to manipulate the process, but on the whole the process was remarkably transparent, and more than $1 billion was raised in sales.

[13] With the probable exception of East Germany.

[14] John S. Earle, Roman Frydman, Andrzej Rapaczynski, and Joel Turkewitz, *Small Privatization: The Transformation of Retail Trade and Consumer Services in the Czech Republic, Hungary, and Poland (Ceu Privatization Reports)* (New York: Central European University Press, 1994), 58.

(3) THE PRIVATIZATION OF LARGE ENTERPRISE. Large privatization covered the bulk of state-owned enterprises. The program was delayed by the practical problems of separating the operations of the enterprises after the breakup of the Czechoslovak Federal State into the Czech Republic and Slovakia. The particular method of privatization fell on enterprise managers, although any worker or citizen could put forward an alternate scheme. Initially, many managers tried to push through insider privatization, but generally those were rejected by the privatization ministry. Some firms were sold by sealed bid offers and some by open auction, while others were sold at negotiated prices to Czech or foreign citizens. However, the bulk of the privatization ultimately took the form of "voucher auctions."

Voucher Auctions. Every citizen of the Czech Republic was invited to purchase, for the sum of one thousand Czech crowns (about $35), a book of vouchers that could be exchanged for shares. The vouchers had no monetary denomination and could not legally be sold or exchanged, except if they were placed with one of the government-licensed, privately owned investment funds that rapidly became established (discussed later). About 75 percent of all adult Czech citizens received vouchers. Each voucher was exchangeable for part of the share capital of a privatizing enterprise, the amount of shares received being in inverse proportion to the total interest in the enterprise. Thus, for example, if 100,000 individuals all offered a voucher in the auction of a firm, then each would receive 1/100,000 of the share capital; if only 10,000 offered shares, each would receive 1/10,000, and so forth.

Enterprise managers generally favored voucher privatization hoping that the diverse share ownership that would result would mean that they might escape scrutiny from the new owners, hence retaining their informal but valuable property rights in the enterprises.

CONCENTRATION OF ECONOMIC POWER. One of the fundamental justifications of privatization is that the financial interest of the owners will give them incentives to oversee management and improve performance in a way not possible under state ownership. An improvement in governance is unlikely if share ownership is diffuse, because the costs of gathering information and acting in unison rises with the number of shareholders. Diffuse ownership and weak oversight seemed likely in the Czech case until the emergence of the **privatization funds.** These financial intermediaries accepted vouchers from citizens and in return offered shares in the profits of the funds. Within a few months 400 such firms were established, and together they attracted about 70 percent of all the vouchers issued. While many were quite small, a few funds amassed considerable purchasing power, and the seven largest controlled 45 percent of all voucher points. Since the average enterprise was expected to sell 60 percent of equity through voucher privatization, the potential for control to be concentrated in a few hands is obvious. On average the "Big 7" funds together own almost 30 percent of every enterprise in the Czech Republic, and concern therefore has shifted from ownership being too diffuse and hindering good governance, to its being too concentrated and giving rise to too much economic power.

BANKING REFORM

The concentration of financial power in the Czech economy has been aggravated by the developments in the banking sector. As part of the liberalization plan, the government chose partial privatization of the state-owned banks, freeing them from direct control, disposing of most of the equity in voucher privatization, but retaining roughly 40 percent of the shares of each in the National Property Fund. However, a problematic development has been the establishment by the banks of their own voucher privatization funds, which have been very successful in attracting voucher deposits. Now the largest banks also control the largest funds, and are not only lenders to industry, but also control much of the share capital and voting rights of many firms. Furthermore, because banks are themselves among the institutions partially privatized under the voucher scheme, some of the banks came to control a substantial part of the share capital of other banks and a system of interlocking ownership has emerged within the banking system itself. For example, Komercni Bank, the largest commercial bank, is 44 percent owned by the National Property Fund (the state), but another 24 percent is owned by investment funds that are controlled by the other four major banks. It is hard to predict exactly what the impact of this concentration of economic power might be, but it gives, at the very least, grounds for concern.

Although Czech banks have been partially sold to the private sector, their management remains highly politicized. Under government pressure the banks made extensive loans to industry, but much of the debt remains unpaid, and this has thrown the banks themselves into near bankruptcy. Komercni Bank reported a loss of about $336 million in 1999, and Spotalna, the national savings bank, lost close to $200 million. These losses are enough to destroy the net worth of the banks, and the government is now faced with stark choices—either refinance them once more or sell them off to foreign financial concerns at close to their net worth, which is zero. The failure to effectively liberalize the financial sector threatens all of the Czech reform effort and underscores the vital role that bank reform must play in overall transition strategy.

THE STRUCTURE OF INDUSTRY

Table 23.10 presents data on change in the form of business organization in the Czech Republic during the first phase of privatization. In 1990 there were almost 3,000 state-owned enterprises (SOEs), covering the gamut of economic activity from auto manufacture to retail, banking, and insurance. Like most enterprises in centrally planned economies these concerns were large in size and highly vertically integrated. The first stage of reform saw a sharp (25 percent) increase in the number of SOEs, as enterprises were spun off into somewhat smaller, more rational units. These were then disposed of in the voucher auctions. However, the vitality of the private sector in the Czech Republic owed more to newly established firms than to those that had been sold from the state sector. Privately owned and financed commercial companies were founded from scratch at a much faster rate than they were created through privatization. In the two years between 1992 and

■ TABLE 23.10

FORMS OF BUSINESS ORGANIZATION IN THE CZECH ECONOMY

	End 1990	End 1991	End 1994
State enterprises	2,945	3,760	1,522
Commercial companies	3,034	25,522	88,424
Cooperatives	2,856	4,070	5,226
Individual entrepreneurs	310,653	902,797	846,285
Individual farmers	127	7,533	91,936
Others	17,219	26,750	85,141
Total	336,834	970,432	1,118,534

SOURCE: Earle, Frydman, Rapaczynski, and Turkewitz.

■ TABLE 23.11

SHARE OF NONSTATE SECTOR IN EMPLOYMENT*: 1992–1996** (AS A PERCENTAGE)

	1992	1993	1994	1995	1996
Total economy	39.8	59.9	64.2	75.5	77.6
Agriculture	68.6	80.4	82.9	91.0	92.3
Industry	31.1	60.4	69.2	90.1	93.0
Construction	61.8	90.7	91.4	96.9	98.1
Wholesale and retail trade	74.2	89.9	90.7	97.7	98.6
Transport, storage, and communications	16.1	25.6	28.6	43.4	47.1

* Mixed ownership.

** Includes private cooperatives and nonprofit corporations serving households.

SOURCE: Data provided by the Czech Statistical Office.

1994, more than 85,000 new private companies were established and about 83,000 of them were startups not privatizations.

The productive sectors of the Czech economy were, by 1996, almost completely privatized. This is illustrated in Table 23.11, which shows the share of private versus state employment by industrial sector. For the economy as a whole, private employment amounted to rather more than 77 percent, while in construction, agriculture, and industry only a tiny fraction of the once universal state presence remained.

DIRECT FOREIGN INVESTMENT

Because of its location, the high human capital of its population, and the confidence that foreigners had in the management of the economy, the Czech Republic

CUMULATIVE INFLOW OF FDI, CZECH REPUBLIC: 1990–1998*

Country	1990–Q1 1998	
	Millions of $ U.S.	Percentage
Germany	2,353.1	27.4
Netherlands	1,142.2	13.3
United States	1,107.8	12.9
Switzerland	884.6	10.3
France	644.1	7.5
United Kingdom	618.3	7.2
Others	1,837.8	21.4
Total	8,587.9	100.0

Last update: June 1998.

*Czechinvest methodology.

SOURCE: Czechinvest Fact-sheet, no. 2.

has been blessed with very sizable inflows of direct investment. Czechinvest, a governmental agency responsible for attracting direct foreign investment, estimated that between 1990 and 1998, more than $8 billion U.S. flowed in (see Table 23.12), a figure roughly amounting to $850 per head of population. The largest source nation has been Germany, and the largest individual firm has been Volkswagen, which has acquired Skoda, a car maker, and invested substantial capital.

PROSPECTS FOR THE CZECH ECONOMY

Until 1997 the Czech Republic stood out as an almost unquestioned star of the transition process. It moved through the dip in output that normally accompanied transition from socialism to capitalism with impressive speed, the contraction being only 15 percent, and growth resumed in 1993. By the end of 1996, GDP had surpassed its pretransition level. During this period inflation was never greater than 4.1 percent, and the budget deficit never more than 3.1 percent. In fact, at the time that the Maastricht criteria for membership in the European Monetary Union were promulgated, the Czech Republic would have met them all, while none of the West European nations did.

Subsequently, however, the situation has worsened on all fronts. The Klaus administration, which had seemed a model of fiscal and monetary conservatism and good management, became increasingly embroiled in accusations of corruption. The banking sector was revealed as a source of great weakness, with political intervention leading to a high proportion of nonperforming loans. In 1996 alone 13 banks failed, and the government was required to sponsor a rescue operation that cost Czech taxpayers over $1.25 billion.[15] Growth was a paltry 1 percent in 1997, and output was virtually stagnant in 1998. Unemployment began to rise in 1996, reaching 5.2 percent, the highest since the fall of communism in mid-1997. The trade balance turned severely negative, and as a result foreign debt rose to over $20 billion.

In this context the fall of the Klaus government in late 1997 came as no surprise, and the country moved sharply leftward. After a brief caretaker government, the Social Democrats formed a government in which there was a large former communist representation. Seven out of nineteen cabinet members had a communist past. While there is no danger of a rebirth of central planning (Vaclav Klaus himself has pledged support for the government while remaining outside it), it is clear that the new policies will be further to the left. Privatization of transport and communication are not now likely. Whether the new government will be able to put the economy back on track, follow through with cleaning up the financial sector, and cut down on the corruption remains to be seen.

KEY TERMS AND CONCEPTS

Big Bang

Central European Free Trade Area (CEFTA)

direct foreign investment (DFI)

Law on Economic Activity

marketization

national investment funds (NIFs)

nomenklatura privatization

Prague Spring

privatization funds

shock therapy

Solidarity

velvet revolution

QUESTIONS FOR DISCUSSION

1. What was the nature of the Polish reforms in the early 1980s?
2. What was the strategy underlying "shock therapy"?
3. What was the planned use of financial intermediaries in the Polish privatization program? What was to be the role of the National Investment Funds?
4. Jeffrey Sachs was insistent that rapid privatization in Poland was essential for success. In effect, a slow pace of privatization has accompanied considerable economic success. Can we account for this?
5. Why might it be that the repression that followed the "Prague Spring" was ultimately an asset in the Czech transition?
6. Outline the strategy and outcome of the Czech privatization program.

---

[15] "East European Bands for Sale: Bracing for a Buying Binge," *The Economist*, 15 August 1998, 64.

7. Why has the Czech economy attracted a disproportionate amount of foreign direct investment?

8. What has caused the amalgamation of economic and political power in the Czech Republic? What threats does this pose?

RESOURCES

WEB SITES

POLAND
Business Central Europe . . . . http://www.bcemag.com/
Embassy of Poland in Washington, D.C. . . . . http://www.polishworld.com/polemb/
Warsaw Stock Exchange . . . . http://www.atm.com.pl/~gielda/
The Warsaw Voice—Weekly Newspaper in English . . http://www.warsawvoice.com.pl/
The Official Website of Poland . . . . http://poland.pl/
The National Bank of Poland . . . . http://www.nbp.pl/home_en.html
Central Europe Online, Poland . . . . http://www.centraleurope.com/polandtoday/
Ministry of Economy . . . . http://www.cup.gov.pl/
Ministry of Finance . . . . http://www.mofnet.gov.pl/
Ministry of Foreign Affairs . . . . http://www.msz.gov.pl/
The Central Statistics Office . . . . http://www.mofnet.gov.pl/

THE CZECH REPUBLIC
Business Central Europe . . . . http://www.bcemag.com/
Central Bank . . . . http://www.cnb.cz/en/index.html
Czech Statistical Office . . . . http://www.czso.cz/
Economic Chamber . . . . http://www.hkcr.cz/en/index.html
Ministry of Industry and Trade . . . . http://www.mpo.cz/english/mpo_uk.htm
Ministry of Finance . . . . http://www.mfcr.cz/scripts/hpe/default.asp
Ministry of Foreign Affairs . . . . http://www.czech.cz/
Czech Capital Market . . . . http://stock.eunet.cz/index_e.html
Embassy of the Czech Republic in Washington, D.C. . . . .
. . . . http://www.czech.cz/washington/
The Prague Post—National Newspaper . . . . http://www.praguepost.cz/
Prague Business Journal . . . . http://www.pbj.cz/
The Prague Tribune Online . . . . http://www.prague-tribune.cz/
Czech Information Center . . . . http://www.muselik.com/czech/frame.html
Radio Prague . . . . http://www.prague.org/english.html
Country Commercial Guide Prepared by the U.S. Embassy in Prague . . . .
. . . . http://www.usis.cz/ccg.htm
Kommercni Bank http://www.kb.cz/01aa1en.htm

Narodni Bank . . . . http://www.cnb.cz/en/index.html

The Czech Economy and Fiscal System described by the Ministry of Finance . . . .
. . . . http://www.mfcr.cz/fiscal/Fiscal0.htm

Central Europe Online, Czech Republic . . . http://www.centraleurope.com/czechtoday/

Books and Articles

POLAND

Angresano, James. "Evolving Socio-economic Conditions in Central and Eastern Europe: A Myrdalian View." *Development Policy Review,* September 1994, 251–275.

Balcerowicz, Leszek. "Transition to the Market Economy: Poland, 1989–93 in Comparative Perspective." *Economic Policy,* 19 December 1994, 71–98.

Blanchard, Olivier Jean, Kenneth A. Froot, and Jeffrey D. Sachs, eds. *The Transition in Eastern Europe.* Vol. 1, *Country Studies;* Vol. 2, *Restructuring.* Chicago: University of Chicago Press, 1994. N. Reviewed by Peter Murrel in the *Journal of Economic Literature,* March 1995, 164–178.

Calvo, Guillermo A., and Fabrizio Coricelli. "Stabilizing a Previously Centrally Planned Economy: Poland 1990." *Economic Policy,* April 1992, 176–226.

"Czech Republic: Statistical Appendix." International Monetary Fund Staff Country Report, Working Paper 98/37 (April 1998).

Ebrill, Liam P., Asaj Chopra, and Charalambos Christofides, eds. *Poland: The Path to a Market Economy.* Occasional Paper 113 (October 1994). Washington D.C.: International Monetary Fund, 1994.

Gandhi, Ved P. "Fundamental Fiscal Reform in Poland: Issues of Design and Implementation." In *Transition to Market,* ed. Vito Tanzi. Washington D.C.: International Monetary Fund, 1993: 91–107.

Jeffries, Ian. *Socialist Economies and the Transition to the Market: A Guide.* New York: Routledge, 1993.

International Monetary Fund, Czech Republic: Selected Issues. IMF Staff Country Report, Working Paper 98/36 (April 1998).

Johnson, Simon, and Gary Loveman. "Starting Over: Poland after Communism." *Harvard Business Review,* March–April 1995, 44–56.

Keane, Michael, and Eswar Prasad, "Consumption and Income Inequality in Poland during the Economic Transition." International Monetary Fund, Working Paper WP/99/14 (1999).

Lipton, David, and Jeffrey Sachs. "Creating a Market in Eastern Europe: The Case of Poland," *Brookings Papers on Economic Activity* (1990): 119.

Pinto, Brian, Marek Belka, and Stefan Krajewski. "Transforming State Enterprise in Poland: Evidence on Adjustment by Manufacturing Firms," *Brookings Papers on Economic Activity* 1 (1993): 213.

"Poland's Economic Reforms." *The Economist,* 23 January 1993, 21–23.

Tittenbrun, Jacek. "The Managerial Revolution Revisited: The Case of Privatisation in Poland." *Capital and Class,* spring 1995, 21–32.

THE CZECH REPUBLIC

Aghevli, Bijan B. *Stabilization and Structural Reform in the Czech and Slovak Federal Republic: First Stage,* Occasional Paper 92 (Mach 1992). Washington, D.C.: International Monetary Fund, 1992.

Dlouhy, Vladimir, and Jan Mladek. "Privatization and Corporate Control in the Czech Republic." *Economic Policy* 19 (December 1994): 155–170.

Eva Marikova Leeds. "Voucher Privatization in Czechoslovakia." *Comparative Economic Studies,* fall 1993, 19–37.

Jeffries, Ian. *Socialist Economies and the Transition to the Market: A Guide.* New York: Routledge, 1993

Myant, Martin, et alia. *Successful Transformations?: The Creation of Market Economies in Eastern Germany and the Czech Republic.* Brookfield, Vt.: Edward Elgar, 1996, 50.

Prust, Jim. "The Czech and Slovak Federal Republic: Government Finances in a Period of Transition." In *Transition to Market,* ed. Vito Tanzi. Washington, D.C.: International Monetary Fund,1993.

Teichova, Alice. *The Czechoslovak Economy, 1918–1980.* London: Routledge, 1988.

INDEX